THE

Nantucket Diary

OF

Ned Rorem

1973-1985

NORTH POINT PRESS
San Francisco
1987

Copyright © 1987 by Ned Rorem
Printed in the United States of America
Library of Congress Catalogue Card Number: 86-62827
ISBN: 0-86547-259-9

1973

This morning while puttering with the crossword (which I seldom try, being slow at it, and never quite getting the point) I fell upon my own name. "Composer Rorem" was the clue. Instantly I filled in three squares with my given label. My immediate reaction was one of relief, since this was virtually the only answer I had found. The second reaction was of embarrassment that most people would complete the puzzle *except* for those three blanks. Finally I felt annoyed. Who am I to be thus immortalized when I haven't done a lick of work all week! I rushed to the piano and began practicing scales.

Someone at the *Times* loves me. Every six or eight months for the past several years I've been featured in either the daily or Sunday puzzle. JH says it's only because my Christian name, like Ava or Ari, is convenient for those short leftover slots.

The pattern of the linoleum on the bathroom floor here resembles welts from bedbug bites. Distant but nagging toothache, or gumache, again. For fifteen years the area of the right eyetooth has been "exquisitely" sensitive. Worry, worry.

Ice-cold Della Robbia weather showers us with sunlight.

4 January

To Steinway's basement for first rehearsal of *Night Music* with Ann Schein and Earl Carlyss, my ugliest piece, and very effective, at least as they played it. An hour earlier, visit to Dr. Schreiber (Mother's proctologist) for the aches of twenty years, aches that fade at the violin's sound.

Madison Hotel
Washington, D.C.
13 January

Shuttled here last night with the Popes and dined with Paul Callaway. Premiere at Library of *Night Music*. The first movement, *Answers*, was no sooner intoned than a female voice, audible and cross, rose from the audience: "What are the questions?" . . . Recorded this morning for Desto.

Later. New York. Dietrich on TV in *Dishonored*, her most perverse, surrealist, nervy film. She is forever more equivocal than Garbo.

24 January

Parties, concert, work, parties. Then yesterday, visit to Hurok offices, later to Tully Hall with Shirley for Elliott Carter's new quartet which we couldn't make anything of, but which got a standing ovation.

Visit to Dr. S., and Dubuffet's tacky sculpture in Chase Manhattan Plaza. Death of Marius Bewly.

28 January

JH's Chapel Concert of Satie and Britten, including his arrangement for organ of *La Messe des pauvres*. Landowska, when asked, "Who's the best after you?" answered, "Denise Restout, of course." I reply to that question, "Jim Holmes, of course."

Sans date

Our cousins, Chester Ronning and his daughter Audrey Topping, came with my parents to dine. (Famous spiced chicken, plus Grimble's cheesecake with a hot strawberry sauce.) Chester and my father, both seventy-seven, look fifty-nine, and suave Audrey in white leather, blondined and booted, hardly seemed smack out of Communist territories. But both, though Norwegian capitalists, are Chinese linguists and, by now, cool and collected with interviewers. After supper Eugene Istomin came over with John Trapp, and we took family pictures.

Chester, when asked no doubt for the millionth time what humor is like in China, replies it's like anywhere else, and illustrates with a joke: A henpecked husband, fed up, exclaims, "I'll die before I let her get away with this anymore," whereupon he drops dead. Now that's not funny in itself, nor hardly just Chinese, the figurative-as-literal being one of the four basic devices of all times.

But there *is* rich-people wit and poor-people wit, French humor and Jewish humor. People *are* different, with their ethnic and national fun, primitive and sophisticated fun. Humor is not exemplified in The Funny Story, since there are too many ways to relate that same plot. Humor is tone based on irony, a Janus head. Children, being literal-minded, have no humor. Which doesn't mean they're pedestrian: they literally see a blue elephant flying, a candy house, Santa Claus. Humor will come to them with disillusionment. By this definition the Chinese peasant probably lacks humor since he lacks training in the nuance of contrast—at least in *our* nuance of contrast.

French: brevity. Jokes about cuckolds.

German: drawn out ("German jokes are no laughing matter"). About food and scatology.

American: sex.

Did Handel have humor? His music's too removed to assess in perspective. Perhaps he was not even great. How long does greatness last?

What *is* musical humor? How wearying to hear forever about Haydn's wit. Play him with a movie on childbirth (as Cocteau played Bach for a suicide) and you'll hear how witty he is.

If Chopin's tunes were better (funnier) than Beethoven's, was he greater than Beethoven?

Have I said all this better elsewhere?

All great art contains humor. Insofar as Beethoven lacked humor he lacked greatness. Children and the insane lack the irony of humor. Ironically, the great are sometimes called grown-up children. They are not. They are like everyone else only more so—like everyone else, but no one is like them.

Humor means seeing three sides of one coin.

Hall Overton's *Huckleberry Finn* failed utterly and for the same reason as my *Miss Julie*, these operas being two sides of one coin. Both composers miscalculated their language: Overton chose chromatic speech for an essentially uncomplicated exterior situation, while my speech was diatonic for a complex inner situation.

Dodecaphonism, inherently tense, has built in too many humorless Luluesque associations to be usable for a Mark Twain book despite its updating to center on Nigger Jim, while diatonicism, inherently relaxed, is incapable of illustrating madness, at least current madness (and Strindberg is more current than Twain). In theater style is all. Even calculated misplacements are risky.

Thus neither Overton nor I by nature of our language could translate the subject matter. Had we traded librettos we might have hit the jackpot.

Fakery in opera is more discernible than in other modern music's modes. Being so slippery in so many ways, particularly in reliance on words, opera cannot depend on rhetoric rather than on expressivity. Opera *must* depend on expressivity. It is hard to imagine one by Stockhausen, since he depends on philosophy, on extramusicality.

Yaddo
11 February

Mostly reading Willa Cather in the warm ease of the Pink Room, while out there lurks the sub-zero weather. But Alvin Ross is here too, pacifying and clever, and doing a still life of a marble cake the model for which, after a week, has, thanks to preservatives, turned hard as marble.

Quaker Meeting this morning with Aileen Ward and Elizabeth Ames. Elizabeth tells the story of Indians entering this very Meeting House with their tomahawks two centuries ago. When they beheld the worshippers, heads bowed in silent oblivion, they put their weapons aside and bowed their heads too.

15 February

Copland concert at Skidmore. Despite the fact that Aaron's Aaron, the performances are no more excellent than when I'm in a similar situation. Aaron, humble star, likeably avoids clamoring students to confer with me & Alvin. Alvin in four séances has finished my portrait to replace the one from 1943. Missing JH. Little work.

New York
24 February

JH's Saturday mornings are passed playing organ at Temple where many an American Jew will not permit an American Gentile to voice an opinion (other than favorable) about Israeli justice—as though that distant war were not a dire concern for Gentile too. (Jews technically are more anti-Semitic than Gentiles. The Jews we mostly know, of Slavic or German descent, bitterly hate the truly Semitic Arabs.)

God sets us a bad example. Those Holy Wars. An Indian Giver of Life.

28 February

Mitchell Wilson's funeral. Vast throng, in which Stella keeps herself admirably invisible.

Another visit to Lillian Libman at the Hurok offices. She will definitely organize and manage two concerts of my music planned for next November in Tully Hall. She feels, however, that it would be prestigious to present these under Hurok's name, assuring me that Hurok himself is thrilled at the notion ("He loves composers! After all, he presented Glazunov, Rachmaninov, and Stravinsky." But how and when?). The hitch is that we must use only Hurok artists. Now, even assuming that any luminous name on the roster would contribute services for the love of new music, none of his singers knows how to sing songs.

The New York City Opera's presentation of *Pelléas et Mélisande* is the best I have ever seen, here or in Paris. Its quality was unquestionably due to the internationality of talents, people who, precisely because they were not French, made a superhuman effort to enter the French brain of the past (of the Dark Ages of Bluebeard, from whom Mélisande had escaped, and of the Paris of 1900, where Claude Debussy lived and loved), an effort not always made by the French who inadvertently sabotage their masterpieces. Frank Corsaro placed the singers in a decor of *art nouveau* (which the French call "modern style") from which New York's Patricia Brooks emerged as an appropriately nubile Mélisande, Canada's André Jobin as an unusually masculine Pelléas, while Viennese Julius Rudel conducted the piece like the symphony it is, a violent reverie, an instrumental tissue with words superimposed.

Elsewhere, Corsaro's knack for turning the stalest chestnuts into *marrons glacés* has earned him the position of the City Opera's chief caterer. Yet, when the chips are down, he is more brash than brave. His directorial reputation is based on presenting "other ways" for the tried and true. Even his *Susannah* was a second look at what had become an established staple. To give hypodermics to old war-horses is to take safe chances in the public eye: what may be lost in taste and tradition may be gained in energy and acclaim. True risks—those inevitably run by directors of courage—are in new works. Yet one feels that under Corsaro's guidance even a world premiere would be an alternate version.

Sans date

Scenario. Curtain rises on an exquisite eighteenth-century drawing room. People of quality assemble around a pink keyboard at which is seated a young lady in a powdered wig. She executes an ugly étude in the style of Schoenberg. Everyone smiles, claps politely, withdraws. Curtain falls.

"Beauty Limps": title for an essay on masterpieces. (Did Cocteau say it, *lu beauté boite*, when the dark angel descended the stairs in *Blood of a Poet*?) Achievement of perfection is for dressmakers, pastry cooks, or performers like Casals for whom the Tragic Flaw would be fatal. The hero, or so-called creative artist, can only strive for perfection. He never arrives. (How far can this be pushed?)

A blocked artist is not an artist. Whoever says, "I shall store this away, let it swell and finally burst like an orchid or a pimple," is not an artist. An artist does not *store away*, he has no future, he blooms now.

4 March

JH's Poulenc concert at the Chapel, including four choruses from *Dialogues des Carmélites*, as grand with organ as with orchestra.

6 March

Visit to Stella Adler, sitting Shiva and staggeringly beautiful. After she received Lulla (who emerged weeping from her *tête-à-tête*) but before she received me, I glimpsed Stella disappearing down the hall in a long white robe, then returning in a long black robe. Very actressy. Yet I felt from the core that she meant it when she grasped both my hands and said there was nothing more to live for.

27 March

Recital last night by Steber at which she sang my old *Alleluia*, and everything else on the all-American program, if not as gorgeously at least as convincingly as in the old days. Party later chez Tobin.

Noël Coward died this morning, making me feel more bereft than seems fitting. He was among the golden few who, though seen but rarely, are so giving, so volatile, so *there* (not looking beyond you at someone more important), that their brief presence is more memorable than certain dear friends enjoyed daily. The quality can't be faked, can't be bought.

29 March

We gave a cocktail today for the following: Mother & Father, Rosemary and three of her children, Janet Flanner and Natalia Murray, Lillian Libman,

Ellen Adler, Shirley, Robert Phelps, Hélène Rémy, Arnold Weissberger and Milton Goldman, Patrick O'Higgins, Hortense Calisher. Four huge quiches, salad, lots of fruit incl. strawberries, and my Orange Cake.

7 April

Death of Picasso. Jane Wilson's exhibit. Jerry Lowenthal records the Piano Concerto in Louisville today with Mester. *A Place in the Sun* on TV.

There are no angelic choirs; there are only the choruses of Bach and Palestrina sung by men. Those choruses are not preparations; they are the last and only word. They are impersonations of what does not exist. Men sing like angels, but where are the "real" angels and what do *they* sing? If there were real angels, we would not have invented Bach and Palestrina. There is no God, there are only proofs of God, and Bach and Palestrina are the word.

Unlike *Superstar* or the Beatles whose propaganda power derives from lyrics attached to the tunes, Stockhausen's propaganda power lies in words extraneous to the music, that is, in program notes which are ultimately dispensable. Except that his program notes *are* the music.

Stockhausen, too, has sold out. He plays to sold-out houses.

Albuquerque
14 April

(Father's in Alaska.) I've been three days at the University of New Mexico. This afternoon the octogenarian composer, Dr. D. J. Robb, drove me to Santa Fe via an Indian reservation. "Look at that beautiful river," said Robb as we passed a brackish pond. "Those gentle faces," as we passed hate-filled stares. "They love us," when clearly they loathed us, as he barged unbidden into their quaint but desperately poor little church. In Santa Fe we had lunch at The Compound where—just as New Orleans reeks of Tennessee Williams, not the other way around—everything sparkled with Stravinsky, because I've just read Horgan's book.

The future, our sweetest possession, melts like ice cream, so the past, though unbearable, sustains us. Aging into the seventies is the bug ascending an ever-thinner reed which bends toward the ground. Dying is the rope dancer vanishing into the sky. Stravinsky has gone and the world's weight's changed.

Britten may be a "lesser" composer than Stravinsky. The fact remains that to vote between the single most extended work (as the clock ticks) of each man, *Peter Grimes* and *The Rake*, is to elect *Peter Grimes*. Britten's opera in all ways surpasses Stravinsky's: technically, coloristically, literarily, and operatically. It is more rewarding for singers, more "inspired," more moving. If both pieces are pastiches—and they are—Britten's works and Stravinsky's doesn't. Which is not to say that *Grimes* is superior to *Sacre*. But staged opera was not Stravinsky's forte. *Rossignol* and *Mavra* are his weakest scores.

15 April

Some notes before leaving:

Concert of my pieces at the university last night. Professional. Ditto the speeches, and also the Albuquerque Orchestra which on Friday did Beethoven's Ninth, the first piece of junk in the grand style.

Kids on campuses ask: "Why don't you use words like the Beatles' and compose music like theirs if you think they're so good?" But I do, why don't you listen! But I don't, why should I, since they do it so much better? I speak my language. I wear saddle shoes.

Teaching sterilizes. After the first year you repeat yourself, and end up believing what you say. I often say that I write music because no one else quite provides what I need to hear. (Not that I need to hear my own music, once it's done, more than once.) But I also compose from a sense of failure, which is probably true of any artist.

I've not composed to "express" myself since early youth. I do it now to make a living—it's all I know—and to keep a clear conscience, to one-up myself. Nothing I've made is perfect, or even good. My so-called best songs seem now an assemblage of concession and imitation. Every work is a new try at what has continually failed.

One aspect of intelligence lies in perception of unexpected similarities, fatal affinities. The amateur sees faces in the clouds, the artist sees clouds in faces. The retreat from standard relationships may seem dubious to outsiders for whom Picasso's faces, Pollock's clouds become frauds. Others will find a rapport even between Picasso and Pollock, as the mill turns full circle unviciously. The scientist finds unlikely relationships and makes them stick. The artist finds unlikely relationships and makes them *seem* to stick.

Amateurs think about meanings, professionals think about means. The beginner's art is a bull session and his social life is very serious. The established artist, taking content for granted, worries (secretly) about technique, while socially he gossips, discussing art mostly as economics.

Skill is suspect when mediocrity is the rule: good writing seems sheer affectation. Economy is deemed poverty by the long-winded. Now, the core of any philosophy can be shown in a phrase, yet such a phrase (the preceding one, for instance) sounds like a mere epigram to the unwashed.

Credibility gap? But there are limitless concepts of Truth which, if it really existed, would be dull, dry, and sad. A politician's duty is to be un-ambiguous; his statement need never be "open to interpretation," for politics is a simple business. But a composer is necessarily ambiguous; his statement is never inarticulate, but *too articulate* for words. He always says what he means, though he never means what he says. It is Nixon's business to tell the truth. It isn't mine. My business is to speak the truth.

Some deplore the *déjà entendu* of discs; I rejoice in it. Ninety times, unfatigued, I have thrilled at the identical twist in a Benny Goodman phrase, at a dragged triplet on Kincaid's flute, at the elegance of Toscanini's slight tenuto—twists and triplets and tenutos that were never quite so good because they were never quite the same when heard live.

As to the intellectualization of music, or rather, the diagnoses around music, when we hear what's talked about we realize that proof of the pudding is not in the recipe. If expressive content in art equals flavor in cooking, today's tasteful music is monosodium glutamate.

Critics of words use words. Critics of music use words.

Performer. His value lies in what can be learned from him. One performer invests those chestnuts with revitalized fragrance. Another makes even the new sound stale because he lacks the vulnerability that is the artist's earmark. Beauty must be ugly to last. He is boring because he is perfect.

Perfection?

After a point, most pianists spend their lives playing the same pieces which they polish and "re-think." Do polish and re-thought produce finer results, or just different?

Suppose an accomplished pianist decides to restrict his repertory to one work. Suppose he practices only Chopin's "Etude in Thirds" five hours a day for twenty years. During those years he examines all editions, occasionally changes a fingering, and may even alter the tempo as he apprehends the various ways to skin his rabbit. Suppose after twenty years he has not grown tired of the Etude. Will he play it better than at first? If he *has* grown tired, *can* he play it better? Is there better? Did Casals play a Bach suite or Serkin the "Hammerklavier" better at forty than at twenty, at sixty-five than at thirty-two or ninety? Prove it. Progress does not equal improvement unless an advancing cancer can be said to improve. How often do our giant classicists force those they interpret to grumble in their graves?

New York

23 April

Spent the afternoon listening to Eugene practice his Debussy group. Those French waters washed me back to Lake Michigan's adolescent waves, waves which were *La Mer* in 1937, and swept me then to Vuillardian parlors where, muskily submerged in *vin rouge* and fumes of Camembert, the composer composed *Khamma*. The Paris I miss most is the Paris of my imagination before I lived there. But it can be summoned clear as a snapshot of the Parc Monceau, and the sound of a series of secondary sevenths is enough for the snapshot to smell of almond leaves.

Offended by the piano playing for *Dances at a Gathering*, Eugene remarks, "Imagine how it would have been with Rubinstein—although with Rubinstein we wouldn't need any ballet." How would Chopin react to the assumption that his works are sacrosanct, vulgarized by Robbins's use for dance? Vulgarity is a part of art (as Beethoven proves), and yes, Robbins is vulgar. So is Chopin. The shock to E. is the superimposition of twentieth century vulgarity on nineteenth-century vulgarity. So much Chopin came from dance!—mazurkas, waltzes, tarantellas, polonaises. Other of his music is sprung from acts of motion: a Barcarolle to inspire boat rowers, a Berceuse to accompany cradle-rockers. You say these forms have been stylized by Chopin? Must they be heard only in recital by rows of motionless freaks? Is it corrupting to move with the sound? The highest compliment a composer can hear: You make me want to sing and dance. All music, from the burial hymns of old Egypt to the urbanities of Varèse, rises from the vocal cords and from the human torso in contraction and release. And musical performance that does not provoke kinetic response is not worth the trouble.

Shirley is distressed when I say that the best music must be nasty as well as beautiful, that it partakes of the gutter as of the altar. It is not a question of whether Beethoven took from the gutter, but of whether the gutter is bad. For Shirley it's bad. For me it's just another place. Gregorian chant had the best of both possible worlds.

There's good music with charm but no character: Federico Mompou, Reynaldo Hahn, John Gruen. There's good music with character but no charm: Beethoven, Bruckner, Berlioz. There's good music with both: Chopin, Falla, Mussorgsky. Now, the music with both is not generally considered the greatest. Is there good music with neither?

Two-day symposium on "Music in the Church" at Saint John the Divine, with Iain Hamilton, Charles Wuorinen, et alia. I read aloud my "Notes On Sacred Music," taking pleasure in stating I don't believe in God. Nobody cares.

Noël Coward memorial. (Skits by Tammy Grimes, Helen Hayes, and such nonsense.) I'd have liked to leave early, since *he* wasn't there. Walked part way home with Lucia Davidova. Proctological concern continues. *Pure Contraption* and *The Final Diary* are both delivered to Holt. Feeling depressed. Seeing people constantly.

To place Beethoven on a pedestal is to miss his point. Place Reynaldo Hahn there instead, for he was ethereal and removed. Beethoven is too all-embracing for the preciosity of pedestals.

The looks of a performer while performing prove something. If he is the real thing, though otherwise ugly he will project an appeal while playing. An artist at his easel oozes sex. Concentration on something not himself is a composer's one refuge from ego, and only a body freed of ego can bear scrutiny. Such carnal purity is never apparent on the faces of audiences at concerts or galleries, who display the stupor of ecstasy or just plain boredom; nor is it apparent in second-rate performers who, with their respect of art, are simply worshipful, hence ego-ridden.

Narcissus was not sensual. Heaven forbid that genius not be ego-oriented! But the *act* of genius is selfless.

(Yet in my old diaries I find the following entries: "Amsterdam, 1951. With great sweetness Julius [Katchen] says that he can never play the Andante of Brahms's F-minor Sonata without an erection, and once during a concert he quite literally came.

"1958. Visit to Mitropoulos, New York Hospital. . . . He maintains that the orchestra members are his children, his 'barnyard of chicks,' whom he fucks collectively at each performance.")

JH for a decade pondered Messiaen's *La Nativité*. Now he proposes to omit an added sixth in one of the final chords, on the grounds that Messiaen would no longer hold to such a cliché. Yet that added sixth may be just what Messiaen most clings to and has never questioned.

It is not trashiness that an artist rejects, or even sees, in his own work, so much as loose seams. He may hate the frame, not the picture. Nothing is riskier than to ingratiate yourself with an artist by showing that you love his work enough to suggest improvements.

Hearing. We do not know how music of the distant past was heard, nor yet of the recent past, nor do we even know how current friends hear single sounds, much less how they hear phrases. We can compare performances; we can define differences between them, but not how we are hearing them.

I love David Del Tredici's new wild *Pot Pourri* for chorus, soprano, rock band, and large orchestra. But what I love there he ignores. I hear long lines where he intends jerks, laughs where he asks for tears. Elsewhere he uses intact Bach's *Es ist genug*. Ever since Berg's fiddle concerto—which David professes not to know—brought us this chorale, it has beguiled me, not for those "enigmatic" progressions but for the straightforward jazz of measures 12–14. The third beat of measure 13 is clearly a blue note, if the phrase is heard as E-major. To David, who hears the phrase in A, that beat is a mere subdominant. If *we* hear it differently, how then did Berg hear it? or Bach himself, who never knew the blues? We four composers may agree only as to the chorale's value, not its character.

We are more unanimous about the fact of merit than about the nature of merit. Tuning in on a Haydnistic piece we've never heard, we're sure it can't be Haydn, not because of the style but because of the quality. You and I concur on that quality but listen to it differently. Good music seems absolute, retaining goodness through myriad massacres.

My first compositional *trouvailles* were notations of misreadings of Bach. To this day the forty-seventh bar of the second movement of Mozart's K. 309 is pure *Salome*, since I learned that sonata the same week I first heard Strauss's opera.

All of us hear all music by comparing it to all the other music in our ken. Such comparison is colored according to the time-space between juxtapositions. If we don't *know* any music beyond what we are presently hearing, our experience is clearly narrow—the case with, say, most rock freaks.

Affection for Lillian Libman and not for Sol Hurok led me to accept an invitation from the former to compose a fanfare for the latter. Since Hurok, in name only, is sponsoring my two concerts next November, it seemed appropriate to offer something built on that name only. The "something" was conducted this evening by Robert Irving as curtain-raiser to a gala at the Met honoring Hurok's sixtieth year of service to the Performing Arts. I called the fanfare *Solemn Prelude*.

Hurok seems not to recall me from one time to the next during my many visits to Lillian. Admittedly, concert managers have no concept of composers (their business is to sell performers, not what is performed), yet one would think that Hurok, with his old-world style, would feign some civility, given his presumed affinities with at least Glazunov. Meanwhile a composer has nothing to lose by blasting management. All an impresario might ever do for him is not to discourage some contracted performer from playing his music (rather than a war-horse) in hick towns.

Nothing about Hurok's vulgarity offends me beyond the pretense of being what he's not: a servant to art. Art (that is, the performing artist) is *his* servant. Now all performers are to an extent whores. Their pimps profit from this. But no pimp, not even Diaghilev, can contain the glamor of the wares he peddles, and the fact that Hurok should place himself above his performers is only too typical of the nonmusical hard sell of our musical world.

Hurok did not thank me for the brass piece because he didn't realize it was played. I'm quite modest though I try not to show it.

JH is being slowly fired, he who in the past two years—all enterprise and no budget—has held together as distinguished a music service as any in a Manhattan church. Now a new vicar has come, Father Williams, avid only to "swing with the times" (substituting rock and gospel for Monteverdi and Messiaen—why not just tear down the church and celebrate mass on the lawn?) and to replace the white choirmaster with a black one. This racism is unconstitutional, but how to prove that? There is less an artistic than a chemical clash. Williams who is black, feels that only blacks have the right to determine Whether Integration; that the service should be tuned to a black tonality. JH feels that it's his church too; that blacks (however one rates their suffering), just as they are Americans and therefore cannot be separatist Americans, must be Christians first and black Christians second or never.

Tomorrow I fly to Paris.

Paris
23 May–10 June

Years after I'd come back to New York for good, I wrote Virgil in Paris to ask if he'd seen my lost youth. "There's plenty of lost youth around," he answered, "but I don't know if any of it's yours."

A city's staying power—its ability to inflict pain—lies less in intrinsic beauty than in the force of faded friendships. Yet Chicago, the town where my every First Time occurred, is no graveyard; it is I who return from the grave into a vital center that has no room left. And so today in Paris, where once I loved and lived, I'm lonely not so much for dead friends as for my own mislaid corpse.

What hits most about a childhood spent in Hyde Park is not specifics, like walking home from the Midway age nine on ice skates because shoes had been lost and being limp with iodized welts for a week, but the sun, the heavy western sun flooding the concrete between Dorchester and Lake Michigan in any season. What hits most about seven French years, with so much to recall that's now congealed into a single flavor as hours and years bubble by, is not famous meals and heads tasted and observed, or heady hearts, but a single stifling afternoon reading *Howard's End* to the smell of tuberoses in Marie Laure's garden, place des États-Unis.

. . . as an adolescent scanning Balzac with a map of Paris to pursue the circuities of Vautrin. Brought up a Quaker, meaning in silence, needing noise, meaning music, and by extension, France (certainly not Germany) and the bejeweled Catholicism of the Mediterranean . . .

Like Guitry's *tricheur*, all unknowing I plucked that poison ivy for the Boy Scout, after he relieved himself in an Indiana glade, to use as toilet tissue. God guided my last Parisian visit in 1969 to say adieu to Marie Laure a month before she died. This week I re-return, three years after her death. Paris: what no longer contains Marie Laure. The presence of her absence is so everywhere apparent. Paris, filled by a void.

"I will love you forever" may be said by one person in honesty to many, since one person *is* many, though not at once. If he is many at once he could only collectively say "I will love you forever," and collectivity isn't love. Take a dozen cherished skeletons, grind to powder, add a quart of adrenaline laced with Chablis, strain and refine until the liquid thins down enough to immerse a metropolis with invisible atomic silk. Observe through tears from a distance of twenty light years, and you'll see Lutèce as it looks this morning.

38 rue des Épinettes. Of course it's as though I'd never left, rain and cold, but a warm supper chez Edouard Roditi and his circle of eccentrics—a mother hen in the Tower of Babel.

It's easier to love the stupid than the bright. The word *France* strikes terror in the hearts of homebound Americans, but there's no rent to pay, taxis are cheap and meals cost about the same while being superior, so I spend dollars on posies for ladies. Exhausted, constipated.

Sunlight peeks furtively now around corners in the seventeenth arrondissement where each humble grocery on the Avenue Saint Ouen upstages with bloody roses and giant tomatoes the equivalent on Madison Avenue. Protective wrath of Nora Auric over the telephone, she having misread a reference to Georges in *Critical Affairs*.

When people ask if during my years in Paris I ever met *Les Six* I like to say, "Yes, I knew all five." How? Through knowing their music—that's the way to a composer's heart. Thus in 1949 toward dawn on a stool in La Reine Blanche I hummed to Auric, whom I'd just met in the bar, themes for each scene of *Sang d'un Poète*. Thus when we played guessing games at Lise Deharme's with Milhaud I tested his tunes by heart to him—tunes he'd forgotten. Thus to Germaine Tailleferre I sang *Madame n'est pas là* on Pinget's poem. Thus to Honegger the theme from *Pastorale d'Été*. And thus to Poulenc. . . . It's not so much that I knew these people's music, or even that I knew it well, as that I was a Young American Composer who knew their music. A Y.A.C., then as now, was a contradiction in terms to the French, and if they weren't particularly interested in my music they were interested in my interest in theirs. And . . . not that I was their type.

I'm 5 feet 10½ inches and since age twenty have weighed seldom less or more than 150 pounds. Dark brown eyes and hair, though the latter was bleached during the early 1950s (the French still think of me as blond). Slim legs have turned skinny, though my shoulders remain good-shaped. Hands, especially the right one, begin to spout liver spots. Extreme nearsightedness such that I've turned—with glasses—quite farsighted, and can read now only with the naked eye. Externally slim ass (internally bloated with what would appear to be swelling brains) and fairly flat stomach. Small nose, selfish lips, as yet no double chin nor much gray hair, but sagging ears and eternal dandruff. Have never had a venereal disease. Was once extremely pretty if you like the type, which I detest. With magnetic charm, which others name crass monopoly, I pontificated forever, having long since coldly concluded that shyness is never rewarded and that I was no dumber than other pontificators in the room. Where's the silver infant who once monopolized by silence? who (so he thought) made philosophy futile in the face of lust? Longing at once to be guiltless and guilty, passive and active, ravished in flesh and dominating in mind, I simply never get laid.

My major weakness during the "Paris Years" was believing flattery (that I was cute, talented, etc.). My strength was in work. But if I never let flattery stand in the way of work, clearly I did work because I was flattered. After a point the goose of Encouragement is more needed than the gander of Fancy. Fancy is the *donnée* of any artist; obviously he would never have been encouraged if he had never produced to start with.

Certain behaviorists claim the contrary—that inside every banker is an artist struggling to get out—and their nurseries swarm with toddlers urged to "express" themselves. But where, pray, are the artists who get out? More cogent: Inside every artist is a banker struggling to get out.

Conversation is neither an art nor a graceful fashion for English-speaking peoples. Americans mean what they say though they sometimes struggle to say what they mean. The French do finally say what they mean though they seldom mean literally what they say. Despite their indirection, their metaphor and irony, the French are succinct; Americans, despite their one-track-mindedness, their clumsy longing for a bull's-eye, are convoluted. This dogma is French but I am American.

Marie-Louise Bousquet has finally died. No American who knew Paris did not know Marie-Louise: the very soil and fluid of two cultures, in her sandwiches and daiquiris, merged every Thursday at the sun-filled flat in Place du Palais Bourbon. American specialists, mainly of *Harper's Bazaar*, learned about general practice by drinking with the French. We met our countrymen (Jean Stein, Thornton Wilder) and those whose country we were visiting (Cartier-Bresson, Josette Day). Not that a party's as good as the guests; it's no better than the host. Knowing who she herself was, Marie-Louise had the freedom to learn about you, and that was great fun for her. But such salon life, never a part of America, is ended forever in France. Marie Laure, Marie-Blanche, now Marie-Louise—*les trois Maries*, as they were called—have flown the coop.

Of all the females of my generation I loved most, during the early fifties, Heddy de Ré. Brief hour in the Orangerie where Degas's *Absinthe* again reminded me of us then, then two hours with Heddy herself. Absent, still pretty, disappointing, asks me nothing of me after sixteen years and, with her friend, drinks Calvados, claims to have forgotten English.

Why when today's so dull should dredging yesterday prove less so? Yesterday, when as an adult I returned to Chicago—that sole shelter and thus sole menace of youth—I was struck not by what my mind once learned there but by what my body had felt: smells of leather in Woolworth's Bookstore, of summery debris in October underscoring anxieties of forgotten homework, and especially of sex forcing itself from behind every door on Kenwood, on Blackstone, in Mandel Hall: every bush in Jackson Park seemed witness to our virginity perpetually lost and found, as every bar on Rush Street hosted our sprees.

Paris becomes the Chicago of my maturity, a maturity which shows nothing of "culture." There from the Reine Blanche (Christ, it's a milk bar!), kidnapped to Morocco by Guy Ferrand twenty-four years ago this month.

Once with Heddy, as we drank deep into the night, we listened wide-eyed while the now-defunct Robert LeMasle (one of several self-proclaimed models for the *Nightwood* doctor) declared: "Hangovers are needles thrust full length into unanesthetized flesh, and I'm a tattoo from sole to scalp with no space left, yet I remember every one."

Friendship for Eugene Istomin led me to hear his Trio play the sort of program (all Brahms) I rarely attend. That they should begin an hour late (because, as it turned out, Isaac Stern had overslept) and then perform routinely (except for Eugene's cohering excellence) didn't lighten matters, particularly since during the wait a couple in my overcrowded loge were necking with a sound like the squashing of hot peanut butter in armpits. Despicable public shows of love! What do they do privately then? In the Théâtre des Champs-Élysées the pleasure of newlyweds should dwell in the complicity of knowing what's coming later or what just came. But to come now, in the open, is to come for us—and we are less jealous than offended: it interferes with our rhythm.

Seventeen years since I permanently left Paris. In October 1957, the Claude episode closed, I returned to America "to start a career," as Virgil put it, revisiting France only in 1964, briefly again in 1969 and now in 1973. Yet during intermission people say, "It's been ages! Have you moved?" And in New York, meeting me for the first time, someone asks, "But don't you live in Paris?"

Slowly, into place de l'Alma, uphill, savoring and withholding, away from the Théâtre des Champs-Élysées (little in common now with the *gratin*, ignorant of our Watergate) into rue Freycinet, disturbed by the shadows. As though I were walking home, like ten thousand times before, with the intention of crying when I emerge into place des États-Unis. But home's now a huge hollow tombstone. How long did I stand there in the inky frost, watching the so-familiar leaves quiver so late in the night over the wall as I had watched the leaves outside Polignac's mansion fifteen seasons ago, watching the still, still, still house behind whose boarded windows no light flickered? All Paris has become a cemetery where this Magritte-like monument dominates and, finally, without life, looks foul. Quickly I walk away and will never return.

Sleepless night, dreams like daydreams, nocturnal daydreams. In blackness the door opened to Marie Laure's house, which became a box of sunshine. Entering there with the white-haired Roro, we walked among white roses wide awake, and way back there another door opened and four beautiful women emerged, two with blond and two with black hair. They strolled toward us but did not (or pretended not to) notice us. Returning through the house alone, I reached the first door which reopened back into this black bed. A cat whined continually. And as if that weren't enough, I kept getting ideas (mostly on how to contain French Music into a definition) and had to turn the light on to record them, then turn it off, then on. A sleepless night— *une nuit blanche*, as the French say.

Nuit blanche. Once in the dear dead days of long ago Gordon Sager visited the Turkish bath of Harlem. Next day he announced, "The only other customers were Caucasians. *J'ai passé une nuit blanche.*"

New York, with the singular virtue of expanse, lacks, by virtue of that virtue, the exterior intimacies of Paris. A French dusk, for instance, is heartwarming: On a rainy afternoon we watch the *tabacs* on the rue du Bac switch on their lamps and fill up with clients pausing for a *coup de rouge* on the way home; later we peek into windows where families sit down quarreling to their lentil soup; or, from indoors, in any season we look out onto passing heads of lovers and sycamore leaves and hear the clink of *boules*. In Manhattan we eavesdrop by phone, nor is it a city of easy cafés, of Peeping Toms, of (as Robert Phelps calls them) followers.

Dull brilliance of liquor, dull pleasures of a sauna, sharp dullness of health. If vice were replaced by intelligence! Yet in a sense, vice *is* intelligence. Along the mall in Central Park, observe the homely Hare Krishna youngsters dancing their uninventive dance. (Mother drops coins in their cup, then asks, "Now will you give me some coins for peace?" They look through her, uncomprehending, and dance off.) A few yards farther, see the health-nut kiosks replete with signs informing you what not to eat so as to "gain a heightened consciousness"—this accompanied by five simultaneous transistors blaring rock.

It proves little that no mutual friends visit her grave (they're permanent residents, after all), or that I, who never do such things, do. But always one to do things halfway I do not, in the taxi to the Cimetière Montparnasse, clutch the cluster of custard-colored roses dreamed of. Nor do I expect, as the caretaker leads the way, to end up at the Caveau Paine-Bischoffsheim (the Caveau Noailles being in another part of the forest) where, if you stand on tiptoe and peek through the vines you perceive not a quarreling family but, next to Marie Laure, the stone coffin of Oscar Dominguez. No morbid tone, no sensation of what Henny Penny called "The Distinguished Thing." Annoyance, on the contrary. To be dead is unlike you, animated witch. Come out from under there, be yourself! Your silence makes a wild noise in me now. You were the only French person who cared about America.

Satie's the most overrated of the underrated composers, yet when you speak with the avid Satilophiles you often discover they've never heard of *Socrate*, the composer's sole piece that might remotely aspire to grandeur, in itself and without quaint appendages, on strictly musical terms. Fifteen years ago Poulenc was in a reverse position but for the same reason: of all the overrated composers he was the most underrated. His piano miniatures and most harmless songs were done to death, yet the existence of his major works (meaning, for once, larger works—the religious and profane operas and cantatas) was ignored, at least in the U.S.A.

. . . like Gide who, the one hour in his life he lay with a woman (on the beach at Hyères, according to Marie Laure), sired a child, Poulenc became the father of a daughter.

. . . the rocky, inexpert French of those longtime expatriate females haunting, drunkishly rich, the rue de Rivoli in 1949. Esther Arthur, Mrs. Forrestal. A language when mastered is mastered in a year or less; the rest is nuance. Yet the nuance already caught by a native child of five will never be caught by you, foreigner. Gift for tongues is unrelated to gift for music.

We each speak our personal sub-tongue. Except for a widening vocabulary, there's no "improvement" past a certain point. Our French is our French. Desiring, when I first lived here, to transport my English to my French—to seek the inevitable equivalent for each Nedism—I merely applied myself. My French is as good as any foreigner's, yet in grade school, seeing no future in French, I was, despite my musical talent (my "good ear"), the worst in class.

From the window, *ô délire*, while writing, I can look over there into another morning window giving onto the court from the rue J. Keller where a man, mirror propped against the pane, shaves, stripped to the waist, biceps at play, black curly hair on scalp and chest, the works, *quoi!*—while behind in shadow the visage of a red-haired woman. The Paris of Gabin, which, having never been known, is most missed like—do you recall?—that May day in 1953 when Georges Geoffroy met James Pope-Hennessy for the first time, yet had dreamed of him the night before and in the dream reproached him for not appearing years sooner, so much time's wasted. . . .

Paris, the place where she isn't. Paris, a disease once had. There remains a glamorous contagion like the perfumed maze through which Gide's Theseus rambled. Heavy rain. Lunch chez Lily Pastré, prey now to gaps of memory, and Boris Kochno, so warm. The ease with which they speak of funerals. Boris retains the guile of alcoholics—their childlike wish to provide antidotes to being a pain in the neck. He's Russian too, of course. The past presses in like a mean tea cozy. I ache to be in this very room as it was years ago. Yet the room hasn't changed. Unless caught quick it's lost for good, but it's never quick enough, and always wrong. Rain. Not a foreign country but a homeland whose patois I've forgotten. Two Mormons just knocked on the door.

The Épinettes is a cobblestone quarter sufficient unto itself, as remote from central Paris as . . . Wooden shoes, window boxes with leeks and zinnias of every color, a bandstand in the adjacent rue Collette. Am vaguely superfluous, like those French journalists living permanently in New York, but are invisible to New Yorkers. Except that their *raison d'être* is to report on the present; mine is the past that grows more labyrinthine than the future. Everywhere mirrors in which to seek a friendly reflection, always more distant, less intriguing.

Robert Phelps, lunch in nearby bistro, rue Lantiez, then, beginning with the Cité des Fleurs, a seven-hour promenade. Manic and vicarious, Robert plays the role of professional loser whereas he's a true winner of sorts, being unique in what he does, which he does well: to fix situations through the lens of the brief word: the French gift, bestowed on a Yankee, of the spoken photo. But the gift's not no-strings, flashed in my vision. Unrecapitulatable is to be these three things: in love, in Paris, in your twenties. Poor Robert cannot be twenty. He sees the city as I saw it then, inconveniences are quaint, all crotches godly, ashcans are Greuzes and advertisements pure Corneille. Thanks alas to (they say) Madame de Gaulle not one *pissotière* remains, so that particularly art-nouveau mystique which represented the compleat eroticism of a not-so-distant day's defunct for Robert.

He asks what three things I'm most ashamed of. Quick retort: (1) Sugar,

(2) certain sexual attitudes, and (3) my best songs—as though what feels good must be contemptible. Yes, expatriation does not make Americans more French, it makes them know increasingly how American they are.

One thing may lead to another but art runs faster than beauty, said Paul Goodman and Jean Cocteau. Well, art may run faster than beauty, but one thing leads to another. On April 3, 1952, the first time I ever was in Grasse, Charles de Noailles invited me and Marie Laure (his spouse) to lunch with Cocteau. Afterward the four of us visited Marie Laure's mother, Madame de Croisset, who lived in a nearby rust-colored stucco villa which contained a Pleyel, so that—at Marie Laure's insistence—I could play the ballet *Mélos* for Cocteau. I recall two things mainly: (1) On arriving, Cocteau announced to Madame de Croisset, "It seems like yesterday that I was bringing Marie Laure back from our outings." (He'd not been in this house since the summers of World War I when the adolescent Marie Laure began nursing the love-hate she never forsook.) (2) Rather than do it herself, Madame de Croisset rang for a servant to open the drapes in the *salon de musique*. Oh, there were other things too. (Cocteau wore a white leather jacket; drank straight gin before eating; talked movies with Charles de Noailles as though Charles cared. Wasn't there also a feeling that, although he'd probably made the brief trip from Cap Ferrat mostly to see me again and to hear the music— we'd met only once before—he was disappointed to find me in the company of the Noailles? As he said good-bye, taking his seat beside the curly-haired chauffeur of the white Porsche, he immediately drew forth a notebook and began to work, having already lost an afternoon with the likes of us.) But what is forever striking is that nothing is as (complex as) it seems. To discover that two people whose milieu is presumably identical have not met on home ground for thirty-five years! An outsider concludes that famous contemporaries spend their lives mutually hobnobbing. (When, the outsider might well wonder, do they do the work for which they're famous?) As for Madame de Croisset with the curtain, it was not I (a bourgeois American) but Marie Laure herself who later remarked, "Couldn't she have pulled it herself?" (M. L. added that she'd not realized Cocteau didn't know English. Her surprise surprised me: how could she not have known?)

That same year I first saw Nathalie Sarraute, at the Catalan restaurant, deep in conversation with a mutual friend, Dora Maar. Marie Laure and I watched from across the room. They later joined us. Sarraute appeared to be what I already knew Dora to be: a no-nonsense hardworking reasonable left-wing artist as contemptuous of frivolity then as women's liberationists are contemptuous of it now. Thus it seemed contradictory, a week later, to receive Sarraute's novel, *Portrait d'un inconnu*, amicably inscribed. Frivolous act.

Twenty-two years later, at George Braziller's in New York, I reintroduced myself to Sarraute, reminding her of that other time and place. She said: "You know, that's the last I ever saw of Dora." For two decades I'd assumed they were friends. Actually I know them both better than they know each other.

Dali exhibit. Exhausted, he now imitates himself to where only the signature, which literally never alters, breathes life.

Petit Palais, exhibit from Maoist China of ancient art works and crafts. Impossibly crowded and reeking. So with a catalogue I withdraw to a sunny cloister to examine photographs of the artifacts that surround me. (This trip's a macrocosm of the experience? In an actual teeming Paris I'm enlivened only by memories.)

Eugene's touching solicitude of ailing John Trapp as they cross Avenue Marceau, holding hands, on way to restaurant. Eugene disabused about Hurok. "Managers do little beyond providing a mailing address. Dates are gotten through personal contact." Professional criticism. My unfabulous but literal memory retains less what critics have written about me than about others. Even when good (even when bad), reviews of my work or words bore me. I already know, deeper than they, how good (bad) the work or words are. If the review itself is literature (Mazzacco on *Diaries* or Flanagan on *Cycles*), I'm more intrigued by how it's written than in what . . .

Five o'clock at Nathalie Sarraute's. In the late sunshine of her wide high parlor, a stone's throw from Marie Laure's, we talk pleasantly about our countries for five quarter-hours and drink Fresca. She doesn't feel cordial toward Susan Sontag (who once introduced her at the YMHA, then didn't stay to hear her speak), but loves Mary McCarthy. McCarthy and Sontag are the only American representatives in Paris at present, but I've yet to find a Frenchman who, in his darling insulation, has heard of either.

Sarraute, when I confess that *Tel Quel* and company is just too thick and cold, suggests I look into Butor's nonfiction, especially his words on music. And kisses me good-bye.

Hôtel Biron, gardens and nursemaids, specter of Rilke. Again, museum as environment, as place to inhabit, but only incidentally to look at pictures in. Rodin's pictures, superior to his strangled sculpture.

"Pour Ned Rorem avec une amitié et une admiration qui pour une fois est vraie." Does he recall having thus inscribed the flyleaf of his short stories in

July 1957? With the same eyebrow-raising candor I inscribed *Critical Affairs*: *"Pour José-Luis de Villalonga avec une amitié et une admiration qui pour une fois est vraie,"* presenting it to him last night in his Neuilly apartment, which has black walls and a mirrored floor, before we went forth with his very new youngish spouse, Syliane, not pretty but with *chien* in gold lamé turban and white lamé pants and plenty of gold-and-silver accessories, and whose baby (not José's) was born last month during a seven-minute labor. (*"Sept minutes d'horreur,"* she adds.) We dined at the Sept, which is "where one dines," and were joined by a Guy Monréal whom José had said *"meurt d'envie de te revoir,"* but who showed no sign of ever having heard of me. Despite this false situation—is it a Spanish situation?—one likes José for his unlikely combination of hyper-intelligence and hyper-chic, not to mention his kind, kind eyes with which through his sangría-colored glasses he once gazed down on us from the screen in *Giulietta degli Spiriti* and now gazed at me, while over there with a covey of young beaux dined ageless Danielle Darrieux in yellow. I'm not what Villalonga remembered; lacking *mondanité* now, I bored him.

Pop music, all of it, here is still in 3/4, so I grow testy, fevered, and they drive me home to the sticks of Épinettes. Retire late with sore gums, sore finger, sore foot.

Familiar streets, Varenne, Grenelle, with no longer a lustful rendezvous while waiting in the rain to cross with the green light—green fire, as the French call it—just dates with sentimental agony, for instance Lise Deharme, bejeweled, the same, all in orange. Invited for tea, yet offered nothing but her husband, Jacques Perrin, kept in a side room, and the plump pink pussycat. Nothing has changed except everything. Old friends are reruns with new wrinkles. Only JH, who phoned last night, remains always new.

Rereading Butor, his essay on music. The question is not does he date—everyone dates—but does he date well. Too soon to know, but not too soon to know he dates soon. His whole tonality, like that of current French music (if one can speak of non-tonal music as having tonality), seems a decade off. Of course this judgment is by the same American scale as in 1969 when I last reacted to the music of Paris, and different lands flower differently, some never. Russia never had painting, but did have the novel-of-frenzy and the music-of-frenzy a century before Germany. Germany never had cooking. Italy never had song (as opposed to aria) and England had no music at all during twenty-five decades, though her poems and pictures then . . . etc. *Mais Butor!* When non-practitioners (even Huxley or Mann or Proust) write about music, musicians (even second-raters) twitch. It's hard to learn exactly what point Butor is pushing as he speaks of music as a realist art. To a professional his essay reads (like Pound's essay on harmony) as an obvious conclusion reached the hard way—by hit or miss. Butor seems to have talked to Boulez or someone and then come home to note his own reactions, naive but hardworking.

"Music is indispensable to our life," says he. Why?

"One need not be concerned with political implications in music," says he, "whereas in other realms it's clearly established," etc. How?

In other realms, too, the stronger the politics the weaker the art.

Butor willfully refutes Stravinsky's notorious *mot*, "music is incapable of expressing anything," while alluding to all music as song. Now, all music is not song, but since all song is a musicalizing of words it does gain literary sense and "expresses" something. Yet Butor goes on to claim that unless we know the convention we cannot grasp more than a part. His statement's right but the conclusion is wrong—that "a man who knows nothing of classical Arabic can still delight in the calligraphy, but he resembles a museum viewer who can contemplate only the shadows of statues." There is no single way to love anything; but as soon as we *comprehend* a language we lose its beauty, visual and sonic. A Frenchman can no longer *hear* French.

". . . transcription . . . the possibilities of literal imitation which music possesses are vastly richer than the onomatopoeias of spoken language." Butor is speaking of musical grammar which has "acquired an enormous range of flexible discourse: the noises of machines in Varèse, the songs of birds in Messiaen." Yes, but do Messiaen's birds fool real birds? Are real machines taken in by Varèse? In seeking "the fundamental connection that unites music and words" Butor becomes the hopeless researcher. Why not seek the fundamental disparity (for if the arts all "meant" each other we'd need only one), or posit a thesis on the rapports between rhythmic shapes and colors (though not meanings) of a given nation's music—which came first, the talk or the tune? "If I hear a Schubert song without understanding German," says Butor, "I may find the music wonderful . . . but only when I have understood the poem's meaning shall I appreciate its fitness to the words." Supposing another composer used the same text with equal, but contrasting, fitness? If Butor insists on "that formative process we call rhyme, which in music is generalized into recapitulation, variation, development," how would he compare music to prose?

"Immature poets imitate; mature poets steal." Eliot in 1920.

Inexorable dirt of the nostalgia is less like Proust than like the going-back sequences in *Our Town* or *Un Carnet de bal*. Or is it that these works themselves are so far away, while the situations within them now return? More quickly than the sight or sound, one can retrieve the smell and taste of a *flic* or *ouvrier* long ago adored and now doubtless decrepit or dead. First hot days, daffodillian, and prenubile girls, as they always have in this season, like white bats swarm the byways squeaking offensively in first-communion garb. First hot evenings, orchidian, and muscled paragons, as never before in old seasons, like butterscotch statues avoid the streets in favor of the working-class gay bar, rue Davy, in their *salopettes*. And one goes to bed, alone, disturbed.

Long ride through torrential downpour to Villejuif in Jacques Dupont's car with Sauguet back-seat-driving all the way. (The reward was Jacques's décor for *Les Contes d'Hoffmann*, yet only the French could feel rewarded, as the French do, about a new production of *Les Contes d'Hoffmann*.) They tell me of my "enemies." Sauguet's right-wing royalism is too extreme to take seriously, yet oozes (as how can any conviction not?) onto his music, sometimes profitably (like Wagner's beliefs) as in *La Voyante* and the *Cello Concerto*, sometimes hatefully, as in . . . Conversations do give hangovers, but they don't make you vomit.

We read papers in the subway; they read books.

Nora Auric has retained a kind of beauty like that of a statue in a garden, fashioned first so skillfully by man, but carved and curled thereafter by nature, by mellowing dews and healthy mold and lively rot. She is alarmed by this diary, mistakes it for autobiography, chides me for being démodé with words like *surrealist*, and yes, no doubt I've hurt them all. And yes, I play at being "older" because of course I don't feel older.

Tired of being tired, do the old welcome death as the young welcome sleep? I think not. The young despise going to bed. And the old think always in terms of tomorrow, even of "tomorrow when I'm dead."

A diary is harmony, a memoir is counterpoint. My words are vertical smacking isolated chords which describe, as snapshots describe, quick moments. But even the horizontal narrative misrepresents, since it's only one man's fancy. (Yet what does it misrepresent?)

What now at almost fifty have I made that counts? The future's not ahead, it's here. Let's go home and work.

New York
11 June

Earlier this afternoon as I sat, three thousand wet miles from where now I sit, at Orly, waiting for Air France's flight 077 to waft me back to this younger land, my eye was struck by a headline in another traveler's *International Herald Tribune*: "U.S. Pulitzer Playwright Inge Is an Apparent Suicide at 60." On the plane I read the obit, and during the whole flight the sentiment of the past French fortnight was effaced by the fact of Bill Inge alive and dead. Going over old letters from Bill I come upon this, written in California:

> Probably you'd better make me anonymous in connection with A.A. I don't care personally, but it's best for the welfare of the organization, which I do respect enormously. I did break anonymity once in an interview for *Esquire*, and I've regretted it. After all, should I ever die drunk or decide to kill myself, it would hurt the organization. It's a responsibility I don't want.
>
> I'm so sorry to have missed seeing you out here. In fact I feel rather cheated. Do come again, and let me know in advance. After all, I've no plans for killing myself, at least very soon. I work pretty intensely and have the most quiet of pleasures.

The date was June 2, 1967.

How did I first know Isherwood? We had corresponded a little in the early 1950s apropos of the pages on pacifism in *The World in the Evening*, but we actually met only in 1961 at Bill Inge's Sutton Place apartment (now occupied by Arnold Weissberger). Don Bachardy was present also, and him I saw several times during the following weeks. I got to know them both better during my first trip to California the next summer. Inge had moved out there too. I recall their asking him about Edward Albee, and Inge telling them (with no acknowledgement that I had introduced him to Edward) all there was to know, like Francis Robinson today who answers all questions, no matter to whom they're addressed. And how did I know Inge? From one of Leo Lerman's big parties around 1958. And how did I know Leo? Leo contends it was in the mid-1940s, but that I was too drunk then to have remembered.

12 June

When Camus claimed that the primal philosophical premise—the question to be settled before further discussion—was that of suicide, of whether life were worth living at all, he skipped a point. If life were not worth living, who would bother to discuss even that question? And surely those successful suicides, of sound mind and body, should be consulted after the fact. The first premise should be whether the question of suicide merits discussion. If it does, discuss it only after consulting the dead.

Thus the initial concern is not whether life's worth living but whether death's worth dying. When it kills, suicide fails. True success is to come

back, to have your cake and eat it. Mishima's cake took the form of an international press release, yet he couldn't eat it since he lost his head. Still, like
Marilyn, he acted out a universal dream by bidding good-bye before too
late, at the height of power and beauty.

Suicide as an art form. Mishima at his peak dies publicly for what he feels to
be truth. Truman Capote at the ebb of his power kills himself publicly for
what he knows to be non-truth. Where Mishima grows ennobled, Capote
shrivels (if a toad puffed up with hot air can be said to shrivel). His sketches
of others are ultimately harmless, but the unwitting self-portrait is putrid as
Dorian Gray's.

All that Truman touches turns to fool's gold. A book may or may not be a
work of art, but it's not for the writer to say so, or even to know so. An artist
doesn't "do art," he does work. If the work turns out as art, that's determined
by others after the fact. Art and morality aside, Truman's work can't work. A
work which names real names but whose author is fictitious? An author must
be true, his characters fictitious.

Yes, the suicides that don't kill you are like keeping your cake. But an artist
too has his cake and eats it. He suffers but is appreciated for his suffering,
and this very appreciation is an appeasement, a parole. Is the pain thus less
intense, less aimless than an anonymous death in an internment camp?
Does a rich person feel less ache, in the absolute, than a poor person with
the same malady?

Art and unhappiness are unrelated. Because an artist sees the truth as a
way out, and can do nothing, he is unhappy. Because he is seen seeing the
way out, he is happy. And he often is willing to market his misery, sweep his
madness onto a talk show and laugh at his own tears. Perhaps finally the
greatest intelligence is an ability for joy. But joy in our land is equated with
money. (It is a truth universally acknowledged that a single man in possession of a good fortune must be queer.)

Unhappy people are all alike; a happy person is happy in his own way.
Every aphorism is reversible. Surely nothing's more monotone than misery,
even the misery of philosophers and especially of lovers, whose individuality dissolves into uniform tears dampening their staunchest friendship. Unhappiness is a privilege of the young, the interresemblant young. But happy
people are as unalike as snowflakes, though more . . . more elastic. Happiness, a prerogative of the wise, rejects nothing. Happiness cannot intrinsically lead to unhappiness any more than clarity comes of navel-gazing, but
it can lead to ecstasy, even to death. Did not Olivier in *Les Faux Monnayeurs*

declare that suicide alone was comprehensible after reaching such heights of joy that anything afterward must become a permanent letdown?

Is even suicide worth it? The small comfort of art. Art has even less "meaning" than life. Art does not outlast life. We've not the least notion of what Bach meant to Bach. Art salves loneliness perhaps, but is no cure for cancer.

13 June

Nausea at the news of a friend's death is balanced by guilty twinges of expectancy on turning to the obits: the disappointment when "nobody" today is commemorated. Yet for survivors each death brings the adventure of a new start. With one less acquaintance to distract them, the road is cleared to fresh arrangements. The world's weight's changed. But soon these losses announce that they're just that, losses, potholes never to be filled, and those ever more numerous dead hail us with one moan that won't soften as it recedes, but grows more touching, ice clear, wished for, out of reach, adorable, tough.

20 June

Admittedly in the case of extended vocal works the searching for and choosing of texts is half the battle. But I've spent *six months* agonizing over what to use for the midwestern oratorio. As usual, JH comes to my aid, after shuffling through the morass of disconnected poems I've been trying to cohere with scotch tape. "Who counts?" he asks. Paul Goodman. "Has Goodman written sequences?" Yes, the *Little Prayers*. That's that. I'll use fifteen of them for two solo voices, huge chorus (i.e., the combined choruses from eleven colleges in Iowa and South Dakota), and orchestra.

People sometimes ask why I don't set myself to music. I set words to music I feel can take a change. As a composer of songs I don't seek to improve words so much as to reemphasize them—to alter their dimension. Music can't heighten the meaning of words, only change their meaning (unless to heighten be a form of change). Occasionally the words benefit from the change; although they might not inherently *need* this change, I must feel that they need it.

Now, to write words with the intention of setting them would be to write words I intended to change. Only a bad text could emerge from so inhibiting a task. Nor could I musicalize words I had written at another time and for their own sake, since those words would not exist if I had been able (at that other time) to express their sense in music. As for composing words and music simultaneously, that is a game for precocious children, and presupposes a third party beneath the skin of the composer-poet: the performer. Ballad-eers are triple personalities dealing in short forms (or repetitive narra-tives). The mere dual personality, the non-performing composer-writer, usually deals in large librettos which he writes as he goes along. Menotti, Blitzstein, Tippett, Nono.

There is already a presumption in a composer who sets a poet to music. To direct this presumption toward his own prose would be presumptuousis-simo.

24 June

Myrna Loy is not the first person I'd ever have expected to become friends with. But when asked to "escort" her (in black tie at 2 P.M.) to the Libby Hol-man memorial in Stamford yesterday I was thrilled. She was punctual and pretty in green & yellow silk, her red hair coiffed squarely as of yore. Driv-ing to Connecticut, we talked about Roosevelt (whose favorite actress she was), movies (especially *Stamboul Quest*, the first of hers I ever saw), music (which she doesn't pretend to know about, but like most secure people—and most good talkers—she's a good listener), and Libby. I reminded her that we had chatted for a minute at a party at Libby's around thirteen years ago, and was surprised to learn that was the only time the two women ever met, as with Sarraute and Maar. Actually I know them each better than they know each other. At Treetops the house and grounds swarmed with rich people who never knew Libby, and Anita Ellis dutifully attempted *Moanin' Low* and other Holmaniana. A cool sense of intrusion on the House of Jon-quils, which only yesterday seemed so warmly livable. (Quandary: Libby bequeathed the estate to Boston University without taking into account maintenance and taxes.) In the limousine back to New York Myrna removed her shoes and told me the story of her life, without a word of gossip, and I kept thinking: behind those eyes—what she knows. After I dropped her off I found she'd left a pair of fawn suede gloves.

Mother and Father come to dine tonight, our traditional Sunday. Visit from Gianni Bates to take a picture for the cover of *Pure Contraption*.

2 July

Weekend chez Morris Golde at Water Island. Twentieth day of rain. Read-ing *A Room of One's Own*. This afternoon, sun. Death of Betty Grable. Morris's *désintéressé* devotion to all the arts, if almost too unprejudiced, is unique in its uncompetitiveness. His suggestions, coming as they do from a non-practitioner, are keen. It would not have occurred to me to set John Ashbery without Morris's prodding.

My need for poetry is utilitarian. I read it not for pleasure but to keep abreast of friends' work or to seek texts for music. I don't dislike poetry, though it is hard for me. Because I cannot understand it I make songs of it. (Did Schumann need poetry for itself alone?)

The only thing bad about songs in English is bad English.

At a party I tell John Ashbery that, having recovered from a love affair, I don't intend to start over. "I'm tired of being shit on."

With concerned disbelief John replies, "You *are?*"

At a party I run into Kenneth Koch for the first time in years. "Haven't seen you in a coon's age."

With an open smile Kenneth replies, "It's been longer than that."

After the party for *The Paris Diary* Frank O'Hara tells Joe LeSueur who tells Joe Adamiak who tells me that my journal "reads like *The Alice B. Toklas Cook Book* without the recipes."

The verbal style of the so-called New York poets resembles to a T their written style. They speak to everyone including each other as though reciting lines from their own plays. Because, precisely, this style attracts me while excluding me, I take revenge (like the cuckoo who lays her eggs in other people's nests) by setting the style to music. Each setting provokes a grave contretemps with the poet, while the few remaining poets I've not set implore me.

6 July

Nancy Mitford is dead. With less shock than resignation (death's no longer surprising), I did what I do ever more often: quieted the ghost by rereading old letters and reanimating old pictures. I like to think that Nancy, who wasn't partial to Americans, was fond of me during our daily summer promenades in the magic hills of Hyères in the mid-1950s. It's hard to imagine that athletic stride, sarcastic laughter, and inventive cleverness as forever stilled.

Why do people write books and music?

To become famous.

Not for self-expression?

That need has worn pretty thin by the time they turn professional. Self-expression is primary: making paper dolls or cherry pies. The reward is appreciation, everyone's first need.

Isn't fame a form of appreciation?

Maybe, but appreciation isn't a form of fame. Housewives don't ask to become famous for their cooking, nor husbands for their wheeler-dealing. With an artist, fame can be separate from appreciation, even from understanding (if he's great, how can he be "understood"?). Fame can be divorced from power too, and this is a twentieth-century phenomenon. Rulers of yore thought of glory less than of force, while Bach thought in terms of doing a job. A movie star has less power than the studio chief.

Why is Zsa Zsa Gabor famous? Is she an artist? Can an artist today not be famous? Could he be urged by humanitarian motives? Would he produce if fame were not his goal?

No.

Britten and Salinger shun fame?

They only shun peripheral vulgarities of fame.

There is no good taste or bad; there's taste or lack of it. Tasteful versus tasteless. Tasteless as opposed to indiscreet.

Signs posted in European trains describe in four languages the nature of nationalities:

> PRIÈRE DE NE PAS SE PENCHER
> E PERICOLOSO SPORGERSI
> VERBOTEN
> DO NOT LEAN OUT

The French keep within the bounds of taste, and are polite. Italians overflow the bounds, but explain. Germans avoid the bounds, and don't explain. Americans ignore the bounds.

If the worst you might say about a critic is that he lacks taste, the worst you might say about a composer is that he has taste—only taste. Taste is merely one ingredient of a creative recipe, and is dispensable to many great works. If taste garnishes the music of Rameau, Rossini, or Ravel (indeed, the entire

Latin sensibility), it is hardly the first element we think of in Beethoven, Strauss, or Ives.

Absence of taste is not fatal to an artist as it is to a critic. Taste presupposes a general, that is, comparative, knowledge, which any good critic needs. An artist cannot keep up with every trend and still get work done. Which is why Hollywood portraits of The Great depict *gaffeurs* who finally shame everyone by creating their masterpiece. The with-it artist (Lukas Foss, Jean-Louis Barrault) is convincing only if bandwagons are his normal means of travel. Well-rounded geniuses are as rare as any other kind.

If having taste means being well-rounded, it means discriminating, too, which paradoxically means delimiting. So taste automatically inhibits—again, good for critics, bad for artists. What the latter feel about the former is sheer bemusement, even when highest praises or subtlest diagnoses are offered. Critics find a meaning, then write it down; artists write "it" down, then find a meaning. Meaning, like taste, is a control which comes after the fact.

Creators thus seem narrower and broader than critics. They "know" less, yet of course they know more. Taste isn't their chief concern. Perhaps even intelligence is not a vital requisite for an artist.

Rhinebeck
26 July

Midweek sojourn at Tommy Thompson's. Lots of guests, incl. Newell Jenkins. Listening to Puccini; long walks; reading.

Auden notes concerning the Renaissance Man: "His attitude is always professional, that is, his first concern is for the nature of the medium and its hidden possibilities: his drawings are drawings, not uncolored paintings, his theater is theater, not reading matter in dialogue. . . ."

But those twentieth-century Renaissance men who touch on music touch on it as amateurs—Ezra Pound, Jean Cocteau, Lionel Barrymore. Noël Coward's pride in not being able to read music can be considered professional insofar as he "dictates" his notes, though his music's durability is no indication of professionalism in the poet's sense.

Elsewhere Auden states: "I myself do not believe an artist can entirely ignore the claims of the ethical, but in a work of art goodness and truth are subordinate to beauty."

Despite Polonius, truth and beauty aren't necessarily one. Yet people talk of the committed artist, as though commitment (to politics presumably) were a requirement for art, as though the hows and whys of art were choices and not dictates. Commitment will not make an artist special, yet being special is what makes an artist an artist. More relevant than the artist engagé would be the politician engagé who labors so that the state will become committed to art.

There is a difference between what an artist says in his art, and what he says he says in his art. Sure, he can be political, but his politics aren't always in his art. If they are, they shrink or expand into propaganda, because statements about actions are not the same as actions. Actions are more politically effective than rhetoric; an artist's statements are directed to the already convinced, and through his work. His actions are made through his body, in lecture demonstrations or street demonstrations. Actions may lead to death, statements never, surely not musical statements.

Music, even bad music, does not inspire ideological behavior. The regular beat of a march may impel men toward battle, but will it impel them away from battle?

Marlboro
29 July

In 1949, before emigrating to France, I was featured in a joint program with Leon Kirchner on the Composers Forum Series (promoted then by Ashley Pettis, who later became a monk). The press treated Leon as more "serious" than I. Now at Leon's warm behest I'm here at Marlboro for a week as one of three Visiting Composers. The other two are Leon himself (actually permanent, being staff) and Barbara Kolb. The site is not new to me, having been the property of Walter Hendricks's family in the 1930s when we estivated here annually during Father's conferences on The Cost of Medical Care. The main house of this little campus is indeed the one from under whose eaves I swiped that robin's egg forty years ago, and those Mock Orange bushes surrounding it are the source of young verses, O God. But now the property contains an assemblage of dorms and practice halls, and the emerging noises are those of any international conservatory, except that they are produced by first-raters.

The hundred nonpaying guests are all successful heterosexual Jewish instrumentalists under thirty. Composers being as anathema to performers as to the general public, Barbara Kolb and I feel like pariahs in Marlboro, albeit benevolent pariahs. Money being the yardstick, composers offer no threat to performers: a performer of the same age and reputation as a given composer makes ten times more.

Rudolf Serkin welcomes me with a bear hug and tears of gratitude. I'd have been more moved had I not seen this routine repeated with others. How crass to begrudge him what I lack, though one hears no whisper of French music, like papa like baby. Serkin sets the tone, that of nineteenth-century Germany with occasional forays into Janáček's Bohemia.

Casals master class. Flanked by a lustrous spouse, who with muscular tenderness rises occasionally to tune her husband's instrument, the Maestro attends young cellists during a heat wave. Boys don't interest him, yet to one bonnie lass (Sharon Robinson) he suggests with a chuckle, "Play more like a man." (Subdued hisses.) To pianists—the "accompanists"—not one word, as though Schumann's keyboard were a mere backdrop. After class, parasol in hand, he makes for his limousine surrounded by an entourage of fifty, including Serkin who lowers the chain so that the auto may pass, but the auto takes another route, leaving Serkin holding the chain.

What delicate composer could remain unmoved by the mealtime mood? In the vast refectory this mob of married wunderkinder, acclaimed the world over for exquisite tone, unflawed ensemble, and superior comprehension, relaxes with pratfalls and spitballs.

Wednesday evening, concert of my chamber works on the Marlboro campus rehearsed for two days only, and impeccable. These kids compounded become like a single Divine Sarah with no need to "know" what they're doing, since what they're doing bypasses the all-knowing creator's capacity.

Saturday in the public concert Ruth and Jaime Laredo played *Day Music* with panache. Afterward at the Kirchners' party, Peter Serkin, a more than merely adroit young musician and Peter Fonda-ish though not exactly dripping with charm, fails to respond. I try all sorts of chitchat but don't get a rise out of him. Desperate, I resort to crossing the room on my hands (the one thing in the world I can do that nobody else can). He melts.

Book music (Notes for an essay on non-musicians who write about Music):
In his powerful and now-famous story "Patriotism," Yukio Mishima (like René Crevel in France forty years earlier) previews his own suicide. In the film version made by the author, he considerably weakened (and inadvertently insulted) this detailed act by overlaying it with a soundtrack of the Love-Death from *Tristan und Isolde*. It can't be proved, but probably Mishima's choice of this sumptuous score to illustrate his stark subject was because of Wagner's title rather than his music. The premise: one Love-Death is like another. Even were this true, symbolic interpretations alter every decade. Since programmatic music conveys only what its composer tells you, verbally, it's meant to convey, a Love-Death by any other name would sound

as lush. Except for the best ballets, wherein choreography is based on the core of the music, mixed-media ingredients don't mix.

By the same token, books could be written citing great novelists who put their foot in it when talking of music. No other art seems so elusive yet so necessary to cultivated amateurs. Other than Mann, is there one author who incorporated music with an educated intelligence, rather than described it—albeit with awe—as decoration? No, not even Proust. The famous final chapter of *Point Counter Point* comes to mind, but again we find not a musician but a marvelous writer. Gide's book on Chopin resembles Pound's on harmony: their insights become bromides to professional musicians. Sartre and Kafka did not pretend about it, while the surrealists were plain hostile to it.

(Françoise Sagan uses music as furniture: the music of her daily life—the rock of night clubs—actually gives sound to her silent novels, a cut above the filmed biographies of long ago. Can anyone forget Cornel Wilde turning to Merle Oberon, who portrays Madame Sand, and saying, "Say, George"?)

Far from being uncomfortable, American authors are blithe about their ignorance—their indifference—to music. Imagine that non-apologetic attitude about painting! Imagine a composer admitting indifference to books, or a painter to music! Of course, and alas, everyone without embarrassment digs pop.

Even Cocteau, master of all trades, took care to subtitle *Le Coq et l'Arlequin*: "Notes Around Music."

(Ezra Pound: If you want to know X's whereabouts don't go to the F.B.I., look him up in the phone book.)

Susanne Langer's written smartly about music, but she's not an author, she's a writer—and European, like Forster and G.B.S.

Some who don't care: Philip Roth, Philip Rahv, John Cheever, Mary McCarthy, Norman Podhoretz, Christopher Isherwood. (Isherwood endeared himself to Stravinsky by falling asleep while the music was playing. But musicians do that too.)

Some who do care, but still put their foot—or at least their big toe—in it: Truman Capote, Paul Goodman, Glenway Wescott, Gore Vidal. Truman speaks of sound for its color, as though it were visual. Paul speaks of music (as Auden does) in technical jargon, and so sounds naive; for artist though he is, he is still an outsider. Glenway writes about the "Emperor Concerto," a second-rate piece, as though it were happening to him, rather than to itself. And take this sentence from Gore's *Two Sisters*:

Of the disappointments of my youth, I recall not so much love affairs gone wrong as those moments of intimacy when at last the dominant theme of the duet was clearly myself, when point counterpoint vain youth and admirer were developing the splendid harmonies of my uniqueness and then, like a non-serial dissonance in a usual work, the music went sour and the other made reference not to me but to self.

No musician could have composed that; the giveaway is "non-serial dissonance . . ." etc. Yet I'm willing to bet he wrote it only after consulting a musician.

Less amusing is an "esthetician" like Stanley Burnshaw who balks at voting a book award to Charles Rosen because he (Burnshaw) can't read notes and therefore can't follow the text. By that standard, poems too should be disqualified as too specialized. (No musical example in Rosen's book is beyond a third-grade child with a proper education.)

Gide likened *Les Faux Monnayeurs* to The Art of the Fugue, but it's closer to the Quartet from *Rigoletto*. A fugue, by definition, uses only the same material, which twines around itself in non-differentiated counterpoint. Differentiated counterpoint is what Gide and Verdi use: various themes that twine around each other. A three-voice fugue, for example, resembles a family of identical triplets in perfect agreement, or a madman talking to himself. Gide's book is a symphony, if you will, but certainly not a fugue.

At the end of *Point Counter Point* (which postdates Gide's novel by two years, and emerges from it), Spandrell, while awaiting violent death, converts some friends to the more-than-human persuasions of Beethoven, specially the "Lydian mode" movement of the Quartet Op. 132 in A minor. Huxley's exegesis is original, canny, free of that ingenuous awe one finds in otherwise wise lay musicians. His argument, couched all in non-musical terms, is indeed so "converting" that the fly in that smooth ointment seems the more gross. His record appears to be a 78-rpm of the Budapest played on an old (1928) crank gramophone. Mark and Mary Rampion, hearing *for the first time ever* this complicated quartet, thrill to its "meanings" despite at each record change (roughly every four minutes) a pep talk from Spandrell. Such things don't happen.
     They were more likely bored. Masterpieces, even when not accompanied by running commentary, are intrinsically boring: too much goes on, the mind gives way.
     To understand a masterpiece is to insult the masterpiece.
     Huxley uses music for his own purpose. As don't we all.

In *Sunday Bloody Sunday* Ms. Gilliatt, needless to say, uses a trio from *Così fan Tutte* to illustrate her eternal triangle. Why can't intellectuals drop names other than Mozart's? Debussy's, say, or Monteverdi's. (They *are* dropping Machaut and Satie now a little.)

Sartre used only an American blues in *La Nausée*. Kafka, nothing: he feared music. Gertrude Stein liked music to "frame" her words. Ditto Tennessee Williams, who speaks of the twelve-tone scale as though it were indeed a scale.

An old fart like Schweitzer lends a meaning to Bach that Bach, historically, could not have comprehended, while nice Jules Feiffer with that worried smile asks me (I'm supposed to know, being a musician) what kind of piece should be used for background in a scene in this movie he's writing where a girl and boy meet in church, Bach, maybe? No, use Messiaen.

One musician's heart sinks on witnessing Allen Ginsberg, presumably oblivious to the TV cameras yet mugging like Dean Martin in slow motion, embedded among acolytes intoning with mindless de-energized redundant unison the stanzas of William Blake. Ginsberg acknowledges he's never studied music, that his settings of Blake are "in a C chord, C-major" (he means in a non-modulating Ionian mode; his tonic is actually B-flat), and that he teaches Blake by singing him "because Blake sang, you know—he was a literal poet."

Formal study would not make Ginsberg a better composer, only a discerning one. He needs more of an ear: his music may be fun to join in, as any college songs are for the tone-deaf, but it sounds colorless, uncommunicative, and wrong for Blake, who needs a rainbow blaze. To counter, as Ginsberg does, that although nobody knows what Blake's own music was like, since it was not written down, but that it was "probably similar to what I'm doing . . . [which] is sort of in the style of Isaac Watts" (a hymnodist who died ten years before Blake was born), is not only to strain the credulity of his students, but also to *know* the past, and to assume that an ugly drone is as valid as the simplisticities being droned. Even if we did know Blake's own settings, why set his poems now in the manner of his time rather than ours? Would rock music embellish those poems? Maybe, but rock has its own words.

Couldn't Ginsberg musicalize his own good verses instead? Of course, then he'd risk the inadvertent masochism of a Paul Goodman whose nonprofessional love for music leads him to believe he's a composer. (Though unlike Pound who turned to Villon—as Ginsberg turns to Blake—Paul sabotages his own perfect poetry.)

Heat wave continues and New Hampshire's windlessness enters the window like mud. There is not among the young here, as among the Serkin seniors and Casalsites, the notion, thank heaven, of music's sacrosanctness. If you master a Beethoven sonata, then you master it. To our elders it was shameful to say we'd finally "understood" a sonata. But not even the universe today is without limits.

Returned to New York to find that JH has adopted a cat. The seven-year-old fifteen-pound Russian Blue was in a frantic state of being discriminated against by a clan of other cats at Gustavo's. JH took pity and brought him here. One gets used to anything. We call him Wallace.

Candid I am, but vicious, no. If I put down others, it's not to hoist myself onto their seat. Leave that to the Nin woman who brings light to those benighted darlings who see as through a glass darkly.

Someone said: It's hard to divorce Camus from his raincoat. We are what we eat and physique is persuasive. As a child I equated wisdom with dry sexless elderly features. Nor could I imagine that someone serious enough to research neumes or Frescobaldian ornamentation could possibly venture toward the fleshly visions that peopled my own disgusting daydreams.

Although for three years Donald Gramm and I have been listed as a team on the Columbia Concerts roster we never get any calls. The composer-singer tandem seems an incredible vehicle even to our universities. Now suddenly we have two dates in two weeks, presenting our American song program in Oklahoma City and in Atlanta. I'm in the unique position of being simultaneously a Columbia Artist and a Hurok Artist, though in fact I'm not an Artist at all—not in the sense that the performing world understands the term.

Parents' fifty-third anniversary. Ancient hemorrhoidal fissure still aches. Intense heat. Death of Barbette. Melon ice cream with angelfood cake. Visit from Patrick Cerza and John West, the latter sounding stentorian, velvety, and wistful as we rehearse *Bertha*.

19 August

Leon Kirchner, Barbara Kolb, and Charles Moss came to dine. Lots of salad & sherbet & picture taking, and talk of other people's music. Leon's enmeshed in the radically high soprano roles for his *Rain King* opera, while Barbara seeks ever newer ways for the mouth to utter verbs. Her Achilles' heel is novelty. So often her exquisite, mystical, telling fabrics are rent by doing presumably "what Lukas would do": suddenly the sung voice starts to speak (which is not solving the problem of song), or an honest tune is interrupted with a literal quote from Chopin.

Sans date

In writing vocal music I have never used special effects—no whines, shrieks, whispers, elongations, nor even word repetitions. My aim toward poetry is, I suppose, to intensify rather than to reinterpret.

In a word, my music is expressivity, rather than novelty. Expressivity is not novel, nor is novelty ever expressive. Yet this is my one trump card, which will either save or sink me, and, being naked, I'm more vulnerable than most these days.

To Juilliard for part of Callas's master class. She is, for me, the sole diva ever to perform meaningfully a meaningless repertory. From the moment she strode onto that Roman stage in 1954 and intoned the words *È forse qui* I've been no less enamored of her than has your average opera queen who knows far more than I.

Yet how can a star teach, except by doing? What Callas imparts (through her handsome mock-humble style of Regular Gal, no-nonsense, let's-get-down-to-work—and she's a dead ringer for Rosemarie Beck) is not more exceptional than what any intelligence imparts: Pretend you understand the words, sing them like you mean them. Alan Rich seemed impressed by her advice for hitting a high C: "Think B!" Why not think D-flat? But I'm not a singer. And not being a singer I learned little, for how much nuance can be disclosed in Bellini?

(I say this, who would not permit some other to say it. I compose song, and my business is not tolerance but self-protection. Stick to contemporary music, mesdames: those fierce roulades in Mozart will wreck your voice!)

No music of any period, when a singer learns to like it, can harm his voice. He must perform the music of his own time to keep in trim for those risky skips in *bel canto* which will otherwise kill him.

Bel canto is the pap of the past as pop is the pap of the present. Being a mere gymnastic sketch, *bel canto* contains nothing not more commendably contained in Bach or Mozart. By stressing the doing over what's done, the shadow before the substance, *bel canto* utterly embodies the superficial. What intellect can admire, for itself on the page unsung, the hurdy-gurdy-isms of a Donizetti? Maria Callas, like Billie Holiday, gave sense to senseless airs, but what is that music without the diva? Bad music needs interpretation, good music plays itself.

Not that *bel canto* is wholly bad, just too big for itself. Like Albert Schweitzer or Zen, like Bob Dylan or Scientology, like Toscanini or Structuralism, *bel canto* is obscenely merchandized. If the past season's Philharmonic display overrated Liszt for his underratedness, the reverse holds for *bel canto*.

People often compare Bessie and Billie as though they were the same thing, like Bardot and Brigitte, or as though they could be blended, like benedictine and brandy. In fact, they were not even chipped off the same old block. Bessie Smith was a big-scale rural belter of Negro-oriented song. Billie Holiday was a small-scale urban "stylist" of songs by white masters. Bessie, a born leader, sang blues. Billie, a born victim, sang pop. Sure, they're comparable, in quality and society, since both were great black vocalists. But generically they're as different as an outdoor stadium and a supper club, different as a Wagnerian diva and a lieder singer.

More than other vocal pigeonholes mezzo-soprano neatly splits in two: the soft sound and the hard. Some are contraltos with a top and make chocolate noises associated with deep sensuality. Others are sopranos with a bottom and make diamond noises identified with high purity.

30 August

Practiced all afternoon with Donald Gramm. *War Scenes* for the November concert, and the American group (Ives, Thomson, Chanler, and Copland) for recitals elsewhere. Except for Phyllis, Donald's the only singer I feel completely comfortable with. There's never anything I have to tell him.

Visit for tea from John Kander and Larry Alpert with whom, despite their dwelling next door for five years, we've not fraternized until recently. John is the opposite of me in that he wants appreciation solely through his work, not through controversy or his name in lights. My need for attention, despite an overwhelming shyness (which no one believes), is probably a rebuff to the boys who beat me up in gym, most of whom are dead or wouldn't remember me.

Fire Island
8 September

At Morris's on Water Island with JH. Visit from Tom Prentiss and Nan, during which an orange rainbow migration: thousands upon thousands of monarch butterflies fluttered by for an hour.

Vancouver
16–19 September

Here for three days to record a program for CBS. Time to spare. Took a cab miles across town to hear Jill Johnston at the university. Drab, ungiving delivery to a mainly female audience sitting on the floor. When I asked a question ("Do you think that as a lesbian you got away with the kind of murder that a gay male couldn't risk when you disrupted that program on feminism by rolling on the floor of Town Hall with your girlfriend?") she refused to answer. So I left the room in a huff, but couldn't find a taxi, and was still waiting out in the cold a half-hour later when the assembly disbanded and tumbled into their cars, leaving me alone in tears in Canada.

Heredity and environment are the same.

So much traveling, yet never blasé toward planes. Those brief hours, from Manhattan to this far shore of Canada, sailing over America (where there still are, as Gertrude said, "more people where nobody is than where anybody is"), demand conjecture. The months it took an early settler! From a valley he saw one mountain, from its peak another mountain, again into the valley, and so on, forever; waves blanked out the future. But we watch that future—that spatial future—from above, before it exists for the landbound. If in fact there is a spatial future, is there not, too, a temporal future, preexisting like a fan before it's opened? If so, when it is opened, can we perceive beyond the ridge that is our death?—not to discover if there's life after death, but to discover if there's life after *our* life? I'm confusing time and space; a plane does move in time as it covers space. What about a helicopter, hovering above a clear view of both spatial and temporal future? Still, the future does not exist. If the future existed, it would not, by definition, be the future.

Perspective depends on your mood of the hour. Monday my host came to the hotel to tape an interview. For two hours I answered fourteen carefully prepared questions. The tape was lost. Tuesday morning I agreed to retape the interview. To the same fourteen questions I gave new answers. Both sets of answers were honest, but on Tuesday I was a different person. I was a different person less by being a day older than by having exhausted a view-point, or at least my examples of viewpoint. Now, if the original interview had occurred Tuesday it could have been the same as on Monday (despite snow, which had fallen overnight) because the questions would be hitting me for the first time. On the other hand, had the second tape also been lost and a third identical interview been set up for Wednesday, I would have re-fused. By Wednesday I would have turned into a teacher. Teachers repeat themselves.

How eerie to be leaving Vancouver after just three days. Not that I feel at home. As in San Francisco there's a personal oxygen which is quickly habit-forming, an ether, this constant private snow, not especially lovable, but lovely and welcoming, like the inside of a halo.

3 October

Florence Quivar did the whole cycle of *Hearing* tonight, plus a half dozen other songs (Bishop, Whitman, etc.), at the Cultural Center. Later several people came over and ate things: Kenneth Koch, Barbara K., Betty Allen, Noel Lee. Also Jacques Dupont and Marc Payen, who are here for a week. The exterminator had made a visit this afternoon, which gave us all a sense of security.

Hilton Inn
Oklahoma City
11 October

Here with Donald Gramm for our American recital last evening at the uni-versity. This morning Donald did his customary master class, then flew back. (My class is this afternoon.) At his session Donald hears a song straight through, then talks about the interpretation from every possible angle, then asks the quivering aspirant to repeat the song, after which he always ex-claims, "See, it's already a hundred times better," but confides to me later that it's never better and usually worse. How can a student absorb all that information, and then apply it so suddenly? We do the program again next week in Atlanta.

23 October

I am fifty. Interview with Robert Jacobson for *Opera News*. Ditto with Win-ston Leyland for *Gay Sunshine*, and wretchedly for *After Dark*. Casals is dying. Bought a Leonid, one of his most beautiful from the belle époque of the early 1950s. Rehearsing continually and going to movies.

Last night at the Cathedral of Saint John the Divine, Alec Wyton offered the birthday gift of a program of my vocal music—as moving as Charles Walker's revival in the afternoon, at his Church of the Heavenly Rest, of *A Sermon On Miracles*, the joint parturience of Paul Goodman and myself twenty-six years ago. Charles's wife, Janet Hayes, performed yesterday as capably as she had at the premiere in 1947.

Phone call from Lillian Libman to announce, in her crack-of-doom baritone, that Mr. Hurok is taking a lively interest in the upcoming concerts. Typical Lillianian euphemism. She burst into tears. Hurok, as it turns out, having seen her ad in last Sunday's *Times*, called in the whole staff to confront Lillian. "Who the hell is Rorem?. . . Why is he using my name?. . . I can't sue you but I can sure sue him!" etc., as though our project had not for months been common knowledge to everyone but that senile bastard.

　　Rehearsals for *Bertha* meanwhile proceed in orderly fashion, thanks to JH.

Sans date

More and more I receive requests (oh, not a constant flaw, but every few months) to dredge up yesterday: souvenirs of the dance, of France *d'après-guerre*, of Paul Goodman and other recent dead. Less and less I care. My life has been based on my life. But isn't it wrong, morally wrong, to eat the past? When we die, our bodies and those shards of our vanity which served as precious bark should be forgotten, flung to feed poppies. Why, then, do I trouble to note this? From habit, it's all I know.

As I lie dying, might the final page of Josquin's *Missa Pange Lingua* help to waft me off? No, death doesn't busy itself with "fine" emotions. Death is disgusting. Nor does death approach, no matter how expected or even desired, with what we call taste. *J'ai médité sur la mort chaque heure de ma vie, et cela maintenant ne me sert de rien!* Thus intoned Poulenc's Prieur from the stage of the Salle Garnier on June 21, 1957, and every hour since then I've mulled those words. Were the Prieur's disciplined fancies finally so far from mine? That as we sink into the winding sheet those sunny others leave for a party to which we're not invited? (Why say *we*? Nothing is less *we* than dying. A priest is no help as he leads you to the gallows.)

Write the tale of a man who all his life dreads death, but on his deathbed he realizes the waste, for death is not dreadful at all.

In Hyères, April 1951, Félix Labisse offered to Marie Laure a house gift in the form of a canny little illustrated tome named *Le Livre du Suicide*. Certain morbid types among the *sous-bourgeoisie* commit suicide ornately according to execution methods of their homeland. Thus in Vanves the fat local butcher and father of seven, after donning a gold wig and fluffy tutu, managed to behead himself with an axe-blade lashed to the base of a two-ton armoire.

By 1954 I had not only confected a libretto loosely based on Stevenson's *Suicide Club* (which I called *The Dying Room* in homage to Graham Greene's current play *The Living Room*), but I actually completed a few airs and trios before shelving the deal as a dull bargain.

I picture everything dead. Over the day I picture the cat, the checkout girl at the A & P, that usher. The melancholy is elusive, not in definition but in whereabouts. I chase after melancholy, desirous, sliding around corners. Later it arrives in this room uncalled-for. Certain things we'll comprehend only after we're gone. The time from now till then visibly shrinks like the *peau de chagrin* and brings a faint smile.

13 November

Alvin Ross at the Washburn Gallery. My portrait exposed. Dentist regularly. Beverly Wolff has come from Florida to rehearse *Bertha*, for which she's ideal in voice and in carriage. Kenneth Koch will "narrate" *Bertha*— that is, he'll declaim the stage directions, which JH thinks will be informative, witty, and theatrical.

27 November

The fray's finished—the pair of Hurok-sponsored birthday recitals are past, and my elation would be total but for the death of Jennie Tourel on Saturday. Before the first concert we agreed that Shelly Gold would appear on the Tully Hall stage to dedicate the forthcoming music to Jennie's memory. For the record, here is a list of the devotedly expert musicians who were more than a composer could pray for: Phyllis Curtin, who with Joseph Rabbai and Ryan Edwards performed *Ariel*, and with me and Beverly did *Gloria*; Donald Gramm, who sang *War Scenes* with me playing; violinists Sergiu Luca and Zvi Zeitlin, who respectively played *Day Music* and *Night Music*, both with Jerome Lowenthal, who also was pianist in *Last Poems of Wallace Stevens* with cellist Jeffrey Solow and soprano Betti McDonald, and in the *Trio* with flutist Eugenia Zukerman and Jeffrey Solow; Kenneth Koch, who was speaker for his play, *Bertha*; Beverly Wolff, who sang the title role; the nine vocalists who surrounded her: Enoch Sherman, Willard White, Grayson Hirst, John West, Kathryn Hinton, Rose Taylor, Lorna Myers, Ruth Sherman, and Betti McDonald; and James Holmes, who cohered it all. Lillian gave me a silver snuff box which she strongly implied had belonged to Stravinsky, and Henahan gave me a dismissive review, which hurt.

At noon today, Tourel's funeral at Riverside Chapel. A pretty good speech by Lenny to the jam-packed crowd, and a record of the Lydian movement from opus 132 which made me cry. Jennie was the most influential mezzo of my life (possibly because she's the first real one I ever knew, even before Nell Tangeman), and her sound, with its unique honey-smooth nasally pure-dictioned gleam, the most satisfying. I will always recall her bourgeois style in contrast to her over-flamboyant (except on the stage) wardrobe, and socially her total self-absorption (even when coaching students) in contrast to the absolutely tasteful yet grand and generous delivery of almost every item in her multilingual repertory.

28 November

Visit from soprano Irene Gubrud who will be one of the two soloists next year in *Little Prayers*. The most extraordinary aspect of this beautiful creature is that she is permanently supported by a pair of crutches the same color as her satiny flowing hair. The voice is clean and projecting, at least in the parlor.

1 December

An old game for judging the new is to guess at survival value. Today we play by asking how many of our "serious" works would retain their vitality if the Vietnam War were to end. Would pieces of, say, Stockhausen's syndrome be forever flushed away like outmoded detergents? Such pieces do serve philosophical as well as musical needs, but when the needs become ends in themselves—when they become *timely*—they become disposable. Not the least of those needs is masochism, which will always play some role in the enjoyment of art. Surely much of the pain we undergo at Modern Music Concerts would seem invalidated by a permanent cease-fire. And surely much of rock, despite grave poetic intentions, has already earned artistic legitimacy through the music's clean, soap-bubble simplicity. We may never be able to test the theory, but very possibly Stockhausen, with all due originality, will not outlast this war, while *Jesus Christ Superstar*, with all due banality, will be around for the millennium.

The preceding paragraph was deleted (with my permission) from an essay on the so-called rock opera in *Harper's*. I have just re-read the entire article. If printed words speak truth to the general reader, to their author they reveal a naked lie; what three months ago in manuscript seemed a conscientious effort now rings false as a forced confession. Not that I am at odds with all I wrote, only with the emphasis. I don't and did not feel the pervading enthusiasm.

What one writes, in words or in music, depends so much on whom one writes for (oneself, youth, the private donor, the well-paying middlebrow journal) that the nature of the financial or otherwise extra-artistic impulse of any given work of the last five hundred years could probably be guessed through the size and nature (though not the quality) of that work itself.

My intuition was that *Harper's* wanted a favorable review of *Jesus Christ Superstar*, a record I might never have listened to without the magazine's commission. The result wasn't dishonest so much as blind, bland, affable, ambitious.

To see itself through, music must have either idea or magic. The best has both. Music with neither dies young, though sometimes rich.

The words on Stockhausen I cannot retract, for he himself has told us how to feel. What sensitive listeners would repudiate this composer's plea for a brotherhood of nations, for an Esperanto of love and all, when he, with those beautiful eyes set off by chestnut hair in an irresistible ponytail, tells them what his music represents? They find themselves attending in good faith to hour upon deafening hour of static, scared to admit that what composers say about their music need not always jibe with what their music says about itself.

Contemporary culture dominated by the avant-garde? A contradiction in terms. How can the advance runner dominate? Yet he does in America, and by extension everywhere, since we now set the international creative tone. We do so by murdering our heroes every few years while salvaging, in the guise of influence, the froth of their output. We throw out the baby but keep the bathwater. (Consider the cold dethronings of playwrights Williams and Albee and of composers Barber and Copland.) Perhaps this has always been so. But whereas assassination was once considered a fine art, today it's pop art; anyone can do it.

If not Stockhausen then who? It's hard to deny the fact of his following, or to assert that The Young have abandoned concert music for rock when they turn up in thousands for Stockhausen. Yet any music that attracts thousands, of whatever age, must have its facile, not to say extra-musical, side, since the majority has never liked to concentrate, and good art is hard work. The mass, as we know, is not always right. But it will replace Stockhausen.

A recent review of an intelligent collection, *The Performing Self*, chided the author Richard Poirier for his article on the Beatles. The review suggested that now, only four years after he wrote it, the attitude of a Jamesian scholar talking of pop music "seems silly," especially his sober appraisal of the campy record jacket. Doubtless jackets of James's first novels would now seem dated too, just like their contents. There is a difference between dated and outmoded. If dated means that style and subject matter can, secondarily, locate the historical period of a work's creation, then all art dates. Something outmoded is merely something which dates badly, something whose primary quality is historical location.

Replaying *Sgt. Pepper* provided such relief that I had an orgy of old Beatles records. Their way with their own tunes, their ingenuity, energy, wit, and contagiously magic charm, present the best gauge for judgment: the music holds up, along with those few huge thrills from childhood.

The catalogue is doubtless closed. Thus the Beatles will have bequeathed us about as many first-rate songs as did Poulenc, say 15 out of nearly 200, a good percentage. My own article on the Beatles published around the time of Poirier's and asserting that they were superior to their competition, not for their meaning but for their melody, now seems so obvious as to be thoroughly outmoded. But they themselves—they date divinely.

11 December

Early this morning on emerging from the County Courthouse where against my desire I had enrolled for jury duty, I bought *New York Magazine* with the faint hope of finding a review, however brief and bad, of my two birthday concerts. In the taxi I read a sizable critique—the sort for which your most indulgent fantasies yearn vainly. Unqualifiedly, Alan Rich takes my defense, absolves me, so to speak, from the crime of being me, and by so doing he not only justifies my "American worth" to critical foes who confound persona with product but admits to a covert longing to *be* me (as I want to be Doris Day). Reaction? Disbelief, embarrassment, thrill. How could I dream that the up-to-date Alan might allow that grammar, rather than language, contains what is intrinsically vicious or virtuous in music, and that I am mostly a grammarian? Still, no one's as virtuous as he claims me to be. I've always found his journalistic horniness enticing, and here he commits himself now in the eyes of the world to one who might not live up to such standards. Like being raped (happily) in the County Courthouse, this second-best review of my adulthood.

Good reviews don't make me feel as good as bad ones make me feel bad. Writing up poems is to write poems. Reviewing concerts is writing down. (Occasionally a Tovey rises high, but not as a reviewer.) What is one to think of, learn from, the contradictions in various professional criticisms of the same music? Allen Hughes talks of me warmly, Henahan icily. Where Schonberg is pecksniffian, Rich is magnanimous. The *Post* reviews most everything I compose, the *Voice* nothing, ever. Being a sometime critic, I know the breed's human. The difference between specimens of the breed is that some write well, some don't. Few speak for the hearer.

Three features distinguish the music reviewer from reviewers of other arts. He deals with the ephemeral. He hears mostly works of the past. He is often a practitioner, as well as a critic, of his art.

Nearly every concert is a one-shot deal: it will not be repeated here tomorrow for another public, or next week, or ever. An art show lasts long enough for maximum attendance. A new ballet remains in repertory till season's end. So it is, too, with movies and (theoretically) plays. But with music the surefirest hit gets heard only once, even with famous soloists. A Gielgud alone on stage reciting Shakespeare fills the hall for weeks, but could a Horowitz have a run with one Beethoven program night after night in Carnegie? The question doesn't arise; it's not in the nature of the game. The music critic, therefore, unlike theater or painting critics, is not a foretaster. He writes epitaphs rather than birth notices.

The contemporary audience of Handel was not concerned with Machaut. Schubert's fans were not concerned with Handel. But today's Music Lovers place past composers above and before present composers. Right or wrong, this is endemic. Bach may thus be correctly termed a twentieth-century musician. I don't mean this metaphorically, that he answers to our needs. We hear him as he never heard himself; we perform him in the now, with mannerisms of now. Our Bach is actually closer to Berio than to the Bach of 1785 and is absorbed with intervening wisdoms and delusions. I knew Billie Holiday before I knew Bach so I still hear him conditioned by the fact of her—his bluesy chords, those wailing tunes.

Familles, je vous hais, said Gide. Music Lovers, I loathe you.

I've never trained myself to listen critically with the intention of forming verbal ideas about music. I hear kinetically rather than intelligently, or else I don't listen at all. (I *have*—though none too happily—trained my ears to turn off.) Response to what I hear is as much reaction as opinion. Trained reaction, not dreams. For a composer, as distinct from reviewer or executant or mere Music Lover, such reaction tends toward what is played rather than how it's played.

12 December

Christmas shopping for Boosey & Hawkes, the sole objects of yearly gifts. A Baccarat vase for the indomitable Sylvia Goldstein, a quart of Poire for the all-knowing Jean Golden.

    Reception at the Library to honor Elliott Carter's papers. Exhibited are an invitation to the White House and *framed* letters from Boulez. Talk about your canonizing the actual: even the sanctified Elliott drops names.

People resent my diary for not divulging conversations with those whose names I "merely" drop. Yet there's nothing to divulge. Artists of stature together talk money and health and sex, occasionally politics if they're petitioning funds for Israel or against Vietnam, but never, never esthetics. Esthetics is the priority of beginners and has no place in the bull sessions of professionals—only in their work. As for the diary not containing what it means to be an artist: that meaning presumably is in my music. The reviewer need not be blamed for ignoring my sixty-odd published essays and four published collections on non-diary matters. But then, what qualifies him as a reviewer?

    When *The Paris Diary* came out, Harold Acton, who loathed it, asked: "What have such horrors as crabs, piles, and bedbugs to do with musical inspiration and 'the crushing necessity to be an artist'?" How should I know? I'm the artist, he's the esthete.

20 December

Spine still ailing. Lillian's put me onto a chiropractor whom I saw today, twice. Now that daylight's so very short I take infantile comfort by drowsing in bed at 4 P.M. and gazing north toward the twelve-story buildings on 71st as one by one their lights turn warmly on. And the Christmas Spirit, which everyone claims to hate, invades me like sherry and reanimates childhood. (Yes, sherry was part of a long-lingering childhood.)

Christmas Day

Morris Golde and my parents bringing posies and incense came for a quiet
Christmas meal of capon with olives and brown rice, salad, and rhubarb pie.
JH did the labor while I lay stretched on the parlor floor. A fortnight ago for
the third time in twenty years I dislocated the vertebrae in the lumbar region and no amount of chiropractic hip-baths dulls the wincing. If this follows the previous patterns I'll be more or less incapacitated for a month.

27 December

Although we've corresponded lately because of the piece Tommy Schippers
is commissioning for the Cincinnati Symphony, it's been years since our last
meeting. His beauteous wife has died and he himself has just undergone
surgery for a spastic esophagus, while I've passed through a critical birthday
and am for the moment a hobbling cripple. Thus when I step from the elevator and into his more-than-comfortable lodgings at 550 Park we appraise
each other warily. Tommy in a sky-blue sweater and white slacks remains
young and handsome but drawn and pained, and I feel a concerted effort on
his part during our three-hour tête-à-tête.

Twenty-two years since we first shook hands in the Bar Montana, rue St.-
Benoit. How different those years have been for each of us. How different
indeed are the various categories of musician who to the outsider appear all
the same. Conductor and composer, doer and maker, are in fact as disparate
in professional duty and personal habit as gardener and botanist. Tommy's
career has been all public and lavish, concentrated labor on other people's
music, and a marriage, which he describes as idyllic, that resolved in sadness. That he should wish me to compose for his orchestra comes as a happy
surprise, since his only (public) reaction to my music has been hitherto
adverse.

Although the weather is pure spring, the sun was setting already when we
parted at four. Despite his fame and fortune Tommy seems an orphan now,
cursed for his blessings by the gods.

To Maggy's on Bank Street for a brief but intense cocktail, then with JH
for another seasonal spree in the new strange-shaped Central Park West
apartment of Claire and Barry Brook where, curved double by the wounded
spine, I collapsed upon a long soft sofa and remained there for the duration.
On learning that Desmond Shawe-Taylor (the *New Yorker*'s most recent
pedant) was present, I asked to meet him. A full hour later, an intermediary
explained that Shawe-Taylor had replied, "Oh no, I couldn't do that. I gave
him a bad review!"

How enviable is the prose of Louise Bogan. In themselves and from start to finish her letters scan, soar, gleam, and not a dumb sentence among them. (The Toklas correspondence has just come out too and is spirited, yes, but not the work of a working mind.) Bogan's letters are true gifts, written for the recipient rather than for herself or for posterity. One believes her when she disclaims interest in such a collection. Yet she takes the time to impart information, to compose her phrases, never to repeat herself. Her prose surpasses her verse.

Also reading with astonishment the galleys of Meyer Levin's *The Obsession*. What messiness compared to Bogan. With all his machismo how much more "feminine" the disarray of Levin's persecution than the steely awkwardness of Bogan's vulnerability. If Louise *thinks* better than Meyer, Meyer remains more compelling. I've never read *The Diary of Anne Frank* (Levin's book concerns her rape by those presumed monsters who denied him use of his own theater adaptation), but while hearing him kvetch one wonders if Otto Frank did not himself author that diary. Could such a document—an intact work of art—have just been left like that? And many a brokenhearted poet has keen financial instincts.

1974

The past days have been spent shuttling from doctor to doctor with X rays of my back.

Visit from Molly Haskell. I'd expected somebody plump with mauve ribbons in her tresses. She's shorn, without an inch of spare flesh. I'd forgotten, if I'd ever known, that she's married to Andrew Sarris. She's intelligent, not shy, and can talk you under the table.

Orchestrating *Little Prayers*.

Letter this morning from Christiane Fourtine in Cugnaux. Henri is dead. He died, in fact, months ago, before my trip to Paris last spring, and after a year of torture from intestinal cancer. In her second sentence Christiane (whom I met only once, years ago, and found to be a shy farm girl) affirms that she tended her husband day and night despite the meanness and neglect he had shown her through their conjugal life. "*C'est seulement dans le malheur,*" she goes on, "*qu'il a compris qu'un foyer était plus précieux et surtout plus solide que les amis de rencontre.*"

Les amis de rencontre. But I was one of them. Indeed, we were, each of us, that life-changing chance encounter which took place in an April dusk of 1952 near the Observatoire garden. "*Un café, ça vous dit?*" he had said. I recall each phrase of our ensuing night in the Hôtel des Saints-Pères, of the next weeks, the next two years, the very very intense odoriferous sex, the thorough snarling satisfaction that has since not been equaled, not certainly in America.

So now he's dead, the paragon. And every shred of that liveliness (the only body that could make my body lose its head) lies decomposing underground. Today it's too easy to write I'd felt it; yet his silence of the last two years made me suspect that Henri was unwell, more indeed than his wife and children of whose maladies he'd written me. It is extraordinary how we allow people to come and go in our hearts and heads, how we reanimate at will the quick and dead, oceans away. Each morning begins the numbing wait till night. The sole preoccupation is: How will these days complete themselves? As an adolescent with Maggy in those West Chicago bars I ruminated that there we were, in the small packed room as in a trap, but a trap that was life and not death, for outside lurked the empty streets, behind them the prairie, and beyond the prairie death, closing in, gradual but sure, and all this glued onto a sphere hurtling dumbly across the sky.

Christiane solicits nothing. She must (she writes) spend the rest of her life providing for the youngsters with her limited resources. Her note exudes no sorrow. Yet how can I know? My Henri was the dessert; she had the main course. With no sense whatsoever of responsibility I keep him alive at leisure here in the flame of this room. These ever-more-frequent black-rimmed announcements make me bristle more than weep. They contain a certain *mauvais goût*.

25 January

Murder of James Pope-Hennessy. The awful image has jiggled before me all day, as I think back to the gentle person that James was. His wit, affability, kindness to Marie Laure (through whom we met twenty-three years ago), the sound of that voice reading from the Queen Mary biography over the Buffalo radio while I washed dishes in 1959, his book on slavery, which so bewitched JH last summer.

Finished scoring *Little Prayers*.

5 February

JH helps me hobble to WOR for my tenth interview with Arlene Francis despite flu and broken back. Chiropractor threatens to sue since I accused him of fraud and refused to pay for cancelled future sessions. Practicing song accompaniments for Skidmore concert.

Yaddo
13 February

Warm, and robin's-egg bright.

As a child I used to ask my parents, Am I worth a million dollars to you?

Why yes, of course, they reassured. After I'd been "bad" I would ask them, Am I still worth a million dollars?

Four decades later, without children and not rich, how would I confront the two-hundred-million-dollar ransom demand for a daughter, as Mr. William Hearst is asked to confront it this morning? From the sidelines the demand at first seems less outrageous than stupid. This money, asked as a benefit for the poor, would be absorbed without a ripple, leaving the poor as poor and Hearst poorer. Still, in the name of the Revolution, the demand's not dumb. The gesture, like the granting of civil rights, is a fact that could burst an abscess. Probably I'd shell out. But then, I'm without children and not rich.

17 February

This noon in the thick rain I carried my lunch pail over to Elizabeth's little house and we sat together for two hours there. Mostly she talked about the vast wedding last month of Marianne, and I was shown the gorgeous bridal gown in the cedar chest upstairs. Maybe she spoke on other things; I can't remember, because as I nibbled raw carrots and wild cherries all concentration was for Elizabeth's right eyelid. Upon it already a year ago there appeared a noticeable darkening, a sort of bruised lump; today it has spread and festered, is redder, oozing. My hostess made no allusion to it nor did I, but as we chattered on, swallowing and bemoaning, I grew hypnotized by that wound, which took on its own life, while Elizabeth's words seemed as remote to me as mine (in her deafness) must always seem to her. Can it be cancer? The smear now swelled to the size of a rotted apricot, extended feelers, and began crawling down her right cheek. Elizabeth, I no longer wish to discuss my own problems, but the Artist's, it all comes to the same but with more generous phrasing. The taut skin throbbed like a timpani, and though the left side of her head remained normal, the whole right side became a pineapple melting onto the lace of her shoulder, and finally into her lap, a sheet of soft taffy in which the running eye was located at about the level of her breast. Yes, she agreed that an objectifying of my concerns is indicated at this time if only I could learn, as she has, to enjoy being alone, compose not for someone but for everyone, and smell the petunias. Indeed, the petunias' rich odor was rampant everywhere, it having been pouring since 3 A.M. when I awoke to the thundering on the tin roof and never returned to sleep but lay entertaining vital clarifications which only, it appears, appear unusually. I was exhausted now, poured myself another cup of skim milk while Elizabeth continued her never unnecessary speaking. The river of her eye's infection had reached the floor, gushing rapidly now, and hairily made its way toward me. Had I met Wallace Fowlie yet? Well yes, and liked him more than I had anticipated. I could do without Yaddo's surplus of mosquitoes and deerflies, but could do *with* a haircut, it's longer than ever in my life, really quite mod. My feet were embalmed in mud; I stood up quickly. Elizabeth! I yelled (for she is also deaf), there's a tree blossoming on your path outside: show it to me, because I must go to work now and the rain's stopped. We walked a few paces together toward the locust tree, enchanted and hung with wet crystals. The sky was clearing ever so slowly. Elizabeth looked well for her unknown age and sprightly, but said she needs rest. So we murmured good-bye, until tonight.

(She explains that her eye condition results from a beautician's accident some forty years ago. A white-hot curling iron glanced her cornea, permanently destroying the oil glands, or something.)

A man never knows quite who he is, but who he says he thinks he is gives a fair notion of who he thinks he is, if not, in fact, who he is.

In Susan Sontag's article "The Third World of Women," two points keep cropping up, as they always do among liberated women. The points are hardly minor, yet are always incomplete:

(1) Need for grammatical changes. Sontag composed the essay for translation into Spanish but didn't specify that the grammar she wrote about applied only to English. How would this read to Spaniards who know no English? That we say "he" when we mean either sex is meaningful only to someone who thinks in English. Admittedly this could stand change and would be comparatively easy to install among our habits, like using "Ms." But although the woman's condition is international, language conditions are not. The mind boggles at how to desexify a Latin tongue. If French doesn't have our pronoun problem, it does have gender for all nouns. Yet a French person born to the language doesn't *think* gender—that is, sex—as we, who have learned French as adults, do. Thus it doesn't strike a French person as funny that, say, most words both slang and medical for male organs are feminine (*la queue, la verge, la bitte*, etc.) while those for female parts are masculine (*le vagin, le con, le sein*, etc.). Diminutives, thought by Americans to be feminine, often turn masculine in French, i.e., *la mouche* becomes *le moucheron*. None of this is true for Italian, which, however, has masculinized such eternally "female" things as the sea—*la mer*—which is *il mare*. That their nouns have gender (and that adjectives and certain verbs must agree) is not, French friends tell me, in any way sexual. As far as implication is concerned, one could substitute red noun or green noun for masculine noun and feminine noun. Agreeing then that gender quit the psy-

chology of European languages long centuries back (just as it abandoned, along with the second person singular, our English language), how would other languages "treat" the feminist question?

(2) For a woman to adopt her mother's family name as her own last name only means that she adopts her grandfather's name instead of her father's. Should you reply, Well, we've got to start somewhere, why not start with a brand-new name, as slaves did after the Civil War?

Why not eliminate Ms., along with Mrs. and Mr. and Master and Miss, and call everyone, as Quakers do, by both names?

French hardware stores sell signs saying *Chien Méchant*. As the case may be, should they not also sell a *Chienne Méchante*?

Asked by "outsiders" what word to use for the gay condition, what do I answer? Gay's not in my vocabulary, I wasn't raised that way. I've the right to say "queer" (but you have not), and "boy" and "girl," using them as the French do for every age. It's how you're brought up. (Chicago jargon used "jam" for "straight," "minty" for "dyke." Nor had I ever heard of garlic, limburger, pastrami, or pizza before moving to New York.) Must we alter vocabulary because the revolution tells us to? Paris may be worth a mass, but who are those who dictate the mass's dialect? All's in a name. Were our own names changed tomorrow we would wither.

Are women who act actors (or is that only men?), actresses (or is that for other species, like *tigress*?), female actors (patronizing distinction?), or finally, yes, *faute de mieux*, actresses? We don't say authoress or Negress but we do say laundress and temptress. We don't say usheress or jeweleress but we do say duchess and seamstress. The French, of course, have the feminine of (most) every noun. But if they do have separate words, as we do, for bull and cow, they don't, as we do not, have the feminine for shark.

Sontag remarks, "I think now, looking back, that I don't really believe all the things I said in the essays I wrote in the 1960s." Where does that leave those whose consciousness was raised by her once novel concepts? Sontag was not, after all, a warm romancer, but a cool cataloguer (catalogueress?) of opinions (many, of course—like those on music—sounding as though she'd come to them yesterday) which she shouldn't belittle, if only for the sake of her converts. Or will the converts follow her bandwagon, not having learned from the early essays to think for themselves?

"The world loves drunks, but it despises perverts," Jane Bowles once sadly wrote. And indeed, alcoholics can always find companions, in crime if not in love. But I drank to find companions in love—or rather, to be found by them.

Crucial distinction. Note the passive mode, *to be found* (which makes me feel sexy because guilty), a mode of Anglo-Saxon parlance but rare to the unguilty French. The unguilty French seldom refer to getting laid, that is, *être baisé*, but place that so-called passive act into the active mode: to get yourself laid, that is, *se faire baiser*. Anyway, strong-willed though I was (I command you to rape me!) I passed myself off as a vulnerable bit of lavender fluff longing to be—*comment dirai-je?*—to be, well, soiled.

The French have no word for straight, as counterpart (I almost wrote opposite) of gay. Nor have they an adjective like gay, preferring a noun or verb like *tante* or *en être*. And they have no words for crooked, shallow, vicarious, urge, or gentile. Crooked, as distinct from straight in its upright meaning, they must call *courbé* (curved), *sinueux*, or *tortueux*. Shallow becomes *peu profond*. Vicarious stems from our Protestant "vicar"—not a Catholic concern (they would say *vicieux*), which also is why gentiles are conveniently *chrétiens*. The closest thing to our verb "to urge" is their *exhorter*. From this paragraph draw no conclusions about the French; draw conclusions only about my conclusions about the French.

The French, however *vicieux*, are of all Europeans the most heterosexual.

Maldoror made love with a shark—a female shark, needless to say.

Women classically take their husband's name. Unmarried artists declare, "My work is my wife," and give their name to their creation. But the creation, no sooner spawned, goes off to live or die independently. Work is not spouse but offspring.

That paragraph reeks chauvinism. Artist implies male artist.

Does a female artist seek a mate? Could she conceivably think of her work as a husband? I, Ned Rorem, don't want a wife in any form (though at times I want a husband), and less and less do I want children—the desire to see my flesh on other bones. My music's not my wife, nor my husband, nor my child. My music is my music. Once composed it is no longer even mine.

You open the *Times* and there, yet again, is the saga of a sex transplant. There, yet again and sober as you please in this bourgeois periodical, you see the photo of A New Woman, muscular calves garnished with ankle hose, spit curls embellishing a receding forehead, and rhetoric proclaiming that now at forty-five she is finally fulfilled—thanks to hormones, penile mutilation, and an official receipt from the government. So you think, Well, poor dear, she must be getting on: no one twenty today seems concerned with sexual differences. Good-bye past, good-bye stardom, good-bye O melting passive heroines enfolded by sculptured biceps of the active heros. What butch male will now defile this fulfilled middle-aged female?

Then you fantasize a bit (though not for long) on possibilities. Suppose a man and woman are deeply in love. Their only "obstacle" is that both are homophilic. Thus, the carnal gratification—the final signature—is by nature denied them. They separate. Now, such is the strength of absence that each one reaches the same sacrificial conclusion. "If she can only sexually be excited by women," says he to himself, "I'll become a woman." "If he can only be stimulated by men," says she, "a man I shall be." But they ignore each other's procedures. When next they meet he is (genitally) a woman, she a man. Are they still in love? Where do they go from here? Are they heterosexual? Who's on top?

You do grow weary of "courageous" announcements of Homosexual Studies—of scientists achieving breakthroughs on this "complex condition." Do the scientists have courses in Heterosexual Studies? Might they then conclude that homosexuality is in fact a simple condition? That problem solved, they could go on to something important, like a cure for asthma.

As for the daring chic of the "new" bisexuality, why not talk of sexuality *tout court*? How about autosexuality for the Paul Newmans of this world? The term is more reasonable than the masturbatory *narcissism* for one who enjoys turning on all the sexes; such a person is not *attracted to*, such a person is *attracted to being attractive*, works well at it, and deserves all that she-he can get. (Not the love of self, but the love of being loved.)

It's been over forty years since in her witty verses on homosexuality Kay Boyle declared it "As engrossing as bee-raising / And as monotonous to the outsider." Like Alcoholics Anonymous, which is swell for stock-market analysts but not for poets, gay libbers are (rightly) more concerned with effects than causes. I couldn't stick A.A. because, being obsessed with the pound of cure, they never asked Why.

Isn't the "homosexual condition" precisely that: a condition—a state to which one is conditioned? Isn't exclusive heterosexuality also conditioned from the day of birth, with those blue and pink cribs? Is one conditioned to "manhood"? Cannot a certain father be, in fact, a second mother? Was it not within a young male's rights to demand courtship privileges identical to those of the most popular girl in class? Could I too not be worshipped? Or was my role to worship?

Maybe the poet too is conditioned—even the first-rate poet. God doesn't make poets, parents do. In days when we believed in God, talent was not thought of as God-given but as a craft, a duty. Bach, Raphael were servants, it ran in their families. Today, with God gone, talent's an enigma; it falls from heaven. And gayness rises from hell.

Deep quiet snow, a "shroud," quite pleasing. Attention span narrower than
ten years ago. I write so as not to write. The diary is an ambulant procrastination, to keep from the task of beauty, that is, the duty of composition. The
duty is the piece for Schippers. It will be Chamber Music for Large Orchestra, with from eight to twelve movements, each movement to be instrumen-
tally composed of small groups—groups not usually found in chambers.
(That is, four flutes, four violas, and four English horns. Or five percussion-
ists, three trombonists, and two harpists. Or three bassoons and eleven
violins.)

Mostly the music will be new and based partially on a harmonic sequence,
like *Eleven Studies* in 1959. But, as with those studies, I'll crib from the
past—in this case from the unused *Panic in Needle Park*, and from isolated
orchestral movements completed here at Yaddo three years ago when I had
no commissions.

When the score's signed and sealed, how far will it have deviated from the
notes—verbal and musical—written here in these sentences and there at
that piano?

Mountain Climbing. One long line punctuated but never severed by many
hazards. Tunes are usually a few seconds long (Beethoven, Debussy), or a
few measures long (Hoagy Carmichael), or many measures long (Ravel, Mozart), or many *many* measures long (Mahler). This tune will last fifteen minutes, continually evolving, no repetition or backtracking, like Gregorian
chant (which, however, does not evolve).

Invent a different weave for each canvas, i.e., for each background or accompaniment. The music won't be heard so much as overheard. The scenes
will reduplicate themselves infinitely: they are acts without action (but with
motion) which never cease, eternal middles. We open a door upon these pictures, as in a *maison d'illusions*, and participate for a while. After we close
the door the movement nevertheless continues, unchanged and unheard,
forever.

Pure Contraption's been available for months, and so have good reviews.
The only sour note is Eugene's mutism. As co-dedicatee with Shirley (they
being, among musical contemporaries, my oldest school friends) he relished the honor before the fact. But according to the *petits amis*, because it

contains a disobliging reference to his friend Casals, he hasn't acknowledged the volume. Had I known of his sentiment earlier, I would have retained the reference but removed Eugene's name from the dedication page.

How does it benefit a publisher to put a book into the world without weaning it first? If literally no one knows the book exists, it will die of malnutrition, and go to the potter's field of shredding rooms. When Shirley says I should ignore these promotional superficialities and go on creating, she suggests I abandon my children once they're born—not guide them into the world. The main food is appreciation. Appreciation comes only through the public's tangible awareness, that is, not through understanding but through fame and cash.

Midge Decter phones to ask for a review of Tennessee Williams's *Eight Mortal Ladies Possessed*. How European, to be taken as general practitioner and not asked to write on only music. Conversely, though we can't yet expect book critics to review music, they should be obliged, for the good of the country, to learn how to review books about music.

26 February

Concert of my tunes at Skidmore last night, plus a so-called master class in afternoon, then a speech, then another class today and another concert tonight. Yaddo contingent ever faithful. Reading Graham Greene's *Loser Takes All*.

Aunt Pearl died. She would have been far older than Mama Miller, whose death provoked in me a flood of tears (was I eight? nine?—it was the summer I learned *Für Elise*), but solely out of sympathy for Mother's flood of tears, Mother who is now, at seventy-seven, orphaned of her four siblings.

Finished a little song based on Jean Garrigue's *Where We Came*, not for myself but for the memorial program Ben Weber is organizing. Now, although I admired Jean's poems (without especially liking them), would I on my own have thought of setting one? Can I yet know if the result is good? A song is as good as the vitality invested by singer and audience and has nothing to do with its composer's inspiration. Some of my "realest" songs have been deemed bloodless by best friends.

1 March

At the end of any year my production display is solid. But when and how it gets done I wouldn't know. Day after procrastinating day drags by as I curl into this corner with a book while in that corner unheard melodies wheeze across the room like cats that want out of the bag. Three weeks at Yaddo have been gracious but sterile. Hard work is hard work. The performance of already completed hard work is not hard at all, as with the recent public sessions at Skidmore, for it involves merely practicing the piano (a thoughtless vocation), repeating a speech, and seeing that the beautiful new velvet suit is pressed. But so time-taking.

It has been agreeable cohabiting with new strangers. But Elizabeth Ames is failing now, and her deafness a strain to all. One can always enjoy discussing abstractions with her, though about current personal facts she is "forgetful." Still, she doesn't experience what the French call *absences*; indeed, her room is alive with ectoplasm of the dead—her mother and sisters and with what she feels to be her active responsibility to Yaddo.

2 March

Tomorrow in Kansas, premiere of *In Time of Pestilence*, six short madrigals on verses of Thomas Nashe. The choice of poetry for these a cappella morsels I owe directly to Allen Ginsberg, although he doesn't know it. During an interview with *Gay Sunshine* long ago, Ginsberg quoted the line composed in 1593: *Brightness falls from the air*; and this urged forth my song. Thank you, Allen. Coincidence is not the word for fine minds functioning together while miles apart; it is the word for mediocre minds finding greatness—which is never. There is no coincidence. So I was not surprised to recall the phrase only last night, isolated painfully, as I reread *A Portrait of the Artist* after thirty years. *Brightness falls from the air*.

Stephen Dedalus recalls the words as he picks a louse from his neck, crushes it between his fingers, and lets it drop shining to the ground.

From the hamlet garden we plaintively watch trains go by. From the train window we enviously see hamlet gardens. Finally enclosed in the actual arms of the butcher we've dreamed about, we dream about the butcher. Go up in flames, go down in flames.

To be a working playwright in America is a remunerative proposition. A busy dramatist of a given age and reputation is far richer than a busy fiction writer of the same age and reputation. Remuneration now being the driving urge in art, successful dramatists if they write fiction do so in their spare time. Most try, but only one turns the trick of shifting at will between staged and nonstaged drama. Tennessee's short stories are finer than his plays—a high compliment to America's best playwright. The stories contain the strength of the plays without the froth; they never read like substitute scripts, with their drum-tight form and functional dialogue. Meanwhile the plays seem like meandering versions of the stories; indeed, after a story by Williams is discovered to have been the source for a play, the play looks less good.

3 March

A diary can't contain much humor: that would indicate an objectivity intrinsically absent from diaries. Humor (irony) is also notably absent from the insane, and from children. Most writing is autobiography once removed. So most writers are insane and/or childlike. Does it follow that most masterpieces are humorless?

Until parents are gone we cannot compose freely. Artists compose freely. Yet it's said they are children (and that in becoming adults, artists shed honesty). By nature a child has parents he wants to impress, yet few children are artists. So the syllogism is faulty, unless we state: artists are never orphans; or, inasmuch as only children can be orphans, an artist without mother or father is an orphan, free now, but creating always for his parents.

Does great work come from the loving child of living parents? Does it come, deflowered, the day of their funeral?

If all the children in Kenneth Koch's famous class are poets, then none are. Poetry is more than free-flowing non-literal juices. Poets are exceptional, but the exceptional child is the one without talent.

Optimism is fundamental to intelligence, though pessimism seems fundamental to logic. Saints and artists, at least during business hours, are not sad. Sorrow comes from love and private death, not from science and politics or from failure in these. Such failure is desperate, not sorrowful.

The first philosophy isn't that of suicide, of deciding whether life is worth living, but of deciding the value of writing about whether life is worth living.

An address book takes more wear and tear than a novel. A good one lasts twenty years before coming apart. By then most of those listed have died anyway. Address book manufacturers know this and are fair, exchanging planned obsolescence for well-planned obsolescence.

Great art works, being unique, are final: they do not open doors, they close them.

Tomorrow, the Trailways back to New York. Although I'm here, I've gone; everything's packed and my brain's been forwarded.

Along with unsolicited manuscripts (mostly worthless libretto outlines), I receive every fortnight or so, with their authors' "compliments," printed volumes of poetry. With a sigh and a gasp I engorge them all.

Poetry's dangerous. Oh, not because it exposes "truths" to the world, no. It's dangerous for the poet: it makes him look sappy to *talk* that way. I distrust the impulse, and shan't read poems anymore. I hate that word. The pomposity of Poetry. I could scream. There's no such thing as Poetry.

Ides of March

Ben Weber phones to acknowledge receipt of the Garrigue song. Dumb-foundingly he says he would like to instrumentalize it, and asks my permission. I never knew he cared. It's been ages since a fellow composer of stature (especially one of such different language) has expressed interest in my work. Ben's proposition illustrates the exercise of camaraderie, like Debussy orchestrating Satie's *Gymnopédies*, or Ravel orchestrating Debussy's *Danse*, or Caplet orchestrating Ravel's *Pavane*. (But who will orchestrate Caplet?)

Visit from William Powers, baritone who will sing in *Little Prayers*. Touch of flu.

16 March

Myrna Loy came to dine. She arrived early, every inch a star (magnanimous, not the haughty breed) in a fox chubby the same tint as her mahogany coiffure. Also, as appropriate *garniture*, we asked Ellen Adler plus Sondra Lee with Harlan Kleiman. Myrna's the only top actress to have been in a movie every decade since the 1920s. She's congenial to a fault (when Wallace bit her hand she didn't complain), and outspoken only insofar as her liberal professional values are disturbed. For example, while she will divulge none of the "secrets," if there are any, about Colbert or Gable or even David Manners, she's quick to despair of Ronald Reagan or Charlton Heston or even (perhaps unjustly) Molly Haskell—not to mention the recent crass biographies of Harlow. I read aloud Frank O'Hara's famous *To the Film Industry in Crisis*, which contains the lines:

> . . . *Gloria Swanson reclining,*
> *and Jean Harlow reclining and wiggling, and Alice Faye reclining*
> *and wiggling and singing, Myrna Loy being calm and wise* . . .

19 March

Visit yesterday from John Gosling, who wishes to commission a piece for the North Carolina Symphony of which he's the conductor. I accept, and will write something long in one movement, as contrast to *Air Music* in ten movements.

Extraction at the dentist's, he messed it up, and sent me bleeding down the street to the clinic where the job was finished. Then to Dr. Webster for more tests. Then Tracy Sterne here to dine. Scrambled eggs.

24 March

The tail end of March. For days, like a mean white lion, the sky's puked hail. This Sunday morning the beast sits on our city and emits quiet icy farts.

Visit from Muriel Smith, our first in twenty years. The always solid frame is somewhat *empaté*, but her handsome head—those fierce eyes, butterscotch skin, slightly buck teeth, blue-black hair—is unchanged from the starlit Carmen Jones. Muriel was the first ever publicly to sing my songs (the unpublished *Doll's Boy*, a Chaucer poem, a setting of Cocteau's quatrain, *De Don Juan*), the first of our Curtis group to defect to big-time in New York, then the first to establish herself in London where, like Tallulah in the twenties, she became the Englishman's idea of American Star. But after she converted to Moral Rearmament in the late 1950s, her musical reputation dissolved.

Sadly, here she is, living with her mother in a Mount Kisco medical compound, sorting computerized prescriptions. Like many another she's reached a point of looking back, of contacting school friends. She's hired a coach to revive her old repertory, yet her career is through, and she senses it. It's all very well to put your art at the service of non-artistic concerns so long as those concerns do not alter the nature of the art.

Before she left, Muriel handed me a booklet that extols "Christ's standards of absolute honesty, absolute purity, absolute unselfishness, absolute love." And she asked if I ever regretted not having children.

25 March

Finished Julien Green's *L'Autre*. As do all his novels this one holds the attention from first to last. Nevertheless it's too long. The emphasis on the sadism of others is itself sadistic. We examine paragraph after paragraph, many of them duplicates of each other like diary entries, exhausting injustice with a self-defeating single focus. Motivations in the characters are questionable, and not carried through, and the Catholicism seems more *mélo* than mellow. This is doubtless the last book by Green I'll ever read.

26 March

At David Diamond's invitation I conducted a seminar at Juilliard this afternoon. The assembly consisted of David, Milton Babbitt, Elliott Carter, and twenty of their pupils. Printed copies of *Ariel* were handed out, the record of it was played, and the next seventy-five minutes were consumed in discussion mostly of word-setting.

Once I'd have been apprehensive about such a meeting: might the young find me anachronistic, treat me with indulgence or sarcasm? Would Elliott and Milton, in their crusty cerebrality, consider me a waste? Today, with the assurance of durability, it all seemed fun. David was hotly concerned (being, after all, to "blame" for me) while the other two were attentive and, on the surface, deferential. The students meanwhile were a disappointment, seeming hardly more evolved than those one encounters in less prestigious schools around the land. Not that it was surprising to hear the same questions (there are, after all, less than a dozen basic queries to any basic *donnée*, and no answers at all), but what a small frame of reference. They found my songs not so much obsolete as uppity, their own choice of texts, when they use words at all, coming from Hesse, or from that *engagé* rock mystique of inventing phonetics as they hum along.

Iterated my usual spiel about how all music, even non-vocal timpani solos or computerized fugues, is primarily a sung expression; further, all music, even the pre-verbal music of Neanderthals, is a setting of texts—wordless texts, perhaps, but nonetheless texts drawn from some extramusical language. For instance (said I), Mr. Carter here is hardly known for his contributions to song literature, yet I contend (nor can he prove otherwise) that his composing impulse lies in the primal speech of his unconscious, a speech whose grammar is particularlized through his string quartets.

Beyond this there wasn't much to discuss, since my music is not discussable, not "constructed," can't be explicated (as Milton would say)—there's nothing to explicate. Unless a composer endorses a system, students, not to mention critics, are at a loss.

JH feels that my recent work (specifically *Little Prayers*) is burdened by rhythmic stodginess. Surely, he says, this comes from too often declaring that all music is tune. Rely on maxim: it springs shut like a trap.

27 March

I first met Elliott Carter in early 1944 at the Forum Group of the I.S.C.M. (This consisted of Miriam Gideon, Vivian Fine, Merton Brown, Harold Brown, Jacques de Menasce, and Lou Harrison.) During the next thirty years Elliott and I have spent a total of nine minutes in verbal converse. During the same period I've spoken with Helen Carter a bit more, around sixteen minutes, always at parties—for the Carters are social, their publicized aloofness notwithstanding. (Impervious to musical trends myself, God knows I'm garrulous.) During those fragmented minutes I've never got the feel of him as a person. Then a month ago, at yet another party, the fates choreographed the pair of us into a corner. For a half hour I was impressed that he should attend my banalities as though they were new to him, that I should do likewise in reverse. Surely he's the fox, I the goat (he feigns unawareness of my essay on his book). Yet even in these roles we fire no contact, do not spar, speak separate tongues. He would seem to have the grim dedication of youth, the one-track-mindedness which is essentially frivolous. Yet humor lies behind that naughty Burgess Meredithian glance and I should like to savor that, for humor is less frivolous than devotion, and I am not frivolous. But it's unlikely that we'll talk again for thirty years.

Too much concentration turns diffuse. Like the gowns of Adrian. Cheapness that only money can buy (as JH says of——).

4 April

Alan Rich and Bruce Saylor came to dine last night (but didn't comment on my delicate raspberry bavarian; also Alan, a cat freak, passed surreptitious scraps to Wallace beneath the table, a habit we don't encourage), after which we adjourned to the Hartford Museum to be on—to *be*—the panel for "Hear America First," Joe Fennimore's estimable baby, despite the right-wing connotations. I gave a pertinent, boring talk too long to transcribe, but which is already incorporated into "Our Music Now" for the *New Republic*.

Later tonight (but it's already night over there) Paul Sperry in Avignon will sing my *Poèmes pour la paix* with Marius Constant, in the string orchestra version devised twenty years ago for Capdevielle, which I've never heard.

7 April

Dinner party for the half-century of Shirley, who looks thirty. We invited Jane Wilson and John Gruen, Eugene Istomin, and Felicia and Lenny Bernstein. JH and I, with the Gruens and Eugene, had pitched in for a delicate gold chain from Tiffany's. What did the Bernsteins come up with? A delicate gold chain. Stew, homemade cake, red glass; Lenny asked where the *celebrities* were. We then all demonstrated what we alone, and nobody else, could do (me walking on my hands, etc.).

Being a computer, I lack imagination and cannot guess at meanings, so I must *learn* languages. I have no intuition and cannot recognize music unless I already know it, so I must memorize each example of a repertory. I have no ear and cannot think up colors or tunes, so to compose I must mimic the great (like the voiceless Chaplin who sings beautifully only when imitating Caruso). I am literal-minded and thus without humor, so I must employ a programmed intelligence that shows me what is truly witty. I explain all this to Felicia, who takes it at face value and offers her condolence.

14 April

Easter Sunday brunch with parents and Morris. Visit at five from Edouard Roditi. Press pants. Check airlines (first class). Leaving tomorrow for the Midwest. The terms of the *Little Prayers* commission are that I will not only attend the two premieres, in Sioux Falls and Sioux City, but that I will grace the campuses of every one of the eleven schools participating in the performances.

Yankton, South Dakota
18 April

In this town for many a childhood summer Rosemary and I dwelt on Pine Street in the house of Granddaddy, the Rev. A. C. Miller, and over there, kitty-corner across the road in the Shakespearian garden, is where I fell from the false balcony, acquiring this scar that still damages my shin.

(Sioux City) The performances rough but honest. The piece monstrous but flashy. The conductors, Trautwein and Kucinski, valiant, as were Gubrud and Powers. Reception last night chez the Wylie Maynes. I despise sleeping away from home, but feel terribly touched to have been asked to compose such a bulky and curious contraption, and gratified to have been able.

New York
24 April

Back from six days in Iowa and South Dakota where on two successive nights the oratorio *Little Prayers* was premiered. Except for the soloists (Irene

Gubrud and William Powers), the performance forces were unduplicated, Trautwein conducting the Sioux Falls Orchestra and a chorus of three hundred on Saturday, and Kucinski leading the Sioux City Symphony and a quite different chorus on Sunday. Previous to these occasions I lectured in widely spaced centers (including the Yankton of my childhood), mornings, afternoons, evenings, and managed to come through without once failing my regulated toilet habits. This region of the Middle West is a latticework of maternal Millers and of Rorems, of Republicans, real Indians on street corners, and lots of homemade pies.

After each rehearsal they thank me for "sparing the time" to give suggestions. Quaint reaction. Of course, since they've never met a composer before, they can't realize that he has more to lose than they by an unprepared performance. But "sparing the time" from what? From work? This *is* my work. From a charismatic life? That life exists only because I occasionally spare time from work for it. (I don't occasionally spare time from parties so as to write a symphony.)

Glamor and temperament, the supposed attributes of a star, are luxury items reserved for the intermission. No true artist—no Auden, say, or Callas—brings a "difficult" side to the scene of work except sometimes as priority to speed up matters; a demanding artist, if he's an artist, is always correct in his demands. Only nonprofessionals bring glamor to rehearsals.

26 April

At Trinity Church, premiere of my *Three Motets* for organ and chorus, on poems of Gerard Manley Hopkins. How can a composer best describe his own music? By playing it. Avoid definitions of style; the music defines itself. Hearers may eventually "locate" the music, but the composer can't guide them in words. (Browning: "When I wrote that, only God and I knew its meaning. Today only God knows.") Sculptors and choreographers may be comprehensibly observed in the act of work. Composers, like poets, can't even tell you about it after the fact.

Vita brevis est, ars longa. I never concurred. Life may be short, but so should art be. Economy is the core of craft, and art lasts only as long as an individual pair of eyes or ears is fixed upon it.

May Day

JH and I flew to Nantucket yesterday and rented a house for the summer, beginning six weeks from now. The realtor, Ann Killen, a Katharine Hepburnish number, not to mention the jonquiline weather, conspired to make the island appear as inviting as it was hostile when last we visited. Killen will have a piano installed, and the cosily bourgeois ambiance is somehow more apposite for us—or for me at my age—than the Fire Island of recent summers.

6 May

Death of Israel Citkowitz. I think first of Bill Flanagan who swore by him, but can't phone Bill in his grave. Then Caroline Blackwood, who I suppose, when we first met at Marie Laure's, was the most beautiful woman I'd ever seen, with those enormous eyes and languorous hand dropping cigarette ash like Danaë's gold all over the velvet carpet. Years later, when she was married to Israel and living down the street on West 12th, I'd see her from my window at the delicatessen across the way, frumpy, wheeling a carriage, still smoking. Now she's married elsewhere.

As soon as an artist dies he begins to date. He dates well or badly like John Donne or Edgar Guest, but he dates all the same: becomes identifiably locked into his period. When an artist of our time dies, we who survive witness the process of dating; smile or cringe at recognizing our own convictions or failings as they prevail or recede. That which is most *à la mode* becomes most *passé*.

13 May

Alvin Ross and Morris Golde came to dine last night. Alvin described his recent barium exam which he saw refracted on the ceiling, like an enlarged embryo moving in blood. The doctors moved their heads together over this phenomenon, but said nothing.

Alvin calls Wallace our "used cat." Depression. Dentist at four. Then we greeted Howard Moss at the Gotham Book Mart, and from there went to *Le Petit Théâtre de Jean Renoir*.

15 May

Temperature of crocus, the first true morning of summer. Between boulders at the edge of the Sheep Meadow I settle myself where a shaft of sunlight forms a hot halo through my gold curls; I loosen my shoulder straps, then smooth the plaid linen skirt around my ankles after removing my spike-heeled pumps and half-hose, the better to forage with clean toes in the as-yet-unseeded earth. With the confidence of noble womanhood (today's my twentieth birthday) yet impervious to the flirtation of passersby (inevitable on warm days when, for a moment, humankind puts forth brief feelers of friendship), I recommence my reading. I'm well into the little paperback of N. R.'s diaries, and though I confess that his arch revelations put me off, I'm captured by the flow, the thoroughly "natural" albeit narcissistic style and the sometimes surreal juxtapositions, which bring to a reader's lips the embarrassed sigh of Oh how true!

On vision's periphery I gradually grow aware of someone hovering. Looking up I see not two yards off a middle-aged gaunt person in sloppy turtleneck and dark glasses who, putting a finger to his lips, seats himself with the words: "Only let me speak for a minute. Occasionally strollers can't help but notice the title of readers' books. Perhaps, after a while, you will go home to commemorate in your own diary the not-too-usual fact that a stranger explained that that which is contained in one's reading can—like a movie—color or discolor one's hours long after the book or film is finished. The sight of myself, for example, may in your eyes not be far from the image of the author you read, though less beguiling, being more actual, leaving nothing to fancy. Yet surely you will remark that the tone of our exchange is not remote from the tone of those pages, by virtue of the fact that . . . Why go on? How can I advise you how to complete your written page, since there are—'" And he gets up and walks away. Here now I sit writing, yet there are . . . .

Week after week after week after aching week, year in year out, the round-robin relay persists: from thudding piles to herpes, to fissures and thudding piles to herpes. That devastating surgery in Fez is only a nightmare of twenty-four years ago. (Only a nightmare?) If writing of it here now could just lend the pain the humor of fiction! Yet this most comic of afflictions is what, in fact, will doubtless finally carry me off.

JH, forlorn, having just left on his annual trek home to Kansas; here I remain forlorn on a heavy wet Sunday. I'd long planned secretly to get drunk today on the Pouilly Fumé filling the fridge, then to go out to Julius' Bar, etcetera, where once I drank when far from fifty. For JH by his very presence is my A.A., and prospect of his absence confuses. Now this morning, sick at the thought of the sickness of tomorrow, I phoned these seven friends who, unbeknownst to them, were to witness (at least at the start) this downfall, and told them to stay home. Here I am home too, wondering how it would have been, yet knowing drunkenness is out of date. Rectal pains persist, and Wednesday I'm scheduled for a thorough proctological exam.

23 May

Gay Rights Bill (Intro II) defeated.

4 June

Dined at Elaine's last night with Ruth Kligman and Morris. Cheap costly food and too loud. (Came home alone, unsurprised at why I so seldom go to famous restaurants, or any restaurants.) When the check arrived Ruth, whose feministic chitchat had crackled with Equal Rights slogans, drew forth her compact and vanished to the ladies'. We waited for her return before we paid, having decided that since Ruth can't have it both ways, the bill should be split among the three of us.

The June weather redeems itself. Daily stroll into the splendors of Central Park. All finally is in full leaf, mimicking La Touche's *Lazy Afternoon*. Yet what one should inhale with a smile—the fat elms, quartz sky, buzzing roses in the Belvedere Gardens, sunning queens spewn upon healthy lawns—seems greasy with melancholy, as with Raid. This reaction's due partly to JH's brief absence (brief?) and to the in-depth proctology (if you'll pardon the expression) which occurs tomorrow. Alvin's condition conditions me.

5 June

After yesterday's long afternoon walk, another long walk last evening with Robert and Becki Phelps through Soho. We dined *à trois* exquisitely (such fresh salad! oh walnut pie!) at The Ballroom, then to Saint Antony's fair on Sullivan Street which annually from a distance looks more unclaustrophobically titillating than it turns out to be. Speaking, as cinquegenarians do, of horrors and habits of health.

Well, my health's less horrible than I'd feared, thanks to the reassurance of today's exam.

Robert quotes Auden: Those who hate to go to bed fear death, those who hate to get up fear life. Aren't these analogies identical? And isn't Auden anyway wrong? Children hate to go to bed, and they aren't conditioned to forebodings good or bad. It's rather a question of halting inertia, altering an aspect of life (for in life there is no death; not even dying is death). I, for one, enjoy waking up and enjoy going to sleep. Dreamland's not a void but a vital geography.

10 June

Alvin's recent barium showed a malignancy. I cannot forget his description of witnessing on a screen the X rays filtering through his intestine, and the interns' heads converging to a point on the film to focus on what looked like a wee embryo moving hazily on a pond—a pool within his body and, simultaneously, there above him. This morning Alvin enters Beth Israel.

Ten weeks since the extraction, with "complications," of the right canine which for years has caused trouble. (The golden post in the root canal was wrongly poised and continually perforated a nerve. Or something.) It's the first tooth, besides the wisdom ones, ever wrenched from my head. Its replacement has been dear in time and cash. Annual doctor bills amount to fortunes to pacify my fancy and the fancies of physicians.

For the first time the radio uneuphemistically reports today's air as "unhealthy."

Could this book be named *Truth*? A better title would be *Tlooth*, except that Harry Mathews . . .

Paradox: There is only one fruit, the raspberry. There is only one jam, the apricot. English does not naturally contain what the French call *olorime*—literal phonetic rhyme (*J'envias janvier*). Yet who becomes free from first-time associations? Antic Hay, Aunty Kay. Lead me not to Penn Station. Sonny laid Matine (for *Sonnez les matines*). In *L'Enfant et les Sortilèges* the armchair's crooning "*un vrai beau gosse*" sounded ever like "and pray for Gus." And at those Chicago football games, "Ever shall our team be victor / Without a peer she stands" for long childhood years remained "Ever shalerteen revictor / Without a pier she stands." Like Christ on the waves.

11 June

Tranquil day in Philadelphia. Not since December of '72 have I visited Rosemary on home ground, and then it wasn't mainly for her but for an orchestra performance. Without the distraction of her family, this afternoon was pure peace. We wandered through the Japanese pavilion of Fairmont Park and among the statues of Schiller and Beethoven along the formal paths, later sipped iced tea in Rosemary's backyard on Hamilton Street and talked for hours. Tan, svelte, well poised in a floor-length brick-colored skirt and peasant blouse, Rosemary looked better than in years. She'd wanted to speak with me, I guess, about her therapy. Indeed, it makes a difference, this process (along with her Zen and T'ai Chi exercises, so removed from my needs). Because finally, instead of—or along with—feeling languid and dismayed at John's dying, she's resentful. How could he have left her in the lurch! She admitted to a resentment of me also, and of Father and Christopher (sixteen when John died), for not stepping in and *being* John. To have said this much in an hour was for Rosemary to have said more than in the thirty-four years since, on leaving high school, we went our very separate ways. During those years I'd always felt from her a stifled sarcasm for what she would term my superficial life. After all, while I was living in the most comfortable home of Europe, she bore six children and functioned as housewife and social worker—functioned, that is, *outside* herself.

Summer has come and Monday JH and I leave for Nantucket where I've sublet until September a well-equipped bungalow. Rosemary, meanwhile, goes to Maine, where for a pittance she has purchased twenty acres of rock. So it goes, the Yin—as she says—and Yang of the Rorems.

Six weeks ago JH planted morning glory seeds on his bedroom windowsill. Already they have shot into an impenetrable lattice of green across his window. Each morning the heart is gladdened by these translucent blue blooms straining toward the city sunlight, transforming the unwashed panes into stained glass.

13 June

Rehearsal at Gregg Smith's of my new *Missa Brevis*, which he premieres next week in Cleveland. For sixteen unaccompanied minutes the sixteen singers remain smack on pitch, and the four soloists, especially Rosalind Rees (Gregg's wife), are angelic.

18 June

On the train yesterday I fell upon Rockwell's review of *Ariel* and felt thwarted. When he's written about my friends I've found him always right. To be belittled by someone one finds always right is bitter. How can he know it? Or what can a composer believe, since what he says is in contradiction to what others say in similar places?

If music could be written about, it wouldn't need to be written.

Today it seems paradoxical that my earliest exposure to what was called Modern Music and to left-wing politics should have been in the same milieu. It was Rosemary who first took me to Max & Cynthia's, a thin seedy couple inhabiting a single room off Fifty-seventh Street between Kenwood and Kimbark. Although not young—late twenties, perhaps—they were the crux of the local YCL, and their pad was a continual come-and-go depot where one heard (here's the paradox) discs not of Red Army songs but of Carillo(?)'s quarter-tone *Preludio al Cristobal Colon* and Milhaud's melodrama *Les choëphores*. The assemblage was unmoneyed and high-principled, and Rosemary and I, to them, were adolescent capitalist tourists. Revolutions never produce revolutionary art. How could one have known then that this depot was indulging precisely what Stalin at that moment was chastizing? How different, from frontier to frontier, becomes the sense of detail, like flirtation or food or the formality of funerals, not to mention the sense of dogma. A rose by every name smells different across the borders.

The most valuable composers are apolitical and aristocratic (Wagner, Ravel, Stravinsky), or bourgeois and bearish and pseudo-political (Bach, Beethoven, Debussy), or just straightforwardly religious members of the status quo, like all those before the Industrial Revolution.

Nantucket
20 June

Airborne, confined to his box, Wallace arrived petrified, in a pond of urine, shit, and vomit. Within twenty minutes he was at home on West Chester, licked sleek, proprietary.

Static-y transistors, unmuffled motorcycles; noise for noise's sake is not the final insult for some, but a surreal burlesque.

Once we were installed in the house, our landlady showed up to show us a few ropes. She turned on the electric dishwasher and left it on, so we talked a little louder. Proudly she turned on the laundry box and then the dryer and left them churning, so we talked louder still. Calm as you please, she switched on the radio (already set to a "good music" station, perhaps for my benefit) to show how she used background music. By the time she demonstrated the furnace adjustments we were all merely answering each other's mouthings, unruffled as in a silent movie.

Conservatives say: "We notice that those in favor of abortion are so often the same as those against the Vietnam War. Isn't this a contradiction?" Liberals reply: "We notice that those against abortion are so often for the Vietnam War. Isn't that a contradiction?" Both arguments are specious, the contradiction being that Vietnam and abortion are unrelated.

25 June

Darius Milhaud is dead at eighty-one. The headline strikes ironically after what I wrote yesterday of Claudel, collaborator in Milhaud's happiest works.

Did Darius die "fulfilled"? Does anyone at that age? Fulfillment comes with youth, while age poses pointless questions. *Faute de mieux*, he did continue and had a following. I, for one, would be quite another musician today were it not for adolescent obsessions with his *Création* and *Choéphores* and the contagious *Chants hébraïques* which Nell Tangeman sang so often and so well.

Personally, I knew Milhaud far less than I knew Auric, but he influenced me far more. How could Auric's music influence any composer? His greatness lies not in his music but in the intelligence that produces the music. Like too many intellectual artists (like Bill Flanagan), he thinks before he speaks, then fails to write it down afterward. Motto: make first, censor later. By this motto Milhaud made junk, but his pile is far higher than Auric's and contains some sizable pearls.

Like great chess players, certain geniuses are social dolts with one-track minds. I doubt that Beethoven was "well-rounded," that Bach was "cultivated." Breeding, reading, and charm infringe upon the necessary narrowness of great acts. Humor is decadence pure. Why suppose that the key composers are any more literary than the monumental authors are musical?

Half the Groupe des Six has vanished.

28 June

Ten days on this island—raw, windy, with ropes of rain thick as the bars in a zoo. Restrained by the weather from the joys of the beach, I've been orchestrating eight hours a day and have sties in both eyes. JH meanwhile has been reading on Africa—*everything* on Africa—and our only company is each other. Mutual entente is somewhat of an invasion of privacy. Yet do I know what privacy is?

Left to my own devices I'm a shell.

At dawn JH went into New York, where he must remain for a week. With his departure the ironic sun emerged, and here am I at loose ends, dreading the virtue (chore) of creation. Two big orchestral works are commissioned, paid for; yet I've spent the morning baking a *clafouti aux cerises*, keeping my mind as far as possible from the needs of my métier.

Clafouti Limousin
1 cup flour
¼ cup butter
2 eggs
½ cup granulated sugar
½ cup powdered sugar
1 cup boiled milk
Pinch of salt
3 cups pitted black cherries

Mix flour, salt, granulated sugar and butter. Add cool milk and eggs, and mix to produce a smooth dough. Line a buttered flan case with half the batter, sprinkle cherries with powdered sugar, cover them with the other half of the batter. Preheat oven, and bake at 400° F. for 30 minutes.

Pears may be used instead of, or along with, cherries. Brown sugar may be used instead of, or along with, granulated.

29 June

The Paris Diary is quoted in Darius's long obituary. ("Rorem described the Milhaud home in Paris as 'a barren apartment on the boulevard Clichy looking down onto the million wild lights of Pigalle's merry-go-rounds.'") What nature of work would I now be most concentrating on were it not for Robert Phelps's perseverance in getting that little classic printed? Could I have written (and published) six more books, thus gaining the authority to be heard as a critic whose quaintness makes other critics climb the wall? Would I have centered more on musical composition? Would the composition have been "better"? Deeper? Idle conjectures. But in the less than eight years of this new career I've become, with the accompanying slight notoriety, sourer. That may be age.

I am growing more superficial. "Why" interests me less than "what." Surfaces are all: the smell of roses or peanut butter, the story line in Kierkegaard. How these things came to be, what *forms* them, no longer intrigues me.

Profundity is for the young. It has little to do with being alive, though it has much to do with being human. (Ironically, sex, which has everything to do with being alive, preoccupies me hardly at all, not even vicariously. In *Deep Throat* the orgies are continually slowing down the plot.)

Will I, did Darius, do people die because they've said all there is in them to say? Style remains. Yes, but that point's been made too.

Last night, alone in this ocean, after a supper of yams, fresh tomatoes, and oatmeal bread (one dollar a loaf), I took a stroll at the hour between dog and wolf, overcoming the honeysuckle and foghorns but not the non-melancholy void which seems to indicate: Why even bother to kill yourself?

This morning I feel all right again.

30 June

Preview last month of Jim Bridges's new movie. Afterward, small party at the Sherry Netherland for the prima donnas, including John Houseman with whom I've always found conversation hard as with a statue. Fate arranged that the two of us leave in the same elevator and, finding ourselves on the same street pursuing the same taxi, we shared the vehicle with strained civility. Houseman, as it happens, is the best thing about *The Paper Chase*. With expertise and diligence Jim Bridges has confected a film which ridicules diligence and expertise. Personally affable, Jim asks that his work also be taken affably. Result: the story is recounted in an antiseptic voice having nothing to do with its *auteur*. I recognize this the more quickly in that the virtue of likability is my vice too. The Houseman character, a grumpily skillful law professor, is made to seem unsympathetic because he places hard work higher than personality interplay.

I blew my nose in the paper napkin, then wadded the napkin and, as an afterthought but within the same gesture, reached across the table to polish some dust off the brass lamp. Jim Bridges reacted only by stating, "Now, that would be filmed, not in three shots, but in one." My reaction, had he done this, would have been: "He blows his nose in G-flat major."

1 July

For whom do I compose? For the listener within me. Sure, I hope other listeners may find a sympathetic point of contact, and I need those listeners. But I don't know who they are. There are as many audiences as there are pieces, and the audiences don't necessarily overlap. "The" audience is neither vast nor wee. Mick Jagger's audience is not *La Traviata*'s, and hers isn't Billie Holiday's, and hers isn't Mélisande's, and hers isn't Berg's, and his isn't Webern's, and Balanchine's isn't Martha's, and hers isn't Twyla's, and Twyla's isn't mine. Does art soothe death or the death of love? Not much. The cause of art is never enough. Art is usually about love and death, but death and love are not art, nor even about art, not even Mishima's. Priority: anyone can die of love, but only I can pen my tunes.

If Nantucket is made up of right-wing Gentiles, comfortable but not super-rich, and no artists, none at all, but some good journalists, is it the Jews of Martha's Vineyard who lend it its higher artistic gloss? They're comfortable but not super-rich either, and Gentile.

The argument of *Equus* comes too close for comfort to the dream recounted on page 34 of *The Paris Diary*, published in England in 1967. The playwright credits his source as being an unnamed man, now dead. Well, I am sort of alive, but the author of my old diary is in a sense dead, though not his copyright.

Toothpick limbs descended from the terry-cloth robe which, when he removed it, revealed a hairless belly looking less like a pot than a pillow case of mauve silk stuffed with mashed potatoes. He eyed us, not cruisily, but with that sidelong Neronic leer meaning "I recognize you but I don't recognize you."

2 July

Our world is mine as well as yours. Anxiously each morning I realize that before nightfall there will be two bombardments of noise pollution from North Church, day after day, month after unquiet month. I do not, as a citizen, challenge the genuineness of motive in bestowing upon Nantucketers these "carillon concerts" (actually commercial discs emitted through loudspeakers). I do not, as a Quaker, primarily object to the Congregational bias in program selection, though it does exclude the island's Catholics, Jews, Buddhists, and atheists. Nor do I, as a professional composer, necessarily resent the quality of the "arrangements" flowing like tasteless treacle through my study.

I do complain that a church can be so arrogant as to presume I enjoy these broadcasts, and that I have no choice in the matter. Whatever other townspeople's reaction may now be, they were not consulted beforehand and are a captive audience. Suppose they in turn, through religious (or even lay) affiliations, broadcast far and wide their personal convictions! Imagine the din! Yet what prevents them? Who sets examples in taste?

Taste is a personal affair; to impose it upon others is to insult them, whether the imposition be that of a rock band or a Bach mass. Painting (fortunately for many in Nantucket) is a silent art: we can look away when it offends us. But since we cannot "listen away" from music, its public emission becomes an invasion of privacy.

Should a vote be cast? Perhaps. But not on whether to continue the North Church recitals, nor indeed on whether they should ever have begun, since most voters wouldn't care (there is too much approved noise everywhere to assume that the inured ear actually listens rather than merely hears, viz, the constant Muzak at the A & P). The vote should be on the more tenuously moral question of whether the pleasure some find in certain public sound is worth the pain this sound causes for others.

Can it now be observed that Schoenberg, like Gertrude Stein, evaded the problem of making art by allowing himself to become snared by his own design for making art?

To complain about the Pan Am Building is to miss the point of Manhattan.

The Pan Am Building doesn't block the view, it *is* the view. By the same token, to complain that one performer betrays the composer while another
illuminates the composer is to assume that there is one way only. The composer himself might be surprised by this. Still, there are differences that
have less to do with interpreting specifics than with music generally. The
difference between Eugene and Gary as pianists is that there is nothing
"wrong" with Gary. His one identifying mannerism is his lack of mannerism. Beauty limps, greatness contains the tragic flaw. Paradoxically, the flaw
of perfection is not tragic.

Tears didn't blind her, they acted as magnifying glasses. Seen through salt
water her own mistakes looked like the faults of others. (Or: Tears don't
blind, they enlarge. Seen through salt water, our own mistakes look like others' faults.) Yes, the world is according to our humor and locations. If I see
that field with my eyes, but cannot see my eyes, can I see the field?

Who is Plato? He is Satie's librettist. Stella Adler? Ellen's mother. Jesus
Christ? a character in a tale by Anatole France. Poppaea? Charles Laugh-
ton's wife.

They've grown diamond-bright and too strong. I can no longer compete
with my imitators.

3 July

Are there, this hot afternoon in Chicago, ten thousand youths masturbating
to Michigan breezes in a blazing room, as we learned to masturbate there
thirty-six years ago? By the average law, my life's two-thirds done.

He has led—*comment dirai-je?*—a dead life. A dead life. How flat falls the
phrase.

The large kitchen has passed from yellow to gray even as I've typed these few
words, and the lanes of Nantucket begin again to resemble those of Tangier
as night falls, with the hills and cranberries charging through the window,
and the hour turns sad again, as though JH, son and father, had died.

One's happiest days are those when one was saddest—that is, most open
to reaction, to new experience and heartbreak, the first long journey away
from home.

4 July

On the beach this morning a retarded (what used to be called feeble-
minded) woman of perhaps thirty-five, flanked by patronizing kin, was pat-
ting her sand castle with unlovely hands and giggling—her drooping lower

lip incapable of enthusiasm, the lusterless mongol eyes unfocused on her work. What does she *know*? Where are her answers? Who guides her?

All day I observe the *va-et-vients* of Wallace the cat, and wait for his secrets. Is he a sage or an idiot sphinx? Maybe just a baby? But babies know what we've long forgotten.

You know that ghastly look some mashed potatoes get, of cheap white soiled satin? Well, that's how my abdomen's beginning . . .

The Cincinnati piece is nearly done. The overall title of the ten separately named sections is *Dreams*.

5 July

We had decided on Nantucket for three negative reasons: no mosquitoes, no need for a car, no social temptations. The positive virtues are those of many a New England area: clean air, swimmable sea, homegrown tomatoes. The house, rented from a Miss Melva Chesrown, charming and comfortable, two floors quaintly furnished, and a geranium garden.

Community is 101 percent heterosexual WASP, non-intellectual well-off Republicans with too many children, of whom the females are prettier than the males. The food (like the painting in the clever wharf galleries) is blandly costly, and the movies are safe, chic revivals: *Million Dollar Legs*, which is surrealism for the unwashed—or rather, for the overwashed—and *To Have and Have Not*, which holds up neatly, Bacall being that contradiction: a human star. Bogart/Bacall has nothing to do with acting, everything to do with presence.

In the Unitarian Church there is a conventional concert series run by cultured behatted matrons who do not know my name. In the charming bookstore there are shelf upon shelf of best-sellers dusted daily by macrobiotic thirty-year-olds who do not know my name. So much for a life's work.

I've been alone here half the time (JH must return intermittently to New York). Black nights no longer afflict mornings' start at eight, and the weather's been perfect: a level, silky seventy-two degrees.

On the new vast sheets of prepared onionskin, with a special soft lead, I've orchestrated forty *tutti* pages; this comes to about five hours a day and a callused thumb. (Oh why, in this large cottage, does Wallace in the middle of the night choose to climb onto the kitchen table and sleep precisely on top of the smudgeable manuscript?)

Of the three books I've finished reading—the Claudel play, *Maigret et le fantôme* (even my precious Simenon seems watery on this island), and *Claudine en ménage*—only the last was worth it. But what worth! In that Claudine series, which readers overlook, the good-natured and all-wise Colette argues a stronger case for women, and two generations earlier, than *A Room of One's Own*.

Gay Sunshine, in a joint issue with Boston's *Fag Rag*, has appeared, containing the interview Winston Leyland taped with me last October. It's inordinately extended, and could surely be as informative at half the length. Yet there's no rule for interviews and, if cut, the content might remain, but my snappish aura would fade with the conversational tone. I do make an issue of how I don't make an issue of homosexuality, and I must say that, within the context of the rest of the magazine (those close-ups of cocks, those manifestos of faggots, those dirty poems), my statements seem reactionary. Yet compared to these islanders I'm an insidious radical.

The islanders, meanwhile, without exception possess the Gentile hemophilic lassitude of the unliterary *gratin* (as opposed to Jewish *nouveaux riches*), which folks like me seldom come across anymore except in Marx Brothers revivals. Yet my loneliness led yesterday to the Harbach's cocktail party at which, through throngs of martini drinkers in the clean old American decor, I was approached by a lady—yes, lady—whose name I didn't catch but whose posture—slim, high-society, handsome, fifty, white marcelled hair and long amber skirt—looked cool as a foaming beer. Heat rose only in a declaration about her native Washington, D.C.: "It's all taken over by the darn Negroes!" I don't necessarily resent her prejudice. I resent her country-club presumption that I, a perfect stranger, share her prejudice.

Depressing fireworks on the public beach.

Why do I write all this? Why persist? For whom? It's not particularly unusual. I write it all because I know who I am, and that is unusual. If from the start *je me suis fait un personnage*, I know who that personage is.

Thus (and I state this seriously) I am drawing for posterity a situating portrait that plainly does portray.

Meanwhile in the oven across the room cooks a Nectarine Crumble, same recipe as for Joe LeSueur's Cherry Crumble, but with the dangerous addition of one egg. Will it turn out?

6 July

For an autobiography, a logical and legitimate scenario could be built from other people's letters, especially love letters. Who has the courage to plunge into those tear-filled trunks? To spend too long there means that one's life is past. Yet such letters, at least in my case, make landmarks. Who was I, or who did I think I was, when A thirty years ago sent those unhappy words, or B twenty years ago or C ten? Alone, the box filled with mementos from

Marie Laure provides a portrait of both her and me at a fixed point in French history.

Love letters are the food of retrospect, introspect, and extroversion. And what about hate letters? And business letters?

11 July

Monet's *Regatta à Trouville* is my favorite painting because it evokes some satisfied geography from my own past, a geography I can't elsewhere relocate. Was it on the beach of Lake Michigan that I first knew that untroubled combination of color and temperature? or the beach at Safi? at Paestum? Saint Tropez? Fire Island? A late-summer cloudless sky, a tulip garden filled with hoopskirts at water's edge, money, calm, a chill in the breeze. Such a scene was this afternoon's at the Nantucket jetties, with JH, recalling the sailboats from Scheveningen beach in 1956, when elegant wolfhounds fled through the snow as the sky darkened.

Other pictures by Monet hold little interest for me. Vuillard is my favorite painter.

Did the Ark of Noah provide for fish, or for the larger mammals of the oceans? It did not.

My favorite painter is Caravaggio because he makes me long to live on his stage. That's the sole criterion by which I can judge art, including the art of tragedy.

18 July

The Cincinnati commission is coming nicely. Nine of the eleven movements are composed and orchestrated. What shall I name it? JH suggests *Music for Money*.

Finished *After Leaving Mr. McKenzie*, which in its lumpy style and subject is identical to *Good Morning Midnight*. No American writer has ever, as Jean Rhys does, centered on the mistreated lackluster female caught in unlikely sectors of foreign cities. (What about Maeve Brennan? asks JH.)

The Sting. Some folks got together and said, Let's make a movie about whores and hire two whores to star in it. There's not a frame of the film that doesn't pander.

Lost Horizon (revival of Frank Capra version). How could we once have so thrilled to this sexist, racist cant, this admonition to "Be Kind" by the same Sam Jaffe who presumably sanctioned a pilot's murder and kidnapped these unwilling passengers to fertilize his Caucasian Utopia, where Jane

Wyatt (who, with Isabel Jewell and Margo, is the only woman of any race in sight) teaches Tibetan children to sing Brahms in English?

Current reviews of Kate Millett's *Flying* make me uneasy about the reception (if there is one) of my *Final Diary* this autumn. Millett is chided (at least by Lehmann-Haupt) for being homosexual ("the book should appeal to others with her hangups") and, worse, for mixing trivia with deep thinking. As though the very nature of diaries were not based on the Importance of Unimportance.

But humor can't go hand in hand with revolution. Humor means multiple viewpoints, which revisionists cannot afford. Humor has always been for the comfortable. Because they are healthy and their world is new, children view with blinders—they laugh at nothing. Humor is the beginning of decay.

23 July

Finished *Eugénie Grandet* late last night in discouraged astonishment. Ineffable Balzac! Without him, would Mauriac or Green or Gide be as they are? Could they even exist without his example of high strain in the provinces?

This morning I again take up Henry James (he in whom I so drowned in the early 1950s), this time with apprehension. To peruse his introduction for *The Awkward Age* is to laugh with despair. Could I really understand all this in 1952? Today Henry James reads like a parody of Henry James.

You cannot write a tone of voice. Nor can a composer compose his interpretation. Hearing today, over the years, those stern words of Miss Burris— that fourth-grade teacher who made me cry—I cry again at what made her make me cry.

25 July

JH returns this evening from four days away in the cold, according to his call last night, while Nantucket finally bursts into a conflagration of good-natured hydrangeas. His voice is always so defeated that I protect myself by impatience rather than by sympathy. Yet if JH's woes are continual, I tell myself that I grow less pessimistic with age, that I have more to hide behind than JH, notably a screen of appreciation without which every infant and man is only half himself. Yet what is appreciation but another transient luxury, while JH's sadness, if I were to admit it, is the purity of logic: a necessity. Our planet has no escape. Hope of outer space? Heaven's an endless cemetery. As far as eyes can see, and forever beyond, shine stars by the quadrillion, each one a tombstone.

Clearly I am not endowed with what once was called a poet's eye. I see what is. Waiting last month on Morris Golde's Water Island porch I observe acres of shrubbery, the beach beyond and the ocean. I find what's there, not clusters of throbbing emerald plush or masses of lavender talcum stained with blue champagne, but shrubbery, the beach beyond and the ocean. Although reared within Freudian metaphor I lacked the imagination to see Mother as Jocasta, buttocks as breasts, cocks as snakes and vice versa, or art as depiction of anything beyond itself. Perhaps such literal-mindedness, coupled with lazy half-knowledge, becomes the specialty that turns into Me.

Morris's shining virtue: wishing to be loved, he's willing to love others by giving them the benefit of the doubt. His shining vice: expecting rhetorical questions to be answered. ("Isn't that the most gorgeous sunset you've ever seen? Hey, isn't it?" "Yes Morris, yes it is.")

Morris, to whom I explain that I never made it to Jane Wilson's opening, answers: "Neither did I. How was it?"

27 July

The obituary page was meaningless once. Now I turn there daily with the nausea of anticipation. If no one has died, I sigh with relief (and disappointment). Yet hardly a week passes but the hyper-private news spits from the public pages, as we tremble from the banality of it. This morning: Parker Tyler. Again the review of a lifetime flies by in a minute, as for a drowning man.

We are not who we think we are. But then who are we? This persona—contrived with our bare hands early—is indeed what we think, though its *effect* we can never be sure of. The difference between sane and insane is that the one knows himself and the other doesn't. Which one? The contrivance, so human, we've forced on beasts. Wallace, our Russian blue feline, the apple of JH's eye—fat, spoiled, and domesticated there on the gray lawn—is *a part of our lives*. He too, when the bomb explodes, explodes. And the *natural* world? We humans precisely have *made* it natural and in our image, reconditioned. We are who we think then.

Parker was seventy. I'd have thought younger, despite his pasty look during our *croisements* of the past year, mostly in the elevator of my parents' building where he too lives—lived. The excruciating familiarity of that elevator where Parker will nevermore set foot. The lavish art nouveau of the Nantucket Sweet Shop on Main Street. I could immortalize it on this page, as in *L'Eclisse* Antonioni immortalized a bus stop where his stars met. The film ends at the bus stop, abandoned, not even haunted, ours now. Should you visit the Sweet Shop, where nightly I now sit, you would recognize that bric-a-brac from my accurate description, but you'd ask, Where's Ned? Nothing remains but place. Finally it goes too. Battlefields of hell bloom bright with posies.

28 July

Over thirty years ago I left Chicago and with it the Fifty-seventh Street meeting of the Society of Friends, into which I'd been bred by converted parents. Because the general past is always golden, because this particular group seemed, to my family, lively and liberal (flourishing as it did on the twigs of Hutchins's imaginative nest), and because every gust but this one from the Windy City has ebbed, what more natural than to retain membership in absentia? This I do with an annual contribution, receiving in return the *Newsletter*, virtually my sole lien. Now, although the *Newsletter* does not purport to be a literary monthly, I see no reason why, when for once I send a message (an articulate complaint against one Reverend Greeley, whose macho pap in an earlier edition had outraged me), this message should be revised by the editors into the garbled smarmy cant typical of this periodical's tone. Etcetera.

That paragraph opens an unfinished missal to the *Newsletter*. But then— sigh—O why? The recipients do not recall the saucy little boy in their halls, do not know "who" he has become, do not see Quakerhood my way, and why bother? Three weeks ago, when Mother and Father were here on Nantucket, we attended meeting (I for the first time in a decade) on Fair Street, and each of us was "moved" to speak regarding the self-congratulatory mood about us. In my case, this was self-congratulation on how un-self-congratulatory I am, but I was proud of *them*. How, they asked, can we sit here and benefit from this peace, which you say we owe to George Fox, when in fact there is no peace?

Having paddled out of the preface to float swiftly now in the mainstream of *The Awkward Age*, I've cracked the nut—or grown a 1974 vintage—of Henny Penny (as Robert Phelps calls him). The novel is camp, so high that Wilde by comparison joins Neil Simon. (Those characters of every sex and age are never at a loss for original *répliques*!) Now, if the text proper is camp, so by extension is the preface, on a stratosphere level—a triumph not only of style, but of style-as-wit. Consider, then, the whole oeuvre of HJ (JH reacts with bored laughter) and how very coarse in his wake become his immediate American predecessors.

Parker Tyler's obituary (he deserves a more comprehensive one) places his major—his *known*—works as from an early period. Shuddering, I realize that most of what most of us have to say is said before fifty. Fortunately, at least in the area of "art," for every Rimbaud there is a Verdi.

How, I've been trying all day to recall, did I first know Parker? Through John Myers during those fruitful *View* years? I do recall that through Parker I met Tchelitchev. Indeed, it was my urging (having, like all nineteen-year-olds, become bewitched with Tchelitcheviana at MOMA) that prompted Parker to choreograph a meeting, realized at the Russian Tea Room, where a fourth joined us (Perry Embiricos?).

Dawn Angel, composed in 1945, predates *The Lordly Hudson* by two years, and is my first post-juvenile song. Before musicalizing the verses, I asked Parker to read them aloud, during which process I recorded in my mind the nuances of his careful voice, then set the poetry according to the poet's personal rises, falls, and pauses.

The chore of correcting two massive sets of proofs just received from Boosey & Hawkes! *The Poets' Requiem* (1954–55, Rome) and *Little Prayers* (1973, New York), my only large works for chorus and orchestra, both with soprano solo, and both—perhaps not coincidentally—on poetic compilations of Paul Goodman. A page of music proof, as opposed to the less complex prose galley, requires about ten minutes' reconsideration. Here are 150 pages. How uninterested I've grown in the old *Requiem* and new *Prayers*, which already have little to do with me.

29 July

Monday night. Robert Phelps phoned late yesterday from Hyannis, where Becki has been hospitalized for a week following a major car crash. (At fifty we change our minds, yes, but if we refuse to change our bodies, engines and oak trees change them for us.) Glad to offer Robert, who ferried over for the day, a perfect temperature, healthy lunch (with JH and Gustavo Vega, who's visiting for a few weeks), and a Chekhovian stroll—*des journées entières passées sous les arbres.*

With righteous indignation we follow the impeachment ceremonies on the clear-cut cable TV with which this house is endowed, while through the window creep new-mown hay and goldfinch chirping—and Becki's bones are broken on Cape Cod. Nixon's initials are mine backward. (My middle letter is Miller, Mother's maiden name.)

The one person on the island—perhaps because I've vaguely known and liked her earlier and elsewhere—with whom fraternity would seem plausible is D. D. Ryan. So when she accepted my invitation for a drink, I went to some effort to prepare for a nice visit. When, after an hour, she hadn't shown, I phoned, to learn she'd simply forgotten. I am very, very, very paranoid, and this is no help.

It is misleading for any workman to pretend that the reputation (whatever it may be) gleaned from his work doesn't grant both carte blanche and noblesse oblige, although these attitudes, in principle, are extraneous to the work. (Protection's needed from too much public if one is to create the very work which creates that public, but one still craves appreciation in order to feel that the work is worthwhile. Only amateurs champion value in a vacuum.) When D. D. simply forgets, what's the use?

The rich make their own rules, more tiresome here than in France where the rich have been rich longer, so you don't constantly have to prove you love them for themselves, as though money had nothing to do with the grooming of those selves. Admittedly, the European rich I once knew were only through Marie Laure's association (though I knew *her*), while in America I know almost none, and those "almost" are past episodes, all female, with marriage in mind.

1 August

Is the theater of the quotidian more active in the rural summer, or just more sharply focused? Mother called to say that Father fell from a curb, suffered a chipped hip, will remain in Saint Vincent's for three weeks after a pin is affixed to the bone. She adds (not knowing I know) that Parker Tyler is dead, that a few mornings ago, as coincidence would have it, she was at Saint Vincent's visiting a patient who said Parker was in the next room. She entered there, greeted Charles Boultenhouse *qui veillait*, and shook the pallid hand of the patient, who *maybe* recognized her though he seemed "lost," and who died that evening.

Mother and Father waited five hours in Emergency before Father was examined—Father, who co-founded Blue Cross and who for forty years was America's most distinguished medical economist, who lies now in a ward, Father who will be eighty in November.

Whatever became of rough trade? Already in the 1960s there had emerged a type far too sveltely masculine to be anything but queer, while the straight hard hat was too potbellied to be appealing. Today—after flower children, "passive" husbands, and unisex—one may well ask, If opposites attract, who is one's opposite?

2 August

Here is your past, pronounced the voice, and a door opened into the gloom of our Chicago apartment. It had been stripped bare, as by bandits.

Before falling to sleep (from which I was, at 2:30, to wake up screaming from that nightmare too clear for comment), I savored the habitual skilled intensity of Pauline Kael in her diatribe against the "moguls." She does skirt one point: that people get (as Nixon got) what they deserve. And though she allows that better movies are being made now in America than at any time anywhere, and reaffirms the obvious—that hits are not to be confused with art—she avoids admitting that the vast movie public never was or can be, by definition, discriminating. (The young, as she claims, may have had their taste waylaid in the past two years, but have they ever really been *nuancés*, as she gives them credit for? On summer beaches now, as from winter porches then, show us one, just one, of those thousand lovely children attending to the Debussy Trio as he would to the rock background. *Le Sacre* could fill their every visceral requirement, but where is it?) Otherwise, of course, she's right about moguls slapping poets for being poets. In music the moguls (i.e., performers' impresarios) are unaware of the very existence of poets (i.e., composers), and the word *artist* has come to mean performer, entertainer.

To be a movie critic is to investigate, as through a telescope, the inherently expanding, because film, no matter how "fine," is by its size construed for *le grand public*—the collective eye. To be a music critic is to examine, as under a microscope, the infinitely small (and how many contracting universes float on that lens!), because a piece of music, no matter how gross, is construed for the unique ear. Only when music relinquishes its function as an aural art (something to be attended) and caters to the whole body (an accompaniment) does it cease being a fine art.

9 P.M. After twenty minutes of *Blazing Saddles* we leave the theater, discouraged. There's still enough calm afterglow on South Water Street for our stroll toward the wharves to watch the sunset, balanced this evening by the moon, which has become a perfect lavender globe. This cheers us up. Then we stop by the Hub to buy ten postcards.

"That's fifty-two cents," announces the salesgirl, one of the prettyish Vassar types who swarm the island in summer to learn about life by getting a job.

"Why fifty-two? How much is one card?"

"A nickel."

"Then if I buy each card as a separate purchase, they'd only come to fifty cents."

"You'd be ripping us off by avoiding the tax."

"On the contrary, you're ripping me off by manipulating the tax."

"Are you speaking to me, personally?"

"I'm saying the policy is unfair. Usually to sell an item in quantity is to lower the price. Here, the more I buy, the more you charge, yet you say I'm ripping you off. The customer as usual is wrong, and I resent it."

Yet I paid what she asked, and went off feeling awful. Returning with Gustavo to the safety of the house on West Chester Street and the purry welcome of Wallace, I finish the peach cobbler made this afternoon and begin the penultimate piece of my Cincinnati opus—a scurrying toccata called *Apples*, for three oboes and three violas.

(That loathsome new verb—*to rip off!*)

7 August

JH returned from New York Sunday with a headache. By last night the ache had turned to what he felt was a cerebral hemorrhage after three days of high fever and near-constant delirium. I waited in the emergency ward of Nantucket's Cottage Hospital while JH was being inspected this morning at dawn. And I inspected the flow of the very young in other emergencies— mostly long-haired children with ticks in their ears or gashes in their poison-ivied toes. One young couple brought in their son Brian, age two, who since yesterday had refused to open his eyes. There he was in his mother's arms, silky skinned, unsmiling and unprecedented, shrieking when prodded, the parents more innocent than he in his sophisticated visual autism. What became of Brian I do not know. JH emerged, after sinus X rays (negative), diagnosed as a flu carrier and told to take two aspirins and rest. He's sleeping now, thank God, silently.

8 August

Twenty years ago tonight I first met P at a long-since-vanished *boîte* in Cannes. Of that, nothing remains, though I can recall, as clearly as though it were a large-print version of the Bible in my lap, each phrase and motion of that two-year episode. But I only recall; I do not reexperience. The body's intact, without the blood. Still, the past looms ever larger as the future recedes. (Is *recede* the word? I mean to get smaller, *rapetisser*.) And if love affairs of the past are unnourishing, affairs of the past stick and twist, entertaining endlessly. Nobody, except JH (who, when he goes off, leaves me bereft), means much today.

We can sympathize with, but not feel and so not weigh, another's pain. The hurt which for days J H has borne is almost too much for me, yet I don't ache. We can "project into," but not adopt and so not judge, the flesh of the opposite sex. No man or woman will ever know from inside what is a woman or man. Nor can we be readers of our own writing, and music composed in a swoon is sneered at. We might know the facts of our youth, but can only repeat them blurred on the edge of an expensive coffin.

What a wind. And so clear. The first morning of a new president's reign, Mother's and Father's fifty-fourth anniversary (to be toasted tonight at Saint Vincent's Hospital), and the day I completed the orchestration on what now is named *Air Music: Ten Variations for Orchestra*. Methodic folly.

Could one wish for more unflawed mornings, windless clovered cobalt air at body temperature? Jane Bowles's *Plain Pleasures* extols the virtue of "simple things," those little joys that make life worthwhile. I wouldn't dare today, as I dared a year ago, to be bored, to wish tomorrow would come, to "kill" time, because the only delights in the present are bromides. Yet such perfect sunlight only helps to focus on tombstones, like naked light bulbs in a concentration camp.

Plain Pleasures, in fact, is a sordid tale, and I do feel at loose ends, notwithstanding Mother Nature's inexplicable splendors, when I've finished a long piece. Which is worse: the distraction of not working or the anxiety of work? Thank God, I've two more deadlined commissions, one for North Carolina's orchestra, the other for harp solo. *Je suis un mauvais oisif*, a bad idler. Lacking the imagination for just living, I'm forced into art.

How can I know if my prose and music interfere with each other? Without the prose would the music be better or just thicker? Without the music would there be a subject for the prose?

Only as a composer am I qualified to soliloquize, since my life is no longer amorous, garrulous, or drunk, and since I've no more friends—certainly no new ones. (Who would they be, and what could they give me that I couldn't find in their works? Except maybe a taxi ride to the hospital in moments of need—moments, however, growing paradoxically fewer as one gets feebler.) Killing time. Now that I am allowed to speak, I have no more to say.

Of my six books published since 1966, none has been reviewed by the national weekly press, and only one, *The Paris Diary*, in the Sunday *Times*. Reasons for this I will never be told. Clearly they have little to do with my two "categories" of book, since Nin's and Muggeridge's diaries are all reviewed by all the press, and essays by, say, Haggin or Porter are also decently covered. Nor is it because of my value as a littérateur, since those who do not review me (*Time, Newsweek, Esquire*) do often quote my opinions, and since those authors who won't supply blurbs for me (Calisher, Purdy, Robert Craft) do often use my blurbs for themselves.

A seventh book is coming forth. The resignation in midstream of Aaron Asher includes most support for my *Final Diary* at Holt-Rinehart. Their logistics to the contrary, publishers who do not show interest in their own books, specifically through advertising, will hardly fire the public's interest, since the public will not know the books exist. With a sigh I see the *Diary* relegated to the also-ran column of the ad brochures, and foresee the usual pipe-smoking disinterest from the *Times*, which prefers its latter-day Saroyans.

With music I have no complaints. Whatever my music *is*, whatever it represents for various levels of consumer (from fellow composers of all persuasions to choir directors in Idaho), it is *available*.

Julien Green's endless examination of faith, tiresome as it is, gives motivation and body to his journal. Green's glue is God; mine is bitterness. I'm not contemptuous of the deserving, or even of the nondeserving (Casals, Schweitzer), in themselves. My hate is centered on the unfocused adoration of gurus at the expense of the intellect.

23 August

Sweep terrace, bake peach pie, empty cat pan, water marigolds, spend long hours at beach without a book—anything to avoid typing these paragraphs. Type these paragraphs, strain for "perception," concoct some gossip, reflect on horrors of creation, think up "telling" epigrams—anything to avoid real work. Really work, spend long hours at keyboard, fill notebook with notes and their inversions, copy and orchestrate, make it legible—anything to avoid that strain of concentration which is the stimulation of a true creative bowel. Stimulate a true creative bowel and forget the pies and pans.

But nowhere here anymore will you find moaning for sex—for wasting time performing the (perhaps) one act worth noting.

To have said this before is not to have said it, since I've not said it at this age. All's the same, but different; the blank page is the same, but the anxiety's quicker, with less time to fill the page.

There are no fascinating people, only their works are fascinating. *Et encore*. I don't interest myself now, only my work does that. *Et encore*. (I pic-

ture her cold eyes falling by chance upon such words, hear her superior sigh
of pity at the poverty of my invention, O friendly diarist. Yet in fact, America
has no art.)

The telling sounds savage, although the "reality" of the dream seemed sad.
Wallace, his Russian blue fur on fire, clenched teeth with his double, except
that the double had no eyes. Slowly he absorbed Wallace, and a single beast
was formed with black bloodless sockets "looking" at the moon, and I awoke
to a bleak whine. Neighbors explained: all local cats were having their eyes
cored by the maniac.

In fourth grade I saved my allowance to buy a tiger-eye bracelet. Within
this bracelet I stored the playing cards (the trading of which was all the rage
with fourth-graders then) and hid them in my school desk. Miss Burris, discovering this, observed that the bracelet was too valuable for such service
and called my home.

I love my friends because I need them, not the other way around, and begrudge each second of the time they take. A composer cannot be a host, at
least not this one. I'm so easily swayed, yet I blame you, not me. Could I live
with just the cat as though he were a friend? Possibly. Provided JH were
there.

Morris Golde has come and gone after an agreeable four-night stay, one
of several we've had since June 17, reconfirming the yawning disparity between a dinner guest and a weekend companion. It's not that I haven't the
time, as the clock goes, to isolate myself while friends are here. It's that I
haven't *the leisure to work*—the ability (so pronounced when I was thirteen)
to shut myself off from family. On the incomparable caramel sands of Cisco
we observe a bevy of muscular red-haired paragons whom I imagine, as with
a scythe, decapitated. Brilliant. (How can intelligent commentators use that
meaningless adjective anymore?)

I am not intelligent, I am brilliant.

And yet we are planning to buy a house. If we do (assuming there's no
crash), and my life savings become land, it will effect my third major relo-
cation in a half century.

24 August

Welcome damp day, early cool, dead maple leaves all over. Fog of churning
butter. Shirley's about to arrive from Martha's Vineyard for an all-too-short
week.

For Shirley's distraction and our emancipation we invited three guests for Tanqueray gin at six: Rosette Lamont, platinum blonde in bright blue, bringing her essays on Ionesco; Eugenie Voorhees, bracelet of gold and silver (a merging which, like brass and bronze or sequences and cloisters, satisfied me utterly), bringing her calm beauty; and Rex Reed, with an expensive red sweater, bringing his brash and never-still tongue. My standards are perhaps no higher than Rex's, but my criteria are different. When he exclaims about Nantucket's being "divorced from reality," I picture him back in Manhattan at those private screenings, those cocktail parties where he's the cock of the walk, those *têtes-à-têtes* with Angela Lansbury.

I tell them I've just finished an extended piece, which Rex takes to mean journalism—*piece* having replaced *article* in literary jargon. Do I, he wonders, ever write fiction? No. My life is fiction.

Herpes simplex is virulently recurring. For two decades, three times a year, it has arrived at an hour's notice—a fragile tingle at the base of the spine; a flowering of pustules that expand into blisters, secrete, burst; a hyper-sweet pain through the buttocks dissolving into a raw wound. The attack runs its course in twelve days.

Cervical *herpes* may lead to cancer, though rectal *herpes* (far rarer than genital *herpes*, or shingles, or cold sores) is, in males, just what it is—a virus with no antidote. Nonetheless, last winter Dr. Webster experimentally subjected me to six smallpox vaccinations in six weeks. Shots in the dark that didn't take.

Before leaving on her ferry yesterday, Shirley strolled with me (like characters in each other's dreams, stunned from the heat in slow motion) through the little pair of cemeteries on New Lane, where the stone-marked graves of the Folgers and Coffins and Gardners revived my Chicago Quakerism. Thirty-five years at most, Shirley contends, and we'll both be stashed in that ground.

JH feels that my condolence letters never quite hit the mark. But what should I write in such letters? That I wished it were me? If we were guaranteed a longer life—another hundred years, say—but knowing what we know, would we accept? Of course. We can quickly get used to anything, including mint-new dimensions.

Brooding on yesterday's cemeteries. The fact that I will not survive is intolerable. Fear of death lies not in that my work might be lost, but that myself will be lost. If the work survives, it will be as misconstrued, or at least as reinterpreted, as Chopin's today. But what of the person, Chopin? The man is superfluous to his art: the art sheds the body like a lizard its skin. People who may love my music look into my eyes and are—what? unaware? dare I write uninterested? Yet I live in this body and am afraid of being abandoned underground. With a magnifying glass let me focus on Nadar's famous photograph and ask, "Who are you? Tell me, who are you? Because your music can't answer any more than mine can."

We are not our art. I entreat the eyes of Chopin. But they do not answer.

Of everyone I know H. B. most plays the genius and has the least to show for it. I wish that barking dog would stop barking so that I could write about that barking dog that won't stop barking.

Allergy frightful. For two years it's been quiescent. Since Mother's hay fever vanished with menopause perhaps here was one change of life for the better. But it returned full force. Chlor-Trimeton and Afrin give all the bad side effects without good benefits. A drowsy numbness fills the soul but my nose remains blocked.

Despite these increasingly savage bouts, which always rage during the pre-frost sodden days of late September, especially on Nantucket, which (though advertised as pollen-free) is adorned with eighteen cruel varieties of goldenrod that go to seed during weather too sweet to be true, autumn is visible, most particularly through the total darkness that now covers the town like a giant tea cozy by 7:30 P.M.

Although antagonistic to dream interpretation, to mysticism, to ESP, even to practical analysis of events beyond the five senses, I've long since ceased being surprised that dreams, far from symbolizing what in fact occurred yesterday, represent fairly accurately what will occur today. Paradox. For the future does not exist. If the future existed it would not, by definition, be the future.

The French, who have no word for mind (as distinct from brain or wit or intelligence), sometimes say soul, as in *état d'âme*, the equivalent of *state of mind*. Thus, when I raised a table knife, not to eat nor yet to test the sharpness but to examine in its gleam the reflection of myself, Marie Laure would say, *"Tu t'occupes moins de ton état d'âme que de ton état de corps."* Preoccupation with a "state of body" has switched now from concern with beauty to concern with collapse. This Nantucket summer has strayed unnoticed when, faithless to work and play, day after opaline day, I keep to my room in suicidal panic, self-absorbed utterly, gasping from all-consuming asthma. With ill health, the first thing to vanish is objectivity—seeing three sides of the same coin, which defines humor. The funniest thing JH, in his infinite patience, has uttered these past weeks is, "Your sense of humor will see you through."

3 September

No one has written, but somebody should, an esthetic history of movie music. Seeing *Of Human Bondage* again (what bromidic marshmallows we swallowed once from the lips of Leslie Howard, yet what matchless techniques had Bette Davis even then!), and all to the afflicting notes of Max Steiner, I realized how inappropriate such music had become. Music makes or breaks the weakest, the strongest, film. The sixties' taste of the European masters: Antonioni used only the sound of factory whistles or "source" tunes from radios; Fellini, only Rota's jaunty scores for even his saddest tales; Bergman, with his sense of the apropos in *Cries and Whispers*, Chopin and Bach; Bertolucci, the languorous Delerue. The most avant-garde use the most arrière-garde music (Satie). Cocteau's taste. Use of jazz in the fifties' tragedies. Why they worked, why they didn't. Etc. Endlessly complex as a study on the employment of form and color in the Renaissance.

Cold, wet, end of a season. The weather smells of Fez twenty-five Novembers ago, the premature African snow, burning logs, dampness that makes my music paper curve and the crackers soggy.

4 September

From Sauguet in Coutras, and from Roro in Majorca where he's bought a house, I learn that *"la grande, la grosse, la bonne Lily Pastré n'est plus."* Well, she'd have been well over eighty, so it's no surprise, though there does come the question, With what do all those recollections rhyme, alone and unversified in my brain, and to be scratched out thoroughly when my body too *"n'est plus"*? It's here in this paragraph? No, sir. The flavor of her lawns—those eighty-acre lawns of Montredon where we played croquet, where I completed the second act of *Miss Julie*, where Lily's indiscriminate generosity was manifest in five full meals a day on a garden table set for twenty and conversation (not probing but still urgent) solely on music, and those granddaughters gorgeous as hyacinths or fawns, and where I was warmed by the sentiment of knowing that she, whom I'd known longer than Marie Laure, would stick—the flavor of those lawns is gone.

Something is seamy about the presence of Rex Reed. Has it to do with high intelligence congealed around projects so flippant, or with his soft black hair framing those unfocused eyes? When I announce I might buy a house here, he says: "You must be very rich. Imagine what it's going to cost you, those shipments from Bloomingdale's on the ferry?" When I answer that I'll paint the rooms white, and that such furnishings as are needed will be found at the local Sears, he gazes at me from those gorgeous empty orbs with disbelief and pity.

5 *September*

Alone again this week, and the temperature's turned almost to freezing. Still, with a sweater on, I water the lawns while the evening stew stews, the invisible sun sets, and out through the door and up to the cloudy heaven floats the simmering onion. My frame of reference, ever narrower, is me, me, me. This diary, though compiled by a sure intelligence, seeks vainly for intelligent observation.

A call out of the blue from Martin Peretz invites me to organize a panorama of the current musical American scene for the *New Republic*'s sixtieth anniversary. This will take me away from myself, thank God.

Since for years I've derided Hemingway, last night, to refresh my mind for future derision, I reread a dozen of his stories. I liked them. Suddenly they're in context, classic, assessable (*Up in Michigan*, for instance, was composed three years before my birth). He wasn't a poet, or even somehow a novelist, but a playwright who didn't write plays. His gift, his unmistakable quality, was a good ear—that is, an absence of imagination.

7 *September*

Despite the continuing knots of rain, Rosette and I went last night to the White Elephant to hear Frank Conroy play piano. This he does with the lean skill of those black thirties' soloists but not (so far as I hear) with much personal necessity. Like his book, *Stop Time*, Conroy's musicality is undeniably affable: it holds your interest even when nothing is happening, which is most of the time. But it lacks the fever of art. His intelligence, his neuroses, his acute sensitivity are all quite predictably normal. His pianism, like his literature, feeds on the past (a narrow past) more than you'd think for one his age—an age, however, more advanced than it looks. For he's not twenty but thirty-eight, with a brief catalogue, and a face which, like Jackie Onassis's, resembles, because of the extremely wide-set eyes, a bewitchingly lovely embryo.

Later. Advance reviews of the *Diary*, just received, are more snide than for previous books. "The self he exhibits," declares the Kirkus Service, "belongs to a world of artifice, finds Rochas cologne truer than roses, and seems to require the diaries for completion." Yes, that is so. I prefer perfume to plants just as I prefer Frescobaldi to folk song. I am not attracted to raw material, but to what can be made from it. More disconcerting is to be taken literally, to have each phrase humorlessly deciphered as though I had *meant* the phrase. "For how much longer can he entice the boys with his black T-shirt?" the review asks (the boys, indeed, as though that slur were still in coinage!), and goes on to say, "An involvement for consenting adults."

But if there's a grain of truth in every lie, there's a sackful in any opinion, no matter how stupid. Perhaps, simply, my book does not give off the tone I intend. With all the contrivance, the tears are real, but I cannot bear to have my sarcasms taken sarcastically. Nor, alas, can I with any potency defend my diary within my diary.

Night. The rain forms a cage around the house. Not with displeasure have I been shutting myself off more and more from all art and all attitude, even from the day. I wait to sleep. Unfortunately for my money-making, I'm no longer convinced, American style, that a "productive" life need be spent in producing. My life's sole variety is in the never-the-same flame patterns there in Melva's grate.

8 September

Shouldn't there be second thoughts on Frank Conroy as for Jim Bridges? Isn't the heel of Achilles precisely his most identifying trait? Could not our faults be more special—indeed, more purposeful—than our virtues? (Cocteau is generally credited with Picasso's famous remark: *"Ce que les autres te reprochent, cultive-le, c'est toi."*) On a Tuesday night instead of a Thursday am I not capable of finding in Frank Conroy's *Honeysuckle Rose* an ordinariness so unique as to become great art? On a Thursday night instead of a Tuesday am I not capable of finding that Jim Bridges's weakness—charm in lieu of statement—is in fact his strength, his statement? Frank says that a person in deep depression, by dint of never giving but ever taking as into a bottomless pit, becomes finally less touching, less fascinating, than (*pace* R. D. Laing) just boring. His piano playing, like his single novel, although both concern madness, is sanity pure, and lovable. As for Jim Bridges's movies, it is only because their obsession with the Practical Joke goes against my upbringing that I chide them and not him.

Can a composer know what his music connotes? Some of my merriest moments have been heard as macabre, while other heart-burning songs are termed (and by paid men of sense) icy.

. . . although at this writing I've yet to attend a first rehearsal. The meaning implicit in the hot live sound may stray from what, even to me, it said on the inscribed cool page.

Wildly rainy, with lightning way out there, yet the sun shines and everything's diffused (is that the word?) in a pink glow. To awaken inside a rosebud couldn't be too different from this.

Insomnia. As though this shimmering bed were the sole wakeful object in the universe, alit, radioactive, shuddering. How to summon sleep! Will sleep ever arrive, like astronauts gauging that frail slit in the envelope of space through which they must reenter Earth's orbit?

Ned Rorem, b. 1923. Like everyone whose birthday comes in the fall, I'm forever recorded as being older than I am—as being, for example, thirty instead of twenty-nine during most of 1953, or forty-two in 1965. Indeed, in 1923 I was reported as being a year old before I was born.

Robin Morgan proposes that in these troubled times women too should be drafted. Well, yes. But if conscription is our world's sole indignity wherein men have it worse than women, why should women apply for equal rights under a stupid law? Would it not be purer to work together to abolish that law? Or is such reasoning pacifist rather than egalitarian?

Yet again this morning the radio talks of "innocent victims," meaning women and children. Is the implication that the soldiers—those teenage boys who have little choice but to fight—are guilty?

The fetus in a repressive society. Suppose a woman were pregnant with what she knew to be, for whatever reason, a homosexual. Has she the right to willfully miscarry this infant, knowing that in the adult world it would eventually be legally executed? In a repressive society, which is stronger: the horror of abortion or the horror of inversion? If a fetus is a creature with rights, why do we not sing a requiem for a miscarriage?

JH came into the room a moment ago and said: "I was just at Grandma Moses's vernissage where I overheard one eight-year-old say to another, 'What junk! My ninety-year-old grandfather can paint better than that.'"

9 September

The sun's come out after two weeks. The sky looks washed. Off for a long bike ride to Polpis.

For Rosette Lamont, when she interviews me as a new resident of Nantucket: The local concert series? It's profoundly superficial—to coin an oxymoron—because in its super-safe concentration on established nineteenth-century German masterpieces the programs become expendable; they go in one ear and out the other—at least my ears. There's really nothing more to get from these eternal hearings of Schubert and Beethoven. Of course, that's why people go to them.

Bitter? Sort of very. But it's glib: a lifetime spent on what is unappreciated. I'd have liked to be, but am not, a celebrity American style. My nature demands it, but the nature of my work does not. There I am. Now it's too late, nor will I concede—for I could never talk on a talk show about all those passing fancies meant to be seen and not heard.

The Final Diary's a grave. I remain living. That book houses a fictitious animal I chose to name Ned.

There is no posterity anymore. Why should I, then, not collect my own letters, and publish while alive my posthumous works?

15 September

Mother and Father went home by way of the ferryboat to Hyannis yesterday after a week of indefatigable talking and walking, though between them they count 160 years while I am forever thirteen. Who could not envy their rapport, the continual conversation and mutual consideration, the active participation in Quaker Meeting and radical politics, when so many couples well before their golden anniversary adopt policies of exhausted silence?

Summer visitors. Those fogbound morning conversations that so eat into the energy of the day. I keep wanting everyone to stop talking, so that I can go write about what they're saying—to stop living, so that I can write about living.

The composer in me could never have written that paragraph. No one can prove, nor do musicians necessarily claim, that music concerns living.

17 September

Everyone's gone. Even D. D. Ryan (the Pop Art devastation on the interior of whose innocently old-fashioned brick house provides, they say, an ideal clue for how to make a sow's ear from a silk purse) is gone. Nantucket now, after the season, would resemble *Death in Venice*, except that only in America will you find a breeze so pure, so rich in bluebell cloisonné, etc., etc.

"Bang, you're dead!" and the fictive victim obligingly falls to the ground during this child's game.

"But what if the fictive victim coincidentally has an infarction and actually does fall dead?" asks gifted little Claudinette while explaining her new novel's plot, and so doing, imitates the fictive victim. But the book never gets written, since Claudinette too falls dead.

Anachronisms in the movies: Jeanette MacDonald's wristwatch in *Naughty Marietta*. The seagull that flies across the lens in *On the Beach* when the San Francisco Bay is supposed to be devoid of life.

JH just came into the room and said: "I've been rereading all of Shakespeare. He doesn't hold up."

New York
20 September

Back in New York I am able finally to play the new Desto recording of my *Night Music*, which was issued several months ago. I put on the record. Displeased, I stop it midway and turn on the radio, where *Night Music* is playing at exactly the point I had turned it off.

It's already been ten years since I've felt a strong need for novelty, for possibilities around the corner—love affairs, world travel. Gradually the efforts outward, the planet's potential, have dwindled, and for several months now the corners I've turned are internal. My living area grows smaller and smaller, from city to armchair to my myopic frosted-over lenses. All my gymnastic is in thought. Unhappily I'm limited to myself, smugly, knowing that just that rose petal there has so much more variety than my poor fancy.

Sans date

Those who say, "Look out, he'll quote you in that diary," are the very ones I never notice. The others, they're safe, they can't win, I don't quote, I misquote. Lurking behind the exquisite monster, I'm capable of guidance—that is, of guiding him. The matriarch's mother.

Who most loathe the diary are those depicted within. What they most loathe is not precious archness, not opinions stated as facts nor the urbane reflections posing as pastorale *pensées*, but seeing their life reduced to anecdote, however crass or laudatory. "I was there," they say, "I keep a diary too, I remember what happened, and you're wrong." Of course there's no such thing as *the* truth, there is only *one's* truth, and even that fluxes with each passing hour. Though I disown nothing, I've come to value discretion, even to claim it among virtues broader than mere truth. Mere truth. Yet in the old days it never occurred to me that friends would feel hurt from my passing verities.

It means nothing that I can't understand John Ashbery's poetry, because I can't understand any poetry. Oh, occasionally after making a song from a poem I may intuit some vague message in the words, through the music— although, of course, the music means nothing either.

All true artists are modest but try not to show it.

Common to all greatness is the sense of vulnerability, and the keynote to greatness is less genius than patience.

Was *Rashomon* three versions of a lie, or of a truth? Are diaries less honest inherently than novels?

Diaries are a sideline, notebooks wherein a person records problems of work and play. Nearly always, though, they are kept with the intention of being read; so like all art they dissimulate by becoming a code. The diarist doesn't present himself, but an idea of himself, and only that idea of himself which he chooses to publicize.

As a literary form the diary is hardly new (it's far older than the novel) except as an indigenous American utterance, public confession not having been our bent until recently. Yet confession risks adopting the features of the very mask novelists hide behind. Our century's best-known diarist, André Gide, during the blitzes of World War Two blissfully notated adventures with Arab lads in his Biskra retreat. To tell it like it is is no more a property of diaries than of fiction. Lives are not facts, nor does the present moment exist; an author can necessarily record the present only after the fact. Of itself truth is not persuasive; even less is it art. And who, including the diarist himself, can prove that the character represented is, in this guise, finally, the *real* author? Does Baudelaire's journal disclose more to us of Baudelaire than Genet's novels do of Genet? Could Philip Roth have composed his complaint in another form without its becoming more rather than less of a mask? To fictionalize the real makes it easier to be honest. The realist novel of the thirties became the unrealistic autobiography of the sixties. Still, each real work of art (be it geometric sculpture, a child's poem, or a report on Hanoi) speaks to us, by definition, with its creator's voice.

A voice is a voice, unfakeable. We cannot lie, no matter what tone we pretend to—or in fact *do*—project, no matter how we try to shade or disguise that voice, no matter what master's words or songs we filch and, like reverse dybbuks, sing through our own lips. No one can lie, the body cannot lie, and the wiliest plagiarism is verifiable. What is not verifiable is why those fingerprints are more amusing than these, or why some standard stolen goods take on a wilder luster on a thief's back. Alas, most thefts are of trash and remain trash.

The difference between a journalist and a diarist is that one reports what happened, the other reports a reaction to what happened. Yet both are susceptible to cries of *liar*. Rightly. Less truthful than a painter, a photographer *is* bias: a camera selects the angle and snaps its subject unawares, especially if the subject is a tree. The tree is a lie, but not the picture of it. If truth is fact, then all art—which only represents fact, and one person's version at that—lies, but by extension speaks true.

Talent to the talented holds no wonder. It is a duty, even a burden, like going to the outhouse or milking the goats. Joy, especially early joy, springs from the talent of others, their books, their songs.

He has spent his whole life in Chartres. Only at twenty did he learn that not every town in the world harbored a big church. That his big church was special never occurred to him. But that children in America or China did not realize their lack of a big church was frightening.

JH confides he's been glancing through some of my notes, and hopes, should they ever be published, that I'll delete a reflection about his voice sounding sad on the phone. Now, I'm as responsive to the desires of JH as to those of any living person, but it is a diarist's nature to include precisely what others would have him exclude. There lies the danger. Estrangements don't come from what people find gossipy about other people, but from what they find incomplete—and thus untrue—about themselves, for truth means only the whole truth. Indeed, for me to read what's written about me is to see a life reduced to several lines—sometimes ecstatic, sometimes sarcastic—and to find myself miniaturized and existing for others who, because they see fractionally, find me peripheral to their own laws. In a diary no mention of a person can be, to that person, the *right* mention, since no mention of anything (even of E equals MC squared) is all-inclusive, and so can be only a lie. My own mention of others, even of myself, means to me only what it means during the moment of mention, since we change pores—natures, reality—each with fluid second.

What is comparatively stable is the sadness of JH's voice on the phone. If this were all that signified to me I would (at his request) omit mention of it, as wrongly I have omitted whimsies or eccentricities or passing "perversions," at their request, of others, thereby diluting the blood—the *truth*, *my* truth, however superficial—of the published diary in the past, because the diary became no longer a biased monologue but a fair exchange. If I mention the sadness of JH's voice it's because I am so vulnerable to the sound; in fact my susceptibility is such that, when we met a decade ago, I understood that for the remainder of my life another person would never fill his special shoes, and that I could (and largely did) renounce a certain sociability without feeling anything but richer. JH is everything, and to write that is to compromise us both far more than any mention of a sad voice. Should he choose that I also delete this paragraph, I shall. Though where then will be my documented verities, fragmented but contradictorily (if only through style) flowing, continual, and in a way necessary because inimitable?

"Seeing that artists tend to make good the year after they die," wrote Paul Goodman, "an artist gives out that he is dead and vanishes. Nothing happens. Twenty years later, in Mexico, he in fact dies, and the year following he makes good."

Yes, but a dozen others die and don't make good. And what about the poor suicide who, a day later, is quite forgotten, and for twenty years and forever? If in fact (though it is no fact) unknown artists tend to make good a year after they die, known artists tend to fade away. For every Plath or Bartók who burst out, a Gide or a Hindemith is not long mourned. What of Paul himself? Was his sudden fame at fifty a sort of death from which he was resurrected (since when he did die at sixty-one he was again comparatively forsaken)? Today where is he? For if friends who count do recall, others don't, and friends aren't what Paul would have meant by making good.

Students don't learn by instruction but by imitation.

Teaching means: to lead a horse to water and to make him drink. A teacher takes joy in other people's self-discovery. An artist takes joy in other people's joy at *his* self-discovery, a joy so acute it is edged in a pain which adds to its value like goldplate on silver. Teachers know; artists do. Obviously the two can overlap. Myself, I've not a Socratic bone in my body.

You can't teach a young dog old tricks. (Ironically, some young dogs are older than me. Among my crop at Utah were those whose idea of the ultimate was to set the words of Brigham Young to music.) Young composers aren't that interested in the past.

Of course a trick is by definition new. When it's old it's a rule.

Nantucket style. A Martha Walters, who has a TV show, inquires about "personalities" she might interview. I tell her that, except she's gone, Francine du Plessix Gray would have been perfect.

"Who?" asks Mrs. Walters.

"Francine Gray, a journalist and religionist who's about to publish her first novel, which is already a Book-of-the-Month selection. She worked here all during August with her husband Cleve, the painter, and their two sons, in a house they rented on Mill Street."

"I love Mill Street," says Mrs. Walters.

In the post office up comes Elsie Wachtel, big cheese on the committee of Nantucket's summer concert series. Without stopping she poses three un-answerable questions: "And what have you been doing?" (Suffering from piles, *ma bonne*, and making cakes; talking to strangers.) "Writing lots of beautiful music for us?" (For you? How much of that beautiful music do you already know, and are you willing to pay?) "Doesn't our summer's series look divine?" (But since there's no American piece in any of the six recitals, how can I care?)

Suppose I expressed myself aloud? Far from taking offense, she would take pity, arrange to have me asked to participate, which I would refuse, so feelings would harden.

At a dinner party sans style a Mrs. Melhado (Floridian and affluent) declares that the *New York Times* has "crucified" Nixon. Without malice I say, "I've heard about people like you but never actually met one." She regards me warily, never having met one of me either, and literally holds back the tears.

Apparently I analyze with some succinctness the art of others, putting a steady finger on how the method provokes rise or fall. What of my own art? Have I principles by which to proceed? Often noted here are comments that I'm composing this or that, or that that or this was premiered here or there (comments quaintly satirized by Howard Moss). But what I preach, or even practice, is best shown verbally in what I say of others. To explain that music must speak for itself is a lame out, since every artist, whatever he may admit, has both a technical and moral angle about the language he chooses to utter.

A diary—a public diary—is no more spontaneously composed than a sym-phony. Yes, themes may come all of a piece from the impulsive and recalcitrant muse, but they are set in gold alone, or sewn together, and forever revised before they are printed. That the expressive (the artistic, if you will) process can be untampered with is fallacy. Abandon takes rehearsal. Sometimes a song, a paragraph (like this one), emerges effortlessly. However it springs forth, art must seem seamless.

The hero of my diary is a fictional man upon whom I've worked hard but who has little to do with me—including the me penning this sentence, who is also the hero of my diary.

The Diabelli Variations: a magic mountain from a molehill.

People need formulas. They ask, "When do you work?" hoping to learn that composers put pen to paper each morning at seven and go on till tea. Now, by the time composers put pen to paper the composing is done; this is the inscription of the act, not the act itself.

Never say "I'm working well"; it brings bad luck. The nightmare—or rather, nightmare's sibling—that composers know too well: insomnia forcing them through the wee hours to jot notes which next morning ring false.

The sorry postponement of writing it down, writing it down . . . because when written down it might not be good enough. Such intellectual trepidation is, if you will, uncreative—and I say "intellectual" advisedly: the intelligence of certain composers impedes them from simply making it up as it goes along. Rule of thumb: Compose first, worry later. Or: Speak before you think and write it down afterwards. Actually, all composers think before they speak. The speaking is the writing down.

Which came first, the punishment or the crime? Was the Inquisition concocted to legitimize the pleasures of torture? Are cruel acts, committed in the name of the Lord or for the good of the people, ever honestly meant for the good of the people or in the name of the Lord? Which came first, lawbreaker or law? In music, of course, rules came after the fact, to substantiate (to justify, *excuse*) what composers made up as they went along. Let a piece flow out, then think up reasons for the flow. Yet what teacher could thus counsel a student? Though precisely the reverse is straitjacketing: to fear the flow because of reasons coming before the flow.

Composers' secrets? Some love to tell secrets of how a piece is made. It shouldn't be how, but how well. Describe form, and form is all a hearer hears. Then observe that fugue of Bach, crystalline, with friendly head or heads intermittently popping forth from the tangles. Tangles? No, tails continually attached. Friends in tangled tails, crystalline, which need not be sliced like Medusa's curls or the Gordian knot, for at the end of tails grow heads again, codas, stretti, logical hoorays.

I am never *not* working, yet I never catch myself in the act. At the end of each year I've somehow produced around an hour of music, and that hour is not a few sheets of penciled whole notes, but hundreds of pages of inked orchestration. Work is the process of composing—making it up as it goes along, which is the only precise description since Homer. The action is at once so disparate and so compact that the actor is unaware, which is doubtless why I "never catch myself," etc. I don't consider as work the postcompositional drudgery (often pleasant) of copying, instrumentation, rehearsal, letter-writing, or dealing with publishers, though all this is time-consuming. Nor do I consider as work the compiling of my books, which is the assembling of prewritten fragments. I do consider as work the answering of this question: "When do you work?"—since it concerns, like musical composition, the placement of notion into order. As to when, and is it daily, I notate when I have a commissioned deadline and don't when I don't: the goal is functional, and its approach makes me scribble ten hours a day. Between commissions months are eaten looking at soap operas.

Every piece is the first. Over the years we learn to put notes mechanically together, yet the blank page remains no less terrifying than for a blocked beginner.

Stage fright. Each time's the first. If over the years I'm geared to play better in public than in private, I'm no less anxious before going to the lions. Still, to be on stage is as exhilarating as sex: I do the work, but *they* are making me do it—they are not passive at all.

Of course, I'm never on stage except as pianist for my own songs. If something goes wrong, who's responsible? To sit impotently in the audience while the songs are massacred up there is the ultimate torment; the composer is held responsible for the singer's unwitting sabotage. I'd rather make my own music than hear it, even played well.

My musical memory is visual. Should the muse approach incongruously— on the subway, in a steam bath—and find me without a notebook, I will quickly picture in my mind the five strands in a staff, snatch from the air the inspiring notes glittering like bats, glue them to the staff, take a snapshot with an imaginary camera and, reaching home, develop the film on actual paper. The result is usually worthwhile, more so than similar transactions in dreams, which next morning turn out to be trash. The music of night is unworked-for, untrue; true music, transmittable music, true ease, is difficult.

For years I've been lamenting at universities the ignorance of their students. "How," I declare, "can a musician call himself that who doesn't know *Le Sa-*

cre by heart?" Suddenly I realized that my moth-eaten score of the master-work (which I, age twelve, stole from Lyon & Healy's) had long since vanished. I bought a new copy and went to bed with it last night. How clean, how Haydnesque *Le Sacre* looks now, with no note superfluous, no pattern complex, no color dirty, no formal section particularly difficult anymore.

"What do you consider your most important education?"
   "Self-taught."
   "But we've read you had a Master's from Juilliard."
   "So I have. I'd quite forgotten."
For a full degree at Juilliard one took nonmusical courses. Having passed the entrance exams with flying colors, I wasn't required to attend musical classes except in piano and composition. What I therefore recall most clearly of that illustrious school in 1946–48 are studies in sociology, American history, physical education and, yes, hygiene (which taught that the human diet needs copper as well as iron, copper being obtained both through apricots and through milk stored in brass vats). Also two semesters of world literature which, if nothing else, did inspire some musical output including songs on texts both sacred and profane, notably *Four Madrigals* to Sappho fragments.

What genius! one hears of the soloist during an intermission. Why genius? He doesn't invent the music, nor does he, as people say, bring it to life. Music exists always, unrendered yet breathing, even on Grecian urns. The soloist is a vessel (an urn) through which preexisting music passes. Now a vessel may be of Steuben glass or a tin can, but a vessel is not the cause of its contents. Genius is a word I don't use. If I did, I would not, surely, apply it to an interpreter. To a composer? Well, vessel is not my word either, but Stravinsky's. Questioned as to the creative process which brought his masterpiece into being, he replied, "I am merely the vessel through which *Le Sacre* flowed."

Brief chat with Stephen Sondheim all about his score for *Stavisky*, which I'd liked. That he knows neither the French language nor the craft of orchestration is eyebrow-raising, not because he's so notoriously adept at Double-Crostics (the various knacks don't overlap, nor do tastes for the various arts), but because one would suppose in him a broader curiosity. Foreign tongues are, after all, puzzles that can be solved; and orchestration is a trade, not an art: anyone can do it. A composer's unique reward is to hear his work take life, to know that all those players must join to activate his flyspecked staves whose sonorous combinations he alone has dreamed up as means of setting into relief—putting into color—his basic premise. To hear this music as "re-alized" by a hired arranger is surely less tantalizing than to hear it as realized by himself. Yet the more money a composer makes, the less he has con-cretely to do with his own élans.

Laziness is due not to too few but to too many notions, all fully realized. They aren't waiting to be born, but to be notated, and oh the drudgery, because they exist, almost complete—at least theoretically—there on the staves of the brain. The hours spent writing them down could be better spent think-ing them up. Or so I reason, and get sick.

"When do you find time to compose?" people ask, assuming that to com-pose is a transitive verb, the action of placing notes on paper (or worse, of rambling over the keys). Time for that action is comparatively minimal: any-one finds time for any action that means anything to him. When do I do any-thing else? might be a better question, since in some way each breath drawn, awake or asleep, is musical; at parties, the A & P, a Turkish bath, in the Metro, reading *Lear*, I'm never not composing, will it or no. Euterpe's a healthy succubus. The action? That's merely the final, boring chore.

The woman across the street (with whom I share an aversion for a little boy at the corner who rides around his front yard on a sputtering Honda) asks: "I hear you're having a piano moved in. Does that mean we'll be hearing beau-tiful music?"

To be overheard composing. This invasion of privacy is more anxious-making than to be surprised by a total stranger while you're on the toilet. The endless foundering of the so-called creative act is more intimate, more unrehearsed, than the surgeon's cut. Over and over and over and over again the trial and error, the error and trial, the in-directed cross-exam, the flop. How can the woman know, who is used to a finished product played by a star on a record? Yet even were I a pianist, she would pose the same question and assume that virtuosos practice inspiredly and up to tempo.

JH has been practicing too much. Practicing and learning are unrelated practices. Learning's highest intensity is in the first minutes of deciphering (or even in the first hearing) of a new piece. Once learned, the only reason for practicing is not so that the piece will get better, but so that it won't get worse.

Once learned, pieces don't get better with practice, though they can get different, and sometimes stale. (I don't swallow Casals' claim that he found a newness in Bach each day of his life. With everything new we find, we lose something old.) Practicing is so that, even if your performance is at its worst, it will be up to your own minimum standards.

Awakened with, still flowing through remembered dreams, Debussy's ever-friendly Trio Sonata. The first movement unmistakably represents quails mating. In these four measures preceding ⬚1 and the seven preceding ⬚5 a female flute preens serenely among flecks of grain in the gravel, while the stupid male viola struts, roughing his ruff. And that harp? Well, the harp's the garden path up and down which they walk making patterns for Amy Lowell whom I've not thought of in decades, but mightn't she have composed those verses during the very months Debussy composed his?

The most sadly seductive key change in all literature is at ⬚20. How carefully the composer, during the five preceding measures, prepares his "unprepared" modulation.

"What a waste of time," I sigh, as the players put down their bows after a performance of Mendelssohn's Quintet, and the hall goes wild. A woman in front of us turns with hot contempt: "You think you can do better?" What does she mean? Better at what? At playing, at composing? No, I couldn't do better, I couldn't do at all. I can't play a fiddle, and I sing a different language from the precocious Mendelssohn. But is the woman there because she can't do as well? Is music's purpose to show us how unexcellent we are? Or are we merely to "experience" music? In which case, if the experience doesn't catch fire, must we keep quiet? Oh, the sacrosanct ordinariness of these Classical Concert reactions!

People suggest that I sneer at musical masterpieces. It's not a sneer, it's awe taken for granted. I won't deny the fact of masterpieces (though some are my cup of tea while others are straight medicine). We are preconditioned to this one, another we "discover," but both kinds, once swallowed, can't stay with us daily, or we'd have time for nothing else—for searching out new masterpieces, maybe composing one ourselves. Since rarely now I sit down and listen to, say, Beethoven's Fifth, the very rareness permits fresh surprise: Why, it *is* marvelous! despite the fact that we *know* it's marvelous.

That symphony's marvelousness is self-contained. In a so-called collaborative venture conclusions are less black and white. I never hear Stravinsky's *Oedipus Rex*, for instance, without the uneasy feeling that the ancient drama more than the music is what makes it tick. Indeed, Sophocles' specter haunts and finally crushes all intruders in his dust. Not Racine nor Gide nor Cocteau nor Stravinsky nor even Freud, while in the shadow of the Greek master, remains more than a dabbler with the Oedipal hangup.

As to that hangup (the now-unrefuted fact of which has shaped and shaded our century), is it too soon to admit I was never persuaded? An appealing conundrum, it still did not apply to me, who cherished my father. The Oedipus hangup was another of Freud's poems, fallacious as the age-old notion of female fallibility.

Barbarity of refinement, ugliness of dinner parties. Words issuing from, as food enters, wet mouths. (Barbarians, in fact, move apart to eat.) Heredity and environment are one.

Ponderous snow, ponderous sunshine, the world crumbles and everything seems to hurt—poor nations, rich Americans, the tomato in the lunch pail, even the rocks. To sympathize and be of no help, there is no help. I'm not the person JH invents for himself. But if not, do I then exist? Can others become those we construct from need, if that need changes daily? Do we invent ourselves as well? If so, do the molecules of our work—our "product"—remain more stationary, more intact, than we do? A Chopin nocturne is more real than Chopin, but its reality exists in as many versions as there are for people to hear it, and each version alters with each performance.

Any lie contains some truth by the fact of being uttered.

No one asks, "Do you think your songs lack strength?" unless he feels those songs lack strength. To think it (though the thought may be in but one head) means that somewhere the songs do lack strength—whatever strength means (since strength is not all force and muscle). Strength means spine. *Placet futile* is stronger than all the sound and fury of *Harold in Italy*.

Would I stand up for what I believe? What do I believe? Not, certainly, generalities, homeland or God or one genre of music locking antlers with another. I do believe in my work (although faith in that work hangs by a thread), and, maybe, in my many loves. But manifestation, proselytization, a raised voice, I shy from, and it's not just Midwestern goyishness. The *en masse* shriek at Chicago football games was always meaningless. Overt enthusiasm or defiance—re art or Israel or E S P—strikes me as common. Yet I'm more "outward" far than JH.

I am not interested in restrictions of participation, nor in composing according to my own limitations. I chant less well than the average communicant, but my mute notions soar high. Because they confuse worthy activity with art, American choruses have a built-in amateurism that discourages a composer.

My first songs were on Psalms. It never occurred to me that they were "appropriate" for church. I'd chosen the verses for their literary worth, not for their rapport with what Virgil Thomson calls "the Jesus Business." Trials of Job, like TV commercials, become too much of a bad thing.

I don't know much about church music from the inside (nuanced definitions of anthem versus hymn, breakdown of the Mass, and so forth), yet always delivered what was asked for, keeping a distance. It worked out that way.

I do know what church music is not. It is not a subdivision of a larger genre. All music is church music in that all music expresses what church music expresses: praise and despair.

Iain Hamilton, lest we fail to make the analogy, hurries to point out that his *Epitaph*, based on lines from Revelations, is "For This World and Time." If the music's not hip, the subtitle is, thereby passing the test of today's swinging clerics, updaters of the rock ritual. Now the Church is not rock, the Church is The Rock. The point of the Church is conservatism. The Church does not change with the times. For when do times change? Each decade? Each hour? Shall Billy Baldwin rethink the Vatican? To wear the latest fashion you must have the right figure.

Charles Wuorinen and I have nothing in common, not even music. Yet for a brief minute, during a composers' panel at Saint John the Divine, we exchange glances of complicity when the question of money is touched. Because as artists we want the rewards of Mammon, we become lambs for those Philistines who believe only in God.

If one cannot serve both God and Mammon, I'll serve Mammon.

"There is no God," screamed Anna de Noailles. "If God existed, he'd have told me first of all."

The sacred and profane styles, so-called, of so many, are indistinguishable. Wagner's *Parsifal* and *Venusberg*, Poulenc's *Mamelles* and *Stabat*, Britten's *War Requiem* and *Death in Venice* are brewed from the same irrepressible perfumes. Composers speak one language only, though they can speak it well or poorly depending on the weather. Or depending on God, who sometimes arranges that their holy music is not "as good as" their sin tunes.

All organ music is implicitly sacred, specifically Christian. Even such "abstract" solos as the Bach and Hindemith sonatas, the Brahms preludes or the pantheistic essays of Messiaen are religious by extension, since the organ sound is equated by everyone with Church. Which is why so many people hate the sound. As I was an attender of Silent Meeting, the sound entered childhood surreptitiously, yet I too steered clear, preferring the neat economical slyness of French musical thought to the blurred expensive obviousness of the greasy organ hues which seem somehow German.

Now, connecting two penchants, Quakerism and music, I'm planning a set of eleven organ solos for Alice Tully and Leonard Raver. Epigraphs from Quaker "thinkers" justify (if justice be needed) these loud homages to the Silent Meeting.

George Fox was right about all religious shams except the biggest sham of all: the existence of God.

Organists hear differently from real people. They spend their lives in echo chambers. At organ recitals an outsider's ears (including the ears of a composer who may have written skillfully for the instrument) try plaintively to part the doubly exposed rich purple flesh of sound and to find the music's bone. For an organist the blur *is* the music.

JH is not garrulous; he speaks when there's something to say. I talk all the time, for if there's never much that needs saying, the exercise stimulates, and "communication" comes by restating what *is*. Art is redundant. JH is really more Quaker than I.

Can silence be an art? A fine art? Silence, of course, is the very yeast that makes music breathe, but silence by itself is just silence, not an art.

"Who hath wrote so much as the Quakers?" asked Francis Bugg. "He that doth not write whilst he is alive, can't speak when he is dead," answered John Bellers in the seventeenth century. Silence as craft, however, is cultivated by Quakers, not to mention Trappists.

The summer stint, because ending, looks to have been good; while it lasted I've never been more anxious: continual nasal allergy aggravated by continual shrieking of the kids next door, plus being trapped in heaven, growing old in both skin and travail. God knows I've never allowed that experience had much to do with what we call creativity, for artists don't need knowledge, they need artistry. (You don't have to know what makes babies to make babies.) But I've not left this small island in nineteen weeks, and all I can see is myself.

Once upon a time when a piece was finished it was finished, *assez!*, don't look back; and ah, the bored bemusement that they for whom the piece was wrought (was finished) should now be taken by it, since I was elsewhere launched! Tonight, three weeks before another birthday, I scan the summer's many pieces like the final shot in *Citizen Kane* panning over the packed-up crockery, and wonder at my inability to duplicate some of them, not because they're bad but because they're good. No thrilling costly architecture proposed by the dentist will I accept now, just let him scrape the gums some, stanch the blood. Not rest, not yet, please. But to escape from the body.

New York
24 September

I'm "doing things" again so there's no time to write about doing things. All summer I dutifully filled these pages, because in Nantucket I was working— working, not "doing things." New York is where we busily idle, pursuing the business around work rather than the business of work. Such as the launching of *The Final Diary*, looking marbleized and feeling like the tombstone it is. Nobody cares, least of all Holt-Rinehart. A book cannot do better than a publisher's interest in it. Prose may be the bagatelle of my life, an appendage to music, but it asks in the public eye to be taken more seriously, being more publicized because more financial, and money's more serious than music. So sourness here exceeds that toward music manufacture, and my heart sickens when I find in store windows not me but Seymour Krim, who has but one dull axe to grind. Celebrity—the "being known" being more important than what one is known for—I may covet, but it doesn't come naturally. So I recoil, cowed, toward the secrecy of what counts, the silence of music.

Holt meanwhile, vetoing ads, conspires for machismo and money. Adding injury to insult, the editor writes me that Robert Craft acknowledged the galleys by stating, "I greatly enjoyed reading it, until page 302," and gently threatens litigation unless one phrase is removed. (Everyone likes everything except the niggardly sentences on themselves.) Perhaps Craft's letter could be used as a blurb.

Back in New York to find Jay Harrison nailed in a coffin. Deaths that "don't come as a surprise" surprise us most. As we expect them, we write them off before they occur. When they occur we're doubly grieved. No gulf is wider than between the almost dead and the dead.

Deaths today of Marcel Achard and of Harry Partch, the arrière-garde of France and the avant-garde of America. Why are we less attracted to a contemporary artist's work after he dies? When friends die, the excruciation is that we'll never see them again. That "never" is what leaves me cold when artists pass away—artists, that is, who aren't particularly friends. That their catalogue is now complete lames rather than quickens interest. (Do an essay on this. These words are too rusty and the idea's shiny.)

Cornell, Iowa
14 October

Here at college for usual two-day stint, recitals and speeches. Judith Raskin is at the same little *pensione* and we have breakfast together. What a charmer, with her two compulsions: (1) the necessity of words, words, words, when singing, and (2) the mastectomy that she's now "allowed"—and brave enough—to talk about. If her stance on stage is delicate, her breakfast style's intense. When I say that she sings my songs more clearly than any soprano except Phyllis Curtin, she answers that it's because she learned everything from Phyllis.

Tomorrow I'll stop off in Iowa City for a half-day with Jane Wilson.

15 October

People justify a belief in God because the universe has no other explanation. If the species were to be seen not as God's work but as a tedious procession of failures, the universe would still exist (presumably) in but one mold. The uniqueness of the universe is "blamed" on God. Now, didn't *we* concoct the notion of Him, who, without our intellect, could not be? The notion lends reason to life—the reason of search, search being meaning, meaning being value. (What's death? "Death is death," said Gertrude.) Isn't life's purpose simply to be alive? Life is life. There is no past, no future. I made the universe. I am God. Pause. And so are you.

16 October

Rain. *Turandot* last night with Ellen. Dress rehearsal this morning of *Death in Venice* (which sounds confusingly different from how it looks on paper, but which I must decide about for the *New Republic*, of which I'm now music critic) with Ellen and Nicholas Maw, then lunch with Ellen and Nicholas and also Jack Larson, Jim Bridges, and Gary Samuel, all fragrant with West Coast innocence.

25 October

Visit this morning from a Kristin Booth Glen, lawyer of the Listeners' Guild representing WNCN, with an affadavit, which I gladly sign. To switch on that station and hear rocky blasts now freezes the heart. But finesse and thoughtful work are as nothing beneath the dinosaur's paw. How does one prove Buckley wrong when he speaks just obliquely? Yet it's hard to credit current statements from the station about phone calls pouring in in favor of the new pop format. Where were these approvers during the picketing? Is their money what props up Starr? No, satisfaction is always voiced far less than discontent; those who marched in favor of the Vietnam policy were few.

Long evening . . . Sharon Mitchell and John Simon came to dine (baked chicken in sherry, rice and carrots in brown sugar, spinach salad, and *bavaroise au citron* in a Grand Marnier sauce). He suggested that some of my *Diary* stories could be more strung out, like the one about Gide passing for Claudel with the Arab boy. His own verbal excursions being, indeed, more ambling than the information they relay, we lift our eyebrows when he takes Moira Hodgson (also present, in brown moire) to task for admiring what he declares are the over-extended Brooklyn displays of Robert Wilson. John grants no benefit of doubt: that Wilson may be the other side of Webern's coin, or Western garb on a Chinese tract. So vehement is John's anti-Wilson stand that, as he speaks, he disintegrates before our eyes into a foaming red maniac clutching at the sofa's arm; then, gradually, subsides, eases back into the skin of suave Mr. Simon.

While we're on musical generalities, where did I note the conversation with Kinsey in 1949 when we spoke of who was and wasn't homoerotic in the musical worlds of pop and classical? Things have changed—except for organists, who remain exclusively one way in America, and in Europe (why?) exclusively the other.

Memorial for Parker Tyler at Jefferson Library. With my parents I listen in horror as Eric Bentley, giving tastelessness a new twist, reads for one hour from *Homosexuality in the Movies*, pausing at appropriate carnalities for us to savor. Finally a man behind us rises to yell, "Excuse me while I go out and vomit!" Later, Mother says, "I couldn't hear too well, could you?"

Fellini starts to pall. The characters finally have no ideas, just bodies. Except perhaps in 8½, where the hero poses thoughtful conundrums, Fellini derides intellectuals (poor Iris Tree in *La Dolce Vita*), and has now come quite to ignore them. So *Amarcord* isn't about anything. It moves not into but around Fellini's past because the actors have no extracorporeal notion. They eat and flirt and argue but there's no argument and so no target. Old Antonioni, Fellini's one-time competitor, used to make movies about duty. Insofar as he dropped his thesis (never having, maybe, realized he carried it) his films too have fallen. Still, the images of both men beguiled the unwashed, even some of the washed, and continue to render film not inferior but superior to the stage.

And what is great art? everyone sits around asking. Can you prove that it's not conditioning? Ives and Vivaldi, Gesualdo and Crumb: Were we not told what to think, what would we think? Even Beethoven, who invented greatness (Bach never thought in such terms), is no absolute, since I for one reject his quartets as yardsticks in this conversation.

No water for two days, the commodes have become cesspools, and David Diamond's due for dinner in an hour.

6 November

A letter from an unknown woman tells me that Joe Adamiak thirteen months ago committed suicide. As though it had happened this morning, I dissolved at how logical it seemed. Like thousands of others Joe had assumed he'd take the world by storm. He didn't. He died.

Now, eight hours later, it's passed, and it's the past. For once I don't feel guilty. Coolly transferred his letter file from the cabinet of the living to the cabinet of the dead. Recovered from the anguish of rereading, now I see the letters as heirlooms.

Cocktails at Gruens' for Lueen McGrath. Not impressed when the guest of honor appeared an hour late (especially since, after everyone had been invited for next Saturday, she'd asked that the party be switched to today). Why do this? For mystery? Her sole mystery is that she's unknown. Rudeness is dated, and never did have class. Sterile virtues, fertile vices.

Nantucket
11 November

Another interview with Arlene Francis yesterday afternoon to launch *The Final Diary*, then flew here to spend a few days in the new house which, until December 31st when the deed is signed, we are renting at one hundred dollars a month. I read Borges aloud to JH as he paints and plasters.

25 November

A week in New York, during which: De Sica died; Margherita Hastings conducted nicely Poulenc's *Figure humaine* (the most taxing a cappella vehicle ever penned); Anne Meacham gave a brunch for Tennessee who's ever more difficult to talk to; John Koch had an exhibition of his troubling oils; I signed an agreement with Georges Borchardt (whose secretary is Willy Kapell's daughter) so now I have an agent for the first time; did a cultural Roundtable on Channel 13 and they want me back; attended Ruth Laredo's birthday party; saw a movie called *Earthquake*; visited the dentist twice; went to Ingrid Dingfelder's flute recital because I'm writing a piece for her; received a visit from Martin Peretz who invited me to write for the *New Republic*, not realizing I've had seven articles in that magazine during the past year; and then flew back here where John Wulp has agreed to lend us some chairs for the winter. Termite inspection by Valero. Plumbing inspection by Ramos.

28 November

Thanksgiving dinner chez John Wulp, who likes to feed hordes but doesn't introduce anyone to anyone. Frank Conroy there. A wonderful orange cake.

30 November

Cold beyond imagining. With Eugenie Voorhees to the Unitarian Church for high culture in the form of a long solo by Viveca Lindfors.

In *I Am a Woman* Lindfors remains handsome, with a continental carriage that works fine in drawing rooms. Her problem is that she can't act. Considering who's barnstormed in the show and knows it cold, how can her evening be ungraced by a sole professional minute? No diction, no projection, no differentiation between roles, and the too-frequent mannerism—a curse also of Cher, Natalie Wood, and many another long-tressed thespian—of combing her hair out of her eyes with her fingers.

We the audience become a collective retina, the accumulation of dozens of pairs of eyes. Concentration is extreme, for we have *paid* to concentrate. We catch all gestures and assume they mean something. To learn that a gesture means nothing is to be had. We are disconcerted when it is replicated in every one of her multifaced monologues, for the gesture (which we hoped was Plath's or Freud's or Nin's or King Lear's) is only Viveca's, sucking us into her ego rather than into her personification of another's ego.

New York
6 December

In my essay for last week's *New Republic* appear these phrases: "Art does not grow from the collective tension of the left but from individual leisure. Sadly, our most liberal politicals are often the least culture-minded. Bella Abzug, for example, makes no statements on behalf of the arts, yet her district alone houses the most concentrated covey of first-rate creators this side of Paris in the twenties. God knows she's for human rights, but only the jaded rich seem to have time for the art of artists as well as for their campaign support." The magazine has forwarded a letter from a congressional press secretary: "Allow me to say that the Congresswoman, among other things, has been an active supporter of Lincoln Center and appeared at benefits there and at other cultural centers in her constituency." Doesn't anyone ever want to get the point?

Prose writing is hardly my first occupation. Yet over the past fifteen years I have published perhaps a million words, not to mention dozens of hours of music of every stripe. Most of the mail I get about music deals in facts (When did you write this or that piece? Should the third beat of measure seven be a half-note or a quarter?), while the mail I get about the diaries is mostly from crazies. To articles in periodicals there's little response, pro or con. Yet I presume that my sentences have style and that my thoughts are neatly parsed, or why am I accepted by such a wide variety of publications? A letter like the one from Abzug's secretary is both amusing and discouraging.

7 December

Eugenie and Shirley came to dine. Later John Gruen stopped by with Lueen McGrath, Moira, and W. S. Merwin. Much discussion of morality and art. (Pique at Lueen abated with her undeniable charm.)

Artists are always telling us they hate to repeat themselves, as though self-imitation were a flaw, but of course they all do it all their lives; they simply choose new molds into which to pour their five or six (seldom more) ideas forever.

12 December

Afternoon visit from Maxine and James Dickey, both three sheets to the wind but looking handsome. James is the only paleface today who's made himself a star in the same way that, on the other side of the fence, Allen Ginsberg has. He wants to do a book of poems *illustrated* by my music—not songs, but sonic backgrounds. That's what he says.

21 December

Howard Moss came over to show us his pastiche of my journals—the parody of a parody, you might say—before publishing it in the *New Yorker*. He calls it "The Ultimate Diary." I had no reaction. It didn't seem amusing, but I'm too close or too far for focus. Then again, maybe it's just not amusing (although JH laughed). Howard, with his catholic verbal gifts, has never struck me as a humorist. But if satire's not my dish, glory is, and to be satirized is *the* glory. Howard himself once wrote: "The parody is an unconscious compliment: to have read someone closely enough to produce an acceptable imitation, to have become obsessed to the necessary degree, requires an attention and concentration the works of most authors never receive."

A reassuring wonder, Howard never changes. In 1946 when we first met he looked fifteen years older than he was; today he looks fifteen years younger. He remains thirty-seven. His poet's quality too is stationary—which is to say high. If there've been no tidal waves, neither have there been droughts, and he's one of the few versifiers who can write prose that's prose (although he can't write theater—or, of course, pastiche). All this—his appearance, his talent's stance—is due, I'd say, to psychoanalysis. With his furrowed Noël Cowardian smile and his unwillingness to utter a banal quip, Howard's the "therapized" model, the precise contrary of the current New York school (all those Anne Waldmans), whom one might call The Pseudo-Unsophisticated.

A souvenir persists. Was it in 1950, after having lived already one year in Paris, that I ran across Howard briefly one summer night at Saint Germain dœ Près and, according to Howard in later years, was cool to his warm greeting? True, expatriated Americans were proprietarily inclined against old friends as new interlopers. But in this case coldness came from being taken unawares (just as we are cold to those we'd prefer to be in bed with, but, from shyness, haven't yet met): I happened to be wearing a black-and-white broad-striped polo shirt which Howard had loaned me three years earlier.

27 December

By pop standards Anita Ellis's nightly concert at the Birdcage is old-fashioned, and so is her vocal style. But everyone loves her because what she does is now rare, and she does it better than anyone.

Her platform manner is without manner. She stands there and sings, in basic black. For occasional emphasis she'll raise a hand like Lenya, close her eyes like Billie, or throw back her head like Piaf, but no histrionics, no sequins, no flailing arms. She's motionless, but what emerges is hot with action. She can shift from a whisper to a roar and back again in the space of three notes and not sound wrong; or hit and hold onto a tone, making it melt from an icicle into a tear merely by increasing her vibrato. The trick echoes Streisand and Garland, but Ellis was *their* big influence; she coined hysteria as a vocal art.

She herself claims to be influenced by, of all people, Fischer-Dieskau. One does detect more than a residue of black women, though all her material is by white men. The selection is small (she's been doing the same twenty songs for thirty years) but classy: handpicked bonbons from the stores of Kern, Arlen, Wilder, or Weill, or from sound tracks of movies she dubbed for Rita Hayworth.

If the repertory of Anna Moffo is deeper than Anita's, Anita is not necessarily the lesser artist. American opera stars could learn a lot about English diction from her. Pop singers do have it easier than concert singers: their vocal range is narrower, they profit from the intimacy of microphones, and their words—"lyrics"—are simpler than the poetry of recitalists. But recitalists too often rely on beauty of voice at the expense of projection of their not-simple poetry. To need to stress that Anita knows what she's singing about is to decry the absence of what would seem to be the obvious goal of singers in any category. (Rock singers have nothing to do with singing, but with recording.)

With pop singers, it's not the song but their way with it. The difference between pop and classical is the difference between playing and what's played. Jazz is a performer's art, classical a composer's art. With vocal jazz, pleasure lies less in what's sung than in how it's sung. True, Billie Holiday did certain good songs often, but she also had a knack for making trash good, for bending tones until the tune became hers. We have *arrangements* by the thousand of pop songs, while songs by Schumann or Poulenc can't be "arranged" and still retain identity. Pop is variable, classical invariable. A classical piece exists in a unique state, there is no question of fooling around. Insofar as a singer takes liberties with a classical song its composer is betrayed. (Insofar as a coloratura *colors* a *bel canto* aria by inventing ornaments to hang on the written phrases, she steals the music, as jazz artists do, and sometimes improves it.)

I've never heard a singer, no matter how proficient, who was convincing in both "kinds" of music—pop and classical. Opera divas have enough trouble scaling down to Schubert songs without adding their hokey rolled R's to Gershwin tunes. As to whether an Anita Ellis could handle an opera role is beside the point; that which is *hers*—the crooning purr, the world as cameo—has nothing to do with arias.

Coincidence this morning delivered the disc *Classical Barbra*. Once I wrote that Streisand could handle certain arias if she wished, but her timbre is geared in other directions. (By the reverse token Grace Moore, and more recently Eileen Farrell, just never had it when trying to swing.) The point now is demonstrated by this record, starting with the title. Except for the

Handel, none of her "numbers" are classical—they are what *l'homme moyen sensuel* thinks of as classical. Streisand's error is to aim at her mass public rather than to put out an edition for just a few thousand dear friends.

The program note boasts that "only one song in the collection is sung in English," as though classical meant foreign, arhythmic, and as though beat or color betray pop leanings. Now, these songs contain a wider expressive range than pop songs, both in tune and text, yet Streisand feels that's exactly what "classical" songs don't contain, for classical means restraint. (Respect without comprehension. No language talent. No musicality, considering how musical she elsewhere is. Etc.)

Argument with JH about whether the two musics will ever be one. He feels that *au fond* they fill the same need, I feel they don't. If they did we'd have the same music. Pop music is erotic, while church music, by removing rhythm, no longer resembles sex. (But who can say what's sexual?) The fact remains that, in our century, although some instrumentalists live by playing in jazz bands at night and symphonies by day, and although some classical "vocalists" can skillfully warble pop, pop singers simply haven't the tools for classical. (Imagine Holiday or Bessie Smith or Peggy Lee convincingly faking even the dumbest Donizetti, let alone Schubert or Poulenc or Christmas carols.) Those with technical equipment miss the point, like Streisand.

Two kinds of music have run forever parallel. Call them sacred and profane, church and folkloric, classical and popular, indoor and outdoor, high and low, isolated and participatory, specific and general. They have always had two definable audiences. Only in recent decades has confusion arisen, a rivalry, a sense of either/or. High prices granted to entertainment industries have allowed these industries a high notion of themselves and thus to feel they're where it's at, they're what the public wants. They're right. But what public? Once upon a time the distinction of entertainment lay in its passive public, while art (even the simplest) presumed some activity from the audience, a willingness to come halfway. Things blur in today's heterogeneous world; good and bad are thrown at us in look-alike packages.

Death today of Jack Benny. Suicide of Amy Vanderbilt.

28 December

With JH this afternoon to see *The Towering Inferno*, an assignment by Channel 13. But oh, the untheatrical attenuation of it all: it just goes on and on. There *is* a feeling of symbolism—those horrors momentarily represent our world's mistakes, and time running out. But the totality (and I do mean totality) starves us. Five minutes after leaving the theater I retain nothing, not even shock, not even annoyance, not even the trumped-up "message."

I've never been a fan of Paul Newman's acting, though I have admired his direction. Yes, he's gorgeous, smart too, and I'm in the minority. But he's embarrassing. That hammy boyish corny hard-earned vanity of our male actors! Newman, even in the fiery jaws of death, manages loving asides to the camera, and through it to his great loving public out there.

Let's put in a bad word for the new National movie theater in Times Square, a sty that looks like a firetrap, a dubious site in which to see *The Towering Inferno*. Yet the owners charge four dollars a seat.

Tonight, *Bluebeard's Castle* at the Met. Tomorrow, Nantucket.

The author at eleven

Fannie Hurst with Rorem *père* at the Commodore Hotel, December 1945, on the occasion of the tenth anniversary of the Blue Cross of which Ned Rorem's father, Dr. C. Rufus Rorem was cofounder. Hurst had been number one subscriber in New York.

Garden of Comtesse Lily Pastré, Paris, spring 1951, on the occasion of the announcement of the Prix de Biarritz given to Leo Préger, Ned Rorem, and Monsieur Spivak for their ballet scores based on the scenario, *Mélos*, by Marie Laure de Noailles.

Standing, back row: Spivak, Philippe Erlanger, Denise Tual, Henri Sauguet, Roger Désormière, Georges Auric, Ned Rorem

Sitting, front row: Comtesse Jean de Polignac (Marie Blanche), Vicomtesse de Noailles (Marie Laure), Préger, Nadia Boulanger, Geneviève Joy

(This picture was given to the author by Henri Dutilleux on April 6, 1984)

Ned Rorem, Quai de l'Alma, Paris 1954

Ned Rorem, 1956 *(Horst)*

The author, February 14, 1956 *(Carl Van Vechten)*

Ned Rorem, Hyères 1957 *(Ninette Lyons)*

Drawing by Jean de Gaigneron, Marseille, 1964

Janet Flanner (right) and Natalia Denisi Murray (© *John Deakin*)

Jane Wilson and Ned Rorem in 1970 (*John Gruen*)

Maurice Grosser, Leo Lurman, Ned Rorem and Virgil Thomson in 1971 (© *Arnold Weissberger*)

Gian-Carlo Menotti, Lehman Engel, Ned Rorem in September 1972 (© *Arnold Weissberger*)

Jerome Lowonthal, Ned Rorem and Phyllis Curtin in October 1973 (*Eugene Cook*)

Ned Rorem with Edouard Roditi at Cluny in Paris, 1973 *(T. Cooke)*

Beverly Wolff, Phyllis
Curtin, Donald Gramm
and (on floor) Ned Rorem
in November 1973
(Eugene Cook)

Counterclockwise: Hugo
Weisgall, John Gruen, Ned
Rorem, James Holmes,
Marta Casals Istomin, Jane
Wilson, Eugene Istomin.
April 2, 1977

Ned Rorem, 1973 *(Gianni Bates)*

Gladys Rorem (mother), Stanley Adams, Ned Rorem, Morton Gould, Walter
Wager and C. Rufus Rorem after lunch offered by ASCAP to honor the Pulitzer
Prize. November 9, 1976

The author, 1977 (© *John de Clef Pineiro*)

Judy Collins and Louis Nelson in Saratoga
Springs, August 1978 *(Ruth Orkin)*

Ned Rorem by Hirschfeld
*(Courtesy of Margo Feiden
Galleries)*

Ned Rorem with his sister, Rosemary Marshall, backstage at the Philadelphia Academy, September 1978 *(Louis Hood)*

With Eugene Ormandy, after premiere of *Sunday Morning*, Philadelphia, 1978 *(Louis Hood)*

Ned Rorem and James Holmes, Nantucket 1978 *(© Harry Benson)*

Ned Rorem at "The Oldest House," Nantucket, Summer 1978 *(© Harry Benson)*

Ned Rorem, 1979 *(Christopher Cox)*

William Parker and Ned Rorem in
Santa Fe, Summer 1980

Virgil Thomson *(© Thomas Victor)*

Sharon Robinson, Lucy Shelton and Ned Rorem in 1982 (© *Gerry Goodstein*)

Ned Rorem, Highland Park,
Illinois, 1982 *(Kitty Reeve)*

Ellen Adler, 1982

Portrait of Ned Rorem by Maurice
Grosser, Autumn 1983

Ned Rorem, 1984 *(© Jack Mitchell)*

Ned Rorem and James Holmes, New York, 1984 *(© Jack Mitchell)*

George Perle and Shirley, 1985

Eugene Istomin and
Marta Casals Istomin
(© *Karsh of Ottawa*)

Leonard Bernstein and Ned Rorem, March 18, 1986 (© *Andrew French*)

Ned Rorem, 1978 *(Harry Benson)*

1975

As of last evening I own this house, the deed having been witnessed yesterday in Grace Henry's sunny office at the brick Pacific Bank. JH grievously burned his wrist making coffee. Last night I dreamed this: Years ago I was swimming east under Eighth Street, literally diving into the cement while Bill Flanagan looked on with a skeptical eye, though he wanted to learn. I progressed slowly with a wide breast stroke from square to square of the soggy sidewalk. With each crack the harmony changed, instructively. Harmonic progressions.

This morning in cold light the island seems empty. Last evening too, Main Street, indeed the whole town and countryside, though decorated with yew branches and glittering lanterns, contained no living soul. We have two more full days of plastering. JH does all the work. I cook, sweep, worry about imminent deadlines.

For twenty minutes at the upstairs window I watched the three trees—my three trees—wave for dear life in the destructive wind as day turned to night, though it's only three P.M., and I wondered what with the sleet if the plane will take off tomorrow morning. For twenty long minutes I stood. Could I have done so if I weren't going to write that I'd done so?

Stymied? The new piece will be so perfect I can't compose it. (Or: The new piece is too perfect to put into notes.) Moral: Perfection impoverishes.

Perils of order. The blandness of heaven where all is perfection. Beauties of perfection at the abyss. The soprano of Adele Addison, before it faded, was flawless, dangerously. A suntan acquired this morning is smooth as a fawn-satin rose: never have cheeks seemed more sleek; yet tonight the dry furrows will be there, and the face in a trice will have aged like that of She.

3 January

Alas or Thank God, I've reached the age where I'm asked to provide letters of recommendation. Four out of five I write willingly. The fifth I write too (how refuse?), but without recommending the "individual" (it's confidential after all), and that makes me sad. I'd lie and say nice things, but too many deserving people need . . . etc., etc.

More frequently I'm asked to write blurbs, and there, four out of five times I cheat, say more than I believe (friends are friends). The fifth time I refuse. Even I am not so avid for glory that I'll fix my name to what I don't at all believe.

New York
5 January

Through sleet to Bank Street last night, with JH and Gustavo, to see Stanley Silverman's new little opera, *Hotel for Criminals,* which lacks the witty energy of his *Elephant Steps*. Pastiche and parody are legitimate expressions and can be funny. But this is pastiche of pastiche (the dadaism of Buñuel and Clair), and parody of parody (Satie and Weill). Imitation of imitation provides no nourishment; one goes off hungry.

Silverman's mimicries are too near for viewpoint and thus for caricature. The literal quotes (from *Sacre* or *Pierrot*) are literal for no reason. Parody usually has focus. The unique voice of Gilbert and Sullivan gleams through their pseudo-Rossini, but we don't hear Silverman through his pseudo-Satie.

12 January

The phone intrudes like the person from Porlock, derailing my train of thought. A tenor, organizing a program around gay themes by gay composers, wonders if I will contribute. Certainly not. I'm a composer, not a gay composer. Sexuality may relate to an artist's becoming an artist, but not to his becoming a good artist. I want to be loved or hated, not for my nature, but for the quality of my nature. Anyone can be gay—it's no accomplishment—but only I can be me. (A concert of straight composers might be a novelty.)

I am not We and am unable to verbalize collectively, much less identify with even such groups as composers or lovers. I can't say "we composers" or "my lover and me," but "lovers are," "composers are," "Americans are," "they are." Do I dread not being unique? With gays, I think Them, not Us. How can They, inherently more diverse than a Zulu tribe or even than an international bourgeoisie, merely magnify, with We, a sole thread of their complex web? I resent vouchsafing individuality even to such a category as Mankind (still, what can you do?), but classify myself as a homo-sapient musician who is sexual. The sexual object is nobody's business, at least in public discussion. So diaries. If the goal of my drive becomes clear within their pages, such a "confession" is intended simply (simply?) as that of a human whose pangs of head and heart seem only too prevalent within the world's common groin.

Unlike negritude, homosexuality is not physically spottable, though gay clichés abound. A black when he's not Uncle Tomming is still black, and he's still black when he solves an algebraic equation. Is a queer queer when out of bed? When solving equations? Homosexuals have options: like heretics they can repent. A black cannot repent: he can only regret, or be proud.

Black Pride and Gay Pride are dangerous slogans, like White Pride or Straight Pride. Gay and black are not achievements but accidents of birth. One must not be ashamed, but that's not the same as being proud. Pride should lie only in what one does with one's blackness or gayness. Even so, has a straight or a white ever done anything to be proud of as a straight or a white?

Nor is the gay condition comparable to the female condition. A female remains so tomorrow. A lesbian (but who is not a lesbian?) may decide—consciously decide—not to be. Can change her mind. For a gay man to long to be treated like an unliberated woman is for him to have it both ways. A woman has no choice, but he can change his tune at any measure and never pay the piper.

How far must we discourage "isms" and promote tolerance? Is it antifeminist to be sexually unattracted to women? Or blondist to dislike blonds? Must gerontophiles in fairness also covet kids? By extension embryos and corpses become fair game. Can we believe James Baldwin when he claims to have reached a utopian state when once, years ago, he was unaware that a friend of his was indeed Algerian until a test moment brought the fact home? Must humanity be so ideally One that we don't (aren't allowed to) distinguish sexually between mentalities, colors, ages, sexes, or even species? We smile when Gore Vidal, to the question "Was your first experience with a man or a woman?" answers "I thought it would be rude to ask." Do I, less young than last year, require gerontophiles? Could my fantasies not instead be for an ancient father embodied in that brawny young farmer there? But if in fact fantasies nourish us to that extent, what prevents the makeshift co-ition with virtually anything—jars of mercury, cobras, dynamite sticks?

Though turnabout may be fair play, men who like to "do anything" are as a rule of average intelligence, generous, congenial, but without much artistic force. Those whom in America we call "achievers" are as a rule carnally self-restricted, play one role, and have a knack for extended concentration on things not sexual. *L'homme moyen sensuel* is by definition less human than the "achiever," if by human we define the logic which differentiates man from other mammals. Sex has nothing to do with logic, but achievers treat sex logically (hence their roles) while average men treat sex sensually.

Just as there is no real literature recounting exploits from the viewpoint of the passive male (the *enculé*) so there is no real literature, beyond the blues of Ma Rainey, describing lesbian carnality. Has any woman related—with the necessity and anxiety and joy of a Goodman or a Ginsberg—the strictly physical charge of lesbianism? Can she? Can, in fact, the "passive" man make art from the trials of Eros? Yes. Since he exists he can be subject as well as object. Forster tried.

14 January

Visit from Emanuel Ax, for whom I'm commissioned to write "an extended work." Probably Études—he can do anything. He's also very bright, but not what we once called intellectual, the way Eugene exceptionally is.

The arts in America do not overlap. Sometimes it even seems that, para-doxically, they exist not simultaneously but on separate historic planes, evolving at different speeds. Practitioners of the various arts often do not know each other, much less each other's work. If as a rule composers (though not performers) are better-rounded than other artists, possibly it's because their area—being the only truly abstract area—needs reaffirmation in "real" logic. (Reword.) It is inconceivable that any composer, good or bad, should be ignorant of the work of the major playwrights, painters, and poets of his time; indeed, his work, when it deals with visuals or texts, sometimes depends on other arts. But it is more the rule than the exception that other artists, without blushing, say they can't tell Bach from the Beatles.

26 January

Over two years since I'd talked with Virgil. Everyone knew he'd not been feeling close to me. Certainly I was moved by his (unexpectedly) kind words on my essays in the *Times* recently. People suggested that maybe the hour had come to warm up; perhaps someone would arrange something. During this long period we'd not once run into each other accidentally.

Taking the bull by the horns I phoned to invite him. Last night he came. (Night *before* last we met on the street, as he was leaving the Gruens', wouldn't you know!) Just the three of us—with JH—all quite cordial, with no references to our rift, and he stayed the proper time, then left, civil if not ecstatic. So we're speaking again.

Like all true artists you are made of contradictions, contradictions embodied in your very name, Virgil Thomson: The Latin poet in you forms frenchness; the anglo-saxon (minus the P for puritan) provides solid fancy. We can hate our debtors. More subtly, we can resent those to whom we are, unbeknownst to them, indebted. I owe you all yet love you still.

27 January

In *Paul's Case* the boy committing suicide witnesses his own dying, until suddenly the witnessing mechanism snaps off, and in blackness all returns to natural order. In childhood I identified with Paul, the oversensitive parvenu who, like Lily Bart, could no longer bear it. At the same time I sensed that Lily and Paul were unfit subjects for grown-up books. To read Cather and Wharton was to indulge a guilty luxury (luxury of vicarious suicide) when my mind, like Paul's and Lily's, should have been on important items like gym class or useful contacts. Adults, one assumed, put away childish things, broken hearts.

One can live and die by literary reference, not so much because one cannot distinguish fact from fiction as because fiction imposes itself forever upon fact, gives fact fragrance and shape, never permits fact to function in the abstract. Unless the very abstraction of fact is itself a fiction.

The "objectivity" of Paul's suicide—his seeing it happen while it happened, his *using* it—didn't make it any less doleful than did, for instance, my tantrums in adolescence, refusing to eat, while noting coolly that the diet trimmed down my figure.

Cocktails at Gethsemane. Peter named Paul, this is Paul named Peter. May we introduce you both to Percy named Mae. And here comes Ebenezer named Archibald along with George called Myrt. But where's Elsa named Charles? and Joan called John?

Over to Juilliard this afternoon for a timpani lesson with Saul Goodman. The North Carolina piece will be a sort of non-virtuosic Concerto Grosso featuring oboe, trumpet, timpani and viola. The lesson may have been a mistake, showing not so much what the drums can do as what I can't. Returned to find the cats had peed all over the armchair. *Young Frankenstein* with JH.

29 January

Everything has ego. Not just cats and plants and that bowl of tortoise eggs, but a pile of pillows, a steel bed, radiators exist there, without moving, ominous, taking up your space. I am not nice. Pretend to be, even try to be. But I'm not. Also I'm dull, though having learned to feign sparkle I get along.

Weary and without illusion, I persist in noting it. Why even write? Why even write"Why even write 'Why even write "Why even write"'"?

If you know you are going to die, if you're condemned and the date is set, nothing—no creed or philosophy, no friendly phrase or stoical recipe— makes any difference. The fact of your near and certain end becomes as all-consuming as love was years ago.

31 January

Miffed by Shirley's remark during intermission at the Boulez concert: "Don't you agree that in the future it will still be Beethoven and Schubert that people listen willingly to, and not all this?" But I too am a composer, and although my musical language is not like "all this" I listen willingly to it, whereas I never listen to Beethoven and Schubert. The same holds for much of the sold-out and youthful audience. Shirley assumed that, first, music must be in some way pleasurable, and second, and that all this was not pleasurable. The remark would not have been made at the opening of a new play: she wouldn't have said, for example, at Albee's *Seascape*, "Shakespeare will surely outlive all this," because Albee is not in competition with Shakespeare. Indeed, no creative artists today are held up in the light of the past— except composers.

Charm. It's clarity. We hear him forever demoted by Debussy, but if we enjoyed Ravel more, can we admit he's better? Perhaps this decade.

Charm, depending on the decade, is fault or attribute. The 1960s saw charm as glib vice until pop's intellectualization made it kosher. The most fearsome masterpieces, with hindsight, can now be given their due as charming (even, occasionally, Beethoven). Some composers have it on the spot, others only in retrospect. French versus German. Copland can't avoid it, even when he tries (as in *Connotations*). Carter cannot acquire it, nor does he try (though in a decade we'll find some—yes—charm in those irritating quartets). Boulez tries not to, but today it shines through. (Alone, Schoenberg will never possess it.)

Carter is uncompromisingly colorless. He cannot pander, there are no "effects," at least in the quartets. The quartet is a notorious trap, the most exposed of mediums where bones forever show through the maquillage. The undifferentiated gray voices of strings paradoxically hold the ear more tirelessly than four mixed hues—of, say, trombone and bongo and bass flute and harp. Ravel, *coloriste né* and model orchestrator, nonetheless composed the last great quartet in France. Can a moral be drawn? For he is also the father (no, the mother: Debussy's the father) of modern French orchestration, which is distinguished from German by its avoidance of doublings, its transparency. Its charm.

Corpus Christi, Texas
8 February

Here on a three-day stint; haven't been able to leave behind headache that's plagued me for a month. Padre Island, bleak, thrilling; classes, concerts, shrimp, receptions. Maurice Peress says the Moss piece is in the current *New Yorker*, so I've bought and read it, cringing. Subtitled "Further Daily Jottings of a Contemporary Composer," it's terribly funny and terribly embarrassing. Can I ever pen another line?

New York
10 February

In her ivorine glory, Moira . . .

Maggy Magerstadt here for tea. Her birthday. Except for Bruce Phemister, whom I've known since nursery school and who, as in Chicago, still lives three blocks away, and Frazier Rippy, whom I've known since sixth grade and who lives in Rome, Maggy is the oldest dear friend I still see regularly (yearly). Brought three jars of her homemade raspberry jelly.

Depression, muted frenzy. Very sore left eye. I've given the centenary article on Ravel to Norman Podhoretz, *tant bien que mal*, possibly because Ravel's vague Jewishness seems not inappropriate for *Commentary*.

11 February

With no special pang, suddenly I realize that except for Roro, there's no longer regular contact with a single person in Europe. Paris has become like

Chicago, a city which once was the world, my sole frame of reference, a globe now withering, receding. It takes a telescope to find it. Finding myself in France tonight I'd be at a loss as to whom to phone.

Deciannual visit from Dick Jacob sporting the identical features as in our Chicago adolescence. Conversation nine-tenths reminiscence. I recall that Don Dalton first introduced us to the voice of Billie Holiday in 1939. Dick grows indignant about Don (dead for three decades), for he had given Don that disc, yet Don took credit for presenting "Fine and Mellow" to South Side's intelligentsia. Similarly today I still nurse grudges against poor Bill Flanagan, who defends himself even less well than when he was alive. This is not especially unhealthy.

The trouble with pornography is no viewpoint. It's not more honest than. It's only simpler than. Blue blue blue blue blue, the Manhattan air takes on airs of whory sentience to beguile us as we prepare to leave for months.

15 February

Wedding of Eugene Istomin to Martita Casals. Proustian convolution.

27 February

Visit from Robert Veyron-Lacroix, here on his annual trek with Rampal. We gave him boned chicken breasts marinated in ale and garlic, baked yams, a watercress salad, and strawberry mousse with framboise-flavored raspberry sauce.

   Since we meet so seldom our rapports cannot center on the present. We know to some extent what we have become, while the past evanesces increasingly. I was interested in whether Roro had ever returned to Hyères. Yes, two years ago, having to play in Toulon, he detoured bravely to the Château St. Bernard. Henri, Marie Laure's caretaker, who now lives alone over the garage, warned Roro that the property would seem a *triste* shock. The once-manicured lawns are yards high in weeds; vines have grown through the windows and rend the concrete floors. The fifty-room house, once filled with Kislings and pianos, esprit and quarrels, hard work and gold wealth, is now an empty station with a cold wind. Roro said it was ugly (that it always had been, but we never noticed), and has been sold to the town to be converted, like Edith Wharton's mansion nearby, into an inn. So there it is, where my only songs for eight years saw the light, every cranny familiar as my pocket, dust now, like her.

Yaddo
3 March

The yellow ice of Saratoga Springs again. As with my arrivals at Hyères every summer in the fifties I fume when the first twelve hours don't bring forth an opera. Momentum of desire, held in check during the urban winter, wants quick release; and since in my head six Romes are already built, why can't they be *realized* in a day? The notation of music is a composer's chief impediment.

5 March

Wasteful insomnia. Those wide-awake nocturnes charged with sterile thought, useless next morning when, exhausted, I go back to bed to reread *Dubliners* for the first time since a freshman at Northwestern (age sixteen in 1940), and retrieve as accurately as in a snapshot each phrase, each indelible reaction of thirty-five years ago when clearly I was more mature than now.

Also reading and am impressed by *One Hundred Years of Solitude*, at Curt's insistence.

6 March

Every time I pick up a magazine it contains a letter of complaint about Dotson Rader. People despise him (as they sometimes despise me), feeling that he twists their words into silk bows which become him more than them. Of course these bows, like all ornaments, finally do not offset his bad features but set them off. He's covered with wrinkles—not new wrinkles—furrows as old as his ego which reveal him for the swindler he is.

8 March

The sky has been of crackling fire and dreamless (I meant to write cloudless) for four days: now this morning a slow fine sleet has fallen for hours on the Yaddo lawns, and I'm wondering if over in Nantucket, where JH is painting ceilings, the planes will as usual be *en panne*: he must fly back to the city tonight for his choir rehearsal. The high points of my annual stays here are his semiweekly three-minute phone calls.

The right thumb, flattened in Paris, May 1961, retains an ache. The ankle smashed here at Yaddo a year or two later is cured. Like a minesweeper my mind belabors the past in useless, timetaking evocation of the thousand places I've grazed. Valueless and sad, perhaps, this store of facts; yet I'm at my peacefullest in cemeteries. Today's Michelangelo's 500th birthday. Frequent headaches. Piercing pain in left eye. Reading Giraudoux's *Choix des Élues* and Arnold Bennett's *Old Wives Tale*.

10 March

The only time an affliction of ennui's not upon me is during the fifteenth waking hour, reading in bed. Nor is there boredom in sleep. My compositional attention span is sporadic, yet I've composed thirty seconds of music a day (working two hours each day) since coming here, and that's huge. The piece is for the North Carolina Orchestra. Boring? Am I capable of boring music? Or ugly music? I try, but I can't write ugly music.

Sad flashes, that begin at four in the morning and continue for hours, about the little time left. Will the end hurt? Then sunlight creeps in, and dutifully drooling like Pavlov's dog I trot through the snow to a breakfast of hot porridge and wholewheat toast.

17 March

Wednesday, after eighteen days, I return to New York where JH, in dental strife, requires stability. I leave with an easy conscience for a change: the Carolina piece is safely under way (should I call it *Winter Music*?), and I've read enough to last a month: Forster as always with awe, and Marquez as a *tour de force*.

To be aware of your own death. Everyone else goes on to dumb festivities, while you stay home alone and die. To say this means in some way to care— that I'm not incapacitated. Yet I've said all I have to say. In which case, such a final saying seems . . . Long nights.

Most of the time I feel lousy. Unable to underplay, I recount my own misery. Why? It's not a pleasure to wonder how I'll kill myself; suicide's not child's play, nor can anyone accept, even for a moment, Freud's verses anymore. ("No man can believe in his own death. And when he tries to imagine it, he perceives that he really survives as a spectator.") Were it not for JH where would I be? The drift of a high-school lass's diary comes back to haunt us.

Elizabeth Ames is sad to see. Her sunfilled drawing room with its cheerful carpet and valuable oils is unchanged as ever, but for Elizabeth the house is peopled with fancies. She imagines her sisters and mother to be staying here; she imagines her duties to the corporation keep her too busy for old friends, all in fact dead. Her deafness prevents her getting the point, and she's unaware that, during the last decade, she was repeatedly operated on for eye cancer. Elizabeth makes me want to cry.

New York
24 March

For five weeks our block of 70th Street has been undergoing major surgery. Gashes six feet deep and fifty yards long flank the roadway and are infected by buzz saws so loud you laugh in disbelief. If I perish from this, engrave on the marble Paul Goodman's translation of the *Duino Elegies*, which I've just been retyping for the publication of *The Poets' Requiem*, and have understood for the first time since the composition in Rome twenty sad years ago.

> *But we have never, not a single day, pure space in front of us . . .*
> *. . . that pure unguarded thing one breathes,*
> *endlessly knows, and does not crave.*
> *A child one day gets calmly lost in it, is prodded back.*
> *Or someone dies, and is it.*

Tonight at Tully Hall, for survivors of the Holocaust, my goyische *Trio* played by the faithful Jerry Lowenthal, Eugenia Zukerman, and Jeffrey Solow.

27 March

Paul Goodman's *Collected Poems* from Random House. After the muse's allotted time, there is no example of revision improving a work of art. You may revise during the process, and for perhaps a month or two after—during which you are more or less the same person as during the process. But years later, coming back, you damage the work of another poet. Rather than revise, write another poem. (Or, as Hindemith did with *Marienleben*, write different songs on the same words.) The saddest example is old Paul Goodman's contaminating tamperings with his youth. This book hurts the fingers.

Differently stated: Revision's a polish which can only be applied successfully within a tight time slot, for quickly the poem is weaned and leads its own life. Paul erred. Thirty years later he snatched *The Lordly Hudson* back from us and swallowed it whole.

We faithful never asked ourselves, on committing some questionable act, What would Freud think? but rather, What would Paul think? He used to say: When one of us dies, I'll go to Paris.

Nature imitates art, and art imitates nature, yes, yes, yes. But if nature imitates nature (ontology recapitulates etc.), art can also imitate art, and I do not talk of influences, healthy influences. Paul pointed out that the use of a prop lute as a real lute in *Orpheus* was a moral mistake by no less noble law-makers than Stravinsky and Balanchine.

He felt thwarted by Auden, the rare poet (with Cocteau) he admired. None of the three, although they knew foreign languages, spoke them convincingly. Like other great poets, who by definition have a way with the written verb—that is, an ear for what is eyed—Auden had not the gift of tongues. His spoken Italian, French, and German were apparently incomprehensible to natives; even his Oxfordian English was trying for American students, not to mention Stravinsky, especially after Auden was fitted with false teeth by Chester's father, a dentist. The same holds for musicians: it does not follow that those with a so-called musical ear have a knack for foreign languages. Some of our greatest composers simply don't get the hang of it, while many a fool speaks many a language with unaccented nuance (though, of course, with the same foolishness in each). I used to think that talent for language was a question of desire mixed with a sense of the ham: Gertrude Stein had the hamminess but not the desire, for, like André Breton who never learned English while in America so as not to "tarnish" his French, Gertrude wished to keep her English pure. But Auden was both ham and scholar.

28 March

Visit from Peter Davis to edit my essay "On Song" for the *Times*. Then Ethan Mordden for *his* essay on American operas. By definition I cannot trust some whom I may like as I can many whom I dislike, if they belong to that indispensable breed, from which, of course, individuals are sometimes plucked who prove more vital than many a necessary composer. I mean critics.

To Shirley's to celebrate the Gruens' twenty-seventh anniversary. Eugene and Martita also, and Lenny B.

29 March

Party for Susan Crile, chez Judy Collins, a stranger to me. Judy opens the door, bestows upon my features a serious, long look from out those violet eyes, breaks into a smile, embraces and kisses me. Impressive, since I was not raised to be demonstrative. (As a family we walked about the house stark naked, but we never *touched*.) Judy too's from the Midwest, so maybe vodka clears the path.

16 April

Brief spell in Nantucket, where Nils Van Vorst, a Rhodes Scholar in Greek, has begun our fence. Back for two more Roundtables. Tomorrow, New Haven for a concert with Phyllis.

20 April

Visit from Taylor Stoehr about Paul Goodman's biography. Then to Sylvia Marlowe's; she plays us the *Goldberg Variations*. JH bowled over by the unfussy grandeur of it all. Sylvia knows what she wants and how to get it, and what the hell if some of the notes fly out the window.

29 April

For the record: recording session this morning for Desto, of *King Midas*, my 1960 cycle on Howard Moss's poems. Sandra Walker and John Stewart, singers, with Ann Schein, pianist. Still sick with sore back.

30 April

END OF THE WAR IN VIETNAM.
   Visit for tea (and my *gâteau au Grand Marnier*) from soprano Joyce Mathis, who wants a cycle but has no money. The midnight phone calls continue from a mysterious woman whose motives may be honest or mad, but who is awfully boring. But spooky.

Philadelphia
11 May

Phyllis Curtin for lunch (egg salad, lime mousse) yesterday, after which we practiced at Donald Gramm's. Today the two of them did a whole concert of my songs in the Walnut Theater here, during which Phyllis's purse, which contained *everything*, was stolen backstage. Instead of being helpful, the management was vicious. Which made me wretched, since Phyllis and Donald were performing as a favor to me, not for the Walnut's measly fee.

27 May

Finished the piece for North Carolina. It's nearly as long as *Air Music*, about twenty-five minutes, but in just one movement. The orchestration, quite massive, is done too, but still no title. Often when composing a large non-vocal work I'm propelled less by a musical format than by a visual pattern or literary plot. (Perhaps sonatas have plots too, but plots without stories.) This propulsion comes from my having always associated music with words and images, and with my feeling most at home while writing songs or choruses or opera—pieces with the impurity of an extramusical requirement. I need an inspirational sight as a dressmaker needs a dummy. But sometimes when the work is finished, to cover my traces I throw away the dummy and offer the music as an "abstraction." (The reverse process is the choreographer imposing a story upon a symphony.)

As I composed, this image persisted in my conciousness: On an endless prairie four individuals—an oboe, a trumpet, a timpani, a viola—stretch their muscles and vocalize. An enormous crowd gathers. The individuals, abetted by their family members, offer themselves to the world. Separately and in combination they mingle with each other and with the crowd, which alternately embraces and ignores them. Finally they go their different ways, toward a career or love or the old homestead or a faraway death. But before they arrive they are swamped and destroyed. And the crowd inexorably fades from the vast field.

Yesterday Andrew Porter came for lunch. I gave him the preceding information, then asked him for a name. Long pause. "Why not call it *Assembly*?" But this morning he phoned and said, "No, call it *Assembly and Fall*."

29 May

Luck was with yesterday, for the weather conspired to become a peachy silk, etc., flowing through the windows into the first party I've given in five years. Of the thirty guests, of whom Stella Adler was first to arrive, not one was a duty. Most memorable vision: In the empty parlor Stella, seated as on a throne, regards the approach of Myrna Loy. Though one would assume they meet regularly, they've not seen each other since *After The Thin Man*. Now these poised beauties examine each other quizzically, then Stella says: "Well, you're still a looker!" She continues, "My bit in that *Thin Man* movie was my film debut. When I saw the first rushes, and *you* came on the screen, I thought you were me. I turned to Harold and murmured: star quality."

Parties, like pimples, infect, grow, burst, exude, fade, and sometimes leave a charming cicatrix. Standing in the eruption at its hottest, I thought: What am I doing here, when I should be home working?

Tonight Myrna came over again, for leftovers, then to the Balanchine-Ravel soirée. Fate allowed John Simon to sit beside us. Myrna later: "If I'd known it were Simon I wouldn't have shaken hands," echoing Jennie Tou-

rel's very words four years ago. At intermission when a stranger asked me to
sign a program, I was embarrassed. "Wouldn't you rather have Miss Loy's
signature?" I asked, but Myrna, forever "calm and wise," said, That's the result of television.

And the last television Roundtable tomorrow. So I put Myrna in a cab, and
am about to collate notes about this evening's performance. Sunday we leave
for the whole summer in Nantucket.

Sans date

Some art dates well, some badly, but all art dates, the worst and the best.
From the moment he writes *The End* an artist's work becomes the past, like
Bluebeard's wife. Even *within* a work of any scope, because time passed
while he created it, an artist may have inadvertently introduced anachronisms; the sole purpose of his technique is to solder these anachronisms
convincingly, to make them cohere in the flow of the work. The work dictates
its own terms, whatever its location in the artist's catalogue or in the history
of the century. Inspiration, of course, does not concern the artist. Even if it
does, there's nothing he can do about it. Nor will a conscious timeliness in
the long run make his work seem inspired. Certainly timeliness doesn't add
to worth. *Lysistrata* and *The Trojan Women* may strike us as ironically pertinent to the present, but *The Birds* and *Oedipus Rex*—as great or greater—
do not obtain to us at all. Paintings and movies from the 1930s are bad or
good, embarrassing or thrilling, junky or skillful, but all are old-fashioned
in both matter and style. Whatever period a work of art purports to depict,
the work itself is situatable only in its own period. Jules Verne's visions of
the twenty-first century are strictly from the nineteenth. Shakespeare's
Cleopatra is strictly Elizabethan, while De Mille's Cleopatra is less involved
with ancient Rome than with ancient Hollywood. Thus Bartók's *Bluebeard's
Castle* is not "about" medieval mores but about the dawn of Freudianism in
Hungary as observed through musical explorations of 1911.

So much of art is patience, merely patience, taking the time to do what
others would never have thought of doing—not because it's so unusual but
because it's so ordinary. Subject matter of itself need not be extraordinary.
For every murder in Edgar Allan Poe there's humdrum heartache in George
Eliot.

For the past twenty-six weeks Channel 13 has experimented with a Critics' Roundtable. Every fortnight Jack Richardson, Alexander Cockburn,
and I gathered for thirty minutes to discuss matters artistic with our host,
Harold Hayes. Richardson would do a solo about a recent play (sometimes a
book), Cockburn would usually review a movie, and I would criticize some

concert or passing opera. After these preambles we performed as a trio, since presumably we had attended each other's "events" and were of catholic disposition. My notes were scribbled just before the broadcasts, then discarded while I "improvised." In the normal course of things I seldom hear music publicly anymore, and never go to plays. But this season, while so uncommonly active, I learned, if nothing else, that not being up-to-date is unrelated to being old. I've just collected these notes into an essay called "A Cultured Winter."

Nantucket
2 June

Hideous hiatus in Hyannis. Plane grounded. Unable to continue because of fog, we spent the night at a Ramada Inn, fixing a cat box for Wallace out of a drawer filled with dirt that was tick-infested, we discovered belatedly. Got here. Hot June clovery morning, and we're already busy with plants, wallpaper, bank accounts and doctors' names. Eugenie has lent me her piano (actually her son Scott's piano) for an indefinite period.

2 July

After a month, no social life except with Hurricane Amy who made her presence felt last night with less panache than her advance publicity. The gardenia tree is ripped asunder, but the weather's seraphic now—the calm after the storm. Movies (sometimes with Rosette Lamont), lots of television, the beach at Cisco and, when I'm alone, at The Jetties. Reading voraciously, working lazily on the piano Études for Emanuel Ax. There'll be eight, or maybe nine, envisaged as always being played together in an assigned order. Each one presents a problem, but the problem's not to be listed in the program any more than Chopin's problems are listed. I've finished ones for sevenths, for contrary motion, for speed-without-pedal, for maximum quiet, for tune-with-filigree. Planning an hysterical and vulgar waltz, a two-part invention (but, as opposed to Bach, each voice being independent of the other; although, like Proust maybe, meeting in midstream, passing, and turning out to be the same persons in reverse), and a final ninth ordeal—perhaps a study in loudness.

Mother and Father arrive next week, our first guests.

10 July

I'm now doing what everyone only plans to do: reading Proust from start to finish simultaneously in French and English. I had read *Swann's Way* twice in the forties, but found it unhandy to complete during a decade in France. The reason: Marie Laure (whose grandmother Chevigné served as model for the Duchesse de Guermantes) always found him a *vieux raseur*, never read him, and didn't comprehend until his death what she'd missed—although as a toddler she had been dandled on Proust's knee and in the ensuing years had had ample access to the author. Result: she denied the very fact of Proust, banished his books, and told me to read more urgent writers for my French education. Like Queneau.

His work is alien to those mighty fanciful flights of other sociologists—a Petronius or a Henry James. His famous asides notwithstanding, the earmark is one-track-mindedness. He eschews poverty, alcoholism, menu specifics, physical cruelty, religion, and details of sexual acts (except the few unconvincing scenes in Jupien's hotel with their farcical coincidences, tough talk, stereotype perversions; an old-fashioned whip of nails is not a torture when the "victim" craves it). Proust describes what is. His milieu is no less familiar to Americans than Melville's to Frenchmen, and, as Paul Goodman never tired of saying (the obvious always digs deepest), "One thing leads to another," which Proust knew well, and Proust knew all.

Is it heresy to suggest that he was not homosexual? Insofar as he was sexual at all, Proust's vicariousness is slanted straight. Marcel's conclusions on homosexuality, even when drowsing in the predawn of our current awakening, are just too touristy. Charlus, that lovable contemporary of Wilde and precursor of Djuna Barnes's doctor, is a marvel when being a learned snob, but a joke when being a fractious fruit. Proust's notion, like that of puritan grade-school principals, is that sodomites are all in a continual state of cruising—that's their defining characteristic—and that even the most cultured of lesbians (like Bloch's sister) will, when left to their own devices, perform cunnilingus in hotel lobbies.

As for Moncrieff, someone sometime must surely write an essay on his famous job. Translation is the wrong word. It's hideously magnificent and has something to do with Proust. Yet, if it has little to do with French, it has a lot to do with English. Any fool can see that *Sodome et Gomorrhe* translates as *Sodom and Gomorrah*, not as *Cities of the Plain*. But if this bowdlerization could be explained by the pristine censors of yore, why retitle the unoffending *Albertine disparue* as *The Sweet Cheat Gone*? As for gay jargon, Moncrieff did use the word "camp" way back then, an exquisite find for what lacked in the original, though elsewhere he merely misleads us by transliterating Jupien's reference to Charlus's cock—*Vous en avez un gros pétard!*—as "Aren't you naughty!" and he quite miffs us by calling a *raseur* a "shaver," whatever that may be.

Will anyone deny that Moncrieff's is a commendable Life's Work in its own right?

Blossom errs. His ear is tin, his balance rickety. One example will do. For the last word Proust reserved the crucial *temps*. To intensify its impact he understandably avoided that word for several previous paragraphs. Blossom sees fit (lest we miss the point?) to inject Time (capitalized) thrice within the final sentence, so that *his* last word falls flat.

Why is Nantucket unsexy? For the same reason, in a sense, that Proust isn't sexy. People here are too well off. All consideration for tastes of coloring and nationality aside, sexiness comes from the financially underprivileged. The rich don't *need* to be sexy. Any Greek waiter or *ragazzo di vita* exudes more carnality than the handsomest duke in town. And if the northern peoples are less sexy than the Mediterranean it's because they are by nature more privileged; that is, by dint of the preserving cold they are less prey to decay: Northerners are inherently permanent, while sexiness is transient. I'm speaking, of course, strictly for the male sex. A beautiful woman, no matter how wealthy, is still underprivileged and by that token sexual.

There are those who thrill at the idea of a Visconti movie, *In Search of Lost Time*, and the prospect of Brando as Charlus. Neither the Absolute General nor the Absolute Particular has ever been filmed convincingly. Kafka's *Trial* is an instance of Absolute General, K. being Everyman—that is, ourself— and thus a Tony Perkins can only outrage our personal fantasy. *In Search of Lost Time* is an instance of Absolute Particular, Marcel being Oneman— that is, Narrator Proust—and thus Visconti's vision can only jar *our* vision of Proust's vision. A ballet perhaps? But Proust is nothing if not French, while Brando, whatever his breadth, is nothing if not American, and oh, the common gratuitous assumption (by an Italian) that American names might depict the exquisite wit of milieux now nearly unremembered even by rich elderly Parisians.

Place de la Madeleine. Given what finally emerged, could one claim that the potential was contained in the madeleine when first tasted? Can a man be potentially an artist (or a dreamer of the past) if he never realizes himself as an artist (or a dreamer)? If the future is contained, literally contained, in the present, supposing a man dies before the future (the eating of the second madeleine) arrives? What becomes of this nipped-in-the-bud future? The world existed in that madeleine not in fact but because Marcel said it did. (Interesting that in an earlier draft his madeleine was toast.)

Unrequited love, mystery of the common cold, hate for a person who's forgotten us, the women's vote, a crossword puzzle. Solutions often come from unexpected sources. Dazzled by the pearly gates, we miss the trapdoor.

14 July

Mother and Father left yesterday by ferry for New York via Hyannis, where they'll visit the Hawthornes. JH was away during much of their visit. I offered them, on different days, Eugenie, Rosette and her mother, Ludmilla, and John Wulp. Mostly we ate plaice fish, and I worked, indoors and out, while they read and strolled. Not sure if they entirely approve of the house.

20 July

Gustavo's here for a while.

Reading James Salter's *Light Years*. The first blurb I ever wrote was for *A Sport and a Pastime*—ending with, "Can be read with the heart, with the mind, and with one hand." It wasn't used. Now, with his second novel, Salter again gives American letters a new tone, a new *gender*: he allows what used to be called "homosexual sensibility" to color his utterly heterosexual material, and since his own morality is (presumably) above reproach, the result rings true. (A James Jones, a Mailer, wouldn't risk so much on women's ornaments at the expense of women without ornaments; much less would they speak of "tea colored soap.") That Salter is surely unaware of this only strengthens my point. A dumb point. The book's depressing but purging. He does in cameo for the Hudson River Valley what Proust does in epic for Normandy: uses the lush cultured decor as a frame, a cause, containing intelligent people who, having everything, invent new traps, snare themselves, and expire without ever discussing those larger world conflicts which nonetheless produced their frustration. Nantucket's a bit like that. The tone's well-off, right wing, educated, un-black, and sexually pretty straight.

11 August

Morris here for a few days, very self-sufficient. I had a bad bike spill because my foot, in old slippers, got caught in the spokes. Shostakovich died today. Neighbors' children endlessly noisy.

25 August

Our blackberry bushes are dense with rich fruit. We made a pie as dessert for our first dinner party here last night, which, decorated with heavy rain and thunderclaps, consisted of, besides me and JH, Eugenie, her friend Robert Hill, and David Halberstam. David is manly as hell, bright and rather likeable if a bit furtive and not especially poetic. Like all journalists he expresses reaction rather than opinion, although he's good at description—and when description's really good, opinion often shines through unbidden. Yet asked if daily confrontation with battle in Vietnam provoked any philosophic change in him, any sense of justice through war or of meaning in death, he seemed never to have thought about it. But then, his vocabulary isn't mine.

4 September

Eye trouble. So I called a certain Doctor Runge—only to be told he died last week. Went instead to Eugenie's former husband, the reassuring Dr. David Voorhees, who tapped my eyeball with a tension hammer.

Shirley here for several days. For her delectation, a buffet at Rosette's with Judge Knapp, and a cocktail at the Harbachs'. Then last night to dine here came Frank Conroy and Maggie Lee, Nils and Joyce Van Voorst, and one Sven Lucan. Shirley made a meat loaf with a cylindrical core of Philadelphia cream cheese. Successful. Joyce went upstairs to sleep during most of the meal, after which they all took Shirley to the Chicken Box.

Continual sieges of hay fever. Nasal hemorrhage.

16 September

Headache, *crise d'angoisse*. Crickets everywhere. JH in NYC. Sneezing ceaseless. Yesterday in this condition received four ladies for tea (made a chocolate cake, which slumped but tasted true, and an orange bavarian): Ellie Bissinger, Myrna Loy, Sascha Cavander and Gerrie Feder. Impressed with each other, as I with them, and, being anxious, they waited on me. Tonight, same group (minus Gerrie but plus Ellie's opinionated daughter Annie and a casting director named Isabel Holliburton) dined chez Ellie on Fair Street, then watched *The April Fools*, a not-too-good movie of Myrna's from five years ago, though she looks comely in chiffon the same color as my bavarian yesterday. Came home early for antihistamine. Copying near-finished Études. Working on essay about critics.

I have always been a lone wolf, never an acolyte or part of a clique, or a champion of this or that mood, nor (except for the vocal series with Bill Flanagan in 1959–61) have I ever pushed music beyond my own. My protectors are not built-in but random, my defenders mainly from the performing world.

No one has ever written a sensible study of my work (my *musical* work; there's *nothing* on my verbal work), and scarcely a dozen superficial studies exist. What's there to write? And of the hundreds of reviews and interviews, each is as ephemeral as the next.

People say I waste precious energy on bitterness; that I should get my work done and let critics get theirs. Indeed, I have not one friend who hasn't sometime been embarrassed by my obsessions. But I have a lot of energy, and criticism is part of my work. If I don't muckrake, who will?

Tomorrow, dine at John Wulp's, again with the ubiquitous Bissingers and Myrna (remember to tell her about *Topaze* at the Tower Theater when I was nine; or isn't this flattering for a movie star?). My last evening here. Friday, since JH is still away, I'll close the house, deposit Wallace at the animal hospital, and leave. Mourning doves each morning.

Thinking about Halberstam. He takes up a lot of room, as the French say. Like Philip Roth, concerned about his manhood, he's not so much threatened by pederasty as by boyhood. Both American and Jewish—the threat. Has no real credo about war, nor about his hobby, fishing.

Doris Lessing's *Memoirs of a Survivor* is very Kafka (even to the cat-dog Hugo, which K. used in *A Sport*), but icier, clumsier, less economical. Is she a good writer? She has a good mind, but littered. Takes too long to state her facts. (Proust never took too long.)

New York
18 September

Flew back to New York this morning, with a copy of *Les Mots*, on one of those always doubtful nine-passenger timpani that Air New England supplies. At Martha's Vineyard who should take the seat beside me but Lillian Hellman, who, seeing Sartre in my lap, asked "How does he hold up?" I told her we'd met before, ten years ago at Virgil's. We did the rundown of mutual friends. She was easy to talk to, but are we close enough yet for her to say about Marc Blitzstein's death, "Well, that's bound to happen, sooner or later, if you like rough trade"? She had her chauffeur drop me off, and we shall meet again. (She and I, I mean, not the chauffeur.)

Dined tonight with Mother and Father. Mother illish and sad. Went to baths. Smog everywhere. *Cafard*. Tomorrow and Saturday Ormandy does *Eagles* in Philly, while I go to New Haven to rehearse with Phyllis for our all-American fund-raising recital at Yaddo next week.

19 September

I am composing a cycle of songs for soprano Joyce Mathis, of whom a not inconspicuous feature, at least to me since I am white, is that she's black. I have chosen to musicalize poems only by women (I mention this now, and never again, since the main point of the poems is that they're good), but none of these women is black. For my music there are no good black female poets. More important, I can't identify from inside with blackness as I can with femaleness: none of my ancestors were Negro slaves, though half of them were women. Artists contain all sexes, but not all races.

Still, maybe Robin Morgan's harsh words years ago were true: "Leave Plath to our sisters, stick to men poets." If I feel no more need for Plath it's precisely because she *was* a woman, and I am not, not even metaphorically. (If I reject Sandra Hochman's plea for songs it's because her verse extols her own menstrual flow, not mine, and I can no more compose from within a bleeding female than from within a black one.) Not that a composer need *feel*, or even respect, a poem in order to set it well. And masterpieces that thrill are more impossible to musicalize than lesser verses that ring a bell. The question of which composers select which poets to set to music, and of how they set them when selected, is endlessly engrossing. A woman's setting of Plath might not be better than mine but will be different, not only because she's another person but because she's female. How to prove that difference? Is there more difference between a man and a woman than between one good composer and another good composer?

It's hard to deal with a woman's poem insofar as that poem dwells on solely womanly problems. Yet I'm writing a cycle on women's poems. From Phaedra to Blanche, great-women roles have been written by men. But in plays, in opera, these roles have been part of a larger pattern—a pattern, however eccentric, we all grow up in. Could a man write a solo lyric poem, *as a woman*, and make it convincing?

On fixed scales we are prone to measure the realities of others by our own needs and experience, conveniently evading disparities of age, strength, class, even era and intelligence. Did the smart lord of Gaul suffer more than the dumb peasant of Maine? Or, given absolute conditions, did the godly old Jew with his prayers suffer less than the young atheistic Gypsy who had no "belief" to cling to in the gas chamber? Widowed, knifed, betrayed, insulted, who suffers more, the wise Woman of Andros or the *Précieuse Ridicule*? And who can resist, or (dare one ask?) *learn*, from pain, while the pain is in action, and after the pain is gone?

If Solzhenitsyn's assertion is correct—that the liberty earned by our forebears is taken for granted by Americans, who compromise rather than sacrifice to retain that liberty—then he is implying the need for an alternative before unworked-for freedom turns to chaos. That alternative is always violence, and violence is always war in some form. Now Quakers alone, of all intellectuals today, claim there is no alternative to peace. So they preach. In theory they practice. Freedom from what? From persecution or from air conditioning? Sacrifice what? Our children or our glibness? What comes of it all? Does the Belsen survivor, once reestablished in Israel, become more magnanimous, more "aware," than a solvent Kansas farmer? In saying that war accomplishes nothing I, in a sense, speak by rote, for I was raised a Quaker yet never suffered what George Fox suffered. Yet neither have I known the anguish of the Belsen survivor nor, for that matter, of Joyce Mathis, Ethel Kennedy, or the checkout girl, or Jean Paul Getty, or my own sister Rosemary. But I am not a fool, my rote is not cant—is smarter than most—and I've survived till today.

The kindness of strangers? It is their hostility or indifference that scares, in supermarkets, buses, neighboring apartments. Daily I reach home in tears. Accomplishment is not a public calling card, fame is no armor, beauty is vulnerable, but dumb beauty's durable. To be intelligent yet to want to survive is the strongest accomplishment.

Saratoga
24 September

Hay fever so devastating that, after the Yaddo staff had spent the morning decorating the hall with a thousand white roses, I was forced to have them removed by afternoon or there would have been no concert in the evening. But things went prettily, not least because the quarter-mile road from the highway to the mansion was bordered with tapers, and because John Cheever's here too and behaves touchingly with Phyllis. Phyllis, whom I'd always thought to be the model of Spartan self-denial and strong as Minerva, said last night, as she stretched out on the white divan in her tower suite, that for five years her bursitis has forced her to sleep upright and that she takes sixteen aspirins a day.

Nantucket
27 September

Last evening, when humanly alone in the house and washing dishes, I heard a crash. The front porch door was shattered. My two simultaneous reactions: something had been thrown in; Wallace had jumped out. I do feel despised by locals who find me cranky about the carillon and are capable of harassment, yet no rock or BB shot was on the inside porch floor. I do know that Wallace had been excited by the sight of a rabbit on the lawn at dusk, but no bloody fur was on the outside grass. A neighbor who heard the noise appeared a minute later, but said she'd seen nobody running off. On the other hand, a cat just doesn't dive with impunity through plate glass, especially a sedentary nine-year-old urban beauty like Wallace who's never been outside without a leash. Yet that's what he had done.

For three hours I patrolled the area with a flashlight. Nothing. JH phoned back from New York, distraught. (Though perhaps no more lovingly attached to the animal than I, he surely is more anthropomorphically so, and for him it was as though an offspring had been kidnapped.) Sleepless night, cups of snot pour from itchy eyes, delayed reactions setting in, visions of Wallace stunned and scraped, devoured by foxes, demented by famine, incapable of coping.

In the thick mist of dawn he materialized on the front lawn, no worse for wear, and I phoned JH who was so relieved he wept. Wallace has consumed two packs of Tender Vittles, and now, at noon, slumbers atop the piano, his nocturne vanished but not my hay fever.

4 October

Last of the blackberries. Weather too good to be true, but allergy persists and no medication avails.

Raleigh, North Carolina
13 October

Premiere last night of *Assembly and Fall*, surely my most sprawlingly undefinable opus, played excellently by the orchestra of which the string section on high notes is more in tune than in certain major-league orchestras, probably because the median age here is twenty-eight. Coincidentally, Phyllis is on the same program, doing the *Four Last Songs* with perfect intonation and pungent sorrow, and the last scene from *Salome*, which is not persuasive. Whatever else, Phyllis is a lady, Salome is not. Which is what also undermines not only her but every diva's assays at, say, Cole Porter. Porter may be upper class, but he's also dirty. Not even Eileen Farrell can counterfeit that highclass dirt.

Spent afternoon with the still exquisitely voiced Penelope Jensen. JH arrived at five (to attend tomorrow's performance in Greensboro), and we went to Chapel Hill, his alma mater, to dine at Jacques Hardré's where Tom had gone to some trouble with a barbecue. Also present, Martha and Wilton Mason (who gave me a turquoise) and Wallace Fowlie. During the meal I had a devastating and embarrassing siege of hay fever and had to be excused. JH told Mrs. Mason that Jennie Tourel's sole memory of Chapel Hill centered around Mrs. Mason's cheese dip, so the Masons have invited us tomorrow to savor it.

New York
19 October

Parents last night. *Le cafard de Maman.* At least once a day, or night, the burglar alarm of some nearby parked car is activated and the piercing screech that ensues lasts from a minute to an hour. You'd think the manufacturers . . .

Continually heavy rains.

At four, visit from a youngish reporter planning a bio of Truman Capote. Disconcerting, the number of years and anecdotes surrounding my tangential acquaintance with that unsatisfactory author, from our first cool meeting with Jane and Paul Bowles in Tangier in 1949, through hectic Paris evenings that fall, then in New York, then in France again with Jack Dunphy, and the ballet *Early Voyagers* with Valerie Bettis, to the last ugly contact in 1968. Today Truman's name is uttered in hushed tones by the likes of Cher and Johnny Carson: he's the poor man's thinker, *le savant des pauvres* who are mostly quite rich. Not that the real intelligentsia is contemptuous, they just have nothing left to say. Truman sold his talent for a mess of pottage. (When later I tell JH how disconcerting it was to dredge up the past, he snorts, "The past? You have no past—you sold it for a mess of pottage.")

(Question of ethics: Should a living subject of biography be paid? Should people being interviewed be paid? The biographer, after all, gets a fat advance and the publisher stands to make a mint off the exploited subject. But we who were there did all the work.)

At six, Maxine Groffsky arrives. She and Gerald Clarke (the interviewer who otherwise works for *Time*) know each other already, and they talk about Maxine's now being an agent. Maxine is also the classiest-looking creature at Heddy Baum's buffet where we then deliver ourselves, but I'll say no more since she'll accuse me, as she did once before, of being sexist.

22 October

Depressingly lovely weather. Exhausted from valium because of JH's jealous outburst. Paul Jacobs called to talk about the death in Paris of Bernard Saby (who must have expired from drugs and drink, not to mention from the weight of Boulez, and from years of barking up the wrong tree. But I don't say so to Paul). A birthday card from David Diamond—telling about his heart attack. And Mother on the phone, still low.

23 October

So I am fifty-two, the age at which Shakespeare, on his birthday, died. Birthday of Sarah Bernhardt, Johnny Carson, Franz Liszt, Miriam Gideon, Maurice Grosser.

Marre de la mort, marre des arbres qui ne rendent pas leur secret, marre de la mauvaise critique pour ce que je'exerce—quoique borné—mieux que quiconque. Sick of death, sick of trees that don't tell their secret, sick of bad reviews for what I practice—however restricted—better than anyone.

To emerge from the sadness of late youth into the smugness of early middle age was to declare that, barring bad health, unhappiness was unseemly after forty. Today it remains unseemly (and ever so boring to outsiders), while becoming the sole logical stance. But keep it quiet, if you can, and stick to your faithful Quaker guns.

Pale hand aquiver on the receiver (for it's anxious-making to phone even close friends, let alone comparative strangers, especially ones we admire) I waited for five rings after which, when he did answer, it was clear I'd wakened him, though it was noon. "Shall I call back later—at two, say?" "Well, I've a tentative lunch appointment; make it after"—but no hint that *he* call *me*, though his tone was friendly enough, and he had suggested we meet when I returned to town. (The only time we did meet, eight years ago, he'd not made it easy either, with that deceptive warm way teachers have of obliging students to make the first pass.) Well, now it's six o'clock; I won't call back. How can I? Let history determine what's been missed.

Maybe there's not always need to meet those we respect. A man's conversation can't always equal, in clarity and condensation, what he's written. But Martin Duberman did earn my admiration, if only because of his public penitence for the awful review he gave, years ago, to Paul Goodman's masterpiece, *Five Years*.

Sometimes I wonder if M's disease has caught up to me, when the smell of a cooked carrot or sight of a mere vase brings on tears.

John Simon phoned this evening to say he was enjoying WNCN's Birthday Salute to me. In the background, behind the phone's static and John's Transylvanian syllables, I did detect the ripple of my *Barcarolles*. Should one tell a composer *during* his music that one likes the music? John does believe in hissing plays, but only *after* a performance.

24 October

Because his gift is richer than that of Solzhenitsyn, Sartre, or Steinbeck, Nabokov is of course continually denied the Nobel prize. Prizes are for What and not How, for general goodwill rather than for that homemade turn of phrase that defines a *maître*. The "humanity" of the above three S's isn't what Nabokov aims at through private keening or public drumming. Perhaps, though, it's an eschewed vulnerability that keeps his work, like Gore Vidal's, from sweep, from grandeur, from a kind of necessary high vulgarity, and finally from greatness.

He constructs musically (like Gide, Proust, Mann, Tolstoy and Forster though not Joyce, Kafka, Dostoevsky or the three S's) but never speaks about music (like Joyce, etcetera).

The ecstasy with which he writes of moths is never attained by his inter-human remembrances. Indeed, a case could be made for him as parodist, or at least as pasticheur. *Speak Memory* could be deemed too close for comfort to *In Search of Lost Time* (mother's ritual bedtime kiss, salty French maid) unless taken as satire, just as *Pnin* mocks academia and *Lolita* takes off our homeland, an outsider's *America Hurrah!* with Balthus as protagonist. If the case sounds demented as *Pale Fire*, it seems safe to say that, like Vidal and Voltaire, Nabokov does stand outside his material, and that such a stance, while divine, can't break the heart.

Those notes were scrawled after a call from the *Times* asking if I'd review the new volume of Nabokov's memoirs. Miffed but honored, I agreed, only to open the package that just arrived and find not Vladimir but Nicolas Nabokov's book. Well, of course that makes more sense.

26 October

Andrew, to whom I'd sent the Carolina program, which relates the anecdote of his naming *Assembly and Fall*, is forced to point out that he'd *not* named it that—he'd named it *Assembly and Four*, and I'd misheard, he like all the English having dropped the final *r*.

Beautiful recital this afternoon by JH at St. Matthew's & St. Timothy's of organ music by Bach and Thomson. (JH, a true performer in all but one crucial sense: he takes no pleasure in showing off.) At the first jarring notes of

Bach's G-minor Fantasia, Virgil, wrenched from his nap, yelled "What's that!" Later, *souper* at the Gruens' with Shirley, Sylvia and Leonid, Maurice Grosser and Virgil, and JH, uneasy at being the center of attention.

27 October

Virgil keeps a vanilla bean in a large jar of sugar. The sugar is used for cooking puddings, or for sprinkling over wild strawberries with *crème fraîche*.

JH says my fatal flaw lies in using my work to promote myself rather than using myself to promote my work. A case in point: the premature publishing of diaries. Etc.

Party of Joe Machlis's for Alger Hiss. I take Maxine, but Father is there too and fraternizes warmly with the guest of honor. Joe is to be commended for spending money intelligently. After forty years of eating other people's breast of guinea hen, he's used the royalties from *The Enjoyment of Music* on a non-residential apartment where twice a week he throws recital-buffets of mostly high quality, and where worthwhile guests convene and make out as they've not been able to since Leo Lerman closed shop on Lexington Avenue.

28 October

Awakened as usual by the predawn gurgle of pigeons on the sill, satisfying tones that swell, melt, dissolve, fade like an aerial shot of Niagara. A loud sloppy flutter, silence again, flush of a far toilet, then a din of traffic starts to grow. Do birds dream? Gulf of insomnia, so all-important during the endless uninteresting minutes, yet so insignificant in retrospect. With luck I'll drift off, but at 8:50 sharp Wallace pads into the room with a no-nonsense *meow!* which officially starts the day.

The life I lived was the life I lived; how could I have known it was history? History—who says? Could not the gardener—if not in name at least in shame or glory—have been fixed there too? If he *is* fixed there in my reverie, does he vanish with my death, though I remain fixed (fixed?) in notes and nouns?

Well, the Joan Little ordeal is resolved, with the defense lawyer stating that only money can assure a fair trial. The judge counters: "Many a poor person is granted a fair trial," but he skirts the real question: How many rich people go to prison?

Nantucket
Halloween

Have I an *oeuvre*? If I die tonight what single piece do I leave? No *Maldoror*
surely, no *Four Saints*, nor even *Little Foxes*—none of those works, like
Shostakovich's First Symphony, penned young and shining. It's not for me
to say that my output, like Chopin's or Janet Flanner's, is an assemblage, letters and preludes, nourishing one-page meals.

Second day of storms, alone in Nantucket with thumping radiators and
the slumping basement, humanoid moans from a crack in the wall all night,
and if that stricture in my chest flings me floorward how long do I lie?

Was that heart ever wrapped in *Serenade*, which this morning I finished
and mailed to Ohio? Must heart always distinguish output? Distinguished
output should *appear* to have heart. Our best work is not always what we feel
deepest but what we work hardest on. This is most true for long-term results
like operas or "functioning" marriages. (The joke is when something we
work on hard also flops.) Pieces dashed off, but dashed off with heart, that
succeed are generally short, like songs.

5 November

Ten years ago the fatal premiere of *Miss Julie*. Could I do better tonight?
Differently, surely, and time flies fast. Works of art, said Proust, are less disappointing than life, for they do not begin by giving us the best of themselves. Yet are not various great works for me now exhausted (some by Stravinsky, for example, which once drained us repeatedly while retaining their
own vitality, or movements of Mozart, or Rembrandt or of Proust himself),
while "life"—indeed the very "affair" with JH—is in continual flowering
with the "best" yet to come, or how go on? Nets were finally flung and for
some months there's been proximity of death. I am death's host, for he in-
habits me, and his guest, since he's provisionally placed me in a transparent
placenta sack which, rather sooner than later, he'll rip open to the world's
air, like a gas chamber's. Meanwhile he parades me about, a corpse on parole, chuckling as I balk at meager deadlines, write tunes but am easily dis-
tracted by television's lure. Death's female to the French. West Chester
Street. Is this a street or some ancient thoroughfare through cemeteries that
now, with daylight saving rescinded, turn blue by four P.M.? Alone on this
island where I know no one, own a house, plain but costly, for the first time
ever like grown-ups, and each evening after supper of lentils and Jello, take
a constitutional through the seasonal mist down Lily Street encountering
not a soul, and return to the dubious welcome thirty minutes later of Wallace the cat. Like ghosts of Hammerfest or Thule, Nantucket is far from any-

where, from America, from even a memory of childhood, though not from plagues that could accompany us to Mars, not from masculine death who glides at any speed. Why Nantucket? Why, when I've never owned a thing, buy a house in this Huguenot anti-art cranberry bog rather than in beloved Provence?

Allergic not just to seed and perfume, but to the smell of dollar bills and newsprint, Kleenex, water and thoughts of horses wild. JH tries to cope with my inability myself to cope. I fall apart, suffocate, scream. It's easy to write this now—but just one hour ago I saw *him*, N R, in flames, and JH at sea.

Yet there are moments every few days in Nantucket—during a flash of light across the page, during an afternoon pause in the Quaker cemetery—moments filled with happiness so clean you'd think they sprang from paradise. But in retrospect, sometimes as soon as one hour after, these moments seem unbearably sad. Is it because such moments, experienced only when alone, are remorse from the comparative passivity of contentment, even the contentment of the intellect at work, in arguments with JH or of trying a new recipe? No, the shock of happiness is so positive it resembles an invasion, burning energy with such speed that the recipient is left flat or, sometimes, dead.

Anyone can close the eyes of the dead, but who can open the eyes of the living?

How much time is left? Will the end hurt?

With Herbert Machiz dying, the hill grows higher. In *War Scenes*: "The whole world, North and South, seemed one vast hospital." Herbert, the only artist with whom collaboration wasn't friction. I recall pleasurably the four or five plays we musicalized together. But what purpose is served by the death of friends, the ever-grander bunch of bones? The same purpose as their living? Are skulls ground into a fertile dust?

6 November

With irony can I claim to merit a continual halo of ruby dust about the shoulders. But what have I? Roaches in the bathtub and a zero in my checkbook, not to mention the (protective) wall of ignorance by outsiders.

Murder in Rome of Pasolini. A plump pair of golden pheasants big as turkeys appeared from nowhere to grace for half an hour the wilting bamboo
patch. They satisfy, as Kenneth Burke used to say, every need in me but the
need of someone else.

10 November

Here alone with Wallace. Working on *Women's Voices* all day, and every evening a stream of TV movies. Summer weather continues. Today at ten A.M.,
seventy-eight degrees and windless. The mouth and the nose, so near, yet
one spells death and the other's harmless. For my ever-clogged sinuses I've
been sniffing Cointreau and sherry and scotch. The fragrances bring back
the old days, but I'm not tempted to taste.

Nearly eight years since I took my—knock wood—last drink. Partly this
is due to JH, but mostly to the common sense of A.A. I was attracted to JH
first because of what was healthy about his attitude, although no one is a life-
saver except oneself. As for A.A, as with Quaker Meeting, I never go anymore, but the tenets are there to be used at all times, alone in the desert.

Alcoholism, like homosexuality, is something outsiders never quite grasp.
But whereas alcoholism is by all standards bad, homosexuality is not. Homosexuality is only a problem to those who make it one. Yet even during the
sixties, when youth practiced tolerance in the antiwar movement, gayety
was never a real part of the scene. Radical liberals have always been more
queasy about sexual "deviation" than have capitalists, while tolerating, even
encouraging, drugs and drink.

Simplicity's difficult. To arrest alcoholism is simple: stop drinking—it's
the only solution. But to effect the solution is hard.

No day passes that I don't thank the stars for a clear head. Yet even at the
most Bohemian teenaged period of my life I detested messy rooms: nowadays, even when for weeks at a time I'm alone in Nantucket, I dutifully make
the bed each morning.

I was, so to speak, drunk and orderly. Order came from chaos. Drink and
recover in order to drink and recover in order to . . .

Title: *Drunk and Orderly.*

18 November

Finished Nabokov review. Made peanut butter. Yesterday, Father's eighty-
first birthday. Today, at 5:05, total eclipse of the moon. Death of Franco.

Cincinnati
5 December

In Cincinnati for the new piece. If sound were taste, Tommy Schippers's version of *Air Music* would resemble the best sour cream mashed with hand-picked gooseberries: smooth without slickness, tart without bitterness, a healthful dessert. An unexpected surprise is that the music does sound like air—like a mean wind through flaming leaves of yew. A barrel of ice cubes flung into an enamel aviary. And so forth.

As curtain raiser—from backstage!—was Virgil's charming fanfare, performed without fanfare, like a far fragrance of lavender.

Why *Air Music*? Because sound goes in one ear and out the other like air through organ pipes or through the laryngeal tunnels of fabulous vocalists, and thus is heard all sound. Wilhelm Heinse: "Music touches the nerves in a particular manner and results in a singular playfulness, a quick special communication that cannot be described in words. Music represents the inner feeling in the exterior air."

More is less. Konrad Wolff once said that in the old days those all-modern-music concerts were so long that he used to add something by Webern to make them seem shorter.

The premiere was at 11:00 this morning. Another performance tomorrow night. Summer weather. Tommy, who knows the piece far better than I, looks drawn and frail. He lives in the house where the staircase scene of *Gone With the Wind* was filmed.

New York
7 December

Last night's performance as good as the first. Flew back this morning with John Ward and a bad cold. Tea at Charles-Henri Ford's; cocktail party at Red and Pick Heller's. Death of Thornton Wilder. Thirty-fourth anniversary of Pearl Harbor.

10 December

Alvin Ross died today. Brooding on what I didn't do. When Alvin called a month ago, after his colostomy, and said he was hurting, I tried to find the right words. But I should have gone to see him. Now all I have are his four marvelous pictures, plus other indelible ones in the mind that trace back to

1943 in Philadelphia: his perverse but harmless humor, his too-gentle stance in a mean city. Dined at the Markhams' (with Lukas and Cornelia, also Claude Samuel *et son amie*), but kept dwelling on Alvin in pain.

12 December

New York premiere last night of *Air Music*. Took Maxine and Eugenie, then dined at the Russian Tea Room joined by Eugene and Martita before going to party chez Tommy, very chic, where no one seemed to know I'd written a piece that they'd all just heard, though maybe they hadn't been there.

No end of horrors. Today Peter Kemeny committed suicide by throwing himself before an oncoming subway train. Deaths this week too of Hannah Arendt, Lee Wiley, James Waring.

16 December

Plays and music are to be booed at or clapped for. Can you applaud a painting?

No one imagines himself to be without humor. To claim that you lack humor is already a humorous notion—humor being an ability to see three sides of one coin, a coin shaped like a tear.

But in music nothing is more elusive than humor. Judging from last night's "opera," *The W. of Babylon*, Wuorinen too is on the wrong path, a path all the more uncomfortable in being paved with coy intentions. (Stanley Silverman aims lower but hits the same target dead center.) Even were his Firbankian libretto livelier, Wuorinen's craggy language would be at odds with it. Just as twelve-tone music, vast in tragic potential, can never be funny, neither can consistently ugly music depict whimsy. (Mozart is ugly only part of the time.) I used to feel I missed the might of Wuorinen's art—it was my lack. But there *is* no might; it's bluff. Or is it still my lack? Like Kosinski he's skilled in the wiles of PR men. His clique, each dead-serious, hairy member of which resembles him to a T, breaks up on cue like a TV laugh track. Of course it's unfair (voluptuously unfair) to judge a man by a single flop, especially if he's had successes. Yet one errant brick can destabilize a monument, and I have loathed upstanding citizens for the sounds they make when swallowing water. Just as John Simon poisons a well-reasoned essay by a gibe at an actress, so, I imagine, do my diaries—or some mere paragraphs therein (perhaps this very sentence)—disqualify a life's work in music.

Can the One Rotten Apple theory apply to the test of esthetics? Can one unfocused moment in the otherwise unblurred intuition of a respected person contaminate the respect, especially if the focus is professionally aimed?

Can Simon's championing of Lina Wertmüller put into doubt his whole work? Can Andrew Porter's nearsighted view of Crumb today raise questions about his farsightedness yesterday? Sadly, one false step can, for a critic, demean his whole *oeuvre*, even as Hugues Cuénod's vocal artistry is diminished by his continually singing with inept accompanists. And what about creative artists? Ravel, the canniest jeweler of our century, never allowed his duds to greet the public; but the posthumous printing of his early forays now casts a gray light—at least for me—upon the perfection of his later masterpieces. Perhaps it's unfair to disillusion the public with professional secrets (those last-minute formal hints by "noncreative" advisers which made whole pieces jell), although most of us, artists and otherwise, are judged by flops and not by triumphs.

I judge all art the same way first: by whether I believe it. If I believe it I'll nudge further to see if I believe *in* it. Honesty of tone preempts honesty of content.

Wertmüller: Not for a second do I believe she believes what she purports to say so much as she believes in the veneer of Love Me, Italian style. Now, because I feel she doesn't believe herself, I don't believe her either, so obviously I don't believe *in* her.

John Simon, in his (justifiable) treatise on the esthetics of the actor's appearance, states: "A homely actress is always driven to *act* beautiful, and this is precisely what no beautiful woman ever does." (By beautiful woman one assumes he means beautiful actress. Nor does he anywhere pose the problem of a beautiful actress portraying a homely woman.) Yes, but a beautiful actress must *act* beautiful too, in a manner different from, even opposed to, her own "kind" of beauty. (Could Margaret Leighton have portrayed Marilyn Monroe?) Beauty's not endowed with built-in confidence, strange as this seems to the plain. Only stupidity provides confidence. Smart beauties are socially uneasy. Despite Simon's feelings to the contrary (and he admits bias toward women; nowhere is there question of men), it's irrefutable that "plain" women can give convincing illusions of beauty, certainly in opera. What Simon bemoans is probably not lack of beauty but lack of class.

"Is nothing sacred?" asks a letter to the *Times* chastising John Simon for chastising Ruth Gordon. No, nothing is sacred. What takes Ruth Gordon beyond criticism, at sixteen bucks a ticket?

26 December

Learning with glee that Cyril Connolly, weary of Wystan Auden's harping that *toilets* was an anagram for T. S. Eliot, had relettered Auden's own name as *A nasty unwed*, I lay awake confecting arrangements for Richard Howard and Maxine Groffsky. The best I could do was *Ira, draw chord H* and *Fame in frog Sky* (with a leftover x to be used in *Foxy skin farm*, which leaves over g and e, to be used in *Sex in frog famky*, which makes no sense, nor does *germ frig*, nor *No sexy fig mark*, which also has a leftover f). Anyway, these two, with Robert Phelps (*spelt bore rph* or *he probes robes*) and Morris Golde (*older so grim*), came Christmas day for tea and were offered the orange walnut icebox torte.

Asked how many letters he writes a day, Richard sighs, "It's not what our friends keep us from doing but what they require us to do." The inverse applies better: It's not what friends ask of us but what they keep us from—though actually the two are one. A letter, after all, is nothing much (and it *can* be literature) compared to the demands of lovers, or the duty of keeping abreast of other people's concerts, politics, books, exhibitions, parties, matings, and funerals.

27 December

The song cycle, *Women's Voices*, is two-thirds complete. A militant dyke asks, "What do you know about women's voices?" I'm forced to counter with: "What do you know about what I don't know about women's voices?"

Mediocre earth, if I don't judge others by myself, then by whom?

Von Däniken's premise is appealing: that Martian giants millenniums ago brought their know-how to earth, bred with "our women," thereby producing "a new race," then vanished. The only flaw is that species cannot interbreed, despite their know-how. (Some species can mix—canaries with sparrows, donkeys with horses—and produce offspring, but the offspring are mules, sterile. Other species can intermate—gorillas and humans—but produce no offspring.) Even if species could interbreed, one trembles to think of "our women" impregnated by giants. But why assume those "gods" had sex, or even two sexes? If they did have two sexes, why assume their males came? Perhaps 'twas goddesses, fertilized by manly earthlings, who, without more pain than a sneeze, gave birth to the missing link.

30 December

Success doesn't make one less cranky, it lends authority to crankiness. As people age and turn more successful, or less successful, they tend to get more central. Tastes don't alter much, but viewpoint softens. Conservatives notoriously grow more liberal, radicals more conventional. In politics this is most visible, but in the arts too. Exceptions like Duchamp or Bertrand Russell only emphasize rules like Gertrude Stein, Stravinsky, Elliott Carter, Schoenberg, who all, it could be argued, evolved in the reverse.

Prizes and praise replace sex. Or rather, they are sex. Any number of public performers, while playing the so-called Serious Masterpieces, reach states of literal orgasmic trance.

Confession for the new year. My growing laziness (and this applies to general life as well as to this special paragraph, its style and content and dubious desire for being) stems from knowing I've uttered all that's in me in as many accents as can be counterfeited. In the half-million words published, and in the thirty-plus hours of music composed, I've probably said most of what I know. Does there remain only to say it all again differently? Were they to announce, "You will stay known and loved, and need never express yourself again; you will be rich and admired, but will never more compose,"would I feel deprived, or relieved?

Having writ this, having professed forever that I can't know how the quality of my nice music or mean prose would hold were they not interdependent, I now believe they wound each other. To write words is finally very bad for my music.

Why persist? When we were children, Mother's father, Granddaddy Miller in Yankton, taught us all to to knit—everything except how to cast off. That scarf was luscious, longer day by day, every week, month upon month, a woolen snake of many colors, I couldn't stop. There it still is, over there, ivory needles still caught in those forty feet of indecision, its option, and only Isadora could have put an end to it.

Cynthia Ozick, Zionist, on learning that as a Quaker I was conditioned to think all war wrong, while granting that certain Arabs have a point, poses the old canard: What if you're being mugged? Isn't that argument's fallacy now clear to all? Person-to-person is not people-to-people. (Lytton Strachey, asked what he'd do if a soldier were raping his sister, answered: "I'd try to get between them.") In theory Quakers turn the other cheek to muggers, and in fact police advise us to play dead. The question is not how Quakers feel about being mugged but how they feel about muggers. They aren't geared to protect themselves so much as to protect aggressors from themselves—to discourage need for war rather than assuming war as solution.

Earth is round, the trinity is round, the concept of the universe is eternally round. Yet although we dine from round plates we humans set those plates on rectangular tables on rectangular floors in rectangular houses on streets and acres and miles, all square. We paint pictures in angled frames and hang them in rooms that are never globes. Does the free animal perceive his world, his human friends, as spheres? Do we contradict possibilities of endless joy by blocking out our life? Could we curve our lives?

Galloping insomnia. Patches of wakefulness, ever larger, form a totally unraveled sleeve. Can't recall not having been conscious.

1976

Paul Jacobs came for a drink last night, but couldn't stay for our dinner party where all the guests were female: Eugenie Voorhees, Lillian Hellman, Claire Brook, and Janet Flanner. Talk of cooking, and of a device about the existence of which I'm apparently the last to be informed: the Cuisinart. Natalia, out of town, had expressed concern about Janet coming alone. Indeed, toward ten Janet began fumbling in her purse. "What are you looking for, dear?" asks Lillian, as Janet's eyes turn at once blazing and vague. She was looking, apparently, for a slip of paper with her own address on it. I've seen Elizabeth Ames like that. It must be racking. Some level of the brain can't help but know that another level is out of kilter. Eugenie phoned today to say that things got worse: Janet had hysterics in the elevator, and was finally delivered all tremulous to her door, while Lillian kept saying, "Don't pay any attention, she's just putting on."

Lunch chez Judy Collins. Dined with parents.

Originally John Ashbery and David Kermani were to have dined here with John Simon, but this morning Simon called to invite us all instead to Ann Gordon's where Lina Wertmüller and her entourage would be on view. (John S. just did a cover story on *Seven Beauties* for his magazine.) I loathe Wertmüller's vulgar films, and especially this last one, which renders the Holocaust as entertainment. But off we went. John Ashbery got quickly drunk, telling John Simon how sexy he found him (and spilling bourbon all over both of them), while on the sofa over there Miss Berenson cruelly teased Mr. Giannini, as Wertmüller's spouse gazed lovingly at JH. Shirley Stoler, meanwhile, says she got a thousand dollars plus expenses for the deal, and that despite wonderful reviews she still can't find an agent.

1 February

Visit yesterday from Byrne Fone and protégé, Charles Ortleb, who plan to
start a gay periodical called *Christopher Street* (good name) about which I
take a dim view. You lose identity in a mass. Still, I've promised them some
diary snippets.

Mother and Father come tonight to dine, despite the endless rain and
sleet.

6 February

Felicia Bernstein's birthday. The invitation promises cocktails at eight, dinner at nine. Shaved and shining I arrive at the Lotos Club promptly, then
grow queasy at that massive stone, that menacing Rolls, that showbiz luxe,
and can't bring myself to go in. Two hours later I return, ashamed, and actually check my coat in the foyer. Yet the thought of effecting a lone ascent
by that curling stair toward the jolly tinkle and thick scents above so petrifies
me that, for the second time, I retreat. Had I been with someone, no problem. But to enter anywhere alone (except onto a stage where the plan is
aloof, formal, prepaid) intimidates me to where I get a headache that lasts
for days.

Durability as proof? Baseball bats are more durable than cloisonné vases,
sacks of potatoes than baked Alaskas, and Merv Griffin has survived Ned
Rorem.

If my oft-uttered contention holds—that we don't change, we just get more
so—then I've always been a crank, even when most *mignon*, and it shows
increasingly through rancor and envy, which I take out on patient friends,
ever fewer. In the cold street those nonlooks we sling at long-lost contemporaries counteract keenly the gentle cruising we once . . . oh, we pretend
not to see each other, for there now without the grace of God go I. All those
missed opportunities (exclusively carnal) from drinking too much become
missed opportunities from not drinking at all; shyness and logic (which
aren't the same) preclude stumbling into the barren boredom of prescrew-
ing chitchat. Last night I finally began *Elle et Lui* (phrase by which Henri
Hell and his boyfriend once were known) thanks to the lamentable TV series
"Notorious Woman." It's about having the time to miss opportunities, and
at least rich Sand could impose rules better than thin Rosemary Harris,
who, thanks to a sterile director and a bromidic script, turns narrow, super-
American, sans class, and terribly petty. Sand was nothing if not French,
had style, scope, talent. She knew how to enter rooms.

14 February

Interview in today's *Post* with Jerry Tallmer, including my recipe for Torte à la Grand Marnier.

Deaths today by cancer and by murder of Lily Pons and Sal Mineo. This famous pair led starlit lives and were, as the saying goes, appreciated; their very nonanonymity is healthy if only by bringing to public light (starlight?) their unhealthy finales. Yet they were only interpreters, so what have they left—that is, left to us? Works of art they performed were at best second-class. It is, of course, bromidic to ask what does anyone finally leave, yet I ask it hourly.

1 March

Premiere of *Book of Hours*, for flute and harp (Ingrid Dindfelder and Martine Géliot). Afterward, at a middle-class party on West End Avenue to which JH and I were conscripted, a mean-lipped woman faced me with the unanswerable question, "What kind of music do you write—do you write Modern Music?" "Well, you just heard some," I uttered, and turned away. "You talk funny," she said. "You talk out of the side of your mouth."

Emanuel Ax played my *Études* for me today. They'll be all right. The premiere's in Washington on the 13th.

With JH to *Souvenirs d'en France* in which Moreau looks and behaves like Bette Davis in *Beyond the Forest*.

Tomorrow we record *Book of Hours* for CRI.

22 March

How often one feels: if only there were a camera for these unrepeatable assemblies. At yesterday's tea party, when I played the tape of *Air Music*, there were me and JH, David Del Tredici and Barbara Kolb, Judy Collins and Eugenie Voorhees, Myrna Loy and John Ashbery. Served a huge version of the Torte à la Grand Marnier, every crumb of which was consumed. People who deny caring for sugar, when confronted, generally succumb.

2 April

Death of Max Ernst.

Rereading the famous conversation (in Herodotus, and again in Plutarch) between Croesus and Solon, the premise seems cantish. Happiness, like love, is at best impermanent for intelligent people and should be defined solely in terms of the moment, not in terms of longevity. Cannot a man *have been* happy (we might ask Solon), although he's not happy now? Croesus with all his riches did fall, but he also rose again.

"Just one minute more: I was about to understand everything." These are the words that Valéry once said he would say on his deathbed. They go Madame Du Barry one better.

7 April

Mass photographic session at Iolas Gallery. Charles-Henri Ford flings us like rag dolls against a staircase where we strike poses for a woman with a camera, surrealist and *demodé*—though anything *demodé* today is sturdier than what's *à la page*. Afterwards Gore Vidal (in America to plug his new book and—who knows?—to run as a White House candidate) takes me to the Plaza for a very late lunch. I tell him with what dismay one reads the recent high-culture interviews with the paltry Wertmüller. "Yes, isn't she paltry," agrees Gore. "Last week in Rome I was at Rossellini's when Wertmüller, just back from New York, telephoned. Rossellini said, 'Lina, *Il Messagerro* tells us that some woman in America who says she's Lina Wertmüller has been advertising herself as the world's greatest *cinéaste*. Look into this, it's bad business.'"

The Sunday *Times Magazine* now solicits an "in depth" piece on rock. Obviously they recall my long lines on that subject, pro and con, a decade ago. But years have passed, I never hear rock, know nothing about it, am not interested, decline edgily, for these are the people who think I still live in Paris.

19 April

Though mostly I awaken in despair. The searching on maps of a lost Moroccan town brings waves (like the Debussy Trio flowing) of sadness, the sadness of sex, of the actual smell of legionnaires back then, in 1949, when we lunched daily at Fez's Café de la Légion, and they were there, thick-thighed steely-satined—*Il était mince, il était beau, il sentait bon le sable chaud*, shrieked *la môme*—and today I dwell longingly on Frenchmen in shorts in Chad, musky hot. But the reality and glory of averageness sputters from the TV tube, each candidate so trifling, and the mere fact of an incumbent campaigning is, to put it mildly, unstylish, although the mere fact of *wanting* the presidency should disqualify a candidate. That boy-scout ambition drummed into American dreams: the will to be A Leader is already the last impurity. The Supreme Court turns thumbs down on consenting adults in private. Gore Vidal claims Sweden's better—Sweden, where police traumatize their most exceptional citizen, Ingmar Bergman.

All is habit, and so is art. Death is the giving up of our last and hardest habit, life. Life is a rehearsal of death. But at the final curtain, the very pain of agony helps to mask the coming horrors.

Eyes and eggs make potatoes and turkeys, and turkeys and potatoes make eggs and eyes. So rolls the hoop forever. Humankind too, reproducing itself, comes up with endlessly undifferentiated models. Only a work of art, even a bad one, grows from a seed toward a singular finish and writes a unique Stop.

JH contends that whereas Virgil's prose is to instruct, mine is to punish.

Instruction and punishment are two sides of one coin (the third side is satire). What we call life is the scattered attempt to get even with those who "misunderstood" us in childhood. What we call art is the disciplined attempt to get even.

It's been seven years since I've smoked, eight since I've drunk, and nine since I first met JH. Has this abstinence (which viewed differently might be named indulgence) recolored me? I no longer get depressed. Saddened, yes, by the reality of a dying planet, but not overcome as with hangovers by my own willfully damaged body. Death's real, but dwelling on death is not.

23 April

With Shirley last night to Hugo Weisgall's new opera, culled by John Hollander from Mishima's *The Hundred Nights*. Wrote Hugo this morning that his opera glowed with passion, beauty, honest theatrics, and a sadness mindful of Resnais movies. Longueurs here and there, and a weak leading lady; but the orchestral writing, especially at the start with those low sensuous cellos, haunts in retrospect. At the reception afterward we chatted (painfully—her English is feeble) with Madame Mishima who has long fingernails painted royal blue, and with Petrassi, whose *Il Cordovano* was cobilled. Hadn't seen Petrassi since Rome in 1955. Unruly eyebrows. We spoke in French, as did Elliott Carter, whose French, I'd never realized, is as good as mine.

Fate led John Hollander to Food City this afternoon, and we chatted in front of Dairy Products. Is it wrong to have signaled a couple of minor technical errors in his libretto so soon after the fact, especially since I recently criticized another librctto of his? Well, John is a genuine, and sometimes readably exciting, poet; what's more, he's one of our two or three clear thinkers *about* poetry.

Flawlessly beautiful day, like a Roman summer. Tonight, the Phelpses *chez eux.*

Sopranos, like cheesecakes, are of two kinds: velvet or satin, vanilla or chocolate, silver or gold. The moist voice of Leontyne Price versus the diamond streak of Judy Collins.

I never answer stapled correspondence. The haughty facility of staplers insults not only the paper by puncturing key words, but also maims the recipients' thumbs.

Tight fairy eyes empty of everything but meanness. Negress/egress. Tigress/digress. Poppies/lobby.

Just as there are no hoary primitives, like Grandma Moses, in musical composition, neither are there child prodigies. Mozart's adolescent works are not equal to Rimbaud's.

29 April

Last night precisely at the moment Judy Collins was ringing my doorbell thinking she'd been invited to dine, I was ringing her doorbell thinking I'd been invited to dine. On such contretemps are funny feelings seeded. Luckily at both ends were interceptors, and we eventually met *chez elle* over odoriferous cans of Armour's corned beef hash, but the evening expanded without energy and *entretien* was meaningless.

5 May

And so I am a Pulitzer Prize winner.

Monday night JH bussed to Nantucket. Tuesday afternoon, undone by the *cafard* that used to accompany hangovers, I went to the Club Baths, "did" nothing, came home joyless at 8 P.M., heard the phone while unlocking the door under which was a telegram, and was struck mute by the news which, like beauty, hurt and made me want to cry. Next reaction: there must be some mistake.

Immediately JH (exhausted) returned by plane from Nantucket "to help with the glory," and co-winner John Ashbery phoned at midnight wondering where we go from here. The Machlis party last evening, originally planned so that Emanuel Ax could try out my new *Études* on some pedigreed dogs, turned into a celebration, with Stuart Pope toasting not the future but, for once, the present.

Lou Harrison, returning to San Francisco from the isle of Manhattan, says, "I've got to fly back to the mainland."

8 May

Rosemary's birthday. And Lukas conducted *Lions* last night in Detroit.

The Prize was apparently not an error, since the house is full of telegrams. My main emotion, beyond elated disbelief, is (though I must never admit this in public) one of vindication, because I'm queer and because I write attractive music—attractive music and queerness being, if not exactly sins, at least silly to the academy.

10 May

Recollection of Apollinaire's Montparnasse after Hearing Poulenc

At the hotel doors stand two green plants
Green but which will never bloom
Where are my fruits
Where plant myself?
O hotel door
An angel's before you
passing out pamphlets.
Never has virtue been so well defended.
Give me forever a room by the week
Bearded angel
you're only in reality
a lyric poet from Germany
who wants to get to know Paris.
You do know our sidewalks
those cracks on which you mustn't step—   [mustn't pounce]
and you dream of spending Sundays in Garches.   [in the Bronx . . . the sticks]
It's getting kind of sultry
and your hair is long,
O good little poet
rather dumb,
much too blond.

Your eyes look very like
those two great big balloons
adrift up there
in adventure's fresh air.

Yes, poetry is that which can't be translated.

The translator's secret lies less in knowing the foreign language than in knowing his own. If we grow aware of how it must have read in the original, if too many locutions appear literally translated, then we are looking through gaping seams upon work poorly done.

A songwriter's secret is the same as a verbal translator's, except that he is not translating from one language into another. He is grafting unrelated media: joining music, which is inherently meaningless in the intellectual sense of the word, to poetry, which is inherently meaningful. His success lies less in comprehending the words he is setting than in feeling them musically, and in being able to convince us of the necessity of his feeling.

The various means of grafting are something many composers take for granted but have never written about. I tried, in an essay called "Poetry of Music." Now those poets who read about themselves therein took offense, without exception, as did their friends. The feeling went: "Since Ned treated each one so briefly, couldn't he have been more flattering, or at least more correct?" I was not appraising them as people, or even as poets (if I didn't admire and need their work I'd never have set it to music); I was detailing "collaborations" to illustrate cases. To bring up one poet's concern with billing was not to belittle his art (though is publicity so unartistic?), any more than to say another "supplied" me with verse was to treat him as a pimp (is it wrong to say that Shakespeare, for example, supplies us with poetry?), or to suggest that a third's misreading of the music's intentions was condescending. Actually, all mention of all persons in all contexts is all incomplete and therefore misrepresentative; and even the most accurate cannot, in its limitation, jibe with those persons' idea of themselves. To berate me for thumbnail candor while chuckling over the sage ferocity of Stravinsky (how he treats Cocteau, or Copland, even Auden!) is to imply that only the Great have a right to the truth.

Janet Flanner once claimed that in my description of an evening with her, every word was false. To me the words were true, and to (some of) you. No reviewer likes to be reviewed. Her vision of herself is not my vision of her, any more than her Paris is my Paris.

11 May

Ella Fitzgerald has a wondrous way of topping a note with a sort of Spanish *tilde* when least expected. This mordant's a mannerism with meaning (as opposed to, say, Sarah Vaughan's befuddling rather than clarifying a text with her self-referential swoops), yet a mannerism all the same. Ella is never less than musical, never tiresome. But our mind will wander. She's bland in the end.

Over forty-five years since Maggy and I went down to the Loop—in the *morning*, a Saturday morning—to hear Ella in person with Chick Webb. *A tisket, a tasket.* Later, the gay bars, Simon's and Waldman's, filled with her sound: "Cootchy-Coo," "Don't Worry About Me," "Stairway To the Stars." That was the same season we saw Dietrich's *Destry* comeback—also in the morning. Names of theaters? The Chicago? Last time I was at a morning movie was with Bill Flanagan for the first showing of *What Ever Happened to Baby Jane?*

12 May

Leontyne, as is her triennial wont, gave a tryout of the new recital in her green plush parlor for ten guests who then ate cookies and talked about her singing. Howard Swanson, Lee Hoiby and I were the live composers included. Of me she did *The Silver Swan, Such Beauty as Hurts to Behold,* and *Alleluia*—good choices (chosen, actually, by David Garvey). The first of these floated from her lips like a gold thread to heaven, the second (on Paul Goodman's greatest lyric) was wrought with as much intelligence as love needs, and the third ended as no one has ended it before, on a solid high-E. There's no one like her, and Lee and Howard surely agree, since when she asked us to make suggestions, we were mute.

Later, strolled through the Village with Lee who claims he was miffed by my review of his opera in the *New Republic* (has it been four years since last we met?). I erred, maybe. I want to keep my friends.

18 May

One trouble with interviews as information (beyond the notorious fact that biography is drenched in the biographer's prejudices) is that the choicest nuggets are unearthed once the meeting is over. Presumably. Or else the interviewee talks and talks, reformulating for the thousandth time those formulas which, by virtue of repetition, he no longer questions. Talks and talks, like Anna de Noailles, precisely to dissimulate the fact that that which makes him him lies not in speech but in work. I don't say this necessarily of non-creative personalities like Pablo Casals or Carol Channing, but of my-self. I talk because I've nothing to say, because my intelligence is no more than itself, filling an empty shell.

How does it feel to win the Pulitzer? Totally satisfying. It's a once-in-a-decade refashioner carrying the decree that bitterness is henceforth unbe-coming. And if you die in shame and squalor, at least you die Official. I never counted on it. Not because I felt undeserving but because academics pre-sumably frowned on my wayward ways. That the judges should prove un-biased fills me with cheer for the Establishment. Except there is no more Establishment. Composers of every size and shape warmly phoned or wrote, though very few performers. That's because doers and makers move in quite separate professional, hence social, orbits. Players face out, com-posers in.

Ironically it was for an orchestral rather than for a vocal piece. My repu-tation, such as it is, has always centered around song, or the various tentacles of song: opera, chorus, cantata. *Air Music*, commissioned by Tommy Schip-pers for the Cincinnati Symphony, is a half-hour work in ten balletic sec-tions, each of which uses smallish and unusual groups of instruments. Yet although all the sections are, as they say, abstract, in that they eschew the human voice and don't "mean" anything, I conceived them as I conceive all music, vocally. Whatever my music is written for—tuba, tambourine, tu-bular bells—it always is the singer within me crying to get out.

What does the Pulitzer mean? It means the kind of honor that allows your basic fee to go up. Beyond that, it's a joy to play with, like a new sled, which you finally put away and go back to work.

You're a most prolific worker, aren't you? In spurts. I will have had seven major premieres in twelve months, but that windfall is mainly due to the Bicentennial frenzy, which already is subsiding. The seven works, though of different sonic species, are thematically related inasmuch as they all spouted from one flow. The first, a grand symphonic affair called *Assembly and Fall*, was played last autumn by the magnificent North Carolina Orches-tra. Then came *Air Music*. *Book of Hours*, for flute and harp, had its first performance in February. One week later in Kennedy Center the coruscat-ing Emanuel Ax premiered my *Eight Piano Études*. *Serenade* for voice, vi-ola, violin and piano, commissioned by a group in Akron, will be heard there this month, as will *Sky Music* for solo harp that gets launched in Albuquer-que. The seventh and last new work, and the closest to my heart, is a large set of songs called *Women's Voices*, which Joyce Mathis will sing here next November. It is, so to speak, an uncomfortable privilege—a pleasurable torture—to sit in the audience and hear a really good performer execute one's intimate sounds, hitherto so private, now hopelessly public.

Your brash, outspoken Diaries *are a public part of yourself too, yet you have vetoed discussion of your personal life in this interview. Why?* My literary outspokenness, if such it be, is a mode of art which cannot extend to published conversation. I'm a very closed person, really, and surely your *Times* readers are above prurience. Besides, the *Diaries* belong to the past, as does that form of brashness which is youth's prerogative. Meanwhile I do have four printed books of objective essays, which no one reads but which are also a part of myself.

You say there is no more Establishment. Where do you fit into the spectrum of your musical peers? You'd have to ask the peers. Or rather, objective bystanders. Some of those so-called peers have no use for me, although I admire them, while others seem perversely overrated. One can't know what people say behind one's back, but by and large composers' opinions about each other's work are no longer voiced *ex cathedra* from rival camps. Rather than belittle each other's dialects, they concentrate on how the dialects are phrased. There are exceptions. If a Boulez, for instance, does not take seriously a certain sort of tonal melodism, I myself am incapable of digging electronics or aleatorics. Anyway, I've never run with the pack, composing according to fashion; I've always been a lone wolf, composing according to need. The Red Queen said you've got to run fast to stay in one place. I stayed in one place. Now it's clear I've run fast.

What one American composer do you most love? Paul Bowles.

What American singers do you admire? How tell the singer from the song? Insofar as we applaud music rather than the glittering bodies from which music issues, I admire Phyllis Curtin because she knows how to utter English, a rarer gift than you might suppose. Let me quickly add Beverly Wolff, Betty Allen, Susan Davenny, Elaine Bonazzi, Bethany Beardslee, Cathy Berberian, Judith Raskin, Jan DeGaetani, Phyllis Bryn-Julson. Fewer known male singers are so special, though Donald Gramm and Charles Bressler come to mind. As for superstars, Leontyne Price is unique in giving even a remote damn about today's music. Indeed, Price is the only American opera diva who has any notion of song, thanks partly to her training as an intelligence rather than as a computerized triller. As representatives of vital music, there are no superstar mezzos in our country. One British Janet Baker equals a dozen Marilyn Hornes. It might be useful to note here that my lifelong affair with songwriting stems from a love not of singing but of poetry. Virtuosity for its own sake accounts for my indifference to *bel canto* literature and perhaps for my failure thus far to create a viable opera in the soap tradition. I'm incapable of musicalizing words whose literary value I don't believe in. The texts of most arias embarrass me no less than the expository parts of librettos.

How about music critics? There are fewer decent critics than decent composers in the U.S. today. Using Virgil Thomson as an absolute, only three or four critics come up to par. They share Thomson's perception, and may even exceed his scope, but none boasts his unquenchable panache—his gift for cracking square center with that perfect little Fabergé hammer. No good critic is now, as Virgil was (and remains), also a composer activated from within the core of sound, endowing his subject with compassion rather than with contempt or, at the very best, with musicological cant. A critic's chief crime, as composers see it, rests in a casual viewpoint toward new music. Admittedly most new music, like most everything, is mediocre and the critic must say so; but let him say so with sorrow, not sarcasm. His problem is partly occupational, for good criticism abounds in related fields. Movie, art, dance and drama critics review mostly the new. Only music critics must still think up phrases for Beethoven because only they review performance equally with what's performed. In other arts the past is exception; in music the past is rule. Music reviewing is music rehearing.

Dare I ask where you think music is heading? Behind that familiar question lurks a modern uneasiness, as though art had a moral obligation to endure (a conclusion which would never have occurred to Bach), while suspecting that only a fraction of it deserves room in a time capsule. There also lurks a modern implication that art, as a value, is precarious—that it should last but won't. Well, a mere composer is the last person to question, since, by definition, he's in no position to see beyond his nose. That answer is evasive, for I flatter myself that I'm more than a mere composer. However, the matter doesn't concern me much. Replies to such questions invariably prove fallacious within a year. Still, trends are clear. For example, scandal in music seems to be gone. Earlier in the century the biggest *causes célèbres* were scandals, and all except *Sacre* were vocal works: *Pierrot, Noces, Wozzeck, Four Saints.* But those sixties firecrackers of, say, Berio and Salzman and Austin spluttered insofar as they offered themselves as outrageous. Perhaps the scandal of Vietnam dwarfed such adventures. In any case true scandal can't be planned and might come today only via the quintessentially pristine. Meanwhile the current example of an *enfant terrible* is not even an Alice Cooper or a loud Lukas Foss, but a muffled Morton Feldman or a gentle George Crumb.

Are you pleased with yourself? My self-assured tone clothes an insecurity. I know my worth, yet that worth lies in past works which now lead their own life and no longer concern me. I feel unprotected and, in spite of dear friends, alone. I no longer smoke, drink, carouse or go to parties. Sugar is my sole vice and reading my joy. My mind is on work, or related elements, twenty-four hours a day, which accounts for the egocentricity of all artists and hides them from their own vulnerability. No, I'm not pleased with myself, because I'm continually alarmed by the ongoing present of which I am a part.

Does politics enter into art? How does it not? Musicians can be as dumb as anyone, but they are surely no dumber, and as a rule they have quicker instincts than "real" people. But as for Big Statements, artists shouldn't bother, since they all, no matter how sterile or derivative, reflect the times simply by dint of inhabiting the times.

What are you working on now? Orchestration of a mini-opera for the National Endowment. The scenario by Jim Holmes is based on Kenneth Koch's *Hearing*, which I set to music years ago. I also have three books in the oven: another diary, a batch of essays about esthetics, and a treatise on song. This summer I'd like to do a long organ piece and think about a new opera. I will never *never* NEVER write another soap opera of sound effects smeared on a European classic like *Miss Julie* (though that's all opera companies take chances on), but I might consider some Forster novel. After that, I have no ideas. Have you any?

My dear Ned Rorem, who are you? Who is anyone? The search for an answer keeps us forever evolving—which accounts for the poignance of Madame Du Barry's last words, "Just one more moment, Mister Headsman." I don't know who I am, but I've a notion of what I am. The *what* is a special fact, distorted through one's personal lens then flashed, for better or worse, into the world.

26 May

Four long Ohio afternoons centering around the premiere, at Akron's museum, of *Serenade on Five English Poems*. Three contiguous events were scheduled: a lecture and master class at the university's music school, a well-rehearsed concert of my chamber music (including myself accompanying two song groups), and a reading from this unpublished diary at Kent State. Each function, decently promoted and served up in halls of three hundred seats, attracted less than thirty-five people (which did not include music faculties, busy elsewhere). Not that I am a draw, or even a criterion for the elite or for the hungry young. But when I, as they say, was a boy, wild horses couldn't have kept me—or indeed kept my teachers—from those visits to Northwestern's campus of cultural luminaries. In New York it's reported that I'm a Pulitzer Winner and Quality Diarist, but to the Midwest most liv-

ing creators are invisible quantities. Kent's trustees meanwhile have allo-
cated a million dollars to their athletic program, while discontinuing the
ten-thousand-dollar annual budget for the Artist Lecture Series.

27 May

Death of Maggie Teyte.

Doctor at two for divers diseases. Then at three, Nan Talese to discuss the
new book. Sunday: to Nantucket for four and a half months.

Nantucket
8 June

Bees. When we returned after a season's absence a swarm throbbed on the
south eave of the house, at once motionless and speedy, like a flying saucer.
A neighbor said it'd been there for days. One hour later the bees vanished.
Two days later they—or ten thousand like them—came back. I was alone in
the kitchen as the faint, all-encompassing whir began. Gradually the entire
lawn grew inhabited, then the house was surrounded, encased in a translucent nacreous tent of yellow aspic, while the drone persisted, meaningless
and purposeful like an Ashbery verse, with a life of its own. . . . Suddenly
they evaporated. Oh, a few—maybe two dozen—hovered around the north
roof, but for all practical purposes they'd gone. (In the basement three stray
fighters buzzed frantically as the sun set, but quieted with the dark; and
when my eyes panned in so close as to join perhaps momentarily their frame
of reference the dying beauties came together, rubbed antlers, then ceased
breathing utterly.)

Illusion. Those sentinels at the north eaves have remained. Indeed, they
work for the cluster now ensconced in the house's framework. By the time
the exterminator arrived you could feel them beating like red hot snowflakes
against the warming parlor wall. Valero sprayed some cursory droplets under the eaves and said he'd be back next week if we needed him.

But the bees have moved in. Their intelligence lives in this house with us
like Hitchcock's birds. It's midnight. I've taken a Valium. Are they in conference? Their pale angry roar continues, although the encyclopedia says they
sleep quietly at night.

Next day, silence. The wall is cool. The bees have disappeared without a
trace.

9 June

Then this morning JH, who had been cutting the grass, came hysterical into the house. "I've run over a baby rabbit with the lawn mower." I went into the yard, and there sure enough were the bloody shards, which I buried. JH disconsolate. "Its mother must be frantic."

Extremely warm, sunny, hazy.

10 June

Like the student reading *Romeo and Juliet* in a Verona park, like the boy reading *Moby Dick* on a bench in Nantucket, or like the lass on the dock of Lesbos reading *The Well of Loneliness*, so the spirit of summer announces itself today with a thrilling obviousness. All the island's embalmed in the smell of wild roses, and the windless mild air has the clarity of gin.

Stella Brooks used to say (in the 1940s, when it was chic to sleep with Negro jazzmen), "I can't tell one white person from another." Virgil Thomson: "I can't tell one young person from another." Well, it's getting so I can't tell one *person* from another. On Nantucket I socialize not at all. Why, when invited, do I sometimes accept? Not to learn anything, but for another kind of boredom, a change of *ennui*. It's nice being alone, or with friends in books or from the past.

26 June

Back from Princeton. The house progresses, JH having laid the new rugs from W & J Sloane and built basement doors. With so much in all ways I remain bowed under and sad. Selfish state, hard to kick. Passion for old lovers and loved places revives during insomnia, but dissipates during actual revisiting of those places and lovers. Thirty summers ago at Janet Fairbank's family mansion in Wisconsin the after-dinner comportment was for men to smoke in this room while ladies retired to that room. We were struck, then as now, less by the archaism than by Janet's tacit acceptance of the archaism—Janet, whose career as singer of modern Americana would even today be daring against all odds.

28 June

Rerun on TV of *Lady From Shanghai*, fifth viewing since 1948 of this opus which grows ever hokier and, by extension, throws light (or darkness) on the holes in Welles's other films which, often as not, seem like arbitrary knots in search of a cohering thread. Deaths the same day of Johnny Mercer and of our staunch Sam Dushkin.

1 July

"There are really four kinds of composition," writes Lou Harrison. "Voluntary, Suggested, Requested, Commissioned. Best of all is when someone commissions an already begun voluntary work."

I want to contribute a major work to the literature for organ, which in America is meager. Although I don't love the organ. You don't have to love an instrument to write well for it; conversely, because you love an instrument doesn't mean you have the magic touch. It's a challenge. Besides, JH is an organist and he loves it. Putting our heads together we came to a scientific approach. Leonard Raver is the organ's most conspicuous champion for new works. I've asked him to ask Alice Tully to commission me to write the first piece composed specifically for the new organ in her hall. Alice agreed.

I've just told Leonard: Nothing pans out precisely as projected, but for the moment I see a collection of études, theatrically joined (though not necessarily thematically), and with programmatic titles drawn from Quaker tenets and/or the poems of Whittier. The esthetic problem will be in justifying the sound of music for one who was raised in Silent Meeting. Incidentally, when I say theatrical I don't mean visual (lights and things); I mean integrally related, like separate characters in the same plot. The same cemetery plot.

14 July

We stayed up to watch—hear—Jimmy Carter's cunningly bromidic nomination speech, after which I dream: Alone now in Paris: Jean Leuvrais arrives to erase uneasy years but is soon guided off by a woman; *Elle t'a envoûté*, I say, but he only smiles, and together they fade into a pasture of cornflowers; I would follow, but the pasture becomes a gymnasium a thousand miles long and the cornflowers turn into boys with guns; I wend my way through them to an unknown Paris *ruelle*, enter a bar, and order a brandy, but the woman beyond the *zinc* hands over a book with gray blood on its pages and speaks my name. *Comment le saviez-vous?* I ask, and she answers, "Oh, you've come to our library before." Awake in tears, prisoner of the present, lie for a while, back aching, stuck in the door of the Hôtel du bon la Fontaine where stands Jean Leuvrais, as young as 1951, whom I can actually smell but never again touch. It's six A.M. Downstairs JH makes coffee before taking off—he too—on the boat to New York.

3 August

A cold August. Everything's early. Hay fever's come with a vengeance. Tiger lilies come and gone. Chill winds. Fatigue from antihistamine pills. Heaviness. Still orchestrating *Hearing*, and correcting, listlessly, proofs of *Air Music*.

6 August

Hay-fever nightmare continues.

New York
19 October

Haven't written in this notebook for ten weeks. Several reasons: many of my notes were transferred into three essays, "Being Alone," "Of Vanity," and "Criticism," for *Christopher Street*. Busy, more or less, on *A Quaker Reader*. Houseguests: parents, then Maggy Magerstadt, then Morris, then Shirley (who broke her foot), then Gustavo. Cleve and Francine du Plessix Gray in Nantucket most of latter half of summer, and I saw them almost every day. Also the Conroys, Harbachs, Rosette, Ruth Laredo, etc. Gina Bachauer and Lotte Lehmann died. No one was born. Lots of movies and TV and reading (incl. *Silas Marner*), and a hurricane named Belle. But all of this now, so soon after, blurs. Overwhelming preoccupation of summer was my allergy. Each page of the notebook proclaims: another bad day; sneezing just frightful; hysterics; bleeding in nostrils. Continues today. Descent of plane into La Guardia brought an electrocuting sinus attack, splitting open forehead. Wondering if it's a punishment for the Pulitzer. Feel always gloomy, in decline. JH a mountain of considerate patience and ministrations. *Rien à faire*. I do cope, but in slow motion, and nothing matters. Meanwhile I feel JH sagging, forced to deal with my tantrums. If he gives way, what's left? Somehow don't care about jotting deep thoughts, chic doings, or vainglorious concerts. Body's anxiety is far worse than mind's.

21 October

Complete run-through of Joyce Mathis's upcoming program, including my *Women's Voices*, for a dozen guests in a private hall. Joyce's vocal coach, Cornelius Reid, does not remain for my songs. That a reputable voice teacher should depart, for whatever reason, before the unveiling of a new cycle is insulting no less to that cycle's composer than to all writers of song today, and underlines once again the indifference to contemporary vocal music, even by those most involved.

9 November

When ASCAP a few weeks ago invited me to a lunch, to honor me and fellow-member Marvin Hamlisch for our Pulitzer Prizes in music, I rebelled. Marvin Hamlisch did not win the Pulitzer Prize in music; *Chorus Line* (to which he was one of many contributors) was awarded a prize. Although it was surely Hamlisch who, being a bigger moneymaking wheel than I for ASCAP, choreographed this, I refused to attend unless the wording of the homages was specific. The Pulitzer Prize is the most important gesture ever made to me and I will not share it with an interloper. The lunch occurred today. Hamlisch and I both brought our parents. We eyed each other warily (to use Gloria Steinem's telling phrase about her meeting with Pat Nixon), the "wording" was acceptable, and pictures were taken of us shaking hands.

4 December

Deaths last month of Man Ray, of Malraux, and then today most hopelessly of Benjamin Britten.

15 December

Not that Lenny Bernstein doesn't sing for his supper, but his long solo (there are no ensembles) is based on the Affectionate Insult, for which a listener has no retort. Verbs emerge from his now-bearded visage with a comet's speed and a diamond's dazzle. But the comet trails allergenic dust, and the diamond lights up a sty. You can't set forth an idea without Lenny's poohpoohing it, then putting you straight by merely rewording the idea in his own style. The style is built around non stop impersonations (of Boulanger, of Giscard d'Estaing, of Rosalynn Carter, of people present), accurate, and cutting—no less than Capote cuts—big people down to size. The content is that of He Who Sees Clearly, anecdotes from the Inside interlarded with the Suddenly Serious Stance about the Great Problems.

Our other guests last night were Aaron Copland, David Del Tredici, Leonard Raver, and George Cree. None was spared Lenny's wounding thrusts, quickly salved with a kiss. To presume to stall his monopoly is, according to Lenny, to draw attention to one's self. After three hours, declaring that since no one would listen to him he was going home, he left, with loving hugs all around. Admittedly Lenny's under a strain of broken connubiality and public exposure. But when is he not, or anyone? Some react to stress with magnanimity, but he no longer even pretends to be kind, only vast. It smacks of smallness. Bette Davis once remarked: The duty of the Truly Grand is to learn how to set mere mortals at ease.

(Lenny's dinner gift—coals to Newcastle—was a big red book on homosexuality.)

And Aaron? He arrived an hour early, asked for something to pay the cab because he'd lost his wallet, then called to where he'd been before and learned that the wallet had been left on the sofa. So he returned there, then returned here, and said, "Guess what! I lost my wallet."

16 December

Is it unfair to have written that about Lenny when, by definition as the world's most vital musician, he's the world's most generous creature? When we first met in 1943 I referred to somebody as having "all the bad points of Jews, and none of the good points." Surprised when he asked if I were anti-Semitic.

1977

Here in style for *Air Music* at the same Orchestra Hall in which my youth was spent, in which the very definition of music was instilled, but in which I've never heard myself represented before last night. Noon today, irrepressible Dolores Fredrickson arranged a lunch at the Arts Club for me to "retrieve" certain people I was never close to in high school (Howard and Roger Brown, Sid Epstein, their wives, etcetera). Who are they, these semi-senior citizens eager to invoke lost years? They are ourselves, united here precisely because, at another time nearly four decades ago, they were united at the University Chapel for graduation. That great group dissolved into other groups, each autonomous: religious, military, familial, collegiate, economic, even musical, with the subdivisions of those. With the computerized accuracy of the brain we recapture in a trice the unity of yore, of U-High (a private institution called Jew-High by denizens of the public Hyde Park High). That June morning in 1940 has more reality for me than this meeting today.

John Edwards met plane Wednesday in time for 3:30 rehearsal, before which I had asthma crisis which symphony nurse supervised with grain of salt. Orchestra, under Guido Ajmone-Marsan, exemplary (except solo cello, pale and out of tune for his big movement). Radio interview with Tom Willis. Took Arrand Parsons to dine with John Maxon. Yesterday: morning rehearsal; interview with Studs Terkel (his energy, his total recall since last we met at Gertrude Abercrombie's and I was drunk in 1966); nostalgic visit with Parsons to Hyde Park; preconcert symposium with Edwards at hall; agitated meal with Paul Fromm; then concert, during which sat with Maxon. Was to have gone with Ruth Page, but she had been mugged—*mugged*, in front of her house on Lake Shore Drive—and was in the hospital.

It's four in the afternoon. I await George Garratt. Anxious, anxious, anxious breathing. (Everything's pollen, even those wallpaper roses, even that snow out there.) Old times. Earlier, another symposium at Northwestern with Willis, another alma mater (let claim me who will), and tonight another hearing of *Air Music*. Then back to the reality of New York, once so unreal, a hazy promised land when Illinois was terra firma and our hearts were young and grave.

New York
9 January

Vagaries of English. Verb, *to put*, i.e., *to place*, and problems for the French both in sense and in pronunciation:

    To put out (as extinguish a fire)
    To put out (as outdoors: the cat)
    To be put out (annoyed)
    To put out for (deliver the goods, usually sex)
    To put up (to house)
    To put up (to bottle or can)
    To put up with (tolerate)
    To put up on (place on the shelf)
    To feel put upon (feel used)
    To put over (to deceive; to put one over on)
    To put over . . . a deal
    To put under . . . under a counter

Put yourself in my place. Place yourself in my put. A put-up job. Enough rough stuff. Enough ruff's tough. Job's job's tough, though thought-through. Boughs in the soughing wind / Wind round the bows bowed and red, / Icy red. I see red when the reed / which I read / and have read as a willow will, / lo!, claim itself as a reed. Was Oedipus complex?

17 January

Saturday at three Robin Morgan brought me her new book. As we sat chatting both my arms grew numb, breath came short, and a sick anxiety overcame my whole body. By the time JH got home I felt paralyzed. No taxis. We walked through the slush to the emergency room of Roosevelt Hospital where, after a gloomy hour of fruitless waiting, I said I'd rather die at home. Walked back. Josué by phone prescribed Sinequan, two a day forever. Meanwhile the ENT specialist prescribes other pills; if in a week they don't reduce the polyps in my nose he'll operate. I hate my body. Death of Anaïs Nin.

Second session of yoga, prescribed by Francis Thorne, in a class of five with a youngish gymnast. The breathing, ease, concentration, straightforward dispensing of ego seems worth twenty doctors (at least today), and twenty times cheaper. Subzero weather.

Interview for *Music Journal*. Dine chez Heddy Baum, where I tell Sam Barber I've just been reading about him—very nice things—in my own new book. "That's a switch," said he in a voice so snide that my evening was ruined.

My feeling toward tea—yes, real tea: Earl Grey, Orange Pekoe, etc.—is not merely one of indifference. I am hostile to tea, and its loathsome insipidity. Vaughan Williams is insipid too, but benign. Laurence Olivier is not benign; his upward-rolling eyes betray some of us into saying he's great.

Beauty limps. All great art is flawed. But the flaws can not be "put in," as by Navajo rug weavers who dare not mock God with perfection, or like old glamor girls with their beauty spots like warts. The flaw defines the beauty: Michelangelo's *David* with those too-long limbs, Garbo's too-long neck. Meanwhile Lana Turner or a Pontiac are in their perfection not beautiful but pretty. Beautiful art is unduplicatable, even by the artist. The *oeuvre* makes the rules, after the fact, and each work conforms to its own law. Everything on our planet is replaceable—humans, platypuses, apples, philosophies, cancers, stones—everything except the work of art, which is unique and cannot reproduce itself. But it limps. Its limp is it.

To contend, as certain aging (and only aging, never young) people do, that sexual indifference to the elderly is discriminatory is logically to infer that avoidance of sex with children is discriminatory. Infantism. By extension, necrophilia should not be discouraged. Well, perhaps it's rationalization, but if the young don't lust for the old there simply may not be that much to lust for. I, for one, feel far less the need for proof, for making out, for taking the hours away from work that sex, any sex, requires.

The flesh stays willing, it's the spirit that's weak.

Nature designed us to be "attractive" from puberty to menopause, roughly thirty years. The gerontophilia so desired by older folks is, on the whole, bigoted: they resent not being loved by the young, but are sexually indifferent to their own age group.

Man, in meditating and in searching for God, does not transcend his human condition, he expands it. All that he does is, finally, human. Inhumanity and superhumanity are human concepts and have nothing to do with God.

God gave man his grand talents; the devil gave man his little ones—though the reverse could be convincingly reasoned. So-called responsible artists always talk about how they won't sell their soul for an easy buck. But their soul is precisely what buyers don't want. The soul is the one part of themselves they're allowed to keep when they reach Hollywood.

31 January

Regular diet of Sinequan and yoga. Polyps in nose shrunk, but this morning saw Howard Moss's allergist, Dr. Earl Brown, who announces that my blood contains six percent eosinophiles, whatever that means. Then sinus X rays with a Dr. Ernest Newman. Then a two-hour broadcast with Leonard Raver on WBAI apropos of *A Quaker Reader*, which we've been rehearsing diligently for the past month. Stultifying cold.

3 February

More than instrumentalists, singers to survive must keep their bodies fit. The best way is not to overtax the mind. Admittedly singers at work can coax a hearer to depths of intellect and passion, for they are hot funnels through which large notions flow. But those notions are not—indeed, must not be—caught and held within the singer: he must feel how to emit them. Singers at work are essentially physical, and highly praised. Thus singers at play are all that they're rumored: given to pseudo-warm self-congratulatory banter.

I penned those words eight years ago but never published them, JH feeling they were at the very least graceless. Have I in any case changed my mind since the visit yesterday afternoon of a brainy young baritone, William Parker, whose French-English repertory is vast and proud, whose diction is second only to Donald's, whose timbre can be tasted as well as heard (marmalade, marble, ebon-blue, sadness), and whose ambition seems propelled less by ego than by a sense of mission?

Meanwhile in the evening Leonard gave the world premiere of *A Quaker Reader* in Alice Tully Hall as the entire second half of his program. (It clocks at nearly forty minutes.) Allen Hughes' pretty good and quite long review in the *Times* begins by quoting the program notes ("Myself, raised in Quaker silence, I craved Catholic sound"), and ends by stating that, precisely because of these extended notes, "the result is a music-literary work that one can listen to and read with pleasure, and, despite its technical difficulty, it will surely be welcomed by organists." In our box—Alice Tully's box, actually—sat Alice herself, Shirley, Judy Collins, and Jerry Oster. Party after at the Poulailler where I learned with distress that Myrna had been at the concert but that, unable to find us, she didn't join us later. While Leonard was playing authoritatively in New York, *Air Music* was being heard a thousand miles away in Minnesota where tonight it will be repeated.

6 February

Where drifts a reviewer sans program note as guide?

Should it not be noted that all the critics on the *Times* are straight (or married—it's a matter of policy), and none is allowed to be a practicing musician?

What is a critic? Anyone who assesses.

What is a composer? Anyone who inscribes notes.

Who is a critic? One who gets paid, or at least printed, and is read by people he doesn't know. These are his sole qualifications. As for who's a good critic, that's forever opinion beyond defining.

Who is a composer? Like the alcoholic, the composer is self-defined. A composer is that if he says he is. As for who's a good composer, again it's opinion. Satie is not very good but he's certainly communicative, while Reger is certainly good but awfully dry, don't you think? Inspiration has nothing to do with being a good composer (everyone's inspired), yet it does bear on what decides a young person to call himself a composer at the start. However, the *channeling* of inspiration has everything to do with being a professional, that is a *good*, composer.

Petrifying cold, and the heat's been off for three days. I sleep at Mother & Father's, JH at Gustavo's. Invited Edouard Roditi to lunch today, but had to take him out to a dump on Columbus Avenue called Genghis Kahn's Bicycle. A paragon. Edouard, who smokes and drinks and gobbles up cupcakes, is cardiac, diabetic, and (he'd have us believe) both pregnant and bilious. Remains prolific beyond measure, and a most original intellect.

7 February

Still no heat. Still more doctors. JH's depression.

Did you, yes or no, on the night of the thirteenth, cry out "I'd like to see you dead"?

You're distorting the words out of context.

Answer yes or no.

I'll answer if you'll answer a question of mine first.

Agreed.

Did you, yes or no, two minutes ago, use the words "I'd like to see you dead"?

Both Sagan and Sartre, while indulging homosexuals from afar—she by casting them as jesters, he by apotheosizing Genet in a giant tome—seem uncomfortable about granting them individual dignity.

Nantucket
23 February

Here alone for ten days. Allergy frightful. To date I've seen five specialists. JH demoralized by my demoralization. Last week for the record: interviewed, along with John Cage, on WNYC by Matthew Paris; John Maxon (& friend) for tea with Bruce; *Fun with Dick and Jane*, a Fonda comedy, with JH; diner chez Emily Genauer, with Mazzola, Katherine Kuh and Rosemary Harris; Valentine's Day with a young photographer named Pineiro who took extravagant pictures; yoga and doctors, doctors and yoga; Rorems to dine; dinner party for Francine & Cleve Gray, Eugenie, Dominique Nabokov, and later Judy & Jerry.

Now I'm pasting a book together for Nan Talese. *An Absolute Gift*. Tonight Maggie and Frank Conroy come to dine with a homemade daquoise. Heavy winds and rains. Rereading *Nightwood* for the tenth time. What a marvelous mess.

New York
5 March

Visit from Millicent Dillon for her book about Jane Bowles. She never met Jane, but looks just like her—has, in a sense, already *become* her subject, which I suppose is inevitable for biographers. Or is it?

9 March

New York premiere of *Assembly and Fall* with Gosling at Carnegie Hall. Afterward, in front of Shirley, JH had a *crise de jalousie* about a stranger who said hello, and the evening's joy was deflated utterly.

12 March

Father this morning, at his age, went to Hammacher Schlemmer, purchased a heavy air purifier, and lugged it in a taxi here. Janet Flanner's 85th birthday, so we're going to Natalia's to celebrate.

15 March

Premiere tonight, by Gregg Smith, four of his solo singers and seven instrumentalists (including saxophone and mandolin), of *Hearing* in the little opera version made by JH six years ago. First-rate and witty performance in Saint Stephen's Church to sparse audience.

Every day I attend either the yoga class or visit an allergist, or both. JH falling lower.

16 March

Breakdown of JH.

17 March

Dined on West 20th chez Nicolas and Dominique Nabokov, and Nicolas's sister. *Soirée française.* In the quarter century that I have known him, Nicolas has never seemed so at ease, so lucid yet so mortal, so not on stage. Doubtless it's Dominique. Small apartment.

18 March

Came sniffling home from the allergist to find a sheet of paper with just one word: "Gone." Snow, sleet, rain. Night fell. Finally the bell sounded. JH collapsed in the lobby. Later, found a suicide note. I talk and talk and talk. He can't hear. I write this in hysterics.

21 March

Composers I mostly see are around forty years old. A new solid crop of twenty-year-olds is emerging in America, but where are those of thirty? Five years ago the concept of art, in the shade of Vietnam, was at once relaxed and political. Relaxed political art can't outlive itself. I've no close pal my own age anymore, as Bill Flanagan and I once so platonically were.

I can't prove it but probably even Elliott Carter doesn't "like" his own music, if one can surmise that God has likes and dislikes. (Though why would God create what he hates?) Carter's music contains more *information* than, say, William Schuman's, but that information seems to me disparate, lacking a center, like the complex formats of rock videos, which are expensive, sadistic, filled with color and tears and meaningful glances, but which don't convey a clear-cut message. Paradoxically, Carter's music is more *personal* than Schuman's (i.e., hotter, more feverish), while being less immediately identifiable. If I tune in late on a Carter piece, I'm never sure who it is.

The Pitchford-Morgans came to dine. Watched a TV salute to Bette Davis. *The Letter*, which I first saw in 1940 with Father at that "art" theater across from the Water Tower, is my favorite movie, with *Sunset Boulevard*. Unlike *Sunset Boulevard*, every frame, and every measure of Max Steiner's score, is correct and needed.

23 March

Yesterday, procured serum for shots for the next several months. JH touch-and-go. Hélène Rémy's exhibit in Soho beneath a deluge of rain and wind. The baths. Today, gloom, Robert Phelps at five, then Judy Collins at seven, and an A.A. meeting maybe. Whatever the highs and lows, never does a day go by that I don't thank God (in whom I don't believe) for the continuing sobriety that permits me to witness, cope with, all horrors, unblurred.

Nantucket
30 March

Alone, working on a small choral affair called *Surge Illuminare*. Morning at Atheneum library, reading on suicide. At the Looms, violet wool shawl, to match her eyes, for Judy on her birthday, and green bathrobe, to match his eyes, for JH's birthday next week: he'll be thirty-eight. The shadow of forty, plus my own shadow, surely accounts for part of his misery, though he denies it. Twice a week I report to the nurse for a shot.

Cornwall, Connecticut
9 April

Last night Leon Kirchner and David Del Tredici came over, Leon in a state about his opera, which after eighteen years will see the light next week. He seems to want my approval, and I'm sympathetic (recalling *Miss Julie*), for only with opera is a composer high man on the totem pole, and only with opera's failure is he thrust from sight utterly, as with Sam Barber's withdrawal after Zeffirelli's sabotage of his *Antony & Cleopatra*. Still, Sam's piece could never by its nature have been the Great American Opera—a title that Leon is bidding for. Can Great American Operas be devised from Great American Novels, as Leon is trying with Saul Bellow? Previous chauvinist contenders have all been on original librettos. Not that viable music can't rise from preexisting literature; it's just that American composers haven't yet added convincing dimensions to classical European plays. Or even to native blockbusters. (Britten has, for whatever reason, dealt more movingly than any American opera-maker with preestablished American texts, viz. *Billy Budd* and *Turn of the Screw*.) Need for the Big Statement, still acute for book critics, has become a thing of the past for most musicians, due largely to inroads of pop where breath is short and inspiration collective. Al Carmines, in *his* choice of librettists like Gertrude Stein and of subjects like World Liberation, bites off a lot. But the music is small-time: he makes molehills out of mountains.

Anyway, this morning with the Borchardts we drove here to spend Easter weekend with Francine and Cleve in their liveable house, every aspect of which is commendable (except the sound system, which ceaselessly bathes us in Palestrina; for a musician, true class is silence), including the well-mannered sons, Thaddeus and Luke, and the emphasis, in deference to my lusts, on rich desserts despite the Spartan bent of our hosts. Conversation very high toned, with Francine wasting nary a second on the Unimportant: she knits while discussing Kafka, and while jogging wears earphones into which Shakespeare's sonnets are intoned.

Philip Roth came over with Claire Bloom, whom I'd never met. I asked if she were intrigued by other versions of "her" roles, Liv Ullmann's interpretation of Nora, for example, adding that I'd just finished Ullmann's memoirs which guiltily discuss the actress's surly and overweight daughter. Have you any children, Miss Bloom? Turns out she has an overweight, surly daughter who plays the oboe. Sunday, big Russian lunch chez Francine's mother, Tatiana, with Alexander Liberman, who dwells nearby. Vast ugly sculptures of Alex. Later, the paintings of Cleve. Worried the whole time about being away from JH who, had I remained in New York, wouldn't have been home anyway.

13 April

Nice unseasonable temperature continues at ninety degrees.

Afternoon dress rehearsal, with JH, of Kirchner's *Lily*. Toward the end, several thousand balloons were for some reason released into the orchestra. JH whispers, "Not even the balloons can save it"—his first lighthearted remark in months. The piece will flop and Leon will have a trauma. *Ainsi vont toutes choses.* Still, much is salvageable. Leon has a bad sense of theater, but a good sense of drama; a bad sense of imparting text, but a good sense of vocal writing (like Bill Flanagan) above the staff where text doesn't matter. Excerpts might turn out to seem theatrical in a non-theatrical setting, like the concert hall.

Dined at the Rudels' with the Manuel Rosenthals. Hadn't seen them since Paris, 1961. Pleasure.

14 April

Disgusting evening. I loathe the theater and I've never cared for Margaret C. But when the latter asked me to the former, some perverse weakness allowed me to accept, despite the stipulation that I escort her to the post-play party. Liv Ullmann in *Anna Christie* was less embarrassing than the conspicuous opportunism at the Plaza where, while MC tablehopped, I was forced to chat with Mr. Sardi, whose cuisine is unfit for beasts. I felt used. So I left, leaving Margaret to get home on her own. Tomorrow I'll send her two dozen roses. Awful sadness.

May Day

Before departing for Nantucket, here's a résumé of the past fortnight:

New allergist acquired.

Saw Altman's *Three Women*, the first movie in a decade to use real music, although Gerald Busby, who did the Stravinskian score, tells me he was paid peanuts. (Has a treatise yet appeared on music's conditioning role in film? Bad music wrecks good movies, good music can redeem bad movies, and any music can radically alter the intention of any given scene. Its "abstract"—though not neutral—force makes music more subliminally persuasive than all other periphera of film, something cinéastes have known from the start. But movie music has now depreciated with the advent of star directors, in Europe as in America. Auteurs employ hacks, as though to join hands with a vital musician would constitute a threat. There is no movie music anymore.)

Supervised a colloquium at Yale for thirty pupils of the Institute of Sacred Music. Attended Eric Salzman and Michael Sahl's semi-successful *Civilization and its Discontents* essayed with jocularity at Tom O'Horgan's. With Morris and JH to Lily Tomlin's show, during which the afternoon *piqueur* swelled my itchy arm to twice its normal size. *Oedipus* and *Carmina* at Center Opera. Rorems to dine, as always, on Sunday evening. Claudine and Manuel Rosenthal came for tea (historic for me: he's Ravel's only pupil, and vital as a puppy); Maggy Magerstadt for tea, then with Judy to Nana Mouskouri's dreary concert, which we quit in the middle to attend Ellen Adler's post-exhibit party in Stella's studio, where Arnold Weinstein—never having met her—embraced Judy instead of shaking hands. Wednesday, Martita and Eugene Istomin came to dine, plus the Gruens, and Nathalie & Hugo Weisgall. Picture-taking, especially of Hugo in the lotus position. Afternoon at the library (with a bad cold) examining the Griffes collection, including his pale watercolors, in preparation for Roger Englander's TV documentary about that composer, for which I'm to be host. Signed fifty copies of the just-published *Air Music* at Boosey & Hawkes, and had another *crise du nez. Et voilà.* My initial projects now are the piece for guitar and flute and the commencement address for Northwestern.

8 May

Elizabeth Ames died a month ago in Saratoga. She was ninety-two, yet I feel more bereft than when certain younger friends have vanished, perhaps because there were more years in which to grow accustomed to her. Then too, "We never said farewell, nor even looked / Our last upon each other," and I feel a bit guilty.

In today's *Times* John Cheever, in a memoir called "The Hostess of Yaddo" (surely not his title), evokes Elizabeth's intuitive glory and speaks quite frankly, as he should, about her senility. He may be pardoned his poetic license—"I remember passing a football to Danny Fuchs and Leonard Ehrlich while Ned Rorem played the piano in the music room and Marc Blitzstein wandered around the back roads singing the score from *Regina*," since I never knew Ehrlich, nor were Marc and I ever at Yaddo simultaneously (and if we had been, it's doubtful that Marc would have sung *Regina* in the back roads)—John may be pardoned his license since he condenses fact, like any writer, though he could have added that Elizabeth and Ehrlich had once been lovers. Indeed, the autobiography that Elizabeth planned but for purposes of discretion never penned could have told as much about the foibles of American artists as any dull *Who's Who* or *Grove's*. Someone now should write the book for her; because Elizabeth was not *une femme insatisfaite*, but, like waiters and bank clerks, or indeed, like a "Hostess at Yaddo," she existed as a servant to others and is thought to have had no personal life.

When Alison Lurie's *Real People*—a portrait of Yaddo, in part necessarily mean and raw—was published I asked Elizabeth what she thought. "Well," said she, "Alison will not be invited back." That's the closest I ever heard to a negative opinion of Elizabeth about a guest, though if the guest were a man she might have paused: she inclined to give the male sex more benefit of the doubt. Still, the Lurie novel, for its very truth, has impact and is better than any other picture I know.

Elizabeth Ames, because she was a convert, was a more devoted Quaker than I. (During our frequent Sunday Meetings, just the two of us, my mind would wander, but hers held firm to "higher" visions.) But she was not a *better* Quaker than I, insofar as, God or no God, Quakers work toward peace, not only in time of war but in time of peace.

Holiday Inn
Evanston
18 June

At Northwestern this morning to receive my first Doctorate of Fine Arts. Elliott Carter, who has received many such degrees, is the one other musician among the eleven honorees, who include eighty-six-year-old Earl Dickerson, Father's colleague at the Rosenwald Fund in the 1930s. The expedient, orderly, colorful, massive ceremony moved me to tears, here on this campus where thirty-five years ago I came drunk to classes and got bad grades. After the folksy "luncheon" (as the meal is called in the Midwest), we repaired to Pick Auditorium. This time Elliott and I were the only outsiders on stage. After we had each been presented with little awards, I rose to give (as had been arranged months ago) the commencement address to these green School of Music graduates. This lasted, as preordered, not a second more than fifteen minutes. Then the diplomas. Elliott, meanwhile, who had not been asked to speak, presumably had attended my words, but uttered no comment on them. Does this make me smile? In all the years we've known each other, I've always been the one to keep the conversation moving, generally with questions about E.C.'s work. He's never asked me beans about myself.

19 June

Could I be dead (rather than dying), given the indifferent motion of shadows emitting perfumes of ginger and formaldehyde? Dead nostrils don't inhale. Nor does dead gray matter recall the skill of a Janet Frame whose nonhero, pronounced moribund, nevertheless arose from an unguarded coffin to walk home, where a distraught but aquiescent mate was unable to accept him as viable, and in the end, years later, the neighbors stoned him to death for real.

Misdiagnosed as dead. Misdiagnosed as living.

To wait alone in the subway is said to be risky, although terms of risk change with the seasons. Criminals once were those sleazy folks who importuned in toilets; today those same evildoers become victims of desexualized muggers. Now during this midnight what will disturb the stillness? No shadow braids the low rows of girders, nothing forbodes. As in the Cordova mosque or Nantucket's graveyard, I've never felt calmer.

Meanwhile I await Art Lange, a young Chicago poet who will interview me for his magazine, *Brilliant Corners*.

Nantucket
5 July

Death of Vladimir Nabokov.

Nothing is funny absolutely, not even within a self-relating culture. A so-called "practical" (as opposed to "intellectual") joke, if funny at all, is funny only in relation to its victim. The pratfall of an uppity millionaire is laughable because it brings him down to our mediocre peg, but to pull a chair from under a poor old woman is strictly delinquent. The so-called sick (as opposed to well?) joke depends on the teller who, by missing a cue, may flatten or inflate the punch. Jennie Tourel, circa 1969, posed this in her Russian accent: "What did Saint Peter say as Martin Luther King approached the pearly gates? 'Look who's coming to dinner.'" The amusement here lies not in the sauciness but in Tourel's substitution of "Look" for "Guess"; and it lies in the very fact of her telling a joke. Witty divas (like baby-kissing presidents) fill us with warmth because they are, for the moment, behaving just like you and me. Actually Jennie hadn't much humor—not, at least, in the American grain—so that her *attempt* at humor was all the more touching. Would this paragraph have the same point if she were alive today?

6 September

So impassioned is the need for dextrose that I have rushed into the drenched yard to pluck with bloody digits a quart of the season's last blackberries, plump and purple, flung them onto a hasty crust confected *n'importe comment* with oleo, brown sugar, oat flour and cinnamon, and thrust the mess into the stove. I type these words to keep torn fingers from removing too early the soggy batter from out the oven. But soon, soon, I shall gobble the entire tart, garnished with opulent dollops of whipped cream sweetened with artificial blackberry flavoring. It is three in the morning.

18 October

Hardly a day goes by, if it's fair when I cycle into town, that I don't pause for ten minutes at the Atheneum, the library where Mother and Father spend so much time whenever they visit Nantucket. It's a protectively quaint old-fashioned structure, and the smells are tantalizing: of pencil shavings, sweat and lavender, moldering paper and hot bread floating through the windows from the nearby bakery. It's nice just to sit there. It's also nice to catch up on periodicals—especially such now-dreary ones as the *New Republic*—that no one buys anymore. Thus with shock I read, in the current *Harper's*, Norman Podhoretz's polemic against peaceniks and fruits. Now, I will tolerate from even smart straights their repulsion for things gay, or in even dumb Jews their fear of more holocausts. But it's scary when a smart heterosexual Jew, presumably with both a sound mind and an artist's needs, becomes an ill-reasoned liberal-baiter. Just last Thursday Norman spoke to me on the phone, to turn down, oh so gently, the "Notes on Death" I'd submitted to *Commentary.* "They're just too personal," he explained, adding, "but I do love them, and we are on the same wavelength." Except that we aren't. Why sneer, rather than cleanly agree, when a poet laments the waste upon the battlefield of beautiful boys? What purpose can this or that corpse possibly serve? Isn't liking obviously better than hating? The question's not sentimental, but a reaction merely. I could wish Norman had accepted the "Notes" so that I could now withdraw them. His article ruined the afternoon.

New York
10 November

Some great music should never be performed.

Back from a labored rendition of Satie's *Socrate* at the new Beacon, where Calder's irrelevant decor stole the show crassly. It's not that I mind a lousy performance in itself (most performances of most things are lousy and one ends up not going); but when the highly literary though non-musical public (Sontag et alia) is hearing this piece for the first time, judging it solely through the rendition, then storing it away among avant-garde masterpieces now known, why do they feel unsatisfied?

I take more pleasure in my own crude renditions, since my imagination fills in the gaps.

Socrates' plea for an afterlife rests on the *donnée* of man's soul: the fact of the soul is as foregone a conclusion as the fact of the body. If there is no soul then all *Phaedo* collapses, except as poetry. But perhaps there is only a soul, and no body.

Scene. During his suicidal preparation (loading pistol, lighting gas, shaking out Nembutal) the phone rings. A friend wants advice: on the stock market, on dealing with new junctures in love, on how to resolve a Neapolitan sixth. He gives the advice, lucidly, wittily, correctly. Then hangs up and kills himself.

Awash in his own blood he wonders: Is a work of art that from which one is safe? Is the poem a bridge to danger? (Danger to the poet, that is. For the public a poem is ever a bridge to safety.)

Does art succeed when it fails? A suicide that fails—leaving the victim alive and therefore an observer of his own "demise"—succeeds. Here I lie in my life's blood grinning, and am I my art? Who takes thus this *coup de théâtre*?

If to suffer from unrequited love is a waste of time, why should the documentation of that love—rendering it as history, as art—be time wisely spent? (Such practical queries! when in reality the world is unreal.)

Nantucket
13 November

In retreat to the country to avoid the calls of town, I begin each day by reading. But books in Nantucket are worse than phones in Manhattan. Hackles rise, and righteous indignation lures me from work.

John Leonard, a stock reviewer, uneasy beyond his ken, asks where the Jews are in Cheever's stories, then quickly replies: Cheever is right to stick to what he "knows," uppercrust suburbia, and to avoid forays into foreign areas, like the homosexuality in *Falconer*. (When the straight mafia docs sanction homosexuality-as-subject, it never occurs to them that the writer just might have firsthand knowledge.) Now, you know and I know and Cheever knows that he does have first-hand knowledge of what it means for at least one person to harbor queer drives. I never thought I'd see the day wherein I criticize an author's material rather than how he deals with the material, but in his new (actually old) collection Cheever's a coward. The hero-genius in *The World of Apples* would, in life, more interestingly have gone off the deep end of pornography, and not ended reverting to "higher things." The story is lessened when grandeur is recontained. As to whether Cheever in "real life" should "come out" more, I can't say. I do feel he should defend his work against, say, Dick Cavett's listing of homosexuality with drugs and murder. Nothing, nothing goes far enough. The Royal Ballet, Steve Reich, even Ingmar Bergman. They're all we've got, so we inflate them. But good critics should tear them down, and stop making do.

Book critics do as a rule base comment on the work in question more than do music critics, if only because a book, no matter how original, is always concrete, music never. The so-called program note is always demanded of composers on the grounds that since they put ideas into notes they must know how to put the same ideas into words. (Is it not through words that we listen?) Now, to provide this note can be both risk and blessing, while refusal to provide it can be fatal. Reviewers rely as much on annotation as on what's annotated, chiding the composer if he hasn't done what he says he's done, lauding him if he has, but mocking him when he's a touch too explicative. Still: no annotation, no review. For critics lack abstract viewpoint. The public, meanwhile, enraged by jargon and lulled by myth (metric modulation and moonlit inspiration being the poles of sound-expounding), is yet disillusioned by the few facts that count: what the composer had for breakfast, who he was in love with, what models he plundered to get him going. The truth is that while there's nothing a composer can say that his music can't say better, his prose does maintain a sociological bearing, even though it's sand in the eyes of historians. Divulge the crude fact that your piece is concocted from scraps of unused juvenilia whose day has come, and listeners say, "It sounds like it," yet that's exactly what most of us do.

17 December

Tommy Schippers died last night. It finally happened, what all expected; one can strew his exhausted flesh as fertilizer now for others. Yet what of the blessed brain, his gift and enterprise and hot spark and waned beauty? They linger awhile, yes, and then linger no longer.

Philharmonic tonight with Shirley for Bernstein *Songfest*. Felicia high up in a box looking ashen, fragile, and so beautiful. Lenny glanced toward the box before turning to the audience to announce that the slow movement of Schumann's Second Symphony would be dedicated to Schippers.

Nantucket
29 December

Busy week before flying here Monday. Rehearsed daily with Donald. The 19th, tenth anniversary of meeting JH, and a party for Copland chez Jack Kelly. Next night, with Robert Phelps, trip through the snow (with white roses and Godiva chocolates) to visit the precious Janet Flanner at Natalia's. Stayed perhaps three hours during which Natalia filled the chasms of Janet's lapses by regaling us with tales of de Pachmann, one of those mad geniuses who, when divorced from his métier, seems merely moronic. Janet's already half in heaven, her every hesitant phrase and gesture being made in souvenir of ancient gestures and phrases, and one feels her hang on. For she forgets who we are from one five-minute period to the next, and after the several times she goes to the bathroom (she has many stiff drinks), imagines herself to be home in the Paris Ritz again. (Like Elizabeth Ames who at ninety talked in the next room with her mother and sister, each gone for fifty years.) Yet I'm at ease and learn from her, and admire her staunchly no less for yesterday than for today. Senility is surely agonizing for them too, who cannot help but know they're lost. . . . Later that evening, with David Del Tredici, souper au Poulailler for Lenny to celebrate the last performance of *Songfest*.

Next day, Wednesday, Rorems to dine. Thursday, eye doctor; recorded *Serenade* for Grenadilla in Rutgers Church; delivered essay on Pelléas to *Opera News*; attended Judy Collins's concert—spirited and stale (needs a change of menu). Friday, Christmas party at Boosey & Hawkes; picked up new glasses; dined at Istomin's with Francis Robinson. Saturday, Maggy to lunch; Judy for tea. Sunday, Christmas in Philly, then flew here.

Vacuumed, because at 6:30 the Conroys, spruced up, came by: Maggie and Frank and the two sons. Tomorrow JH flies back to New York, while I stay on for a week.

Rain. JH abstracted and very low. Night falls by 3:30 P.M.

New Year's Eve

Foraging through old treasures I come across these meaningless Sitwellian verses from a novel called (blush) *The Door to Sorrow's Chamber*, penned at age fifteen:

> And the sterile herons stare
> at the gold in Miriamne's hair

(Miriamne would have come from *Winterset*, which beguiled us then.) I go on with these notes:

> Why not:
> And the steriled branded heralds stare
> At the brandied bran in Brenda's hair (or: *brittle bran*)

(Pentameter, but not iambic, thus not heroic)

As the frigid herons stare
at the ridge in Brigid's hair,
barren bridges bear her,
bare as bugbears of Alaska,
dove I'll ask you is fair fair?
Alas! Q is fare for fairies fair,
Al Askew is far from fair
though fair to fairies, and fairies' fare.

Why keep a diary? I never write about the essential—my own music—because it, so to speak, writes about itself. Then do I keep a diary through notion of order, even posterity, to prove to myself there's a reason to have lived, though I only pretend to be talented—whatever that means—as people jump through hoops, and though the world too, and life itself, are fraudulent, adding up to a pointless zero? Whatever the purpose, I've writ here little this past year.

Glancing through the 1977 yearbook, on nearly every page is noted: JH depressed; tristresse de JH; JH in decline. Or: cats provoke sneezing; allergy attack; *crise d'éternuement*. Clearly Jim's breakdown dominates the year. Most of my writing's been in letters to him; we rented out the house for half the summer (while I went to Yaddo and California), so we were apart. What a different tone those letters have, on both sides, from our daily contact or from this self-directed journal. Well, toward that "notion of order," here are meager souvenirs, lacking the heat of on-the-spot recording:

May. Joan Crawford died. Sessions with Nan Talese (likeable and intelligent pawn of Simon & Schuster) for the new book. Recital by Steber at the Waldorf Hotel where Joe Machlis whispers, "It's like bumping into your best friend at a whorehouse." *Air Music* played twice in Saint Louis, and first proofs of *A Quaker Reader* corrected. Frequent visits with David Del Tredici and the Phelpses, and with Dr. Cohen for allergy shots. Death of John Maxon. *Annie Hall.* (Woody Allen's "deep" films are nice, but at the funny ones I sit like the Black Fairy at a party.) Beacon Baths.

June. Nantucket. No society, except for a fugitive hour with Mimsi & Robin Harbach, or with Frank and Cynthia Stewart of Cincinnati, who are Music Lovers. Three days back in NYC for Griffes taping on *Camera 3*, Peggy Jory, Roger E., etc. (Couldn't read my own script from the prompter *sans lunettes* so extemporized, more or less.) Nantucket again. Rain, rain. JH made a nonpareil ginger cheesecake. Morris in hospital. Evanston, for Northwestern ceremonies, then back here. *The Passenger* and *Network* on TV. Flew by private two-engine plane (Charlie's Flying Service) for 24 hours in East

Hampton to speak about my *Serenade* (well done by Elaine Bonazzi, etc.) in
Guild Hall; stayed with Heddy Baum and saw the Griffes broadcast, then
flew back in the same little plane skimming the waves through fog and thun-
derstorms next to a pilot who smelled bad. Visit from Anne Roiphe who
looks, but doesn't act, like Jane Bowles.

July. New York again. Ferocious heat. Doctors. Massive blackout on the
13th during which long, strange walk with JH and new friend K. Parents.
On the 16th noted: "Record heat wave continues and so does JH's unhappiness." Anxiously left him with K and flew to San Francisco. Two weeks as
Composer-in-Residence at Forest Meadows Festival at Dominican College
in San Raphael. Pleasant memories of seminude trombonists rushing to rehearsals amidst nuns in full regalia. Lectures, rehearsals, clinic for shots,
perfs. of my music incl. a ballet, by Stuart Sebastian, based on *Eleven Studies*, seminar with the would-be-crusty but actually docile Martin Bernhei-
mer, interviews, classes, the usual plus excursions into Sausalito and to Bo-
linas (to visit Don Allen and Bill Berkson) with Russell Oberlin. Indeed,
becoming friendly with Russell after all these years of admiring his sheer
musicality and magical voice (except for him, I can't abide countertenors any
more than boy sopranos, Donizetti, broccoli, leather pants, poodles, dominant sevenths, and Malcolm Lowry) was one of the two most agreeable California experiences. The other was Jessamyn West. We'd corresponded for
a year about her writings which were of such immeasureable help to the
composing of *A Quaker Reader*; without her epigraphs the music could have
been quite other. Yet, like so many literary folks she's immune to Euterpe;
she claimed already to know my diaries, but not my music. Resembles a
svelte squaw though like me is a Hoosier. Passed a day and an evening with
her family at their rambling house in the drastically parched Napa Valley. At
first the conversation was drawn solely from information better stated in our
books, with nothing left to say that we'd not already written. "I'm a book-
worm with a tin ear, except for words," she said, "so I wish you'd give yourself full time to composing on the typewriter."

Forlorn letters from JH, but with the courage at least to put them on paper. A brief paragraph from July 21st: "I cannot tell you how much I hope
the Elavil will be of help. You have seen how desperate I've been. I've even
thought the last several weeks of a lobotomy or something. The half-life of a
placid cow is a better alternative than destructive madness. My 'states' are
mostly a reaction to others, an obsessive concern with the effects I have on
them. I think that if Elavil can lower my level of concern that others approve
of me, then I can get out of the trap or quagmire of depending on others to
rate and grade me. Above all, I hope it might help me to inhabit my own in-

ner kingdom again. To 'return home to within' and to allow you to do so also."
(The reference is to the tenth movement of *A Quaker Reader* which has a
quote from the fifteenth-century Richard Howgill: "Return home to within,
sweep your Houses all. . . . The Groat is there . . . and here you will see
your Teacher, not removed into a Corner, but present.") That was five
months ago. Today JH is much worse, grinding not groat but sowing wild
oats with a teacher in the shape of the promiscuous and dangerous K. My
long years of drink do not inure me, any more than a parent, to JH's dalli-
ances—his making up for lost time, which is never made up, in the shade of
middle age.

On the 31st, after a pre-noon staging of my *Fables*, Russell and I dined in
Tiburon with Martin Frick. They then deposited me at the Hotel Jack Tar
on Geary Street (where the desk clerk called up to ask if I were *the* Ned Rorem), after which I went, dutifully and dreamily, to both the Liberty Baths
and Jack's Baths, and at dawn caught a series of vehicles that whisked me
from the Very General to the Very Particular, across the entire width of our
famous land to the few square yards six floors above 70th Street. Californians
are WASPs acting like Mexicans and consuming wheat germ to combat the
earthquake.

August. On the third—the dead of summer—gave a dinner party to introduce Cleve and Francine Gray to Molly Haskell and Andrew Sarris. (Can't
recall whether JH was present, and neither can he. Already then, as now, he
was away most nights at K's, although K was often elsewhere. For that morning is written simply: "Cut toenails, heat continues, sadness, sadness.") I
would never have thought Francine had her equal in electric no-nonsense
culture-chatter, commitment and concern to things that can't—or maybe
they can—be changed. Molly gives her a run for her money, and Andrew
too. The Sarrises, energy-wise, outshine the Grays.

From the 7th to the end of the month: Yaddo. Harnacks gave a party; Hortense asked, "How's Jim?" and in front of everyone I started to cry. Hortense
cool, inscrutable, because her daughter . . . Other guests included Nora
Sayre, Mary Cantwell, Daniel Fuchs, T. J. Anderson, Max Zimmer (Cheever's protégé), Patricia Blake. Frustration at being unable to help JH. I
wrote him: "Finally, of course, the help will come from yourself, as various
threads are re-gathered and start making sense again. Our brief separations
give me a clearer head, and probably they do the same for you. Try not to
resent them. I drink a lot of tea. Reading Margaret Drabble with disappointment. My love for you is the stabilizing factor of my existence, however it
may seem to you. I need your help as much as you need mine."

Finished two essays—"Notes on Death" for *Christopher Street* and

"Paris in the Spring" for *Antæus*—and the piece for guitar and flute, in nine movements, called *Romeo and Juliet*. Death of Elvis Presley. Announcement in the *Times* of an antiviral serum called Adenine Arabinoside for Herpes Simplex Encephalitis. Bought two small oils from David Vereano. Read Ambrose Bierce, Plato, Cervantes. Continual insomnia. Mary Cantwell claims that her cats were of great aid during her postpartum depression, and that Wallace could be JH's salvation. On the 21st, noted: "I am the oldest guest presently at Yaddo." Gave a big going-away party, as is required of any resident of The Pink Room, and left by car with Daniel Fuchs on the evening of the 24th.

The 28th, a Sunday, another heat wave with foul air. Touched when JH said that my parents, foregoing their habitual Friends Meeting, showed up at his Episcopalian Mass. Mother, probably more than anyone (certainly more than I), is in a position to empathize with JH's distress, as she was with Bill Flanagan.

September. Death of Ethel Waters on the 1st. During the next ten days, visits from: Pia Gilbert; the Rorems; David De Porte; K frequently (but JH bad off); Wilder Burnap; J. Cheever to say he'll be in Wauwinet this month; Judy Collins; Barbara Kolb with Charles Moss; Nan Talese. Visits to: Boosey & Hawkes; the baths; A.A. meeting on East 76th (a gay meeting, self-conscious, self-congratulatory, low-class); dentist; Nan Talese at Simon & Schuster, which resembles a lavish set for an Astaire-Rogers film but where (because of my modest advance?) I'm screened like a hijacker; Joe LeSueur; George Mendelssohn at Vox; a movie called *Crià*, which I liked but left in the middle of. Then to Nantucket. Deaths on the fourteenth of Stokowski, Robert Lowell, and Gustave Reese. JH arrived. On the sixteenth, death of Callas. Rorems arrived for a dark week, and when they left I missed them awfully. On the 27th, back to NYC for "The Listener's Room" with Seymour Barab, George Perle and Ben Weber, dress rehearsal of Musgrave opera, and Scola's movie *Una Giornata Particolare*, all in one day. Musgrave's premiere I've written of elsewhere.

October. He wants to play house with everyone, but won't see it through. Once he's wrenched a commitment he loses interest, surrounded by would-be (or he would have them be) Penelopes.

Ormandy does *Pilgrims* in Philly. Seymour Barab's all-American cello recital, with my three unpublished bonbons, *Andante* (1950), *Sifting* (1971), and *In Memory of My Feelings* (1959). Seymour, the instrumentalist, has influenced my string writing more than any composer, just as Nell Tangeman and Billie Holiday—their way with a song rather than the song itself—influenced my sense of vocal arch & ebb.

Six-day *séjour* of Pierre Quezel [PQ of 1957], as grave, charming and intelligent as of yore. A French-speaking *goûter* for him involving Helen Bishop, Tom & Nan Prentiss, Ellen Adler, and Richard Howard. *Pelléas* at the Met (Levine, fatally slow) to stimulate article for Robert Jacobson.

Nantucket for the second half of the month, rain, rain, rain, rain, until the 23rd and my 54th birthday. Visit to Loring Hayden's India Street abode, which makes the Collier Brothers' house seem like Craig's Wife's. Persistent aches in chest.

November. Accompanied baritone Bruce Fifer in Rorem recital at Frick estate, then long meal at the Popes's in Great Neck, during which JH, exhausted, fell asleep. Party at Machlis's for Alger Hiss, after which Club Baths briefly.

On the 12th, visit to Paul Jacobs in his marvelous new apartment on Riverside Drive, he played me Busoni; after which dined tête-à-tête chez Lenny Bernstein and spent the next six hours examining his weird, semi-successful cycle *Songfest*. One extraordinary aspect of Lenny (an aspect that almost defines him) is his willingness to expend on one person and without witnesses as much violent energy as he expends on an audience of thousands. Before playing the tape he lectured me on his intentions, on the "layers" of meaning of the poets (O'Hara, Millay, Whitman, Aiken, Stein and others), on the structure of the piece, on the need for an entire orchestra to frame the fragile verses. Like a cheetah he studied my every reaction—except I never react. I liked the music, with all its earthy pomp, although it suffers from inflation. Lenny cannot not be theatrical, yet his format demands a simpler accompaniment.

Paul Callaway's program at Riverside Church, then tea chez Charles-Henri Ford. Sunday the 20th, took Judy and my parents to hear my *Serenade* at the Guggenheim Museum, cordially reviewed by Rockwell. Flew to Nantucket the next day for Thanksgiving week. JH too, and K.

Frankenthaler and Balthus exhibits. The 28th, tea for Jan DeGaetani and Philip West, for whom I baked a Grand Marnier cake that made me sick. Snow. The 30th, tea (or rather lemon with hot water) for Francine. Later, Richard Howard came for meat loaf. I wanted Richard to explicate Wallace Stevens's *Sunday Morning*. For the past six months I've been working on the commission from the Saratoga Performing Arts Festival, an eight-movement symphony (which Ormandy will do next August) vaguely modeled after Stevens's eight-stanza poem, with unsung fragments plucked from each stanza as epigraphs ("Green freedom," "Passions of rain," "Indifferent blue," "Death is the mother of beauty," "Our insipid lutes," etc.). But I don't know what the poem means—because I don't know what any poem means, and Richard is supposed to. His canny approach was psychoanalytic: "What does this or that line remind you of?" "I think it reminds me of this or that." "You're absolutely right."

December. Finished *Sunday Morning* on the first day. Relapse of JH. With Shirley to party chez Machlis for Lukas Foss. Eightieth birthday dinner for Mother with Aline and Charles Boultenhouse. The Graffmans' silver wedding anniversary at Joanna Simon's; made them an elaborate anagram based on their names. Visits from Joel Thome, Barry Laine (to discuss a reading for The Glines), Paul Callaway. Visits to the dentist, the Borchardts, the *Nutcracker* with Morris, and the Philharmonic for John Corigliano's staggering and too-attractive Clarinet Concerto. (Too attractive, because it draws attention away from itself by drawing attention to itself.) Party for Alexis Weissenberg at Arnold Weissberger's. Buñuel's *Obscure Object of Desire.* Serkin at Carnegie Hall, unimaginably flat. Dined at Jerry & Ronit Lowenthal's. Rehearsed with Donald G. for recital next month in Texas. *Serenade* recorded for Grenadilla. Etcetera. Little of this was in the company of JH. Little of anything.

1978

Alone on Wesco Place. Bleak afternoon. Fat pheasant family in yard. A drink with Eugenie at the Benchleys' on Pleasant Street. Door to door, it's 670 paces (i.e., double steps, left-right, a bit less than two yards) from the back door to the A & P.

An unalloyed pleasure is to play and replay, on the old piano Eugenie's lent me (a Henry F. Miller, Boston), the Bach *Inventions*. My Kalmus edition, edited by Bischoff, is disgusting—so flytracked with ornamentation as to camouflage the notes. I never observe ornaments in Bach. I disapprove of ornaments, which pollute the pure line. A complete program of twenty-four Preludes, minus the Fugues, from the Wohltemperierte Klavier, balanced by Chopin's twenty-four.

Music, like blondes and then brunettes in movies, or masculine and then feminine actors, or vogue for circumcision, seems during the past two hundred fifty years to have alternated generationally between contrapuntal and harmonic periods. We've just emerged from emphatic counterpoint (Carter, etc.) into harmony again (Glass, Del Tredici, etc.).

Last night we invited to dine: Elliott and Helen Carter, Shirley Rhoads, and Russell Oberlin. Between their ringing of the downstairs doorbell and the arrival of the Carters at our sixth-floor apartment, JH had a relapse. On the phone with K, he began screaming, then weeping, then collapsing, and was hardly in a position to play host. In the middle of the meal he left the table, washed the dishes loudly, then left and didn't return until this morning. A strain. I recall little of the conversation, but the guests were models of decorum. Elliott's setting some Elizabeth Bishop poems. Which annoys me, though it shouldn't. Elizabeth doesn't belong to me. Yes she does.

10 January

To see again *Orphée* (as was the case last night) for the first time since its opening run on the Champs-Élysées in 1949, is to see Cocteau no less grand but far more funny. It's a broad farce, partly inadvertent, with Marais, electrically untalented, behaving like the grandest of fin-de-siècle prima donnas. Alas, poor Auric, I knew him as too smart to be right. His music, here as elsewhere in Cocteau-land, is far afield and too prevalent.

18 January

Dined at Elliott and Helen Carter's on 12th Street. (JH refused to go.) Guests, including me, all models of decorum. Home by cab with Paul Jacobs, whom I like more and more, the only musician I've ever known who, in growing older, has broadened rather than narrowed his outlook. In Paris during the fifties he sneered at Boulanger and Poulenc; today he laments what he missed (although he still lauds Boulez). He's also the only New York musician with whom one can discuss French (as opposed to German) culture. Elliott meanwhile is socially, with his quiet and generous manners, the reverse of his angry snarled muse. Yet his early ballets, heard now, are bland, characterless, thinned-down Copland.

Austin, Texas
28 January

Here with Donald for a recital on the campus and a series of classes. Party last night chez Paul Schmidt, who's on the language faculty. Visit to the extraordinary library, and view of the tower whence that man shot all those people. Tomorrow Donald flies to San Antonio with Robert Tobin (who came for the concert), and I return to New York.

Funny how in the twenty years we've worked together Donald and I have not become close friends. Yes, we're staunch colleagues, and he's the most satisfying of interpreters. Yes, while on the road we do take a meal or two together and exchange confidences. But mostly he keeps to his room, never goes to the post-concert party (which is often the *reason* for the concert), and lets me do the interviews. In New York my milieu, if I have one, does not overlap with Donald's, which is one of performers—mainly extrovert

singers. When we find ourselves together, it's nearly always for practice. Socially he seems wary of me, probably not so much because I so often chide
him for his right-wing politics as because he feels I don't speak his language.
Far from being lovers, which some outsiders assume (as they always assumed, wrongly, of Poulenc and Bernac), we retain a cool and exceedingly
fertile attitude of mutual respect. The fertility has produced healthy results,
so whatever we do have between us is for the best.

1 February

Went with JH to his shrink, Dr. Wood. Violently upsetting. I wept, while
they sat there and watched.

8 February

The first time I ever appeared before a Manhattan audience as an author
rather than as a composer was last night at the so-called Glines in the bowels
of the Bowery during the season's worst blizzard. (Shirley nobly accompanied me. JH didn't come.) Avoiding essays on art—The Glines is gay-
oriented, after all—I chose entries from the early years of this diary, about
the baths, Cocteau, drugs, Claude, alcohol, love, chichi stuff as befit the ambiance, and felt both at home and off center. A diary is by its nature not designed to be read aloud, much less read aloud by its author to a disparate
audience, as though it were literature. Yet my songs are a diary too, and so
are Brahms symphonies, and *War and Peace*.

16 February

Anita Ellis came over, late in the day, in order to say hello to Judy whom she'd
never met. They put on a great show for each other, effusing, looking theatrical and vital, like apples or gazelles. Then Judy took me to hear *Adriana
Lecouvreur*, of all things.

What could have led one (her fat photos?) to imagine that Caballé was
stentorian? She's a two-ton cuisinart exuding only egg whites, and the adu-
lation around this tedious invention only reconvinces me of the average opera buff's misdirection. Or am I misdirected in feeling that all feeling for all
music must be focused on, and judged from, the composer's vantage? Yet by
any vantage Caballé, since her vehicles are so weak (i.e., choice of repertory
and physical stamina), should be billed as no more than a latter-day Stich-
Randall.

Visit from a young clarinetist, Richard Stoltzman, whom I'd chatted with at John Corigliano's birthday party a few nights ago. Possibly because he's the picture of vulnerable credulity, like a bunny rabbit aspiring to both glory and anonymity (at Marlboro in 1973 he used conspicuously to sit yoga-fashion on the lawn and eat yogurt with closed eyes), I found myself meanly generalizing about the hopelessness of solo careers today, especially for woodwind players, whose vulgar repertory didn't amount to a hill of beans. He left sadly, and I later felt good and horrible.

1 March

Premiere of my *Romeo and Juliet* in Alice Tully Hall, with Ingrid Dingfelder playing flute, Herbert Levine, guitar. JH did come too, and Shirley and Judy, after dining here at home.

18 March

Three days last week in the sleet and slush of Virginia. Then, just now, three days at the NATS Convention in Chapel Hill, from which I returned tonight to find JH collapsed.

2 April

Low Sunday. JH's 38th birthday. We attended a pretty good performance by Golden Fleece Ltd. of my *Three Sisters Who Are Not Sisters* at a sordid little theater in the Ansonia Hotel.

7 April

Last winter Francine Gray invited me, and I accepted, to join her panel, called "Women and the Arts in 1920: Paris and New York," which was to take place this week at Rutgers during a two-day Conference on Women. Thus, although I generally arise at nine, I managed to find my path in a gentle rain across Central Park to the Libermans' town house this morning at eight, thence to drive with the Grays into Jersey. Francine's other guests were Thomas Hess for painting, Elizabeth Kendall for dance, and Cheryl Wall, who spoke for the Harlem Renaissance. We'd all met at my house last month to coordinate our acts (I made a huge pear tart and espresso coffee); now here we were again. After my speech—a formal twelve minutes of which I'm proud, and which Francine will ask her father to print in *Vogue*—who should show up but Geoffrey Hendricks, whom I'd not seen since we were pre-adolescents in the Friends Meeting of Chicago. "Hello Ned, from one gay Quaker composer to another." Tom Hess drove me back to New York, feeling put out that no one had warned him to prepare his lecture (he had rambled), and I went to a screening of Jim Bridges's new little movie—chamber music, in a way—about James Dean.

8 April

Funeral of Nicolas Nabokov this morning at the Russian Church on East 93rd. Arriving early, the only person I know is Elliott Carter. I've never been to a Russian funeral before, so what must I do? One stands. Hardly an hour for small talk, and Elliott turns away. The room fills. Madame Stravinsky arrives, glamorous, grief-stricken, is given a chair, bows her head. The service is moving and endless. Flowers into the open coffin. I feel out of place.

Alone to *What Price Hollywood* in the evening.

14 April

At eight A.M. Ormandy phones from Philadelphia, and since one never makes excuses to conductors, much less to Ormandy, I spend the next hour, without having used the bathroom, checking through the score of *Sunday Morning* measure by measure. Reassuring to discover that he knows it so much better, or at least differently, than I. The rest of the day was monstrously sad. JH: another catatonic crisis.

Although titled *Sunday Morning* who knows, including the composer, if this "tone poem" is unqualifiedly about anything at all? Music is music, not literature, and thus its pictorial and emotional targets are verbally non-describable. Even such broad terms as *sad* and *happy*, when applied to music, are mere conventions and constantly changing. If the minor mode meant merry in the Middle Ages, the major mode was obscene to the Spartans; in our time Kurt Weill uses spirited tangos as background to horror even as Poulenc uses jazz harmonies to illuminate high tragedy. With nonvocal music it is impossible to assert that a composer meant this or that, even when he calls a piece *The Pines of Rome*. Play *La Mer* for someone who's never heard it, tell him it represents three scenes of Paris—the market at dawn, traffic at noon, the Tuileries at dusk—and he will "see" these landbound images forever after. As to whether a composer's music is necessarily injected with his mood of the moment: that too is unprovable. A professional can compose love music when he's not in love just as he can compose a funeral march when he's on top of the world; he composes not from immediate impulse but from what he's learned about impulse.

16 April

Sunday. Shirley's Ravel recital at the Maison Française this afternoon, at which I joined her at the keys for *Ma mère l'oie* (and also accompanied tenor Joseph Porello in the Greek songs plus some of mine). Packed hall included, thank God, JH. Shirley looked pretty, and as a pianist she has everything—clarity, taste, a gentle power, precise fingers, sense of devotion—everything except confidence. Or, if she has confidence, it doesn't come over as exhibitionism, which every professional, even Serkin, possesses. (Glenn Gould has confidence but hates the public.) Like JH, who's as good a practitioner as Shirley, she doesn't relish showing off. Yet I would heed Shirley, as a critic of music of any period, ahead of any paid reviewer there is.

Reception at Tom & Helen Bishop's, after which I joined Rosette on 67th Street to view, yet again, *The Little Players.* I'm a minority of one, but this pair of marionettists, with all their cult and culture, always embarrasses me. Too coy.

17 April

Another young clarinetist, affable and very ambitious, named Stewart Newbold, has been after me to write him a quintet, and this evening he invited a bunch of people to hear him chez none other than Lee Radziwill. Her apartment turned out to be huge and red, with fifty gold straight-backed chairs; the bunch of people turned out to be rich know-nothings (except for Sam Barber, at his most ill-mannered, perhaps as put off by my presence as I by his); and Miss Radziwill, who reeled in at the last moment to give a little welcome in which she pronounced Mozart with a soft z, and who appeared unsure as to what this was all about.

28 April

Last night Lukas, with his Brooklyn Philharmonia, conducted my *Six Songs for High Voice and Orchestra* which hadn't been done complete since 1954 in Paris. Geanie Faulkner, who sang in Kirchner's opera, was the pretty able soloist. Despite my continuing bad cold and sore throat, we fly tomorrow to London.

Waldorf Hotel
London
13 May

Retracing the fortnight, our stay has worked, considering we're not used to sharing one room. (On a couple of nights I toted the mattress to the bathroom because of JH's snoring.) Considering his condition, he's been orderly and thorough about sightseeing, with and without me, especially to the Tate for his beloved Turners and to the Hotel Russell, which he's drawn to because of Bloomsbury's mystique. We've quarreled just once. JH feels I should relax about career, while I feel that Boosey & Hawkes is family. We've seen in some detail Russell Oberlin, who's here for the winter, John Lehmann, Ginny Becker, Jack Henderson, and a couple of plays: Joan Plowright in De Filippo's *Filumena*, and Gielgud in Julian Mitchell's *Half-Life*. Lunch at the Pig 'n' Whistle with Tony Botha of Johannesburg, who assures us that his land's malodorous reputation stems from media slander and that the Negroes are happy down there.

The very young Simon Rattle conducted a contemporary program, including a drabbish version of Messiaen's *Oiseaux exotiques*. On my own, visited Basil Horsfield and John Dayeen in their double house (across the road from the park in which on that very green grass the murder was perhaps committed in Antonioni's *Blow Up*) and gave a class in my songs to ten young British singers at the Guildhall School. (When they intone my settings of Tennyson and Blake, who am I to tell them, as I do in America, that it's inappropriate to roll their *r*'s?) Pleasant outings with Tony Fell and Tona Schercken. Tomorrow, before catching the afternoon plane, a three-hour taping at the BBC with Anthony Burton, and with mezzo Margaret Cable in a dozen songs. Too tired to write more.

New York
16 May

Hugh Hefner, attending shrieks of women (objecting to being objects) who dare him to wear a bunnytail attached to *his* behind, should reply: If bunnytails turned women on, sure men would wear them. Men as a sex would be only too happy to be used as objects if women wished it.

No: in fact, women do use men as objects, but differently, since their needs are different. If this difference—this admitting that pears aren't peaches but are just as tasty and as quick to rot—were brought into the open (rather than the fact that women don't act as men act in making the other sex abject or merry), the question could be broached. For women are just as good and wide, just as evil and narrow, as men.

But women are simply not passive. In grammar school we learned that a snatch is the most preemptively dictatorial of organs (is it an organ?) and calls the shots. (A wound, a constantly infected, unhealable wound, versus the rectum, a wee scarlet target, a strawberry bullet hole, if that's your dish.)

Two vaginal jokes, recalled from childhood:
1) First fairy: "Why is it called a cunt?"
   Second fairy: "My dear, haven't you ever seen one?"

2) Whore to the Innocent Boy: "Just examine closely. See, there aren't any teeth."
   Innocent Boy: "Of course there aren't any teeth. Look at the state of those gums."

19 May

If asked, "Who in France would you most like to see?" I would unhesitatingly answer the Aurics. All through the fifties they were daily neighbors in Hyères and stalwart companions in Paris. Georges was surely the best-rounded musician I've ever met, Nora the most personable painter. I last saw Georges in 1964, but I met with Nora in 1969 and again in 1973 during returns to Paris; both times she chastised me (no doubt rightly) for brief paragraphs about her mate in my books, both times I apologized and we kissed and made up.

This morning as I quit the studios of WQXR, who should arrive but the Aurics, in New York for the ballet *Tricolore*. My excitement is quickly tempered by these non sequiturs from Nora: "What you've written is mean. You're not in the phone book, but we couldn't have called you anyway; we're into a mad round of interviews, and none of the interviewers has ever heard of you." When I don't react, she repeats, *"Nous voulions te voir, mais on ne te connait pas"*—this with a smile, cutting me down to size by informing me (lest I not know it) that I am unknown in my native land, while her husband is the toast of the town. This meaningless cattiness left me less annoyed than sad at the prospect of two fewer people to call up when, if ever, I go back to France.

Came home to rehearse with Will Parker, in front of Joe LeSueur who sat with a cup of tea. Then back downtown to dine at Maggie Paley's with the Pitchford-Morgans. Gustavo's cat, Nemra, died today at the vet's.

27 May

A well-made journalist's title . . . (bad beginning).

In journalism a well-made title contains a key word that opens the door to a reader and lets him step down into the paragraphs.

Some people ask if I still keep a diary. I never did, and yes I do. Diaries are by definition daily; there's no definition as to what they contain, but usually they're "personal." No, I don't still keep one—at least not in the sense that I can still with a straight face inscribe a love affair (if I had one). Once there is the strong possibility that one's current diary will soon see print, it's not quite feasible—and not quite kosher—to write "Be still O heart" for a stranger's eye.

Some people feign astonishment at what they term my total recall: that I remember not only occurrences but exactly when they occurred. Yet why live, if only to forget each large or small happening, if only to let days flow in each end and out the other? Of course, much of my memory of experience lies not so much, perhaps, in the actual experience as in what I've written about the experience. Yet is that so different—the having written—from "merely" having lived? The past is a maze of conjecture, even about your own yesterday. Still, I'm disturbed that *they* are undisturbed that they can't remember, even incorrectly. Perhaps I *do* have a knack for reverting, for becoming again the historic person I was at any given time according to whom I'm with. (With Howard Moss, for example, I always act as I did—photographically. Etc.)

Visit from Edmund White bringing Simon Karlinsky, the eminent Russian specialist. The latter reminds me—since I, with my famous total recall, cannot recall—that he was in Honegger's class with me at the École Normale in 1950; remembers further that I said he had no gift as a composer and advised him to plough other fields. Well, I've blocked that out. Was I, even at my most arrogant (and shyness pushed me to say anything in order to say something), also so rude, so dumbly knowing? Today I apologize, embarrassed. But Karlinsky politely protests that my remark caused him to become what he became.

Passing remarks, like the Coctelian snowball whose casual cruelty was ignored or quickly forgotten by the remarker, shape us all. Karlinsky remembered too that I entered class that first day in a white raincoat. I *do* recall that coat. Jerry Robbins gave it to me, the coat Man Ray photographed me in two years later.

31 May

An Absolute Gift being officially published, Nan Talese invited us to dine in her beautiful house with Gay, John & Barbara Chancellor, Henry & Beverly Grunwald, and Grace Mirabella. Nan, with her pearly skin, Etruscan eyes, tactful voice, and exquisite habit of looking at you when you talk and not over your shoulder to see who's just come in, offered meal and company with a style that must make up for the budget of zero that Simon & Schuster plans for my book. This is not to reflect on Nan, whose patience and interest has been supportive, but on the crassness of the whole publishing racket.

7 June

Silky weather italicizes the inability to communicate with JH. From 9:00 to 1:00, recording of *A Quaker Reader* in Tully Hall by Raver for C.R.I. Haircut. Baths. Death of Romola Nijinska.

9 June

At Paul Jacobs, recital for a few friends of all the Busoni sonatas, which for all their "daring" are dry as dust. Later, Billy Masselos brought two students over (I'm not certain why), whose playing dazzled but who are shadows of their unique mentor. Tomorrow Nantucket for most of the summer, and things will be better.

Nantucket
28 June

A Ms. Barbara Rowes, on behalf of *People*, came last week and noted my every move for forty-eight hours. I am to be the subject of a four-page spread in that subtle magazine, but only if I discuss my financial status, which interests readers more than music.

Today photographer Harry Benson appeared and "shot" for five hours. We asked the Conroys for lunch, to lend a high moral tone, and JH also willingly posed. K is here too.

10 July

Evening picnic at Jetties Beach. Before we sup (but we have forgotten the mustard, forgotten the coffee thermos, indeed forgotten all staples) JH tests his new kite. Slowly he unwinds the long slack cord, fifty feet, a hundred feet, two hundred, until the thing floats high in the darkening sky. A flock of seagulls swoops past and one of their number is caught in the string, jerking and falling fast. The others withdraw shrieking to the beach where they alight and sit like a chorus.

JH is marvelous with animals (is that the word? he's comprehending, treats them as peers). Gradually, gradually, seeing that the great entangled gull now struggles in water and may drown in panic, he rewinds the cord, wading through the shallow surf toward the bird even while easing the bird out of the deep toward him, tensing the cord, talking and talking and talking so softly. Like Androcles with the lion JH tends the nearly inextricably snared wing and legs, cajoling, soothing, fanning, releasing, and the bird knows a friend when he sees one and does not lash back with his beak, except lightly by reflex, unhurting. The snarls unwound, JH plucks the creature from the sea, carries it ashore like an offering, releases it. The gull stands poised, hops a few paces, then flies low over the sand toward its brethren. They all take off and fade into the night.

13 July

Arrival of Paul Callaway for twenty-four hours to discuss projected performances of *Letters From Paris* in Washington this fall and of *A Quaker Reader* at Trinity in New York. For sightseeing we take him to the town dump, brightly smoky like Moroccan wastelands, then to lunch at The Porch in Sconset, and to dine at India House.

How more-than-grateful I am for Paul's continuing interest since our Chicago meeting through Leo Sowerby when I was sixteen. Others have three Marys, but I've always had three Pauls—Goodman, Bowles, Callaway—as models whose approval I've sought since adolescence and in whose work my interest stays unflagged. There is no truer musician than Paul, standing always behind and not in front of the score.

Finished review of Shaw's music reviews for the Chicago *Tribune*.

Call from Saratoga to ask, out of the blue, if I'll dedicate the *Sunday Morning* premiere there next month to Nelson Rockefeller. Mr. Rockefeller, I'm informed, has been a stalwart friend of the Performing Arts Center, and plans to attend the Philadelphia Orchestra's performance there. Telling them to call back in an hour, I consult JH. "Well, Lorenzo de Medici had his Attica too, but was good to the arts." So I tell SPAC okay. Still, I'm apprehensive that the billionaire's mere presence will spoil the show.

Brief week in NYC to edit tape of *Quaker Reader* and to discuss with Bob
Jacobson (over lunch, *Café des Artistes*, of a spun-gold omelet, *baveuse*,
with cheese) the possibility of something on Bizet for the next of what have
become annual tracts for *Opera News*. Dined with parents, with Joe Le-
Sueur, with the Graffmans (took Judy; there were also the Istomins and Shirley), and had a rehearsal with Robert White and his sweetly clangorous and
accurate tenor, during which Gustavo arrived in tears, agitated and abandoned, to have me cash a check so that he could take a bus to anywhere. Visit
from Jeanne Kirstein, the Cincinnati pianist who, with her cellist husband
Jack, has commissioned a double concerto to be played next year with their
city's orchestra. It's madly flattering to be invited, so soon after *Air Music*,
to compose another big piece for that group; yet Mrs. Kirstein and I do not
see eye to eye, and I wonder why they chose me? JH in Provincetown with
K. My flight back to Nantucket Sunday was cancelled at the last moment
without cause by the piggish Air New England, so shuttled to Boston and
took Nor-East.

Chavez dead at 79. Ruth Laredo, resembling a Wee Queen of Israel in
skin tight tangerine silk, played her annual recital last night at the Unitarian
Church with enviable aplomb, especially her signature, *La Valse*. She's a
Romantic, in that her left hand consistently anticipates her right and in that
she is unaware of this. (Perhaps Classical pianists had this mannerism—who
knows?—but nobody did when I was growing up.) Ruth is staying across the
street, so we see her constantly and happily.

John Myers came by ferry from Oak Bluffs with Arthur Cady to spend a
long hot day, out of place in a rural setting, and insisted on trimming the let-
tuce and scallions before I made salad. Cady's a dead ringer (a live ringer) for
Herbert Machiz. *Plus ça change . . .*

Francine Gray and Cleve are very much here again this summer, Francine
doing an "in depth" portrait of the island for *Vogue*, to be garnished by the
photographs of Inge Morath. Their voguish entourage, again on Mill Street,
includes Richard Avedon, about whom, when I ask if he's straight or gay,
Francine answers curtly, "Oh, straight"—as though to suppose otherwise
were an aspersion. Indeed, it's hard to know what to make of Francine's out-
of-date compulsion for being up-to-date and not wasting a minute, when she
comes out with: "This morning while taking my bath, and knowing I'd be
seeing you later, I asked myself how I'd feel if one of my sons turned out to
be homosexual, and answered that I'd be disturbed." A tasteful remark? Yet

I'm fond of Francine; there's no one like her, with that anorexic panache and ski-jump nose.

JH, meanwhile, lives on the edge; the more unhappy, the handsomer he grows.

Birds that come daily to feed from the pan of grain in the backyard: red-winged blackbirds; crows; song sparrows with slightly crimsoner wings than the city variety; goldfinches, which sometimes arrive in flocks and flutter among the bank of ten thousand daisies; grackles (or starlings), whose scrawny children, bigger than they, screech to be fed; bluejays (occasionally); one male cardinal; mourning doves; ring-necked pheasants (one scarlet-bibbed male with as many as five females, rain or shine). Also gulls by the dozen, not for grain but for the more elegant garbage; similarly young robins, for the worms. Rabbits too, which as in Eden join the pheasants but remain aloof from the other birds.

> *Archibald*: With a voice like . . .
> *Pamela*: Like what, dearest?
> *Archibald*: Like summer clouds I guess. Like purple caramels, like love.
> *Pamela*: Oh my.
> *Archibald*: Sing do.
> *Pamela* (singing): I prefer sour mustard
>   to gold lemon custard
>   and would take a case of scabies
>   to a roomful of babies.
>   I hate a stiff dick,
>   and rather loathe sex.
>   I like folks who are sick
>   and adore broken necks.

A soprano asked what the clarinet signifies in *Ariel*, and I couldn't answer. Yet it's an important question. (If I had a pupil, he wouldn't be permitted to use an extra instrument with the voice without a reason.) The clarinet signifies the alter ego, I guess—Plath's blurred otherness—though I didn't know this eight years ago, when the piece was composed.

Richard Avedon, to whom I say his book of portraits is perhaps cruel, an-

swers edgily (he's heard it before) that the book is not cruel. Yet that's not for
him to say, it's for the book to say. Himself meanwhile is chic as Sondheim's
Ladies Who Lunch, ladies sneered at by their very inventors, unfairly I feel.

15 August

Avedon, to whom I'd expressed jitters about the *People* piece, phoned to say
it's out, nothing to worry about. Rushed to the Hub, grabbed a copy, read it
with horror. The caption: "Composer, Author, Critic, Matter-Of-Fact Gay,
Ned Rorem Is an American Phenomenon." (What will Mr. Rockefeller
think!) The Benson photos are warm and artful but the text is trash.

Visit from Inge Morath to take pictures along the back fence, joined two
hours later by Arthur Miller, with Francine and Joel Conarroe (of Modern
Language Association), also Eugenie. JH made an almond-flavored cheesecake. Miller, sexy, intelligent, unmusical but aware of his work's musical
potential.

Yaddo (Saratoga)
26 August

Unusual week. The familiar Pink Room of West House, but my position
here is no longer as inmate but as guest, Curt having used the *Sunday Morning* premiere as publicity for Yaddo, giving a cocktail in my honor in the
Mansion on Tuesday for The Rich—eager folk with a genuine wish to witness Creation (though wishing does not comprehension make). The regulars
treat me as an outsider, which in fact I am, being off campus much of the
time. But Patricka Blake is here, and Stephen Dixon, Donald Justice, David
Vereano, and Ruth Orkin with her camera. Yesterday at dawn Judy, *toujours
fidèle*, arrived with her bearded companion, Louis Nelson, to stay at the
Gideon Putman Hotel where the Ormandys too are staying, and Sylvia
Goldstein also drove up with her friend, Julie Horowitz. The final rehearsal
(the only one I attended) unfolded *Sunday Morning* as a work of such glittering orchestral professionalism that I hardly realized it was by me. Ormandy, as always, deferred, asking for suggestions, and, as always, I made
none, knowing that suggestions would be an insult. In fact, there weren't
any to make. Much had been settled at our pre-rehearsal confab when (as
with Schippers, two years ago, who asked permission to remove the most
difficult movement of *Air Music*, and I refused) the Maestro, among other
things, asked permission to delete the seventh section, "A Ring of Men,"
saying it was just too complicated rhythmically. How could I comment on
such a truncation except by saying, "You and only you can pull it off, Mae-

stro"? Indeed, at the performance last night this six-minute timpani solo in
7/4 embellished with ever-more-loudly shrieking trumpets that climb to orgasm and then wilt into a grotesque morass, was pulled off sensationally. At
the performance Nelson and Happy Rockefeller did show up, amidst a Niagara of flashblubs and secret service men, after which, ensconced in their
box, they were apparently well behaved. (It's said that Rockefeller, like most
dyslexics, can't sit still for more than a minute, even at baseball games.) And
yes, the program did contain a conspicuous announcement of the dedication, portraying me, at least in my eyes, as *arriviste* and fool. Dined with
Hortense and Curt and sat with them during my piece, after which I rushed
on stage to take a bow, bending so low that my glasses slid conspicuously
from my breast pocket and into the front row.

In the Green Room, Emanuel Ax, who had played the Chopin F-minor,
said he planned to record my *Études*, a cloying untruth.

Party then at the Patrons Club consisting of three factions: my entourage
of impecunious Yaddo geniuses plus Judy and Sylvia; Rockefeller's entourage; Ormandy's. When I entered, Happy, a handsome strapping lass in
blood-red velvet, approached and, gazing down at me from her considerable
height, spoke with great ease about nothing (during which all I could think
about was her mastectomy), then introduced me to her spouse. At which
point everyone pretended to go on talking, but actually quieted down so as
to hear what *we* would say, attending with sidelong glances. (Stephen Dixon
later said he had heard Rocky exclaim in his best Hey Fella manner, "Say,
I wanna meet that guy.") Well, what do you talk about with Rockefeller?
Painting, mostly, and his Albany mall which I saw last Sunday, and one mutual acquaintance, Philip Johnson, but not music, which he's smart enough
to avoid. He's attractive, radiant even, in the way that The Enemy can be
radiant. "Happy tells me you write books, too." I offered to send him one,
but when I asked where to, he said simply, "Any of the addresses will do."

This morning Sylvia and Julie, Judy and Louis all came out to Yaddo to
sniff the rose garden and to have brunch with Curt and Hortense. Discussion mostly of copyright and finance, in which Sylvia shines and with which
Curt is preoccupied.

After two minutes in the new Saratoga Bookstore I had to leave. The place
was well stocked and with pleasant ambiance (a fire blazed, a woman with
braids sat reading Kafka), but the radio blaring country music was too intrusive for concentrated browsing. In New York too I've noticed this: hangouts
like health stores and head shops you'd think would be opposed to such
digestive hindrance to hearing yourself at any price.

I don't know why, but young people today who read their Kafka (as well as

Shakespeare) and who like de Kooning (as well as Raphael), do not listen to the "equivalent" music. Never in a bookstore or art gallery do we hear Monteverdi or Machaut or Webern or von Weber. Ideally, of course, one would prefer silence in these locations, and I'm opposed to Rizzoli's policy of "good music" as background for buying.

O the dithyrambs I confected around the Beatles years ago! Today I'm more than indifferent, I'm hostile. Pop is inherently wrong by being preemptive. Each summer the Schaefer Festival in Central Park not only drowns the contiguous opera concerts in another part of the forest (like a great sow who, oblivious to her runts, smothers them), but forty thousand West Side families become captive audience to the din. This is no comment on the quality of the music, although overstatement is always suspect.

Virgil Thomson (calmly to Hortense, who is annoyed that guests ignore him): "When I find myself among those who don't know my name, I know I'm in the real world."

New York
18 September

The past month in Nantucket was a period of work, mainly on the *Double Concerto* for the Cincinnati people. Weather continually sapphirine. Saw Francine often. Now New York. Today at noon in Tully Hall, "A Remembrance for Felicia Montealegre." At five, Tennessee at the Gotham Book Mart. At nine, *The Eyes of Laura Mars*.

Philadelphia
Barclay Hotel
23 September

Here for the Philadelphia premiere of *Sunday Morning*, with the orchestra playing on home ground. Holly Stevens came down especially from Connecticut and is staying with the Buttels (he's a Wallace Stevens scholar) on Front Street. She reminds me in her forthrightness of Jessamyn West, is tough and likeable, drinks, and claims to have all but forgotten the poem, *Sunday Morning*. Refuses to be photographed. When the name Ives is mentioned as a contemporary of her father, she says, "Dad thought Ives had no talent."

This is the fifth work of mine Ormandy has championed and, since he's twice taken my pieces on tour (*Eagles* and *Pilgrims*), tonight makes about the fiftieth time he's conducted me. Yet we scarcely know each other (he still calls me Mister Rorem), have never broken bread, nor in twenty-two years has he ever expressed an opinion about my music. In this he's similar to Steinberg who, before he died last May, also played much of my music but never said what he thought of it. I adore this rapport—this mute, cold love— with the vanishing breed of absolute monarch, European stars. After the concert I introduced Holly to Ormandy, but he was unclear about her identity, as he probably is about the identity of her parent. Then we all went to the Buttels', we being Rosemary & me, Morris, Kit & Sonia Davis, Stuart & Doris Pope. (JH came down for yesterday's performance.) Good reviews. Back to Nantucket on Monday so will miss the third performance.

> *Nantucket*
> *3 October*

Dream, night before last: Robert Phelps, conniving with Richard Cumming, murders two French prostitutes and shifts the blame on me. He attends my trial, silently.

Dream, last night: Richard Rodney Bennett, playing four hands with Debussy (who later becomes Debussy's widow), ousts me from the room and onto the stage, naked, where I am shamed then finally forgotten by all of Paris.

Titles from a dream: Coming Back as Mary

> *Rire Jaune*: Laughing Yellow

> The Relief of Failure

In England surrounded by people with big granite thighs who drop their *h*'s. As a rule women don't commit bloody crimes but they perpetrate them. Judith or Lizzie Borden aren't the rule, but the torsos of prostitutes discovered in Times Square hotels are. Would another woman have . . . have *caused* such torsos?

With a buccaneer mustache and sideburns shaped like Italy. The room glowed strangely, happily, like the inside of a cantaloupe.

Call this diary *A Night Book*, or merely *Night Book*.

Titles: Alan Dreaming

Poem: V.S.O.P. is just N.G. to the W.C.T.U.

> While DNA is TNT to the D.A.R., 'tis true.

> Is the E.R.A. what the N.R.A. once was, U or non-U?

> I long to swallow a leech and a needle, I want to F, don't U?

The fact, my dove, that we forget your name because you're not as famous as your mate, must not imply that you won't fetch as high a price on God's auction block.

Nantucket's the mainland to Tuckernuck.

4 October

Dark rain out there, vaporisers buzzing in here. Alone in Nantucket with television, falling leaves, books, and orchestration. My society is in watching the arrogant pheasants from the kitchen window and in speaking by phone with JH for four minutes each afternoon at six.

8 October

Valium for insomnia. Rain. Working on the concerto. Also writing a statement called *Messiaen and Carter on Their Birthdays* to be uttered aloud into a microphone for the BBC next month, then printed in the TLS. Tonight, watched Leontyne's concert at the White House. She sang *The Silver Swan*, and Jim Lehrer, the announcer, grossly mispronounced my name.

Cleaned house, changed sheets, shopped, because tomorrow, ah joy, JH flies here. Then Rosemary on Wednesday. She'll stay in the house while we're away the following week.

12 October

The opposite of a hoarder of pieces of string, I need to clean out, throw away, empty ashtrays, spit. Once they were transcribed neatly, I used to incinerate notebooks and manuscripts, proud of my beautifully inked copy, which served for eventual publication. Then I learned, for posterity and taxes, to keep all. It goes against nature, but today I clasp, ghoulishly wondering where now are those masses of deep-felt letters to Joe Adamiak, to Henri Fourtine, to Marie Laure, notes to dead lovers, which when reread so come back to life (the lovers, not the letters).

Letters to myself, like this diary, I treasure but don't covet. A diary's an embarrassment we love, like a pet spaniel humping a stranger's leg. Or old poems, like the "Sestina for Old Odors" from 1957. Is there a sestina by anyone that says anything, or even that works virtuosically? We speak of certain finished works as being deceptively easy. The sestina is deceptively complex—anyone can compose one on the spot with a semblance of meaning, although no sestina has meaning not more clearly stated in prose. (And no, this isn't true for all poetry.) Maybe music's the final home for the form. If it is a conceit to title a musical piece *Sonnet*, as Liszt did, it would not be so with *Sestina*. Music can't rhyme, but like a sestina it can have literal echoes, and even, should you want them, iambic meters.

For an autobiography, a logical and legitimate scenario could be built from other people's letters, especially love letters. Who has the nerve for plunging into those tear-filled trunks? To spend too long there means life is past. Yet such letters make landmarks. Who was I, or who did I think I was, when X thirty years ago sent those unhappy words, or Y twenty years ago, or Z ten? Alone the memento box labeled "Marie Laure" provides a portrait of both her and me at a fixed point in French history.

Love letters are the food of retrospect, introspect, and extroversion. What about hate letters? And business letters?

Many of the greatest books have happy endings. *Middlemarch. A Room with a View.* Any others?

How is my actual death conceivable when my idea of death exists only in— indeed, was conceived only by—myself, never in you (even if you *are* Death), and must, so to speak, die with me?

22 October

Three days last week doing a dance at Coral Gables—several dances, actually. The most impressive, least depressing, corner of Florida seems to be Parrot Jungle, which was shown to me only an hour before I took the plane back.

Some people twenty or forty may seem to be thirty or fifty, but no one fifty or thirty truly looks forty or twenty. JH insists that we all look our age, but some look it better than others.

People say my face belies my years. Why is it a compliment to look young? What's wrong with looking one's age? True, to "look old" is to slim down the chances of getting laid. But what are these "chances"? Are they American only? Is sex just for the young? Yes, maybe.

And so tomorrow, at the vast party planned by JH here, I turn fifty-five, and not only youth but the past as concept slide into a new dimension. On the day you discover that grown-ups don't have the answers, you yourself have become grown-up.

Francine and I are both now hesitant about losing our heads through our bodies: great sex takes so much time. The more fools we, in our flight from folly.

Insomnia's the negative side to that coin which depicts the fight betwixt the flesh and the intellect of a single person. Sex is the cure for insomnia. They say.

(Sketch a profile of Francine: her suave naïveté, her "Malheurs de Sophie" nose, her literary wisdom and lacunae, her beauty at forty-eight.)

24 October

Then last night, from 5:00 to 9:00, JH gave an enormous birthday party—about a hundred souls—for me here. Promptly at five when the doorbell rang (it turned out to be the caterer with the cake) JH, in his eagerness to answer, deeply gashed his head on a cupboard door. Ice cubes and peroxide were of some help. I was preoccupied for the next four hours (mindful of last January 6). No one seemed to notice, but later Linda Asher offered in vain to take him to the hospital. Today the wound looks ugly but healthy. As for Wallace, we allowed him free rein, and he was the life of the party.

Washington D.C.
Chez Callaway
30 October

Paul tonight conducted his small chorus and orchestra, at the over-resonant Coolidge Auditorium of the Library of Congress, in a flawless version of *Letters from Paris*. Janet & Natalia were to have come (indeed, the Library presented a vast exhibition of Flanner papers in glass cases during intermission) but at the last minute Janet's health gave way.

Nantucket
8 November

Warm. Beach at Pocomo with JH. The swans . . .

Robert phoned to say that Janet Flanner died last night. Write on how this occurred only a week after our piece was played and sung in Washington. On how JH says that she was our best journalist because, although without ideas of her own, she transliterated the ideas of others into a language of her own. On how I cried. Because all those candles that flicker so high and so very bright (though not at both ends, in Janet's case) must be snuffed utterly.

9 November

What do they *want*, these women? I mean the unliberated types like Schlafly or our bright new Miss America. How can it benefit them to remain unequal? Although even they are for same pay for same job, they do seem to fear being drafted into the military while relinquishing home economics to "their men." Well, these women are no wilting lilies, are tough, are even maybe brave, so it's not passivity they seek to preserve. What they want—what they want to *preserve*—is, of course, power, the privileges of their sex, which are exemption and dictation. Anita Bryant's pathological horror of male homosexuality (she never discusses female homosexuality) is fear of being forsaken, of being useless to men, of being unable to dominate through feminine wiles. Lesbians solved the problem of "their men" by ignoring them, while liberated straight females, presumably without manipulation, socialize with gay and straight men on an intellectual basis. But Bryant even frowns mockingly on what we used to call male bonding between heterosexuals.

"It's not enough that I succeed, my friends must fail," was Maugham's notorious phrase, and all artists nod uneasily. Or does this contention merely reveal my stingy spirit? John Lahr's new portrait of Joe Orton revives like yesterday that uncommon yet logical murder-suicide of eleven summers ago, the acted-out extension of so many thwarted dramas. (Bill Flanagan ideally would have killed Edward Albee before killing himself.)

When I attended Orton's posthumous play, *What the Butler Saw*, I was pleased to find it fine. Am I good in being pleased? In whose eyes—yours, mine, or theirs? What is the stimulus? Would it be bad to find it bad?

The play is good; alas! there will be no more.

The play is good; thank God! there will be no more.

Suppose the play were bad? Would it matter then that Orton is dead? But if he'd lived, he might have improved.

Should one be sad it's good, because the fount's shut off, or glad it's good, because at least (so sadly) he completed it by curtain time?

Is posing these questions—of which twenty more convolutions might be turned—a sign, as people say, of an ungenerous character?

Finished review of Cosima Wagner's *Diaries* for the *Washington Post's Book World*.

15 *November*

Bright spring day. Death of Margaret Mead, a frequent communicant at JH's church, St. Matthew's & St. Timothy's. Made a pear sherbet in the blender with: 5 peeled pears, ¾ cup sugar, 2 tablespoons fresh lime juice, 1 egg white, 1 pint heavy cream. (For non-alcoholics, a dash of Poire Williams adds zest.)

Jack Kirstein in Cincinnati, to whom I sent a progress report describing the piece as a divertissement, replies: "Divertissement seems to indicate something frothy, light, charming. Jeanne's performance fortes are poetry, elegance, liquidity, nuance, color, insight and dramatic power. I am serious, emotionally profound—although, alas, not sufficiently profound intellectually—and I am most comfortable with material of substance. Do we have a problem here?"

JH advises me simply to change the title to *Concerto Profundo*, since the Kirsteins and I, though perhaps musically sympathetic, don't speak the same English, and since music (which is never too vague for words, always too precise) only means whatever the composer tells you, in words, that it means. Meanwhile, what's wrong with froth, light, charm? Emotional profundity is for sophomore bull sessions. Since everyone imagines himself to be emotionally profound (as opposed to unemotionally profound?), conscious frivolity, i.e., comedy—which, at its most "profound," comes only through, and thus comprises, tragedy—is what must be cultivated. Depth is there or it isn't, but it can't be bought.

Make an essay on the virtues of superficiality, on whether art cannot be snared and frozen in a sad clean ray of red light or in a tight flock of feathers as well as in a Greco crucifixion or in a Bach mass. No one's glibber than he who sees forever deep. Tragedy examines two sides of one mask, but comedy examines three.

Re frivolity: the moment—the *value* of it—can never come again, whether it be savoring a pear sherbet in Piazza Navona as we gaze into each other's features, or learning the horrors steaming on Three Mile Island. The star of an Antonioni movie is not the groaning heroine but the waving trees.

27 November

The island weather has grown inclement, though only a week ago there was still a mass of peppermint-colored roses in the pink of condition on the back fence, and crabgrass was heartily thrusting forth its mean green tongues, asking to be mown. Then the sky clouded over, chilliness set in, and I had to "bleed" the clogged radiators in preparation for Thanksgiving. Alone for two weeks working, I also saw Dr. Voorhees regularly for my shots and for Valium. (The shots have definitely suppressed the sneezing, even the anxiety of suffocation, and longing for the first frost. Yet JH recently said that his own decline began when, two years ago at the height of my frustration, I groaned, "I hate Nantucket." With those three words his defense crumpled—his optimism about this house, and his sense of me as a support, now a whining rag.)

On the 21st Mother and Father arrived, and also JH. Next day K came too, preemptive as ever. Thursday we fixed an ambitious meal—turkey, squash pie, etc.—during which the heat failed. Harbor Fuel Company, to its credit, arrived within the hour. Heavy rain Friday. Next day JH left with K. So I'm here with my parents. We too would normally be gone, but the sky forbids.

Last evening, as we watched with disbelief the unfolding of the drama in Guyana (Jim Jones and the colossal suicide), Father spilled his aperitif all over the coffee table. As I tidied up, he began to sob terribly. When he regained control, he said, "I'm not crying because of that"—a gesture toward the TV set—"but because the whole world seems sad. Even love seems so tenuous." Mother said nothing; but she and Father are the center of each other's world. An hour's respite. Then we cheerfully ate leftovers.

Today, packed and bundled up, we taxied through sleet to the airport, hung around, all flights cancelled, returned here, unpacked, walked to The Thistle for a wretched supper, and have decided to wait it out. They, and I too, are too old for such exhausting false alarms.

How old were Rosemary and I—eleven and ten?—when Paul Tillich had his "date" with Mother? It would have been in the mid-1930s when Tillich reached Chicago from Hitler's Germany for a semester at the university. Father, as was often the case, was on the road, but completely approving of Mother's sortie with a staunch colleague from the theology department. I was theoretically asleep when Tillich brought Mother home; but as it happened, on that very day grades had been issued, and I'd flunked three courses. So when Rosemary tapped on my door I was wide-eyed and worrying. "Come out to the kitchen," she said. By pushing the swinging door a fraction we got a peek at the parlor, where Professor Tillich was embracing Mother exactly as John Gilbert embraced Greta Garbo, while Mother laughed and protested ever so mildly. With our innocent voices we called out. Mother, angry, chided us for being up. Tillich, a gentleman, quit the premises. My sole remark: "If you don't tell Father about my bad grades, I won't tell him about you and Mr. Tillich."

New York
5 December

Arnold Weissberger's party to honor Vera Stravinsky on her ninetieth birthday. In the cab JH and I secretly hoped it would be a movie-star party of the kind Arnold's notorious for, but feared it could be a bid toward musical ambiance. I had brought as a token—what do you give to a famous widow you do not know?—a ten-dollar ceramic box, prettily wrapped.

It turned out to be a movie-star party, with Madame Stravinsky seated beautifully in the midst of it all. Next to her were female Russian suppliants, plus Robert Craft who eyed me warily (we've recently altercated within the pages of the *New York Review*). "What's in that box?" he asked, "a big eraser?" The box duly presented, we withdrew to talk with movie stars so that Madame Stravinsky could receive other homages. But the guests were intimidated; nobody spoke to her much. And when we departed an hour later we observed that nobody else had given her a present.

11 December

Premiere of Elliott Carter's *Syringa*. Loathed every note. Based on John Ashbery's disturbing, complex yet direct verses, the music is truly pretentious: Elliott has superimposed (or subimposed) a Greek text that runs parallel to John's—so cultured and so superfluous. Why not allow the words to sing themselves—and allow the singers to *sing*? His premise for word-setting is too opposed to mine for me ever to see things his way. Nor do I believe that the audience believed in what they so dithyrambically applauded (during which Elliott neglected to acknowledge John). Party later at Joe Machlis's where Helen—though not Elliott (God isn't grateful)—thanked me for the BBC birthday homage. Perhaps Elliott's displeased at being linked to Messiaen; he once did allow in print that Messiaen's music is "worse than vulgar," and vulgar for Elliott is bad. Or perhaps he sensed that my phrase "I love the music of each one" is a lie. Well, it wasn't when I wrote it, because as recently as last summer I was still brainwashed by the global reign of terror propounding the myth that Carter is the one Important Composer of our time. The cause, or need, for this myth will be the subject for another sermon. Meanwhile, I'm now not embarrassed to admit that I've never found an ounce of real music in his entire catalogue.

While on the subject of homages: my little memoir of Janet Flanner just appeared in *Gaysweek*, with a beautiful layout of pictures, music, and prose.

And while on the subject of word-setting: I've been examining Miriam Gideon's earnest *Questions on Nature*. So strongly do I feel about a composer's repetition of words not repeated in the poem he is musicalizing, that once the rule is transgressed I am (doubtless unfairly) deaf to the result. In seven sonic strophes Miriam has set—for voice, piano, oboe, bells and gong—seven charming prose queries about the universe as presumably voiced through a child, using sentences (chapter headings, actually) by a twelfth-century English philosopher named Adelard of Bath. The straightforward words are straightforwardly pitched and arched and elongated until the sixth stanza, which begins, "Why we hear echoes. . ." Miriam, in a choice so dangerously obvious that I blush, has repeated thrice the word *echoes* (and she does likewise four lines later with "joy"). If she must echo "echoes," could not the human voice hold the "o" while the other instruments, one by one, echo the syllables, perhaps in inversion, at other octaves? That is a *musical* solution, which does not ridicule the author. Still, even as the greatest singers (Lenya, Holiday, Tourel, Piaf) just stand there and get the words out without recourse to hand movement, much less to "meaning" on each adjective, so composers need only to set words in a manner to make them comprehended at one hearing, without italicizing their sense.

15 December

When anyone mentions the Six Million I stop listening. Until it becomes the Ten Million (to include as well those brothers and sisters of mine who also vanished) the phrase will seem preemptive, exclusive, and cruel.

Henri Fourtine's daughter Véronique, whom I met but once when she was three, has written recently with voluminous enthusiasm (the hysteria of adolescence) to say, *en me tutoyant,* that she approves of the relation I once had with her father, that the world must be free, and that she wants to come to America so that she can "learn" from me. Though I'm touched, I dare not answer. What a far cry from the vitriolic letters of P.'s mother twenty-four years ago.

21 December

Shirley is in New York Hospital, room 520-M. When I saw her there yesterday I was shocked to tears, not realizing that she was anesthetized. Today she's her old self, or almost, and interested in outside news.

Christmas Day

Final rehearsal yesterday of three unaccompanied choruses, *The Oxen, O magnum misterium* and *Sing the Glad Tidings,* which will be premiered tonight at nearby Saint Stephen's Church, which commissioned them. Fairly decent performance.

I try to see or to speak with Shirley every day. Elsewhere quarrels and tears, quarrels and tears, quarrels and JH and I don't seem able to hear each other. Third week of stomach cramps. Heavy warm rain, luminous and bruised, so that a fugitive hour last night in the steam room could as well have transpired in Times Square for all it delivered.

Morris this afternoon, with a gift of two cashmere sweaters.

28 December

Tuesday, finished long review of Stravinsky book, mailed it off to the *Washington Post*, then met Ellen at the New Yorker Theater to see Dassin's movie about a modern-day Medea. It's really very good, both in idea and realization; even Mercouri, with her usually embarrassing vulturous presence, is deliciously cast as an actress with an embarrassingly vulturous presence. The end is wrong, though, unless I misunderstood it. Just as I misunderstood Malick's *Days of Heaven* this afternoon. But then, I never understand anything—not just Ashbery's poetry but any poetry. Maybe artists aren't supposed to "understand." Indeed, I had already completed my little opera on Gertrude Stein's text, *Three Sisters Who Are Not Sisters*, when I told Father that I didn't understand the title. Father, with the sober logic that I've always longed for but will never acquire, after a brief examination of the score, explained that the three sisters were indeed sisters, but of other people, not of each other.

30 December

Never less than tasteful, combining Djuna's doctor with the Collier brothers, Quentin Crisp held the stage at the Provincetown Playhouse for two hours by admonishing us to be ourselves at any cost (or rather, at no cost) by freeing ourselves from freedom. First half, a set of loose-knit epigrams posing as cynical but actually horse sense. Second half, a question period with the new questions (as is always the case) being old wine to our host. I itched to ask, after establishing goodwill by introducing myself as blurbist for his book, who Crisp thought he was in relation to us: preacher, guru, what? since aphorists are hard to pin down. He wants to be both Mama and Prophet, epigrams can be stood on their heads. Etc. He's actually a nice person. But I kept quiet, for fear, as usual, of embarrassing JH.

Awoke sharply from a dream of flying at 5 A.M. with fierce pain, as though by an electrode, in the right testicle. Now, seven hours later, the ache still echoes there.

New Year's Eve

Evening passed with JH's acquaintance S, in a mansarde of the East Village. Also a pair of irresistible month-old female kittens, one black, one white. We left before midnight so that JH could join K. But K never showed up. So I went home, while JH in the subway sped back and forth through the cold city, aimlessly, or so it would seem, wondering how to divide his existence.

1979

To be moved by music anymore! For we are usually moved by association: by the words to Our Song from high school, by visuals (the ballet sight recalls former Prince Igors), and, for me, even the odor of Russian Leather revives old sounds. How, though, does "pure" or so-called abstract music move us, a Beethoven quartet, a non-programmatic Debussy sonata, indeed any non-vocal piece which doesn't pretend to tell a story? Does it provoke us sexually? inspire tears? make us sick?

Sick? Once when our friend the musician Noah Greenberg was presenting *The Play of Daniel*, we went to see and hear it at the Chapel of the Intercession. Midway through, one of the twelve angelic choirboys began to vomit, copiously, in view of hundreds, all over his white robes and the altar steps. While cymbals and trumpets continued inviolably, an older angel helped him beneath her wing into the corridors, hiding his humiliation and physical pain. Meanwhile not even the strewing of sawdust on the puddle of puke could quash the stench rising stronger than incense through the church to remind us that the boy's emotion toward this theatrical reality had moved us more than the music pure.

Now, could the child have reacted thus to a *straight* piece, without God, or choruses, or superimposed "meaning," or, above all, without his direct participation?

We would have been around six and seven when our parents, on some holy occasion, took me and Rosemary away from Quaker service and into the noise of another church. There we beheld wild-eyed women in veils running through the aisles and heard from the balconies the thunder of choirs, and I was sore afraid. My first brush with ritual, with music as fear, and with sound as a heightener, crucial as water.

Thirteen months, and a leaden sadness has settled over JH and me, an es-
tranging deterioration that sometimes seems beyond repair. Yet the strange-
ness of his strife seems ever less strange, snared as he is by chivalric infatua-
tion, and it hurts. His tears and vomit, which spew forth in lieu of ire and
fury, spew not from a congenital unnamed seat but from quickly traceable
altercations with K.

Once I wrote: "*L'homme moyen sensuel* is by definition less human than
the 'achiever,' if by human we define the logic which differentiates man from
other mammals. Sex has nothing to do with logic, but achievers treat sex logically (with their restricting rules) while average men treat sex sensually."
Today I would add: If intelligent people, by virtue of their preoccupations
with the workings of culture, are less "good in bed" than "real people," they
are also given to more drastic suffering about non-vital problems such as
love. JH is the most intelligent person I know, and a friend without whom I
could not go on. Still, our headiest of frequent disputes center on the irrational, and he will reproach an interviewer for stating that Wallace is my cat
when in fact Wallace is his.

Serenade has just come out with an ecstatic orange cover. Hour at Boosey &
Hawkes signing copies. Later, John Margulis, young director who's reviving
Miss Julie in early April with the New York Lyric Opera. We've auditioned
dozens of singers, and will continue. Extraordinary, how many good vocalists are willing to perform for nothing. The production, on a shoestring, in
the new one-act version that Kenward and I have concocted, could be better
(which isn't saying much) than the City Opera's in 1965.

Bank. Snow. Baths. Insomnia.

JH, whom I ask how Virgil gets those plugs in the *Times*, answers, "Well, to
young critics he's pope." Pause. "Of course, like all popes, Virgil doesn't
know what's going on." He's referring to VT's proclamation that there are
only three sorts of music being written today: the Carter-Sessions kind,
which is too complex for many acolytes; the John Cage kind, which is so easy
to imitate that it's not quite respectable in academia; and the "spiderweb"
kind, made up of graphs and numbers, like Stockhausen's, which is not too

easy but not too hard either. Now, all three styles have been out of date for ten years. Virgil may not realize that "realistic" music (like his own) is today once again acceptable.

At Bill Flanagan's Memorial Virgil Thomson declared "Another August" to be a major American work, and his reason, if I recall, was that Bill treated the coloratura not as color but as content. Well, Virgil is the one critic whose opinions I heed, and whose opinions are always—even when wrong—literature. What do *I* think of "Another August"? It is Bill's most realized piece, yet imperfect. I don't object that it seems too short for its opening promise, nor that its language is too close for comfort to a Messiaen version of what we used to call Movie Music, since the length is, after all, imposed by the text, and the corn is overwhelmingly tasty. I *do* feel that although the composer may well be illustrating the poet, James Merrill, he is not comprehensibly setting Merrill's strange poem. Not one word of the singer can be comprehended, and this because, precisely, Bill does what Thomson said: treated the coloratura for content and not line.

7 January

Lunch of quiche and lots of tea for Francine and Cleve who bring Ethel de Croissset. Marie Laure's mother's second husband, librettist Francis de Croisset, produced a half-brother, Philippe, whom I recall meeting only once, around 1952, when he lunched at the place des États-Unis with his intimidatingly cold and stylish American spouse, Ethel, née Woodward. Here now she is, eating heartily at my table, still stylish with short hair and glasses, but scarcely intimidating. She says that Marie Laure always frightened her, which may explain the first impression. Ethel lives in Paris and loves music. (I note the two facts as contradictions.)

Took leftovers down to the Rorems' tonight, along with three jars of Maggy's homemade raspberry and apricot jelly, through the sleet and rain, stopping en route chez Jerry Oster to return his manuscript about which I told him the truth. Tomorrow, Nantucket for five solitary days during which I'll have a thorough checkup with Voorhees.

When Francine calls Jane Bowles a minor writer, she seems surprised when I say that, by and large, I prefer minor art to major art—that I have more *need* for, say, Fauré than for Beethoven, while admitting that Beethoven digs deeper. It seems never to have occurred to Francine (any more than to up-and-coming freshmen) that so-called secondary artists could be more satisfying than those making the Big Statement. Of course, my examples are frail; how can one argue two composers of such different time and place? And maybe I am missing something. But don't we all miss something by not being each other? Still, in art the Big Statement is often a political blinder. (Does Beethoven dig deeper?)

Dinner party for: Judy Collins & Louis Nelson, Ellen Adler, Lenny B. (who arrived an hour late with the cellist, Larry Lenske), me & JH, and later Jack Larson & Jim Bridges. Played tape of *Sunday Morning*, which Lenny, following the score and conducting wildly, found mistakes in and said he'd like to do.

Yesterday John Cheever to lunch. Chaos. Too complicated to write about now. Later Vincent Persichetti, the picture of adjustment, came for tea so that we could go over some thirty scores for the A.G.O. choral contest. Icy cold out.

Today at six o'clock, Bob Holton (with Lee Hoiby, etc.) to fill in the details of Ben Murphy's hideous death last summer.

Call from David Diamond. I've been elected to membership in the Institute of the American Academy & Institute of Arts & Letters.

At the Barclay for two days with a toothache and the flu, preparing the all-Rorem program, which took place tonight next door at the Curtis Institute, the second of my three alma maters, in whose hallowed halls I've not set foot for 144 seasons. Wonderful performances (especially of *Eleven Studies*), as so often happens with the slave labor of dedicated students. Visits with Jim McLelland, Rosemary & family, and especially the faculty (Sokoloff, de Lancie, etc.), who may be feeling me out.

Tea chez Henry McIlhenny with Stephen Spender. We talk of Saul Bellow. I mention that Bellow is, well, a bit too heterosexual for me, if you know what I mean. Spender answers: "Yes, Bellow does treat women horribly, doesn't he!"—then goes on to equate male homosexuality with the feminine side of man's nature. Stephen being Stephen, this is surely not stupidity so much as academic hypocrisy.

New York
1 February

Bronchitis. Elbert Lenrow and Dominique Nabokov for tea, during which the picture purchased last month arrived, a Jane Freilicher still life of peonies which "in person" looks even more scrumptiously edible, and more (as I always find Jane's work) melancholy than on the wall at Fishbach's. One enters her realm and breathes there. She's my favorite painter, except for . . .

To Elbert, the English professor from my third alma mater (Juilliard, in 1946–47), I owe the revelation of the texts for my opus 1, the *Four Madrigals* of Sappho. To Dominique, fifth and final wife of Nicolas, I owe the charm of her Parisian outlook and the expertise of her photographic portraits.

Nantucket
9 February

Past week in a nutshell: Friday, Board Meeting of the American Music Center with Peggy Jory in afternoon; dine at Stella Adler's with JH. Saturday, Maurice Grosser's exhibit at Fishbach; dine with Kenward Elmslie and John Margulis; later, the opera *Mary Dyer,* to see how Lyric Opera productions function. Sunday, dine with parents at their friends the Littauers', with Jean Behrend and my niece, Mary Marshall. Monday, to Nantucket with JH, cold and bright and windy; baked chicken, salad, peaches and cream. Tuesday, bacon & eggs and apple pie; later The Brotherhood—one of JH's hangouts. Wednesday, darkish, then heavy snow; codfish with butternut squash. Thursday, sun and snow, shot at the hospital. Today, cruelly cold but bright. We return to New York by Nor-East Air.

A happy family is rare and singular, but unhappy families are all unhappy in the same way, unless the unhappy family happens to be yours. Misery blurs identity. Write of how JH still writhes in the platitudinous mysteries of romantic love. The single, but powerful, tiding at turning fifty-five is the new talent for avoiding such useless tortures. Or is it that I'm able to avoid them precisely through the example of JH? Claude seems a thousand years ago.

At The Brotherhood, Nantucket's one bistro that in the subzero evening stays open late, for the first time I sit still, with JH, and watch the scene where everyone knows everyone but no one knows me, yet *I* know "everyone"! Except that I know only peers, and grow invisible to the young, other than those (few) who know *of* me but are either too intimidated or too pushy. Less lonely-making's when I'm all by myself, even late at night in Nantucket with wolves howling as I scramble eggs and think on work to be done, then do it, and look forward to midnight television.

JH just read the above paragraph, inadvertently left open, and was disgusted. "Why do you always have to be the center of everything? Why can't you just go to The Brotherhood and think about someone else for a change? I'm sorry I took you there."

13 February

Pre-Valentine's dinner at Edmund White's on Lafayette Street, where I was the center of things (or so I thought—that's all that matters) mainly because I was the oldest by more than a generation. We each (six of us, with Douglas Gruenau, Alfred Corn, Sandy McClatchy and Christopher Cox) were given a red heart, magnetic so that it attaches to a metal object anywhere, for instance, to the triangle on the wall of my bedroom where now I gaze at it.

Ed plays Maggie Teyte. Listening again after decades, knowing what I know after living where I lived, having once adored her, then disapproved (those aggressive affectations!), now Teyte seems inevitable, flawless, and very, very touching. Can any French soprano pronounce the language, as well as speak the sense of Verlaine, as persuasively as this *Irelandaise*? The best interpreters of any country's culture arrive from beyond the borders. (This is simply not true: Americans can't act Shakespeare, the English drown in Tennessee Williams, and no European begins to know what jazz is. What *is* true is that the greatest interpreters of classical French music have never been French. Is there technically such a thing as classical French music?)

Ed also told of the recent death of his father so vividly it could have been transcribed from a novel, except that every spoken predicate rang true, and he lent a new (to me) dimension to the definition of this finally ugly condition. So much for Ed. So much indeed. I mean that phrase not glibly. A rich future is his.

To everyone I recounted my ambiguous annoyance with Cheever.

18 February

In 1966 in the wake of *The Paris Diary* I became, briefly and to a meager bookish milieu, America's official queer, goyim division. (Allen Ginsberg and Paul Goodman had already come out in print.) Thus John Cheever, on

seeing me again at Yaddo—we'd met there four years earlier, when I broke
my ankle—decided I should be the first (so he claimed) male he would embrace. Of our week-long idyll I made notes in this book while it was taking
place, and during the urban months following while it decayed and died. Of
all the infantile authors I've known, John was the most likeable.

In 1974, when *The Final Diary* was in galleys, the publisher's lawyer prepared a list of presumably actionable paragraphs. These included references to both Cheever and the Baron de Charlus. Leaving Charlus to cope,
I toned down the Yaddo affair. When the book came out, John, safe in knowing it was too late, said, "You should have left the part about us, I wouldn't
have minded, I'd have been proud," just as during the fatal period he would
often say, "They're spying on us, they *know*, they watch us leave for our picnics, but I'm glad, no I'm not, yes I am,"—this in that inimitable mid-
Atlantic accent as he swigged gin from a thermos. Too much time has
elapsed to fill in details here. Simply, John once loved me, or so he said, but
I was scarcely the only one, and hardly the first. Looking back, what I
learned from him was behavioral, never literary, always inadvertent. He was
an overgrown collegian, like John Leonard, now out running the world. No
phrase of his, in speech as in writing (both in letters and in fiction), was so
exquisite—so "feminine"—but that it needed to be tempered by a reference to hiking or football. Unlike Leonard (straight literary critics will sanction gay behavior in a novel but not in the novelist), Cheever was obsessed
with homosexuality, as though hoarding lost time. Learning about my orgasm fantasies (squalid, narrow and sadomasochistic), he was anxious to
show that *his* were elating, like being on a crimson staircase toward a silver
tower that bursts open to a sky of golden stars. John's a born writer, a real
writer, and mostly an honest and technically solid writer. But he's not a re-
markably intelligent, certainly not an intellectual, writer. I never heard him
utter a canny literary judgment nor saw him approvingly nod toward any but
Yevtushenko. Nor has John ever been especially generous, beyond amorous protestations, except for his pixie charm and, of course, for the fact of
his books, which I suppose is generosity itself. He never wrote me a blurb
("I don't know anything about music," he'd say, like all authors), or expressed concern about *my* drinking problems, or interest in my work, although he *was* wonderfully attentive to Elizabeth Ames. On the whole, I
was flattered by John's attentions, while also a little bored. I have never been
sexually drawn to famous people, even beautiful ones. It's been years since
we've met.

I recount this now because, a month ago, dizzy from the international
hype that Knopf's weaving around his new collection, John phoned from

Westchester to say he'd be in town on Tuesday and longed to see me: I was "the only homosexual" he knew in New York. Well, I was not to be here on Tuesday, couldn't he call again? Call again he did, and on the 19th came to lunch. I specifically asked JH, who has never met John, to be present, although JH (who is mostly at K's these days) has problems too, and violent stomach cramps.

John arrives early. No sooner in the door than he drops his pants, pleads, whispers how lonely he is; I'm already in a state about JH's depression—JH, who's to arrive in five minutes—and about the quiche in the oven, and John like a bull in a china closet chases me about, like a Mack Sennett comedy, until I lock myself in the bathroom. "Please come out, I'll be good." So I come out, and we sit nervously on the sofa, John still with his trousers around his ankles, when JH comes in.

Transformation. At the sight of JH, John becomes calm, contrite, angelic, in love.

We have lunch, discuss his emotional isolation. JH offers to take him to the baths; no, he just wants to sit on the sofa for a while with JH's arms around him. I do the dishes. Before John departs I give him a signed copy of *An Absolute Gift*. He forgets to take it. Next morning he calls to say how much better he feels from having spent a platonic hour being held by JH, and do I mind if he calls JH? Apologizes for never being able to empathize with the anxieties or needs of others, but asks not one question about my relationship to JH. Suppose I went to his house and made passes at his spouse while at table with them both? His locker-room notion that we're all boys together and don't need to observe the niceties of suburban domesticity; after all, all gays are at all times horny and indiscriminate, free of principle and long-term commitment. (For the record, this is not a teenage farce. I am 55, JH is 38, and John is 66.)

That is a month ago. JH, with the air of Florence Nightingale tending the wounded, has seen John often, and found tranquility therein, the way maniacs are said to find tranquility as babysitters. JH, I think, is pleased that the great author enjoys his company, as they dine in the Edwardian Room and then play backgammon in John's chambers at the Plaza. (JH does however think less of John's work than do I. "Of course he's misunderstood by the world—the world thinks he's a great writer.") I do not begrudge them the comprehensible pleasure of each other's company. But John's resultant disregard of me is wounding.

There, that's off my mind.

20 February

Produce today, comprehend tomorrow.
Artists make fact. Critics make rules after the fact.

Women's Lib and Gay Lib are diametrically opposed, the one being deductively formulated, the other inductively. Women, like blacks, want acceptance not as women or blacks but as people. Homosexuals ask to be accepted as homosexuals first, and then presumably as individuals. Women want general behavioral rights, not women's rights nor the right to be women. Homosexuals want specific behavioral rights, and acclaim for what they are, as if the generic label were itself an accomplishment.

In self-consideration an artist must proceed from the broad to the final particular, or perish: it's a matter of priorities. I am not a homosexual, I am a composer. I am not a composer, I am Ned Rorem. I am not Ned Rorem, I am my parents' child.

More then Jews, blacks, women, or homosexuals, artists in America are second-class citizens. Yet to proclaim this would provoke disdain not only from the Silent Majority but from Jews, blacks, women, and homosexuals. For *artist* is a dirty word to us. If both Revolution and Establishment concur that art is not among the First Things First, they ignore citizens of poorer lands who sell their bread and name their streets for art. The poor remain with us but the artist has gone, too late to organize an Artists' Lib.

Nantucket
26 February

Alone on the island for ten days. Eclipse. Heavy rain. Seven pheasants. Still more rain. The golden pheasants seem to need the rain. Who'd have thought the old sky had so much blood in't? *Too Hot to Handle* with Loy and Gable, made just before *Gone With The Wind*. JH left after only two days because K, back in New York, is presumably ill. Horrors in China and Vietnam, Russia and Iran.

Enjoying with ho-hum tinges Edmund Wilson's successfully aged criticism of a half-century ago. But is Wilson *creative*, ho-hum? On Henry James, for example, he's like a wee woodpecker worrying an unwieldy oak. Generally Wilson's right, but he is wrong to judge a genre as, in itself, right or wrong (e.g. James's reluctance to "get inside" a character, or his tendency to waste space with "gratuitous meaningless verbiage—the *as it were*'s and *as we may say's*"). James is James, and right, and not necessarily "inferior" to Tolstoy. Wilson is not unique.

Turning to Ron Padgett: I find him creative, oh yes. But the poems don't hit home, being too close for comfort to Frank O'Hara, too wilfully whimsical without a true ear; one can't believe him. Padgett's not unique.

A genius may be of *genus homo* but he's then only one of his species, and the race expires with him. (The race is won forever, you might say.) Indeed, the genius, alone of men, produces what is an end in itself, rather than merely a grandson, a better mousetrap, a stable democracy, a nectarine.

Sans date

I began this diary in 1945 as a release from shyness, to investigate on paper what I could not say aloud. Over the years the journal absorbed more than mere outpourings of love, vicious envy, or depressions oozing from the gray corners of alcoholism; it grew into a travelogue, a recipe carnet, a social calendar with notes on works in progress. Indeed, the book became a catchall for my virtually every preoccupation except the main one: musical composition. I was a musician who happened to write, not an author who happened to compose.

Thus the diary, being random and bloody and self-indulgent, answered to different needs from the music, which was planned, pristine, objective. Or such was the case until 1966 when my first book, *The Paris Diary*, was published. At that time I had already been a professional composer for twenty years. Suddenly I discovered that the reading audience was far different from the listening audience, that the two did not overlap, that neumes and nouns excite separate nerves, and that a composer's notoriety will never equal an author's. The "public" ascribes less responsibility to a composer than to an author, for literature can wound where music cannot. True, when Proust lamented that the upper-crust fauna to whom he mailed galleys of *Swann's Way* never reacted (Madame de Chevigné, the model for the Princesse de Guermantes, confessed that she "caught her feet" in Proust's prose), Cocteau pacified him: "Do you ask ants to read Fabre's studies in entomology so as to learn more about themselves?" But I had written of people by name and was stunned to learn they didn't appreciate it.

Did you originally keep a diary in order for it to be read? people ask. Everything written is meant to be read, if only by the author at another time. But if I were to continue to publish words, I realized that I would have to bear the consequences. Gradually, like amoebas merging and then separating, or like two Ned Rorems passing each other as they enter a mirror from opposite sides, my joint professions exchanged focus. If the writing today has become more planned, pristine and objective, the music, though not exactly random or bloody or self-indulgent, is, I like to think, more imbued with the kind of ugliness which is as crucial as beauty is to art. Two careers run parallel. Can I really know if they infringe upon each other, any more than general practitioners can know where the path of specialization might have led them? Most who read my words have never heard my music, while musicians are usually surprised that I have written books. Books about what? The question is academic. Those three diaries, which brought a brief but golden fame, are out of print, as are the earlier collections of essays. Meanwhile musical life prevails as it did before I ever published books. Yet I still write prose, branching out now beyond my navel, with articles mainly on matters artistic commissioned by, and tailored to the requirements (sometimes even aping the tone) of, specific periodicals. And I still keep this diary—though what author's work, or indeed what composer's, is not to some extent a diary? The mood is quieter. After a certain age, certain subjects become embarrassingly dull and nobody's business. One of these is sexual intercourse, the other is the injustice of personal sorrow. Could the same be said of a composer's palette? Will I hold to such a principle a decade from now?

The diarist years later cannot be sure if he is recalling an actual occurrence or what he wrote about the occurrence. The composer endures no such confusion: he never knows, in vision or in verbs, what he's composing "about."

Do I still hold to those neat paragraphs? Yes, on the whole. A diary is a book about how hard it is to write a book, fragmentary by its very nature, forever unfinished. At least that's one definition for Gide's archetypal tome, although there are as many definitions as there are (admittedly few) people who publish diaries.

Actually, this diary takes little time; it's not composed with a sense of order, and its form can't be predetermined—only postdetermined, after I'm dead. Nor is there any drive for revision or polishing. Thus, at the end of any given year, I probably haven't spent more than a few dozen hours on this book, in contrast to the many dozen weeks composing, copying and orchestrating, not to mention the excruciation over the making of essays.

What do I choose *not* to write about here? Looking back through the nonacademic entries (excluding, for example, the formal sketches in 1975 for TV commentary), most of what's here is just slightly enlarged versions of minutiae from my yearly date-book. But why do I decide to mention seeing this person on Friday, but not that one on Saturday? or read these books in March but not those books in May? By arbitrary choice more than by bind-

ing compulsion. Compulsions of the fifties—liquor and love—no longer obtain, and occupations of today—friendship and career—take care of themselves. Am I trying to impress anyone beyond myself? if so, whom? and are
they impressed? What's elemental gets lost. I speak with Shirley oftener
than to any other friend and would probably turn toward her first in a moment of crisis. But who is Shirley? And who is Sylvia, what is Stuart Pope or
Boosey & Hawkes with whom I deal daily, the salt of my earth? The comings
& goings represented here are a mere calendar without italics; where's the
anxious cloud of JH's nervous breakdown that has darkened the past eighteen months? This journal does not represent my life, how it's spent. But
yes, it does, because it's my journal. The essential, by being omitted (how
do you represent music in words?), omits me. But there is no me. Such superficiality that sets your teeth on edge—meals, rendezvous, ailments,
theater—is sheer. But no, it's not: we are what we eat, and the irretrievable
passing glance is the staff of life.

Gide, in an April entry for that archetypal tome in 1918, chides Cocteau
yet again: "I do not claim that he is wrong to believe that art breathes freely
only in its newest manifestation. . . . [But] I do not seek to be of my epoch;
I seek to overflow my epoch." Can't one likewise chide, say, Susan Sontag
today? Today, sixty years later, has either Cocteau or Gide overflowed his
epoch? Had I to choose betwixt them, I could not.

New York
2 March

Beautiful performance tonight at the MacMillan Theater of my thirteen-
year-old *Water Music*, with Anahid Ajemian and Stanley Drucker playing
the solo instruments under Howard Shanet. Rectal woes anew, anew. Valium. Correcting the parts for the Cincinnati *Double Concerto*. Jack Kirstein's asked if I can make the cello part "more showy." I'll try.

Penelope Gilliat, nothing if not experienced, nonetheless flaunts the novi-
tiate vice so repugnant that I am turned off by the first paragraph of most of
her writings. This vice is the indulgence of the first-person pronoun in a context that asks for impersonality. She seems unable to compose a review or an
interview without quickly interpolating a "me" or an "I." The pronoun is not
used professionally ("in my opinion") but socially ("Nabokov and I were talking"; "Graham Greene said to me"), lest we forget that the writer rubs elbows with the great. But who, in the line of her duty, is the writer? What are
her credentials, that Nabokov should tell *her*? She forever deflects our attention away from her subject and toward her self, without that self being

integral. When Phillip Ramey objects that I do the same he misses the point of the medium: of Gilliat's "me" versus my "me." The point of a diary is to include the self. The point of a review is to (seem to) exclude the self. When I write a review I omit entirely the "I."

12 March

In his folly JH has adopted one of those twin kittens from New Year's Eve, the white one with dark spots. Her name is Princess because she's such a tomboy and her table manners are so gluttonous. She plays up to Wallace, either pouncing playfully upon him or waiting for hours for him to be a "role model." But Wallace will have none of her; he merely waddles about or, mostly, naps.

Hours at the dentist again. Heddy Baum came to dine, after which we went to the Met (as usual, third rate) to see *Norma* but, since Verrett had cancelled, we stayed for one act only.

15 March

Fog, melancholy, JH in Kansas.

Moira Hodgson gave a dinner party, and we were eight, with Howard Moss, Daniel Lang, John Rockwell, Lueen McGrath, and two women whose names I didn't catch. (Their names, according to Moira on the phone just now, are Melinda Love and Alice George.) Of Rockwell, who is rangy and self-confident and whom I've never met, I asked: "Can you recall every review you've ever written? For instance, can you recall the two opinions you've penned about me—one good, one bad?" "I remember the good one," he said, "for your *Serenade*, a few weeks ago." "But in 1974 you wrote to the effect that if Ned Rorem is the best we have in American song, we don't need any worst." He was embarrassed, and so was everyone else, including me.

20 March

Preview of Christopher Isherwood and Don Bachardy's play based on *A Meeting by the River*, which both JH and I loved. Party later. Got as far as the door, then decided not to go in.

Rehearsals well under way for *Miss Julie*. The extremely young conductor, Peter Leonard, appears prepared beyond the line of duty (where is that line?), and Margulis, if unadventurous, is solid and thorough and knows music, although knowing music is irrelevant to effective, even to expert, opera direction.

5 April

Last evening at the Academy, annual pre-induction dinner. Although this included painters (Larry Rivers, etcetera) and writers (Susan Sontag, etcetera), only we composers (me, Ulysses Kay, and Henry Brant) were required to confirm ourselves by providing entertainment, for which we were paid. In my case, a group of songs, including the setting of Elizabeth Bishop's "Visits to Saint Elizabeths," with me accompanying Will Parker. The last thing a roomful of well-fed drunken geniuses wants to do is listen to music, even geniuses who know and care about music, which of course is not the case at the Academy, or anywhere else. But the food was marvelous, the ambiance luxuriant, the company warm. Virgil called at dawn this morning and said, "Welcome to the old man's club."

Tonight at 7:30, premiere of new production of *Miss Julie*.

10 April

The four performances of *Miss Julie* are now of the past. So is the recording of "Highlights" for the Painted Smiles label which transpired over eight hours, yesterday and today, at Holy Trinity on East 88th, with the string choirs beefed up. The double cast—Ronald Madden, William Dansby, Beverly Morgan, Judith James, and Veronica August—was flawless, and the one-act one-hundred-minute version was superior to the expensive two-acter, except for Donald Gramm and Elaine Bonazzi, who in 1965 were at their heights. "Everyone" was there, I took Alice Tully, Kenward gave a party (at which Father lost his multicolored cane), and reviews were good. And Larry Rivers has already designed the jacket cover for the disc: a skeletal face, over which is superimposed a yellow right hand with a razor slicing the wrist of a yellow left hand (Clarice Rivers' hands posed for this), from which gobbets of dark red blood leak onto my name and onto Kenward's.

Tonight, after the taping, we went to Jim Bridges's new movie, his best to date, about a leak in a nuclear reactor—uncomfortably close to the reality of Three Mile Island. Other than too many dirty words, nothing amiss except the end. How can you morally show the horrors of nuclear power unless the reactor *does* explode and wreak havoc? Here, at the last moment, all is saved.

16 April

It turns out that American instrumentalists are as blindly specialized as singers, judging by the audience last night at Bert Lucarelli's oboe recital. I recognized not one face. Flutist Paul Dunkel, with whom I sat (we were two coppers in a panful of garnets—is that the image?), said he felt out of place with this swarm of oboe students. Waiting in line to pick up my ticket I overheard an exchange between two post-adolescent females:

"I went to this opera down at NYU by Ned Rorem. *Miss Julie*."

"Oh. How was it? His songs are okay."

"Well, some of it was godawful, and some was okay. The oboe player was okay."

25 April

A week's respite in Nantucket where, aptly enough, I worked on *The Nantucket Songs*, a cycle commissioned by the Library of Congress. One condition is that I accompany the cycle myself, with a singer of my choice, in an entire recital next autumn. My choice is Phyllis Bryn-Julson, and probably the recital will consist of half me, half Debussy.

Flew back Saturday, went to a party chez Judith James for the *Miss Julie* cast (took a huge chocolate cheesecake from Grimbles), then went straight to New Haven where Phyllis Curtin and I did a half-program of Virgil's songs, and delivered an essay called "Thomson as Teacher," on the occasion of Virgil's papers being sold to Yale for a rumored hundred thousand. At intermission Phyllis in her silver gown drove me to the station to catch the late train, so that I could receive a visit from Ms. Jill Dunbar, who wants me to read in her Three Lives Bookstore in the Village, and attend this evening with Miss Alice Tully a Musica Aeterna concert in her hall followed by the usual reception au Poullailer.

27 April

Rain rain rain. Worry and throat constrictions. Kenward's birthday celebrated in Tribeca, after which came uptown by cab betwixt the blonde warmth of Ruth Ford and Stella Adler—a heady position. Shall I tell which of them wins?

Tomorrow, Nicholas Maw, whose triennial visits are a sober treat, partly because he's among the few real composers of his generation and partly because he speaks the Queen's English with a sexy intelligence which to my American ears seems fresh as rain.

30 April

The gathering last night at the Gruens' for Jane's birthday (I took a silver mirror) included Angela Lansbury and her daughter Dierdre, both of whom exude immediate warmth, not to say interest in things beyond themselves. Invited us to see *Sweeney Todd* next week.

Went to Dr. Weisman, Judy's ENT, for throat tension. Then *Picnic at Hanging Rock*, the most interesting movie in years.

5 May

Sweeney Todd Thursday was so unpleasant, the music (except for Jonathan Tunick's opulent and telling orchestrations) so pretentious and non-infectious, the melodrama so gratuitously ugly (I remember being scared by it when I was nine in Brattleboro), the text so vulgar, that we would have left at intermission but for the promise to see Angela after. And what a charmer she is.

Last night, my reading at Three Lives. Packed—there's room for only sixty sitting on the floor. Judy came with us, then JH went elsewhere after. Seeing young Victor Cardell, Virgil's secretary, browsing (he'd not been allowed in because of the crowd), I asked him over to watch VT on the Cavett show, after taking Judy home. Invited Ed White and Chris Cox to dine, with Robert Phelps. They came tonight. JH a touch testy with Ed, who is a flirt. Starting tomorrow, a fortnight in Nantucket.

Nantucket
10 May

Ben Weber is dead. Shirley called this morning and broke the news. "Well, you won't have to listen to Ben on the phone anymore." Immediately I got in touch with Polly Hanson, who was unable to say more than a few words; her reaction, like mine, was one of instant incoherence. Ben's the first of us—Chicago expatriates from thirty-five years ago—to die. His death is both no surprise and a sad surprise. What happens now to his dogs, whose barking it was that informed the world?

Reading Elizabeth Hardwick's rather thin *Sleepless Nights* with disappointment.

Irene Gubrud, from somewhere in the west, phoned to say she'd been engaged to sing *Sun* with Maazel in Cleveland next season and hopes we can go through the score together next time we're both in New York. Curious choice for this piece.

One of the poems I'm using in *The Nantucket Songs* is John Ashbery's *Fear of Death*. Despite immediate intentions, humorous or thrilling, every piece I write would finally be named *Fear of Death*.

New York
22 May

Cafard de JH. Nevertheless he came to Joe Machlis's soirée for Rosalyn Tureck, thence at 11:30 P.M. to supper at Angela Lansbury and Peter Shaw's. Just the four of us; Dierdre (who resembles a very tall Jane Bowles) was leaving to meet a boyfriend in the Village when we arrived. I'm more and more impressed with Angela: she and Peter have been listening frantically to "classical" music so as not to seem like fools in front of us, or so she claims, not knowing that show-biz people are a thrilling mystery to me. I tell them I've always longed to be an actor (or, more correctly, an actress), but that specifically I don't know how to act. "But your whole life's an act," says JH.

Angela's made a cheesecake, smooth as silk and faintly almond-flavored. We talk of Agatha Christie, forty of whose books are stacked up there, because she's to be Miss Marple in England as soon as the *Sweeney Todd* run is through.

We talk too at length of Dierdre and her problems. I give the Shaws a copy of *The Final Diary*; they give me the record of the show.

23 May

Inducted officially this afternoon into The Institute of Arts & Letters, along with Ulysses Kay and Henry Brant. Came home and collapsed. At which point the phone rang; I'd quite forgotten Lehman Engel's dinner party. Took a cab across town, and there were Brigitta Lieberson (whom I hardly see every ten years, yet next to whom I'd sat at lunch today at the Academy), Tom Shepard, and others.

I ask Shepard how his opera's coming. It's based on Schwarz-Bart's *Le Dernier des justes* (which Lenny B. longed to use but couldn't get the rights to), and deals with the Holocaust, straight and simple. Shepard says they're having trouble finding a producer, because the cast and orchestra are so huge. "Why do you need so many?" I ask. "Because," answers Shepard, "it's a big subject." Which is why, I suppose, Britten used only thirteen instruments for his *Turn of the Screw*? or Beethoven just four for those last quartets? or Bach a single string for the Cello Suites? Brion Gysin, not finding a canvas the size of the Sahara, paints the Sahara on six-by-eight inch clapboard.

Listening to the record of *Sweeney Todd*, undistracted by the sordid images on stage, the music seems more solid, replete with echoes; there are some good tunes (some terrible), and Angela is irreplaceably musical. Inconceivable that her role be taken by a true diva, though there's talk of it, opera (in all its trashy glory) being a sacred word to Broadway.

3 June

High tea for Red & Pick Heller, Alice Tully, Rosalyn Tureck, and Judy Collins, a motley crew. I play the tape of *Sunday Morning*, during which Alice falls gently asleep.

(Spent an hour this morning cleaning the bathroom and scouring the toilet bowl. Yet not one of the guests remarked "Oh what a clean bathroom, Ned, and what a nicely scoured toilet bowl.")

Tomorrow, Lukas at five. Then Catharine Crozier plays *A Quaker Reader* in Tully Hall.

7 June

Dined last night at the Waverly Inn with Mother & Father, Rosemary and her son Paul and Paul's girlfriend, Lynn. It's been eleven years since I moved away from the Village with JH, and visits there now are nostalgic, evoking a thousand and one nights of industrious debauch as well as of youthfully hard work. Now my only friends there, besides Maggy, are Mother & Father. Everything they do is the reverse of the norm, like their retiring to Manhattan.

Today the recording of *Serenade* came out.

Visit from Stephen Greco for an interview for the *Advocate*. Tomorrow a photographer from the *Advocate*, Gene Bagnato, will appear; also Chris Cox to take pictures. (There's no such thing as looking photogenic anymore. After the age of fifty, Marie Laure allowed herself to be photographed solely from behind.) Then, in the evening, Alec Wyton with Walter Hussey, the Very Reverend Dean of Chichester Cathedral.

12 June

Une journée pas comme les autres. At one, perused songs with Judith Blegen who lives around the corner: from her bathroom you can see my dining room. At four, a photographer named King Wehrle, on behalf of Milton Goldman.

At seven, at Trinity Church, a tribute to Alice Tully, the second half of which consisted of Paul Callaway playing (grandiloquently) my *Quaker Reader*, during which performance Alice and I were made to sit side by side with our backs to the altar, facing an audience of a thousand. And as we listened, a man in the audience died, and was removed, but the music did not stop.

Tomorrow, Nantucket for the summer.

Nantucket
14 June

If everything is art then nothing is art. That's okay, so long as I'm not made to suffer the conclusion. But why must the conclusion be reached by others than me? Why should the National Endowment make the rules as to what is art? The confusion is that so-called populism and elitism are deemed two sides to the same coin, and thus that outgoing monies must be fairly divided between them. In fact, these are separate ventures—separate esthetics, if you will—as unrelated as medicine and literature.

With Rosemary last night our voices rose, then rose higher still, as we disagreed about who deserved subsidy. She feels that reaction to art (the stimulus of mutual "creation," the making of street plays and psychodramas, and the betterance of the lot of Harlem children) is just as important as what I, in my presumptuous isolation, am doing. Yes, maybe it's just as important, but it's not comparable. What I am doing results from individual accomplishment—whatever that's worth—and aims at producing a work: an end, so to speak, rather than a means. Communal grooving is great, but the means is the end, and there's nothing to show for the effort but good health.

Potential should be encouraged. Accomplishment should be encouraged. But potential is not accomplishment. Therapy is not art, nor is comprehension, nor is education.

Difference between art and entertainment is, I suppose, not one of degree so much as of purpose. Entertainment confirms rather than challenges. Entertainment, when participatory, is inherently passive: it doesn't ask, as art does, that you bring more than visceral goodwill. Art meanwhile never functions as background to other activities, especially talking. (I'm always amused and annoyed when I go to dine with cultured laymen who, for my sake, play tapes of cultured music softly, like sonic wallpaper.)

Does that claim hold? Probably not. I'm sick of art, anyway. Not to mention entertainment.

18 June

For months there's been a flutter in the wall, more irregular and forceful than the bees two years ago. Gnawing termites? Scurry of rat paws? If, as 'tis said, a cat's mere presence discourages rodents, then we have no rodents, or Wallace (admittedly quite deaf now at thirteen) is not a cat, and neither is Princess. But yesterday morning on finding the stovetop strewn with what resembled caraway seeds we finally decided, against our will, to set a trap.

(Against our will, for who are we to contrive the eradication of fellow mammals?) Last evening, not thirty minutes after placing the bait, there sounded the terrible snap. We paused long, fearful of what we'd find: sprayed blood? splayed bones yet still gasping? Together we went, and there sure enough was a mouse, limply dead. JH assured me it was killed before it knew what hit it, even before savoring the fatal Brie. The mouse was not of urban hue (not solid gray; indeed, like our mouse-colored Wallace, the royal Russian blue), but a clean goldenish mauve merging into sugar-white on the belly, with wide-open garnet eyes. We put it down the toilet but it wouldn't flush, kept belching back to haunt us like the corpse in *Purple Noon*. So we sealed it in plastic and flung it to the garbage, and wondered when its nest of starving offspring would start to rot and stink. The episode undid me, no less than the morning *Times* detailing tortures in faraway Persia or the faraway boatloads of Vietnamese. I went to bed.

During the chaotic-seeming composites of dream after dream (which in fact are sanity pure, including surely the dreams of the insane) there was a melding revivification of Vietnam and Persia, and of the mouse. If this morning I invoke the limitations of John Donne—since all men *are* islands who forever and vainly seek to play kneesies beneath the surface—I'd rather commit suicide than have it proved I'd ever been willingly physically cruel. I say physically, because all is fair in the "mental" game of broken hearts, nor is the will ever brought into play where love's concerned, love throbbing as it does beyond the frontiers of time as in an ice-cold bubble where we breathe forever and don't grow old.

Nantucket
25 June

Dear Paul,

Here am I alone in the middle of the house in the middle of the island in the middle of the ocean, sunbeams rolling like giggly peach-colored sapphires across the carpet, though it's already eight in the evening and Quaker ghosts start to stare in at the windows. Hardly a noise, no neighbors, no distant transistors, just pheasants scratching on the lawn, and on the stove a simmering vegetable stew. (I never eat meat when by myself.) The afternoon was squandered in concocting a cantaloupe sherbet, which I'll have for dessert along with store-bought cookies, while meditating on Madame Porte's pâtisserie in Tangier. Does she still exist? Nantucket, while host to a fair share of zonked-out swingers, is still puritan enough to think in terms of salt instead of sugar, so first-rate cakes and pies are hard come by. But since I no longer smoke or drink or fuck or use foul terms my sole indulgence is sweets.

Now, during the half-hour before adjourning to the porch, there to spread a yellow linen on my lap, leaning forward to read the propped-up book (Spender's wartime essays, better than I'd thought or hoped—indeed, the terse pages on *Poetry and Revolution* are the clearest statement I've ever seen on that subject) while dining, I thought it would be proper to type you my semiannual letter.

Little new news (and no catastrophes) re mutual friends since last we wrote. Aaron ever forgetful but very feted. Sam Barber in "remission" and in Italy. Morris Golde thinly tawny and often in Mexico. (It just occurs to me: wasn't it just 37 years ago this week that we met *chez Magda et Gilberte* in Taxco? Remember? I was with my father, whom no one believed was my father, and Gilberte had made a golden gateau with fudge frosting.) In April Phyllis Curtin and I performed a small recital of Virgil's songs, in his honor, at Yale where, as you doubtless know, he "gave" his papers in exchange for . . . *one hundred thousand dollars*! I'm not even jealous. Anything a composer can glean from this blank society becomes grist for the mill. (Is that the expression?)

America nonetheless lusts for culture but aims low. New York in particular feels the need to canonize artists, though always on extra-artistic terms: for being Jewish or queer or female or—worst of all—new. The three saints currently in highest place are Elizabeth Hardwick, Steve Sondheim, and Woody Allen.

Hardwick's thin tome (have you read it?) is good, but not *that* good, and adds up to less than the sum of its parts. Snippets strewn through the *NYR* and *Prose* magazine during recent years read exquisitely alone, but sewn together they don't mesh. They seem, hmmm, well, feminine—yet not feminine in any urgent way, like Jane's writing. For example: "Is it true," asks Miss Hardwick, "that a bad artist suffers as much as a good one?" More, wouldn't you think? A bad artist has no release through true appreciation, while a good artist (even if later he commits suicide), during those moments when he's working, can "get it out," and does know real love. However, the personal suffering of artists, good or bad, makes little difference even to the connoisseur, much less to art. That it does make a difference to Hardwick relegates her to the level of an Anaïs Nin.

Sondheim's *Sweeney Todd* (have you heard it?) is okay, but not *that* okay, and is being bruited as the breakthrough for opera. In any context but Broadway the complex tunes would sound puerile, if not flatly derivative of Sondheim's betters (mainly Weill and Bernstein), and the sonic seduction lies actually in the lush orchestration, by Jonathan Tunick. The plot of Sweeney, what's more, is irredeemably villainous. *Your* operas are more novel and more likeable (just as your musical comprehension of Lorca is more telling than George Crumb's. But that's another tale).

Woody Allen's movies (have you seen any?) are smart enough, but not *that* smart, and they try too hard. Never having been a comics buff, putting Groucho above Garbo, I sit poker-faced through Woody's movies like the black fairy at the ball. He really hasn't much humor. New Yorkers root for him because he's a professional Jew whose style, like the style of twenty years ago, is to deride the chic of the moment while being oneself the chic of the moment. His latest, *Manhattan*, I saw here on Nantucket only last night, and although the audience of Bostonian WASP warts were primed like a laugh-track, they didn't know what they were laughing at. The film does contain the likeable Mariel Hemingway, portraying what's presumably a nymphet although everyone feels she acts like a virgin. Whatever that means—since certain worldly types, such as Marie Laure or Theda Bara or even myself, when you get to know us, turn out to be quite sexually naive.

Well, America longs for genius and is willing to pay. But America, not the genius, makes the rules, so you can't win. If you're scratching your head at all this fine writing ("giggling sunbeams," indeed), know simply that time passes slowly now that I've given up Being An Artist, and you across the Atlantic are my outlet. To assume you don't know what's up over here is to forget I lived in Morocco three years myself; but that *was* in another era, and now the wench is dead. Did the book and record, supposedly sent months ago, arrive?

Hey, my stew is boiling over. Write quick.

Love,
Ned

26 June

The tone of a letter as opposed to a diary depends on its particular reader. Now that particular letter, although written to be included in this diary, was also written for Paul Bowles, precisely so that I could unburden without literariness certain moods of the moment, then include it here. My own voice changes according to whom I write; even the weight of an anecdote changes.

As for Spender's book: one is tempted to wonder if Stephen's passion for knowledge might not be finally detrimental to him. The unstillness, the knowing everyone who is anyone, the persistent questions on the highest level, the keeping the eyes ever open: all this makes for fairness, for being well versed on Judgment Day. But can it make a poet? Can it not also freeze the eyes? Can it not keep him from plain thinking? Not plain thinking in the sense of assimilating, of sorting out this morning's rich experiences, but as cleansing the mind of cultural debris, as forgetting "truth" for once and opening up to the reasonableness of non-events. Meditation? Why, no. Art? The art of solitude. Animals.

Ah, but suppose meanwhile the truth—the final mystery, the meaning of meaning, "the horror!" of Conrad, "The Great Good Place" of James, the dissection of God, the Ultimate Answer, yes, The Truth—suppose that we were to be granted the resolution of all philosophy, and that, the endless curtain of heaven being rent to the blare of horns, it revealed only a vacuum into which a camera entered and focused (way down there in the lefthand corner a billion miles away) upon a copper walnut engraved with but the one noun, *boredom*? Just suppose. Well, my own truth, should I choose to reveal it, would be my obsession not with art nor with love nor with beauty nor (like Stephen) with friends, nor with death, but with the sheer mediocrity of this whole bag of tricks. I cry. Yes, I cry real tears. Anything brings tears: coffee boiling, sunlight, the lampshade, the dead mouse. And I think about Father crying.

I am a camera's mirror, no less selective, no less transient (quasi-false, if you will) than the lens itself, and, like a luscious pool luxuriating in its own rolling flesh, I preen my wings of peacock blue in anticipation of Narcissus's exacting eye. Yet we cannot win, we who occasionally, with pain or with pleasure, find ourselves on this side of the clicking shutter—we cannot win against the instrument; his choice is final, seeing as he wants to see, arranging in a trice penchants and prejudices ingrained for decades. Sometimes, though, in losing we are favored, although whom cameras love die young.

5 July

Vogue has published Francine's piece on Nantucket, a mean, dishonest portrait. So shackled is her straw horse that Francine's habitually flowing style turns crabbed, and she repeats locutions too singular to bear more than one stating (e.g., *cutesy-pie*). Wrote her a letter, decided not to send it, wrote her another about why I didn't send the first. Since her essay is presumably documentation (for non–cutesy-pie *Vogue* readers), and not a novel, and since I know where she's strained facts (especially re Quakers, homosexuality, and what art "should" be), I will never—although continuing to like her—trust Francine again.

Colitis. Depression and tears. Took Princess to the vet, because of her continual scratching of ulcers behind both bleeding ears and to have her spayed. Now she's home, her abdomen bandaged, and JH has devised a little bonnet to protect her ears. How sweet she is, already energetic, and without (unlike me if I were her) feeling sorry for herself.

Tonight Madame Tureck comes to dine. Later Rosette. Lawn mowed, posies plucked, rugs vacuumed.

10 July

Mimsi and Robin Harbach come for a drink, so I bathed, and shaved for the first time in days. Discussed Francine's article, which remains upsetting. My name's in the crossword again. Deaths of Arthur Fiedler and of Cornelia Otis Skinner. Finished *Hilda Lessways* by Arnold Bennett, a curious, "feminist," exciting affair that no one seems to have heard of.

Tomorrow Madame Tureck is due again, this time with the young guitarist Sharon Isbin. They're coming at 5:45, the hour at which a violent chunk of hardware called Skylab in outer space is scheduled to whirl into our atmosphere and crash, probably on Nantucket, splattering our teacups and innards.

17 July

Wallace had a fit. I was working at the piano, JH outside mowing the lawn, when I heard a raspy flopping in the kitchen. Wallace had fallen from the high shelf where he naps and was convulsing on the floor, foaming at the mouth. I called JH, who held him. Gradually calming down, his eyes empty and brilliant, he let out one shriek, then staggered to his feet. Ate voraciously and slept for several hours. Was he stung by a bee?

Stifling, steamy weather continues. The beach at Pocomo. This evening, a cooling-off. Reading John Gardner's *Grendel* with a mild interest, mainly because he's rumored to write librettos.

23 July

Still the glistering heat. Stepped on a bee and have a swollen sole, but no epilepsy like Wallace.

We invited to dine Frank and Maggie Conroy and Robin and Mimsi Harbach. Cold cucumber soup, JH's beef burgundy, and a stunning lemon meringue tart by our houseguest, Billy Moscato. In their yellow open auto called "Good Intentions," Mimsi (in her applegreen shift) and Robin (in his Harry Truman jacket & slacks) lugged a humidifier the size of a rain barrel in homage to my hay fever.

28 July

The heat's almost undone me.

Rosalyn Tureck has this month been a neighbor across the island, at Quidnet. I accepted her dinner invitation on the condition that she garnish this with a private concert. I arranged myself carefully among the rather tough cushions of an antique pink sofa, and she began to play. It was the same dusky hour as JH's adventure with the kite last year. Although the closed windows in Rosalyn's vast "piano room" are, like most windows, three feet up from the floor on the inside, on the outside they're flush with the lawn. The music, which I'd never heard or even heard of (Bach's D-minor keyboard version of his A-minor violin sonata), was unutterably touching, and while it unwound the semi-wild fauna of Nantucket fluttered or scurried over the grass toward the glass panes and gazed through the sunset into my features. The sound, like all controlled perfection (is perfection by definition controlled?), seemed inscrutably tragic (generally I'm not given, when speaking of music, to metaphoric adjectives) and all the more satisfyingly so in that the ravens and rabbits conspired contingently to found a Peaceable Kingdom, choreographing a composition beyond their earshot. The sonata was followed by a Chopinesque adagio, again from a fiddle suite, and by two sinfonias. When Rosalyn had finished the mourning doves were lowing and the sky was filled with stars.

She feigned comprehension when I declared that, because my first exposure to Bach coincided with my first exposure to the blues, those baroque harmonic sevenths formed by the characteristic contrapuntal sequences resemble the canvases upon which Billie Holiday etched her plaints. Put another way, music smells good or bad according to its setting (those Renoirs in the Polignac music room did distract, though not necessarily "wrongly," from the formal sounds at hand, and a celestial cavatina turns hellish when you have a hangover), and Bach beneath Tureck's hand changed meaning in the very process of unfurling tonight as civilized background to the animal kingdom.

Her forte is precision, and, in a sense, that's all that counts. One is never uneasy. She never travels with the score; her fingertips house ten lilliputian brains with their own infallible memories.

10 August

Back from eight days in New York, mainly for first rehearsal of *Nantucket Songs* with Phyllis Bryn-Julson, who was three hours late. In 1951 Hugues Cuénod was equally cavalier about a first reading of *Cycle of Holy Songs* (it was at the Gouins'; we had to sit through an entire lunch on a silver service

glazed with Parisian chitchat before getting to the music about which I was
so eager), but the reading more than made up for the wait, Cuénod, then as
now, being not only a consummate sight reader but one who in *sight-
reading* can give a performance more excellent than any after. Bryn-Julson
is no letdown either, but less for her sight-reading than for her ear: because
of her pluperfect pitch she can give a perfect rendition at first reading, but
the perfection is robotic—she sings the notes, not the relationships among
notes, much less the words. Thus, unlike Cuénod, who interprets immediately through instinct and intellect, Bryn-Julson can only improve. She
stayed for a cold supper with my parents and Chuck Turner, for whom we
then gave a complete performance. (Yes, she'd improved. After all, she'd already known the piece for two hours.)

With John Gruen to the Bolshoi's *Stone Flower* by Prokofiev. Took Shirley
to *Every Good Boy Deserves Favor* by the poor man's Prokofiev, André
Previn. *Miss Julie* was rebroadcast on WNYC. Planned next sixteen-month
schedule at length with Stuart Pope at B. & H. Ovenlike humidity seeped
into a second hopeless month; took to bed with chills from heat prostration.
My newish *Surge Illuminare* ("Arise, Shine") had its first NY perf. on the 5th
at Saint Thomas Church. Visit to Eugene & Martita, and philosophical discussion of the death of Mrs. Istomin. Older now than most of my friends, I
remain the only one not an orphan—the only one who can still weep into his
mother's apron.

On the 7th, listened to a baritone, Dick Frisch, on behalf of Shirley; then
submitted willingly to Gene Bagnato's camera. Then Alice Tully took me to
dine at The Lion's Den on East 77th and told me the moving story of her life.
I never am with Alice, even for a moment, without being touched by her
generosity of spirit and awed by her knowledge of opera (much wider than
mine).

Back now on the island, and so for a week of good company is Chuck
Turner. Small hurricane this morning. Parents' 57th anniversary. Made a
nectarine-and-pear pie. Then we drove through the rain in our big ugly blue
pick up to Sconset where Chuck showed us the house along the bluffs where
Sam Barber composed the first act of *Vanessa*.

Advance copy of Sunday's *Washington Post Book World*, which contains
"Being Ready."

16 August

Perfect, cool day. Chuck has departed by ferry, while Stephen Koch (on behalf of the Phelpses on the Vineyard) arrived by ferry to spend the night.
He's a tall eager enthusiastic manly intellectual, an intimate of Susan Sontag

whose up-to-dateness he reflects (he gave me his paperback about Andy
Warhol's world, called *Stargazer*, with the Coctelian *dédicace*: "To Ned—
who gazes, and *is* one, both"), but I like his way of making absolutely no differentiation between me and JH when he speaks to us. Now he too's gone,
and Russell Oberlin's come, in his own boat with friend Tom; they're cruising the East Coast from Hatteras to Halifax in this wooden apparatus of no
more than forty feet. We went to Swain's Wharf this afternoon to have a drink
on their deck, and I got claustrophobic, despite the vaguely friendly swans
who approached with irreproachable smoothness to cluckingly solicit our
soda crackers with camembert. "*Ma pensée est un cygne harmonieux et sage
qui glisse . . .*" I've never seen Russell lose his temper, or indeed behave
with any but the highest good humor. But he's surely too intelligent not to
be testy sometimes, especially cooped up in the middle of the Atlantic.

Blackberry bushes ever more copious. We pick quarts every day.

Cruelty in the name of truth, serpentine candor entwines the pillars of society. To tell someone (whether or not "for his own good") that someone else
has slandered him, or that his nose is grotesque, or that his sister is a dyke
(which maybe he never knew), is to relate facts (when in fact these are only
facts), not truth. Fact is the odd side of fiction, while truth is the odd side of
lie. A fact is not necessarily necessary; even truth need be called up only to
set a fiction straight, when that fiction has been uselessly disruptive.

The contempt I can feel for even my closest friends.

Most of what we think about each other we don't say. Curiosity, hostility,
lust, those suggestions "for his own good," or, above all, boredom—these
impulses, with the years, are kept more or less consciously quiescent, while
amenities increasingly satisfy. The surface delight of regarding those bright
persimmons on that deep blue plate, of regarding them with or without you,
seems more urgent than falling in love again or than working for justice in
the world. Do I want to know you better? There is no better.

19 August

Lunch yesterday with Olga Carlisle who gave me a pile of her books, which
she wants back soon. (Spent last night relishing her exposé of Solzhenitsyn.)
At five a man who had called from the mainland to ask for my autograph
stopped by with his wife, and I gave him my autograph. *Dîner chez* Rosette
with Seward and Joyce Johnson, stopping off en route at her marvelous brick
house on Main Street to return Olga's books.

The fact of Stephen Koch sent me back to the Sontag photography book. All
writing, first and foremost, evokes. Some bad writing draws forth a "how

true" while some good draws false conclusions. But the false and true are reactions to what the writing evokes of our own—not the writer's—experience. Scanning Susan's last essay, I read: "The primitive notion of the efficacy of images presumes that images possess the qualities of real things, but our inclination is to attribute to real things the quality of an image."

Darius Milhaud in the late 1960s, humorous and alert in his wheelchair, had long since given up on medicine. Milhaud's current consultant, a sort of diviner, was able by means of a scanning rod to examine a group photo in the day's paper and determine not only who among those featured had what disease but even diagnose those (unseen at the extreme right or left) who had been cropped from the portrait. He did stress that the picture had to be not only recent (the image of a person now dead was useless) but reproduced by a small-circulation press—the more editions or replicas, the more evanescent the subject's "readable" specter.

Swing Band men of the thirties were famous through recordings. When hired for a hotel dance they felt obliged to recheck their own discs and to imitate by rote their recorded improvisations, so that the college kids would not feel cheated by living variations.

". . . our reluctance to tear up or throw away the photograph of a loved one, especially of someone dead or far away." Aren't we equally reluctant to throw out letters, or books, or quilts, or locks of hair? Yet we do—and are instantly less bereft, more secure in what we call our memories.

One page of Susan elicits this page from me. If her evocations in themselves are not particularly sentimental, the reactions they call up, at least in me, are strong, and that is good for us both.

22 August

Rosemarie Beck, most precious, arrives by ferry from the Vineyard and we have a big lunch plus a tour of inspection. Cool, very cool, and damp.

With sadness I discovered, on finishing Richard Gillman's defense of a possible draft resumption (today's *Times*), that he writes not with irony but with the simplistic zeal of a scoutmaster. "The military system was a human system," says Gillman of his 1950 idyll as a draftee, "its other-world appearance [being] little different from what many of us perceived when we entered the educational system." He quotes Karl Shapiro: "Nothing is expected of you except your obedience. . . . The army can't hurt a good poet," and lends weight to this claim by noting that Shapiro "had not only survived World War II combat but had emerged with two extraordinary books of poems."

Are books of poems, even extraordinary ones, worth a war? Can an intellectual still fail to realize that, as Quakers say, there is no alternative to peace? Can he still buy the notion that good citizenship resides in compliance with the army right or wrong, given examples like George Fox or Gandhi whose reverse passivity moved millions? Can one rationally posit the military system as human when precisely its purpose is to dehumanize by removing options, as distinct from the educational system which by definition offers multiple choices? What does it mean to say that "the military can't hurt a good poet," in the face of Wilfred Owen or Siegfried Sassoon, when the army can quite simply kill good poets? Should not the phrase rather read: "The military can't kill a good poet's poetry"? But would the poems be nothing without the military? Can it kill bad poets? or non-poets? or do they matter?

It seems to me specious, in this age of push-button warfare, to romanticize the draft by suggesting it's as good a way as another for trying, as Gillman puts it, "the innocence and pluck of the great majority of young men and women."

28 August

Yesterday I was called by the John F. Kennedy Center–Rockefeller Foundation International Competition for Excellence in the Performance of American Music. The purpose of the contest is to spur interpreters from all over the world into playing and singing American music, and it is held in successive years for pianists, singers, and violinists. This year it's singers, and the first prize is high beyond imagining: $75,000 (which includes a record, a New York recital, and matching budget for any group that will hire the soloist in his or her bizarre program). Would I, the representative wanted to know, come to Washington next month to give a little speech while the jury retires after having heard the three finalists, and then to hand the check to the winner? What will I be paid, I inquired, for preparing the talk, etcetera, since you are the Rockefellers? On learning that I would be paid nothing, I said no. Now I've prepared the following statement, sent to To Whom It May Concern at the *Washington Post*, the *Star*, and the *American Music Center in Washington*, as well as to the Foundation, and anyone else I could think of:

Yesterday Ellen Buchwalter, representing the competition, phoned to ask if I would come to Washington to present the three winners with their awards after the finals on September 15th. It was hoped I would also give a short talk. Why me? Because my songs were so liberally featured in each category of the contest, and by implication I and the ceremony would be mutually honored. When I asked about the fee, Buchwalter explained that

although expenses would be supplied, the notion of payment was "unprecedented." Now, since I cannot afford the energy and time for a round-trip
from Nantucket without a token of at least $250, I suggested that she and her
colleagues reconsider and call me back. Meanwhile I wrote the talk—an appraisal of the unhappy state of American Song, and a felicitation for the pro-
motion of such contests in the face of impresarios who loathe contemporary
music. (I like to get paid for speeches too, but was willing to throw this in
free.) However, when Buchwalter phoned again, the verdict was negative.
So I won't be going to Washington.

It's an old story to us composers, but it still comes as news to everyone
else, including well-meaning instigators of competitions for national music:
the notion that composers are somehow independent of, rather than depen-
dent on, the music they produce. In America a well-known person is assumed to be well off, since fame equals money. Well, my name for the moment may be more familiar within the wee coterie of Modern Music Buffs
than the names of the upcoming contest winners, but I have never, not even
for an opera, received such fruitful rewards as theirs. If my reputation, such
as it is, centers around some two hundred published songs, proceeds from
them during any ten-year period amount to less than what certain singers
earn for a single evening's recital, a recital which may contain a group of
those very songs. Now, the singers are often reluctant to pay to the Performing Rights Society the small sum legally required for the programming of
music not in public domain. The poor composer! Only too anxious for his
work to be heard, he keeps his own voice unheard. For him a performance is
its own reward. But not for me—not any longer.

Surely the accompanists for this contest are being paid. Surely rent for the
hall is being paid. Surely the organizers, including Ellen Buchwalter, are
being paid. The judges too are being handsomely paid, and for all I know the
audience is plunking down cash to attend this second Kennedy–Rockefeller
International Competition for Excellence in the Performance of American
Music. Indeed, money is what the whole thing is about. Why, then, does the
budget overlook a minimal fee—let's call it "for awards presentation"—to
the composer whose presence is desired for sheer prestige, and without
whom, along with his brothers and sisters, the competition could not exist?

The burden of this plaint, uttered on behalf of all makers of serious (i.e.,
non-commercial) music, is that we deserve the just rewards of our labor.
Such an utterance in the eyes of the world, or even to the ears of the Rockefeller Foundation, still at this late date appears avid and crass; worse, it appears unromantic. Creators aren't supposed to think about money.

Does not a wry note sound from a situation wherein a composer is invited, without remuneration, to act as purveyor of a large check for singers, to encourage them to sing his songs?

4 September

Shirley's been here for the past week (losing her suitcase promptly on arrival), and she just departed with her friend D. in his private plane. We showed her off to Wynn and Bobbie Handman, to Ann and Paul Sperry (the latter of whom helpfully sang through all six of the Debussy songs I've been practicing for the Washington recital next month), and to the Conroys. Shirley's quandary about which suitor to renounce, D. or G., inspires in an outsider the same small amount of envious pity he may have felt on viewing *Daisy Kenyon*, wherein Joan Crawford was forced to opt between the gorgeous Dana Andrews and the divine Henry Fonda, especially since it's obvious that Shirley will choose G., with whom she has everything in common, and live happily ever after.

6 September

As far as anyone is ever cured, JH is. As far as anyone can judge such things. The two-year stress, fanned by my own surrender to allergies (I've been taking shots just twenty-four months now, and I am doing better, thanks) has abated, due as much to illness running its course as to a fortieth birthday. He functions. What more can one note about any friend? It's feasible to resume the *égoisme à deux*—the mutual solitude—as the French name marriage.

He functions too as translator of animals, being himself a thoroughbred, with psyche tuned to sea urchins no less than to bank clerks, exasperating bank clerks. My own loneliness has not in a decade been linked to the waiting for a silent phone to sound. Question of priorities. The solitude of work, during which all priorities (happiness, death, taxes) are suspended, resembles, like love, that cold bubble.

7 September

Over and beyond a scientific interest, does an entomologist develop or inherently possess a sympathetic, a *human*, rapport with insects similar to the sentiments of a zoologist with apes, or, indeed, to the affections of any pet owner?

Despite the ever-cooler afternoons the hydrangea in the front yard blooms greener and greener, sheltering (among a million more microscopic invertebrates) a lost mantis all foamy white and sea-colored and shivering, crippled, on a leaf. Did it or did it not feel differently about me from the way it might about some other person, as I aided it, examined it at point-blank range, purred to it about its pair of dear eyes that turned from right to left? Insects do make choices.

New York
9 September

Party for Ed White on lower Fifth Avenue. I sit talking with Stephen Koch who tells me that Susan Sontag is in Europe. "Then what's she doing here?" I ask, gesturing toward a figure over there in a white jumpsuit, shoulder-length tresses of sombre hue, and a slouch—because, although not wearing my glasses, my nearsightedness has eased with the ebbing years. "That's not Susan," says Stephen, "that's her son, David." I haven't seen David since his mother, thirteen years ago, brought him to dine at the Waverly with me and Joe Adamiak, during which, since she was off to France in a day or two, Susan was noting all the dirty French verbs I was teaching her. I remember this, because I wondered whether it were proper to teach dirty verbs in front of a preadolescent.

I invite Stephen to leave the party with me and Virgil, who hates parties because of his deafness (because of his ears he'll miss the point, like me with my eyes) and to have peach cobbler on the terrace of the Fifth Avenue Hotel. After which we come back here to hear music, I think.

15 September

The song competition was broadcast live tonight on National Public Radio, the three finalists (all baritones) each presenting a full recital, mostly of American music, from the Kennedy Center. Apparently my crank letter of August 28 was reprinted in all the papers and is the talk of the town. Thank God it can't sound like sour grapes, since I was well featured on two of the three programs, winner Will Parker and runner-up Leslie Guinn both having sung *War Scenes*.

18 September

The Elephant Man with Morris, after which he takes me to sup at that magic Mecca, Sardi's. The seeming cynicism of the management is not weaker than the A & P's. My Old-Fashioned Chicken Salad resembled, in taste and sight and smell, the week-old leavings from the floor of a better *abattoir*.

The grocery store meanwhile sells me a two-dollar carton of cottage cheese, dated a month from now, which when I get it home turns out to be blue with mold. I'm unable to complain, to make public noise, except by letters to the editor. (Even that letter to Francine I didn't mail.) What is moral? Should one complain? at the expense of being conspicuous and splitting a blood vessel?

At Doubleday's. Tennessee Williams: because he never looks at you while you're talking, you talk more and more, not knowing if he's listening, and you end up saying *n'importe quoi*.

Judging by her interpolations in Sunday's interview with Menotti ("Toe the line, Buster"), and by her opening the season with *The Merry Widow*, Beverly Sills bodes ill for coming opera. Her vulgarity would be salubrious if it weren't paradoxically linked to the palest conservatism.

Suicide of Jean Seberg in Paris.

Nantucket
2 October

My pacificism was not rote, but it *was* rather unthinkingly ingrown. As a birthright Quaker I never doubted that war, all war, was wrong, then thought no more about it. Thus in the early forties (I in my teens) I did not feel that I was wrong and you were right, but the other way around—this, in the face of the world. Would I feel that now—be unconvinced that mass killings can settle matters? do they ever? The conflict was whether I should believe, like my sister Rosemary (for no reason at all except "bohemianism"), that Russian Marxism was the answer, or c.o. camps, or writing music, or getting drunk, or "knowing life." The crass query from strangers (inevitably women) of "Why aren't you in the army?" was not guilty-making, just uncomfortable. I learned to lie ("I'm being called up next week") for simple survival.

In all the brouhaha around whether Jerzy Kosinski does or doesn't write the books credited to his name, no one has yet pointed out that the true author, whoever he is, is not very good.

3 October

What is more alarming than a dumb bigot? A smart bigot. More discouraging than a fool's bigotry is the bigotry of a sage. That way lies despair. Mary

McCarthy's new novel, although admirably unsentimental, is mostly fair and thorough and compassionate about most human foibles. But, as in her previous novels, all references to homosexuality are sneers, and she outdoes Anita Bryant in the assumption that queers (as she still calls them, although she now says *black* instead of *Negro*) all covet young kids. The only extraneous roles in the otherwise tight and full-blown cast of *Cannibals and Missionaries* are "the 'boys' from Antibes," for whom she shows only contempt, using them as superfluous window dressing. It's not that she's a bitch (that's her style) but that she's stupid on the subject; coming from her, stupidity, like the several grammatical confusions that have slipped into the otherwise well-trimmed, thought-through text, catches the reader short. Didn't she learn anything during her marriage to Bowden Broadwater? Would she object that homosexual is not a grown-up thing to be? that in these troubled times there are more urgent matters than Gay Lib?

In none of her books is there talk of music. This must mean something. An intellectual who gets into deep water by using musical padding (viz. Sontag) makes a musician uncomfortable. No one does this more than Styron, who obviously dotes on music yet drops only the tired, old, expected names: Schubert, Beethoven, Mozart, other Germans. Does no one, Jew or Gentile, even in France, ever use French music as mood-setter? Styron, meanwhile, although his scattered references to homosexuality rather touchingly treat the "condition" as a *pis aller*, does reveal his most courageous character to be a lesbian. Could he have done as much with a male without sounding touristy?

12 October (Friday night)

Of all the weeks of my life this one's been the most anxious. Finally finished (a bad piece of work) the review of Shostakovich's presumed memoirs, though how honest the transcriber, Solomon Volkov, has been is anyone's guess. Yet the anti-Soviet stance is less distracting than the sloppy work. A tone of voice is not a tone of page, and literal jottings are annoying to read.

Meanwhile the Pope. Oh horrid Church, feigning progress to disguise conservatism, Mass in the vernacular but no rights to women, a rock-and-roll service but an equation of violence with sex.

And I, who must go, must be on display over an array of geographies during these many weeks to come.

> *Que me veulent toutes ces pieuvres*
> *Qui feuillent jusque sous mon toit?*
> —Cocteau, *Mon chef-d'oeuvre*

Ungratefully (for if I were a young composer I'd be curious to see and learn from me) I grow panicky, terrified of the crowd, the anonymous motel bathroom upon whose floor I lie bleeding.

Love is a puzzle which when solved is forgotten. To scrutinize a heightened experience is to kill it. This is no less true of honeymoons than of hallucinations. And it can be true of art, although art is presumably less ephemeral. Or the scrutiny may itself become art, replacing what it kills. Discourse on the current scene often seems subtler, more persuasive, than the scene itself. We read with respectful relish about the qualities of, say, certain obscene books, only to find, when referring directly to them, a dull red herring. The real experience was in discussion of the experience.

13 October

Angela Lansbury and Peter Shaw's daughter Dierdre did phone, and last evening she came for a chat. A handsome and open blonde Juno, she's also a vulnerable and scared infant seeming to want to be an actress yet, oddly, having no sense of what that implies (the way Rosemary as a child learned about applying wigs and mascara but never read plays). We took a stroll on Columbus Avenue, which is now as romantic and *mouvementé* as yesterday it was sordid and stagnant, stopping at O'Neal's, where I left her playing the pinball machine. I've been in her shoes, the ones that slosh for days through bourbon on an empty stomach; but I always had music at the end of the line, a diamond-hard core around which even my most squalid years revolved. With all my imagination, it's difficult for me to put myself in Dierdre's place (just as it's been difficult for the past two or three years to see through JH's jaundiced eye). It takes one to know one, yes, and I am an alcoholic. But I am not "one."

It's difficult also for me to converse with tenors, even such unusual ones as Gedda with whom in a black limousine I rode this morning to Yale where Phyllis Curtin had devised a panel on opera. After lunch at a place called Mory's, the other panelists—Robert Sherman, Phyllis, John Alexander—and I repaired for three hours to a platform where earlier this year we sang for Virgil's supper and where now we discussed the subject of opera, to little avail, before a hundred souls.

Baltimore
18 October

I write this on the last of three days spent in a two-story structure, empty but for me, called Nichols House on the Johns Hopkins campus; because of a hotel-room shortage my hosts at Peabody could find no other lodging. The usual: roundtable, master class with singers, beautiful performance of *Water Music* by Comissiona, composers' seminar. But the most memorable hours have been those extracurricular, fugitive ones spent with David Sachs and Norris Embry, identical in style and content to Chicago forty years ago, except perhaps physically. Even there, David's scarcely altered except for some silver threads among carroty cowlicks atop the laughing bust of Socrates. Norris looks like something the cat dragged in: vastly eager, with eyes that still light up at words like Garbo, Ravel, Plato, truck driver, and Libby Holman, but with his body in shambles from drinking and suicide attempts. Norris, an outpatient at Johns Hopkins's loony bin, lives in town in a one-room first-floor walk-up the bathroom of which has not been cleaned for years, the same years that produced the unique pictures, in oil and chalk and charcoal and collage, that festoon the walls from ceiling to floor. Norris speaks with a sometimes incomprehensible hoarseness because of his near strangulation, a few years ago, by a hospital warden. I bought three two-by-three-foot red-green-and-purple fantasies as gifts for JH. David, meanwhile, resides most properly in a not-yet-furnished (except for a couple of Norris's fantasies) set of three rooms out across from the campus whereon he commands an office which he showed me at midnight. It was moving, very moving, to retrieve old friends, and to *savor* them without discomfort after so much time.

Later (*New York*). Returned by Metroliner which, just before Philadelphia, stopped, and remained stopped for three hours. Elaine Bonazzi in same car. We chatted, *nous aussi*, about the good old days, exhaustion overcoming us finally. (*Sun* is being heard, tonight and tomorrow, in Cleveland.)

24 October

Nadia Boulanger died in Paris yesterday, on my birthday. Visit from Michael Di Capua. Then a festive dinner at the Gruens'. Returned home and made a pineapple mousse for today's lunch because Phyllis Bryn-Julson's coming to rehearse for five hours. Insomnia as usual.

Wallace since last summer has had two more seizures, both frightful to behold. Clearly it was not a bee that set off that first convulsion; rather it seems to be a steady, regular rhythm, like a lawn mower or typewriter. JH thinks it stems, along with his deafness, from that first traumatic plane trip in 1974, when the Delta crew at La Guardia left him caged out on the tarmac beneath a screaming jet engine.

25 October

Phyllis Bryn-Julson is reassurance personified. Vocally she can do anything (including a steady trill between middle C and high C, should you wish), and do it, square on pitch, with any tone or dynamic required: dewy, vicious, joyful, steely, yellow, navy blue. Nor does she distinguish in value between genres. Boulez uses her because without whining she can learn all that stuff overnight, yet she has no sense of condescension with Reynaldo Hahn. We'll open with the twelve songs of *Women's Voices*; then the three from the first set of Debussy's *Fêtes Galantes*; intermission; Debussy's *Trois Poèmes de Stéphane Mallarmé*, which neither of us has ever heard before but which I've been so long longing to bring to noisy life; and we'll end with the premiere: the ten-part *Nantucket Songs*. (Three encores of mine, incl. *Visits*.)

What wild perversity goaded JH and me to attend, this afternoon, a party at Harpers to honor the new book of Norman Podhoretz? JH defiantly donned a clone outfit, a lumberjack shirt and a visor cap, which the scandalized Sylvia Marlowe, meeting us in the foyer, insisted he remove. Midge was all welcoming warmth, as was Norman, kissing me ostentatiously: he's not ashamed. But what were we doing there, without a protestation? for Norman is The Enemy. Still, not going would have proved nothing either.

27 October

If I grind axes as a composer in the world, as a composer composing I do not. In composition I've no method, have invented naught, have offered to the world no *means* for producing; indeed, I allow myself to produce according to that most dangerous of all means: tailored impulse. Neither leader nor follower nor textbook maker, I am judged only as good or bad, not by whether through learned exegesis I conform to my own graphic system. Since critics don't know bad from good, they have difficulty assessing me, not to mention (and this is the critic's chief chore) describing me.

Long slanted sideburns like guillotine blades . . .

Have begun a little memoir of Ben Weber for *Christopher Street*.

6 November

A week ago tonight, in the Elizabeth Sprague Coolidge Auditorium of the Library of Congress, Phyllis Bryn-Julson and I finally presented our Debussy–Rorem recital. Finally—because every day for six months, as I practiced, I pictured myself at the Library's Steinway before the small but canny audience, and the reality was photographically identical to the advance image. Except that I had a temperature of 103°. The result was that delirium, for two hours controlled by mind-over-matter, gave way to nerveless clarity: I seemed to be playing while hearing myself play (among the canny audience!), and smiling at how "in charge" I was of both ensemble and sonority. Yet the next day I grew worse, and now my uvula's swollen like a great useless phallus limp in a nest of crimson barbed wire.

I could never be a pro performer. For the five or six times each year spent in far-off cities I worry, for months ahead of time, at the very least how I'll find an hour to use the bathroom, and at the very most that I'll be lying, bloody and incommunicado, on the floor of that bathroom. (Auden often expressed the same fear, which became a reality.) There's so much more to a performer's life than performing: being *nice* to the identical strangers, missing planes, wondering where to practise.

Meanwhile, *The Nantucket Songs* seem to have found their way. And never, month after month, did I once weary of working on the Debussy.

8 November

Abed, befevered and raving, what notion is dwelt upon? Hot fudge sundaes? Dismembered torsos? Massive erections? None of the above? Once I asked (in *Paris Diary* apropos of Balanchine's sometimes symmetrical choreography) if art were odd- or even-numbered. Rorschach's inkblot would seem to be even-numbered, yet does not the separating line—that point where your nose meets the mirror, the svelte moth's body 'twixt his widespread identical wings, the palindromic "r" splaying forth and back its galaxy of letters ("Able was I ere I saw Elba")—does not that line, of itself, make symmetry paradoxically odd-numbered? In music can this discussion even be argued, since symmetry exists in space with visually simultaneous directions, while sound by its nature does not go backward?

Well, the *composition* of music exists in space, on paper, so how does a composer, should he want to, locate and notate the central point in a 4/4 measure? Is it thus between the second and third beats:

But *where* between them? Here?

No. Well, then here?

No. There is not a notation for the infinite moment when the guillotine crashes through the exact middle of an even-numbered measure. The precise middle of a 3/4 measure is, of course, the second beat itself:

But the center of 4/4 can be located only by concocting a compound rhythm:

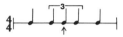

That, raving and befevered, is the notion dwelt upon.

13 November

Weekend in Saint Paul, at Saint Catherine's College, housed in a nunnery; attended a concert of my tunes. Returned for Lenny's *Fidelio* with Shirley, after which a giant party at Mendy Wager's surrealist loft.

Today, a visit from Sheldon Rich, who runs the Santa Fe Chamber Music Festival. Wants me to write a piece in time for performance next summer. Voice, piano, and three or four other instruments. (I must be the pianist and be present for a week or two out there.)

Meeting at the Academy, after which JH joins me for one of their succulent dinners where a mass of distinguished characters act silly. Postprandial program of slides.

Nantucket
19 November

Last week, Losey's film on *Don Giovanni* which I loved. Visit from Christopher Davis. Father's eighty-fifth birthday at the Littauers'. Flew here yesterday. Voorhees for my allergy shot today (the last shot was October 4). (Less and less I like to note here my divers diseases. It's a bid for pity, pity from myself, a pity that can't be bestowed.) Parents due on Wednesday's eight-o'clock ferry with Paul Marshall, for Thanksgiving.

20 November

Rushing to the bathroom I grabbed the first book that came to hand, which turned out to be *The Age of Innocence*. There I read again those masterful (hmmm . . . *mistressful* isn't quite the word either) last paragraphs where Archer withdraws from a longed-for reunion "lest that last shadow of reality should lose its edge"—remembering when I'd first read them a quarter-century ago. It would have been an autumn afternoon (like today in Nantucket, warm and russet) on a café terrace, rue Galilée, and I closed the book, moved, and filled with a Paris evoked by Wharton some thirty years earlier, fictional even then, and so real.

We have the choice, the passing choice, of returning and ruining, or of refraining and keeping. If we keep too long the living person in our heart (imagining that person in a firelit room across the ocean), that person will die. Which is the case with my Paris now. I can go back and rekindle in that same café the rekindling that fired me twenty-five years ago as I evoked Archer rekindling his past. But I cannot close the book—that physically same book—and rise to keep my date with Marie Laure (who was tolerant of lateness only when the need of a book retained her date), because Marie Laure lies underground. Yet, maybe fortunately, for me the power of places has always been stronger than the power of persons.

The older I get the aloner I feel. (But one can grow only so old.) The solitude, classically divorced from company or place, is hinged to a knowledge, recognized even by children, that we rise to heaven unaided. *"Car le joli printemps/C'est le temps d'une aiguille,"* sang Fombeure through Poulenc's lips. Our springtime's but a point, a needle point, in time; but rich and poor can pass with equal ease, though forever single file, through the needle's eye. (I never knew whether that needle's eye was the same as Gide's *Porte étroite*—the "strait gate" to paradise?—mentioned by Saint Matthew.) Those hundreds who perished "simultaneously" at Guyana really died, as the clock ticks, separately.

New York
1 December

Joyce Carol Oates last night, and husband Raymond Smith. (JH's pot roast, my lemon bavarian.) They are Midwestern, not glib and New Yorkish, a touch bland, hard to talk to insofar as they are anxious not to offend. Joyce asks that uncomfortable question, Are you still keeping your wonderful diary? and I must answer no, and explain why. (Explain why.) We talk of prolificity, of which both Joyce and I are so often "accused," as though the accusers had the formula of Art which we're too greedy to heed. Now, prolificity is the very kernel of any so-called creative person. Writers produce; what else should they do? That, for example, Duparc composed only sixteen songs in his lifetime makes him a lesser artist than, for example,

Fauré, who composed exactly the same kind of songs but more of them. Told Joyce that her epistolary account of a composer adored, then menaced, by an anonymous fan was one of the best stories I knew by an American. She claimed to scarcely recall it.

Practicing Debussy's *Villon Ballades*. Show again how much of Debussy's method for development consists merely of repeating, literally repeating, short phrases. His much-touted formal imagination—his structural innovation—is just not there.

3 December

Kenward's *Grass Harp* yesterday afternoon at the Church of the Heavenly Rest. If it cloys, so does Truman's too-coy text.

Visit from Earl Wild and Michael Davis, Earl's first visit here since 1967 when he sold me his Baldwin as we took over his apartment. Later, Ken Fuchs, young composer from Florida last year, who wants to go to Juilliard.

7 December

Mother's birthday last night; we dined at the Waverly.

Tonight, Alvin Ailey. Ugh! Twenty years ago dance was at its zenith; today, when dance is considered by the great unwashed to be at its zenith, it's at its nadir. Music's the first and foremost impulse for dance; without music, dance is dead. Where are the composers today for choreographers? Such music as was used this evening was taped. People paid sixteen dollars for a dance concert that omitted an essential ingredient, live music. As though a gourmet restaurant had served Miracle Whip. Of course, audiences take what they get, gullibly, but would they listen to Isaac Stern play his concertos with a taped orchestra? Ailey apparently pays thousands to an orchestra *not* to play. Union regulations. This money could go toward commissioning a young composer's ballet for just a couple of instruments. (Type this up coherently and send it to . . .)

"What's the matter," asks my dentist when I kvetsch about the wall-to-wall muzak, "don't you like music?" Of course I don't; I'm a musician.

9 December (Sunday)

Churches. Yesterday, *The Play of Saint Nicholas* at Saint John the Divine. Today, memorial service for Harold Brown at Rutgers on Seventy-third. Shirley crisply played his Preludes, which we hadn't heard for thirty-five years, and, sharp as snapshots, they defied time, familiar as one's own feet. Afterward, tea at the Dakota chez Charles-Henri Ford, back from two years in Katmandu and Goa. He defies space, in that no amount of exotica deflects him from—charming though it be—his small-time self-promotion. Not a sentence uttered that doesn't advertise some aspect of his career, generally from the past. Yet, as in the past, he's all for the present, criticizing me for my indifference to The New. Quality seems not to concern him (yet he's known the best), and, unlike me, he refrains from moral judgments.

Finished, after five weeks' labor, the review of *Misia*, and it's no better than the better critics could do in a day. But the weeks did take me back, profitably perhaps, to a time I never—but almost—knew. Question (moral judgment?) as to *Misia's* final "importance." That she was peripheral doesn't make her less important? Yes, it does. I've often thought it would be fun to compose a monologue from the standpoint of the beau at the other end of the wire with the jilted heroine of *La Voix humaine* (assuming that the beau could get in a word edgewise). But Fizdale and Gold, with *Misia*, have already written such a work: great artists seen through the other end of a telescope.

10 December

Since Eliot used an epigraph from *Heart of Darkness* for *The Hollow Men*, does it follow that Conrad might have used an epigraph from *The Hollow Men* for *Heart of Darkness*? This is Coppola's conclusion in *Apocalypse Now*, with the justification of musical impurists when they claim that "if Bach had known our piano he would have loved it." Being an impurist, I love Bach on the piano, though *he* probably wouldn't have; time, sound and space are no more transferable than the meaning of experiences from century to century. However, the Eliot quote (which would have been senseless to Conrad) is more pretentious than provocative in a movie that is elsewhere madly effective but could have been more so with less money. Financial limitations, like censorship, do not make for trammeling of art, they merely make for a tightening of form. Etc. (Also: Absolute evil, presumably represented in Kurtz's camp, is not absolute at all. The picture ends upbeat. Absolute evil is absolute hopelessness: the entire planet as concentration camp.) *Apocalypse Now* absorbed me, even the leaden Marlonian ending, although it wasn't depressing. By depicting the undepictable (which Daphne du Maurier, say, or Tennessee Williams, like Conrad himself, were smart enough to avoid with their invisible personifications of Bad Beauty in *Rebecca* and *Suddenly Last Summer*) Coppola miscalculates. Severed heads strewing the campsite like rotten poppies are horrible, yes, but not The Horror, for they are not our poppies but theirs, and are finite in number. (Lieutenant Calley is as remote as Madame de Farge.) Yet to define, as I would, The Horror as the final loss of hope when our entire planet becomes an anonymous prison without legacy, without even a Hitler, is again too personal, and so probably is Sartre's "Hell is ourself" (or is it "Hell is others"?), though that does hit home. If the self must die and leave no trace, what difference if a few poppies rot, or indeed if the whole world caves in? If we each must die, what difference if ten others die, or a quadrillion? (The Sartrian "self" never dies, and that's *his* ultimate Horror.)

Stephen Koch says I said when I met Peter Hujar at The Dom seventeen years ago I found him handsome and sexy but that when I saw him recently I found him handsome but no longer sexy. Not to alter physically is to be a building, bright in morning, and in the evening the same building in shadows. Sexiness is, and maybe should be, a concern of youth. Older folks have, and maybe should have, other concerns, like, I suppose, The Horror. A magazine headline at the A & P: "You're Not Too Old to Fall in Love." We buy it, having translated the slogan "You're Not Too Old to Be Fallen in Love With."

War, war, unbelievably again the daily threat. War: the attempt to coerce the so-called enemy by mortifying the flesh of Earth. Does it help, truly, that my children's bodies, my own body, or the limbs of tillers of the soil across the globe, be torn asunder, and that the soil itself be poisoned (the rotten poppies), for peace to prevail? So ingrown a pacifist am I by training (which also accounts for my love life, and perhaps, it could be argued, my art, or at least the texture of that art) that no fighting, none at all, can ever seem persuasive in the light of logic. Many a "thinker" disagrees. But if intellectuals can be bigots about homosexuality, they can with equal conviction be hawks. The contradiction—so obvious as to seem naive—that's never explained is: Thou Shalt Not Kill, followed by Kill. (1944, Hate Japs. 1945, Love Japs.) Even the legal system: The time and care and cash dispensed on the "fair trial" of some "nobody" who, though evading the electric chair, is legally slain a week later on the battlefield for ten thousand others.

12 December

The Christmas season. Between the Jews and the Italians last night the Jews won out. Big dinner party chez Lenny Bernstein for Zeffirelli, whom I've not seen since writing the score for his *Lady of the Camellias* in 1963. I never admired him then, and I still don't: he tries for Latin sweetness but is hard beneath, like his productions. When I say I liked his version of *Lucia* (with Sutherland in Paris years ago), but that the opera itself means nothing to me, he regards me with scorn. "Ah, but the sextet, that is great music. And many great musicians have praised *Lucia*." The opera doesn't need his defense. Why does he not, instead, ask my reasons for disliking it? Does he even remember that I am a musician? Italian, he has no irony, and therefore no humor.

Irony is the great Jewish defense and the basis of all humor. Lenny, pontifical and beguiling and irrepressible, accompanied Mendy Wager, Stella Adler, Adolph Green, and especially Peter Ustinov in a varied song recital that was hysterically successful in its professional amateurism. At the piano, he can do anything. As host, with all his dictatorial crassness, he is sweetness itself. He does more than sustain the center of attention by out-shouting everyone else; he does it by out-talenting everyone else.

Extended condolences to the beauteous Betty Comden for the recent loss of her husband. (Once while drunk at a party like this one, I asked her if she'd marry me when I grew up. "But I'm already married," she said, and I said, "Well, he doesn't have to know.")

Christmas Day

Virtually every day of the past fortnight has been filled with dentists, parties, rehearsals, deaths (Peggy Guggenheim, Roy Harris), visits from acquaintances old and new, and family. If I don't develop it here, it's all fast in the yearbook. Just a note or two before leaving tomorrow for Nantucket, very early, with JH:

Enjoyed practising with Will Parker on the 12th, then a party for John Myers at Margot Stewart's, and a supper at Mendy's. On the 13th, all the banks with JH, the American Music Center's party at the Astor Gallery of the Library, then at six Judy, whose apparition delighted Gustavo, whose birthday it was. The 14th, Sharon Isbin's party. The 15th, lunch at Shirley's with her mother, Rae Gabis, and my parents. The 16th, a much-too-crowded "Performer of the Year" thing for Angela in a disco, where we stayed twelve minutes. The 17th, yet another meeting at A.M.C. of the publication committee, where everyone loves to talk, but no new music magazine will emerge because no new music magazine is needed. In the evening to dine, the cherished annual tradition of Maggy Magerstadt and Joe Rosner. The 18th, soirée of French Song provided by Thomas Grubb et Cie. at Alice Tully's comfortable pad. The 19th, heavy snow. The 21st, dentist, party at Boosey & Hawkes (Doris Pope's sensational Christmas pudding), and East Side A.A. meeting at six. Judy & Louis. The 22nd, dined at Heddy

Baum's with the McNeil Lowry's and the Sheldon Riches. (Sheldon wonders if trumpet, oboe, and/or bassoon with percussion might not be apt for my new piece.) The 23rd, a most sympathetic tea party here, with Susan Davenny & Yehudi Wyner, John Gruen & Jane Wilson, Robert Jacobson & Robert Phelps. We listened to tapes of the Washington concert, then my homemade tangerine torte and coffee (no tea). Dined at Earl Wild's. Then a vast party at Gregg Smith's. Last night, Gustavo to dine, then party at Naomi & Percival Goodman's, then party at Lenny Bernstein's, then JH's beautiful Midnight Mass at St. Matthew's & St. Timothy's. Today, to Philadelphia (where I visited Rosemary and all the Marshalls and took them spiced cherries) and back. At the end of the year a check from the Merrill Foundation will provide the substance of support for 1980.

Americans, wrote Tennessee Williams in 1949, suffer from "a misconception of what it means to be . . . any kind of creative artist. They feel it is something to adopt *in the place of* actual living." Couldn't the reverse be posited? The act of making art *is* the artist's actual living, and the humdrum needs of life are a byproduct of that art. The best artists, by and large, lead what outsiders would find dull lives; those whose "actual living" is overly gaudy just haven't the time for art, even when such living forms the art's very material.

1980

Elliott Carter thirty years ago told *Time* that after long writing music in the popular idiom so that it would in fact be popular, it didn't turn out to be popular, so he decided to write (like Ives before him) the "unplayable" music that was truly in his mind. Now history shows that Carter's unplayable music is more played than anyone's.

I say today that, since no one plays my "difficult" music, I'm going to revert to what's always been truly on my mind: lean, popular tunes. Except that no reversion's required. I've never (almost never) been a whore, in the sense that I've performed what I didn't wish to perform: written what was *supposed* to be written.

Nowadays, as so many complicated sheep coming round to simplicity's fold they find me already there. But do I get credit, any more than non-smokers get credit for not smoking during those long decades when now-reformed smokers were up to no good?

Like the Prodigal Son, a person who renounces is more commended than a person who never practiced. Rochberg who retracts his evil ways by reverting to flagrant tonality is more worthy to news-hungry critics than am I. Not that I never wanted to be a whore; I just never had the makings of one who does what he doesn't want to do.

People wonder at my retentive memory. But why live, if only to forget? How do I remember, in fact? By dates and geography and food.

Virgil comes to dine, and as always his table talk shimmers. Afterward when we all adjourn to the parlor he as always falls asleep. Conversation turns to classical music. Virgil awakens.

"What are we discussing?"

"Beethoven."

"Top drawer," says Virgil, and drops off again.

Sun broadcast from Cleveland on WQXR with Lorin Maazel and Irene Gubrud. Orchestrally its best performance, glamorous yet precise. Vocally, also pretty fair, except that Gubrud has, with my reluctant acquiescence, lowered to an A the high-C toward which the first movement, bit by bit, directs itself, thus imposing *coitus interruptus* upon *orgasmo liberatus*.

Sprained ankle in Central Park. Cold and coughing continue after three weeks. Dietrich's *Dishonored* on TV again, and again a surrealist treat.

13 January

Angela Lansbury and Peter Shaw came to dine, also Judy with Louis Nelson. All went well until the last course. Seldom anymore do I have contretemps with friends; elongated misunderstanding is a luxury of youth, and life's now too short to begrudge the ways of our dear ones' indoctrinated styles. (Even lovers' quarrels seem expensive.) But in the past month I've had two—shall I call them setbacks?—both with women, and both about cake. The first was Shirley's last-minute command to bring a chocolate torte to a lunch she was planning for her mother, my parents, plus George and her son, Paul, the last-named quite able to have gone shopping. The second was tonight when Judy, on being presented with an ample slice of my homemade Golden Walnut Kuchen drenched in Grand Marnier, refused it and brooded for the rest of the evening, although there was an alternative non-alcoholized dessert, an apricot whip. I didn't have any cake either, and for the same reason. But Judy overreacted. The Shaws, meanwhile, exemplary.

19 January

Mammoth birthday at Arnold Weissberger's. Arnold and Milton behave as always toward me & JH, in all our modesty, with the same deference they would show to the Empress of Cathay. Indeed, Arnold credits his success as an attorney to the fact that he doesn't differentiate, so far as his comportment's concerned, between, say, my parents employing him (as they did) to make their last will & testament, and a superstar's million-dollar lawsuit. Arnold, with his thrilling smile, white gardenia, Magritte-covered walls (in this Sutton Place apartment that I recall from the days when Inge owned it), and bowler hat, is the image of He Who Has No Enemies. My favorite Weissberger story: When Clay Shaw, in deep trouble at the time of the Kennedy assassination, consults him, Arnold says, "The first thing we must do is find a good lawyer."

Judy for a meeting. Then Erick Hawkins at the Whitney. I've known Erick kindly since those snowy hungover mornings during the war thirty-five years ago when I played for his sessions at Martha Graham's. Now he is someone, but I find many of his dances pre-sophomoric and humorless, like self-expression classes in nursery school. Years ago I asked Edwin Denby, "Do you take Erick seriously?" Edwin gazed back unflinchingly and replied, "Mustn't one?" Still, Erick is the sole American choreographer continuing the tradition of always commissioning new music for new dances (his work with Lucia Dlugoszewski is alone enough to warrant his name in history books), and his sense of *what should be*, although diametrically opposed to my own, is honest and touching.

Sad. Glimmers of war.

23 January

Seated amongst my peers in the oaken meeting room of the Academy of Arts & Letters, sobered by the near-mythical agglomeration, it came to me that in the bad old days I had nevertheless dallied with four of the forty there. (Or, to change the viewpoint, with four of the twenty-eight males.) Rasputin, surrounded by the doting widows, belched, "*Je vous ai toutes eues.*"

Back in the war years John La Touche used to call Donald Fuller his drunk composer. "I want one too," cried Bu Faulkner. "Well, there's always Ned Rorem," everyone said. I was thrilled—not for being ascribed a drunk, but because for the first time I was labeled a composer.

Visit from John Myers. Talk turns to money and to the artist's notorious humiliation in procuring any. He recalls for us La Touche's anecdote of yore. Always skilled with rich dowagers, Touche had an appointment with one he'd never met, in order to solicit funds for a show. The butler, explaining that Madame would be in shortly, bade the guest take a chair and withdrew. Touche was aware of a squeaking crunch. He'd sat heavily upon a Pekingese and killed it. Immediate reaction: There goes the money! What to do? Opening the window, he flung the creature to the street. What would you have done? (Did he get the funds? Yes, he did.)

The Dietrich festival continues. *Blonde Venus*, which I wasn't allowed to see when it came out, is a wonderful mess of the sort that children should not be allowed to see, or they'll grow up like me. Except that I never saw it.

26 January

JH's fairly professional and highly therapeutic production, with piano, of *The Apple Tree* at his church. I sat with K. Exhausted, after rehearsing all afternoon with Will Parker. Yet insomnia as always. Just to get through the night is a minor victory, or Calvary, depending on how you view it.

My ten-movement Double Concerto for Cello, Piano and Orchestra, tentatively rechristened *Green Music*, has been cancelled for May in Cincinnati. The reasons make sense. Jeanne Kirstein, the cellist, died. Walter Susskind, the conductor, died. Jack Kirstein, the pianist, suffered a heart attack, after which he wrote me a long letter telling of his horror at my music, a letter containing this phrase: "But to be served cream puffs when you've ordered steak—even though the cream puffs are *absolutely* extraordinary—is something else again."

28 January

Joyce Carol Oates and Raymond A. Smith this noon for lunch, at which I served a huge mixed garlicky salad, hot croissants, and a rather grainy chocolate mousse from page 272 of *The Alice B. Toklas Cookbook*. They plan to publish both "Lies" and "Being Alone" in *Ontario Review*. Joyce, with her black stockings, spit curls, and soft voice, belies her vicious fictions. (That is, *vicieux*, meaning mildly vice-ridden.) They are not gossips.

Tomorrow Will Parker records *Mourning Scene* with the Columbia Quartet for New World Records.

1 February

Wednesday, Albee's *Lady from Dubuque*, of which the first of the two acts is from a strictly verbal standpoint agreeably fugal. JH still suffering after a massive toothpulling session. Yesterday, party for Ed White's new book, followed by a motley dinner collection at the Dardanelles: me and Gary Clarke, Stephen Koch and Robert Phelps, James Salter and Barbara (Mrs. Larry) Rosenthal and her daughter, Nadia, a molecular biologist. Cold. Later, Dietrich on TV in the giddily artistic *Scarlet Empress*. Today, dentist and bank. Tomorrow, Nantucket. Working on the Santa Fe piece for this summer, a sheaf of poems by the whimsical yet solid Witter Bynner, for baritone (Parker) and piano quartet.

Nantucket
7 February

It's hard to believe that only yesterday we took a quiet ride across the island to Eel Point in the blazing sun. This morning JH flew back to New York just before the blizzard hit. Now I'm closed in by snow, snugly alone with the furnace and the piano, working on some very lively songs. Tomorrow I see Dr. Voorhees for my last shot and to get chest X rays; the cough, plus blood and hoarseness, persist.

JH meanwhile retains more than a residue of suffering from his teeth as well as from K. He weeps occasionally. But this does not impair a clear eye on matters beyond his navel or the handsomeness of his person. Still, like this spit of land on which we now pass so much time and where, because of the Gulf Stream, winters are milder and summers more moderate than in New York, JH's metabolism, though it no longer sinks to utter despair, never rises to elated heights. He's neutral.

Oughtn't someone to blow the whistle on Elliott Carter? Since I'm a colleague I'm not the one. But why did I once—more than once!—write admiringly of him? Because I too was duped, unable to believe that so many people, less intelligent than I, could have left me on the wrong boat. In fact, *they* were on the wrong boat. Of course, critics, who invented Carter, must be faithful to their own inventions (although where now are their dithyrambs to Crumb?). Perhaps it's time therefore to blow the whistle on Andrew Porter and on the whole mystique, which has tainted even the singular the *New Yorker*, of allowing Europeans to come here and hand out grades. Andrew has yet to give an English composer a bad review, much less to give him no review at all. Well, maybe I'd do the same if I were a permanent employee of a major London magazine. But can you imagine England permitting an American such a permanent post?

Opening phrase: No one enjoys Carter, not even Carter, but I can't prove it. (Have I writ it before?) At least one Carter biographer finally gave up on his definitive treatise because he couldn't stand the music any longer.

Let's blow the whistle too on Balanchine, and on Hitchcock, and on Chaplin. And on Liza Minelli, for whom understatement is anathema. Unable just to sing a song, she must forever belt and sell.

10 February

This evening JH and I took Alice Tully to Alice Tully Hall to hear Will Parker's all-American recital—one of the Rockefeller Prize bonuses. He opened with *War Scenes*, dramatic in theory but unhappy in fact; the audience isn't yet primed for such melancholy theatrics.

JH wonders: if Miss Tully were to marry Mr. Hall, would they call it Alice Tully Hall Hall?

New York
12 February

Because of my conspicuous review in *Book World* of Gold & Fizdale's *Misia*, they allowed me to attend yesterday a publisher's party. I enter, garbed in blue velvet, as Jean Stein comes forth from the loud and surprisingly heterogeneous (Sylvia Marlowe, Mick Jagger, Anita Loos) crowd and begins a conversation. After a while I turn to chat briefly with Stella Adler, then turn back to Jean who is now speaking with a tall gentleman whom she doesn't introduce. He seems to be Maugham's biographer—yes, Ted Morgan—so I ask if he knows David Posner, and one thing leads to another until he says that Maugham's mansion's being turned into a hotel, and I say that so is Marie Laure's house in Hyères. He looks at Jean and says, "Marie Laure— she was the one who was so helpful to Ned Rorem." We all stop to blush, because it turns out I am Ned Rorem. Now I say that Marie Laure's house had been next to the Château Saint Pierre, where Tony Gandarillas smoked opium, and he says Tony had been the lover of his grandmother, Maria de Gramont, so I say that I knew Maria in the old days; and who was she to Sanche de Gramont? We stop again and blush, because, nom de plume aside, *he* is Sanche de Gramont.

13 February

JH after three years still flinches from, indeed is periodically floored by, his rapport with K. This, paired now with major oral surgery, has again demoralized him. And though he "copes" with the daily grind, he is not happy, not "realized," and seems paralyzed at the prospect of collating his dangerously overdue business affairs, not to speak of setting down (before it's too late) the little memoir of his beloved early violin teacher, Rhetia Hesselberg (Joachim's pupil who settled in Joplin, Missouri), she to whom he owes his musical career and the mere mention of whom makes his eyes shine.

JH defines professional as the ability to concentrate on creative work, even in adversity, and he cites me as example. By this description professional doesn't necessarily mean high class, only consistent. Oscar Wilde or Chopin or Verlaine or even Oley Speaks are thus professionals, while Emily Dickinson or Duparc or Jean Rhys or even Judy Garland are not. This shuts me up, does not allow me to complain, but is it the case? Yes, probably; whatever it's worth my catalogue is long, "Thro' every passion ranging."

Well, we have our trip to France to look forward to, in less than two months. Gerard Souzay and Dalton Baldwin have promised us their apartment, rent free, and we have the whole of Paris as once we had London.

Notre Dame, Indiana
23 February

A strange pair of days is drawing to a close for me on the campus of Saint Mary's College as guest of the affable musician Roger Briggs. Not only was I nearly felled by flu and saddled with a full speaking schedule, but I was lodged in a sort of nunnery where, because the ticking of the nearby hall clock was so maddening, I dragged a mattress into the bathroom on both Thursday and Friday nights and groaned there sleeplessly.

28 February

A TB test. Judy brought over forty dollars worth of Chinese cuisine, and with JH we quietly consumed this, discussing meanwhile my coughing blood, the dubious X rays, and my possible lung cancer. Judy has new fluffy hair.

1 March

The "spot" on my lung turns out to be identical on another X ray from five years ago. What's more, it's a spot that only people reared in the proximity of the dust from the dried excrement of Chicago pigeons are graced with. This dust, though harmless, is imprinted within many a midwestern chest.

Visit from Tim Dlugos with young artist friend, Duncan Hannah, who brings a portrait of me painted from photographs. I strike a pose, but the damage is done.

Learned of the deaths of both Tom Keogh and Charles Mather—Tom so staunch from the Paris years, and Charles from kindergarten. The past grows larger.

Exceedingly cold. Tomorrow, Hattiesburg, Mississippi.

5 March

Although certain members of the faculty are high in intelligence, charm, and information, and although the climate is intoxicatingly ugly and mysterious, the musical performance level at the University of Southern Mississippi is not first rate, and I'm glad to be home.

Spent this evening in the weird but appealing, and as yet half-unfurnished, flat of Michael Tilson Thomas and Joshua Robison on East Tenth Street. We supped *à trois* on a mocha cake, which I brought from chez Dumas, then listened to a tape of *Sunday Morning*, which Michael was noncommittal about. I'm not comfortable with him. He seems anxious to show you (You, meaning the great TV audience) how, like Lenny Bernstein, his very veins are conduits not of blood but of heaven's music, and this may be so. But you've got to be Lenny to pull it off, and Michael lacks Lenny's charm. Still, there's nothing he's incapable of; he exudes talent and inspires formal sound. (Joshua: cute, supportive, an ex–circus performer.)

7 March

John de Lancie came for lunch yesterday and firmly offered me a job at the Curtis Institute beginning this autumn. (During the whole decade of Serkin's reign there, no composer was on the faculty. Shame.) Then today from his sickbed Sam Barber phoned to say I should, *must*, take the job—that it's "we" and not "they" that need occupy such positions. He added that he hoped Chuck Turner might be useful on the Curtis faculty, and probably he's right. Tonight Mother and Father came to dine; they are anxious for me to accept Philadelphia.

9 March

To the Pitchford-Morgans' at their house on lower Third Avenue for one of Robin's spectacular meals. Kate Millett too was there, and as so often happens when one meets someone known only through their work, she turns out to be not formidable, even soft-spoken, but keen about what she believes. She'd just returned from behind the Iron Curtain. JH was less annoyed than amused by everyone's farfetched claims re female pornography (e.g., Linda Lovelace's predicament derives from male coercion, and there but for the grace of fate goes every American woman, nay even unto Ms. Millett), and Kenneth was perhaps too quick to defend the cause of women rather than letting *them* speak. It's disheartening to regard Kenneth's violent passivity when he could be frying other fish, like the gay liberation he so championed ten years ago. The fact that I musicalized the verses of both Kenneth and Robin, back in the midsixties, attests my esteem. Are they uttering anything now that could be—needs to be—sung?

Are there animal rights? Would the women's movement laud the female spider, which devours the male, or suppress the male lion, which permits his harem to forage for him? If they counter that ecology and the law of the jungle make for a needed balance of nature, then could the same not be said for human relations? By that token, of course, the "need" for war must be allowed. Yet I am human too and feel no such need, and surely my feeling is not based solely on pacifist rearing.

They will not touch on the rape of men. Yet what is it but rape when men, as a sex, are—against their own will, not to mention the Ten Commandments—drafted to be killed?

25 March

I never go to A.A., except once or twice a year when, at their request, I introduce anxious acquaintances into the society. Nor have I ever spoken out formally—never *qualified*, as they say—at an A.A. meeting; in the early years I was never sober for the stipulated three months; in later years it's because I've simply been out of touch. (My last drinking was in 1967; my last drink was in 1972.) But now I've been invited to address the "Renewal East" group tomorrow night, and so I asked Judy over this afternoon to "audition" for her my variations on these points:

(1) My name is Ned and I am an alcoholic. That phrase still makes me wince. And yet I'm proud to be alcoholic. Knowing it, admitting it, has helped to sort out priorities, to stabilize aspects of my nature, and to teach me who I am.

(2) State of sobriety: The snug feel of not-being-drunk, which no outsiders can know. (Outsiders, curled up with hot buttered rum.)

(3) Born during Prohibition. Huck Finn's father. (Little did I know that in ten years, after one drink, I'd sell my own mother.) Repeal. Fear of being slain, on the way to school, by a drunk. First whisky, a straight shot, like the fires of paradise.

(4) Just as at fifteen I assumed all the other boys went home after school to write music, so at twenty I assumed that everyone at the cocktail party was going to have, like me, a dozen martinis.

(5) Psychoanalysis is to alcoholism as wheat germ is to a broken leg. Alcoholism defined: In that parlor game of stating quickly, in two words, who or what you are, my reflex is to answer: musician and alcoholic. A friend says, "You're not an alcoholic. My uncle Jake was alcoholic. You don't drink like him." There is no absolute medical definition, nor abstract lay definition. An alcoholic is self-defined.

(6) France: (a) Everyone, from the age of three, is always slightly drunk,

because wine is a food. (b) Not to accept a drink is to be suspected of vene-real disease. (c) There is no God, except for drunks. (True: drunks don't often catch the flu, or get beaten up. But they do get robbed. And their "state" masks a hundred ills.)

(7) Morocco and Utah: Not alcoholic countries. . . . I was incipiently al-coholic, and incipiently a composer, from birth. My sister was not.

(8) First brush with A.A. in 1958. Bill Inge and Charlie Jackson, glittering proselytizers, both committed suicide all the same. Thus with my *Paris Di-ary* (1966), when Virgil Thomson said to me at the publication celebration, "You're not supposed to get drunk at a party for a book about getting drunk," I realized that one can't *get rid* of an illness within a work of art, any more than through a single A.A. meeting. The therapy must be repeated forever.

(9) Liquor and success. (Alcoholics are not all failures.) Success, with its abnormality (especially in America), is as hard to swallow as rejection. Be-sides, who thinks of himself as a success?

(10) Waking up with strangers in distant hotel rooms. Once too often. This made me turn literally cold sober. Sobriety brings reticence.

(11) Regressive when drunk.

(12) Moderation for me, as for most drunks, is impossible. A drunk's ex-cessive by definition. When I went on the wagon, I was, so to speak, exces-sively moderate.

(13) Liquor makes fools think they are artists. It also turns artists into fools.

(14) I am glad this is not a Beginner's Meeting. Because what I'm stating is not the surest route to follow. If I have been "cold sober" for nearly ten years, I seldom go to meetings. One can observe the sacraments without having to pass roll call.

(15) If I wasn't ready in 1959—if I had to wait another decade—it's be-cause I kept wanting someone from outside, a lover or a doctor, to make an ultimatum, to say: you must stop drinking for my sake, or for the sake of your physical health. But no one else will ever make you sober.

(16) I drank to stop time.

(17) When I first came into A.A. there was a movie everyone talked about, *The Days of Wine and Roses*. The title came from Ernest Dowson's verses:

> They are not long, the days of wine and roses:
>> Out of a misty dream
> Our path emerges for a while, then closes
>> Within a dream.

Well, I don't know about the roses, but the days of wine seemed to last forever. Perhaps the roses, with all their thorns, are the days we are now passing through.

26 March

The evening didn't pan out quite as planned. JH, who's never been to an A.A. meeting, agreed to come along for moral support, and so did Ann Thorne. We picked Ann up an hour early, and immediately I broke out crying. The idea seemed so futile, so ugly, of reviving all that garbage from yore, in front of JH who never knew me then, and in front of strangers; and of reviving too the gluttonous masochistic carnal *pleasure* of having been a drunk, of having dwelt so long so close to murder, the risks run, without my seeing them as risks. But the tears were cathartic. The speech was smooth, in control, bordered on sentimental, objective, a touch show-biz. Afterward the three of us had corned beef at a Lexington Avenue deli.

I shan't repeat the number (because it *is* a number; which some members perfect and offer from group to group around town, tuning it as to a laugh-track or a soap-opera rerun, while admitting that the very repetition is healthy, even crucial, the way the Holocaust is continually italicized by Jews—as it should be also by gypsies, homosexuals, and all the tortured pariahs).

Considering how this diary once centered around drink, it's remarkable how, except for this entry, the subject has simply slipped my mind, or rather my body, for the past fifteen years. Yet alcoholism remains as close as a Siamese twin. So does the memory of Marie Laure, about whom I never write anymore either.

6 April

Easter, crackling sunlight in cloisonné heaven. A review of the past few days before cousin Sara Watts, because of the ongoing transport strike, comes by in her red & white auto to deliver us to the Boston shuttle.

Annual lunch last Wednesday (same day as the A.A. trauma) with Robert Jacobson at Café des Artistes to discuss an article on the Met's upcoming triple French bill. Of all opera buffs (a breed foreign to my nature), Robert is the most finely tuned, the least dogmatic.

Visit from David Loeb who, with me, will constitute the composition department at Curtis. Visit from a Ms. Krebs of Dayton, who's writing a biography of Tommy Schippers. Visit from Tony Angarano and Rod Hardesty about my doing a piece for the latter, notably a piece for countertenor and double bass. Morning visit same day (Saturday) from John and Andréa de Lancie, and in the evening dined with parents. Phoned Souzay in Paris to discuss keys, furnace, etc.

Sunday, the Istomins *chez eux*. Left shin aches sharply again as it did a fortnight ago.

Monday, rain and sleet, and March goes out like a lion. Wallace had another convulsion, hideous to behold, his fourth since last summer. Shin hurting still.

April Fools' Day, delivered finished score of *The Santa Fe Songs* to Boosey & Hawkes. Saw *Tally's Folly* with Morris. Lanford Wilson is not my cup of tea—too bourgeois, cloying—but skillful. Fumigated.

Wednesday, JH's 41st birthday.

Thursday, visit from Tom Steele of *Christopher Street* asking me to experiment with a monthly column therein. I shall. Later, Rorems and Rosemary on Charles Street. Also doctor.

So we're off to Nantucket, whence JH returns to New York on Friday. Then we'll join up again a week from today at Logan Airport and, if all goes well, board TWA flight #810 for France. Shirley's daughter, Daisy Rhoads, will occupy the apartment, feeding the cats, while we're away.

Nantucket
13 April

As usual, fog hovers ever thicker over Nantucket. Eternal quandary: Will the plane leave for Boston in time to connect with JH (who's flying up from New York) at TWA? To want something so much you can't possibly have it. Plane won't leave, ever. But if it does, what of Paris? The streets will be as I remember them, like a photograph, and the smells, the conversation; yet old friends and their heady wit, former lovers and their lewd odor, are now mostly underground. (Elaine Lorillard decides against buying a Jane Freilicher oil because she—Elaine—doesn't care for green.)

26 rue Freycinet,
Paris
18 April

The city is in mourning. Sartre's death this week is tragic, not because (as the ever canny JH points out) an existential hero is gone, but because a Hero is *publically* gone. Sartre, expiring in the limelight, becomes a Thing, and his existentialism flies out the window.

Arrived five days ago, exhilarated and exhausted, into perfect weather. Guy met us at the airport and drove us here. Gérard Souzay has lent us (he's in Japan) his apartment for three weeks, vast, disordered, convenient, with an oriental piano and a locked room in the rear that emits a faint sound of sobbing. Paris: not disappointment, just detachment; the town is as unrelated to me as the faint sound of sobbing. The Flore is identical, but my life has a term. Used to miss my lost youth here; now if that youth reappeared, what could it be used for? Together in Paris with JH for the first time, I see everything through his eyes. Still more odd: Souzay's flat is a half-block away from my old home, the Noailles' now-gutted mansion in place des États-Unis. I know the neighborhood *comme ma poche*, but when JH asks, "Well, where do we buy croissants and toothpaste and shoe polish?" I'm at a loss; the servants did all that! He's come to know the *quartier* better (or differently) than I ever did. Continued insomnia, both of us. Chestnut and sycamores severely pruned, though the morning market already offers large Spanish strawberries, flavorsome as roses, and tomatoes that taste like tomatoes.

Marcel Schneider, cultivated and caring, thought Maugham was the author of *Catcher in the Rye*, and they all still see America in terms of Hemingway and Gershwin. Gavoty (a.k.a. Clarendon), for whom I was, a quarter century ago, *the* American, responds to a phone call with frantic disinterest, and can't make a date because (a) he has new blood pumped through him three times a week, and (b) my absent host dyes his hair. When I protest that Souzay's the greatest of baritones, Gavoty replies, "*Il l'était. Mais il faut du nouveau.*"

What's new at the opera? Why, they seem to be doing a divine production of *Les noces de Figaro*. At the theater? Hmm. Well, the Comédie Française has a marvelous *Tartuffe* at the moment. And . . . oh yes, there's also a great revival of *En attendant Godot*.

19 April

Dine chez Noel Lee. Plays us a record of Dutilleux's *Deuxième Symphonie*, the sweeping first movement of which sounds as necessary and true as any music in a long time. If Dutilleux isn't finally "as good as" Messiaen, it's that he lacks the added zest of dementia.

20 April

JH arose at 5 A.M. and made a tour of churches. Mammoth Saint Eustache, former home of Langlais, empty, bereft of an organ. The Madeleine intoned simpering tunes for fat cats. Saint Merry, closed. Trinité sans Messiaen. Notre Dame, smudged tone. Only at Saint Sulpice, home of Widor and Dupré, was there a lively service.

Is the French cat, by virtue of living among the French, ever so slightly different, evolutionarily, from the Kansan cat? Look at Foujita's etchings of cats versus the cat of Manet's Olympia, or the cats of Chicago's Gertrude Abercrombie, not to mention those old Egyptian statuettes, and realize that the creatures themselves may sense a mutual remoteness.

Dined chez José (Henri Hell), with Richard Negroux and Robert Kanters. José pontificates as though he were the sole authority on Poulenc, leaving no room for argument.

Lise Deharme is dead. I learned this months ago in New York, but no one here seems to know. It takes outsiders to bring home news. Kanters, himself now nearly blind, said: "Ah, Lise est morte? Elle a dû se piquer."

Juliette Gréco is regarded as an old lady. In pop music, women have vanished (are banished)—not, like men, allowed to age. Youth mostly hears American disco. Weirdly, everyone knows Satie. He's played on pop programs, on radio, in movies and in jukeboxes, and his name is in a category with, say, Mick Jagger's.

23 April

Dîner chez Sauguet. Also Raphaël (resembling Jacques Dupont, whom he never knew), his great dane, Coeur, and Jeanne Ritcher looking frail. Flawless four-course meal by Mohamet. Cheese soufflé, *sauté d'agneau* with carrots and turnips, three cheeses, green salad, a non-sweet apple tart. We took seven roses (two pink, two red, three orange—fifty-six francs), but found the many small rooms already crowded with lilacs from Coutras. Sauguet, fairly fit at seventy-nine. His venom re Boulez. Recording of his hurtingly nostalgic *Sonatine Bucolique* for saxophone and piano, uneven as always. JH leaves early for . . . elsewhere. Raphaël and Coeur walk me to the Clichy métro via the rue Fontaine with its old-fashioned whores.

Chartres. I can't concentrate on history unless I read it, nor on architecture unless I hear it. The cathedral is unaccountably dirty—dusty statues that could be (but haven't been for decades) vacuumed in a trice. And how long can you consider a rose window? After seven minutes, or three hours, or a year, do you clap? (At the unveiling of Chagall's ceiling at the Opéra in 1964, nobody knew how to react.) Of course, JH's disinterest is contagious, and the icy rain is no help. Still, even in 1949 when Guy drove me here, the two most memorable moments were the Proustian sighting from miles away of the silver *clocher*, and the consuming of apricot sherbet in a nearby cafe.

The apricot sherbet, in turn, brought back the apricot sherbet of Geneva in 1936. Has France more to teach me, beyond teaching me more about itself than about myself?

25 April

Salle Cortot last night, concert devoted to Les Six and l'École d'Arcueil. Despite the attendance of such *maîtres* as Sauguet and Auric (seated directly behind us with the beauteous Nora, whom I do not acknowledge, her eyes like red pokers scorching my nape), the performances were eighth rate. The French spawn technicians who can *solfège* us under the table, but they do not spawn pretty voices. The long program of mainly songs had the renditions it deserved: when all is nose-thumbing then nothing is nose-thumbing, and the thin gruel that lies between, except for Poulenc's *Bestiare*, tastes flat. If this concert of the earliest work by France's two schools of current octogenarians were pitted against a program of, say, the oboe concertos of Jean Françaix and Jacques Ibert, Ibert and Françaix would win hands down. Yet who ever plays them now?

Boulez, it could be argued, is as nose-thumbing as Les Six, with as little to say. French music seems either too complex or too simpleminded, never just right.

May Day

JH has flown back to New York. The streets of Paris no longer remind me of trysts years ago with now-dead lovers but of trips with JH weeks ago.

2 May

Seventy minutes yesterday drinking Coke with James Lord (unchanged· tweed jacket, red polo shirt, yellow socks) on the terrace of his clean wi penthouse, rue des Beaux Arts. Why does he remain in Paris, persisting in his life's work, *A Life of Giacometti*, when the rest of us long since went home to sink or swim? Because he can't bear to align himself with his ugly nationals. Here, if he's a pear in a barrel of apples, his identity is clear at least to him. Nor is he concerned as I sadly am of surviving his epoch through his work.

Then two hours, just around the corner on rue Bonaparte, with affably keen Betsy Jolas, whose rich art seems more snarled than I'd anticipated. Complicated and theatrical, unmeasured and without tonal center, it's perhaps too willfully up-to-date. It's all there on paper, it all *sounds*, and a true poet did pen those notes; yet if a work of art is its own definition (the sole possible version of itself), then Betsy wavers.

She certainly has me pegged as a conservative, which is how I peg her but for opposite reasons. Indeed, France flamboyantly longs to *conserve* the notion of avant-garde. When I ask Betsy how her students at the Conservatoire would take to me and my music, she waits a full minute, then says, with measured tact, "I think they'd be quite interested in what you have to say."

Dined with François Valéry at the Ministères in rue du Bac where thirty years ago we dined better at a tenth the price. He remains the visual carbon of his great father. Very *bavard*, his machine-gun French is lavish though not generous. He speaks anecdotally of trends and of friends but proffers little of himself and asks you little of yourself. I question him about the eighty-year-old Jeanne Voilier, who last Saturday at Jean Chalon's claimed to have been Paul Valéry's one love. "Yes, she does possess those thousand letters she boasts of," says François, "and four hundred unpublished love poems. But they aren't very good."

Of his friend Callas he says: She didn't really care much for music, including her own little repertory. She hated Puccini, including *Tosca*, and liked only *Norma*, parts of *Il Pirate*, and the baritone aria that opens the third act of *Don Carlos*. If she lamented the advent of Caballé—"*C'est ça, la nouvella prrrima donna?!*" (her French was apparently Greekish)—she did admire the young Tebaldi. She despised male homosexuals (biting the hand that fed her), except maybe for those who, like Pasolini, made firm political points. Humorless, self-involved, her force was her indefatigability, and she ate a lot at odd hours: rare steak at teatime, two or three Eskimo Pies at the movies.

Few people anymore, says François, can speak of even Gide, let alone of the brainy hostesses—now all dead—of bygone decades. As he drove me home through the storm he gave me news of Claude.

3 *May*

Visit from the American pianist Jay Gottlieb who, with his twin, percussionist Gordon, was born on my birthday in 1949, six months after I first landed in Cherbourg. With relish, indeed with gluttony, he gives me a recital, as I had requested, of his modern repertory. He goes at the ivories with the agility of a twenty-pound spider, and I'm dazzled by the métier while finding the selections an undifferentiated mishmash. Is he moved? Does he cry? Yes, and he replays the last page of Messiaen's *Étude* to prove it. Does he play "normal" music too? Yes, and he begins to limn the opening of Ravel's *Trio*, which is much too *interpreted*.

Jean de Rigeault shows up, we have tea, and they accompany me to boulevard Saint Michel where I buy a huge tome of Hindu pornography and a magnum of champagne as house gifts for Gérard and Dalton.

Rue de Seine, exhibition by Léonor Fini. Pastiches, seemingly of Jacques Callot, outlined like neon in thrillingly faint orange or rose strokes. But the subject matter, coming from her, offends me still, as it offended me long ago: males intercopulating.

Long walk, past 75 rue de Vaugirard, and thoughts of Henri (who with P. was the most sexual man I've ever known), to meet Jeanne Ritcher and Robert Veyron-Lacroix and dine on boulevard Montparnasse. Robert, France's leading harpsichordist and my exact contemporary seems trim, even thin, and does not, like so many middle-aged Frenchmen, color his very gray hair. Jeanne is ravishing but ravaged, her skin transparent as La Tour's virgin. Although we don't say it when we kiss good-bye, we know we'll never meet again.

4 May

Déjeuner et séance d'écoute chez Jean-Pierre Marty. *Les Mamelles.* My Concerto. Dominique Barthe and friend from Toulon.

Fugitive hour chez Brion Gysin overlooking the Beaubourg piazza. His bathroom with colostomy utensils. His wish for extinction. His frightening features. What is the worth of his famous simpleminded stroboscopic lamps, his linoleum paintings, his mudpie collaborations with Burroughs, his baby-talk songs with Stephen Lacey? And yet . . . the Lacey songs stay in the mind, and so does the sight of Brion's wrinkled brow, tense good humor, and view of the fairground from the dirty window of his small Moroccan pad.

All the dead friends. And so many of the quick, when once our lusting bodies were locked onto each other like horseshoe crabs, are now, as they say, old parties talking only about medication.

5 May

Two hours a day I've practised, on Gérard's Yamaha, the repertory for July in Santa Fe. That is, on the new *Santa Fe Songs*, which Will Parker will premiere, and on the French-American program Will and I will do there and in Seattle. Oh, Poulenc's exasperating sloppiness (that's the only word, for it's not mannerism but oversight) in the accompaniments of his fast songs: notes, notes, notes, the want (unlike Chopin's fast pieces) of a fixed pattern!

Repeating a figuration with a slight difference: not a difference that makes a difference—as in a variational quirk of tune—but a difference that makes merely a difficulty.

New York
7 May

A dead man in the subway. At first he seemed perhaps drunk, propped against a bench, sitting as at a picnic. But then his sightless eyes, the look of surprise at realizing his radical state, the red hole in his forehead, and the three policemen scribbling reports made me, like the other pedestrians, want to recoil, and I felt guilty—but why guilty?

Oh, someone to hold doors open for me, and light my cigarette! Except that I've given up smoking and never go through doors.

Bemidji, Minnesota
14 May

Here for seventy-two hours of the usual stint. The choruses of the north Midwest are the best in America: these unpaid Lutheran children with their sweet-potato-hue hair and trusting eyes, knowing what the words *mean* and how to impart them. The professional choirs of Manhattan cannot hold a candle . . .

JH's rare perception. Yet his habit of leaving lit cigarettes poised on the edge of Chippendale chairs or over wastebaskets filled with paper!

We know the effusion of compliments from our friends, but we don't know what they don't tell us—and what they don't tell us, *c'est nous*. By the same token, the world doesn't know what we don't give to it. But if the world is unaware of our witty broadcasts, it is also, fortunately and by definition, unaware of our stillborn children.

I haven't accomplished a thing today.
    You just gave a concert.
    That's dissemination, not production.

New York
19 May

Pre-concert dinner chez Flora Irving in honor of the American Composers Orchestra. Judy Collins and I are seated at a special side table with four others: Aaron Copland, ex-mayor John Lindsay, our hostess, and Ann Thorne. Aaron breaks the ice by asking Lindsay, "Have you ever been at the same table with two composers before?" Unconscionably long silence, pierced by Mrs. Irving: "Judy's a composer too." Judy widens her violet eyes and says, "I was waiting for someone to mention it." Aaron turns toward Judy with a surprised gaze not unlike that of Marilyn Monroe observing the juvenile heir in *Gentlemen Prefer Blondes*. No reaction. We dine and converse and things flow smoothly (although I tell Lindsay that my mother hadn't voted for him because he advocated the draft). Twenty minutes later Aaron asks Lindsay, "Have you ever been at the same table with two composers before?"

26 May

Gave a reading for The Glines at the Actors' Playhouse in Sheridan Square. A crowd, for a change. All dolled up in my London suit with bell-bottoms, a broad wool scarlet tie on a cream-colored shirt, and new (tight) shoes. I thought I cut a sophisticated figure, but Elliott Stein assured me I looked as though I'd come from my Bar Mitzvah. Later, supper at Duffs with Chris Cox and Ed White, Felice Picano, JH & K.

Warm, very. The *Suite for Guitar* is now in print, prettily, the cover in sparrow-gray stock with dropped-out white characters.

Practicing with Will Parker, of the virile velvet voice and an intelligence that doesn't question a genre but only the quality of a genre. From the standpoint of American composers, he's our best baritone today. (But on off days he's unpredictable, letting out squawks he's unaware of.)

29 May

Long visit from Jon Bradshaw, a Californian who's planning a biography of Libby Holman. Then Will Parker. Then David Del Tredici, with whom I attend the A.C.A. reception for Joe Machlis and John Duffy. Then, with Joel Conarroe, to the Juilliard Orchestra, which played David Diamond's Seventh Symphony.

30 May

Dick Cavett's researcher—or segment producer, as they're called—Lynda Sheldon, came for two hours this morning. By coincidence, she lives across the street; we've been using the same Food City for years. A likeable curly-haired blonde, she is thoroughly prepared, knowing more about me than the F.B.I. I'm to have a double segment, that is, a two-part interview of two half-hour sessions, on June 19th, and they'll be broadcast the following week. My only stipulations are (1) that we begin with a few minutes of live music, and (2) no talk about queerness or money. Lynda can't guarantee the second: Cavett (who, yes, will have read my books) never likes to meet his guest until the last moment, and believes in surprises. But for the music, we agree that Will Parker, with me accompanying, will sing three of my songs as a curtain-raiser, even though a piano will have to be brought in, and Cavett will doubtless decide that music at the very start will kill the show. But then, why am I on?

JH comes into the room for a minute and asks Lynda how many programs they've taped and *not* broadcast. Answer: three out of thousands. (Will mine make four?) Lynda and I are to meet twice again.

At 2:00, posed for Fred Plaut's camera. At 5:30 a runthrough at Leontyne Price's. (Three songs of mine.) Copying parts of *The Santa Fe Songs*. Very tired.

Nantucket
8 June

Henry Miller just died. Anaïs Nin can come to meet her maker.

Quiz for a composer: select a sequence of notes—a harmonic phrase or brief "paragraph"—from one of his own works. If he is unable to identify the sequence out of context, he is beheaded.

Rheumatism of left shin again.

17 June

Mostly I've been practicing for Santa Fe next month, working out of doors, reading. Not composing. Tomorrow I fly back to New York for forty-eight hours to do the Dick Cavett thing, for which I've bought a tan summer suit, tan shoes, and a yellow tie. The two "days" will be filmed back to back, that is, in the studio (the same studio where five years ago we did those thirteen cultured roundtables) from 1:00 until 2:30. I asked JH what I should do that nobody else has ever done on the show, and he answered, Walk on your hands.

First Day of Summer

A composer is a composer only when he's composing. Yet there I sat in my party clothes, with my special charm (or lack of it) and knack for talking *about* my work. Isn't that talk hot air if the work can't speak for itself?

The taping went briskly, with Judy backstage massaging my neck, and Lynda, calm and all-knowing, presiding. Will and I dispatched the three ditties, after which Cavett, without preamble, asked, "What do you have against Beverly Sills?" From then on, smooth sailing. I spoke about what matters—the demystification of composers, the economics of art—so there was scarcely a second to interpolate sentimentality, much less personal habits or even whimsy, until toward the end, when Cavett (who's the spitting image of Artaud, from whom he couldn't be more remote) pulled forth Truman Capote's remarks about me in an old *Esquire*, and I declared, "He's a liar." Cavett persisted (I later was told he was goading for a retraction, fearful of another lawsuit). So I changed the subject with, "Would you like to see me do the one thing that no other Pulitzer Prize winner can do?" Whereupon I stood up, removed the lapel microphone, took off the new jacket and shoes (as Cavett gaped with a half-smile, as though I might pull a gun), and proceeded to walk about the studio on my hands as the audience went wild.

For Cavett's guests the show is a means to an end; for himself the show is itself the end. The point of Cavett is to be on the Cavett show; he has achieved that goal.

A man is homosexual if he says he is.
    Or if he's caught in the act.
    Suppose it's the first time he's performed the act? Who makes the rules?

Cavett to Tynan (as one effete straight to another): "Have you ever?"
    Tynan (feigning—but not really feigning—a limp wrist): "I've tried. Lord, how I've tried."

To Saul Bellow: "Do you think Shakespeare was homosexual?"
    Bellow: "Oh come on Dick, let's give him *some* credit."
    Cheever ignores the issue, but doesn't protest when Dick lumps homosexuality with murder, rape, alcoholism, and other of Cheever's recent subjects.

Alcoholism is more socially acceptable than homosexuality.

Nantucket
24 June

Reading Sono Osato's memoir. If I ever write one, surely I must include the influence of her mother, Frances Osato, on my life. The Wooded Island . . . dancing with Perry O'Neill . . . Teru and Tim . . . meeting Sono backstage, as Odalisque with safety pins. (Don't I mention, many pages back, meeting Mary Wigman?) Frances in New York . . . Teru & Vince in Brooklyn Heights . . . Bertelin, and the Basque Songs (influence on my *The Call*) . . . Frances, who willed her music to me.

And shouldn't I refer to the 1936 diary, when we took the train through Germany (from France to Copenhagen was it?), how our parents shushed us when we comically shrieked *Heil Hitler* out the window?

Am planning a cycle, for one vocalist and several instruments, to be called *Eight Songs for a Sane Queen*.

26 June

Melon ice cream. Cisco beach. First swim of the season. Rorems arrive by ferry from Hyannis.

10 July

The summer is not, as in the city, made of climaxes and dips. Except that it is: high points are meals, or cutting your foot, or the minimal social life (tea with Olga Carlisle, say, or the beginning by Nils Van Vorst of the carpentry on the new side porch). A low was the airing of the Cavett show throughout the nation which set off in me a fit of hysterics. Not because it was embarrassing (it was professional, witty and informative) but because it was public. That Ned there on the screen, so sure of himself, has nothing to do with me.

Tonight, Mimsi and Robin Harbach come to dine. Next week, New York again for a few days before embarking for Santa Fe.

Santa Fe
31 July

A hundred and fifty years ago Composer and Performer—hitherto, often as not, the same person—began, for whatever reason, gradually but inexorably to turn their backs on each other so that they now face in opposite directions. That situation is unique to music, the other arts having kept pace with the moment. Books reviewed in this morning's *Times* were published this year; movies showing around town are by definition contemporary; most choreography today is by living persons, and most galleries exhibit mostly living painters. As for theater, "legitimate" and otherwise, it is so regularly the work of active playwrights, that when a drama of O'Neill's comes along we speak of a revival. But we do not speak of a Beethoven revival where Beethoven is the rule. Music's the sole art that hovers over the fading past. That this predicament should forever come as news—bad news—to the pedantically powerful peddlars of musical flesh who presume to know what audiences want is degrading to living composers, on whom it has formed a deep wound.

The wound has been temporarily salved for me this exceptional fortnight in Santa Fe, where I've been a "public guest" of Sheldon Rich's Chamber Music Festival. Old and new works of mine have been maximally rehearsed and glitteringly dispatched by first-rate general practitioners, as distinct from first-rate Modern Music Specialists so often met in academe. I've also been displayed, for better or worse, as pianist and speechifier, and surely got as good as I gave. With a kind of morose joy I've discovered that general practitioners, no less than the general public, when they think about composers at all, still think of them as in the grave.

The Santa Fe Songs, tailor-made for baritone and piano quartet, was premiered. One stipulation by the commissioners was that I myself act as pianist in the first performances. During an open discussion rehearsal for the nonpaying public I announced that although I'm vastly experienced in hearing my music performed and in performing myself as accompanist to singers, I have never, never played with a chamber group. (Whispers of disbelief from the audience.) Turning to my string-playing colleagues, Ani Kavafian, Heiichiro Ohyama and Timothy Eddy, all pretty experienced themselves, I asked if any of them has ever performed—not coached, but actually played—with a composer. Silence. (More whispers of disbelief.)

The unusual inclusion of a live composer at the open rehearsal did strike both artists and listeners as so uncoercively logical that I was momentarily regarded less as a talking dog than as a functioning member of the musical community. That such a community in America should be an exception and not a rule is outrageous.

Sheldon does things right. I've been lodged in a four-room cottage on the estate of Edward and Mary Jean Cook who stock the kitchen each morning with, among other things, their own handpicked raspberries. There've been daily interviews and publicity, not only here but in New York. Rehearsals have been more than ample, and the various halls are jam-packed for every performance. I have both bicycles and chauffeurs; an endless array of parties; the bonus of the opera company ten kilometers off; a signing of my prose & tunes in the local "better bookstore" called The Bindery. And landscape tours. Plus the fee.

I recall a lunch with Noel Ferrand and David Amram in Taos, where John Giovando drove me. An evening meal with Earl Wild and Michael Davis in the gorgeous house (half in, half out, Japanese style) of Diane Jergens. The recital with Will Parker of two Debussy cycles plus *War Scenes* in an Indian church. Sunsets.

It's late afternoon. I write this—yellow pad on my lap, bathed and garbed in the tan summer suit—while awaiting Brigitta Lieberson and Paul Wolfe. We'll dine at The Compound on Canyon Road, thence to the final concert consisting of two Bach suites for solo cello, and in between them my two suites, *Day Music* and *Night Music*, for violin and piano. *Day Music* will be performed by Franco Gulli and his expert spouse (they have all the good points of Italians, but alas, none of the bad ones), and *Night Music* by Daniel Phillips and Edward Auer. Then a party at Sheldon and Alicia's. Tomorrow at dawn, departure for Nantucket. Surprisingly, there are no nonstop planes.

With all of this, I still don't dig the fact of Santa Fe. I miss the point when people, *rich* people, oh and ah over this melancholy site which to me resembles a giant mud bath. Why here, and not the south of France?

Nantucket
9 August

Very very very very hot and muggy, rare for Nantucket where weather extremes are usually softened by favorable ocean currents. The precious cats, as always, Wallace (whose seizures continue), Princess, Sam, and also as a brief pensionaire, K's Calypso.

Stephen Koch's been here for the month, a pleasant presence on Pleasant Street, with Peter Hujar. Also Frank & Cynthia Stewart of Cincinnati's upper classes, and *comme toujours*, Rosette, the Harbachs, and . . .

12 August

How impressed I was last month when Edward Auer, in Santa Fe, complimented me on my piano-playing: "We all spend hours every day practicing trills and scales. But you cut through all that, and play the music." I don't know what he means, but I know what he means. Like Helen Hayes, who's a real actress but a lousy one, in contrast to Maureen Stapleton, who's not an actress at all but a good one. And he said, apropos of *Day Music*, "Your music's like architecture in the sense that it's filled with cornices which jut into midair, then stop. When you've said what you have to say, you shut up."

How do you write a piece? I don't know. What you don't know won't hurt you, but a little knowledge is a dangerous thing. A lot of knowledge is dangerous, too, though what you know doesn't always hurt. Yes, but how does one write a piece? I don't know. I do know—and all composers will concur—that every time is the first time. That blank sheet!

Next month, partly to please Mother and Father because Curtis is such a distinguished school (distinction makes up for the small salary, I'm told), I'll start teaching again.

The first problem is to find a problem. If the notorious suffering that results in good music were a suffering of the heart—of passionate compassion and of experience—then millions would be great artists by eighteen. Music is plainer than that. It results from a formal suffering quite self-involved: the pressure of discovering the sole solution to a given problem. If the problem cannot be disentangled like a spiderweb and rewoven into the five straight lines of a staff, as by a Palestrina, then it must be shattered like a safe, as by an Ives, who scattered debris but froze the basic lightning in crystal.

But first comes the problem of inventing a problem worth solving. Given the state of our world, such musical puzzles are worthless, even senseless, yet their pursuit is compulsive. The need to find meaning in the compulsion has always caused pain, even to the great who were otherwise happy. And isn't the state of our world senseless too?

The questions children ask us are the same we ask ourselves until we die.

Like the foreign language student who finally understands everything in a phrase except the point, so a composer knows all about music except the essential. He alone hits the nail on the head, but even for him the head remains invisible.

"Your songs are flowering dewdrops," you explain. Aren't they also drops of blood gushing from center target? If so, would you or I know it? You ask such questions, but what to answer? A composer has the first word, never the last.

20 August

My *donnée*, or raw notion—the spark that's lit in the night—usually ends up as an accompaniment. If the notion is for a song, it's offered gratis as a canvas on which I must later paint the melody. Orchestral notions given in dreams are for sonorities, not ideas: a gift of background. Conscious sweat pays dearly for the foreground.

I can't remember how I wrote this or that. Even if I could, the secret must stay mine. A composer's methods are personal, no matter how public he would make them. For the public, what he tried to do is less pertinent than what he did do.

If the span of a second contains indivisible billions of segments, and each segment contains indivisible billions of segments forever, a life can be measured by the width of a thought. But we humans standing apart from this hive are impotent to catch and sustain one such segment, for, except under drugs, we can't freeze time. The greatest composer, like the least, concocts his music not according to sonority but according to time, and his concept of time is rough compared to the philosopher's, the theoretician's. Bach's seconds, not "infinite" but gross, are conceived to be perceived and relished in relation to each other, as a flow. (The flow, of course, exists only for some, passing in one ear and out the other of others.)

Possibly a composer's whole *oeuvre* balances in some way his metabolic pace. For instance, Fauré never wrote intrinsically fast music; his fast music is really slow music speeded up.

Young composers, if they're going to study with another person (rather than on their own), must study with a successful composer, one who knows what it means to hear his own music played well and often. To study with a Scalero, as I did at Curtis in 1943, is not only to combat the embittered, but to deal solely with Theory. Nadia Boulanger is the exception proving the rule. (Among performers, there are numerous exceptions.)

14 September

Since last writing here I've covered the map. First, New York for four days where with Gary Clarke I saw the Peking Opera. Long interview with Irving Kolodin for *Saturday Review* about my joining the Curtis staff. (We'd last met in 1954 in Aix-en-Provence, dining at the Roi René, he with Nan Merriman, I with Nell Tangeman. He remains charmingly sad.) Dined with parents, taking them the *Piano Quarterly*, my picture on the cover.

On the 16th Ruth Sumners drove me to Kennedy where I boarded a vehicle for Seattle, there to repeat in miniature the triumphs of Santa Fe: a signing in Dalton's (few showed up); a lecture; a tea at the Boisérie of the museum with Wesley Wehr, where a friendly stranger approached our table and later left threatening messages at my hotel, so that police were summoned; a Poulenc-Rorem-Debussy recital in Meany Auditorium with Will; a Composers' Workshop; the Seattle premiere of *The Santa Fe Songs*.

New York again. Judy for tea; later Chris Cox to dine; Rorems to dine; on the 22nd deposited with B. & H. the finished score of my summer project, the suite for unaccompanied cello, *After Reading Shakespeare*, for Sharon Robinson; bought a sky-blue dress shirt for the concert on the 25th. That day Francine and Cleve came to dine, bringing fruit, wine, quiche, greens, little carrot cakes. Although to be with her is to be with an original presence vital and bright, I will never really believe in Francine again, because of her Nantucket piece. The bloom is off our friendship. JH arrived from Nantucket. Then, with the Grays, we hied ourselves to Tully Hall where I played the piano part again of *The Santa Fe Songs*, broadcast live, reviewed next day by Rockwell who called it my masterpiece. (Does that mean it's *a* masterpiece, or just *mine*?) Party at Walter Trampler's. On the 26th, came to dine Elliott Stein and Robert Jacobson. On the 27th, Will's and my "pre-concert" recital in Tully of Debussy. The 28th, *Day Music* played at Tully. The five-day season in New York of the Santa Fe Chamber Music Festival is a virtue rare, and fair to me.

Flew back here on the 29th. Beautiful weather. Island's quiet after Labor Day. Squawking crows. Hot. Sharp pains in left shin again. Spider bite. Drought. Death of Harold Clurman.

The first summer without hay-fever shots since 1976. So far so good. Monomoy by bike. Bright sky, like mauve enamel. Struggling with an essay on Song for *Christopher Street*, and with a bonbon for *New York Magazine* on "What I Most Like about New York City" (it's the area of my zip code, 10023). Reviewing the scores of the two prospective Curtis students.

Nantucket
15 September

When I'm here alone—which is currently the case, JH being in New York for the past week—I dine vegetarian. A baked yam, a garlicky salad, maybe a piece of fruit, but always a major sweet. For, since I do without smoking or drinking, I deserve dessert once a day. I never go to restaurants. So much of my lost youth was dissolved in them, and they're now so expensive and loud. But also I dread being mocked by strangers as I dine alone. "He has no friends," they seem to be giggling behind their fans. (Though in my ill-described brief encounter with Noël Coward, *he* was dining alone, and quite aristocratic. Noël's one of the only three famous people I've ever consorted with. Explain why I can't—couldn't—sleep with the celebrated or the rich. Not that it's anyone's business. Except that it's interesting.)

Tonight I went (alone) to *Dressed to Kill*. David Halberstam was there, but I didn't say hello because Maxine once told me he "doesn't like fairies," and I didn't want to embarrass him. How's that for adjustment?

How do people talk to each other? Looking across the festive gymnasium at that group laughing over there, I'm wondering how they communicate so easily. I never know what to talk about.

New York
22 September

For the first time in ten years, thanks to John de Lancie, the composition department is reopened at the Curtis Institute. (Shouldn't the composition department be the foundation of every music school?) There are only three students: David Loeb has one and I have two. It has become illegal to request photos of applicants; thus I initially gauged these boys—these young men—solely through their music. They turn out (now that I've spent the day in Philadelphia) to be of nice refinement, deferential, upper-middle, personable. A responsibility. Returned depleted to Manhattan in time to hear—what madness!—a viola recital at Merkin Hall.

23 September

Arthur Laurents came to dine *tête à tête* and to discuss the possibility of our collaborating on an opera. He retains his aggressive, highly intelligent, and rather vulgar demeanor, which I like, but we'll never see eye to eye on theater, mainly because he's right and I'm wrong, and I'm not especially interested in what he's right about.

25 September

Yesterday, five hours with the "Planning Committee," at the French-American Foundation, with Arthur Peters, Steegmuller, etc., about a massive Cocteau retrospective for 1983. My contribution is to be an essay about J.C. and music. Today, lunch with Weissberger, then C.J. Everett at B. & H., then Leonard Raver at 4:00.

26 September

Spent the evening with Shirley at George Perle's, whose view of Central Park from the west is no less heart-stopping than Alice Tully's from the south. Talk of Chicago. I contend I first met George through Hatti Martin in the little recital hall in Lyon & Healy when his Trio for Flute, Piano and Viola was heard—or was it at Steuermann's recital in the same hall when the pianist for a surprising *bis* played Ravel's *Ondine*? George contends we met through my parents, who had already befriended his wife, Laura Slobe, and maybe it was 1939, or 1941, but he scarcely recalls his own trio, or the fact that Steuermann performed *Ondine*, although he (George) did arrange the Steuermann recital. Anyway, I knew George years before Shirley (though not before Ben Weber), although George would probably claim that I've got even this wrong, as were most references to him in previous diaries. And of course he's right, from where he stands (west of Central Park), since a diary, or any referential work (or, indeed, *any* work, including George's own music which is, among other things, a private viewpoint, a vantage) is Rashomonian.

George is less altered by the years than anyone I know, in body and mind, both of which are guarded by a consistent diet: the body by rare lamb chops, raw red pepper, cauliflower (consumed as we gazed), and no dessert, the mind by regular doses of Berg and Proust, two thinkers who on the face of it would seem to have nothing in common. I never picture George as concerned with timely gossip, Proust notwithstanding, or with French music from any period. As to his own music, more than any musician of his years he seems to have wanted, at least subconsciously, to tread the bridge twixt the tonal and the untonal, and so doing he convincingly becomes a sort of daft Stravinsky who sounds more like Bartók than like Berg. When I tell him that he's the only twelve-tone composer capable of writing fast music—music that is intrinsically, *kinetically* fast—and that I don't know how he turns the trick, since kinetically fast music derives not from wild scatterings of hemidemisemiquavers but from a rigidly rapid beat that by definition implies ostinato that in turn implies tonality of the simplest sort—when I tell him this he answers, fairly politely, that he's *not* a twelve-tone composer, and he wishes people would stop linking his music with his musicology (he being, now that Leibowitz is dead, the world's leading specialist on Schoenberg and Berg). Of course I, too, despite our long but irregular relationship, was in the same trap as "people."

27 September

Lunch on Amsterdam Avenue with Charles Wadsworth to discuss the piece for his Chamber Music Society. The length, degree of difficulty, choice of instruments, and deadline resulted from this discussion. Since it's tailor-made for him, the piece will be a half-hour multi-movement virtuosic quintet for clarinet, bassoon, piano, violin and cello, to be premiered early in 1982 during the Society's Haydn–Stravinsky festival. We also agreed that, for an extra sum, I'd give a speech to the subscribers apropos of Stravinsky's birthday. I complimented Charles, then, on his personality-filled pianism long ago in Paris as accompanist to Doda Conrad in Sauguet's *Le Cornette* (incorrectly listed, I note, in Grove as *La Cornette*), although I dislike the servile term "accompanist" unless it's used too for the soloist: singer and pianist *accompany* each other through the adventure of a song.

Charles paid the bill, and I returned home to offer tea to Tom Steele, Tim Dlugos, Paul Jacobs, Shirley & George, and Joe LeSueur.

Nantucket
30 September

Yesterday, to Philadelphia for second session at Curtis. Exhilaration on leaving the train at Thirtieth Street and being in a safe city, a *removed* city, ninety minutes and ninety light-years from Manhattan, walking the sunny twelve blocks to Rittenhouse Square, as though I were still a student in that privileged vicinity.

Flew here this morning. Watched Arthur Miller's *Playing for Time*, which, though original, healthily depressing, and not Jewish especially, is a third too long for its own good. Vanessa Redgrave extraordinary: my favorite actress, with Bette Davis, yet they're alike as Proust and Berg.

Spend time here finishing piece for doublebass and countertenor, a one-movement affair on a fifty-four-line disturbance by Thom Gunn called *Back to Life*.

New York
15 October

Moira came at six last evening for a bite, after which we went to hear *Wintereisse* as ventured by Gérard Souzay and Dalton Baldwin. Moira surprised me by stating she'd never before attended a lieder recital, a statement all the more distressing when, after the fifth song, Gérard quit the stage of the YMHA, then returned alone to announce that he couldn't continue, then walked off again, then returned with Dalton, and continued. A ploy—for he gained our sympathy, though the voice was rough. But the voice was also beautiful, telling, very German (in the sense of hot, expressionistic, even with Gérard looking eccentric, wild-eyed), and very intelligent, while Dalton's pianism remains the velvet upon which rubies are offered, the landscape against which portraits are sketched. That's saying plenty, since Schubert, though admirable, is unnecessary to my well-being, and seldom moves me.

Today, after the dentist, went to Gérard's exhibit (yes, he's a painter, too) of exquisitely geometric japonerie at the Bodley gallery, and thence to the City Opera's ill-begotten "American Trilogy."

In the *Opera News* article on the upcoming French Triptych at the Met I mention that Eugene Istomin used to liken the looks, on paper, of Ravel's *Trio* to Greek columns. Of course, Eugene also hears what he sees. How does a score look to one who can't read notes? Elliott Stein says Bach resembles Klee. Upside down, Bach is still Klee. (In every edition?) To me, upside-down music is quite different from itself: I can't even tell the language of the score, yet I've been dealing with notes on the average of four hours a day, every day of the year, for forty-five years. George Perle, if I remember rightly, reads (prose) as fast upside down as right side up.

The most impeccable piece in Ravel's almost impeccable catalogue might be the brief unaccompanied *Trois beaux oiseaux*, were not the words perhaps a touch coy. Ravel wrote them himself and, although apposite, they have a *pis aller* ring, rather like the doggerel of "Tea for Two," or of *Old Joe has gone fishing / And you know has gone fishing* which Britten (two steps ahead of his librettist) made up to fit the music until the real thing came along—which never came along.

Poulenc's chutzpah. Not only to be so Offenbachianly campy in *Les Mamelles* but to use the same principles, in slow motion, for the serious *Dialogues* (though *Dialogues* has few set numbers).

My old essay on Ravel closed: Nobody dislikes him, and nobody disapproves. An essay on Boulez could begin: No one likes him, but no one disapproves. The time has come. I disapprove. Everything about Boulez's music works except the music itself.

(Such an article encroaches on composing time, and composing encroaches on prose. Result, I permit paralysis and have done little since last summer. The fear of composing music. The fear of involvement, as with a love affair. It can take as much time and concentration to compose terrible music as great music.)

Autumn clarity. Depressed. Then less depressed. The wind, the wind . . . anxious and morbid. Prostate, teeth, Dr. Voorhees, Tranxene and aspirin. Reagan–Carter debate. Came here over a week ago. Judy phoned, thinks

I'm punishing myself for *good* reviews. Mr. Norton repaired the chimney. Sunday, fly back to New York, as JH flies here; housesitting, bedwarming, to delay permanent transfer of Wallace and the other cats back to city. On November eleventh I'm supposed, because of the hit of the first round, to do a second pair of interviews with Dick Cavett. This time Sharon Robinson will be my protectress, previewing three excerpts from the new cello suite.

New York
5 November

Visit from Donald Collup, young baritone from Curtis who wants me to write him something. Reagan elected. Visit from Eric Gordon who's doing a book on Marc Blitzstein; then from Lynda Sheldon to finalize the Cavett format; then from Chuck Turner, and we go to see Godard's tough and homophobic *Sauve qui peut*. Tomorrow, dentist, Roz Rees, then dine chez Heddy Baum.

7 November

Such a crowd at the Ken Russell movie (we'd wanted to hear the Corigliano score) that Chuck and I gave up and took a long, long walk instead, with Earl Wild and Michael Davis, who had also been waiting in line.

The empty spaces in this diary represent ninety-nine percent of my existence when I'm working. The frugal entries do not represent deep thoughts, merely landmarks.

11 November

Does music make me cry? No. But yes. Not music itself, but music's evocations. (What's the difference?) Actually, I never cry.

Early last evening, home alone, hungry, *grippé*, anxious about doing the Cavett show this morning, vulnerable, I began to play through some Poulenc songs. *Dans l'Herbe* has for thirty-five years struck me as one of Poulenc's most touching. I knew Poulenc, and he is dead. I knew Louise de Vilmorin, and she is dead. The poem is about a dead youth, beneath the grass. And these words, these notes, these blades of grass like golden filaments, extensions of Paris streets that exist no longer, seemed to extend across the ocean, calling me back through time and space in a manner that no Beethoven quartet could ever imitate. I wept so spasmodically that I dissolved on the keyboard, buried my head in my arms, and gave over to the voluptuous anguish. The wind howled outside. Then at my feet I felt Wallace whining and threw myself onto his twenty pounds of sky-colored fur, and together we purred.

George Plimpton "hosts" a "show" about migrating caribou. True to his caste, he drops the internal *r*, which he reattaches to vowels at word ends. "Herds between Canada and America" becomes "Heuds between Canadar and America."

If I cause one heart to break, I have not lived in vain.

I'm not a gay activist, I'm a gay pacifist.

12 November

Thom Gunn for a drink. His foreignness comes not from being English but from being Californian. Attractive, ill at ease, he's one of America's (England's?) three true poets, and, I suppose, flattered by my setting of his verse, although classical music seems hardly his forte. Perhaps he'll turn in his grave, as might I, when the screechy rasping piece is finally heard.

Have a bad cold. It was already fomenting at the Cavett taping, to which Shirley accompanied me yesterday. During most of the first segment Sharon, in a very scant gown on a little platform over there, had to wait in the drafty studio, cello poised, before her turn came to show off, and she doubtless has a cold worse than mine.

14 November

Wallace had another brief fit. Visit yesterday from Jim Gaines (of *People* magazine) who's compiling a book about the piano, to which I've agreed to contribute an essay. Cancelled dinner at the Institute. Visit today from guitarist Joseph Breznikar. Did not attend concert at the Met Museum where the Ciesinski sisters sang my *Gloria*. I note this with a fever and chills.

22 November

Returned from three nights in Chicago at the Allerton, which in our youth had a *louche* reputation. My hosts were Art Lange, of *Brilliant Corners* magazine, and his milieu of poets who arranged speeches and songs by me in Thorne Hall. Thursday, an hour's taping with the indefatigable Studs Terkel, then a long and moving evening in memory lane with Dick and Ruth

Jacob. Friday, the ever faithful Dolores Fredrickson for lunch at the Arts Club, a *dîner en masse*, and a recital consisting of a reading, a question period, intermission, and the cycles *Women's Voices* and *The Nantucket Songs* with me accompanying Dorothy Keyser and Elsa Charlston. It was especially touching to find in the audience not only Ruth Page and John Von Rhein, but Jean Edwards, the irrepressible light of my pre-adolescence, now the mother of eight and not about to remember with glee the days when we spit in the fudge, and worse.

Breakfast with Arrand Parsons, who drove me to the plane. Without a nap, tonight, with Rosalind Rees, I performed again, for the Copland marathon at Symphony Space (mob like sardines, winding halfway around the block) where at the last moment I was asked "to say a few words." For two weeks I've been practising the piano for these occasions, but "a few words" come hard.

Mae West died today.

Tomorrow, Nantucket again with JH.

Nantucket
28 November

Mother and Father came for Thanksgiving, and also their friends the Sprengers from Hyannis with their difficult smartass daughter. They've all just departed on the ferry in the driving rain, and we fly, if the rain's willing, back to New York tonight.

Whatever became of rough trade? Already in the sixties there emerged a type too sveltely masculine to be anything but queer, while the straight hard hat was too potbellied to be appealing. Today, after flower children, "passive" husbands, and unisex, one may well ask: If opposites attract, who is one's opposite?

Copulation is a limiting term in that it excludes sex involving less or more than two.

8 December

John Lennon was murdered two blocks away, at the Dakota. The entire neighborhood and half of Central Park seethes with as many mourners as carried candles at Kent State, just ten years ago.

Returned from Philadelphia last night (Curtis classes continue smoothly; I now assign the same poem to all the composers, then compare their settings against mine) in time to catch myself on the Cavett show. During the quarter-hour in the post office this morning I am recognized twice. (Andy Warhol's fifteen minutes!) *Lulu* tonight at the Met (after a cocktail gathering at the Thornes'), from which (because Stratas canceled) we retreated in time to catch the second Cavett installment. It is immeasurably rewarding to see oneself on television, and immeasurably irrelevant.

Black-tie affair at the Plaza for Juilliard's seventy-fifth anniversary. I'm seated between Elliott and Helen Carter. To Helen I explain that the most troubled moment of my life was the eighty seconds between the time they rang the bell and their appearance at the door a few years ago. She, essence of tact, claims to have been simply concerned that JH was ill, when he vanished, but found nothing amiss. Meanwhile, the dinner tonight is so loud, the "entertainment" so vulgar, that this can't, surely, be an occasion for the subtlest musicians of our country.

Evening with Lenny Bernstein at the Dakota where, since the Lennon shooting, cops guard the gates. Lenny says that the building's notables must come and go by a side entrance.

   Lenny is so rude he takes my breath away. During the meal (Harry Kraut and Tom Steele are there too) I veer from a topic I believe to be exhausted. Lenny: "Ned, you're so superficial, always changing the subject to make dinner-table chitchat." JH calmly pursues the previous matter, saying something about how young composers today, being born in the shadow of nuclear destruction, have no incentive to become more expert than they are. Lenny ecstatically concurs, playing us against each other. Would I have got up and left if Lenny were not going to conduct *Sunday Morning* with the Philharmonic in six weeks? The unvoiced conundrum that he forever offers with his affectionate viciousness, not only to me but to all those on his plane (i.e. those strong enough to protect themselves), is: What geniuses you are, you idiots!

21 December

Lulu on television last evening with the woman who substituted the other night. It's *the* medium for opera; surely Berg would have agreed. *Lulu* has never made more sense, and George Perle agrees. Lear overwhelming as the understated Geschwitz.

Tonight, took a poinsettia to Stephen Greco and Barry Laine on Henry Street in Brooklyn.

Tomorrow, a long tense session at the dentist.

Finished finally the "Parade" essay for *Opera News*, a strain. Nantucket on Christmas Day.

23 December

Because of its dreamlike anonymity the activity in a sauna has come to be compared to suspended animation. It is the opposite. To suspend animation is to jell life. In the sauna you suspend niceties of living, not life, which is released full force. Because the force seems aimless, like toadstools which spring up anywhere, we esteem it nonreproductive. In fact, the force is no less indiscriminate than the helter-skelter sperm cells of heterosexuality. Everyone weeps after sex, not from fulfillment but from pointlessness. How ugly, really, the rubbing together of even the most beautiful bodies.

1981

People are given to believing that an artist (or a homosexual, for that matter) is what he is by choice. Well, choice may be there on some childish level insofar as the vocation is practiced, but insofar as the urge persists there is little choice, and even less, alas, for the quality of results. Often I hear, "Why did you become a composer?" I *was* a composer. The question is, Why did I persevere? Perseverance comes from applause, for which the need *chez moi* is no stronger than with Casals or Schubert or the Curies who, despite loneliness and self-sacrifice, were, after all, aiming for the attention of their fellowmen. Without tangible appreciation—performance, publication, money, comparative fame—who would persevere? Nothing's madder or sadder than stacks of unplayed scores. And the unknown genius is anathema to our age of speed. Why am I a composer? To dazzle those virile paragons who bullied me in gym class. Have they noticed? But now the ball's rolling and it's too late to stop.

Asked JH why it is I can't write fiction, as with the aborted novel last year. "Your diary is your fiction," he explains.

How do you make good coffee? After 365 tries a year for four decades I still don't know.
   I'm No Angel on TV tonight. Tomorrow, the city. Snow.

Trains canceled, so my habitual Monday in Philadelphia is postponed until the 16th. I don't write much here about Curtis, probably for the same reason that there are blanks during professorial stays in Buffalo and Salt Lake City.

Life is compartmentalized. Certain compartments are so thoroughly explored while I'm in them that there's not much to add in retrospect. Also, I am more a part of the students' lives than they are of mine; what I give is presumably new to them, but not to me. Thus, what could be written except a textbook? and that's unlikely since I don't believe in formal teaching. (Yes I do.) As to personal feelings toward the students, it's curious, and probably correct, how little they count, once roles are established; I know nothing about their lives. Just as I've never had a hotel-room tryst during forays around the land, so it would never occur to me to be tempted by—to get involved with—a student; we are of separate categories, different species. (Title: *Sixth Species Counterpoint*.) This said, I'm as satisfied with their work as with my ability to incite them properly, and the tone of the Institute is at once fertile and lulling.

With Shirley through the filthy snow to Barbara Kolb's program on East 11th Street.

15 January

Dimly recalled, uncredited . . .
    To be a saint one must have been a sinner.
    Qui a beaucoup peché sera beaucoup pardonné.
    More and more I wonder if it's precisely because of sin that my body seems so regularly racked, my dreams so cursed. Sin means liquor, anonymous sex, bitterness, envy of or indifference to others. These "vices" aren't necessarily vicious, but I've made them so and am flogged.

17 January

Finished article on "The Piano In My Life." Working on article about Cocteau's relation to musicians, JH helping me with bibliography. Exhibition today of Arthur Cady's expert if dryish pictures of Long Island, followed by party at Margot Stewart's with John Myers presiding. (John returns Wednesday for more investigation of his malignant kidney, yet tonight he seems cheerful as a lark. If I could be half so . . .) Chatted with J. Ashbery for half an hour, the one person on this globe with whom I feel uncomfortable. Bleak and cold. Continuation of what feels like an inflamed urethra, but which doctor says is probably prostate although he detects nothing.

22 January

Boisterous dinner at Ellen Adler's with, at one big table, her, me & JH, Aaron Copland, Adolph Green & Betty Comden, Lenny B., Phyllis Newman, Sefronis Mundy, Dominique Nabokov, and Joan Ungara. A pot roast nonpareil with carrots underdone French style. Aaron talked the least, seemingly overpowered by extroversion.

23 January

Sam Barber died today. Chuck called around noon, sounding calm and relieved but exhausted and sad. Not unexpected. Yet, considering how cool our relations have been for years, the fact of Sam's disappearance is upsetting. Rancor drains away in a trice, and his value replaces it.

25 January

Visit from Gerald Cook and Fred Koester, bringing photographs with which to garnish my piano article. Gerald adamant on not being interviewed for Libby's biography, feels that nothing but voyeurism is the issue. Still, a copy of Fred's old poster of Libby will probably adorn the cover. Gerald meanwhile accompanies Alberta Hunter down at the Cookery, and remains as trim (and strong-minded) as when we were children together—and rival prodigies—in Chicago.

26 January

After a full day at Curtis I cross Rittenhouse Square to rest at Henry McIlhenny's. Scheduled to dine *tête à tête* with Henry, but there is a houseful of male guests, fresh from Barber's funeral. Atmosphere shrill and dark, with the jitters that come at wakes after one drink too many. Chuck Turner and I, with Valentino, walk over to Panama Street to spend an hour with the Ettings, then return to dine with Henry (plus John Browning, Phillip Ramey, John Corigliano, and three others I don't know). During the meal Chuck suddenly turns on me: "What right have you to be here? You've always said mean things about Sam." Which makes me feel wretched. Took a cab to the station, reached New York by ten, and here I am, about to swallow a sulfa pill.

5 February

The Bernstein program at the Philharmonic consists of three American works: Copland's *Old American Songs*, Schuman's *Third Symphony*, and opening with the New York premiere of my *Sunday Morning*, which is in eight titled movements. Tonight was the first of four scheduled hearings.

Sitting in the upper left box between Aaron and Bill, I gazed down upon the stage where Lenny seemed caught in a stifled paroxysm while conducting my third movement, called *Indifferent Blue*. Quietly he lay down the baton and left the stage. Silence in the house. Silence on the stage. A minute passed. Two minutes. Three. Aaron whispered slyly, "I hope you know how to conduct, Ned." The musicians didn't move. After an eternity Lenny reappeared, picked up the baton, went on where he left off. But the momentum was shattered, the piece sagged. Later in the green room Lenny told us, as he chain-smoked with the insouciance of Dietrich in the thirties, that he'd submitted to a small biopsy of the throat this morning, which made him cough this evening. It's the first time he's ever stopped in mid-performance. With whom does one commiserate, me or him?

12 February

Monday was the last of the four Philharmonic performances, each attended side by side with Bill Schuman whose landmark symphony I grew nightly more intimate with, as with him, and we each grew progressively suaver with our bows. If Ormandy clocked *Sunday Morning* at twenty-two minutes, Lenny stretched it to twenty-six, perhaps kneading rather too much *meaning* into the dough so that the yeast turned flat. My music, as a rule, doesn't require interpretation. At each presentation I brought different guests, mainly family, and finally Miss Tully whom I took to Mendy Wager's huge party. Betwixt: acupuncture sessions with Josué Corcos.

Dark and wet; still feeling bad, though less so maybe. Yesterday, visit from Sharon, who played through the whole of *After Reading Shakespeare*. Today, Arthur Peters and Schuyler Chapin about the Cocteau thing. (Schuyler clearly withdrawing from the project.) Tomorrow, Mary Cantwell. Then Robert Veyron-Lacroix.

21 February

Norris Embry is dead. He died last Tuesday (according to today's *Times*) of a stroke in Louisville, but of course what did him in began long ago. I feel too sad to note anything beyond this: Among the first poems I ever set to music, Hopkins's *Margaret, are you grieving*, Gibbons's *The Silver Swan*, Goodman's *Rain in Spring*, and a dozen more, including in 1944 a verse of Wyatt's, I became acquainted with because of dear Norris. Generally he'd scribble them onto the back of a menu in a bar where we were drinking; his memory was phenomenal and accurate. He was fifty-nine. I'd known him all my life.

Washington's Birthday

At the Philadelphia Art Alliance, Sharon, to a mob like sardines, played *After Reading Shakespeare* with inspired excellence, succeeding a speech by me. (My pupil, Norman Stumpf: "I hadn't realized you were articulate.") Present were Rosemary and her family, Sharon and hers.

27 February

My little opera *Bertha*, on Kenneth Koch's incomparable playlet, is already thirteen years old, but it is seldom heard. As I did not want to attend a "revival" tonight (and tomorrow), presented by the Golden Fleece Company, because I was dubious about the viewpoint, JH went instead as spy. His worst fears were verified: the action was changed to transpire in an insane asylum, so that not only Queen Bertha but everyone around her are manifestly mad. Which betrays the humor and pathos of Kenneth's (and my) concept. Apparently the singing was fine.

28 February

Lehman Engel phoned early this morning to say that Arnold Weissberger was dead. What a shock.

At noon JH and I went to the Cat Show at Madison Square Garden where despite the dander I did not sneeze once. Of the two thousand felines there displayed, not one, none, was equal in feisty charm and eccentric loveliness to our precious Wallace.

It seems unfair to judge by first reactions, yet for me, in matters of art, those reactions seldom alter with time. Occasionally I'll come round, as for Brahms and Beckett. Though whenever I stab anew at, say, Faulkner or Berlioz, I'm baffled, not at what they are in themselves, but at what other people—delicately wise people—find in them.

Last night masochism urged me to reconsider *Le Partage de Midi*. Claudel too remains what he always seemed: a sophomoric *composeur* with no sense of shape. The lavishness of his banality, the sexist simplicity of his Catholic heart, pushed to such limits turn triteness to fright. That he allowed no abridgments of those redundant *ohs* and *ahs*, that he lived to such a ripe age, is due to the fact that he "got out of himself" by sitting through his endless plays (only economists die young), while the audience feared for its own vanishing youth.

Unlike inspired cuisine from mediocre staples, a good production cannot hide faults of a "literary" play; it can only heighten them. But wow! that marvelous *mise en scène* at the Comédie Française. Was it 1954? There, like yesterday, stands Edwige Feuillère, whose slightest pattern moved mountains, and there is Félix Labisse's set. Was ever decor more apt? Balthus's maybe, for *L'Ile des chèvres*, or Noguchi's for the Graham dance about Saint Joan? Or Bill Ritman's for the second scene of *Tiny Alice*?

4 March

Noon memorial for Arnold Weissberger at the Royal Theater. He would have loved it. A full house attended, as on the stage in a neat row Orson Welles, Ruth Gordon, Garson Kanin, Martha Graham, Louise Rainer, Douglas Fairbanks, Jr., Meryl Streep, Alger Hiss, Beverly Sills, Michael Moriarty, and Lillian Gish each rose, one by one, to offer a five-minute remembrance, succinct, precious and personal. After exactly one hour everybody went back to work, feeling better. If it was Milton Goldman who choreographed the affair—and surely it was—there's proof that press agentry on occasion can be not only tactful but love-filled.

Returned in time to meet with Hilda Harris who, though diminutive and overly pretty, possesses a deep mezzo as mocha-colored as her epidermis and a diction like the very best engraving fluid. We choose songs appropriate for her to render next July in Nantucket. She's currently at the Met singing the title role in *L'Enfant et les sortilèges* under Manuel Rosenthal. If her English is a touch too Negro (which I like), her French is far too Italian (which I don't): she *interprets* the infinitely pristine *Air de l'enfant* which cannot withstand even the slightest bending without sounding inappropriately sophisticated.

7 March

Blizzard. Manuel and Claudine Rosenthal came last night to dine, with, as garnishment because they speak French, John & Jane Gruen, and Eugene & Marta Istomin. What Manuel has done with the Met orchestra, in an otherwise uncommendable trilogy called *Parade* (which misrepresents with American innocence—despite Dexter and Hockney being English—both Ravel and Satie, although Poulenc's *Les Mamelles* isn't bad), is to render the instrumentation radioactive. From start to end the sounds from the pit are illuminated from within, leading an independent life, both original and necessary, under a baton that itself glistens. No one has ever interpreted French music according to the demands of my metabolism except pianist Paul Jacobs and conductor Rosenthal.

Tonight at the Y, the dance troupe of Lillo Way, which, among other piquant chinoiseries, moved to a group of my songs sung live.

Tomorrow, Colorado, for three days of classes at Fort Collins.

Ides of March (Sunday)

Brunch at Joan Peyser's ample and unusual house on Charlton Street where I complimented Jacques Barzun on his Bizet scholarship, when in fact it's on Berlioz. I do have a block against Berlioz. At 3:00 met JH, my parents, and Shirley & George at Tully Hall for the public premiere of *After Reading Shakespeare*, which Sharon, placing it at the theatrically favored moment just after intermission, played with clarity and passion. George was impressed, after the concert, by the sight of Mother and Father, in their mideighties, trotting vigorously toward the subway.

Tuesday, reception for Chinese composers at ASCAP.

22 March (Sunday)

This afternoon at Carnegie Hall, Leontyne Price did "The Dance" (William Carlos Williams) and "Ferry Me across the Water" (Christina Rossetti), both from *The Nantucket Songs*. "The Dance" is not her cup of tea, despite the glittering high C, because, whatever else her singular virtues, high camp isn't one. But her singing of "Ferry Me" was the most satisfying rendition I've ever had by anyone: the final G sharp, plucked from the air like a firefly, became a timeless non-vibrating silver thread suspended confidently from here to Arcturus, as David Garvey, without hurrying, altered the "meaning" of that tone with each descending luscious change of chord.

24 March

Réunion musicale chez Alice Tully. I accompanied a young bearded baritone named Robert Briggs in *Flight For Heaven*, after which Rodney Hardesty and Gary Karr gave the first hearing anywhere of *Back to Life*. It's my weirdest piece, though the weirdness stems less from my inventive powers than from the inborn rasp of the double bass and the inherent screech of any countertenor—but please don't tell Gary and Rod. If the dense beauty of Thom Gunn's words came through to you I cannot know, because I know them. But to me they worked.

A late supper followed, Alice presiding over a catered meal at a table of twenty guests, all male, whose banter, were it not tempered by the wit and wisdom of Hugues Cuénod, could have seemed unseemly.

30 March

Saturday, all-Rorem concert in Hartford at Trinity Church, arranged by the irrepressible Tony Angarano. Last night, Rorems in the evening. Today, assassination attempt on Reagan. Stinging urethra persists after three months, but hope too persists. (It all began while reading Tim Dlugos's article in *Christopher Street* about amoebic parasites.) Have stopped taking vitamins.

2 April

JH's 42nd birthday. Party at 6:00 at Doubleday to celebrate Gary Graffman's clever and informative memoir, *I Should Really Be Practicing.* "Shouldn't you be home practicing," asked Gary, "since you're playing a concert to-night?" Indeed, a year ago, when Rose Plaut—beloved of us all—heard a broadcast of the 1979 Washington recital with Phyllis Bryn-Julson, she took it into her head to have the identical program reproduced live in New York at the YMHA, at some expense to herself and great *remue-ménage* at the Y. I've been practicing an hour a day for months, with and without Phyllis, and sending out reams of brochures with handwritten coercions. Tonight was to have been the night. But Phyllis got laryngitis and cancelled six hours ago. The date has been tentatively reassigned to early summer.

It seems a poignant moment, now that he seldom performs anymore, to mention that Gary is one of my four favorite pianists, at least of those in our generation. (Leon Fleisher seldom plays now either, nor, of course, does Julius Katchen, which leaves just Eugene to carry the day.) Is it really thirty-eight years since I first heard Gary in Curtis Hall effortlessly dashing off the A-flat Ballade? Ever since, it's been Chopin I most identify with him—Chopin with humor. The new autobiography too is drenched in humor, Naomi's as much as her husband's. One suspects she's the ghostwriter. I wish I saw the Graffmans oftener. Of everyone I know they are the least morbid.

7 April

Yesterday (Morris's birthday) was spent, as usual on Mondays, at Curtis. John de Lancie brought his oboe to class and gave us a lesson, plus anecdotes about Richard Strauss whom he knew in Germany at the end of the war. (He did the premiere of the final revised version of Strauss's Oboe Concerto.) John's recording of Ibert's Concerto and of Jean Françaix's little *L'Horloge des fleurs* is oboe performance at its highest.

Today, Shirley's birthday. Went with her to a late afternoon screening of the documentary about Britten, *A Time There Was*, from which we emerged in tears, thence to George Perle's where JH met us, and we consumed, with Jo Carson, a healthy meal.

8 April

JH off to Nantucket this morning.

From six to seven P.M. we (me, Garrick Ohlsson, Adolph Green, and Betty Allen) taped what's called a dry run of a quiz show at CBS. I loved the company, especially Roger Englander's sexy and adept cajoling of us—his flock of *idiots savants*—but the performance struck me as a catastrophic replay of "Information Please," and can't possibly succeed. George Whitmore came over for a late and improvised repast.

Rain. Alone. Still feeling wretched. Trying to work on the quintet, provisionally named *Winter Pages*. Rain.

10 April

Six weeks ago, as I awaited the eighth and final acupuncture session in the anteroom of Josué Corcos's office, my head buried in the *Times*, a male European voice exclaimed, "Why, hello Ned." When he identified himself, although we've not met in a quarter-century, I quickly recognized Claus Bulow, the once-handsome structure, now covered with shadows. "I'm *au courant* of your various doings," said he, "through John and Alexandra." "John?" I said. "Yes, John Simon." After a few seconds the dawn came.

It had never occurred to me that "the other man"—the wealthy Dane—that John Simon, like a lovesick adolescent, discusses so freely as his rival for the favors of Alexandra Isles (two on the Isles—as he puts it) was simply good old Claus. I hadn't even realized Claus was in America, but now it all seemed so logical.

A few days later, the memory of those many summers during the early fifties in Hyères together, when Marie Laure would refer to his annual fortnight there after meager winters in London as *l'engraissage de Claus*, and the vision of him then—clever, soft, balding, *mondain*, indolent, intelligent, a touch obsequious and aiming at targets other than mine (money & style, versus shattering of the cosmos with music)—led me, merging nostalgia with practicality, to pen him a little note enclosing a flyer for the April 2nd concert. Claus replied by mail that he could not attend the recital, adding: "John Simon, with the kindness for which he is famous, quotes you as saying the most horrific and slanderous things about me. When you have set them to music I shall come and listen. Meanwhile I find Dr. Corcos' needles more soothing than Saint Simon's barbs."

JH was no less upset than I by these words, advising me to answer: "Fond Claus, I regret if what I may have said has been used to wound you. This was far from the intention of any remarks."

Today this came: "Not to worry. I was really picking on J. Simon rather than you. I am afraid I always find a good story irresistible, and so a good many stories have stuck to me. I think it was Voltaire who said *mieux perdre un ami qu'un bon mot*, and I assure you that you have not lost . . . ton ami Claus."

16 April

At 10:30 this morning, of all strange hours, I gave a talk at the Huntington Hartford Museum to the mostly female Associated Music Teachers League, then performed a batch of my songs with the dependable Roz Rees. At midday, with JH, visited Cat Cottage on West 81st in search of a cat sitter (which we found) for while we're in Nantucket all next week. Although I never anymore go to ballet or theater, it seemed necessary, for my Stravinsky article, to check out Paul Taylor's *Rites of Spring*, so Morris took me tonight.

Just as the terror of Sophocles pure resounds more purposely than any updated contribution, even by Stravinsky, so Stravinsky's *Rite* will forever defy choreographers. The ballet's undanceable, partly because the story is always taken at face value but mainly because the score smashes all contenders. True, Paul Taylor, avoiding the risky "pagan" tone of every version since 1912, has made a good go at it, though he does ape Nijinsky's knock-kneed profiles. But Taylor's success owes much to the four-hand reduction: the black-&-white keyboard offsets the black-&-white comic-strip yarn in black-&-white modernistic decor; and the Nijinsky stance is brash allusion, not sober homage. However, the music's glamour rests in orchestral color; were Taylor dumb enough to use the full score, his *Rite* would turn from comico-spooky to monotono-silly, like Béjart or Pina Bausch. (Disney's technicolor stab wasn't bad. He inclined, as they say out there, to Mickey-Mouse the music, but he had the right.) Just as Satie's *Parade* is too weak for a viable ballet, Stravinsky's *Rite* is too strong.

Nantucket
25 April

A good week here, installing homemade window boxes and cramming them, perhaps prematurely, with the rich brown loam that reeks of childhood, and then with multicolored impatiens rootings. Sky stays nearly white with brightness as each afternoon we take a drive—to Sconset, to Cisco, to Pocomo—and gather heavy rocks for borders. At night we watch TV (Verdi *Requiem* via Muti, not bad), or go to movies (John Corigliano's *Altered States*, although strictly "movie music," is, in its apposite descriptiveness—mostly of acid trips—and enviably risky orchestration that works, movie music at its most exemplary). Perfect weather for *Winter Pages*, which progresses daily and will contain thirteen movements.

New York

7 May

Returned ten days ago to see Indiana University's version at the Met of a Martinů opera about Greece (why him and not one of their own?); then a trying day at Curtis in Philly, followed by a rerun of Ann Thorne's last year's benefit dinner for the American Composers Orchestra (with, again, Judy Collins and John Lindsay, but no gaffes); on Tuesday, parents to dine; Wednesday, chez Ed White with the alert and fabricating Richard Sennett; Thursday, a meeting with Maggy, then Fellini's failed *La Città delle Donne*; Wednesday, broadcast of Philip Glass's opera in Sanskrit, for which the music has viewpoint and drive and a certain scarifying color. Sunday, after JH's service, saw *Atlantic City*, for which John Guare's text—considering how literary and ornately scripted it is—works surprisingly well in the hard-boiled decor.

Monday, after spending hours with a certain Dr. Downs where both JH and I (and half of New York) are being tested for what may be amoebic dysentery, we visited Ann Thorne's charming (that's the only word) exhibit, thence to Janet Flanner's memorial at the Maison Française. The memorial consisted of statements by Virgil, Brendan Gill, Natalia, Shirley Hazzard, and myself (I recited the little portrait from *Gaysweek*); then a good film in color, made over the past few years, which quite captured Janet in all her bigger-than-life bright-eyed scolding humorous intelligent cogency. Supper at Helen & Tom Bishop's where Gill reminds me (I'd blocked it out) that two years ago I sent him a polite comment on his comment in the *New Yorker*: "*La Cage aux Folles* . . . may be none too singingly translated as 'Cage for Crazy Ladies.'" Having checked the files, here for posterity is what I wrote: "May it not be considered impertinent to suggest that *La Cage aux folles* might be more 'singingly translated' as *The Queen's Cage*. Yes, *folle* does mean crazy lady, but in slang it means male homosexual, as is the case here. Indeed, in France *folle* is more often used in its gay-argot meaning than in its 'correct' meaning (like bitch in English). Meanwhile, the untranslatable *aux* (the plural contraction, of course, of *à les*) must be rendered as 'of,' not as 'for.' Thus the title could also be Englished as *Cage of Queens*. (Queen's a better word than, say, fruit or faggot, since it's an 'inside' term without derisive overtones.) Pedantically yours . . . " This is called setting straights straight.

Now Mother, after a fall at the elevator on Charles Street, is in room 403 of Beekman Hospital with a splayed femur, and her leg is being operated on. Joined Father there at four, and we had a cup of lukewarm mushroom soup in the dreary cafeteria. Father stayed on for the evening, while I met JH for a dinner in Joyce Carol Oates's honor at the Bobst Library.

9 May

We attended, at one of those gentrified little stables on West 42nd, a review called *Ah, Men* based on the prose of some twenty authors and their depiction of "the male condition." Included was a soliloquy, the one on Turkish baths, from my *New York Diary*, the only token queerness on the bill. As we perused our programs we eavesdropped on three young men behind us perusing theirs. "Who's Bertrand Russell?" asks the one on the left. "Oh, he's, you know, that pacifist," answers the one in the middle, obviously the brains of the trio. "Who's O'Casey?" asks the one on the right. "An Irish playwright." "Who's Ned Rorem?" "That faggot composer." For this I have sculpted a long, long life. My feelings were hurt, and the hurt flew to the ailing groin, rendering me more homophobic than ever. I start to sweat. I hate my body, it keeps me from my mind.

Visited Mother this afternoon. Hazy from anesthesia. Rosemary, whose 59th birthday was yesterday, arrives. Tomorrow JH takes all the cats, Wallace and Sam and Princess, to Nantucket, while I go to Philly to finish out the scholastic year at Curtis. Then I too will fly to Nantucket.

Hyatt Hotel
Louisville
23 May

This hotel is disgusting. Every last room opens onto a funnel-like court, like a prison, from which all day the tremor of an all-woman tea-dance ensemble rises, echoing against each door, and over the balconies of which all night an assemblage of Jaycees hang screaming until dawn. Complaints are registered but not heeded. This morning I refused to pay a third of my bill, on the grounds that I'd dwelt in a sty, and the management, without fuss, accepted my terms. I advised Roger Sessions to follow suit (he was at the checkout desk too, and had spent a sleepless night), but he was too shy.

Sessions, however, was a positive attribute of the soujourn. His *Fourth Symphony* and my *Air Music* have just been performed and recorded here under our supervision, and his company has been sweet, cordial, intelligent, and humorous. (We've never met before; I'd always been put off by his physical resemblance to Ralph Shapey, who's as ingratiating as a Jaycee at four A.M.)

Peter Leonard's able conducting of the average orchestra gets the lively results he got with *Miss Julie*, and society has been otherwise entertaining, with parties and interviews and sightseeing and such. Except that late last night, at a restaurant called Casa Grisanti, I was stricken with diarrhea, due to the rough regimen of powerful pills prescribed by Dr. Downs. In an hour I return east on the plane with Roger, he to Pennsylvania, I to Massachusetts.

Nantucket
26 May

Even Balanchine's feet have turned to clay. Apparently he staged "The Spellbound Child" as *L'Enfant et les sortilèges* at its Monte Carlo premiere in the 1920s. He's restaged it often since. Judging by last night's televised version (why is such a work not reviewed by musicians, but instead by TV critics who miscall it a "ballet," an "operetta"?), it's time for him to cease. Even if it were stageable, one can't, as Balanchine does, tamper with Ravel's timbre. To use the strident nonvibrating voice of a preadolescent male in the key role meant for a mezzo is no less misrepresentative than casting a twelve-year-old boy as Queen of the Swans. Obtuse and misaccented English, when a flick of the translator's pen could have shifted a verb here, a clause there, into an easy colloquialism that would have been both better English and, by extension, better Colette. Perhaps Balanchine's ear is not tuned to English. Stravinsky's Russian ear was not either, viz. *The Rake's Progress*.

31 May

JH, because of his church duties, commutes on summer weekends, an exhausting and expensive process. He usually arrives on the midnight ferry, so Sunday evenings my routine is geared toward meeting him—watching various late programs (especially "Sneak Previews" on WGBH), then walking to the docks beneath which eels dart among moored boats in the floodlights, until the glamourous moment when the *Uncatena* or the *Nantucket* appears around Brant Point, lit up like a yellow birthday cake, and glides toward the wharf all throbbing with life.

Tonight I finally finished copying *Winter Pages*, then concocted an elaborate program note and tied the ten pounds of music into a neat package which tomorrow I'll insure and send off to Boosey & Hawkes. Now I'll venture into the dark.

3 June

Mornings I usually spend practicing—on that same damned program with Phyllis B.-J. now rescheduled for June 16, and on the Bach Inventions. JH's working on the patio, an idyllic bricked-in intimate corner, flush with the kitchen, for which he's just finished building four steps. I seldom go swimming, he never.

New York
11 June

Flew back Tuesday, dined with parents. Yesterday afternoon, Dr. Downs, and start of second twenty-day regimen of powerful pills.

This evening I invited, sight unseen, Robin Holloway for a meal. As a fellow contractee with Boosey & Hawkes, as a lover of America both North and South (he's just traversed the Amazon alone), as a writer of music boasting both pathos and wit (David Del Tredici, whose Westbeth apartment he sublets during this first brief trip to the USA from Cambridge, is the only other Anglo-American composer who manages that Gallic combination), and as a ruddy non-narcissist whose turtlenecked likeness I've relished in *Tempo* magazine, he seemed worthy of hospitality. He's eager, gifted, quick, and consecrated (his only real conversation is about music), and his visage expresses as much innocence as any Englishman's I've known; although do the eyes of even the most gullible Europeans ever emit the open candor of even the wickedest American?

16 June

Beyond belief! The song recital with Phyllis Bryn-Julson, postponed from ten weeks ago, was to have transpired tonight at the YMHA. Last night Phyllis, after returning to Essex House from our somewhat fuzzy rehearsal, phoned to warn me that "her chest was filling up"; this morning, nearly voiceless, she phoned again to cancel. I told her to inform Omus Hirschbein (I couldn't face it), who quickly called Donald Gramm, but Donald's bedridden and can't pinch-hit. So for the second time—after a remailing of a thousand conning flyers—the concert's off. Shamefaced, I phoned some thirty ticket-holders (including Myrna Loy, who had organized a party) to say "Stay home." It's the price of jet travel. Only last Friday Phyllis was over-taxing herself with Boulez in Paris. I feel worse for Rose Plaut, who subsi-dized the function, than for myself. Omus feels we can't commit ourselves to Phyllis for yet a third go, but that we can aim for another program with another singer, perhaps two, next season. Meanwhile JH, who flew in from Nantucket especially, and who because of fog got stranded for three hours in New Bedford, was not amused. We've passed a post prandial hour at back-gammon, as we do every evening of the year. Tomorrow he flies back to the island, where I follow a day later. The heat wave devastates and the air con-ditioner hums.

17 June

At four Francis Thorne stopped by with score and tape of his *Eternal Light*, all aspects of which are imaginative and satisfying except for the not insig-nificant flaw (to me) that he sets words in Italian, a language not his own. Is it conceivable that an Italian would set English? Francis is only one of many (viz. Harbison, Crumb) who avoid their native tongue. We build better bombs than other countries, but have an inferiority complex about our language.

At six, buffet on Barbara Kolb's roof two blocks away, where imbibers who could have been assembled by Holly Golightly except for the lack of levity (a rabbi, a priest, an Italian filmmaker, a female Modern Dancer with lank hair and parted lips, Stuart & Doris Pope, Robin Holloway . . .) never quite jelled.

At eight, taking Robin with me, I gave another reading for The Glines, this time on West 49th, poorly attended. George Whitmore gave a caring introduction.

Nantucket
5 July

Eva-Maria Tausig, coordinator of the local summer series, has arranged for the first of this year's six concerts to be all-Rorem, and she's done it adeptly. My prized executants are Daniel Phillips, Edward Auer, Ani Kavafian, and Hilda Harris. The program: *Day Music, Night Music, Serenade*, and a mis-cellaneous song group with me accompanying. Daniel arrived on island last night in a drizzle, and I fed him scrambled eggs, salad, and a green pistachio cream pie (really). Hilda came today. JH arrives tonight on the Hy-Line and Sylvia Goldstein tomorrow by plane.

8 July

Last night was, so far as performance is concerned, of high order, and so was
the Wachtels' reception on the water at Shimmo. Sylvia adjusts to the household with stylish cool and hosts a little sun-tea party in the new patio today
for Ursula Colt, and for the good-looking Margaret Mercer & David Dubal
who appeared incongruously, far from their urban crowd.

12 July

Usually I turn first to the obits in the daily *Times*, but today en route my eye
was caught by the Headliners column: "Christmas Murder Case. If Claus
von Bulow tried to kill his wife, he was very patient about it." John Simon on
the phone filled me in on the whole sordid business. Well, though we were
never awfully close, I despise the thought of Claus in trouble. Surely he's
innocent, if only because he can't have been that dumb—to twice make the
same inane mistake—though perhaps there are no rules. Marie Laure
would have been dazzled. I consult the old agenda . . . Yes. On October 18,
1955, Maggy Magerstadt and I at 6:30 in the evening had a drink chez Claus
at 27 Belgrave Square. During our genteel converse he asked us if we'd care
to see his whips. As another might stash in neat rows his billiard cues, so
Claus stashes his cats-o'-nine-tails, some with jewelled handles, upstairs in
a special chamber.

Saranac Lake
19 July

Here in the Adirondacks since four nights ago, guest of Gregg Smith and
Roz Rees. The first hours were limbo, lonesome, long. Also, like the pea
with the princess, the Hotel Saranac seemed too creaky and confining ("Elliott Carter loved it last summer," they informed me), so I was transferred to
a private home, which became still more problematic. But by the second
day I was dazzled with mountain air, with the earthy cordiality of the Smiths
on their tiny river island, and with the excellence of performance. No other
small professional chorus in the world surpasses Gregg's in precision of
pitch, inevitability of arch & ebb, and scope of repertory, although he does
ask for and get from his sopranos a nonvibrating choirboy sound that I dislike. I'm just not a pederast, hating especially *solo* boy sopranos, with the
result that certain otherwise respectable, even beautiful, works become off-
limits, nothing but mean shrieks to my ears: Falla's *El Retablo*, for example,
or Bernstein's *Chichester Psalms*. If I can take Britten's *Turn of the Screw*,

it's because the little boy therein is meant to be a monster; in *Peter Grimes* he never opens his mouth.

The program of my mostly choral music last night sounded balanced: *Three Motets, Water Music, Give All To Love* (world premiere of this two-part chorus and piano affair, on Emerson verses, sung with the antiphonal choreography of which Gregg's so fond), *Hearing* (the four-voices and nine-instruments version), and finally *Letters from Paris* of which the fourth movement brought tears to my eyes, not so much for the beauty of the music as for the aptness of Janet's text about the funeral of Colette, which could as easily have been her own, with its picture of "the palatial tree-filled Palais Royal Garden, at the opposite end of which she lived for many years, and where she had died suddenly, and painlessly, in the evening, after a small sip of champagne."

Nantucket
30 July

> There always comes a moment, just before the moment of composition, when a subject seems stripped of all attraction . . . even bare of all significance. . . . Losing all interest in it, you curse that secret pact whereby you have committed yourself, and which makes it impossible to back out honorably. In spite of this, you would still rather quit. . . .
>
> I say "you," but actually I do not know whether others feel this way. It is probably similar to the condition of the convert who, the last few days, on the point of approaching the altar, feels his faith suddenly falter and takes fright at the emptiness of his heart.
> —from Gide's notebook, *The Journal of the Counterfeiters*

Wanting something "episodic" to peruse, I snatched up Gide's book on the way to the john this morning. The passage's *déjà vu* was only too ironic, in the light of my writing a review of Auden's biography which now causes me such anguish and which, to protect myself, I've lost all interest in, while allowing (at least that's how JH feels) my body to demolish my morale, still, after seven months now. But also in the light of the Royal Wedding, of which we watched a replay last evening on our new color TV. Suppose that Lady Diana (or even Prince Charles) were to decide, while in the glass carriage en route to Saint Paul's, that she couldn't go through with it, and that, making fact of desire, she fled. In a sense, this was the Duke of Windsor's plot.

Years ago, Shirley told me that the night before her second wedding she had such misgivings that she would have balked had not her mother spent so much energy preparing the reception.

Nantucket
7 August

Still beautiful and windy.

Still on Meprobate, three a day, which Voorhees prescribed to calm my frenzy three weeks ago.

Still agonizing over review of the Auden, due imminently at the *Chicago Tribune*.

Lenny B., in his big thesis called *The Unanswered Question*, is seeking an innate musical grammar during which he finds flagrant syntactical flaws where'er he looks. But he makes his own syntactical flaw on the very first page. His audience for these lectures, he tells us, was mixed, with "experts in music who cared little for linguistics, vice versa, scientists with no interest in poetry, vice versa . . . " Vice versa what? Linguistics who cared little for experts in music? Poetry with no interest in scientists? Throughout the book he does have such a grand time with unusual words—anaphora, chiasmus, rhopalism, polysyndeton—that one hesitates to tell him he's not a Thinker, like the earthbound Chomsky whom he forever uncritically praises, but an airborne doer who doesn't need to prove how smart he is.

Dined tonight with the forever affable and enthusiastic Danny Pinkham, and also Andy Holman, on Westminster Street. Thirty-five summers ago Danny taught me as much as I still know about the harpsichord. In what dusty valise lies the little (actually quite big) *Concertino da Camera*, composed to his recipe, that allowed me in 1946 to pay that famous visit to Landowska? Danny, on his good days (though he has been wrongly tempted by vogues), still writes better tunes than anyone.

22 August

Morris Golde's been here for several days, untiring and self-sufficient. (Statistics: Morris showed me New York at nineteen. JH never knew me before forty-three.)

This afternoon in Saint Paul's Church on Fair Street, memorial for Robin Harbach. His demise last winter didn't come as a surprise, yet habits are hard to break. Thoughts during the informal ceremony: his owlish gaze. His Floridian clothes (so seeming to us know-it-all Manhattanites) as he walked past our house each morning on the way to the Hub—lime-green pants and rose-pink shirts (or was it the other way around?), a sweater looped over his shoulder. The potent grain of self-destruction nursed by so many—though not all—sensitive souls in the light, or the dark, of our malignant moon. His

ASCAP-founding parent. His alcohol intake. Half his name was Bach. Mimsi once said that she and Robin almost never quarreled, and when they did they were sick for days. I believe her. Their community seemed, despite good-natured ribbing on both sides, peaceful and nourishing. But now the peace, the nourishment, must come to Mimsi only in the retrospect of dreams, for Robin's dead. But dreams are nourishment too. Even in the best of times they're all we have to keep us going. So, to her tonight, sweet dreams.

24 August

Morris was absorbed into the mob of the 5 o'clock ferry for the Vineyard. At six we went to Monomoy for a drink with Connie Bessie, so haven't had time yet to miss Morris. Feeling wretched. We've summoned an arborist about our five coveted eighty-foot Chinese elms, which seem blighted.

Tonight, finished the article on Stravinsky, which goes to *Opera News* tomorrow and also will be my lecture next month to the subscribers of the Chamber Music Society. Thus I get paid twice for the same work. Except it's not the same work: *Opera News* pays for the writing, the Society for the lecturing.

30 August

Every professional musician receives daily requests for his time, his money, or the use of his name on a letterhead. These are mostly consigned to the wastebasket. But I've allowed myself to get depressed by the solicitation of something called "Artists to End Hunger" and its pious lay-notion of art. As a Quaker I'm hardly immune to the world's wrongs, but this bunch's propaganda is naive and crass. It's naive to accept hunger as an abstraction (whose hunger? where?) that can be assuaged by "art." Hunger isn't eased by concerts, but by planting crops, planning birth control, meeting of nations. Music doesn't change people, but the sight of suffering might. It's crass to use hunger as a promotional device: to construe the personal elation of pianist Ilana Vered—whoever she may be—as a service to humanity. Rather than a glossy photo of her, why not one of emaciated children? Throughout the prospectus is talk of "creating opportunities for artists," "media publicizing," "seeking government support" for musicians, but no mention of how the proposed program will benefit the hungry.

Like a fool I sent these reactions to the "Artists to End Hunger" board along with the wish for my name not to be linked to their self-serving organization. They answered, stating that my "points stimulated much thought. . . . We discovered that our Purpose and Intended Results were not as clear as we had thought," plus goobledegook about "will" and "commitment," and enclosing a letter ("Dear Ned") from a Marguerite Chandler who begins, "As a fellow Quaker and as a member of the board of 'Artists to End Hunger,' I feel moved to speak to you," following with long pieties which shift the meaning of "hunger" to suit her purposes. Again like a fool I answered:

"To speak of 'hunger of the human spirit' is to use the word metaphorically. It may be that 'majestic music,' as you so sentimentally put it, feeds the spirit, but your group's policy is presumably to feed the body. I will not be convinced that an Indian child, numb from lack of food, can be 'nourished' by Beethoven; nor will I listen to a person who asserts the contrary unless that person has literally starved. To draw no distinction between music and bread, and to claim that a starving human is eased by one as by the other, is cruel.

"You inadvertently insult me when speaking of 'we who are the appreciators of art.' I am a practitioner, not a mere appreciator, as you should have known before soliciting me. Meanwhile, to contend that the aim, and thus the financial profits, of art should be toward ending misery is to invent rules for your convenience. But taking your contention as solid: why should an artist donate financial gains *as well as his art* to the poor? Most artists themselves are poor; nor has their art ever in its history existed for purposes of financial gain, or even been profitable compared to the works of munitions makers or, indeed, to Quaker businessmen. Don't talk to artists about 'impoverishment of the human spirit.' Talk instead about nuclear disarmament. And don't talk about 'the *really* poor' until you yourself have physically starved.

Sincerely . . . "

Shrink all this to half a page.

What's the purpose of art?

Well, I don't know the purpose. But the function (and there's a difference) is to satisfy that indefinable area within us that can't be satisfied by the senses, or at least by the *grosser* senses: taste, touch, and smell. It's indefinable precisely because, were it defined, it wouldn't need to be. Art is its own definition. Are words then art? Tough question. Poetry, yes. But is a novel art— or is it high art?

The nauseating conclusion of the "Artists to End Hunger" people is that art is necessarily ennobling. Now, there is no example, ever, of its being ennobling, and few artists are themselves noble—whatever noble is.

The Quaker woman writes of the starving Somalians who nevertheless retain "great dignity and courage" and she asks herself "Who are the *really poor?*"—meaning us affluent pigs. One wonders how she'd react to starving people who were not, in her eyes, dignified. Do they get demerits?

But the *purpose* of art?

JH says: to make money.

6 September

Scattering of society, agreeable, not worth detailing. Maury Newberger's here, cheerful; dined at the Languedoc. (Today in NY, broadcast of Bernstein version of *Sunday Morning* on WQXR, and on WNCN, a midnight broadcast of interview with Matt Biberfeld.)

Working mainly on new organ suite for the AGO convention next summer. Reexamining the scores and cassettes, mainly an orchestral *Triptych*—full of gift and truth, but so crosshatched with chic notation and special effects as to be self-defeating—of Daron Hagen, the new student at Curtis where I return in a week (after a flu shot). (Once I noted that Rex Reed, contrary to a taffy-apple which is unhealthiness congealed around nourishment, was intelligence congealed around flippancy. Hagen's music is, for the moment, pleasure camouflaged as pain; therefore it *is* pain.)

New York
15 September

Passed yesterday in Philadelphia; nice to see again the previous students, plus the new one from Madison, bearded, bright, and seething with a desire to please. Tonight, visit from Tom Steele, then the keen and funny *Cloud Nine* with Morris at the De Lys, in the rain.

17 September

Within the Chamber Music Society's contract, dated last February, it is stated: "On Thursday, September 17, 1981, you will provide an amusing, sophisticated lecture focusing in some way on Stravinsky." Since I always do what I am told (or I don't do at all), this lecture was duly provided to the packed Bruno Walter Auditorium at six P.M.; it lasted five-sixths of an hour, after which for ten minutes Paul Jacobs and I performed, as a curtain-lowerer, both of the four-hand Stravinsky suites. John de Lancie was there, and so were Mother & Father, William Schuman (who cringed, so he claims, at my question, "Does not a songwriter who repeats phrases not repeated in the poems he is setting threaten that poem's integrity?" since he's always doing just that, but quickly added that he had received special dispensation from Archibald MacLeish), and Eugenia Zukerman who, according to Shirley, dutifully took notes. Then Shirley and I joined Robert Phelps and Stephen Koch for a hamburger at O'Neals.

20 September

Roger Englander stopped by for an early snack, then to the Bernstein-conducts-Stravinsky concert. Bowled over by Lenny's and Michael Tilson Thomas's four-hand rendition of *Sacre*, the very epitome of glamour, yet a glamour that didn't interfere with the score's vicious integrity. My whole notion of M.T.T. has altered for the better. (Still, at the party chez Lenny later, amidst the chitchat and tinkling ice cubes, Michael sat at the Steinway and oh-so-casually played Gershwin, as sophisticates in thirties movies did, but the role doesn't fit him—though, yes, he gets the chords right.)

Watergate Hotel
Washington, D.C.
24 September

Straight to Washington from Philadelphia Tuesday, after teaching at Curtis and suppering with Rosemary. Paul Callaway, bless him, met the Metroliner (which was an hour late) and wearily deposited me at the Watergate toward midnight. Since my reservation had been confirmed by Martita, but since the only space available was the Presidential Suite, the hotel was legally bound to place me temporarily there. Entering with the bellhop—following him meekly through room after room as he flung open casements onto balconies and displayed various bars and baths stocked with Jack Daniels and Jacques Fath—my sole concern was how much tip to bestow.

Martita Istomin must be commended for her series of concerts by visiting composers, not only because it's worthy in itself, but because she, Martita, left solely to her heart, would probably prefer Schubert and Bach. After rehearsing in the Terrace Theater yesterday afternoon, I invited my invaluable performers—Sharon Robinson, Jerry Lowenthal and Roz Rees—to savor briefly from my suite the view of the Potomac, knowing that at four I'd be ousted in favor of Arabs. At 4:30, my new lodging seemed okay in itself, but the clattering radiator turned out to be unfixable, so I ended up down the hall in the only remaining space, a maid's cubicle. The concert went well last night, although Martita hesitated to confess that it was papered with inmates from a reform school. Now I await Eugene for breakfast, after which I shuttle to New York with Sharon and her cello, in time for a date at four with Aaron Asher at Harper & Row.

Visit from Harold Hayes whom I'd not seen since our TV roundtables in 1975. An agile mind, clear writing style, something of the "professional amateur," like George Plimpton. He finds the creative musical character a mystery which must be solved, doesn't understand that the subject is humdrum to "musical personalities" themselves. That's why he's here: to talk about Beethoven's deafness. Because his analytic mind is made up, he won't get the point when I say that the question of deafness in a composer is not amazing to a composer, since most composers, good and bad, compose in silence. Harold, as a layman, is like those psychiatrists who are forever avid to snare and embalm what they themselves can't do, refusing to agree that the so-called creative act is nothing more nor less than hard work. If the work breathes and bleeds, that's beyond the creator's power to guarantee, but he hopes, like any pregnant person, it will *seem* to live. Meanwhile, a composer's physical ear can actually get in the way of what he ideally hears. In the long run, what talking dogs say is more interesting than the fact that they talk; it might be more pertinent to decide whether there is a difference in kind, rather than in worth, between what Beethoven wrote before and after his deafness. As for the famous treatise by J. W. N. Sullivan about Beethoven, which Harold proudly lent me, it turns the stomach with its Moral Majority dicta ("the life that includes love, marriage, friends, children, was withheld from [Beethoven]") and its conclusion that the denial of these bourgeois privileges caused the suffering that produces great art.

After he left I watched Gielgud in Resnais's mildly amusing *Providence*, then made an outline for the upcoming year's twenty analysis sessions at Curtis.

With Ellen tonight to the Whitney to witness *Histoire du soldat*, starring, in the spoken roles, Virgil, Aaron and Roger Sessions—a delicious concept in theory, a theatrical catastrophe in practice. All three kept losing their place.

Phyllis Bryn-Julson and her husband, Donald Sutherland, invited me for a two-day stint ending in this afternoon's all-Rorem concert at Bradley Hills Presbyterian Church. Last night, after the class in French vocal repertory (at which Rose Taylor, who had a bit part in *Bertha* eight years ago, sang the *Chansons de Bilitis* as beautifully as they'll ever be heard), I was left to my own devices, called Paul Callaway, and we went to a local bistro. He came again, with Paul Hume, to this afternoon's concert, a memorable aspect of which (over and above Phyllis's *Nantucket Songs* and a young baritone named David Young's *War Scenes*, both with me at the ivories, plus other solos and choral pieces, and Donald's five excerpts from *A Quaker Reader*) was the presence of police in the crowded audience. Over the past few years I've received love-hate letters (unanswered) from a stranger whose address seems to be a mental hospital in Maryland, and the last letter hinted he'd be present today with a gun. I alerted the Sutherlands, who alerted the ushers, who alerted the cops. But nothing happened.

I now await Paul to drive me to the shuttle. Tomorrow, the students in New York, then evening plane to Nantucket for a month.

Nantucket
8 October

Assassination of Sadat. Reruns of my Cavett interviews. *Chinatown* again, a favorite film. Dark and cold. Sam fell into the turpentine and became quite ill; we've scrubbed him with shampoo and swathed him in heated towels from which his head emerges now as he finally purrs. Reading *Loon Lake*—charmless. Tomorrow JH leaves for nine days.

His smoking is an agony; two to three packs of unfiltered Pall Malls a day, deeply inhaled. He smokes always, everywhere, on the beach, mowing the lawn, at the A & P, and he has a built-in hacking cough. Despite a plethora of ashtrays, JH poses—and then forgets—glowing butts on the edge of sinks, bureaus, oil tanks. To worry aloud about his dying before I die, or even about the dangers of cigarettes, is forbidden on the premise that I'm projecting a death wish! There's a vague Freudian logic to this, though of course the true reason is that he too is scared, hooked, up a blind alley. I brood, unable to vent my frustration; but the tone of connubiality isn't sundered, as with an alcoholic. Yet, *justement*, the quiet of tobacco, as opposed to the noise of liquor, is what's pernicious, and doubtless more physically wounding. For what it's worth, I stopped smoking, as well as drinking, almost from the day we met, while the smoking of JH (who was never even remotely tempted by booze) has, if anything, been aggravated.

13 October

Finished the organ piece, for better or worse, xeroxed it at "The Poet's Corner," and sent it in a scroll to Maury at Boosey & Hawkes, who in turn will forward copies to John Obetz who's scheduled to play it in Washington next June. It's called *Views from the Oldest House*, is in six titled movements, and contains this program note: "For many years now I have lived in the shade of Nantucket's Sunset Hill, site of the island's most venerable landmark, the so-called Oldest House, built in 1686 by Jethro Coffin. The hill's southwest vista gleams with variety, especially during summer evenings when it is my habit to stroll up there while supper cooks. This habit echoes through the following pieces, which may be performed separately or as a suite."

Arthritis in both legs. Full moon. Bergman's *Autumn Sonata* on the telly—wise and tough. Insomnia.

18 October

In anticipation of JH's return I yesterday swept the house from cellar to attic, cleaned the bathroom (and took a bath), watered all plants, bought a chicken, made a chocolate pie, and then for relaxation watched Eisenstein's 1933 movie, *Thunder over Mexico*. Some relaxation! I was no less sickened by its power now than when as a child I saw it at Chicago's Oriental Institute. Despite the now-corny symbolism of crucifixion images, the scene of the trampled heads is as depressing a depiction of man's inhumanity to man as . . .

JH just now called from Hyannis to say that his plane would be late, arriving around seven. I told him to pick up Ruth Ford en route from the airport—Ruth having phoned this morning to say she's on-island, making a movie and staying in a Touch-of-Evil-type inn on Swain's Wharf. I asked her over to dine tonight.

25 October

Golden week. JH planting, and painting kitchen furniture. Wildflowers still vital and ripe for plucking. Struggling with Cocteau essay. Turned clocks back last night. And this night Ruth Ford came for supper again (vegetable stew), saying she'd be responsible for dessert, which at nine was duly delivered (by its maker, a Ms. Mary Coughlin, who works on the crew of Ruth's movie, and who turns out also to be a seamstress, so we've engaged her to sew some much-needed curtains), a carrot cake in honor of my 58th birthday two days ago.

Ruth definitely sings for her supper: trembles with energy, laughs delightedly and at the right time (throwing back her handsome blonde head), can talk about anything but is unafraid to say she's dumb on some subjects, listens well, is bigger than life, generally stagey, and contributes without

being overbearing. In fact, she projects in the parlor better than over the
footlights, being rather brighter than an actress ought to be. There's something incongruous about such an urban creature with her southern accent
here on a faraway island. Nor have we seen her except after nightfall.

New York
6 November

In the current *New Yorker* George Kennan's piece on nuclear armament is
so soberly reasoned that one can imagine Reagan and Haig reading it and
changing their policies overnight. Or would that be like telling hawks to understand themselves by examining Audubon lithographs? There is no such
thing as a purely motivated ruler; just wanting to *be* president is already
corrupt.

Returned to the city on Halloween and have been active, compared to the
unvaried island routine. Parents to dine; session at Curtis (individual lessons, plus class, dissecting Copland's *Variations*); endless minutiae—bank,
B. & H., Patelsons, phone interviews with Cincinnati journalists; David
Diamond's ambitious *Secular Cantata*; and Thursday Moira Hodgson and
Ed White came to dine, with John Wulp and a friend (not a happy fusion).
JH came back yesterday and saw Dr. Downs. Today we went to the Frick (his
favorite site on earth), and later to Ken Fuchs's operetta, which had some of
the direct bluesy appeal of Paul Bowles's old songs.

8 November

Paul Jacobs tried out his program in a Central Park West apartment for a
batch of listeners of whom I knew none except Leighton Kerner. The *clou*
was Elliott Carter's new *Night Fantasies*. With the single score laid upon our
collective knees, Leighton and I (were we the only ones to read notes?) followed the music as best we could for twenty thorny minutes. At the end,
knowing that I would confirm his reaction, Leighton muttered in complicity, "What a wonderful piece," as though we'd just heard a Chopin *Nocturne*.
In fact, for me it was chaos, and I quit the premises, sullen.

Typing poems that I have set to music, which I'll present tomorrow to
Robert Convery, Daron Hagen, and Norman Stumpf for *them* to set to music, so that in a week we can compare results. I'm forever disconcerted not
only by how few, if any, songs (or, indeed, any vocal music at all) young composers compose, but how, when confronted with the assignment, how vague
they are about where to look for (or what to look for in) a "settable" verse.
Maybe if their notions jibed more with mine, there'd be no need for me.

Yesterday, rehearsal here with Kristine and Katherine Ciesinski, during which James Lord showed up. So we sang to him a gloomy section from *Gloria*. The Ciesinski sisters are like nothing else: ripe as yellow plums, brilliant but without intellect, poised, mutually considerate, and with vocal hues and diction that leave little to be wished for. Unlikely that in a million years their tracks would have crossed James Lord's except for this fortuity. James, meanwhile, forever cool but mellowed, keeps deep in Giacometti. We broach the question of Marie Laure's biography, which we've both been approached to do, which neither of us wants to do, but which someone has to do.

Today, visit from Lester D. Brothers, of North Texas State University, who's continuing a thesis on my music. Later, dined at Sharon's with George & Shirley, Bob Steiner, and a Paul Rorem who turns out to be a cousin, but of what remove only Father can tell after consulting the family tree.

Terrace Hilton Hotel
Cincinnati
14 November

I have just done something, or rather refrained from doing something, for the first time: heard the world premiere of a major piece of mine, without having attended any rehearsals. Partly from laziness, partly from fear of being far from home, and partly from curiosity about the risk I was running, I arrived in Cincinnati too late for even a consultation, much less a dress rehearsal, of the *Double Concerto* which finally had its first performance yesterday. I'd never met the soloists before—pianist Lee Luvisi, cellist Peter Wiley, conductor Jorge Mester—and shook their hands only five minutes before they went on stage. During the next half-hour each of the ten movements emerged identical in speed, color, timbre and suppleness to what I had envisaged (is that a word for music?) when composing the piece. Proving that, whatever the piece's value, my notation is expert and so are the players. David Huntley, representing Boosey & Hawkes, met me here and stayed for the second performance, and we've shared breakfasts of French toast garnished with orange slices (in the buffet of this weird hotel that begins on the upper floors of an office building), while David describes with skill and pathos his family saga. We return to New York at noon.

After the premiere I told Mester simply that a certain twenty measures in the first section were too expressive. That was repaired by the second performance—as good a one as the work will ever need. (Jack Kirstein, for whom the piece was originally intended, was apparently present at both presentations but did not say hello.) Mester wants to repeat the work at the Juilliard festival in January with the school orchestra and student players. But we agree it's not a concerto. Should the title be changed to *Double Music*, which Lou Harrison's already used? Or to *Green Music*, which is the name of the tenth movement? Or to *Remembering Tommy*, which is the name of the third movement? (According to the terms of the contract, the piece is inscribed "To the Memory of Thomas Schippers.")

Insofar as anyone, including the composer, can presume to endow musical statements with concrete emotions, I suppose this "concerto" is the merriest piece in my catalogue. Yet the four last months of 1978 seemed morally quite bleak when the work was concocted and orchestrated. So much for the link between an artist's life and his work.

17 November

Father's 87th birthday, for which I got him a cardigan sweater.

Dined chez Molly Haskell and Andrew Sarris on East 88th, with Cleve and Francine. Also present were Ross Wetzeon and Kay Larson. Felt, as I never have before, that certain subjects were avoided because of my presence.

18 November

Miriam Fried and Garrick Ohlsson played *Day Music* at the Y. Two egos retained their identity while meshing into a happy marriage. That is, Garrick did not play like an accompanist, but with a limpid forcefulness. I felt wonderfully well represented.

Tomorrow, Nantucket for ten Thanksgiving days. Then we'll bring all the cats back.

29 November

Death yesterday of Lotte Lenya. Dined with parents.

Death today of Natalie Wood. Rehearsed with Sheila Schoenbrun.

1 December

Performed *The Nantucket Songs* tonight with Sheila on Barbara Kolb's "Music in New York" series down on East Eleventh.

3 December

Public roundtable at the Maison Française in honor of Virgil T., with me, Barbara, David Del T., and Hugo Weisgall.

Whittier, California
6 December

Mother's birthday, for which it seems appropriate that I find myself in this Society of Friends. The project that brings me began to ferment a year ago when Professor Orpha Ochse wrote: "We are planning a festival featuring performances of your *Quaker Reader* by Catharine Crozier, and recognizing the outstanding contributions you and Jessamyn West have made to the fields of music and literature. We will also be celebrating Whittier College's Quaker heritage."

Two programs of my music, plus roundtables on Quakerism and on "Art and the Church" (uniting old friends like John LaMontaine and Pia Gilbert, as well as, of course, Jessamyn, who's taken a gentle *coup de vieux* since our last—and first—meeting in Napa) led toward the main event. This event, which occurred last night and was repeated this evening, consisted of Catharine Crozier performing on the organ all eleven movements of *A Quaker Reader* interspersed with the spoken and expanded version of the eleven paragraphs that I had drawn from Jessamyn's collection and used as epigraphs. These were narrated by Peter Mark Richard, who in 1956 had portrayed a child in the film of *Friendly Persuasion*. This rendition, complete with intermission, was over twice as long as my music by itself; if it worked dramatically, that was none of my doing. Crozier is a marvelous organist, and I wonder if her train of thought was broken, as mine was, by the interpolations.

New York
9 December

An hour yesterday as David Diamond's guest for one of Juilliard's regular Tuesday sessions. Room 539 was stuffed with bright-eyed composers in their twenties. The occasion: to hear, then collectively to analyse, David's new Violin Sonata, his most lively and likeable piece in years. The only comment I could think to make, after David's own sober exegesis and the learned questions from the bright-eyed composers, was: Why, in twenty minutes, is there just one pizzicato?

Today at 6:30, offered coffee etc. to Joe Machlis, Chuck Turner and Phillip Ramey, in exchange for their patiently attending the tape of what is now called *Green Music*, during which Milton Goldman entered and began to talk, not knowing "one doesn't talk" during music, but he described with poignance the circumstances of Arnold's death.

10 December

Now Sylvia Marlowe too has died. A relief, after the physical horrors she underwent—herpes of the eye, emphysema, an iron lung—yet one can't help feeling cheated. The lacuna represents the end of a breed (of which maybe Sylvia was the sole example). Tough character, a delicate instrument—though in truth Sylvia was not tough, and the harpsichord can withstand fierce abuse. Leonid. Living music on a dead instrument.

14 December

Judy's annual concert Friday opened, at my suggestion, not with one of those moody modal folk things, but with the driving breakneck "Hard Losin' Lover." Still, it didn't come off. The scoring was sloppier than on the disc, and Judy cast a coolish spell from the Carnegie stage. She needs a friendlier stance vis-à-vis her players, a more intimate hall, and a new repertory.

During the class today at Curtis we talked about Schoenberg and his "system," which attracts them, at least objectively.

Twelve-tone music is too easy. The formulas can be grasped in an hour, anyone can write it, and it all sounds like the same composer. When everything is dissonance, nothing is dissonance, and little variety emerges from this maximum saturation. I tell them how there can be no "indigenously" rapid twelve-tone music, nor can there be witty twelve-tone music. (Humor is necessarily the resolution of tension.) I don't know how to criticize serial music, since all serial music is "well written." I can respond to none of it. None of it.

Am I a good teacher—or even a teacher? So many composers who are teachers (Sessions, Luening, Finney) tell me that they never express their own taste to, nor analyze their own music for, pupils. I do nothing but. Well, if I haven't Socratic bones, I do have a flair for who a young composer thinks he is, and for how to take the scales from his eyes. Teaching is a contagion. It is leading a horse to water and making him drink, because you too have drunk. But I can't get interested in teaching basics, nor in appraising a language unsympathetic to my own.

Singers can be permanently ruined by a wrong teacher, composers merely frustrated—assuming there's such a thing as the teaching of composition. Compositional advice is the one method that can be applied only after the fact. The fact is a piece, or a stab at a piece, by the student-composer, which the teacher-composer assesses with pointers for remolding. The pointers must refer strictly to the dialect of the piece (and there's no such thing as a faulty dialect, only faulty grammar). Amazing how that stab is anathema to performers who've never tried to write music: they cannot deal with the *fact* of composing. Once the piece is honed—once it exists on its own—it seems inevitable to the outsider, whether it's a piece of pop junk or the opening downbeat of Beethoven's *Fifth*, which was settled after weeks of trial & error. We can't have error without trial. But trial is foreign to performers, because that which is obvious, i.e. the solution to a problem, exists before the fact for singers and pianists and fiddlers.

20 December

Visit from Nadia Turbide, of Canada, who is doing a book on Eva Gauthier. Again I dredged up memories. Madame Gauthier would have been ninety-six. In the 1940s she was my salary, not to mention friend and mentor, since, hungover or not, I showed up nearly every day, at three dollars an hour, to accompany her class in the tiny flat of the now-vanished Woodward Hotel. Her azure hair, pink pillbox hats, unreliable memory, her having sung with Debussy, Ravel, Gershwin and Griffes, her *menschlichkeit*. Everything I could remember I told to Miss Turbide. Including the call I received at 3 A.M. from one of her baritones in the Tombs. He'd been arrested on a morals charge, and I had no recourse but to phone Madame, who duly, in person, bailed him out. Most of her students were ex-G.I.'s in the Theater Wing. Three anecdotes: (1) To a tenor who'd just sung Fauré's *Prison*: "Bear in mind that this poem was written by Verlaine in jail where he'd been put for cutting off van Gogh's ear." (2) To another tenor, who was explaining that a touch of flu made him sing off pitch: "Be glad you're not a soprano who, during her period, spurts blood onto the stage with every high note." (3) To me, about to accompany her in a demonstration of a scene from *Pelléas*: "Just omit the rests, it's the mood that counts."

Yet she knew the repertory, her enthusiasm was transferable, and if she couldn't read music she could talk it. Eva Gauthier was one of three or four teachers of French vocal repertory in New York. Today there is not one.

Is it better for a biographer not to have known his subject personally? There are as many definitive portraits of dead artists as there are good painters, but there can be no one right picture, no absolute. Biographers, like diarists, give a version of a person or an occurrence; but biographers, unlike diarists, invariably represent that which has occurred (as distinct from that which is occurring), and generally they weren't present at the occurrence.

The three biographies of Cocteau which came out a dozen years ago depicted three separate people. The best of these biographies—Steegmuller's—was nonetheless tainted by the author's having once, briefly, been in Cocteau's presence. His whole notion of Cocteau was colored by the incident. A biographer should either have been a friend of his subject, and then compose a memoir, or never have met his subject at all. (The latter term is easy if you're writing about Magellan or Cleopatra.)

Party chez Gruen-Wilson. Took them *The Piano in My Life*.
Solo display by Tom Steele at a bar called Snafu, then a party at his place.

22 December

La Femme d'à côté, a Truffaut potboiler, but with the edible Fanny Ardant (and the more edible Depardieu). Rehearsed with the Ciesinskis. Then *Death Trap* (my one play this year), starring Marian Seldes, after which we took Marian to the Algonquin for supper. The play is empty, but Marian's full of defense of it, as befits an interpreter. Like Ruth Ford she's a bit too actressy to be an actress, though she has more presence on stage, and more intellect off. Neither of them could ever convincingly play a dowdy housewife (both have tried)—though who cares? Talked of Jessamyn West, whom she adores. Her brother is Jessamyn's agent.

23 December

Stravinsky trilogy at the Met. The *Rite* is a joke (pow-wow-type nonsense) and the *Oedipus* humdrum. But David Hockney's set and costumes for *Rossignol* were transfixing. After thirty minutes in a realm of cobalt, slate, azure, ivory and mauve, the blue calm is rent by the appearance of the blood-red giant Japanese nightingale—a *coup de théâtre* matched in my life only by Mary Wigman's gongs and sequin skirt when I was nine.

Christmas Day

Yesterday afternoon, Boosey & Hawkes annual noonday office party with Jean Golden and Doris Pope being "useful" and everyone else quite joyful; Steve Rorem (a far relative) & friend at five; at seven, the Percival Goodmans' traditional reunion, crowded, but I knew no one except Shirley & George (Paul Goodman obviously wasn't there, and he, in a way, is the point); then JH's midnight mass at St. Matthew's & St. Timothy's.

Mother and Father and Rosemary came for Christmas dinner here at five, also Morris. Judy and Louis showed up for a minute with gifts. Touch of flu.

27 December

Late evening. The reason I'd put off Nantucket until tomorrow is because, months ago, Joel Conarroe had asked me to participate in the convention of the Modern Language Association. This I did, in the guise of a reading, a few hours ago, introduced by Gary Schmidgall in the Murray Hill room of the Hilton. My reading, however, witty and naughty and wise and pert as planned, fell flat. The audience squirmed, and after twenty minutes, as I was "doing" the turkish bath number (I'll never do it again, the time has passed), Allen Ginsberg rose and approached the microphone which he tapped for a while, then said, simply, "Speak louder." We later learned that the PA system in the Murray Hill room was connected to a sound system in another room on another floor.

With dismay I note that (not counting the dentist) between January 20 and December 22 of the past year I paid twenty-four visits to eleven different doctors and imbibed eight brands of medication (not counting vitamins *en masse* and magic infusions), from Pyridium to Bactrim, and including a forty-day ingestion of Diodoquin, Carbasone and Doxycycline, all for the symptoms of NSU, which remain no better and no worse than before. Among these specialists was one in Chinatown, recommended by Judy, who over a six-hour period administered two acupuncture treatments, inadvertently leaving a tiny needle in my ear which became infected. JH feels I'm ruled by hysteria. Hysteria's expensive.

Taxi zum Klo ends Proustianly, and no other end is possible. What shall I do with my aimless life? the filmmaker seems to ask. I'll make of it a work of art, and here it is.

1982

Correcting galleys of the North Point reprint of the *Diaries*, I refrain from the (not very strong) urge to "improve" here and there. Yet when I mention to people that the new edition is imminent, they all say, Well, I hope you're going to change this or that lie. George Perle, for example, nearly every time we meet, waxes indignant about the mention of him "which is in every way false." But his false facts are my true souvenirs, and besides, I'm not the person who wrote *The Paris Diary* thirty years ago. Change every "false fact," and I'd have a new book. If I have factually misquoted, the misquotation is me—I'm not writing history. Were Bach to tell Berg, you misquoted my chorale *Es ist genug* in your *Violin Concerto*, what does Berg reply? Were I to print this very paragraph in a new diary and George were to confront me with "You've misquoted me by writing that I found your mention of me 'in every way false,'" what difference does it make? George Perle is my Bach Chorale.

What is it that makes so-called experimental prose more unviable than experimental music or pictures? The fact that language, already imprecise and metaphoric, cannot lend itself to distortion the way notes and images can? Notes and images mean themselves. Language symbolizes something beyond itself. The appearance of versified poetry (though not necessarily its sound or its sense) can seem dumb—dumber, certainly, than abstract pictures.

The art of the written word, even of the spoken language, is less susceptible to fooling around than other arts are. Print (speech) is already a *representation*, which no other art is (music's final state, unlike literature's, is not in the printed score but in the execution of the printed score), so we don't need symbols of symbols. Because of this symbolism every reader visualizes (symbolizes) his own scenes: the same words evoke different pictures for every reader. With movies and paintings and music one viewer or listener may react and interpret differently from another viewer or listener, but what he sees or hears is identical to what another sees or hears.

3 January

It is raining.

Richard Dufallo phoned to ask if I'd be Composer-in-Residence at Aspen this summer. I've been expecting this call for, let's see: about eight years, and am happy.

New York
9 January

Susan Davenny Wyner came to rehearse, during which Donald Collup dropped by and listened to us with one eyebrow raised.

Dined at Maggie Paley's. She's at work, like everyone else, on a novel.

11 January

Bitter cold. Nonetheless I hied me to Philly to appraise the students' ever-expanding catalogues. Assigned texts for songs: the one word *Alleluia* and Roethke's *Orchids*. Went through the score of my Double Concerto, now called *Remembering Tommy*, in preparation for their hearing it live in a fortnight. Spent a moment with de Lancie suggesting additions to his voice faculty (Parker, Addison, Raskin, Lear).

12 January

Gregg Smith recorded *Give All to Love* with his small chorus in the unheated Holy Trinity Church of East 87th Street. The pianist never showed up, so I pinch-hit with blue fingers.

13 January

Snow. Noonday concert of my music by the boys' choir at Saint Thomas Church. The flock of ten-year-olds was all the more adorable, in their long robes, in that they sang square on pitch.

Visit at four from Noah Creshevsky with tapes of his music whose language (overlapping of spoken voices, dirty words, etc.) is so unsympathetic to me that I simply didn't know how to react. He sensed this, and was hurt. The pieces are made, he says, "with great care, and took time to produce," as though such considerations (common to every professional) necessarily guarantee high worth. Still, I felt badly at being mute. Our work is sacred, and his is as important to him as mine to me.

15 January

All day yesterday and today was spent on 156th Street with the music committee of the Academy: Lou Harrison, Milton Babbitt, Leslie Bassett, and Louise Talma. Comfortable feeling of divine right, seated at the broad cedar table, gazing at and listening to score after hopeful score (seventy-two in all), as across the street the cemetery where Audubon lies grows darker and darker beneath the slush. The lunch bestowed by Maggie Mills is unnecessary but appetizing and fun. I learned a lot—mainly that scores by the young today, compared to fifteen years ago, look neater, sound tamer, seem more tonally construed, and are technically far more proficient. All the submissions are good. None are *very* good. What looks effective on paper often disappoints; what looks nondescript sometimes sounds exciting. Also, we're inclined to judge by the first twenty seconds; indeed, those first twenty seconds are inevitably all it takes.

24 January

Lecture at the Bloomingdale House of Music, after which I accompanied Roz Rees in a dozen songs. Gregg's auto got stuck in the ice and we almost didn't make it. Shirley smiled from among the anonymous Upper West Side audience, and the songs took us back to the pre-Paris forties: *The Youth with the Red-Gold Hair*, *The Lordly Hudson*. Backstage, two young men who run their own printing press spoke appealingly of their craft and of their accomplishments: limited editions of, among other authors, Isaac Singer and Edouard Roditi. But they've never engraved music, and want to talk about it. It's what would have enthralled Paul Goodman (pride in what your hands can make), and so it does me.

31 January

Cornucopian pair of days. Morning radio interviews on Friday and Saturday with Arlene Francis and Robert Sherman, then afternoon rehearsals at the Y and in Tully Hall. Friday saw the New York premiere, again conducted by Mester, of *Remembering Tommy*, with extremely agile young soloists Jon

Parker, piano, and John Sharp, cello. Saturday at the YMHA the twice-
postponed song recital finally took place, not with Phyllis B.-J., but with
three other sopranos, Katherine and Kristine Ciesinski, and Susan Davenny, each beautiful sounding and looking, with me at the keys. To precious
Rose Plaut, who so valiantly sponsored the occasion, I offered a Tiffany rose
of silver.

Today, sorted and sent photographs to North Point Press. Began orchestration of *After Long Silence*. At seven, the ballet (*Agon, Magic Flute,
4 Seasons*).

5 February

Fugitive conversation late tonight with Gore Vidal, on a respite from political efforts in California, at Camilla McGrath's. I admire him unqualifiedly,
as author (fiction and non-) and as statesman. It's the latter hat that he's now
wearing (in spite of recent surgery on his scalp which he says was horrific,
but now all is fine), and I wish him well. Yet how can he win? He means what
he says.

Except for Paul Goodman, Gore is the only homophile of his generation
concerned with politics pure, that is, politics for freedom of homeland and
for betterment of all people, as opposed to politics centering about gay justice. Cultivated American male homosexuals, at least before the recent "liberation," were understandably carried by narcissistic interests on a road
away from general politics. Even the European Gide's dalliance with the
USSR now seems a mere flirtation (although it was he, with André Dubois,
a major statesman, who in 1940 organized the vast Franco-Jewish exodus).

Do not be too quick to understand me, said Gide.

12 February

Paul Jacobs stopped by at five yesterday so that we could decide what to
converse about at the public *entretien*, which would occur one hour hence
before subscribers of the Chamber Music Society. Paul coordinates the
monthly *entretiens* whose purpose is to display some live musician (for a
hundred dollars) featured in an upcoming concert. We talked about *Winter
Pages*, of course, and about our relationship to each other—how, so to speak,
we went to different schools together. We would seem to have led similar
lives, both being Francophile American musicians of roughly the same age
who spent the 1950s in Paris. In fact, our paths seldom crossed there; he was
mired in Bouleziana, I in the pastiches of Les Six. But around five years ago
he said to me, with that slight eager whine he adopts for serious matters,

"You know, I really regret never knowing Nadia Boulanger; it would have been so easy, and now it's too late." Such an honest turnabout, for someone so deep into Schoenberg, is rare. That, plus his way with Debussy, makes me feel warmly toward Paul, despite his cool veneer.

This morning, first rehearsal of *Winter Pages* (at least, the first to which I was invited, and I brought JH) seemed rough. But this afternoon on the stage things went smoother. Each of the five players—Gervase De Peyer (clarinet), Loren Glickman (bassoon), Jamie Buswell (violin), Leslie Parnas (cello), and Charles Wadsworth (piano)—is separately super, but they know how to meld, too, like a deck of cards, or rather like frantic amoebas. Tomorrow they preview the piece at the Paula Cooper Gallery.

Dined with Mother & Father. Then listened to *Miss Julie* on PBS. (Will Parker sings *War Scenes* in Wigmore Hall tonight.)

17 February

Since the last entry there have transpired four public performances of *Winter Pages*: the tryout on Saturday at six in Soho, during which I introduced the piece to a large crowd sitting on the floor, after which Joe LeSueur took me and Tim Dlugos back home for a meal on Second Avenue; the premiere Sunday at five, after which a party at Joe Machlis's; the second performance, Monday, before which Rosalyn Tureck in all her glory came for a light collation (and before that, the Curtis students); and last night, when I attended with Ellen Adler and JH, after which The Ginger Man. The thirteen movements take close to forty minutes and are accompanied by my program note, which is almost as long but fairly clever, describing the work as a memoir, an autumnal (or winterish) dwelling upon my teens in Chicago and twenties in Paris. All my non-vocal works are songs without texts; indeed, so firmly do I rely on the poor singer within me longing to get out that the music feels almost like verse without words.

The critics naturally grasped these straws, and flailed around them to confect their generally laudatory reactions.

18 February

Last month at WOR I told Arlene Francis and Jean Bach that it wasn't me but my father they should be interviewing, C. Rufus Rorem being, at eighty-seven, America's leading medical economist, and his book, *A Quest for Certainty: Essays on Health Care Economics, 1930–1970*, having just been published, complete with commentaries by four of our nation's main medical-care specialists. Accordingly Arlene, essence of grace, hosted Father on her program this morning, and Father—although overly nervous, because of the commercials, despite his years of public speaking—acquitted himself lucidly. He was still excited when I dined with him and Mother this evening.

Received, as she had warned me, a formal questionnaire from Rosalyn Tureck about how I hope my music will be performed in a hundred years. Obviously she's defensive about playing Bach on a Steinway and wants the buttressing of various composers.

Well, the future will take care of itself (I tell her), and I'm not really concerned about what instruments perform me, as long as they perform me. But the future can't be judged by the past. Tapes made today will indicate our viewpoint—earpoint—to future generations. However, I don't believe in authenticity, whatever that means. (We know today everything about the nuances of Bach performance except the most important thing: how listeners of his time reacted, and their notion of music's purpose.) Nor do I believe in feuds between harpsichordists and pianists, the harpsichord being again a modern instrument.

19 February

With George Perle to Juilliard's conscientious production of Roger Sessions's *Montezuma*, a concerto for two xylophones and orchestra with incidental human voices. That the voices were incidental is fortunate, the text (by Borgese) being as stilted and puerile a libretto as ever was penned. Sessions lived with that text for twenty-two years! His piece is a mess, charmless, without music.

21 February

Alone in the city. Finished *After Long Silence*. Called Chuck and we had a glass of ginger ale in a Columbus Avenue bar, watching the drizzle reflected in the plate glass as the sun set.

26 February

Two nights at Yale as guest of Gene Cook and of Phyllis Curtin, who is Master of Branford College, in the overheated tower of which I was lodged (but I changed rooms in the middle of the night). Class with young singers. Class with young composers (guidance of Martin Bresnick) who I feared would be sassy, but who, some of them, dream of becoming not Babbitt but Sondheim when they grow up. The more things change, the more they change.

Ash Wednesday tea, hosted by Gene and Phyllis. Then in the echoing paneled refectory of Bradford Hall, the audience *accoudé* at ketchupstained tables, Phyllis and I gave a Poulenc–Rorem recital, relaxed and enjoyable. Phyllis at 60 sounds marvelous, and her frail mother, Mrs. Smith, though wistful, continues keen and fairly self-sufficient at 93. Returned from New Haven last night in time to hear H. K. Gruber's adorable *Frankenstein!!*, a "pen-demonium" for chansonnier (himself, in English) and ensemble.

3 March

Wallace on Monday had his first fit in nearly a year. Went to Curtis, gave the Stravinsky lecture, stayed overnight at the Barclay, came back and had tea with Maggy. Then today Wallace had yet another violent seizure. Tonight, *Winter Pages* at the domed theater of Rockefeller University on York Avenue.

8 March

Visit from Eugenia Zukerman. Talked about her morning show on CBS. She came with me to the Vincent Astor Gallery for the exhibition of Gene Bagnato's photographs of composers. Then back here and talked some more. Eugenia's presence, like her flute-playing, is nuanced, gorgeous, calculating, with both the ice of silver and the heat of gold. I'm being literary; in fact her extreme vulnerability is glossed by an amicable hauteur which makes me feel funny. She has more brains than the world expects, with not quite the organization to combat that world.

Tomorrow, fly to Ohio.

The fascination of Kosinski's would-be fascinating *Cockpit* is its lack of fascination. Persistent perversity can't add up, since each example is a retelling of the previous example, not a new slant or freshly growing layer. A theme but no variations, and always too doggedly heterosexual for my taste. Kosinski errs by claiming his evil hero to be a "symbol of our time," since any book reflects the time it's written in; the point must be made not through explaining but through presenting the protagonist. The author clearly has as much fun inventing his chilly anecdotes as Antonioni, say, or Fellini once had in creating their decadent capitalists, all in the name of righteous objectivity. But those films developed, like song cycles, whereas Kosinski's book merely collects, like this diary. He is a master of public relations, but his public product rings false and bears no kinship to craft. This is the fourth and last of his books I'll read, since each one is the same. Each book of Jean Rhys is the same, too, but they all so nicely break the heart, while Kosinski merely hardens the heart—and to what purpose?

Oberlin
14 March

Five days in Oberlin, where during the early 1930s we spent summers eating kohlrabi and "taking piano" with Aunt Agnes, the musician of our clan. Her daughter Kathleen Thompson became First Viola of the Toledo Symphony and married the First Flute, and their son Ross Harbaugh is the Cello of the New World Quartet. Cousin Olga, Agnes's oldest child, lived with us in Chicago off and on for many seasons, especially during Mother's depressions—for Olga was a nurse both in title and in spirit, platinum blond, excessively pretty, overweight, a lover of movies. Oberlin College is Father's alma mater, to which in 1940 I applied (at his goading) but was turned down because of mediocre grades. I've not set foot here for forty-five years; now I return as a V.I.P. and rub it in. And Olga is here, too, seventy, still on Professor Street.

Each hour of each day was accounted for even before I arrived, except, of course, the time required to switch from an unacceptable hotel room to an acceptable one. The plane was met by three student composers, cute ones (one female, two male), with whom I dined then was whisked to a concert and a postconcert party for Simon Rattle—extrovertedly sensitive as ever and looking like Peter Maxwell Davies—who led the Cleveland Orchestra in Mahler's Tenth. I cherish particularly my hours with Olga (still deemed a "character" in town, with her eternal white shoes and white nurse's cap), who seated me on a divan strewn with cushions and placed a plate of tangerines beside me, then asked, with eyes agleam, "What's Dick Cavett really like?" She states that there are absolutely only two glamourous people left in the world: me and (I was supposed to guess the other, but couldn't) Benny Hill.

Speeches, coaching, lunches, meetings with composers young and less young, interviews (most importantly with Richard Miller of the NATS Bulletin), local broadcasts, and three concerts of my music, the last featuring my Piano Concerto in Six Movements rendered with grand sloppiness.

Like Masada, Oberlin is an unaccountably liberal enclave in a vast hotbed of rednecks. After the song recital Friday evening I was guest of the Gay Student Union—where half the faculty showed up.

New York
24 March

JH has gone to Puerto Rico, specifically to Guayanilla, where Gustavo Vega returned two years ago, then married and now has a child of whom JH is godfather. I remain in New York with Samuel (Gustavo's irritating but smart Siamese, who's been boarding with us for nearly three years), Wallace, and Princess.

Thus alone I prepared and served a meal (rare filets, underdone carrot strips, huge mixed salad, rice, cheese & black grapes, lemon bavarian with Sacher torte, espresso), served with the Etruscan silver that Mother & Father—after its being *en famille* for half a century—just bestowed on me, to this assemblage: Alice Tully, Betty & Schuyler Chapin, Naomi & Gary Graffman, Moira Hodgson & Michael Schulan, and, later, Andrew Porter and Lynda Sheldon.

Conversation anecdotal. Alice, hair its true color and very red lipstick, is of the 1930s in appearance and taste—her taste being for song more than opera. She nonetheless holds her own, far better than I could, in opera-banter with Betty. (She also mentioned in passing that poor so-&-so had just had an eye removed with great courage, not realizing that Moira, also with great courage, had had an eye removed.) I have twice proposed Alice to the Academy for the Award of Distinguished Service to the Arts. In vain.

Gary, like me of the Curtis faculty since the new regime, commutes bi-weekly to Philadelphia. Schuyler is the very definition of tact and style, although he has confused Cocteau with Giacometti (they do look alike in the Stravinsky documentary, which Schuyler supervised), and this indifference is doubtless why he's withdrawn from our Cocteau committee. Andrew sits on the floor, though chairs are available.

27 March

Visit from the two young men of backstage last January 24, Steven Miller and Ken Botwick. Discussed possibility of their Red Ozier Press publishing the three Blues written with Paul Goodman. Since 1947 those songs have lain fallow, too weird for the concert hall, too square for the pop stage, and designed for a voice that doesn't exist: a male Yankee Piaf.

Dined at Becki and Robert Phelps's.

30 March

After the Curtis students departed yesterday (they now alternate with my visits to Philly by coming to New York), I joined Chuck for the Steve Reich concert. In the absolutely full house we recognized not a soul, the audience being made up of well-off heterosexual swingers each in tan leather and a single silver earring, smoking pot and grooving at the maximally rehearsed and metronomic ostinatos full of sound and blandness and signifying nothing.

At noon today, *Victor Victoria* with JH, then visit to Paul Woerner (recommended by Milton Goldman) who, since Arnold's death, is our new lawyer. Woerner is young (as lawyers should be), good-looking, and quick, and he tells us that the one other musician represented by his firm is named Meat Loaf.

31 *March*

Two weeks ago I phoned Coward McCann and spoke to the editor, Tom Miller, about a correction in my blurb for *The Christopher Street Reader*. As an afterthought I asked if he'd like to publish my new book. Yes, he said, then he saw Borchardt and they reached an agreement. Tonight we shared the evening meal to discuss the assemblage of essays and diary snippets, which he will publish as *Setting the Tone*. Tom is unusually tall and gentle, and fairer of hair than even Moira.

April Fool's Day

Glory and quality do not finesse make, when the glory and quality concern an individual's work while the finesse concerns his social comportment. When inducted into the American Academy and Institute of Arts and Letters, my first vision of Olympians-at-the-Feast was Ralph Ellison unsteadily demanding a public apology from President Barbara Tuchman for touching his arm in request that he sit down; then, more sadly, Lillian Hellman, unable through her inch-thick spectacles to read aloud the eulogy of Janet Flanner, and resembling a version of herself as seen through the far end of a telescope, all tiny and wasted with a whisky glass in which floated a sodden cigarette butt.

Today at the meeting, which precedes the annual spring dinner to greet new members, I did speak up before my peers, heart racing as it used to when I'd raise my hand in school. I wished to oppose the new Strauss Livings bequest of over one million dollars intended to provide annual stipends to certain prose writers. Members of the Academy-Institute are invited to propose authors "on the verge of public recognition and having published at least two books" (what does "verge" mean for a published author?), who will each receive for at least five years an annual tax-free sum of $35,000, but the members themselves are not eligible. Is it not perhaps tactless to ask these members, many of whom eke out a living through forty-hour-a-week teaching jobs, to recommend writers for such glittering prizes? If all that keeps a member from qualifying is his little rosette, I'd resign in a minute.

Except for George Perle, who echoed my plaint on the obscenity of it all, not one voice made comment, before all adjourned to cocktails 'midst the Childe Hassams, thence to the Zinfandels of the dining room. Well, at least two of my nominees, complete with my citations, will receive awards from other sources: Jane Wilson ("Her world is at once optimistic and melancholy, casual and thrilling, personal and universal. Whether depicting landscapes, people, or interior arrangements, she lends to the everyday a mystery which, in conceding not at all to short-lived trends, becomes as necessary as it is rare.") and Edouard Roditi ("There would seem to be no area of culture that he, over the past fifty years, has not inspected in one or another of his eleven languages. Yet, despite the well-worded wisdom of his stories and the frightening intellect of his essays, it is finally through poetry that his knowledge is dispersed.").

3 April

Two o'clock at the Ear Inn on Spring Street, gave a reading for Tim Dlugos's series. Returned to dine with JH and Frank Benitez. Party at Ruth Laredo's.

Larry Rivers has agreed to provide a four-color lithograph for Red Ozier Press's publication, which will be called *Paul's Blues*. This will contain a facsimile in my hand of the music, plus a prose prologue and epilogue by me about Paul Goodman, hand-lettered in special type on acid-free cream-colored stock in a plain brown wrapper with black lettering on the cover. A hundred copies, plus ten "author's copies" on lighter stock. Then the mold is destroyed. It will take a year.

6 April

Returned by train last night, before the great snow hit, from two full days in Bridgeport where I was presented in the Andre and Clara Mertens Contemporary Composers Festival. There were two crowded concerts of my music (of which the performances were passable), plus lectures and sightseeing and the affecting company of Clara herself—affecting because while her husband was living their time was spent promoting interpreters in the Columbia Artists mill where the composer was anathema. She feels she's now seen the light.

This evening in a blizzard (robins are freezing) Chuck and I trudged to

John Corigliano's to hear a tape of his fabulous Flute Concerto. Fabulous is
the word: it's all about the Pied Piper, and in one anarchic scene wherein
rats, trillions of them, are pyramided upon each other, John has concocted
sonorities of such vigorous transparency that even as one shivers in horror
one admires his métier. Métier is what the piece is mostly about. The most
telling moments are the sparsest—as when the soloist (James Galway) in-
tones a lean, high, folky refrain—but such moments are few and far apart
between the gaudy effects.

Night after wakeful night, slashes in the ice of sleep overflow with thoughts
of dying. Across the street at 4 A.M., behind those shutters on the second
floor shadowed by the shuddering elms, there drowses deeply some open-
mouthed fool. Yet the longed-for sleep is not a rehearsal of death, as some
contend, but life at its most active richest.

To be beside yourself is wrong, is bad for you. To be *outside* yourself is
good, insofar as it (like suspended animation which, though you have cancer
or a broken heart) stops pain during the so-called Creative Act—though
when it evolves through alcohol, that too is bad. Tonight, beside myself, I
drew closer to drinking (so as to get outside myself) than I have in years, but
I didn't.

Epigraph for a memoir: *Le beau temps où j'étais si malheureuse.*—Madame de Staël

9 April

Howard Kanovitz's paintings at the Rosenberg Gallery absorbed me, in the
vital sense of drawing me into them, as pictures haven't for years. He is of
the Long Island School, whatever that is (it's portrayals of Long Island), but
with a troubling surrealist overlay: the people, none of whom I know, tremble and seem to speak, while behind them colors make *sounds*, and the
waves are distressingly gorgeous.

Rehearsed with Katherine on *After Long Silence*. At five, Noel Lee for
tea.

Snow again. David Huntley brought over the scores of *Arabella* and *Rosenkavalier* (my current annual assignment for *Opera News* is on Strauss) and
stayed for supper with Stephen Koch, Morris, and Chuck.

Easter Sunday

Paul Jacobs has GRID (Gay-Related Immunology Deficiency).
Dined with parents *chez eux*, but my mind was on poor Paul.

14 April

Mother & Father find it increasingly hard to operate on Charles Street. They've hired a helper who's more or less helpful for eight hours each weekday. But that leaves sixteen hours when Father must supervise Mother, who vacillates between vagueness and a willful imperviousness. Neither of them walks well. With Rosemary, we all discuss the possibility of a retirement home, but Mother's fearful.

Spent Monday night at Henry McIlhenny's forever beautiful house in Rittenhouse Square, preceded by (with Henry) the unstaged version of Robert Convery's little Shakespeare opera called *Quince's Dream* at Curtis. Arose at dawn to return to Westminster College (I was there in June of 1976) for a full day of classes & concerts around my choral music. Joyce Carol Oates and Raymond Smith attended. This morning, a literary breakfast with Joyce and Ray in the very likeable house of Ed Cone. Returned exhausted and confused to New York (I was put on the wrong train), to find that Frank had crashed his car. He and JH and I accordingly went to see Scola's *Una Passione d'Amore* which, in its hammered perversity—an ugly woman with money forces her love on a handsome soldier, who ends up loving her—resembles an Oates novel.

15 April

Visit from Alan Titus to settle on our program for July in Santa Fe. (A half-program of half my songs, the other half Stephen Foster in my arrangements). He's brighter and mellower than I'd imagined, having heard him only at his early narcissistic triumph in the Bernstein *Mass*, but with that unctuously modulated and slightly overloud if friendly speaking voice of all baritones. He can talk, and talk well, about other subjects than music.

Later, visit from Stuart Ostrow and also Kenneth Koch. The former, a month or two ago, presented me with the idea of somehow fabricating a Broadway opera from Kenneth's book, *I Never Told Anybody*, about teaching poetry writing in a nursing home. I loved the idea and promised to bring the two of them together. Meanwhile Kenneth prepared a careful synopsis with Kate and waxed all the more enthusiastic in that he figured, as did I, that we'd get a hundred thousand dollars down payment. Our hopes were dashed when Ostrow explained that in show biz—unlike the concert world where one works on commission—one works on spec. Well, Kenneth and I are both too old for that.

Later still, having a date with Judy at the Church of the Heavenly Rest, I took a cab to Fifth Avenue and 90th, stood in front of where I knew the church should be—no church; walked ten blocks north, then ten blocks south, still no church; came home and *phoned* the church; Judy met me here, and we went to dine at Victor's (loud) Café on nearby Columbus Avenue.

20 April

Back from two days in Highland Park where on Sunday I accompanied a recital of my songs (John Vorassi and Joan Gibbons, both good), followed by a supper involving John Edwards plus long-ago friends from high school. Phoned Gladys Campbell, my beloved English teacher in 1939 (she must be ninety now), who remembered me and Rosemary and hoped I was "doing well." Monday, two two-hour classes in my vocal music at the American Conservatory, now on Michigan Avenue (between which, visit to the Art Institute *en face*), then supper with the indefatigable Dolores chez Bill Ferris and Vorassi, then American Airlines night flight 564 back East.

Donald Gramm came over today to rehearse our "segment" on WNCN's marathon tomorrow. An hour at the eye doctor's at four. Thursday: Nantucket, where I'll spend nine days trying to finish the commencement address for Curtis (a recycling of the one for Northwestern five years ago) and the agonizing review of Boulanger's biography for the *Times*.

Nantucket
25 April

Very fair weather. Jonquils in high bloom, from the nine varieties of bulb planted last fall by JH, bursting out in seemingly random patches all over the side yard, little clouds of chiffon: gold, lemony, orange, some pure white, a total joy that obscures worry, at least for a moment. One *tastes* them, like a mountain stream.

Still struggling with essay on Nadia Boulanger, but nearly finished settings of *Three Calamus Poems* for Donald Collup.

Music cannot lie, though it can speak a banal truth.

The profoundest statements are always the most obvious. To put down Rod McKuen as "America's most understood poet" is less witty than dumb. Whatever McKuen's worth, the concept of comprehensibility as suspect is old hat. Great poets don't argue against clarity.

The wisest are never wise to themselves. Difference between critic and reviewer? You can be a critic, but not a reviewer, of your own work. If a writer does have the right to find his own work mawkish years later, he doesn't have the right (even years later) to claim that his work "just misses," much less that it succeeds; it's not for him to know what vibrates for others. A claim is wishful thinking; even when concocting *War and Peace* the author can only keep his fingers crossed.

27 April

Instead of surgically excising, as the New York optometrist longed to do, Dr. Voorhees yesterday injected cortisone into the cyst beneath my lower left lid. By this afternoon the cyst had shrunk considerably. Inclement icy rain. JH made bacon and waffles in the new waffle machine. Insomnia, discouragement, impending flu.

New York
4 May

Returned Friday, coached flutist John Ranck and harpist Barbara Allen in *Book of Hours*, which they accordingly intoned at the Third Street Settlement on Monday, after which "dined Chinese" on Greenwich Avenue with parents. This afternoon Clara Mertens took me on a tour of her ancient-instrument wing at the Met, the decor wherein one is transported not only into a past that never was, but toward a peace that cannot be; impossible to remain here, we're both going to die. This evening, with JH to New York premiere of my *Suite for Guitar* at Merkin Hall by David Leisner, who strums with nuanced precision and nectarlike sound. Later, with Chuck to Il Cantone on Columbus Avenue for orange cheesecake.

5 May

Interview this morning with the *Lancaster New Era* in preparation for my visit this weekend.

Spoke at length with Paul Jacobs, who has a form of GRID cancer known as Kaposi's Sarcoma, and was so disconcerted that even as we talked I seemed to witness lesions on my own thighs.

Scribbled at the entries I'm revising for the American Grove's (on Bowles, Flanagan, Harrison); corrected proofs of early Sitwell songs (for which B. &

H., after thirty-five years, has finally procured publication rights); and rehearsed with Alan Titus on a group of Ives (with which we'll follow the Foster group this summer). But my mind raced, and in a panic I phoned Larry Mass, the only doctor I know who knows about GRID, and pleaded with him to see me today.

Concert tonight of the American Composers Orchestra (major works of Perle, Diamond, and Schuller, which went in one ear and out the other) from which I took a taxi at 11 P.M. to present my body to Larry Mass on West 17th. Well, I don't have lesions—simply a hint of varicosity, complicated by "a diseased mind, and the horrid fears of encroaching old age" (Koch's *Bertha*, scene 6). With lighter heart, taxied back uptown to Joe Machlis's party for the A.C.O.

Lancaster, Pennsylvania
10 May

In France I know—indeed, I intimately *learned*—the topography of both Provence and the Île de France, and to a lesser extent the variegated countryside that rolls between Toulon and Rouen, because I kept my eyes open (even during drunken nights) with a compulsive sense of Don't Miss Anything; in America, since returning here to stay, my eyes have been closed, on the not unfounded grounds (yes, they are unfounded) that there's little to see. So I was unprepared for the exhilaration of this antiseptic landscape: the pale-hued barns in the rain-green fields, the absolute cleanliness of the Amish style (far from the hedonism, near to the anti-hedonism, enmeshed in my Quaker-Roman soul), the dearth of telephone wires, the scrubbed pink brick and right-wing bookstores of the Revolutionary town.

My passive function here is as the twenty-second recipient of the Lancaster Symphony Orchestra's Composer's Award. Since the sole touchable recompense is an engraved gold watch, worth around $300, I somewhat loftily asked for and was granted a limousine to fetch me from New York. Now, after two full days, my duties duly dispatched, I wait here at the Brunswick Hotel (my room as usual had to be changed because of noisy neighbors), not for a limousine but a cab to the train station. Meanwhile, *Eagles* was conducted (very well) two nights in a row by Stephen Gunzenhauser, and I got the gold watch and gave a gracious acceptance speech ("In a world wherein the performer is deified the composer has become an endangered species etc. . . . . It's to the credit of the Lancaster Symphony that they put the horse before the cart etc. . . ."), but didn't stress that you can't eat medals.

The Amish mystery is that there is no mystery, no subterfuge or gloss. It's hard to grasp, but I do approve.

New York
11 May

No sooner off the train than another long session with Alan Titus, his "seasoned" baritone, his diamond-sure enunciation. This afternoon, interview into a machine for Yale's Oral History department. Then an exquisite hour in John Kander's patio next door, drinking Perrier with lime and comparing our lives. Summer's in the air, sparrows flutter in the vines looking for nesting paraphernalia, and we could be in the country, for the lack of traffic noise. John's the least hyperthyroid and most educated sample of the show-biz world I know. He too has had a cyst removed (but with a scalpel) from under an eyelid.

The Barclay
Philadelphia
14 May

Last night my protégés, Norman Stumpf, Robert Convery, and Daron Hagen, had me to dine at Daron's on Spruce Street while Mahler played in the background. The meal climaxed with a hot apple tart, after which we heard tapes of their music composed over the past nine months. This morning, after breakfast of blueberry pancakes and maple syrup in the hotel with my intelligent niece, Mary, I donned some academic finery and delivered the commencement address at Curtis; half of the address was punctuated by a whimpering infant until its unidentified mother was asked to move into the lobby. There were two dozen graduating students; I received an honorary doctorate.

Nantucket
20 May

We drove to Hyannis in a rented car Monday with all the cats, Sam meowing exasperatingly the whole way, then switched to PBA for the twelve-minute hop over the water. Tulips, multicolor and sumptuous, are already fading, and the daffodils are gone, but the large crabapple tree by the back porch has blossomed into resplendent coral.

Working on a chorus & organ setting of Blake's *Little Lamb* for Trinity Church in Princeton. Cool, misty.

23 May

The Boulanger article appeared on the front page of the *NYT Book Review* today, and I'm proud of it. Horowitz on TV from London, playing, with great authority, just any old notes, fingers flat on the keys.

Cold and raw. Rain. Hemorrhages of rain, rain.

29 May

JH to New York for the weekend, but Frank Benitez here. No social life except for occasional exchanges of meals with Eugenie Voorhees and her household.

Window boxes planted. Basement flooded. The rain.

2 June

To Dr. Voorhees for another injection in left eye.

More than composing, I'm practicing the piano for the various commitments of the next ten weeks. Movies every night on TV, some good.

6 June

Shirley and George were married in New York today, after a whirlwind courtship of thirty-five years. We sent them a bright soup tureen from the Emporium. For their soup. There's a Proustian logic to all this—not that the Perles in any way resemble Madame Verdurin and the Prince de Guermantes—simply because what fifteen years ago would have seemed odd, even outrageous (and not just because they were espoused to others), now appears pacific, even necessary.

Key Biscayne Hotel
Florida
13 June

Miami's New World Festival of the Arts is perhaps misbegotten in that "the arts" seldom mix well, too many events occur almost simultaneously at great distances from each other, the advertising misleads ("Come to Miami where surfing and culture co-exist"), and the very choice of June in a southern city seems infelicitous. But as a four-million-dollar gesture toward makers rather than toward interpreters, the venture is unprecedented and valiant. A sizeable number of works by many an eminent American may never have seen the light but for the commissioning project. Certainly my *After Long Silence*, for the specialized combination of mezzo soprano, solo oboe, and string orchestra, would not have occurred to me except for these circumstances.

Katherine Ciesinski and I have for five days dwelt at this hotel. I now wait for her to pick me up (in the rented car we've shared all week) and to drive me first to a farewell brunch organized so that all the visiting stars can greet each other, then to the airport.

On the night of arrival we went to Robert Ward's new opera, *Minutes to Midnight*, which deals with the world's greatest physicist who has unlocked the secrets of cosmic energy; his conflict is between delivering his discovery to the military or publishing it in a scientific review for the peaceful betterment of mankind. As the wife of the preoccupied genius, who never has time even to bolt down his meager lunch, Evelyn Lear is given the evening's best line: "Run, run, run. Always on the run." The music echoes this singsong triviality for three hours (sans hard-edge of Weill or spookiness of Penderecki), but we stuck it out, mainly because Bob and Mary Ward were seated directly behind us. In fairness, both of Bob's other operas, *Pantaloon* and *The Crucible*, hit the nail on the head, and the second of these is among the few urgent American operas, if only because it both heightens and changes the text for the better.

Edward Albee's virtuoso solo turn for Robert Drivas, *The Man Who Had Three Arms*, although well shaped with a core, a solid wrapping, and an outcome, is mean-minded, self-pitying, small, vulgar and tired. He attempts what should be beneath any artist, the punishment of his critics (I do it too), and of course he fails. Afterward, because I so seldom see him anymore, I tried to find nice things to say, but Edward's never very forthcoming, at least with me. Needless to say, he didn't attend my performance.

My performance was the premiere of *After Long Silence*, and the orchestra was the Camerata Bariloche from Argentina. We didn't know until the last moment if they'd make it, the Falkland crisis being at its peak, but they did, and they were overwhelmingly dear. The oboist Andrés Spiller and his sixteen string-playing colleagues (all of whom play standing up except the cellos and without a conductor, and most of whom, though of Spanish tongue, have German names) have spent weeks learning the music, without knowing the sense of the ten texts they would be accompanying. These texts are all except for Dickinson from England—Queen Elizabeth the First through Blake to Yeats, Dowson and Thomas Hardy. Before our first rehearsal the players listened, watching with their wise black eyes, as I tried to impart the sense—mainly about young love, old love, and death, intertwined with the scent of roses, vital and sick—of the poetry. Katherine then joined them, they raised their arms to sound the viol, and voice joined with bows in a lean, radiant rendition which made me happy. How fitting it seemed for Argentinians to be linked for this brief moment to British poets. The concert was repeated last night and will be again tonight (after I've gone). Meantime, Fassbinder died, and Katherine and I, in the unthinkable heat, visited the zoo where a giant Bengal Tiger burned bright in an artificial Floridian forest as children looked on.

New York
17 June

Ninety-six hours in New York. Monday, taped an interview with Gordon Spencer for WNCN. Dined with parents on Charles Street. Later, called on Paul Jacobs who appears thin. We had blueberry sherbet made in his new ice cream machine.

Tuesday, practiced with Katherine. Signed fifty just-published scores of *The Santa Fe Songs* (ruby type dropped out on burnt sienna stock) at B. & H. Stopped by Patelson's for scores of Mahler's 9th & 10th symphs. and discs of Judy Garland & Lena Horne. Then parents again. Rosemary there too. Mother had a hysterical seizure, like epilepsy, lasting close to an hour. The shuddering subsided after Father gave her two yellow Valium, although Valium is possibly also the cause. We each held her, until finally she dozed. During this I called Dr. Grange, leaving a frantic message that Mother had a heart attack. Grange showed up eventually, cool. They can't go on like that, Father being perhaps the worse off.

Yesterday, recorded *Women's Voices* for CRI with Katherine, in about thirty "takes" over three hours. Chuck Turner turned pages. Took Tom Steele to Virgil's where we dined *à quatre* with Chris Cox. Virgil perfect, as always when there's just a small group. I never come away from him without having gleaned some useful data—in this case, the best way to skin a tomato is to dip it for a second in boiling water; that Hemingway and Gertrude Stein were quite possibly physically attracted to one another (which accounts for H's aversion to Alice Toklas); that the secret of good cuisine lies in shopping and chopping, just as a painter's subject matter depends on real estate (you don't use the same still life in a fifth-floor walk-up as when you get rich and move to East Hampton); and that orchestration texture depends on nationality: the French don't double, the Germans do.

In an hour, via the Eastern shuttle and PBA, leave for Nantucket. (The gold watch from Lancaster has vanished. The velvet case is still there, but the contents are gone.)

Nantucket
19 June

John Cheever died yesterday in Ossining. Sent condolences to Mary Cheever, whom I never knew, although I'm not especially moved. I last heard from
John less than six weeks ago ("I've battled cancer all winter and when I go to
the podium these days I lean on a stick and am bald as an egg. . . . Please
give my best to Jim whose kindnesses I remember vividly"), yet despite the
diagnosis it's hard to feel he didn't die of something else—of withdrawal
from cigarettes and alcohol, not to mention withdrawal from lack-of-guilt.
Like Paul Goodman, John was born just ten years too early to fit his homosexuality less shamefacedly into its proper nook. Of course, Paul was Jewish, didn't drink, was political and a pioneer. They both loved participation
in sports, perhaps for the same reason. Will it ever be agreed that Paul is a
far more "important" writer, even though he had less of an ear, than John?
     JH is in Puerto Rico with Frank. He'll be interested in this news. Mean-
while, here with the cats alone in the rain. Mother was supposed to phone,
but hasn't. Not that she can't get herself to phone; it's more, I think, that she
doesn't care, one way or another, despite always talking tearfully about the
need to "share ideas." Those ideas are the ones she shared seventy years ago
around the hearth in South Dakota before her younger brother Robert was
killed, for no reason, at Belleau Wood.

23 June

Spoke with Mother. She had another fit (as she calls it), and I picture her
with those huge Garbo eyes and sleek salt-&-pepper hair, suddenly losing
control, the way Wallace does as his trembling is set off by the click of a typewriter or a rumbling truck. As I note this, the kitchen glows with the smell
of whole wheat toast, mixed with the smell of Mother's old sachet bowl floating from upstairs where I left it open a while ago to give a twinge of fragrance
to the bedroom.
     Something made me get out Bill Flanagan's song on Donne's "Send home
my long strayd eyes to mee,/ Which (Oh) too long have dwelt on thee," which
with all its imperfection after all these years (beauty limps) heads right toward the heart, especially as Regina Sarfaty once so achingly sang those
verses. Bill in his folly felt close to Mother, as Mother did with JH during his
breakdown, and all three knew a horrid country that I, even at my most dissolute, never visited.

3 July

Writing an essay on Paul Jacobs for *Christopher Street*. (Less an essay, really, than a noncritical appraisal, a valentine.) Writing also something called *Thirteen Ways of Looking at a Critic*, to be uttered out loud in Santa Fe, end of the month.

The organ suite, *Views from the Oldest House*, received its first hearings last Tuesday and Wednesday under the hands & feet of John Obetz at the American Guild of Organists convention in Washington, D.C. Obetz and I met only once, years ago, but he asked me recently if his son Peter, a photographer, might visit Nantucket for a few days in order to take pictures of the various sites I've musically described in the suite's six movements: "Sunrise on Sunset Hill," "Elms," "The Nest in Old North Church," "Spires," "Rain Over the Quaker Graveyard," "Sunday Night." John hopes to make a video around the piece and sell it to PBS. Young Peter Obetz has accordingly spent the past three days here, bringing a tape of the Washington performance. He has been well-bred, self-sufficient, and extremely busy taking hundreds of pictures. Now this morning, after three nights and nine free meals, he's gone. During his stay I asked him quietly two or three times, if he could, when he had time, take a photo of the house, and perhaps a quick portrait of JH. But he never did.

Perfect weather. Long talk with Father by telephone, and also with Rosemary in Maine. As usual, Mother is so-so.

9 July

Roses at their peak, color of blood and milk-of-bismuth. While reading indoors I heard from outside the pallid squeak that means, O God, Princess is torturing a baby rabbit. Rushed into the heat of the side yard and, sure enough, found Princess delightedly pouncing around a furry darling with its belly slit open. The little rabbit was petrified, and my heart was beating. What to do? Smash it with a rock? Take it to the vet? I managed to scoop it into a cardboard box from which it immediately leapt, an intestine flowing behind. Princess dashed toward the poor creature as it sped lopsidedly toward the fence, the two of them doing a sort of *pas de deux*. Shaking, I simply turned back into the house, to let nature take its course. Was I wrong?
   Visit to Dr. Voorhees for another shot into the bothersome left eye.

14 July

For an hour or so, around three o'clock, I went down to the back lawn and lay in the yellow plastic chair trying to read (Prokosch), drowsed, gave up. It's rare that the heat grows so thick on Nantucket. Procrastination is par for the course. With Sam on my lap, Princess preening nearby and Wallace wheezing over there in JH's basement hideaway, I simply watched through heavy eyes the motion of buzzing clover, the bumblebees, the perspective of cats, the burning sky where fat pink clouds reflected the peonies' perfume, which just managed not to be sickening, and thought of La Touche's *Lazy Afternoon*, and of the dead, and of Mother and Father and Rosemary where they are today—or yesterday, in South Dakota fifty years ago. An exquisitely satisfying moment. To note it here is, in a way, to defile it.

The Inn at Loretto
Santa Fe
30 July

Week in Santa Fe. So far as sympathy with the scenery is concerned, this visit has made more sense than 1980 when I was lodged far from the madding crowd. The suede adobe, the clean dirt, the endless O'Keeffiana (she's to Santa Fe what Burchfield is to Buffalo: everyone wants to *be* her), the very social culture-lovers yet the non-admixture of Indian culture—all this makes the town more real, perhaps even more dear.

Arrived in Albuquerque on the 22nd, was driven to S.F. with Vivian Perlis (who had been on the same plane) with whom I had an ice cream in the central plaza near the hotel. We've seen each other regularly since then, and she's a warm acquaintance, efficient, caring. Morris has been here the whole time, too; also the Popes.

My every move was filmed, as were the moves of Copland, Schuman, and Harbison who preceded me. The one hundred fifty filmed hours will be whittled to two for PBS programming next spring.

Public rehearsal of *Winter Pages* (with a new cast, less tempestuous but slicker than the New Yorkers), repeated twice in concert, and the recital with Alan Titus—this accounts for my compositorial representation. At the opera, *Der Liebe de Danaë* (with a glorious gold set by Ter-Arutunian), and a dress rehearsal in the driving rain of Rochberg's *Confidence Man*—worse, if possible, than Ward's opera, because in aiming higher it falls lower with its willful simplemindedness and hickish attempt to swing. Rochberg has nothing to say.

Contiguous with the Chamber Music Festival has been the National Symposium of Critics, and every musicologist in the United States is here. When Sheldon Rich last winter requested that I participate in one of the Critics Roundtables at Saint John's College, I agreed, on the condition (because I'm timid and dislike shouting) that as a prelude I be allowed to deliver a prepared statement. Accordingly, on Monday I read *Thirteen Ways of Looking at a Critic*, a twenty-minute relation of the composer's view of his reviewer. Although this is one of my most reasoned and compact articles, not one of the questions it raises was developed by my betters during the ensuing shambles.

My essay didn't bring up the *NY Times*'s explicit policy of not engaging practicing musicians in their music department, nor the implicit policy of engaging only heterosexuals, or at least legally marrieds. God forbid that I should wave a flag so that gayety's sometimes salubrious shadow might taint the art of the *Times*, but neither will I speak against it.

Nor did I mention that critics never mention (is it too frivolous?) what an interpreter looks like, even when such mention would seem to bear on performance. Is he crunched, like Glenn Gould? Décolletée, like Sharon Robinson? Jennie Tourel's *gowns* (singers never wear *dresses*) were crucial to the pre-recital excitement (Will she wear the canary yellow tonight, or the Schrafft's pink?), as was her arrogant soubrette deportment between the stage door and the crook of the Steinway; a dumpy woman, she gave the illusion of high beauty by dint of posture and conviction, even before she opened her mouth. On the other hand, I remember that when only an adolescent I already wondered at the propriety of a blue-haired soprano, swathed in silk and emeralds, singing *Noël pour les enfants qui n'ont plus de maisons*.

Nor did I add: Critics, we can live without you, but you can't without us. Despite our weakness and your power (from the *New Yorker*'s mock-humble force to the *New York Times*'s lofty force), you are merely our parasites. Not one of us in America earns, *as a composer*, a salary commensurate with the best-placed of you, yet you remain live fleas aggravating thoroughbreds.

In an hour Morris and I board the plane for Denver and from there go to the Aspen Music Festival.

Aspen
2 August

Between Santa Fe and Aspen I'd choose Santa Fe. Yes, Aspen's breathtaking, with the peaks and the town's grill layout and the fresh air and the absence of poverty; but by those tokens it lacks the history, the interesting dirt, the religion, and the hate of New Mexico. But if Aspen has no conflict, it does have a welcoming ambiance. Thanks solely to Richard Dufallo every department of the shop is working on every aspect of my oeuvre.

Arrived Friday with Morris. My apartment has three rooms, a piano, and a waterfall just beneath the porch. Red & Pick Heller had us to dine on arrival, with Jan DeGaetani and Philip West, and Pia Gilbert. Since then, not a minute to grow lonely in. I fear the minute to grow lonely in.

Yesterday afternoon Edo de Waart conducted *Remembering Tommy*, with Lee Luvisi again and cellist Laszlo Varga. When I heard a tape, years ago, of de Waart's *Air Music*, I wrote him of my great pleasure. He never answered. When I introduced myself before the performance yesterday, he acted cold as ice. Yet he conducts my music with enough preparation and seeming love (though he may despise it) to satisfy me utterly. Reception after at Pia Gilbert's. JH arrives tomorrow, and I'm as excited as though I'd not seen him in thirteen days. Which is the case.

6 August

A wind is blowing through the rooms. It is nine in the evening, and JH must return to New York after our five days together here. Every such parting (and they seem continual) is agony, and the scrumptious meal he has just fixed— egg salad, ratatouille, raspberry cream pie in a store-bought crust—is like The Last Supper. But the wind blowing through the rooms is peaceful, the sunset was ravishing, and soon we'll be playing backgammon, during which time will stop.

Every afternoon and evening that he's been here there've been seminars, concerts and parties. Tuesday, gave the Stravinsky lecture. Last night we invited the Popes and the Hellers to dine, also Morris, and James Salter. I performed *The Santa Fe Songs* with Leslie Guinn, and Kristine Ciesinski arrives tomorrow to prepare *Sun* with Richard.

Conversation in a dream:
"Twenty martinis in a day?"
"Well, yes, but not just one after another. I stagger them."
"I'll bet."

7 August

After JH left I strolled into town, bought the *New York Review of Books* which I've not seen in months, and sat on a bench in the park beneath the ski lift to read Robert Craft's latest pronouncements, this time on Croce's book about dance.

Just as all that Truman Capote touches turns to fool's gold now that he's solely a pet of the rich, so a distant bitter stench rises from Craft's writings now that he's not bolstered by Stravinsky, dead already for ten years. With all his demolition of anyone whose taste does not coincide with his, Craft is hardly one to let mere taste color his forever patronizing wit about gays. "Taste is for pederasts," he has elsewhere quoted his mentor as saying, "and for most other people it is simply a matter of familiarity." Since Craft is "most other people," yet one who, thanks to his connections, has rubbed elbows with the great, including Auden, and by remote control with *the* tastemaker of the century, Diaghilev, how can he still hold to the touristy notion that homosexuals (which homosexuals?) "identify emotionally" only with cod-pieces, and respond to human emotions only on the "puppy-love level" (but is Romantic Love ever adult?)?

Since Craft presumes to know about what homosexuals identify with, surely I can presume as much about heterosexuals, having dwelt among a rather large number of them since my birth. So I sent off a crank letter to the *New York Review*, hastily reasoned and handwritten (there's no typewriter here), but *bien sentie*, as Parisians say, and right.

Craft is a creature of novel perceptions, and of novel clarity in voicing those perceptions, but his Achilles Heel is a spite so malignant that he will bend any context in order to paint an intelligent rival as an idiot. The margins of my copy of *Stravinsky in Pictures and Documents* are speckled with notes on his careless (and ungrammatical) contempt. Still, I reviewed the book favorably, and an extract from the review was the most prominent feature of ensuing ads.

The reason for this lengthy preoccupation with Craft's ill will is doubtless because of his ambivalence vis-à-vis myself. Five years ago, when I presumed to inquire (again, in a letter to the *NYROB*) into the interesting and never-asked question of what languages Stravinsky's various interviews were in and also to point out mistakes in French in the then-recent Stravinsky-Craft *Obiter Dicta*, Craft, in a reply that required three times the space of my inquiry, began by stating that my "subject [was] of too little consequence to merit the expenditure of time and newsprint." He then proceeded, through a sarcastic misreading of my intentions, to disqualify my very existence to a point where readers might wonder why he allowed his publishers, both before and after this occasion, to use my quotes on his dust jackets and publicity. When *Obiter Dicta* was republished in *Pictures and Documents* he incorporated my corrections and answered my queries (without, of course, crediting me). He has it both ways.

11 August

Final morning in Colorado. A dozen of my pieces, big and little, have been well presented. Most sparkling was Dufallo's conducting of *Sun*, with Kristine's voice swelling from inaudible at the dress rehearsal (when we considered miking) to stentorian at the performance. Most touching was the evening of vocal chamber music plotted by Paul Sperry and Adele Addison, in the Episcopal Church on North Street. At the very end I was covered with gooseflesh when everyone present—soloists, pianists, page-turners, the whole audience—stood up and, in unison, sang *Early in the Morning.*

Nantucket

24 August

From Aspen to Nantucket for six days. From Nantucket to Saint Paul for twenty-four hours where, on Stuart Pope's advice, I adorned the "Schmidt New Music Materials Clinic" by partnering two young singers in forty minutes of song—cold, with no rehearsal whatsoever. From Saint Paul to New York to check up on Mother & Father, who are seriously considering a retirement home, probably the Quaker enclave, Cadbury, near Camden. From New York back to Nantucket where I am: immersing myself in Strauss, especially *Rosenkavalier*, for next season's *Opera News* assignment; writing prefaces to *Setting the Tone*, and to *Paul's Blues* for Red Ozier Press; practicing *Last Poems of Wallace Stevens*; correcting proofs of *After Reading Shakespeare*. Wet and dark. Picking corn and blackberries. Frank visiting, but leaves tomorrow for the Bronx as JH leaves for Kansas. I try to speak with Father every day and to discourage Mother's ingestion of Valium, but anyone can give advice, and I'm not the one who's living inside the boiling problem.

Exhibition, on Straight Wharf, of Mary Heller's photographs. No people in them. Yet their excruciating detail of landscape, every cranny illuminated, gives the feeling that nature had *posed* for Mary. Her portraits of Provence—*my* Provence—bring sadly back to me the sound of locusts and the hot smell of brioches and lavender, and the long happy summers with Marie Laure.

30 August

Deaths of Lehman Engel and of Ingrid Bergman.
Watched Joan Crawford in *Rain*, as it rained outside.

4 September

Back in Nantucket after forty-eight hours away, first New York to meet JH and rent a car, then Cadbury with parents, to look it over. We pray that they'll be accepted, now that their decision's made.

Giant cocktail party for eleven minutes at Peter & Mary Heller's in the heavy mist of Sconset. Today, Denny Koch's vernissage of sea-green cabbages and cattle twenty feet tall, followed by *Mommie Dearest* on television.

15 September

Sylvia's been here for her annual rest, during which she never rests, but walks about and attends by phone and letter to the functioning of B. & H. Her presence, a needed excuse for socializing, brings Eugenie, Rosette, the Conroys. Outing at the Wood Box. She left yesterday, and I'm alone for the moment in the rarified post–Labor Day ozone.

Visit from David Dubal and Margaret Mercer. Death of Grace Kelly. Haircut. Death on motorcycle of John Gardner.

Preparing a little speech for the Rockefeller Song Competition, the one whose wrist I slapped three years ago. I consented this year (a week from Saturday, in fact) because: (1) it now takes place close by in Carnegie Hall, and (2) they pay the same fee to everyone. My duty will be to present, with gracious words, checks to the three finalists, once they've been determined by the judges. I agreed also to give a copy of the "gracious words" to the judges beforehand, because the Rockefeller people are a bit leery.

Reading Noël Coward's diary for the *Chicago Tribune*.

17 September

Death of Vera Stravinsky.

New York
24 September

Life begins anew. Curtis curriculum. Visits this week from Zaidee Parkinson and, separately, Richard Dufallo about the same subject: their incompatibility. From Shirley & George with Bill Brown. From Richard Howard and David Alexander. From Chuck Turner, with whom I go to Tom Miller's birthday party where we know no one and are by far the oldest. (I take Tom a flask of *eau de vie de poire* with a real pear inside.) From Edouard Roditi.

Visits this week to B. & H., to discuss, among other things, a commission from the Gay Men's Chorus. To Mother and Father, from whose apartment on Charles Street we move some hefty furniture. To Richard Sennett (I, wearing my apricot linen shirt and apricot satin tie) in Washington Mews for his party for Ed White's new book.

25 *September*

My prepared speech for the Carnegie-Rockefeller Vocal Competition, which occurred this afternoon from one o'clock until six, states: "America is the only country on earth where singers specialize in every language but their own. America is the only country that has not for three decades produced vocalists who are primarily recitalists. As a result, American composers of song have long since turned elsewhere. Indeed, the medium would today be moribund had not the present contest rescued it in the nick of time. It is my pleasure to present . . . ." A copy of these words was in the hands of all seven judges when they withdrew at six o'clock to determine which of the three singers—two American sopranos and a Welsh baritone, each of whom had just presented a full recital of mostly American songs—should get the main honor. (Two of these, as was the case in 1979, had sung works of mine.) Twenty minutes passed. Forty. An hour. I mingled in the lobby, twiddling my thumbs. Finally an usher appeared with furrowed brow to summon me backstage. There, like Joan of Arc, I stood before the very imposing judges, all of whom I knew except the last: Judith Raskin, Peter Pears, Carlisle Floyd, William Warfield, Maurice Abravanel, Phyllis Bryn-Julson, and Elizabeth Schwarzkopf. Unsmiling, they said, "You've got to change your speech. First prize goes to the Welshman. The sopranos will share equally the second and third prize." Once we had all taken our places in a long row onstage, I realized that, like a messenger before his beheading, this was the most painful duty of my career. When my moment came, I dispensed with all pretense of depth or wit and, so as not to attenuate the singers' wait (after all, everyone on stage already *knew*, except them), I announced firmly, "Third and second prize will be shared by the sopranos, first prize goes to Henry Herford." Flashbulbs, cheers, bemusement. It was unpleasant, handing checks to the crestfallen women.

This said, none of them deserved first prize, or rather, all of them did. Herford, true, had the clearest diction (his Ives was as persuasive as any American's I've ever heard, but my *War Scenes* was lackluster). I did find a moment to tell Madame Schwarzkopf that I heard her not only in *The Rake's Progress* in Venice at the world premiere in 1951, but a few seasons later in Paris when, with Igor Markevitch, she sang Florent Schmitt's *Psalm* in a gray satin gown with a vast gray fox collar. "I hope you remember the music too," she replied, with that smile. I do remember the music, but it wasn't important.

Nantucket
6 October

Silken weather, day after day, with profusions of hot red roses still throbbing with life. Feeling well, but sad. Feeling sad for Mother who no longer enjoys *Walden*, her favorite book, and for Father who quotes "Old Man River," "I'm tired of living and scared of dying." Next week, back to the other island, to help them move to Cadbury.

Reading Ibsen, and following the Bette Davis festival on TV.

New York
17 October

Wednesday morning a moving van came for what's left of Mother's & Father's furniture. JH and I then drove the folks to Cadbury, in Cherry Hill, helped them settle in for several hours, then left. And so the traditional Sunday suppers with the Rorems are now a thing of the past.

Thursday I ventured to Hofstra for thirty-six hours, the first of my six Phi Beta Kappa "residencies," which I consented to do last spring before I had time to reconsider. Maybe it's a good thing, but what a lot of energy for so little money, and just a small number of people, all academics. I'm presented as a professor from Curtis, rather than as a composer; nor are my hosts from the music department, but from Phi Beta Kappa, which represents all departments, and is vaguely right-wing. Shades of *The American Scholar*.

Yesterday morning, Evelyn Lear for coffee. Still the shrewd diva with sensible thoughts about her now-waning career. She seems to know who she is. The reason for her visit (I think) is to assure me that she "believes in" contemporary music, despite what I said about her in the *Times*, seven whole years ago: "Evelyn Lear, biting hands that feed her, repeatedly states, 'Thank God my coach forced me to give up modern stuff; it almost wrecked my voice.'" She claims others had misquoted her. Well, maybe. Anyway she's likeable, and even a touch glamorous, considering her preemptive lovey-dovey pose when singing duets in public with her spouse.

Tonight I go by car pool to Great Neck for Hugo Weisgall's 70th birthday party. As a gift I've devised a little collage—a musical anagram—juxtaposing the scale-letters common to both our names. In fact, there's only one: E.

20 October

Giant party at the Astor Gallery to launch Joe Machlis's novel, *Lisa's Boy*, in a blurb for which I declared Joe "the optimist's Malamud."

Rosenkavalier at the Met. We stuck it out, all five hours, and wept. But, having spent the summer inside that piece, there will never be an ideal performance except inside my head—not even the performance inside Strauss's head.

23 October

My fifty-ninth birthday, so we invited nine people over to listen to the tape of *After Long Silence*, and to savor three kinds of cheese, three kinds of cake, and lots of fruit and coffee and tea. No one had alcohol. Shirley & George brought a Cocteau biography; Andrew Porter brought a jar of thick blueberry preserves in green cellophane; Tom Miller brought three Coward-McCann biographies (one of June Allyson); Diana Trilling brought a collection of essays by Lionel; David Dubal & Margaret Mercer brought homemade drawings; Stephen Koch brought a carrot cake; and Rouben Ter-Arutunian didn't bring anything except his stageworthy genius because he didn't know it was a birthday. JH gave me an oriental rug for the front hall, a maroon silk scarf, and a huge box of Godiva chocolates, all of which are eaten (the chocolates, not the rug and scarf).

Suppose there weren't any more ideas in our galaxy. Yet insofar as no two people are the same, any old idea in a new head takes on a separate—an original—gloss. Whether the gloss is inspired, or even very diverting, is a moot question. But everything is always new under the sun.

27 October

Lectured for an hour yesterday at Collegiate College on West End Avenue (oldest "day school" in the country) to high school males between fourteen and eighteen. Discussion as to whether music represents anything, as painting does. Came home to find Wallace in another paroxysm.

This morning a representative from Australian Broadcasting came by and paid me to speak into a microphone for ten minutes about Nadia Boulanger. At six, visit from Kenton Coe and Jean-Pierre Marty. Kenton's now the composer laureate of Tennessee, and JMP has *déménagé dans le Midi*. At eight, a Speculum concert with Shirley.

Extreme allergy again, with uncontrolled sneezing and Niagaras of mucus.

3 *November*

Beloved Parents—

It's hard to believe this weather, isn't it? A bitter winter—the bitterest since the Ice Age—has been announced. Yet day after sunny day seems June-like, not a bit autumnal. Monday from the train to Philadelphia the landscape was breathtaking: the trees were not only every shade of gold and lemon and green and crimson, but magenta and even sometimes blue. In Europe the fall is never so lavish, mainly because they don't have the same kind of maples we do. As usual I walked to Curtis from 30th Street, the air was so warm, and gave three very good lessons. Indeed, I give the students such good ideas that I have none left over for myself. The teaching's exhausting, but also, in a sense, rewarding.

It was so convenient having Mr. Johnson pick me up. And I was so pleased with how well you both seemed, and "adjusted" to Cadbury. It's the only place to be—I'd even like to live there myself someday.

The trip back to New York was strange—because the bus at night has no lights, and there are only glimpses of factories and distant towns, and occasionally farms; the rest is silence. When I got back home (JH being still in Nantucket) I looked at Mortimer Adler's program "On Beauty" on the television. Have you seen Adler's series on esthetic principles? It sort of annoyed me, oversimplified and smug and also incorrect. For example, he stated (correctly) that though Beauty may or may not be absolute, you still can't compare one genre with another—you can't compare a Gothic cathedral with an Egyptian temple, you can only compare it to another Gothic cathedral in deciding which is the more beautiful. He also says that "experts" in taste are useful to consult, even for him, in areas he's not closely acquainted with. BUT he goes on to say that, as an adolescent, he loved Tchaikovsky's Sixth Symphony, but later grew to see that there was "better" music, notably Beethoven and Schubert and Bartók. That's faulty, since these composers, being of different periods in history, represent different genres. Since I am an expert, I say that Tchaikovsky is equal to Bartók, and Stravinsky certainly thought so too. I do resent Adler's easy thinking, which comes over as profound for the unwashed.

Did I remember to thank you for the sixty dollars in traveler's checks? Thanks. And yes, I do have copies of the previous letters. Spoke at length with Rosemary on the phone last night, after I came home from hearing Kristine Ciesinski sing my *Ariel*, wonderfully, in nearby Merkin Hall. Rosemary seems to be thriving.

Perhaps I'll phone you tonight. Next Sunday I go away on that damned Phi

Beta Kappa tour, for nine days, to Alma, Bucknell, and to Middlebury, Vermont.

More soon, love forever—
Ned

Barclay Hotel
Philadelphia
23 November

Have now completed four of the six Phi Beta Kappa stints, which had me darting about the land—Hofstra, Alma (Michigan), Bucknell (Pa.), and Middlebury (Vt.)—and they're disappointing. If famous universities are no more sophisticated musically than these small colleges, at least they collect an audience for visiting firemen. With Phi Beta Kappa I'm guest not of one department but of the whole campus, which doesn't really know or care about music. The notion of what music *is* is vague, even to the English department; when they learn you're a musician, the assumption is that you're a pop performer, and in it for the money. This is never their assumption for writers or painters or physicists. The inadvertent error, if error it be, lies in Phi Beta Kappa's planning. I'm the sole artist from among this year's roster of twelve Visiting Scholars (the other eleven are all listed as Professor—of Astrophysics, of Mathematics, of the American Enterprise Institute for Public Policy Research, etc.), one of whom is selected, as from a grab bag, by each of the eligible colleges.

Middlebury was the best, the people were brightest, likewise the weather. During a spare hour I stopped by the library which houses private assemblages of Robert Frostiana and of Thoreau. They own all of Thoreau's personal book collection and also his inkwell. Asked how they knew it was his inkwell, they replied that the donors were trustworthy. Well, we take Luther's inkspot on the wall (when he was chasing the devil, if you recall) on faith too, and God is never wrong. Yet even God had his Achilles Heel. Or maybe Achilles had God's Heel. Berenson used to authenticate a Rubens, then decades later say, No, it's the *school* of Rubens, leaving the collector holding the bag (or holding the Rubens) after spending a fortune. Picasso once said, There is no love, there are only proofs of love. Maybe there is no Rubens, only the school of Rubens.

Since returning from Middlebury I've tried to work quietly, but New York isn't quiet. Fassbinder's sordid, riveting *Veronika Voss*. Robin Morgan's book party at Doubleday's. Hélène (Rémy) Valentin's expo. Visits to Curtis. Interview with Swedish Broadcasting. Visits to Cadbury, and to A.A. with

Z. P. A calm hour with Dalton Baldwin, who then accompanied me to B. & H. where I signed a hundred copies of *Two Poems of Edith Sitwell*, just published in a pumpkin-colored cover, inside of which is a little essay on the songs' bizarre history. Dined with JH at Earl Wild's. Dined with Rose Plaut & gang in her Chinese bistro on Second Avenue. Tea party for Chuck, Robert Phelps and Morris. Nantucket now, for the next eight days, will be static, fertile.

Daron Hagen and Norman Stumpf, last night at Curtis Hall, offered a carefully spaced and quite well performed (under these composers' batons) program of entirely their own symphonic works, three by each. Inasmuch as these works were brought to fruition with my guidance, and inasmuch as the boys hustled pretty much on their own to swing this unprecedented (for Curtis) event, I feel proud of myself as of them. Their pieces are every bit as solid, and a good deal more "vocal," as any I've seen by other first-class students around the country, and the orchestra—which they said rehearsed with comparative good will—sounded professionally lustrous. The de Lancies invited me to dine beforehand with Emlen Etting at the Art Alliance; afterward, a glass of tonic with Daron's parents who'd driven clear from Milwaukee. Who should show up but Mrs. Gessel, my landlady above the florist shop on Locust Street in 1943, when I was in Daron's student shoes!

I fly directly from the Philadelphia airport. Deep fog.

Nantucket
25 November

Thanksgiving alone with JH. This morning the thermometer dropped thirty degrees, the sky cleared, and a crystalline sun now streams over the backyard where the pheasant family (crimson-bibbed patriarch with his five spinster daughters) peck about, looking for seedlings which the recent rains have brought to the surface. Actually, in Nantucket I enjoy any kind of weather. *C'est toujours ainsi à la campagne.*

28 November

Because Robert Phelps thinks it might make an opera (and it probably might, if Garbo were twenty and could sing), I've just reread *Nightwood* for the twelfth, and probably last, time since Chicago in 1938 when I knew it by heart. It does still pack a wallop, yet I'm not sure Djuna's a writer; or if she is, that she constructs; or if she constructs, that she knows what she's saying; or if she knows what she's saying, that she says it. Yes, there's nothing like her, and the book seethes with energy, humor, originality and pathos. And yes, it is about something—about, I suppose, the destruction of love by children, a kind of Latin *Billy Budd* or WASP portrait of Odette and Albertine.

Is it mere coincidence that later in the day I finally played Schoenberg's *Trio*, Op. 45? The record's been lying there for years. It's not as though I haven't given him a chance, since I've known Schoenberg for as long as I've known *Nightwood*, and I've earned the right to ask: Is there a reason to listen to Schoenberg? Does his *Trio* say anything? Once I wrote that he was a genius without talent (the opposite of Boulez, who has knowledge without wisdom—but also no talent). I still feel it—though one is not supposed to wonder about the rocks, for Schoenberg's a *fait accompli*. But he doesn't help matters by stating, as quoted in the unsigned liner notes, "I am somewhat sad that people talk so much of atonality, of twelve-tone systems, of technical methods when it comes to my music. All music, all human work, has a skeleton, a circulatory and nervous system. I wish that my music should be considered as an honest and intelligent person who comes to us saying something he feels deeply and which is of significance to all of us." Now, honesty and intelligence do not great music make, nor, of itself, does the utterance of something deeply felt. We all feel deeply, after all, and we're all intelligent and honest. But Schoenberg's chief error is to add "which is of significance to us all." It's not for a composer to review his own music, nor to assess, or even to know, what it contains. But perhaps he means that the "person who comes to us" is of significance? No matter, the proof of the pudding . . . etc.

I am not a fool. But I maintain that nobody sits down to enjoy (even to enjoy the terror and ugliness of) Schoenberg—or Boulez or Carter. And that is because the music, as music, does not say anything. Thus there is no reason to it. Can you, for that matter, listen twice to Lukas Foss's Quartet (which Seymour Barab contends is what music must sound like to a dog)? What it says is said as convincingly in words. I'm no less embarrassed by all the manly exponents (Harold Rosenberg, Barnett Newman) of the vastly expensive movement of Abstract Expressionism. What a self-congratulatory joke.

New York
30 November

The current *New York Review* (Dec. 2) prints my words of last summer on Robert Craft's homophobia (is that too grand a word for his glib stance?), followed by Craft's response, which opens, "Rorem will distort any text, apparently, for yet another of his exhibitionistic effusions," and closes in a diatribe which starts, "Enough of Rorem's sentences without subjects . . . ," and which itself turns out to be, fifty-one words later, a sentence without verbs. Like William Buckley, Craft evades the issue—in this case, that a minority can be wounded by casual generalities—with specious nitpicking.

"On what authority can Rorem call Ravel 'queer'?" he asks, as though I'd made some vile accusation. Well, it takes one to know one, and we have a mafia, didn't you know? But what's the problem? Would he have reacted thus, had I presumed to suggest that Ravel was, say, Jewish or Blackish? Elbert Lenrow suggests that Robert's letter was nasty because he'd been under a strain—as though if Vera Stravinsky were still thriving he'd be his usual dear self.

A year or two ago I wrote here, apropos of Podhoretz, that one thing more sinister than a dumb bigot is a smart bigot. But Craft isn't smart. He simply doesn't see.

Straight men get nervous because they always think you have eyes for them. However, most straight men, like most gay ones and most women and most everyone, are physically drab. Thus, after that initial split-second Yes or No by which we all size each other up on first meetings, they should relax and go on talking about whatever people talk about. Still, they do worry.

Yes, I too am forever aware of, maybe swayed by, who here is old or young or sexy or not, or Jewish or too thin or swishy or too fat or female or rich or talented or useful, but I never *never* think about whether they're white (unless they're not) because no white person ever does.

Heterosexuals worry because homosexuals are demonstrably more promiscuous than they. The two reasons most often given for gay promiscuity are, one, since they exist peripherally they have no responsibilities and two, their one-night stands indicate an inability for fulfillment—a need to seek ceaselessly. Actually, the anonymous bang can be so totally satisfying that a repeat performance could only disappoint, like the same Cordon Bleu meal two days in a row.

Probably no heterosexual, no matter how well-meaning, can know what homosexuality "is," any more than whites know black. What difference does it make, since love has nothing to do with understanding, and understanding can even bring an end to bodily love? (Zeus and Hera quarreled, each claiming the other's sex was more capable of gratification. To prove the point they called in the hermaphrodite Teresias. "Who has more fun in bed, Teresias, man or woman?" "Woman." In fury Hera struck Teresias blind. In compensation Zeus bestowed foresight upon him.) The homosexual artist, in a sense, has the edge, since he or she intuits nuance, thanks to a lifelong immersion in a straight element. But again, vocabulary here misleads. Before Freud, or even just one generation ago, people didn't talk of, say, the "ho-

mosexual" plays of Shakespeare or Marlowe or Wilde or Wilder or Williams
or Inge. No one, including the homosexual, has yet come up with a definition; and not one of the thousand homosexuals I personally know seems
queer for the weary psychoanalytical reason of strong mother and cold father. Nature lets her chips fall everywhere, but whereas those chips fell
upon precise terminology millennia ago for women and Jews, in *Lysistrata*
and Moses, only yesterday was *homosexuality* coined.

2 December

Maggy Magerstadt and Joe Rosner came for our annual *repas à quatre* tonight, Maggy, very blond, bringing five jars of her homemade apricot and
tomato jellies, and Joe bringing his wry and heterogeneous knowledge. We
spoke with frustration of AIDS, the new term for GRID.

4 December

Last summer Frankie Schuman called to invite me to make a spoken comment about the MacDowell Colony—oh, nothing more than two minutes—
for the annual December dinner. Tonight, accordingly, at the Metropolitan
Club on East 60th, I arose at the appointed moment and, in front of all those
rich donors, delivered the following two-minute comment:

> The critic Harold Clurman once considered dedicating *The Fervent Years* "to
> my wife, Stella Adler, without whose constant absence this book would never
> have been written." If our strongest urge is to be with those we love, our second
> strongest is to get away from those we love. For the artist the second urge is ur-
> gent, but he seldom finds legitimate ways to satisfy it.
>   Today, when art is not a necessity but a luxury, what artists most lack is that
> luxuriant necessity: the leisure to be artists. The pressures of want, like the
> pressures of glory, are induced for an artist by the extracurricular chaos of for-
> tune and misfortune, families and phones, persons from Porlock and dirty
> dishes, all of which erode precious hours and derail trains of thought.
>   For certain creators, though, one escape exists—an escape into reality, you
> might say. This is the MacDowell Colony. Most guests will agree that two
> weeks' work up there equals two months' work in the hurly-burly. It is as though
> Proust's cork-lined chamber had expanded over a thousand emerald acres. On
> various occasions in that Spartan Paradise my sanity has been restored. When
> I am there my best tunes are composed, and when I'm far away the fact of the
> place allows me to breathe more easily.

The Colony represents that golden limbo between Stella and the studio, where we put aside the actual pleasures and doubts of love and society, in order to write about the doubts and pleasures of society and love.

Cadbury
Cherry Hill, N.J.
5 December

There is no redeeming feature to growing old. Mother & Father are less serene in their new home than I allow them to think I think. But since for the past two years Mother's been dwelling more and more in a world of her own, and since for the past six months she's been suffering from the undiagnosed *petit mal*, like Wallace, every week or two, there's no alternative to Cadbury. (I'm staying here overnight with them before going to Curtis for the day tomorrow, then with JH to Puerto Rico.) They're lonely, sad, and Father especially, because he's so alert and cultured, is a bit bogged down by Mother's constant demands. She simply gets no fun out of anything, doesn't even cry but sits for hours going through old address books, looking up numbers of people long gone. She snaps out of it, knows where she is, but isn't interested in much except bodily functions. I can literally *see* her living in her girlhood. In a way it's bad for me: I identify, and am hypochondriac. JH must put up with my endless complaints and high doctor bills, and I hate to see myself sinking into . . .

Just wrote these reactions to David Diamond, who, of all people (and not just because of his poor sister Sabina, who seems to be in Mother's state), seems geared to empathize. Precious David. It's thirty-eight years since first we met at the Washington Square show where Allela was standing by her paintings, making quick charcoal sketches of passersby, with David sitting near her on a folding chair in the wind, his long white face, exactly as today, with the melancholy of Petruchka's, expressing the stark seriousness of it all. "I was twenty and a lover / And in paradise to stay . . ."

Parador Quebradillas
11 December

Puerto Rico, so poor and lush and cultureless. But the beaches! They bring back all the other thrilling beaches of the past, at Paestum and Nobadir and Caleta and Lake Michigan . . . Heat . . . Our fifth and final morning on this island, where hotels, rundown and haunted, are like a tropical Miss Havisham in Noon City. Gustavo, the only time in ten years I've seen him in his native element, has the inborn elegance of European tillers of the soil and plays the host touchingly in the mysterious Guayanilla of his birth.

Vacations confuse me; I'm a bad idler, don't know how to do nothing. But it's curiously pleasant for JH to be the guide, and to fantasize about the incongruities of lurking in Guanica's forest preserve if ever war should come. I like Yauco, the beach at Boqueron, the university at San German and also the Portocoeli church, the nocturnal meal at Parguerra to the peep of the rare tree-frogs near the phosphorescent bay, the fair at Guayanilla, and the long trek to the north coast through those steep hills with mango groves.

My sole reading during these Spanish days has been the new *Salmagundi* devoted to "Homosexuality," all 426 pages and 21 authors (mainly outsiders), which I perused consecutively, like a novel. It's foul-smelling, with a preface by George Steiner that "means well" but—as with so many of the other "brains" of the magazine—sounds square. Like Robert Craft, they just don't get the point. It's a good idea for a straight quarterly to put out a gay issue, but with a choice of twenty-one other authors, equally reputable, they'd have a sounder result.

In San Juan I stopped for a moment into the Casals museum to escape the heat. There on the air-conditioned second floor of this town without tourists, I watched a little documentary starring so many old acquaintances that I suddenly didn't know where . . .

Suffocating sunlight.

New York
13 December

Sleet. Death of John Button.

At six last night George Tsontakis conducted two of my difficult choruses, *Praises for the Nativity* and *Surge Illuminare*, before the not especially musical public of his Greek Church of the Annunciation. Later, buffet at Heddy Baum's.

Tonight, meal at Richard Sennett's, with Jon Gachiok and David Parker of the *Nation* staff. Richard's fast and witty, a voguish nonfiction writer but a usefully disturbing novelist. Good cook, three-story apartment, big fuzzy cat. Said he won a Pulitzer, but when I got home I found no trace in the Pulitzer listings. As in *Time and Again*, perhaps his name was eradicated by someone else's excursion into the past.

Death of Arthur Rubinstein.

The superstar in the driver's seat is as lopsided—as meaningless—as the British running India, yet the condition prevails. Fortunes are dispensed on a Sutherland performing music of the past while composers of the present go unheard. The new Horowitz biography will sell far more than any book on a live composer; but who is Horowitz compared to, say, Stravinsky?

While Rubinstein's obit rated a big picture on page 1, Barber's rated a small picture on page 30.

There is no such thing as the inevitable performance. There are as many valid versions of a Mozart rondo or a Stravinsky capriccio as there are players able to hit the right note with the right tone at the right time. Notions of right change every twenty years or so, and even the composer, if still alive, can be hard put to opt for this way or that—and his option is not necessarily right for all. Similarly, there is no better than, there is only different from, and, like rightness, the sense of difference alters each generation. Thus the age of a pianist (as we hear him on a record) is usually locatable according to his style.

However tiresome the mannered Maggie Smith may elsewhere be, her diction is so clear (with that Bette Davis way of holding onto consonants—"I donn'ttt wwanntt tto") that one could wish singers like Sutherland would learn from her. But a little goes a long way.

Madly uneven: Dostoevsky, Christopher Smart, Melville, Ives.
Madly consistent: Beethoven, Milton Babbitt, Kafka, Picasso.
Sanely uneven: Mozart, Proust, Cézanne, all biographers.
Sanely consistent: Bach, Henry James, Jane Austen, Ravel.

Literary dinner Saturday at Diana Trilling's, with Dennis Donahue, Jonathan Lieberson, Moira & Michael, and a woman named Daphne. Diana cooked; ambiance mostly congenial. But when Moira and others began championing pop music, and when I said nothing *happened* in pop (although I wouldn't object if pop weren't so preemptive, and if intellectuals like them wouldn't play the dumb game of either/or), they told me, sweetly, that I had no right to judge since I didn't *know* the music, although I said, correctly, that I was raised loving the equivalent music of the forties—

Benny Goodman, Billie Holiday, and all. JH asked, Well, how many of you know Carter's music, or indeed, Ned's music, or any such music (except Philip Glass's) well enough to recognize it at a glance of the ear? No one raised a hand. Later, Diana brought up the question of Singing in English—how ungrateful it is. To which I retorted: I've spent my life writing songs in my native language, and I'm sick of generalities about other tongues being more *grateful*—the only thing bad about Song in English is bad English. At which Diana bit her lip and shut up. JH later told me I was just plain rude, but the matter's so close to my heart that I recite a set aria when anyone brings it up.

Today, a long and moving note from Diana, at the end of which, as an afterthought, she explains that she hadn't been voicing a wholly untutored opinion. "I didn't become a writer until I was thirty-five—it was a second-best career. I had been studying to be a singer when suddenly I became very ill; for ten years I could do nothing. I was an extraordinarily good singer, but that statement counts, obviously, for nothing; a singer who doesn't sing is like a writer who isn't published. What I was doing in my illegitimate way was generalizing from my own experience of long ago—I found it harder to sing in English than in other languages."

Mother's been moved to another wing of Cadbury. So they'll be living separately for the first time in sixty-two years, although Father can visit as many times a day as he wishes.

Christmas Day

Thursday, midday party at B. & H. Early evening party at the Fosses, from which I depart with Lenny who drives me in his comfortable car back to the West Side through Central Park—ten minutes, in which we commune on the fate of our globe. Late evening party at Gregg Smith's.

Friday, tips for all. Brief visit from Jeanie of Cat Cottage, to finalize her "sitting" schedule when we leave town. Summer weather, so that Midnight Mass in St. Matthew's & St. Timothy's evoked the semitropical Bethlehem, although the sermon was a cool rebuke of our bourgeois ease in the face of poverty.

Today, warm mist and rain. Intimate brunch at Rosalyn Tureck's, with George & Shirley, Sharon Isbin, and Stewart Warkow. Eggs Benedict, espresso, and lots of expensive mints of which I consumed two dozen. As her "gift" to us mortals, Rosalyn offered a friendly lecture, and then a Bach recital on her clavichord. The assembly lasted from 11:30 A.M. until 3:00.

From *Das Wohlentemperierte Klavier*, which daily after decades I admire unqualifiedly, the Preludes bring more pleasure than the Fugues. Is this because all fugues, no matter by whom, become, after their initial statements, rather predictable, being propelled less by inspirational sweep than by device? For fugue is device, not form. And even fugues by Bach—for whom the device was more a need than for, say, Reger—on patterns dictated by angels can only go here or there, not just anywhere, while his preludes lead thrillingly where angels fear to tread.

Nantucket
30 December

I do not wish to be cremated. Decision reached after half a century of mild rumination. Thus, before he returned to the city (I'll be alone here for the entrance of the new year), JH agreed that I could buy a cemetery plot.

How do you buy a cemetery plot? The phone book is no help if you look under C for cemetery, P for plot, or D for dead. I ended by calling Mrs. Norton, who was born on the island. The person to contact, she says, for non-Catholic burial arrangements, is the mortician, Richard (Ricky) Lewis.

Lewis arranged to meet me this afternoon at three at the new Prospect Hill Cemetery—that is, the annex a half-mile away from the beautiful central site. I bicycled there early and strolled about on the cold, unfurrowed, hard-as-rock ten-acre field studded with but five or six tombstones. In a cemetery I'm always cheerfully tranquil and feel protected, not by the past but by the casualness of the present. No effort is made there, not even by the summery gardener mowing the lawns, the gardener more beautiful than his roses. I, who so dread death, find nothing fatal about those lawns, just peace. (Maeterlinck: The dead would not exist if it weren't for cemeteries.)

Mr. Lewis appeared on the horizon and approached, his feet crunching the glassy soil like the spectral creature in *Night of the Living Dead* but his face all affable, wreathed in "understanding." What does a grave cost? fifty dollars? fifty thousand? We decided on a twenty-by-twenty-foot plot priced at $1250, which will be tended for perpetuity and which provides room for eight coffins (*caskets*, as they say in the business), or for twenty-four upright urns.

Dusk. Supper's simmering—a vegetable stew. Outside the last birds screech before dark. Over there, across Wesco Place, the Nortons have turned on their lights. Sense of well-being.

1983

Finished writing a little memoir of Sam Barber for *Stagebill*. Relieved, partly just to know it's done, partly to reemerge into the present, away from the contagiously neurotic but always skilled sounds of Sam's craft, and from the souvenir of his always sly and often unpleasant character. Nantucket, alone on a white, damp morning, is the present. Await Bertha's taxi for the airport with the same uneasiness that every islander knows in such inclement weather.

Two hundred miles southwest of Nantucket the snow has changed to slush, through which David Huntley, Sylvia Goldstein, and Janis Susskind trudged to tea here this afternoon. Janis is the promotionist for B & H's London office, young, smart, and likeable, American despite her accent, and the widow of Walter Susskind. I served huge strawberries and three sorts of chocolate, but it turns out that Janis is indifferent to sweets.

All day at Curtis where Rosemary picked me up at four to drive to Cadbury. Back to Philly to catch Amtrak to NYC. It's the middle of the night, insomnia, a shuddering silence.

Daron Hagen's mother has died. She died, in fact, just weeks after our meeting at Curtis last November. Daron's concert was evidently her final supreme effort. I still see the transparent skin, the eager eyes like candles as she leaned across the table in the Barclay bar, pride subduing fever. Daron at twenty-one now lacks the protection that I at fifty-nine still retain from my parent, *tant bien que mal.* Is his musical composition, for being unprotected, of necessity stronger? Does our music display what we feel, or what we know about having felt, or what we know about other people's feelings? You can't write tragedy with tears in your eyes, they smear the ink.

What have these nuances to do with my mother today, with her knot of puerile concerns? Even as I note this at 3 A.M., she continues to live her own life, goes on, thinks, breathes, feeds her complicated secrets, sighs, is.

30 January

Thumbing through the January agenda I note that I visited, or rehearsed with, the same people, or others like them, as last month or last year; that I went to the same concerts, or others like them, and saw the same movies and plays as last month or last year, and ingested the same meals and reacted to the same stormy weather. That I love and need my friends, doctors, and interpreters almost as I need and love the blessed hermitage of work. That I shut myself apart emotionally (as they say in college) with more frequency. That I have fewer "deep thoughts," no anecdotes, and I worry about the fate of the world more than about my own. Why write? From habit, from order, from terror of being forgotten, like the sultan who, in his wistfulness, was attended by a scribe who noted his every inhalation and excretion. (Why not three scribes, or forty? What do you leave out?)

For the record, I enjoyed, as I did last year, two full recent days with the music committee at the Academy among colleagues (Arthur Berger, Leslie Bassett, Miriam Gideon, Ulysses Kay, Donald Martino, and Louise Talma) and felt rewarded that they saw fit to bestow on my two nominees, Hagen and Convery, their Charles Ives Fellowships.

My one other thought for the month is this: The nighttime soap opera, *Dynasty*, would be morally offensive if for no other reason than that, week after week, ninety million viewers obediently watch the chief protagonists meet in a place called La Mirage, when, of course, it should be called Le Mirage.

1 February

Gave a reading last night for the Academy of American Poets at the Donnell Library. Edmund White introduced me.

Today, emergency dentist, Roz Rees rehearsal, tea with Conrad Cummings of Oberlin. Roz was still here when Conrad arrived, and we both examined with dismay the score of his new opera. In his up-to-date anxiety Conrad has denuded his palette of any semblance of himself. The music's too close to Rameau for even discomfort.

The specter of the New is corrupting utterly. Nobody, not even Susan Sontag, can know what is new *as it occurs*: by the time a phenomenon may be seen to have been new, it's too late—the phenomenon has settled in. With perspective, newness in itself counts for nothing: in a century, in ten years, Glass and Carter will sound alike to our conditioned ears.

If it weren't for his grandiose claims, Philip Glass's music would be attractive enough as far as it goes along its humorless path. But since, like Carter, Glass is God, he believes his own hype. And like Ezra Pound two generations ago who, because he was bright but had no musical schooling, discovered by lugubrious hit-or-miss certain basics that any formal fool can learn in an hour, then proclaimed these basics as *trouvailles*, so Glass tells the world that his music, which may sound repetitive, is not repetitive, because of subtle metrical shiftings which people don't bother to listen to, though in fact these shiftings are apparent to any layman with ears. But so what? The shiftings are naive in themselves; to point them out (except to his hip fans) is an embarrassment in the light of Stravinsky, Bach, or the complex Hindus who, as they have hosted Allen Ginsberg, have hosted Glass (one wonders with what silent sarcasm). Like Pound-the-musician, like Robert Wilson, Glass speaks the truth of freshmen. His audience is not made up of thinking composers who, while cringing at his simplistic pretensions, are naturally jealous of his success. Glass's success has nothing to do with breakthrough in opera (there are no breakthroughs in art, ever; and *Einstein on the Beach* is no opera anyway, but old-style ballet) so much as a lowering of barriers. Anyone can dig it, just as anyone can dig video. Wilson is sometimes marvelous, but not a bit new. I once dissected his *Letter to Queen Victoria* into strands, each one of which led directly to an available source. Like Poulenc, Wilson is a shameless magpie robbing the nests of his betters but weaving the strands into something identifiably his own.

As for Elliot Carter—"My music may sound like confusion at first, but if you hear it often, it isn't really as confused as you might think"—he's saying the same thing as Glass. To be able to unravel and reravel is flattering for critics, who confound their ability with appreciation and their appreciation with a sense of making order from chaos. The order, in and of itself, must be art, or why bother? But the bother is the bother of vanity.

Nantucket
8 February

I speak with Father nearly every day, and the experience is as sapping and, in a sense, rewarding as trying to write a piece. He scarcely attempts to dissimulate his loathing: Is this how one winds up a distinguished career—surrounded by self-centered Elders who should be urged to commit suicide? Father asks if they ought not be left on a mountaintop, then chuckles (so as not to shriek) as he answers, "This is our last home," and adds that he's depressed. Father has never openly been a pessimist. But we wonder if Mother's three sets of shock treatments over the decades could have led to this. Mother, the incomparable, the glamorous, who presently sits, demanding, yet drifting off, in what they call a "posie" (a straitjacket) that "secures" her into the wheelchair. Never anymore does she ask where Father's been, when he skips a day, three days, or seven, but protects herself from the Great Outside by living obsessively within the minute.

Last night I began *Joseph and His Brothers*. It has been exactly forty years since I read, at Eugene's urging when we were all undergrads at Curtis, *Buddenbrooks*, and cried when little Hanno died (and forty-*four* years since I read *The Magic Mountain*). Today I teach at Curtis, urging my pupils to read Mann. But have I myself reread him in those intervening decades? Does he, like Dostoevsky, fall apart as one grows on? No, he hangs together. And then some.

I also began *Slaughterhouse Five*. I'm reminded of that Steve Reich concert at the Met Museum. Other composers are not buying Reich, any more than they buy Glass, probably because he seems to have less to do with excellence than with popularity: he pens best-sellers. He is the Vonnegut of music and, like Vonnegut, relies more on manner than on style—both with their endless et ceteras. Reich does nothing that Lou Harrison wasn't doing forty years ago. Both composers prepare exquisite canvases, but Lou paints a good picture on them, while Reich merely leaves the background in all its glory.

11 February

To Storrs, Connecticut, with Joe LeSueur, Jane Frielicher, John Ashbery and others for a two-day symposium on Frank O'Hara. I disliked it, partly for the crass planning (records of my songs on Frank's poetry were played as *background* for various functions), and partly because I was never that close to what John Myers calls the O'Hara Syndrome, and so felt *à côté* and ill-tempered while everyone else had a merry time. Left before the end, was driven to Hartford, took a train which, because of a heavy snow now covering the East Coast in twelve feet of soiled ermine, was five hours late into Grand Central.

Circa 1949, I had just arrived in Europe and asked Norris Embry, "How's the sex in Florence?" Shirley, overhearing: "You boys! You cross an ocean and all you wonder about is sex. Aren't there other wonders in Florence to interest you besides that?" No. The best way to learn a new language is in bed.

13 February

How long since I've had that weak heave in the stomach, or invested another with powers he can't possibly have (like expecting a Neanderthal, or a Venutian, to react in a modern earthly manner)? Meanwhile Mother rests in Jersey, aflame with an undiagnosable syndrome, and I think on her less than I ought. Yet I think on her every minute, with the impossibility of being able (like the Neanderthal, the Venutian) to help a little.

Albion, Michigan
26 February

Three nights in this college town, with fever and deep chest cold, and a schedule covering twelve hours a day.

Death of Tennessee Williams. Instant switch of attitude from impatience and boredom to pity and impotence. Will it be seen—*dans un mois, dans un an*—that Tennessee's best work was not in the theater at all, but in his stories? The plays, even the best, with their panache and stageworthiness and "truth," pander, as plays must, to a disparate public. The stories, because they never have any but a small "inside" audience anyway, cannot cater: they are the seeds of the plays, the seeds before they fester. Anyway, the thought of poor Tennessee choking in a hotel room is both insufferable and somehow inevitable. The thought will take focus in a few days.

New York
4 March

At Sotheby's Thursday we gave a half-concert for Charles Schwartz's "Composers Showcase." I accompanied Will Parker in *War Scenes*, Katherine

Ciesinski in *Women's Voices* and (with Kristine) *Gloria*. Frightful acoustics, at once too dry and too wet.

Last night, dinner at the Zukerman's at one table with eleven other guests, most of whom I don't know. Spacious, friendly apartment. Richard Sennett, as court jester, makes outrageous statements about "things gay" which fail to shock, which are harmless, maybe even useful. My own outrageous statement is that superstars never play contemporary music, to which Pinchas (spacious, friendly) retorts astoundingly, "Well, at least I don't fit into that category." Eugenia, gossamer and wise and ill at ease, for dessert serves six different flavors of sherbet.

Suicide of Arthur Koestler.

At WNYC this afternoon, a two-hour interview with Tim Page. I'm reminded how thirty-nine years ago last month (Mozart lived and died in less time) I had my first public New York performance in these very studios.

(This morning, at Doctor Photos, X rays of the lower abdomen, during which I vomited. Tomorrow a woman, friend of the Ciesinskis, is coming to give me the first of three treatments according to the Reike method.)

8 March

A beautiful organ program last evening by Leonard Raver, at Ascension Church on lower Fifth Avenue, included the local premiere of *Views from the Oldest House*, and Barbara Kolb's unusual *The Point That Divides the Wind*.

Three hours at the dentist's. Deaths of Cathy Berberian, Igor Markevitch, William Walton.

9 March

Dined at Emily Genauer's. Guest of honor, Segovia. Also Virgil, and Harold Schonberg whom I sat next to—and we got along fine, now that he's retired, despite all his snippy reviews of yore. And despite the fact that I don't care for the guitar, much less for living legends, Segovia comes across (like Casals and Rampal) as a likeable, peasanty diva.

Dwelling on Tennessee, reviving lost time. Although for seven years I had known Tennessee the artist, having attended the historic opening of *The Glass Menagerie*, I never knew Tennessee the man until the afternoon of November 1, 1952, when I woke up in his bed after a Halloween party at Jane Bowles's, the first of a dozen bleary meetings over a span of several years, here and abroad. Then in the fall of 1957 John C. Wilson hired me to com-

pose the incidental music for *Suddenly Last Summer*. It's not certain how
confident Tennessee was of me now as a colleague, given our previous
blurred rapport. It *is* certain that once the rapport was on a professional
plane we were never again at ease together; even in the best of times Tennessee was hard to talk to.

In 1964 I composed the score for the second version (the one with Tallulah) of *Milk Train*. The production failed, but our acquaintance succeeded
because of what it taught me. If Tennessee socially was hard to talk to, sometimes appearing inarticulate, that's because he listened to you. He attended, intensely, or abstractedly, or impatiently, but always as though considering, "Can I use this?" At business meanwhile he was verbose, molding
raw material with a paradoxically extravagant economy. Inspirationally he
resembled both Schubert (who could write a perfect song in a single sitting)
and Beethoven (who would belabor the details of a symphony for months).
Before rehearsals for *Suddenly Last Summer* Tennessee slaved each morning with Herbert Machiz, trimming and padding in what seemed a hit-or-
miss manner. What began as a rambling monologue for Anne Meacham
ended as a pair of what can only be called arias for female voices divided by
an hour's worth of exposition. A dozen references to the sky as "a great white
bone" were shaved down to two. The original title, *Music in the Twelve-Tone
Scale*, was dropped when I explained that the term meant nothing, either in
itself or as reference to the contents of Anne's soliloquy. "But can't you at
least write some background music in that scale?" the author pleaded; "I just
love the sound of those words." His approach to music was not even instinctive so much as plainly visual, or at best, intellectual, metaphoric. For example, he asked that Anne's entrance be accompanied by Corrida trumpets;
he *saw* what bullfights connotated aurally as connected to the dark death of
his unseen demi-hero. We tried it musically, but the association was too
personal, too "poetic," to work. In the end Tennessee left me to my own musical devices which, I admit, were influenced by those of Paul Bowles, who
had almost singlehandedly created what must be called "The Tennessee
Sound"—that suavely aching underwater bluesiness we have come to link
with passive heroines. (Alex North used that sound too in his music for
Streetcar, later choreographed by Valerie Bettis, and Lee Hoiby used it in
his opera *Summer and Smoke*.) Tennessee also kept out of my way on the set
of *Milk Train*. Not so director Tony Richardson who dolled up the play to
within an inch of its life with irrelevant japoneries. My score, which could
have as convincingly accompanied a Kabuki pageant, was at least salvageable as a concert suite, which is what we composers always aim for.

In retrospect neither *Suddenly Last Summer* nor *Milk Train* seem politically solid. The one depicts the male homosexual as an inevitably profiteer-

ing mama's boy; the other portrays The Artist as Victim, whereas all artists, in mirroring the very society that supposedly victimizes them, necessarily have the last laugh. Did the music, by its nature, soften or harden these dramas? I can't say. But Tennessee—although like many literary people he never went to concerts, or talked about symphonies, or listened to records other than pop—did sense that music was as crucial to his plays as to Shakespeare's: it tightened the dream, gave logic to folly. Then are his plays what people like to call musical?

The difference between Tennessee Williams and Edward Albee as users of language is that one is a poet, the other a musician. Albee has claimed to be more influenced by composers than by playwrights (which doesn't mean he's more influenced by music than by theater); in fact, he never personally knew any playwrights until he became—as we say in America—successful, though he was acquainted with lots of composers. Albee is a well-informed Music Lover, while Williams was tone-deaf. Both have utilized moody musical decor for their less naturalistic plays. But when it comes to adaptations of their actual words for singers, Williams lends himself admirably to song and opera, Albee not at all. Williams's prose, being poetry, is easily set to music; Albee's prose, being music, is impossible to set to music.

JH feels that Albee's weakness lies in avoidance of characterization. A Williams drama, even at its purple worst, always shows wounded or laughing individuals moving through the mismanaged argument. Because they are individuals they lived (or died) yesterday and last year, too, and are brought back tomorrow and next year by their maker in other plays. They people his *oeuvre*. But Albee writes plot before personality; his characters live only in the actors portraying them.

Yes, Williams's stories at their best are better than his best plays because they necessarily avoid the vulgar paraphernalia that our theater seems to require: laugh lines, etc.

After *Milk Train* (which coincided with the death of Frank Merlo) encounters with Tennessee became sporadic and were never in the line of duty. The last time we met was at the Gotham Book Mart a few months ago. He acted vague. I was uncomfortable. Yet on reading his obituary last week I felt I'd lost a close friend. Thus it is when artists die.

10 March

Harold Schonberg's defense of his never hobnobbing with professional musicians during his heyday as a critic lies in the notion that the public would not trust him. "Would you," he asks a student of Beveridge Webster, who has criticized Schonberg's aloofness, "ever believe anything I wrote about

Webster if you knew we were friends?" The student sits down, defeated. Applause.

But, as JH points out, Schonberg mistakes the purpose of criticism. Is it to judge Webster, or to disseminate information? Of course we try to speak well of our friends, but I, for one, have lost friends with professional criticism. Nor can a critic really be *used*, as Schonberg maintains that Virgil and the others were used. And anyway, so what? Nor was Schonberg a composer to be used.

12 March

After a week of stewing I phoned *Harper's* to say I just can't review the Horowitz book. Since this is the first time I've ever missed a deadline, should I tremble that, like murder, it may grow easier? Yet to invite a composer to write about a virtuoso is like asking a man to feed a rich neighbor while his own household starves. On the face of it such an invitation is divine justice. For half a century the interpretive and the creative musician have been turning ever more in opposite directions, the one upsetting the other's logical place in the nature of things, so now seems the time to reinstate the horse before the cart. Yet how? The cart has *become* the horse. Today one can claim (to change horses in midstream) that Yeats's once-troubling koan, "How can we know the dancer from the dance?", is merely academic; so far as the public is concerned there is only the dancer.

Being a composer (as distinct from author) I am no Music Lover, and when I turn to prose it is to defend my brethren. Of my five-score essays on musical matters over the years, ninety-eight have been on general esthetics or on specific composers. The other two did happen to be on pianists, Julius Katchen and Paul Jacobs, but only because of their service to the music of their time.

For a composer to discuss a superstar performer with charity is a waste of precious space. Our Pavarottis and Perlmans are elsewhere praised too much for a composer to need to add his word. They earn in an evening what he earns in a year, and the evening's fee depends on their personal glow more than on what they illuminate—which is never the work of a living composer. A superstar, and by extension any performer who wants to make it today, is a package of sugarcoated chestnuts.

Since he is 78 and I am 59, chronologically I am nearer to Horowitz than to my twentyish students. However, I'm separated from him by World War One which, since I did not then exist, is vaster than the second war which divides me from them. Also, since they too are composers, the students' woes and prides jibe with mine, while his are those of executant artists who, along with managers and critics, ironically are "the enemy." Yet when Horowitz performs Debussy with that casual precision of the nineteenth-century boulevardier, I am ready, as the French say, to give him the Good Lord without confession.

There is no one way to play a piece, not even the composer's way. There are as many good ways as there are good players. However, Horowitz's right way coincides with my pulse, and one forgives him his reactionary repertory precisely because he *is* a nineteenth-century boulevardier, whereas there is little excuse for the identical repertory of today's prodigies, who are the age of my students. If all works by living composers were suddenly unavailable, there would be absolutely no change in the programs of our most famous soloists and orchestras.

The love–hate reactions in the preceding five paragraphs are all I would have been able to say had I written the review.

The one thing laymen most want artists to talk about is inspiration. The one thing artists most avoid talking about is inspiration. Artists know only too well what Music Lovers don't wish to know: that art is not experience, but the distillation of what is recalled of experience. Art is hard work. We are all inspired but we are not all artists. An artist is like anyone else, but no one else is like him. He is like anyone else, only more so. Inspiration—that is, extreme joy and sorrow—is what an artist checks at the studio door, the better to labor in limbo where his tears won't smudge the ink or his laughter fog the etching plate.

13 March

Switched on the telly just as a young man, labeled simply Gay Activist, flails in the net of another, labeled simply Religious Fundamentalist, and my heart bleeds for both. The G.A. argues that for every stone flung in the Bible there is a gentle word for sinners, while the R.F. contends that to be homosexual is to be more sinful than to be black, since it's a decision more than a condition, and he wouldn't sublet to gays because the majority of Americans are offended by their necking on the front stoop . . . or something. Neither one proposes what to *do* with the poor dears who are still, one supposes, God's creatures. Actually, the G.A. in arguing on fundamentalist terms becomes as coerced as his foe: there is no out.

Slice through the Gordian knot. My tenets, social and moral, are not based on ancient Hebrews translated whimsically by Wasps four centuries ago. Yet the Bible belongs to me as much as to you, and my interpretations are as true as yours—you who also throw stones at the very Jews who stoned queers. It is poetry, not law—certainly not my law, who never harmed a fly. The Bible means whatever its readers choose it to mean.

The question is not what the Bible means. The question is: Why even invoke the Old Testament, which treats the minor question of homosexuality so rarely and so obliquely, rather than invoking common sense? Answer: It suits our purposes. To persecute is satisfying, and the larger the persecution the less need for justification. The great lie carries more weight than the white lie.

14 March

My "condition," as we've come to name it, prevails. Except for insomnia the nights aren't bad. Day scares. I'm less concerned with getting through the night than with getting through the day. I take walks, long walks, in order to detach, to excrete, the pain. It helps a little. But when I return the pain's still there. Are we our shadows? Are our pains us? Or are we the shadows' lodging? With death the shadow remains, but the pains disappear. This evening Dr. Photos will reveal the results of the blood count.

Daron and Robert came to New York for their lessons. Norman, intermittent. He's half dropped-out, after a sort of nervous breakdown several weeks ago.

Long walk in Central Park with Rosemary on this gorgeous day.

Phoned Photos while still at the dinner table with JH and Rosemary. Blood tests okay. I feel suddenly light.

Tomorrow, from dawn until midnight, Stonybrook, for a speech, a class, and a concert of my chamber music.

18 March

Third and final recording session with Roz, twelve hours in all, and twenty-eight songs in the can. The disc will be called *Rosalind Rees sings Ned Rorem*, balancing her Bill Schuman disc of a year ago.

Visit from Gary Miller, founder of New York Gay Men's Chorus, to whom I present finished copy of *Whitman Cantata*. Have I mentioned here that the combined Gay Men's Choruses of the United States are to convene in Manhattan next September for a series of concerts, mostly in Tully Hall, and that for the final concert I have been commissioned to write a piece for *all* the choruses together—about a thousand male voices—which will be in Avery Fisher Hall on September eleventh? The most sensible choice of text seemed Whitman, and the most sensible choice of instruments seemed twelve brass and timpani which (I pray) can hold their own against all those men.

23 March

Last night and again tonight, with Sharon Robinson and Lucy Shelton (both in creamy lace, I in blue velvet), performed *Last Poems of Wallace Stevens* on Jaime's chamber series at the YMHA. Both women sounded even better than they looked, and it's been a joy working with them these past months.

24 March

Searching the *Times* for a review of *Last Poems* I find instead a write-up by Henahan of *The Mother of Us All*, and adjacent to that the ritual paean to Virgil Thomson, by John Rockwell, which seems to appear ever more frequently. Even eliminating the possibility that Virgil will outlive us all, do we really need such frequent puff pieces? If we do need them, why the same old lamentation that his two "great American operas" have yet to be produced by New York's major companies? Why doesn't Rockwell pick up the phone and call Levine and Sills, ask the reason, then write a news release? Maybe the operas just don't belong at the Met.

Inasmuch as I am what I am I can call my sisters faggots and queers if I choose (which I don't) without being accused of bigotry, but I cringe if straight friends use those words (which they don't). Similarly because I'm white I won't say nigger in front of a black (will I behind him?) although if he's queer I may call him a queer to his face, without his cringing. The fragile frontiers beyond which one does not, should not, step. (See Colette's *Le Képi.*)

27 March

Robert Jacobson has forwarded, without comment, a batch of hate mail received by *Opera News*, responding to my article on Strauss. Far from laughing it off, I'm depressed at being misunderstood: are my notions really so unacceptable, or worse, so unclear? Approbatory essays seldom get a rise out of strangers, but from the moment you dare to print a word questioning the inviolability of their *idées reçues* you are punished. "What right has Ned Rorem, that third- or even fourth-rate composer, to criticize Beethoven?" If

I were merely second-rate, would I have the right? If I were first-rate or, indeed, the equal of Beethoven, would I have the right? But if only peers have the right to criticize each other, then what right has the reader to criticize me?

We all have the right to criticize—which doesn't automatically imply we wish to dethrone this or that idol or miscreant so as to put ourself in his place. Music Lovers are frightened of the possibility of clay feet, even in Beethoven. These Music Lovers are often the same that, a priori, hate "modern music."

I'm taken down a peg by one reader because I don't "know how to write—but since he's a composer, he needn't be expected to excel in every area. He doesn't realize what every freshman is taught—that you can't compare nationalities." Well, you can, because I do. My point was not to be dogmatic about countries, but the opposite: I wished to give a new slant (and admittedly a highly personal one) toward an appreciation of Strauss.

28 March

Full moon. JH already left for Nantucket. Phone calls, pick up laundry, buy tea-party goodies.

Visit yesterday from Yvar Mikhashoff and Tom Halpin (the violinist who, at sixteen, sixteen years ago, premiered and recorded masterfully my *Water Music* with the Oakland Youth Orchestra) to discuss a program for next fall in Albany.

This afternoon, delivered corrected proofs of *Whitman Cantata* to B. & H. (they're going to publish it at breakneck speed, octavo format with lavender cover, so that, as decreed by the contract, the thousand male singers will buy their rehearsal copies), and signed fifty comps of *After Reading Shakespeare*, which has just come out in a gray cover with white lettering.

David Drew for tea. He touched not an ounce of the mass of pastries, strawberries & whipped cream, and other offerings. But we spoke exhaustingly of life and its ways, as well as of Kurt Weill.

Tomorrow, Robert Sherman's "Listening Room" in the morning, then the 3:30 plane for the island.

Nantucket
5 April

More and more the daily news is death. Everyone seems to be croaking. Gloria Swanson, pictured on the front page this morning, is recalled for having stated "I'm not much for the past, I'm concerned about tomorrow and what's going on between dreams." An individual's view of his own life is never "wrong"—is, indeed, what gets him through that life. Thus it is not wrong to dwell "too much" on the past. The future, as the clock ticks, shrinks, while the past fans out with its myriad connotations swelling hourly vaster. What we feel about the past therefore swerves with every breath, until we die, when death freezes. What would Paul Goodman, gone eleven years, have made of his theories—though he goes uncredited—being thrown about as dogma? Those theories are now credited to Paul's idol, Wilhelm Reich—who hitherto was uncredited, too—at least this week, because, like Norman Mailer, his book is in the news.

More and more the daily news is sex. It still seems news that, as Reich and Mailer tell us, sex means life, regeneration, the affirmative orgasm. Yet for some, sex means death. Literally. More and more in the daily news is AIDS, and, as with homosexuality itself (about the "cause" of which even the wisest spin no persuasive fact), theological allusions abound. I am wise, wiser perhaps than even Jerry Falwell, yet cannot help wondering (I who don't believe in God) if some chastisement is at work, some cosmic pendulum.

Maybe I've had my share at nearly sixty, but how about the young, the poor old young, since Sex is Death?

Why call them poor, since they, as we once did, will dictate their own rhythm and form new rules, moral and medical, for the end of the century?

New York
8 April

Although Jerry Lowenthal, its Onlie Begetter, played my *Piano Concerto in Six Movements* with a dozen major orchestras around the land during the early 1970s, the piece has lain fallow since then. But we've all known for two years that Jerry was finally signed to give the New York premiere next November with the American Composers Orchestra. Suddenly last winter a squib in the *Times* declared that one Rita Bouboulidi was scheduled to play it May first with the American Symphony in Carnegie Hall.

And who is Rita Bouboulidi? Schonberg told me enough about her, that night at Emily's, for me to feel queasy, but Rose Plaut swears by her genius. Anyway, the piece is published, anyone with an orchestra has a legal right to perform it, and Bouboulidi's swung the local first-performance date.

Today at four I visited Madame Bouboulidi on West 58th to run through the Concerto on two pianos. I was praying she'd be a monument of technique with no feeling. Alas, she was all feeling with no technique. The fast movements were each a third slower than indicated in the score ("But Mr.

Rorem, you don't know the beauty of your own music; if it goes too fast, that beauty will vanish"), and the slow movements were molded out of shape. I was wretched, cool as ice, and she felt it. I told her to practice, and left.

Allegheny College
Meadville, Pa.
13 April

On tour. The semi-chic pudding-faced wives with their graying teased hair and purple wool pants-suits, their marvelous popovers and walnut pies, their utter deference to their husbands and their need for assurances of heterosexuality ("Is there a Mrs. Rorem?"). The singers as mosquitoes, with their female staff accompanists who play forever mezzo-forte and can scarcely stretch an octave. Same scenario north and south.

Aching and feverish, I've been here two days, the penultimate assignment of the goddam Phi Beta Kappa agenda. Tomorrow I'm supposed to materialize somehow at Knox College in Illinois.

Since the hard work on these campuses is quite out of proportion to the fee I usually receive for such visits, the least Phi Beta Kappa should assure is a cordial reception, if not a decent-sized audience. This college is the low point thus far (though I passed a pleasant week here in the spring of 1967, as guest of the late Wright North and his extraordinary chorus). The music department, perhaps at its own request, has been my sole host during the visit. For the speech on Tuesday evening there appeared perhaps thirty-five souls in a hall that seats five hundred. Mr. Robert Bond of the music school met me at the plane, and no representative of Phi Beta Kappa has shown up at any time to say hello.

Poulenc's *Fleurs* is another instance of his improving on that which he shamelessly rifled, in this case Debussy's *De fleurs* from *Proses Lyriques*. Griffes's *Clouds* (1916), meanwhile, glides very close to both these works, and also presages Poulenc's *La Grenouillère* in both tune and harmony.

I weep at Poulenc (but not at Ravel or Couperin or Chopin), because I knew the man.

New York
14 April

Again AIDS, again Mailer. Last night, felled by flu, I canceled Knox College—the first time I've ever put off a professional engagement at the eleventh hour (as last month I canceled the Horowitz review)—fled Meadville, boarded U.S. Air in Erie, and flew sweating back home to New York. On the plane, annual perusal of *Newsweek* and *Time*, the former containing a cover story on the malady, the latter on the novelist.

What is one to make of AIDS, philosophically or morally, or even Moral Majority-ly? Does the smart Gay posit viewpoints more viable than the dumb straight's? Has the bigot yet posited a viewpoint, so stunned must he be by the Lord's literal justice? For natural violence (like the ominous rumblings of the San Andreas Fault about to engulf wicked Hollywood as AIDS now slaughters Sodomites) is ultimately more convincing than humanized violence (like Catherine de Medici engulfing Huguenots as Turks later slaughtered Armenians). By this token the Agadir earthquake which swallowed fifteen thousand needy citizens in fifteen seconds is persuasive: do earthquakes ever swallow the rich? Heterosexual intercourse literally spawns life. But if getting pregnant was to old-fashioned maidens what AIDS is to modern Gays, at least their stigma brought babies, while ours brings corpses.

Time too makes cheerful reading, as in Mailer's remark: "My feeling is . . . homosexuals want to become heterosexual. If you're homosexual, you might have to ask what God thinks of you." What does that mean? Can Mailer, our most famous writer and an alleged thinker, make such claims with neither wit nor nuance? What did I ever do to him? How could he presume such feeling . . . unless . . . but no, perish the thought.

Ah, of course, I'd missed his point. It's irony.

That smart Mailer should rationalize a dumb viewpoint places him in the class as, say, the Podhoretzes whose beliefs one doesn't for a moment believe they believe. But if they don't believe what, as devils, they advocate, why do they advocate? To attract an attention they could not otherwise attract.

16 April

Why has the gay press never, not once, declared the obvious: that *Torch Song Trilogy* is as ghettoized as *The Boys in the Band*? The same critics who today praise Fierstein fifteen years ago at the first flush of the Revolution were quick to quarantine Mart Crowley. If the two plays had historically appeared in reverse order, would we have not found *Torch Song* a stigmatizing of the gay scene, and *The Boys* an amusing, indeed brave, portrait of a period? I've been around but have never known, or even met, a drag queen (except T. C. Jones). Crowley's play is better written, better shaped, and— the main blessing—shorter than Fierstein's sprawling paean to himself.

Fierstein (as evidenced in that abject *Hustler* interview, and elsewhere) is bright in a bratty high-IQ sort of way but has no intellect, no ideas. Crowley had a sense of structure, a sense of contrast. Today's he forgotten. The one interesting thing about *Torch Song*, perhaps inadvertent but still very strong, is the question of a Queen who is also a Jew. Yet now that I think of it, Crowley's pivotal character was a Queen-Jew.

When correcting the proofs for the new edition of *The Paris Diary*, which I have not looked at for a dozen years, I did recognize the author as myself and recognized the unbroken line from there to here. But I also saw what the author was up to, and I did not especially take to him. I—he—painted a self-portrait of an *arriviste*, which in fact I've never been, not at least socially. My chutzpah was buttressed by alcohol, not self-confidence; like most intelligent people I'm scared. The perhaps curious thing about the portrait, however, is the representation of an angel rushing in where even fools fear to tread. Or am I in my dotage simply not recognizing the prerogatives of youth?

22 April

All day Monday in Philadelphia, because the boys, who had a noonday concert of their worthy songs in a church on Walnut Street, later invited me to dine. Meanwhile, tea with Henry McIlhenny, and later with the Ettings.

Is Henry the only American who's rich in the same grandly casual manner of the French in the 1950s? He doesn't pour his own tea (the butler does), or slit open his mail, or, of course, wait on table. On the other hand, he makes no apparent distinction between a bore and a baron, a hustler and a Hapsburg, a famous poet and a student violinist, an old woman and a young man, insofar as these people are guests *chez lui*. Each is given equal time. Even *tête à tête* he's not prone to expressing biases about other humans—at least not negative biases. Of course, taste will out. Virgil once said that a good critic does not voice opinions, he describes; if his description is succinct, accurate and imaginative, the opinion will automatically shine through. Henry's a good critic. In his house, among the Delacroix, Cézannes and Toulouse-Lautrecs, there is no painting by a living artist.

If in the thirty-one years I've known him (through, I think, Stanley Hollingsworth) there's been little hint of how Henry feels about me or my music, he alone is responsible for my early dealings with Ormandy, for which I'm eternally beholden.

Yesterday, big cocktail at Astor Gallery for Elliott Carter, apropos of Schiff's book about him. When I saw Paul Jacobs, alert but hideously ravaged, my impulse was to recoil, so instead I kissed him, in compensation.

Visit from the young men of Red Ozier Press with mock-ups and proofs of *Paul's Blues*. Sylvia to dine. Then to Symphony Space for theatrical program of Peter Maxwell Davies.

25 April

Yesterday afternoon, Sunday, Catharine Crozier's organ recital at Saint Bartholomew, including the *Messe de la Pentecôte* of Messiaen, the composer closest to JH's heart. This is the best performance he's ever heard. Why? Because Crozier makes the music sing and dance, and has the fluency to avoid all that profundity most organists bring to it. Ecstasy may be profound, but it's also freedom and lets you cavort out of your body.

Later, visit from Robert Phelps whom I'd hoped could adapt some texts for the impending Pittsburgh Oratorio as he once did so expertly with *Letters from Paris*. But Mark Twain's prose doesn't seem as urgent for singing as Janet Flanner's. Later, went alone down Central Park West in the rain to Claire Brook's party for the Peter Maxwell Davies machine. *Everyone* there. Judy Arnold, Davies's no-nonsense Maecenas, graciously shoved me aside so as to snap a picture of Max (as he's called) next to Lenny.

Simultaneous visit this afternoon from Daniel Brewbaker and Sheila Silver, youngish composers neither of whom knew the other would be present. I've reached the age where such creatures want my approval, I don't know why; they'd do better with high-powered performers, and I must budget the hours. Tapes of their colorful offerings, Brewbaker's perhaps a bit too Spanish for his Yankee blood, Silver's a touch too willfully modernistic, but both full of music.

26 April

At 3:00, cousins Kathleen and Ted Harbaugh with their son, cellist Ross Harbaugh, and Bernice. Discussion about where a composer's ideas come from. (Experienced performers are as innocent about composers—the very composers they play each day of their lives—as are lay listeners.) Well, I know as much about where my ideas come from as I do about how my insides function, i.e. nothing at all, but try telling this to outsiders who long to hear about inspiration rather than about gossip or facts!

At 7:00, Finnish opera at the Met with Robert Jacobson.

Feeling lousy. (My insides.)

27 April

Maestro Moshe Atzmon, of Israel, who will conduct my concerto Sunday, stopped by to go over the score. I hinted that he might turn it into a Concerto for Orchestra with piano obligato.

At 6 P.M., world premiere by Donald Collup of my *Three Calamus Poems* in Town Hall.

28 April

These people here tonight: Allen and Nina Hughes, Jerry and Ronit Lowenthal, Fred and Rose Plaut, George and Shirley Perle.

Allen's not a bit *triste* at being on the brink of retirement. Fred extinguished, rusty, contributes with difficulty. Rose lovable in her frenzy at "promoting" Poulenc. Nina: suave. Ronit and Jerry: stalwart. (Jerry in a sense is "my" pianist, the way Ricardo Viñes was Albéniz's.)

Talk of City Opera's plans to update *Carmen*. Miss Sills announces that we can't live in the past among museum pieces—"though, of course, we won't touch the music." Why *not* touch the music? Is it so much more sacred than the words?

Incidentally, doesn't the female *Carmen* chorus, "*La cloche a sonné; nous, les ouvrières,*" remind you of Alice Faye's singing of "Every night at eight, when the moon is high"?

A pedant once claimed that the ear cannot follow more than three simultaneous lines (or was it four, or five?). Wouldn't this depend on how terse or how dense each line is, and how differentiated from the other lines? When each line contains the same information, as in a fugue, is that easier or harder to "hear" than the sextet from *Lucia*? Three simultaneous lines of music, which are meant to mesh, aren't the same as three simultaneous lines of spoken conversation.

One earmark of Ives is his use of two contradictory *kinds* of music at the same time. (Donizetti's lines, though differentiated, are not contradictory.) Has Elliott Carter merely carried Ives a step further? Suppose we dismantle his *Symphony for Three Orchestras* and play the sections separately; does it become less of a problem?

Carter as thickened Ives.

May Day (Sunday)

My essay "On Nearing Sixty" in today's *Times*.
Summer weather.

At 3:00, New York premiere of Third Piano Concerto in Carnegie Hall (Bouboulidi, Atzmon, American Symphony Orchestra), better than feared.

At 7:30 with JH to surprise party for Judy Collins at La Pomme at East 61st. Our gift, Isak Dinesen's biography. Dessert, an alcoholized cake, vindicating the Grand Marnier torte I served Judy two or three years ago.

Balanchine died yesterday. Nell Blaine's exhibition at Fischbach.

Friday the thirteenth

Returned from a week in Nantucket but decided against hearing my Flute Trio at Bruno Walter Auditorium. I've heard it. Cold weather. *Setting the Tone* has arrived, handsome, intelligent, with a black & gold cover.

With surprise I read (*Tempo* 149, page 36) that Dallapiccola in honing his three Latin texts for his *Canti di Prigiona* made them very short "to achieve maximum comprehensibility through repetition." With words, repetition does not produce comprehension but rote, and finally gibberish. Shakespeare does not repeat a phrase as Bach repeats a phrase. With words, once tells, twice is questionable, thrice is amateurish, four times is silly. With words-&-music the composer must compromise. There is no example in contemporary song where repetition of phrases not repeated by the poet produces a stronger effect, or a surer "comprehension," than the single statement. Not even in Britten or Perle. Choral music necessarily stretches this rule, since more than one voice (often five or six—or forty!) is stating the same verbal phrase at different, sometimes overlapping, times.

19 May

Saturday, Bronx botanical garden with JH and Frank.

Sunday, drove to Yaddo with JH (his first glimpse) for the inauguration of the Nichols studio, and spent the night but couldn't sleep for JH's snoring. Curt, Hortense, etc. Dark, rainy. Arthritis in both legs.

Monday, fund-raising orgy for WNYC.

Tuesday at 6:00 with Roz gave a little concert, organized by John Myers at Jane Kitzelman's, of songs as memorial for Arthur Cady. John, in tears, maintains that Arthur died from pneumonia contracted during the blizzard at the O'Hara memorial in February.

Wednesday, annual confusion at the Academy, attended because Convery and Hagen were bestowed with Ives awards. Dined then chez Chuck Turner with Monroe Wheeler (at eighty as entrancing and intelligent as when we met at Marie Laure's thirty years ago) and others.

Today, lunch (quiche and salad) with Faith Sale who has replaced the fired
Tom Miller, as far as my book's concerned, at Coward-McCann's. Which
means *Setting the Tone* could sink from sight: what's in it for her? At 3:30 Jack
Shoemaker showed up with copies of *The Paris and New York Diaries* which
look and *feel* sumptuous in the acid-free North Point Press edition. Jack and
Faith exchanged my books. At 5:30, visit from Frank Campbell, Richard
Jackson, and Thor Wood, cast of the Library of Performing Arts. They'd like
to have my papers, but only if I sign a guarantee. It seems that Virgil deposited *his* papers with their library, then withdrew them when Yale offered
cash. At 7:30, dined at Virgil's.

24 May

Friday, with Chuck Turner to Ensemble Studio Theater, in the wastes of
West 52nd, in search of plays to be turned into librettos. These plays (snap-
pily sordid vignettes by Mamet and Ringkamp) are too tight, self-sufficient
and earthy to need singing. You sing when speech is no longer enough—
about love, death, the weather; nothing else.

Saturday, *Quérelle*. Totally faithful to the novel in that each scene is scru-
pulously emulated; totally unfaithful in that the essence is Germanized (despite the American hero). Fassbinder's as strong as Genet. Loved every
minute.

(Sunday and Monday Charles Wadsworth, for the record, performs *Winter Pages* in Charleston.)

Monday (last night) these came to dine: Jaime Lardeo & Sharon Robinson, Earl Wild & Michael Davis, Lillian Libman & Alice Tully. Alice was an
hour late, having lost the address, and her arrival changed the complexion
of the assembly from casual to respectful. I'm a bad host. A party should
either be an occasion for settling questions (questions of making out, sexually or professionally), in which case it needs a referee like Diaghilev, or an
occasion for old friends to gossip. This was neither, lacked center, fell flat,
and I'm no m.c.

Today, visit at four from David Kalstone to discuss Elizabeth Bishop's ar-
chives at Vassar and to provide him with a stash of letters. At eight, Otto
Luening's concert at the old Juilliard on Claremont, with at least one wondrous piece. Twenty-two flutists arranged themselves in a circle around the
audience, then began to warble, entering one by one, consecutively, until
all twenty-two had turned the hall into an aviary of whistling delight. Then,
one by one, they dropped out, and all disappeared.

JH has driven to Nantucket with all the cats in the new truck. Tomorrow,
with Rosemary, to Cadbury with a large box of candy for Mother who, un-

derstandably because of the acceptable but bland institutional diet, craves sugar. (Was it fifteen years ago?—Maggy Magerstadt asked us all to tea for which she'd made a cake, accidentally using salt instead of sugar. Before Maggy had noticed her error, Mother, then on a salt-free diet, gobbled the cake up with alacrity.)

"What effect is this music meant to produce on the audience?"
   "The effect this music is meant to produce on the audience is the effect it does produce on the audience."
   This is my remembrance after thirty years of an exchange between Pierre Boulez and a member of "the audience" at a program of electronic pieces in the MacMillan Theater. *Malin.*

Nantucket
1 June

On the plane here this afternoon, read the huge piece in "The Magazine Section" by Tim Page on David Del Tredici. A plum for DDT, and a plum for Tim who's not yet corrupted by it all, not quite. Yet criticism sags today because of preoccupation with trends to the exclusion of individuals. DDT doesn't think of himself as a New Romantic any more than John Ashbery thinks of himself as a New York Poet. But critics cram these artists—these individuals—into a pigeonhole, then assign themselves to define the pigeon rather than the artist. What once may have inflamed a critic and caused him to write tellingly—his enthusiasm for the unique élan of a single soul—is replaced by an assignment: cover the general movement, not the singular statement. And criticism dulls.

My suicide note will read: Can no longer bear the mediocrity. That I myself may (in life as in art) have contributed to that mediocrity in no way lessens the burden. But my standards were high.
   The *noise* of mediocrity.

Dined last night with Francine and Cleve Gray and the Borchardts in Andrée's Mediterranean restaurant on East 74th. Francine as unaware sexist: "Just as homosexuals were on the verge of universal acceptance, along comes AIDS. A doctor from Penn says that in three years, AIDS will have spread to the general population." Meaning: there are homosexuals, and there is the general population, and "they" will give "us" AIDS. One wants to answer: "Like you gave us syphilis."

3 June

Such identity as we have left to the world is, bit by bit, being dissipated and replaced. "We," of course, means those few—those happy few—singers who know the art of song. Such as Donald Gramm. Who else?

Last night Shirley phoned to say that Donald Gramm was dead. Today, more calls, plus the cold, confirming obit in the *Times*. I'm no less puzzled than sad. Why Donald? If the world seems still brimming with heavenly voiced superstars who, as far as glamour and panache go, sing rings around Donald (but this isn't true: he had panache and glamour too), there is not one living male singer active in the world today with his repertory and with his intelligence in projecting that repertory.

As I felt eleven years ago at Paul Goodman's funeral—Who's left to write poems for me to set for Donald to sing?—so I feel now with Donald. Who's left to sing anything? Of course I know that, in the realest sense, for all of us, music will be the sole salvation tomorrow. Yet today I feel that, with Donald out of the world, there is no music left.

18 June

Nothing to write about, for the simple reason that I've been writing the only thing that matters, music (the big Pittsburgh Oratorio, with anxious pleasure), and music can't be written about, since it writes itself.

Usual procession of delicious or torturous pre-summer days, more or less undifferentiated, except that now, out of the blue, Peter Mennin has died. I remember meeting him at his first appearance in New York, when he won the Gershwin Memorial Award in 1945. We've been irregular but staunch colleagues ever since. What happens now to Juilliard? Peter was exactly my age.

Reading *The Tragic Muse* with a rekindled feeling for Henry James. As a model for every corner of life in the theater it could have been written yesterday, and in style it's a model not only for Proust and (ahead of his time) Balzac but, yes, Ronald Firbank. How else can we take Gabriel Nash's first *réplique* when we meet him in the museum: "But surely we've diverged since the old days. I adore what you burn; you burn what I adore"?

One oddly wondrous aspect of Marie Laure, among her myriad wondrously odd aspects, was that she was, so far as I could ascertain, the sole French person who had not only *heard* of Henry James when I first knew her in 1951, but was reading him systematically, in English (was he even translated then?), volume by volume, in the so-called New York Edition in green leather, which was kept in a special case on the south wall of the smaller library of her Château Saint Bernard in Hyères. Marie Laure's enthusiasm infected me (before then, I'd read only *The American* and *Turn of the Screw*), but I scarcely matched her, in either speed or depth, as she came to the end of the two-year feat and then began all over again.

1 July

Reading *The Asiatics*. It's too close for comfort to much of Paul Bowles's early prose, not only in tone, which is of the cool American adventurer in the hot carnality of utter exotica, but even in mirroring certain rare images (for example, a Ceylonese house surrounded by ten thousand leeches, erect and slithering toward the front door), yet Prokosch's book predates Bowles by a decade. Suddenly, and perhaps unfairly, Paul's writing, which has always dazzled me, seems diminished.

Nanctucket
The Fourth of July

The French have no sense of humor, David Susskind and Anthony Burgess are all too quick to agree. The proof? Some literal-minded Parisian critic who was not amused by a generality Burgess wrote about the French many years ago. Much as I freely criticize the French, I resent another who has not, as it were, earned the right to do so. Can stodgy Mr. Susskind truly claim that the land of Molière and Jacques Tati, of Fernandel and Feydeau, lacks humor? It's like fraternity hazers who, inflicting tortures, admire the pledges who can "take it"—who have a sense of humor. When we reproach another's lack of humor, what we really mean is that their humor isn't our humor. Is there, in fact, any individual, let alone nationality, devoid of humor? If humor means seeing three sides to one coin, of finding irony even in horror, then surely such objectivity isn't the same for Arabs as for Parisians (although Jews did invent the sick joke). Even "advanced" nations, as well as families within these nations, are disparate in their whimsy. Americans like jokes about excretion (the word *shit* is always good for a laugh), the French about infidelity (whereas *we* scarcely know the word cuckold), and the Germans about food (ach, a German joke is no laughing matter). Burgess has maybe earned the right, and he's quick and smart, if repetitious, and he does now live in Monaco. Yet when he asks Susskind if he knows the definition of an Irish homosexual—"a man who prefers women to drink"—no one knows quite how to react.

Laughter. Do I laugh? Sometimes still I'll get the giggles, with JH or Shirley. But rolling on the floor? The last time I recall having an uncontrollable *fou rire* was in 1951 at Maurice Gendron's cruel imitations of friends (cruel, because literal). Well, Maurice was French. Yes, but he was also Jewish, or so he claimed. Though of course laughter, in itself, has nothing to do with humor.

Eulogies at funerals should stress the gain as well as the loss. If X, in leaving us, leaves also a vacuum, the fact of X's contribution is (since we love and miss him) an unduplicatable fullness: his art.

10 July

The process of selection of text, in choral writing as in songs and opera, is for me half the battle. Musical composition comes easily; it's what to compose *about* that's the rub. For the Pittsburgh Oratorio, as I'm settling on Early American words that will form a stream from childhood through middle age to the grave, I'm stumped by the childhood part. Witty, childly verse existed in nineteenth-century England (Lewis Carroll, Edward Lear) but not in America—or at least my senses don't recognize it. Emerson claimed that "as we go back in history, language becomes more picturesque, until in its infancy, when all is poetry." Couldn't one argue that poetry has nothing of infancy? Poems are the ultimate skimming off. Pure sparseness, which children never possess, defines art. Removal and irony are needed for poems, and the art of old America was still too young for youth.

   After deciding on texts the composition was not—never is—a problem, merely a chore. What didn't I use? Sarah Orne Jewett, Henry James's *Tragic Muse* (perhaps a harangue therefrom), Richard Howard's Baudelaire translations, Oscar Wilde. But I did use Twain. That ragged chunk of prose torn bleeding from *Life on the Mississippi* attracted me for its *déjà vu* rapport with my play, *The Pastry Shop*, about the doctor's obsession with his patient's insides. *Plus ça change . . .*

There are three sorts of program notes as supplied, after the fact, by the composer: the inspirational, the analytical, the gossipy. All three are suspect, since musical actions speak louder than words. But gossip is doubtless most useful to historians because it doesn't purport to explain what only the music, by definition, can explain.

If we must speak of inspiration, let's say: Art starts where inspiration stops. Art is the freezing of, the distilling and dispensing and forgetting of, vulgar inspiration. The freezing cannot be effected while under the giddy spell.
   Perspiration, fever, ice.

An artist declares: "I never repeat myself: that way lies sterile boredom," and the public thrills: an artist never repeats himself! Well, you know and I know and *they* know that the declaration is pure bunk. An artist may consciously try to avoid self-imitation, yet it's not for him to know, finally, whether in fact he succeeds. There is no new thing under the sun. Not to say the same thing twice is impossible, although it can be said in different ways. The best of us have no more than four or five ideas during our whole life; we spend that life chiseling those ideas into various communicating shapes. That sentence states one of *my* four or five ideas, and I've said it over and over.

My own four or five? They're different in prose from those in music, since prose deals with thought and music does not. To some extent I judge a composer by his scope, and his scope by his speed. He who can write fast- and slow- and medium-speeded music (music, which is *inherently* these) is more estimable than he who can write only inherently slow, or fast, or . . . etc.

Pauline Kael phoned from Great Barrington to approve of the vignette in *Harper's* where I defend Lenny Bernstein from the canards of one Leon Botstein. (Odd, since Pauline let Lenny have it for *West Side Story* and no love's lost. Then again, not so odd.) Botstein, who happens to run Bard College, is maybe too young to know that he takes the same moralizing tack that friends and foes have taken for forty years: criticizing Lenny for being Lenny—"if Lenny didn't spread himself so thin he might amount to something." Botstein's "accusations" are posited as givens, and along the way he pulls some specious boners: that Lenny's view of the past is necessarily an affectation because he did not personally *know* the past; that he has done less for music than—of all people—Stern and Serkin; that his service to contemporary music is limited; and that he "reveals no passion for permanence, only for applause." Nothing is easier than to criticize an artist for being what he is not and for small fry like Botstein to lay down the rules to which his betters must bend. *Harper's* printed my little note revealing Leonard Bernstein through a broader lens.

How do I see myself? Just as when, in writing music, I've never—not even in the fever of youth—been especially explorative, but have tried instead to keep my head above water solely through the plying of my unique expressivity, so, when writing *about* music, I've never sought to pass as a Thinker (like, say, Lenny, who takes a year out of his life to crack the code of music's origins—and ultimately of music's arch-meaning—complementing Chomsky's code for language); I've tried instead to gear my verbal statements to muckraking—that is, to setting matters straight. These matters do sometimes graze a Thinker's proposition, which I feel impelled to question. (For instance, when the poetic Lenny quotes the pedestrian Chomsky's *zeugma*, "The whole town was populated by old men and women," an example of "transformational deletion" presumably negotiated internationally by the Collective Unconscious, which automatically supplies the adjective "old" to women as well as to men, and when Lenny proceeds to show us how a page from *Petrushka*, without words, parallels this *zeugma*, I must point out that the verbal phrase has no equivalent in French, where both men and women require a separate adjective modified to their genders. Thus Chomsky's linguistics topple, and Bernstein's Unanswered Question remains unanswered.)

More often the matters are personal quandaries (How can a whole planet become brainwashed by a Carter or a Boulez?), or personal enthusiasms voiced in analytical love letters to this or that musician and published in *Opera News* or *Christopher Street*.

But thinker or muckraker or letter writer, I'm first a composer who writes, not a writer who composes. If as a sometime teacher I have learned by arranging my thoughts into verbally communicative order or by simply shutting up and listening to pupils, or if as a prose writer I have learned by dint of research or self-questioning into and about love and death and the weather, this learning has not—no, not ever, not the least little bit so far as I consciously know—altered the quality or even the shape of my music.

26 July

My first songs were not, as I've oft stated, the setting of Cummings at Northwestern in 1940, but settings of Bruce Phemister, of Amy Lowell, of my own puerile verses, circa 1937. Among the latter I recall the Frostian

> I walked around our grounds last night.
> Nothing's new except the gardener's dead.
> As Mother said,
> "We'll have to be getting a new one soon,
> the tulips haven't grown."
> And he's alone.

And I recall my own mother's gentle anxiety on reading the poem.

Cynthia Ozick's essay on Forster is worthless because, beneath that intimidating didacticism, her conclusions are not based on logic but on a knowledge of God's will—*her* God—and because she purports to know Forster's unstated thoughts (and to offer them as proven displays) about his own guilty trembling in the face of a heterosexual Almighty.

She does bring up the interesting but never-much-discussed question of an outsider's responsibility toward minority persecution. "I am not a homosexual," she writes; "if I had been in England in 1935, should I not have been disturbed by the law that interfered with the untrammeled publication of *Boy*, as Forster was? . . . Liberalism, to be the real thing, ought to be disinterested." (She is talking about Forster's magnanimity toward heterosexual concerns in his books before *Maurice*.) "It is no trick, after all, for a Jew to be against anti-Semitism, or for a homosexual to be against censorship of homosexual novels. The passion behind the commitment may be pure, but the commitment is not so much a philosophy of liberalism as it is of self-preservation." Well, what's the difference if the results are effective? Yet she certainly denies Forster any benefit of the doubt. Has any Gentile worked with the zeal of an Ozick on the ramifications of the Holocaust? As a matter of fact, yes: Sartre. Also, Gide and André Dubois were instrumental in the escape of multitudes of Jews from France. (But perhaps their motives were impure, since both were goys and both were gay.) Do any straights work with honest commitment for gays? Why yes, even today in government, with the AIDS question. (But perhaps the motives are impure, since the work is for the protection of heterosexuals against the dread disease.) Does any Professional Jew make sensible statements about Professional Gays?

Once I wrote to this effect: It's easier to do good deeds than to think good deeds. Actions *do* speak louder than thoughts.

In which of these resides the weaker virtue: the convinced anti-Semite (or anti-Gay) who, in his guilt, labors against the suffering of the minority while retaining his conviction; or the unprejudiced citizen who, in his untainted magnanimity, never does more than sign petitions? Who is less despicable—the paternalistic slave-owner, or the abolitionist who neglects to work for the underground railroad?

Ozick's essay dates from 1971, and a lot of water etc. Would she now be more, or less, virulent?

"Be fruitful and multiply," we are admonished. Well, I am more than just fruitful, I am a fruit. And surely the dozens of works poured forth each decade are multiplications of myself; if they in turn do not reproduce that is because, like any work of art, they are self-contained ends in themselves (although, taken up by students and historians and other composers, they spread their influence—their *seed*—and one thing leads to another). Has Norman Podhoretz reproduced himself?

Meanwhile today, 1983 (*Christopher Street* 73), Seymour Kleinberg writes of "The Jew as Homosexual." Very persuasive, original (to me). Needs expanding. His frightening statement that "the position of homosexual men and women in America has begun to resemble the condition of Jews in Europe before the rise of fascism" is not too clearly substantiated. Although he speaks of rednecks in general, the only *individuals* (all intellectuals) he chooses to cite as homophobes are Jews: Podhoretz, Epstein, Greenfeld, Decter, et alia. Are these Jews the pre-fascist threat he invokes? Who are the gentile homophobes? I doubt that capitalist literary goyim are, on the whole, very concerned with homosexuality one way or the other.

Since writing the above I've pulled out the few long letters from Cynthia of seven years ago. What friendliness they exude, what energy. And her stories—what wild plotting, what precise insanity. But I'd forgotten how our correspondence abruptly ceased because of what she termed "a conceptual polar vastness yawning between us." When she wrote, apropos of my review of *Jesus Christ Superstar*, that "the Judas figure has been the curse and filth of Western so-called civilization," and that "the passion play instantly suggests what historically it accomplished, instigation of pogrom, massacre, slaughter, fire and blood," I answered that Christianity did spring from Judaism, and that no genre is in itself invalid. Did she know that within Eastern Orthodox sects Judas is considered the greatest sufferer insofar as he was forced to execute, against his logical will, what was prewritten? And then despite this act, he was denied sanctity, though he performed God's will? Cynthia said, "The art invented by Ilse Koch—lampshades made of tattooed human skins—is invalid." Of course I wouldn't call that an art, or even a genre. And God forbid that I argue anything in the name of God, Christian or otherwise.

It would be nice to see Cynthia again. I can only love anyone who refers, as she does, to "the good ghost of Paul Goodman."

Jews, more than Catholics or American WASPs, seem to feel a loathing for homosexuality, and the reason "we" give is that they are weaned on the irrational (poetical?) Old Testament. Yet I too feel homophobic at times (to persecute is satisfying, etc.), as, indeed, I feel heterophobic, although the phobia is strictly toward the bodily act which, in each case, when viewed from afar or from a-near, is less ugly than just silly. Penile or vaginal or anal close-ups on the big screen resemble bowls of fruit or twisted ears more than

carnal rapture; and anyone "in sex," like anyone in love, be it Beethoven or
Betty Boop, is as dull to outsiders, be they straight or gay.

But misery does not love company, nor do minorities wish to share their
martyrdom. Gore Vidal's wise admonition notwithstanding—that since
Jews, whatever their prejudices, "are going to be in the same gas chambers
with blacks and faggots, I would suggest a cease-fire and a common front
against the common enemy"—Jewishness and homosexuality appear mutually exclusive. An unquestioned unity of the two conditions becomes a
trouvaille, as in *Torch Song Trilogy*.

Why so cranky?

O dear, am I? I thought charm was exuding. Possibly through public notes
and private prose I'm getting even with those kids who beat me up during
gym, although today, like those outside Hawthorne's "narrow circle," they
remain unaware or are dead. As to what lies ahead: Once I posited the banal
notion that Strauss, though older than Debussy, closed the nineteenth century, while Debussy opened the twentieth. Actually Debussy, like each one
of us, marked the end of a certain kind of thinking. Is there reason to doubt
that our whole millennium, since the advent of notated sound, is at a close?
Yes, there is reason, for no one perceives his own history.

Nantucket
1 August

Am returned from three nights in the dreamlike steam of a summery Baton
Rouge where Martin Katz and I (although we scarcely had a moment to greet
each other) conducted what are named Master Classes in the dying art of
what is called Art Song. During my spare minutes, and on the plane, I read
Russell Baker's memoir the title of which is just one word short of Paul
Goodman's classic *Growing Up Absurd*.

Russell Baker is the most famous man on this island. Nevertheless, at my
"signing" in Mitchell's Bookstore a fortnight ago Russell waited dutifully in
the (short) line, having paid cash for both my new volumes. Since I hardly
know him, I was touched, and naturally I bought *his* book. How different we
are. Wholesome Russell, raised in that irreproachable Lincoln-like poverty
which in America is in itself a medal; decadent me, representing—as Philippe Erlanger once said—everything a mother would not want her son to
grow up to be. Yet his anecdote, germane to "our" generation (indeed he's
twenty-two months younger than I), about selling the products of Curtis
Publishing is not far from mine. When Father wanted me to get a sense of

responsibility, I too had my loathsome paper route. Father at first accompanied me from a distance, later advising me to change my spiel: "You don't want to buy a *Saturday Evening Post*, do you?"

Wallace is pushing eighteen. His bones show, his epilepsy is still triggered by any regular hum or beat, and he's deaf as a post. Yet his charm shines through the slow brain like a star of good hope, and he never, unlike Sam and Princess, complains. Are those flea eggs behind his ears—those specks resembling coffee grounds? JH says that during his breakdown several years ago, Wallace's compassion was his sole consolation. When JH embraced Wallace then he embraced also the fleas. Are fleas our brothers? Where to draw the line? Perhaps the whole universe is just a fat tear in the eye of a giant too vast to perceive.

4 August

Why, asks Moira, is there no index to your diary?

Answer: For the same reason's there's no dedication. Such accoutrements imply a finished, self-contained work, like a novel or even an anthology of other people's poems. A diary is without start or stop, that is the genre. Even if I felt that my example of the genre is self-contained and finished—which I do—the illusion would be shattered by an index. (In 1966 when *The Paris Diary* first appeared, Lenny Bernstein did say there should be an index of people, with a plus or a minus sign beside each name.)

6 August

A young composer came to call, bringing a sheaf of scores and cassettes, for he hoped to be accepted at Curtis. My heart skipped a beat at the sight of this six-foot Apollo with his guileless intelligence arrayed before me. Alas! the music showed no promise—flat, military, Haydnesque. I was not encouraging. After he left, the room retained his outdoorsy smell, and the smell of his disappointment. But was I not once him? No, for I had something to say. Still, I felt badly, and missed him. We'll never meet again.

> I undertook to overtake
> the undertaker taking over . . .

This in a dream last night, wherein it mattered so.

Critics dish it out, but never seem able to take it.
(Write of tiffs with Virgil, with Henahan, with Rockwell.)
I long for silence.

Peace piece.
Walt's waltz.
Fortunes for tunes.

11 August

Virgil Thomson, comparing Carter to Copland in the role as Great Man: "When Aaron reached the top, at least he sent the elevator back down."

Re the expensive confusion of heterosexual doctors in their current battle against AIDS: They ask Haitians "Are you homosexual?" rather than "Have you ever had homosexual relations?" The two states can be mutually exclusive. Certainly Moroccan males, most of whom have had many same-sex experiences, never consider themselves homosexual. Ditto the macho Haitians.

(Baton Rouge) Re the DEKEs' trial for pledges: with their football cleats they stamp to death hundreds of baby chicks, covering the dining room floor with blood. That's North American macho.

Until an Absolute is established as to what defines "good music," I will retain my right to call trash certain works of Beethoven: The Emperor, the Appassionata, the end of the Ninth.

1 September

I'm so insecure that I won't approach my post-office box unless I'm armed with letters to be mailed (which could, to outsiders, look like letters received), for fear that the box will be empty and that people will point a finger and say: Nobody writes to him. Actually, the box is often jam-packed. (Actually, the box is often empty.) Actually, the box is often jam-packed with junk mail. (Actually, I loathe getting letters, since I'm compelled to reply to them all on the spot.) Actually, knowing that these sentences may someday be read by other eyes, I can claim I'm insecure and not be believed. But I *am* insecure.

Why, with all of Gay Lit's foraging for "sisters" of yore—specifically with the exposé now of Mann's diary—have they not cited Stefan Zweig, and especially Zweig's troubling and persuasive *Confusion des sentiments?*

2 September

Marie-Laure's been more than usual in mind because of the Weill essay I'm trying to compose, and because of James Lord's unusual "A Giacometti Portrait" which, on being reread, revives intact a valuable scene of yore.

In 1952 Marie Laure spent most of her days trying to keep Oscar Dominguez sober and most of her nights trying to get him drunk. Anxious to hold him at all costs, and sick with jealously, she tried every ploy that her wit and fortune and no-longer-young-but-ever-naïve body could drum up. I will never forget an image manifested toward two o'clock one summer morning in Hyères. I was still in the downstairs salon orchestrating, the sliding doors drawn shut against mosquitoes. I assumed Marie Laure was long since abed, or perhaps up in the tower studio with O.D. I raised my head at the squeak of the doors sliding open just wide enough to frame the Vicomtesse, blue hair askew, ashy face unsmiling, cobalt peignoir swathing her mad dignity. In a child's voice she announced: *Oscar m'a enculée.*

Back from our biweekly trek to the town dump which always reminds me of the moonlike beaches of Safi thirty-four years ago or perhaps of our entire continent thirty-four years hence. Am reminded too of that afternoon when the poet picked me up at the airport. As we drove toward town in his tiny Toyota—him at the helm, jet-haired and emerald-eyed and cherry-lipped and butch, with ruddy heterosexual biceps—I grew aware of an excremental odor. Realizing that this was the poet's breath, pervasive even when I turned away, I dreaded his every utterance of golden verbs.

A colleague farts. He is a thin, intelligent pedagogue, learned and likable. But yes, he farts. He does so silently every four minutes, and, when conferring with him for any period, there's no getting away from it.

During the Cavett years I twice observed actresses (once Lilli Palmer, the other time Diana Rigg) attempting wit through scatological or halitosisical description. Sex and overeating in a pinch will just do, maybe, but foul odors never. Those actresses are forever tainted in my mind, and so would be—if I did not know him—the author of these three paragraphs.

Labor Day

Summer's suddenly vanished, and what's there to show for it?

Well, during July, I finished *An American Oratorio*, or at least the piano-vocal score. (During the next several months I'll copy and orchestrate the monster—a vast, hand-wrenching chore.) July, as it happens, contained a houseful of guests. Like eighteenth-century female novelists I was constrained to create on the sly. Thus, because the act of seeking the inevitable note is so intimate, I avoided the piano and composed mostly in silence, with the train of thought continually derailed. (Conjecture: If artists concoct in a certain way according to circumstances like love or ulcers or houseguests, would their results necessarily be otherwise without these distractions?) One of the guests was Robert Page, head of the Mendelssohn Choir and commissioner of the piece, who made a special trip to check on the progress. (Between his phone call and, a fortnight later, his arrival, I wrote most of the music.) He approves. A relief. With JH we agreed on the title, which despite emanations of 1930s patriotism, seems the most fitting of the dozen we played with.

Besides Page there's been Sylvia, Chuck, George Cree and Leonard Raver (who's writing an essay on my organ catalogue). Also Frank's sister, Judy, and mother, Mrs. Benitez, thoughtful, discreet and helpful. Daytime guests have included, of course, Eugenie, Mimsi Harbach, Danny Pinkham ("Are you Jewish?" he asks Mrs. Benitez, who is black), Rosette, Maggie and Frank Conroy, Henry and Olga Carlisle, Mary Heller, Martha Lipton, and Frank and Cynthia Stewart of Cincinnati.

The zinnias came and went. So did a photographer who took my picture among the roses for *Vanity Fair* next month, apropos of my birthday. Edwin Denby committed suicide rather than drift into the indignities of old age.

Read Barbara Pym, but not exhaustively. Lots of movies and backgammon. Trouble, as always, with left eye and elsewhere. Visits from John Wulp who, with Mimsi, is plotting a party—which makes me uneasy—for my birthday.

Thursday I return to New York for the premiere of *Whitman Cantata*, and then to Philadelphia to get the Curtis classes under way.

New York
9 September

Where do you find space to rehearse nearly a thousand singers plus a brass orchestra with drums? On the top floor of the Statler, that's where, and there I went this morning for the first combined runthrough of the nine Gay Men's Choruses, each of which has presumably been rehearsing *Whitman Cantata* for weeks in its respective city.

The music was already under way when I arrived. Seated in a series of connecting salons with their doors thrown open was an army of men, their backs to me, singing my sounds as I made my way through them toward the podium where Gregg Smith was weaving his able arms in an effort at mass hypnosis. When I was introduced, the assembly rose as one and applauded with the force and the warmth of a great minority celebrating one of their own. The effect was more than one of mere appreciation: it was erotic, like being embraced by a vast male cloud. I was all the more moved in that every one of them was a non-professional, and for some the learning of my piece (to them difficult, even incomprehensible) could have seemed a burden.

The festival, which has been running all week, is called C.O.A.S.T. (Come Out And Sing Together), and my work was commissioned for the final concert along with ones for more modest forces by Libby Larsen and Calvin Hampton. Later in the day I twice observed, in different parts of town and from a distance, members of these visiting choirs whom I recognized by the lavender scores they were carrying. (B & H rushed the music into print several months ago.) By this sign shall ye know them.

Not with *l'esprit* but with *le remords de l'escalier* I wince at facts destroyed: the witty pornography of Bill Flanagan's letters in the 1950s and 60s because I thought it might be incriminating; the tape on which Joe Adamiak professed his love and that he sent to Utah in 1965, because I thought it might be incriminating; the many, many pencil manuscripts which, once copied onto transparent music paper, I tossed into the incinerator, because what more use had they? Living voices dead.

Setting the Tone has appeared as the lead front-page feature of both the *Washington Post*'s "Book World" and the *Los Angeles Times*'s "Sunday Book Review," not to mention dozens of other reviews across the land, all of them "sellable." Coward-McCann, meanwhile, far from having spent one nickel on an ad, has not even sent me copies of these reviews (I know about them from faithful friends), much less a one-sentence message of good will.

18 September

The premiere of *Whitman Cantata* occurred as climax to tonight's too-long program in the jam-packed Avery Fisher Hall in the middle of a heat wave. I will never forget the sight as, slowly, close to a thousand men emerged onto the stage like a hemorrhage to intone this work with twelve brass and timpani. What did I learn? That the instrumental group could more than hold its own against a thousand voices, and that a thousand voices are not ten times louder than a hundred, only ten times hazier. The most beautiful sounds were the hushed dewy unisons.

19 September

When Daron announced that Norman Stumpf had killed himself, my instant reaction was guilt: had I pressed too hard? Not listened enough? What did I know of Norman since he dropped out last winter? He broke down in the Curtis lobby a month or so after the pressures of the November concert and was an outpatient during the second semester. I saw him for only two or three lessons, during which the task of writing music—of putting notes on paper—seemed insurmountable. The world in which he lived was to me a mystery, and it drew him fatally closer, who can dream at what cost in suffering. I've written his parents, but what good's that. The school seems in a cloud, and the thought of Norman's youth so tormented, and the trusting eyes, is . . .

22 September

Tuesday, stopped by the Kurt Weill Foundation for scattered bits of data for the *Opera News* essay. The foundation's run by Lys Bert Symonette who was almost the first to sing songs of mine in public four decades ago. Today we both teach at Curtis. . . . Visit from a mezzo named Nelda Nelson. Then from Edouard Roditi whose precious annual stopovers are coveted.

Wednesday, with Morris to *Galas*, my first Ludlam experience. Truly funny, truly sad. (Truly, because the wit was integral and developing, as in *Galas*'s competitive audience with the Pope, or in her seemingly narcissistic, but actually arch-generous, need for death.) We laughed, something I seldom do.

Today, started my sittings for Maurice Grosser's brush and canvas.

24 September

Yesterday autumn began. Rehearsal of *Winter Pages*, with brand-new set of instrumentalists, for the Friedheim competition.

Tonight, Virgil T. and Maurice Grosser came to dine. Also Frank Benitez. Our paintings are dulling, so what should we do? I'll show you, said Maurice, and, dipping a soft cloth into a bowl of one part vinegar and five parts cold water, he cleaned a square foot on the lower left-hand corner of Leonid's *Dawn with Mussel Cultivators*. Like most specialists (and his three books on painting are the best in the business), Maurice doesn't mince over his craft. But now we're stuck with this clean square foot on a canvas of nineteen other square feet that are dirty, and we daren't start rubbing them ourselves.

25 September

Death of Paul Jacobs.

Nantucket
1 October

Have come to the island via Indiana State University in Terre Haute, where a three-day festival of modern music (annual even there) unfurled works by me and three "younger" composers, Jan Swafford, Donald Grantham and Larry Stukenholtz. Two big cycles, *Poèmes pour la Paix* and *Women's Voices*, were intoned by Nelda Nelson (wife of John Eaton), and William Henry Curry, assistant conductor of the Indianapolis Symphony, did *Sunday Morning* (its best performance so far) with that orchestra. When I learned that no mandolin was available for the crucial "Our Insipid Lutes" movement, I insisted that a mandolinist be jet-propelled from Indianapolis. I enlarged the part for him, and the enlargement will stay. Lectures, classes, panels, interviews, rehearsals, meals with faculty. What I like best about these stints is the final visit to the best house on campus, in this case the President's, filled with friendly "folks" and suites of wide rooms.

The summer's been thick with musicians' deaths. Other than those mentioned, there've been Claus Adam, Carroll Glenn, Nadia Reisenberg, Jerry Morross, Willy Horne.

6 October

My observation, that European opera has always been composed by their "advanced" chromatic composers and American opera by our "reserved" diatonic composers, is continually substantiated. Not Elliott Carter nor yet John Cage, but Philip Glass and Stephen Paulus keep the ball rolling here.

Heavy feeling in pit of stomach as I come across unanswered love letters and sexy snapshot from intelligent M.H. in Holland. Is it too late now to reply, thirty-two years later?

8 October

Far from receiving first place in the Freidheim Awards this evening, I am given next-to-last place—an honorable mention. George Perle phones to tell me this at midnight. I didn't recognize the winner's name. Thank God I didn't go to Washington to attend this farce, where established composers are played off against each other like Miss America contenders. After a point there is no "best." George and I are not "better than" each other, for the simple reason that we are doing different things.

10 October

Rosemary has gone, this morning on the ferry in an icy fog, after three days of fraternity and communication on a non-verbal level. Verbally I seem compelled to pooh-pooh her enthusiasms in ways she can't refute (verbally), as I do with pupils. Is it arrogance or sadism or anxiety lest she not "admire" me? But, in retrospect, my style is inexcusable. She is, after all, at sixty-one, just trying to get along.

Rosemary wonders if perhaps she wasn't "loved enough" as a child. Does anyone ever feel he was loved enough? The reason first chapters of all autobiographies are boring is that they center on the sensitive unloving childhood of the author. Nobody's ever loved enough, or even loved, on his own terms. We learn what to say: it gets us through life; better, we learn what not to say.

TV documentary on Balanchine. The time has come for somebody to decry the unchallenged sanctification of this man. Why is he so ordinary? Where's the invention, or even the viewpoint, that makes his "steps" for Gershwin different, if they are, from those for Mozart? Turn off the sound and it's the same thing.

Occasionally I have "come around" to certain artists: Brahms, Beckett, Ingmar Bergman. But only two artists have I long admired, then felt the admiration abate: Paul Bowles (via Prokosch, who eclipsed him), and Balanchine.

New York
18 October

Were it not that it's how I earn a living, I might with conviction renounce composing vocal music—the forcing of words to my sounds; something about it feels illegitimate, a hoax even. For the same reason I might give up all composing, and by extension all paragraphs like this one (except that such paragraphs are, as we used to say, self-expressive, which music now is not), and simply spend the remaining years or hours like Baudelaire's *vieillard*, watching the clouds flow by, *les merveilleux nuages*.

J.-F. Revel states: "Proust might have adopted on his own account the sentence that Kierkegaard in *Either/Or* attributes to the supposed author of *Diapsalmata*:

> Alas! The door of happiness does not open inwards, and therefore it does not help to throw oneself at it in order to force it; it opens outwards and there is nothing one can do about it.

With this difference, that Proust never said 'alas.'"

Now I ask: are we (who seek happiness) located within or without the en-closure for which the door opens outwards? and anyway, how does Kierke-gaard (or the supposed author of *Diapsalmata*) know which way the door opens—or even that there is a door?

An essay in the *Times* describes the great tradition of Song from Monteverdi to Kern, from Schubert to Sondheim, from Brahms to the Beatles. No men-tion of the French tradition. Nor is the corollary correct. It's like saying from Jane Austen to Jacqueline Susann, from Rimbaud to Harold Robbins. Not like saying, correctly, from Schubert to . . . well, Rorem, or other so-called art-song composers, whatever their value.

23 October

This evening between five and eight, during a long thunderstorm, John Wulp and Mimsi Harbach in honor of my sixtieth birthday gave a party in an East 91st Street town house (except that Mimsi at the last moment was de-tained in Florida), a party after which I felt . . . not sadness, exactly, but a kind of hopelessness. One reason is that, although I'm fond of the hosts, I'm not close to them, the house was foreign, I didn't have complete charge of the guest list, and everyone seemed ill at ease. I was myself a guest where I'd have liked to be host. Well, maybe next year. Afterward, with JH and Frank and Shirley, we went to a corner restaurant (for real food wasn't served at the party) which seemed comparatively cosier with the rain beating on the windowpane.

Paragraphs after a Birthday

Sans date

My musical childhood seems literally caught in amber. As a little boy I used to sit for hours at Mother's dresser, pondering the objects thereupon. Two of these gleam vital after half a century: a tiger-eye signet tipped with the family initial, and a Spanish comb with five prongs. I can still feel the scorch of sealing (which I thought was ceiling) wax gumming the fingers as I squan-dered scores of R's like neumes across expensive stationary. The wax had the same cidery hue as the comb whose spokes became a musical staff when the Chicago sunlight refracted them onto the blue rug. Notes and staves bloomed everywhere then (and to this day sonic notions come to me visually more than aurally) as for long minutes I would run the comb through Moth-er's hair, and longed to sing both Pelléas and Mélisande when I grew up.

Have I grown up? Sixty, like forty and twenty, is what happens to others. Actually, the flesh stays willing but the spirit grows weak. My distinguished father, eighty-eight as I pen this, says he still dreams anxiously about having to face the world when he "grows up." Meanwhile Mother, who had no special ear for music (though neither parent ever questioned my un-American madness in choosing a non-remunerative career), did have a gift for peeling oranges so that the golden bark—same color as wax and comb—curled like a cello's scroll with a pungency that still fills my studio. Of what use now are these yellowing niceties to Mother who drinks frozen juice and sends her mail uncacheted, or to the very composer whose trade, as they say, spans the ages?

I used to think that all my classmates rushed home after gym, as I did, to make up preludes in the styles of Varese and Delius. Hawthorne wrote: "It is a good lesson for a man to step outside the narrow circle in which his claims are recognized, and to find how utterly devoid of significance, beyond that circle, is all he achieves, all he aims at."

My sexual childhood seems also caught in amber, which at certain hours melts into tableaux to be gazed upon, fondled, even sniffed, across the decades. Did not most of my male classmates dash home after school, as I did, to ruminate guiltlessly—indeed, to agitate the body with olfactory notions of their other male classmates? No? Well, if Hawthorne's remark as easily pertains to homosexuality as to art, and if I have (across the decades) been more dismayed by the solitude of music than by specialized sex, I have never suffered *socially* from my gifts and tastes (although privately I've sometimes envied peers and cursed lovers). That is because my blessed parents, even way back then, did not consider me a freak, either as carnal creature or (far worse) as composer.

It is said that artists are children—that insofar as they grow up they cease being artists. Well yes, artists are children in that they see without subterfuge, and they like approval more than appraisal. But unlike children they construct categorically, pruning and shaving, and they realize, indeed they seek, the advantage of seclusion for these acts.

Perhaps I too today, no less than those dozens of youngish (or so they claim) petitioners in the gay press's pink pages, long for the pungent embrace of some ruddy farmhand; for yes, it's not the flesh that grows weak, and the gods misplanned a structure that maintains undying lust even as it turns repellent to others. Yet is the lust so actual? I can't know. Even as an adolescent, while undergoing the telling puncture, or what Hart Crane termed the "warm tonsilling," my mind would stray to sealing wax, or to the idea that, oh, I'm actually experiencing what for days I've hotly dreamed of and it's not all that great. . . . I'd rather be writing music.

During World War II Paul Bowles was classified 4-F when it was learned he was a composer. "Writes symphonies," noted the army psychiatrist, and they rejected him.

Composers today, and not just for military shrinks but for many a lettered mandarin, are less often symphonists than pop musicians—an image out of sync with the intellectual picture of other kinds of artists. If in the public mind Lillian Hellman and Sam Shepard balance congenially with, say, Sheridan or O'Neill as Jane Frielicher and Larry Rivers emerge from Rubens and Sargeant, or Elizabeth Bishop and John Ashbery from Chaucer and Dryden, what current composers do fans of Telemann and Schubert listen to? Why, to Joni Mitchell and Stevie Wonder. And these fans are exceptional. Most Americans are only peripherally aware of musicians in any form; when occasionally they do meet one of us, their thought is: "Why not write a hit show?" as though fortune were the final goal. They do not distinguish in musical creation between the autonomous genres of so-called classical and so-called popular. Today's classical composer does not figure in the cultural ken; his product cannot be peddled like a playwright's or painter's; he is not an investment; he is not needed.

There are sports. If Reich is the Vonnegut of sound, his fans being people not otherwise "into" music, Foss is the Sontag of sound, his up-to-dateness being an end in itself. John Cage is the Erich Fromm of sound, his easy philosophy being, that music, like love, is where you find it (though where all is music, nothing is music), while Elliott Carter is the Jacques Lacan of sound (there is no American counterpart), his explication being so crucial to appreciation. These composers have been—can one say for extramusical reasons?—absorbed into the workaday unconscious.

Has Gay Lit, like Sport Composers, been absorbed into a workaday unconscious?

Because he knows I'm culling these notes from my diary expressly for *The Advocate*, and because with heavy heart he's just perused a heap of Gaysiana, JH hopes I'll say that gay press rhetoric is becoming—has always been—parochial, if not incestuous, thus producing no first-class or even memorable work, despite good intentions. Gay Lit (says JH) is Us vs. Them, while first-class writing, whatever its text, is always Me to You.

A glance at the reviews in a local gay rag confirms the giggly complicity beclouding literary issues. Like Critic Equality, founded a dozen years ago by Rex Reed and taken up by others like Arthur Bell ("I'm every bit as good as this puffed up star I'm interviewing"), Reviewer Equality quivers between gays and their subject ("I can be just as lewd as this book"). Tell what happens, don't editorialize. "Only Connect" should become "Only Describe."

It obtains as well to the "sensibility" of "creative" works. Do I show my age in being baffled at the fuss over *Torch Song Trilogy*? Is that old broad fruity camp still getting the laughs of forty years ago? Wouldn't any craftsman argue that nothing is said in four hours that can't be said better in three, or two, or one?

Maybe it takes one to know one. Would I myself adopt a new tone when aiming toward a straight periodical? I don't mean to let myself off the hook, the better to impale my brothers; but age commands priority by virtue of being just that, age: a self-referring specter of ever-recurrent history. Still, maybe the priority's unearned. The stupid don't get more intelligent the longer they live. Do you recall in *Gulliver's Travels* the country whose inhabitants never die, just wither and babble, growing dumber and dumber?

Do you still keep a diary? Did I ever? No I don't. Yes you do. The hoary truism about sperm emitted through the pen no longer obtains, now that we use typewriters. But to read of the objectifying of their ills by Sontag or Cousins or Beauvoir, or to talk with friends who are, in fact, dying, is for me to be ashamed of my giving up, yet I persist in making life hell for those around me, and I don't know where to turn. The Première Prieur from her bed: "My life has been spent in meditation on death, and now that I'm dying, the meditation is as nothing." But what about the man reading the Bible in his cell? Before being taken to the gallows he places a bookmark between the pages.

Is a diary anyone else's business? I've never had the answer. Are works of art anyone else's business? They were, in the days when we believed in God. But did Giotto or Machaut think of their works as Art? There's an insolence, like kids with their mud pies, in showing off—in exposing, the French say—your new paintings, or poems, or pieces. While typing these words I'm aware that I'm less aware of my body. *Sois sage Ô ma douleur*. Would Sontag's stoic control allow her thus to quote Baudelaire, or is my pain a pygmy beside hers?

Writing by its nature is rethinking; and rethinking by definition causes change, even sometimes the change of a good person into bad. If writing it down doesn't get rid of it, at least writing it down changes it. Reshuffling eases for a while.

Marie Laure used to say that my diary did not reflect a state of mind so much as a state of body.

Twenty-one years ago in Buffalo, when, along with writing music, I first began writing about music, there came a dusting off of intellect, a putting of thoughts in order. Writing music is communication, yes, but not intellectual communication, much less literary. But writing about music, like teaching, although not making you a better composer, does, like LSD, show you where your faults lie.

When Reagan claims of his balletic son, "Ron's all man; his mother and I made sure of that," the implication is that Ron's not gay. But if he were, would the implication be that he's part woman? A further implication, then, is that Woman is part male homosexual. But since Woman is made of Man, and since a "real man" is not male homosexual, a true male must in some sense be lesbian. That can't be right.

To write about your life is, from one standpoint, to stop living it. You must avoid adventures today so as to make time for registering those of yesterday. The hardest of all adventures to speak of is music, because music has no meaning to speak of.

If music could be translated into human speech it would no longer need to exist. Like love, music's a mystery which, when solved, evaporates.

What purpose does the nuance of thought serve—those trillion rarities hovering around and nursing upon each of the quadrillion memories of our ever-shifting past—when the whole mechanism is snuffed out in a trice? Estelle Winwood, on her hundredth birthday: "I wish something wonderful would happen."

That which is wonderful, of course, is anticipated love. Nothing else so sets the brain a-tingle (except, I'm told, money). Father says that at Cadbury flirtations are no less prevalent than in high school.

Even the most wretched human, insofar as he is human and not a catatonic vegetable, does not desire to die.

Self-perpetuation through children seems the final (reactionary) explanation of, and consolation for, death. But anyone can have children.

Truths of the past are clichés of the present. Proustophile J.-F. Revel notes: "One is sorry to have to point out that Proust regarded Maeterlinck, the Comtesse de Noailles, and Léon Daudet as geniuses, and not Max Jacob, Apollinaire or Jarry." Revel takes as given, and assumes we concur, that the last three authors are superior to the first three. Well, I rate the chilly ambiguities of Pelléas higher than Ubu's rowdy camp, and the dated Romance of Anna higher than the dated Dada of Max. If I agree that Apollinaire is "better than" Daudet, can this be more than a matter of taste? If I hesitate before Proust's high placement of Reynaldo Hahn, can I in fact be "right", or is Revel righter? Until absolutes are unanimous there will be no final judgements in esthetics. But absolutes shift with the decades (especially in painting, where money's involved), and—who knows?—perhaps in 2001 Beethoven will be out. One may hope.

> I am old, I am an old queen. But I still have the power of my childhood
> Contained in my office. If I should lose my office, no more power would accrue
> To my aged and feeble person. But even supposing I keep my power?
> What chance is there that anything really nice will happen to me?

Thus, like Estelle Winwood centuries later, mused mad Queen Bertha of Norway through the pen of Kenneth Koch. And thus she sang in my little opera in 1968.

In 1951, among the earliest paragraphs of *The Paris Diary*, this appears: "Youth is beautiful, age ugly. But is the wisdom of age beautiful? We know nothing old we did not know as children; we merely submit essentially unchanged reactions to wearier refinement. I detest sublety, I like strength. Strength is never subtle in art or in life." I was twenty-seven. I'm now sixty. Do I still agree about strength in art? Do I remain blind to the benefits of aging? There are no benefits

Look around you. Earth is a hecatomb of decaying friends. With or without the aid of AIDS we are all slaughtered unjustly, or at least felled enigmatically, in the sense that we don't ask for, or desire, or comprehend our death. We expire passively always. Death comes to us. Murder comes to us. Suicide is active perhaps, but still . . . we can't choose its opposite: to live forever.

Nothing is caught in amber, neither childhood nor music nor sex, and the amber itself melts like lava into each passing hour. It's hardly news to state that memory shakes, even dumb people wear disguises, some smart-looking folks turn out to be stupid, as if you didn't know, and don't judge a book by its cover. Our youngest cat, Princess, with eyes like the Virgin Mary's, shreds baby rabbits who then hop across the Nantucket lawn dragging their sunset-colored hearts behind them. The Sioux Indians, reserving their most frightful tortures for certain captives, throw them to the children. Prisoners throughout our land petition governors to hire guards older than eighteen.

Rosemary and I, though physically alike (they say) as twins, having veered long ago at a radical crossroad, are only today—partly because of our parents, and partly because time does, except for death, knit up dropped stitches—becoming staunch allies. The one thing that doesn't change is the supposed prostate which still affords a nagging discomfort daily—almost like a friend—after three years.

If all death is incongruous (why do we live if we must die?) as well as humdrum, the death most difficult for mourning survivors is the death that, as we say, does not come as a surprise: our grandmothers, for instance, or war casualties, as opposed to stricken infants or horny lovers. Because really, as the Première Prieur teaches us, all death comes as a surprise. The habit of life is hard to break; the difference between the almost-dead and the actually dead is wider than our universe and is the only difference worth noting.

   Yet I love my work, and if I don't do it, who will? And I love the details, not the philosophies, of living; baking pies, reading, selecting texts for song, abiding near to JH. My most irritating anxiety—more than money or envy or prostate—is that there might not be life after death, for how will I pass the time?

New Haven
25 October

The day after the birthday fête I came here for two days as guest of Vivian Perlis (to continue the Oral History taping for Yale) and of the Symphony (which tonight under Murry Sidlin did a stunning version of *Lions*). Before the concert, dined with Holly Stevens, ever energetic and opinionated and referring always to her mythical father as "Dad," at Mory's, a school hangout, so remote, with its sawdust and pipe-smoking savants, from the crass of Manhattan.

New York
26 October

At Symphony Space, a most affecting marathon memorial for William Kappell. Every pianist we know performed: Shirley, Jerry, a dozen more, and, perhaps most extraordinarily, Billy Masselos, who agreed to play the Copland *Fantasy* on the condition that a stand-in could lurk in the wings. For years Billy's been queasy about playing, even in private, because of his Parkinson's, or whatever it is. And his apparition on stage was unreassuring. From the moment he sat down, placed his left hand like a focusing vise over his right and, extending the central finger, whammed it like a spike into the lone E-flat that opens the piece, we knew that all was more than well for the next half hour. I was present when Billy had given the world premiere of the

Fantasy ("dedicated to the memory of William Kappell") at the old Juilliard in November, 1957. Tonight brought back the old days.

Indeed, the marathon was affecting not specifically because of the living presence of so many friends who played this evening, but because of the presence of Kappell himself who was evoked like a genie. What was evoked was the sight and sound of Willy. I heard him often in the 1940s; even now as I write I can still hear his *way* with a keyboard: that purposeful, shining, pliable strength, like Damascus steel, yet gentle as a child—a *good* child. I knew him, not well, through Eugene Istomin. (Though what does "know well" mean? Willy seemed so dynamically alert that an hour with him was like a week with anyone else.) What I retain is the force, the almost-sexuality, of his attention. I once played some songs for him, intimidated, but egged on by Eugene. After one hearing he knew them, words and music, better than I did, plying me with questions, not letting me off the hook (as, with his pocket comb, he nervously scraped at the eczema on his wrist). He cared.

Like most composers my interest in any performer lies ultimately in his interest in new music. Willy was the first—and, alas, the only—bigtime American pianist for whom, repertorially, the present was on a par with the past.

What a mistake, after this enchantment, to have stopped off at Jean Stein's party ("In honor of Norris and Norman Mailer" the invitation said). I never see Jean anymore; this might be a perfect moment. But the apartment was so jammed with anorexic ladies and heterosexual sissies—"like a rat-fuck," as Francine, who was there, genteelly put it—that I fled without greeting my hostess. How remote the musical world is from the literary, or even from *le monde*.

30 October

Back from forty-eight hours in Washington, D.C., where Virgil and I were decently treated on Alan Mandel's Music Ensemble series. Lunch yesterday with Alan, and with Joseph McLellan, after which I took them (were they disconcerted?) to my co-signing, with author Karla Jay, at Lamda Rising, Washington's chief gay bookstore.

This afternoon, Earl Wild recital at Carnegie.

This evening, the ninety-minute TV documentary on the Santa Fe Chamber Music Festival filmed two summers ago. In the flame-colored shirt I look pretty good (so do we all—Harbison, Schuman, Copland, and the pretty players), and what I say isn't dumb; but every statement is lopped off. Even the music's truncated, with no piece played straight through. The film's not about music, it's about a music festival.

Halloween

Sono Osato had not been able to come to the birthday party. This morning she stopped by with a nineteenth-century etching of Bach, surrounded by views of Leipzig, matted in cobalt blue and framed in gold. We talked for two hours, mainly about her mother and father and sister and brother, all of whom I knew, and all of whom died unpleasantly. Sono survives, she says, on lithium; *tant mieux*, since, at least outwardly, she's as piquant and vital as when, forty years ago, she gleamed out on a crowded stage like a diamond in coal.

Tonight we served dinner to Francine & Cleve, Diana Trilling, and Mary Cantwell. Afterward, adjourned to the parlor where Francine took out her needlework and awaited cultured talk. I asked, "What do straights say about gays when gays leave the room?" Everyone seemed taken aback. Yet the question interests me; I've never asked it, and I don't know the answer. Mary's the only one who finally gave a half-reply: Straight people, at least women, or some of them, feel cheated.

8 November

The week's been largely aimed toward last night. Wednesday, a talk, sponsored by Ann Thorne, to patrons of the American Composers Orchestra. Thursday, meeting and later dinner with JH at the Academy-Institute. Friday, another conversation with Tim Page on WNYC's wavelength. Saturday, party at his office for George Borchardt's thirtieth anniversary in the agentry business. Sunday, preparations for a party in honor of Jerry Lowenthal. Last night, second New York performance this year of the Piano Concerto, with breathtaking and thunderous accuracy, by Jerry Lowenthal with Dennis Russell Davies and the American Composers Orchestra. (Jerry's memory is phenomenal. At the rehearsal for the premiere, thirteen years ago in Pittsburgh, he did not use the score or even have it with him.) Afterwards we gave a party for about thirty people, incl. Lukas Foss (whose strange *Exeunt* was also on the program), Rosalyn Tureck, Sono & Victor, Pia Gilbert, the Popes. JH to Nantucket at dawn, for thirty-six hours.

Another *séance de pose* for about three hours yesterday at Maurice Gros-ser's. Still sitting for *his* pose when I arrived was a Mr. John Sheehan, direc-tor of the Opera Ensemble of New York, stark naked.

Today, visit from Jack Mitchell (and an assistant) to take pictures, at his request, for about three hours. From the standpoint of the poser, the cam-era's more tiring than the painter's brush; the photographer's viewpoint is, yes, just as personal, but the subject daren't bat an eye.

It is easier to distinguish good from bad than to distinguish good art from bad art, and good intentions do not a masterpiece make.

If the pop music of my youth, as much as the "serious" music, so swayed me, why do I despise today's pop music? Not because it's bad but because it's preemptive. The sounds even of Eden sour when we are their captive audience.

The Foss case.

JH, on hearing Lukas Foss's String Quartet (the one Seymour Barab said was how music must sound to a dog), called it "airplane music," meaning mu-sic written in a plane en route from there to here. If you don't have time to write a good old sonata, just write whole notes studded with fermatas in largo tempos—it will last just as long and cover only one page.

Like many other composers, Lukas in interviews never fails solemnly to state that "I try never to repeat myself. Each new work presents new prob-lems." Delusion. Yes, each new work presents new problems in that we are older with each new work, and each work is (presumably) for another occa-sion. Our ideas for saxophone are not the same as for cello. Then again, they are. It is not for us to know we're being new. Anyway, what's wrong with re-peating ourselves, that we feel so guilty? Who does not repeat himself? What great artists, even Stravinsky and Beethoven, have had more than eight or ten ideas in their whole lives?

Bill Flanagan, on the subject of Lukas's chameleonic bandwagon-jump-ing: "If all the music of our century were destroyed except Foss's, future his-torians would be able to reconstruct every artistic trend of our century." That witticism was meant as a put-down. I read it today as merely a defini-tion. There is no one right way to compose. Lukas's very trendiness is him; when he lands on the bandwagon feet first, he glitters.

Ce que les autres te reprochent, cultive-le, c'est toi. (Cocteau)

Morning. Strangers glance at each other for two or three seconds, maybe four or five. They are more than, as we like to say, each other's type: they are each other's ideal. But they must catch different trains.

Night. Each revives the image of the other. They never "meet" again, yet remain faithful to each other over two or three years, maybe four or five.

An indisputably straight man is confronted with this ultimatum: you must have sex with this unlovely seventy-eight-year-old female, or with this handsome twenty-four-year-old male. Which does he choose? So much depends. What does unlovely mean? Or handsome? What act(s) would be performed? And how do the others feel about it?

Were I forced to the choice (and choice of acts) between an unlovely seventy-eight-year-old male and a handsome twenty-four-year-old female, there would be no hesitation.

12 November

Peter Grimes at the Met. Each time (once or twice a year) I come here I'm shocked anew at the sloppy fare proffered by this most self-congratulatory of houses. Tonight, not one voice was on pitch, nor better than your average church choir member even on pitch.

Virgil Thomson's music cannot be assessed on the same expressive basis as any other music I can think of, even Satie's, since his music—the best of it—more than any other of the past millennium depends on words. If Virgil never has a bad review (or, except for the Stein operas, a really good review), it's less because the critics are intimidated by Papa as that they don't know what to say about this seeming inanity. In fact, the inanity is sophistication at its most poignant. Like Debussy's apparent and perpetual recitation in *Pelléas*, which is really aria-in-microcosm and wildly tuneful, so Virgil's concert songs are cantilena-in-a-microscope, built from but two or three intervals. They differ from folksong in their ambiguous accompaniment and eccentric literariness. The songs made from Kenneth Koch's poems, *Mostly about Love*, are America's best, as are the ones drawn from Saint Francis and Saint Augustine. They have never been sung right (except perhaps by Betty Allen a quarter century ago), and Virgil, despite his extreme sparseness, needs to be heard to be believed. His is not *augenmusik*. Yet the ear, the critic's ear, is not often given to hearing them, even in imagination.

What I owe to Virgil is incalculable, though often in the past I've begrudged him this. It's a sense of being able to codify simplicity, of *wanting* to codify it the way others have wanted to codify complexity. Art is economy.

Just as even the most emancipated among us think of waiters as waiters, actors as actors, and even mothers as mothers, so critics are not people, they are critics, and they in turn probably think of composers as strictly composers.

They seem unwilling to locate a new piece except as to the slot it occupies. The slot is of their making.

There is the same space—thirteen years—between Debussy and Ravel as between William Schuman and me. The same space (almost)—twenty-nine years—between Virgil and me as between my father and me. The same space—thirty-nine years—between Beethoven and Schumann as between me and Daron.

Romanticism again. Will you define it? Camus: "Classicism is nothing but romanticism with the excess removed."

Shouldn't definitions, when using comparisons, refer to that which precedes rather than to that which succeeds? Romanticism is overweight classicism—or classicism with the fat still on.

In fact (if fact's involved), isn't there a more radical separation? Isn't classicism (at least in music) that which looks from inside out and is abstract, romanticism that which looks from outside in and is representative?

Mother so touchingly in her own world. Father, astute and subtle as ever, is he to whom I still most often turn. What has he in common with those scores of matrons *bien coiffées* whose goal is the evening's Bingo game? Tonight Father asked, "Shouldn't your mother and I have merely been placed on a drifting iceberg?" but he went on to say he was rereading Anatole France, and put great store in his three daily naps and his walks up and down the plant-filled halls.

Albany
18 November

Am here at the strange but comfortable Fort Orange Club as guest of Yvar Mikhashoff who arranged an invigorating all-Rorem recital that occurred this evening. All I've previously known of Albany is the bus station as stop-off for Yaddo, and distant visions of the Rockefeller mall—a mixture of Bologna and Alphaville. Tonight the gentrified back streets seem more like Liverpool, and Yvar's entourage is good-natured and gifted.

Delivered my liner notes, for the forthcoming Ravel/Boulez album, to

CBS records. Still struggling with the *Mahagonny* essay, due on Bob Jacobson's desk next week.

Visit from Richard Buckle, tea and talk of Paris in the old days.

Train in an hour. Party tonight at Joe Machlis's for Aaron.

Philadelphia
22 November

Just had breakfast here at the Barclay with Dick Jacob who, except for "drawn" features (pulled traits, as the French say), retains the identical baby stare, reinforced by straight-faced whimsy, as in Chicago during high school.

Last night at Curtis: Daron's new Violin Concerto, caringly bowed by his girlfriend Michaela Paetsch; his ambitious cycle, with orchestra, based on ten poems of Anne Sexton, caringly sung by his girlfriend Karen Noteboom; and his affecting memorial symphony, based in part on Norman Stumpf's song "The Waking." Poor Norman's parents were present, amiable but lost, like Bill Flanagan's parents at *his* memorial long ago. They wondered what to do with Norman's manuscripts, which might one day be worth something.

What is a song cycle? Who knows? As with sonata, there are as many definitions as there are examples. However, few will disagree that a cycle consists of two or more songs in an order predetermined by the composer. As with opera, "lyrical" instinct is less crucial than theatrical flair. Sequence is all. Half the battle rests in finding the right texts, then in interrelating them. Change the order and you'll not only change the meaning, you'll weaken the very music. Play *Die Winterreise* backward and hear its force ebb.

Anne Sexton is to Plath what Michael Tippett is to Britten: the same thing, only later, and less good.

Bill Flanagan once confided that, for a period, he modeled his life on mine: after all, he was as good as me—why shouldn't he get the same attention? He wore the same sweaters, saw the same people, wrote the same postcards, feigned the same look.

The sole method in this world that escapes generality is the care and feeding of artists. What turns to gold for Jack, turns to dust for Jill.

Nantucket
1 December

Over a year since Mother and Father were installed at Cadbury, and probably it was the only thing to do. Amongst the pile of books passed on from them to me I recover the magical *Norse Mythology*, each well-thumbed magic page and colored image as familiar as it was fifty years ago. How much I've based standards, calculations, opinions upon those tales which Father, so proudly Scandinavian, encouraged me to read!

Thor's hammer. Like most kids I was embarrassed by deviations, let alone eccentricities, in my family: father aping a Norwegian accent, cousin Olga's wearing too much lipstick, mother's left-wing pacifism. How weird I myself must have been strikes me only now. Yet no "personality" has ever been quite right, let alone perfect. Thor's hammer was a mistake: through his tragic flaw the weapon's handle emerged too short, and remained so forever. Perfection palls (beauty limps), and every star has something wonderfully wrong: the identifying property. A star risks, and is a risk. Observe Horowitz as contrasted to Van Cliburn, Monroe contrasted to June Haver, Lenya in contrast to Diana Ross. There is nothing wrong with Ross, and that's what's wrong.

When Bernard Holland in today's *Times* muses on the stern lack of beauty, the no-nonsense stance, in much of today's music, he puts it down to the times—the painful times, since pain is so clearly in our world. Yet wasn't pain, that is "clearly in our world," the crux of every note of, say, Kurt Weill, whose pretty music was shocking and depressing by its very listenability? As for Messiaen's *Quartet for the End of Time* reaching, as Holland declares, "above the pain and ugliness of the composer's German concentration camp," suppose I aver that, no, the Quartet *is* the pain and ugliness: a perfect painting of it. Am I wrong and Holland right?

Music, with all its reflections, has nothing to do with any of this. (And I've always suspected that Messiaen's dating of his work, *terminé au Stalag VIII A Gorlitz*, was a theatrical coup. Can one—except maybe Messiaen—really compose in concentration camps?) Well, now that the end of time is a real proposition, my own music gets lighter and lighter. Surely there's as valid a reason for that as for Milton Babbitt's sternness. But maybe my music isn't light: it's only I who say so, and I don't know, I only write it.

Speaking of pain: finished Louise de Vilmorin's 1941 novel, *Le lit à colonnes*, which, if less sophomorically crafted, would rival *Ethan Frome* for excruciation. The improbable tale is more than one can bear: a composer, unjustly accused of murder, while serving a life sentence has not only his opera but his love, and every shred of hope, appropriated by his jailer, who becomes famous. Does even this seem paltry in the light (or dark) of the *fin des temps*?

2 December

I'd foreseen every reaction but the reaction of Henahan re my Piano Concerto: no reaction. It is within his right to add a snigger at each mention of my name, as he usually does. But his device of ignoring my concerto while discussing all else on the program comes, I feel convinced, not from his disliking my music as from his disliking me for having once written disobligingly about him. He's been dishing it out to others for thirty years; but that another could presume to criticize *him*. . . .

For the record, Peter Davis in *New York* devoted the bulk of his column to the concerto, or rather, to my place in the scheme of things.

When I told Andrew Porter that we all think *Montezuma* is unmusical, untheatrical, and unskillful, and that we have ears and aren't fools, I am careful to add that the years may prove us wrong. He responded, "Yes, the years will prove you wrong." I did not know then what now I know—that he's writing a libretto for Sessions, on *The Emperor's New Clothes*, which seems appropriate.

3 December

Am attempting again to read Giono, this time *Joy of Man's Desiring* in the so-so translation and beautiful North Point edition. But as in the old days, despite his power and originality, Giono is just too noble and healthy for my decadent spirit. He's a sort of unneurotic Hamsun.

11 December

Dined last night chez Maurice Grosser, with Virgil, Paul Sanfaçon and Claudine & Manuel Rosenthal. Maurice is still doing my portrait. In the exactly forty years we've known each other I'd never before tasted his well-known cuisine. Clam chowder with chopped bacon. A Russian salad (including lima beans, celery, apples, and large slices of smoked ham). A French apple tart made with mace—perhaps too much mace.

Manuel is here to conduct Poulenc's *Carmélites*, which he does luminously. His secret, he says, is that he treats the orchestra members as individual virtuosos. Actually, he's better, indefinably, than they. He makes the score shine. I complain of Poulenc's orchestration, especially of his thickening the "Ave Maria" with useless timpani strokes. Manuel says that Poulenc didn't do his own scoring—that Poulenc's education (as I'd known anyway) was haphazard, slipshod. Elsa Barraine and another were hired to do the scoring. (Not, of course, of the chamber music, where anything "sounds" well.) I'm not sure I believe this.

14 December

Once a reign of divine right is entrenched, it's not easy to get people, even nonbelievers, to see an alternative. Like Renata Adler on Kael some years ago. When such a respected Thinker as Michael Steinberg, who, in his MacDowell Colony address, thanks Carter for not patronizing small intellects (i.e. for presenting problems that are challenging to solve), when such a Thinker is on Elliott Carter's side, how to contradict him? But nobody "likes" it, any more than they like Boulez or Sessions. It's crossword puzzle music—the fun is in the solving. Since I'm a composer, it's not my place to put down Elliott. But someone should.

The matron from Des Moines asks Picasso to please stand aside, so that she can take a snapshot of the Eiffel Tower.

Virgil is to be feted on the 27th with a television relay from the White House. In my agenda I note: VT on TV, which isn't quite a palindrome: that would be VT not on TV.

Doorbell and phone ring simultaneously. On the phone, calling from London, is André Previn, whom I do not know. At the door is the super, Manuel, with a box of monkey wrenches. I have time to explain to Manuel only that it's the left faucet that needs tending, and I hurry back to speak at length with Previn about the new piece. Not wishing to run up Previn's bill nor to make a weird impression, I can't supervise the bathroom work. Result: Manuel ruins the functioning sink faucet and does not touch the offending tub faucet. We'll be without hot water for a week while waiting for the entire sink to be replaced. But I did become acquainted with Previn.

22 December

A few weeks ago, browsing in Endicott's, I leafed through the biography of Barbara Hutton, *Poor Little Rich Girl*, by one David Heymann, just long enough to see that a sizable paragraph from *The Paris Diary* was reprinted, without benefit of quotation marks, and attributed to Hutton herself. On the next page another paragraph, this time properly accredited, blazed through a dishonest context, namely that Ned Rorem (an "indefatigable diary-keeper . . . and American musicologist") was "at the same party" studying Miss Hutton as she danced moodily with Aly Kahn. I bought the book, xeroxed the offending quotes, sent them to Borchardt, and forgot about it.

A week ago when Edwin McDowell of the *Times* revealed a lawsuit by a doctor against Heymann and Random House, JH (who generally is against my making any public noises unless questions of fact are at stake) took it upon himself to deliver the plagiaristic evidence to McDowell, who published it next morning. As of today my position in this distasteful business has been reprinted in seemingly every periodical on our planet, shedding upon me a light, briefer but brighter and more sordid than any I've basked in since 1954 when I was kicked out of the Rome Opera, simultaneously with Stravinsky, for not being in formal dress.

Several frantic letters from Philip Van Rensselaer in California indicate that his published memoirs were much more abused than mine in this affair. More important, however, is the *tone* of Philip's words, touching, vulnerable, nostalgic, which makes me want to see him again, when this nonsense has blown over . . . in a day or two.

24 December

Week's résumé:

15, dined chez Gaby Rodgers. Vincent Canby there too. For dessert, a kiwi tart.

16, buffet at Heddy Baum's.

17, Zaidee Dufallo's farewell party for Byron Belt. (Saw Byron a few days later on the street. He said: "Forgotten, but not gone.")

18, the Plauts.

19, press showing of Santa Fe TV program. Sixteen years ago JH and I first met.

20, visit to parents at Cadbury. Took candy.

21, final session for portrait at Maurice Grosser's.

22, rain.

23, party at B. & H. Took candy. Party in evening at Gregg & Roz's.

24, long conversation, warm as a Christmas tree, with Oliver Daniel about his book on Mitropoulos.

26 December

Rosemary drove up through the cold, with Mary and Paul, on Christmas Eve for JH's midnight Mass which, as every year, was a model of mind over matter, of Jim's energy and sense of cohesion in making The Jesus Show function. But the incense brought on an allergy relapse, and later in the street I had an attack of chills, so that Rosemary had to drive me home, then locked her keys in the car, and, because the cold fell to a record-breaking zero (even in Florida, it seems), all the Marshalls spent the night on the floor, and Christmas morn was passed phoning locksmiths.

Eugene and Martita came for High Tea at five, but touched little of the massive display of Sacher tortes and white chocolate bonbons (so JH, who because of Midwest ice storms canceled his trip to Kansas, and I later stuffed ourselves). I gave them Tony Kuerti's big Whale Book (I'd have preferred giving them my new Cello & Piano Suite, finished only yesterday, so that I could inscribe it "A Partita for Martita"). I'm never uneasy while discussing Casals with the Istomins, although they know that I know that they know how I feel. Eugene, who like Martita is more *au courant* than I about elderly decay (my nearly nonagenarian parents still thrive bodily), plans to be prepared for suicide "when the time comes." But isn't senility precisely what keeps us from suicide? Do we ever know when "the time" has come?

In the evening, with JH watched the well-done documentary on Britten which had so touched me a few years ago. JH is extremely uncomfortable at overtly emotional scenes; hates real tears for the camera; not the tears, but the fact that those tears were edited to be displayed. As we chatted, Joan Miró, on the other side of the ocean, died.

                                                                    29 December

Would my music, or even these fugitive paragraphs, be better or worse or in any way different if my concentration were not shattered every twenty minutes by telephone, doorbell, stacks of mail, the petition of those thousand others each believing he's the center of my concerns? In Nantucket are my chores less fragmented, harrassed, pure? Do the Yaddos of our world make for superior, as well as necessarily more prolific, palettes? Actually I have little social life (never go to theater or parties), and my schedule could be whatever I allow it. I do allow distraction. Another, with more apparent distraction, does not allow it: does not stop working while in the maelstrom. But maybe neither really do I.

Yes always we remember differently. Visit from young Brad Gooch this afternoon, for an interview on "Gay Life in the Fifties" (the fifties, when he was a toddler). He has talked to me, Richard Howard, Jimmy Schuyler, Joe

LeSueur. Now, we are hardly representative. We are *geniuses*. Nor did we once say to each other, "Since we're gay, and it's the fifties, let's remember it all for interviewers thirty years hence."

Sleep in a nest of flames. Baudelaire. Ask Ch.-H. Ford.

There is no truth, there is only fact, and even fact—after the fact—becomes a Rashomonian tangle. Division of epochs into periods (even the notion of epochs), like the "periods" of Picasso and Stravinsky, are conveniences for outsiders and no concern to Picasso or to Stravinsky (or to epochs), for whom time is not discontinuous.

John Myers's memoir, *Tracking the Marvelous*, has just come forth. The three passing references to me are each inaccurate. Harmless, but they could as well be accurate. Yet inaccuracy of fact-in-retrospect is different in kind from on-the-spot inaccuracy of fact (as in diaries). The past is always golden, the present never. The difference lies in responsibility. Yet my facts aren't yours. To edit old diaries to suit survivors would be to write another book.

31 December

Malcolm Boyd, in a mini-review of *The Later Diaries* in the *L. A. Times*, quotes three or four of my glibber jewels. Then, while allowing that I am "candid and precise," adds that I play at being alive. Now, the only person who can play at being alive is a dead person, unless one is speaking meta-phorically, which Boyd is not. What Boyd really means is that I play at being a thinker (or perhaps at being a *serious* writer). Well, of course I'm not alive in the sense—denied to mere mortals—that he is: a running-with-Jesus latter-day out-of-the-closet courageous creature filled, like Anaïs Nin, with the richness of experience and the ability to stare life in the face. Taking my own side, while being fair to the (sexy) Boyd, I am simply a paleface to his redskin.

(Thumbing through the pages now of *The Later Diaries* I see that I myself wrote "I play at being alive." So Boyd can't even claim that *aperçu* as his own.)

In February, for Paul Jacobs's memorial, Will Parker and I will perform De-bussy's *Promenoir des deux amants*. Practising today *Je tremble en voyant ton visage* I see, as though it floated before me, the visage of Frances Osato who, with her strained inexpert soprano, first sang this flawless song for me forty years ago. It is from her copy that I now work. At her death in 1954 Tim Osato mailed me a variety of objects, including this cycle and a volume of Basque songs. Osato *père* is dead long since, and Teru—well before her mother. Tim too now, of suicide two years ago. Sono alone prevails. Reading their letters today, how long ago they stem from—the Jackson Park of my fourteen years, when I longed to become David Lichine.

Violent nightmare from which I awoke at 6 A.M. The inability (as when under mescaline) to speak anxiously, or to show alarm anyway, to friends and police, although when they would depart, the murderer lurking in the closet would tear me limb from limb.

1984

In the order of things twenty years ago I'd be soggy with a hangover. Clear-headed, the weather neutral after a week of arctic chill. The cats scared stiff at midnight by the petards in Central Park. (Except for Wallace, now totally deaf.)

On the grounds that if I'm to be critical I should at least know what I'm crit-icizing, and also from fraternal curiosity, I borrowed three cassettes from B. & H.

Druckman's *Vox Humana*: being a choral piece, it's hard not to hear what *I'd* have done with such texts. But again, I'd never have used such texts (ap-parently in Hebrew and Latin and Sanskrit—why must Americans forever avoid their native tongue?). Exceedingly colorful, even glamorous, con-stantly overwrought, a fusion of *Lost Horizon* and Carl Orff, especially the Orff of *Die Bernauerin*, his opera in Bavarian dialect which I saw—heard—in Munich on March 9, 1954. I remember being overwhelmed by the effects of the mass intake of breath, a collective shouted gasp, as the chorus from a bridge observes a man drowning below. This gasp effect is acquired by Ja-cob, and his piece leaves the impression of being mostly effect and very little straightforward tune. Sounds hard. Could he have gotten the same effects with less difficulty? Druckman does use an attractive harmonic motive—that of a pair of major thirds succeeding each other at the distance of a minor third, thus overlapping, like the pair of trumpets in the first movement of Shostakovitch's Sixth Symphony.

Listened carefully to Carter's *In Sleep, In Thunder*, both with and with-out score in hand, and with (I think) an open mind, but can't make sense of it. It is without sense. Not that I'd have done so differently, in the vocal line, with such texts (and I could have used such texts), but the jumble of instru-ments is incoherent. Like Jacob's piece: when all is overwrought, nothing is overwrought; perpetual drama, in lacking contrast, makes for no drama at all.

Ben Lee's Concerto Grosso for Brass, Choir & Orch. made no impression. A hearing, chez lui, of George Perle's new *Serenade* for piano and a dozen or so instruments made a strong impression. Strangely, it's the only piece of the four with even a shred of charm, a quality George would doubtless shrug off, yet a quality that in the long run is all that matters, and that, in my definition, is the one quality that makes any work last.

The startling lack of charm in all of Carter's music, early and late, when he himself possesses so much of it. To say that his music "reflects our time" and can't afford charm is to know all times. You who know all times, tell us: What time was ever without anguish? (Tom Prentiss in his latest letter: "Concerning repetition: E. Carter declares his dislike of it, which is just as well; we need listen to his work but once.")

The blithe way in which critics from the little sticks praise Carter makes for comical reading, as though they had been programmed like The Stepford Wives by critics from the big sticks. Warren O'Reilley states (*Washington Times*) that it is ironic that a national treasure like Carter, while widely played on the Continent, is virtually unknown on his native soil. (Is this untruth perpetrated by EC's press agent?) Meanwhile Scottie Ferguson (*The Advocate*, Jan. 10, '84) plunges straight out: "The greatest composer of our time, Elliott Carter. . . ." But what does that mean?

If, as I always contend, nobody enjoys his music (enjoys *listening* to it), that statement would be hard to prove. What, people ask, is the secret of his success? The success is due, probably, to the fact that the music flatters critics and performers. Having scanned, parsed, and otherwise dissected the non-sensual challenges, the critic feels he's accomplished something, while the performer, in working harder than he's ever worked before, both as to his own virtuosity and to the trials of ensemble, feels the same. Both confuse complexity with quality. In fact, anyone can write in the IRCAM style (the tenets of integral serialism can be imparted in about thirty minutes, as compared with the tenets of "classical" harmony and counterpoint, which can be imparted in about four hours), and anyone can understand, insofar as understanding means seeing how one thing leads out of and into another. But nobody likes it.

Nantucket
4 January

We flew here New Year's Day. The upstairs bathroom, which was supposed to have been finished three months ago, is still *sens dessus dessous*.

Violent allergy to something, sneezing and sniffing all day.

5 January

Am simultaneously deep into Jonathan Schell's solemn essay in the *New Yorker* while re-rereading (as Cocteau says) Whitman's "Specimen Days"— the entries concerning the Civil War—hoping to find as coherent a blend of texts to set for The King's Singers as I found, fifteen years ago, for Souzay with *War Scenes*. The effects of these two authors, so closely meshed in my mind now, are not at all disparate, Whitman being, one hundred twenty years ago, no less immediate than Schell, though Schell's fate (the fate of the earth?) is, as the clock ticks, nearer to mine. Both are satisfactory logically and emotionally, but neither always hits my esthetic nail on the head. For example, when the intelligent Schell refers to "monumental crime—Hitler's genocidal attack on the Jewish people being the most monstrous in memory," why not include gays, gypsies, cripples and such, who constitute millions more? Or when the compassionate Whitman sums up "those three years in hospital, camp or field" and makes his sole reference to being "among the black soldiers, wounded or sick, and in the contraband camps," why not tell us a bit more about precisely who and where those black soldiers were?

7 January

JH and I give Margaret Mercer two jars of marmalade for her birthday tonight.

> Margaret is a lamb,
> she's beer
> and Brim and bread, a dove.
> But she's not jam,
> so here!
> From Jim and Ned, with love.

8 January

Calm evening chez Leonard Raver, whose birthday it is.

Full-page ad for Martha Graham in today's *Times* (what's the cost? twenty thousand? forty?) announcing each ballet of her coming season, including the new "Rite of Spring." Yet not one composer's name is listed. Martha, bow your head in shame.

Long phone talk with Father this morning. Last night he watched *The Magic Flute* on the new color TV we took him on Saturday, and, he says, he burst into tears when Papagena removed her old woman's mask. (Mother's mask remains, we'll never be young again, music moves, etc.) Meanwhile, I was watching Depardieu as Martin Guerre around the corner, and I burst into tears when he "returns" and all is better than before. Anything's possible.

JH hotly against my using Whitman's prose—yet again!—for The King's Singers. He says it's lazy to fall back on this but offers nothing in its place. *En fin de compte* is any text "legitimate" for song? Whitman's prose, heavy and honest and butch and narrative and pacifist and ever so American, feels ideal for The King's Singers who've specified that they don't want yet another Elizabethan pastiche. Besides, it's close to my heart, and my heart in this pressing case must come before JH's not always infallible instinct.

Westmoreland, that physician of the soul, declares: "The oriental doesn't put the same high price on life as we do." Ergo: we who are sensitive can plow in and kill them.

Leontyne gave the traditional run-through of her "new" program last night chez elle, as she does biannually, and now at 57 she is no less a fountain of purest silver than thirty years ago. Sitting in that small green parlor and hearing the notes pour forth, one wonders: is that sound there within her, like the web within the spider, when she is not spinning it forth? But one may as well wonder if the composer's work is in him when he's not working. Leontyne's choice of my song *Snake* is wrong for her and unrepresentative—all by itself—of me, but one doesn't say that to a diva. Lee Hoiby's new setting of Wallace Stevens, however, is pretty good in most ways. I took along Rosemary (she's in town for visas, etc., in anticipation of her visit next month to India) who was no more dazzled by Leontyne's entourage than they by Rosemary's pacific forthrightness.

The clue for ROREM in the current Dell Crossword Puzzle Magazine is: Late U.S. composer.

How long has it been now—five years? six?—since the death of dearest Elizabeth Ames? Virgil, who never cared for her (the feeling was mutual), compared her style to that of a hostess in Schrafft's.

14 January

Copies received of *Opera News* containing "Notes on Kurt Weill." Astonishingly, no misprints. Before I finish checking it Abravanel phones from Utah to say *"C'est la meilleure chose qu'on ait jamais écrite sur Kurt,"* then proceeds to set me straight—yes, straight—on details. Weill never slept with another man, he despised homosexuals (which may have accounted for his mistrust of Blitzstein), but he did have starlets and, late in life, a regular mistress. He never mentioned his Jewishness, at least to Abravanel who is Jewish and Weill's dearest protégé. Lenya was Catholic, non-Jewish, and had many lovers, and, when Abravanel reproached her for deceiving Kurt, she answered, "I'm not deceiving him, since he knows all about it." Both Madeleine and Darius Milhaud disliked Lenya, it turns out.

A pleasure to speak with Maurice. He and Lucy were of course the cultural center of an otherwise arid period in Salt Lake in 1965–66. Despite a major heart operation (more than one), and cancer of the prostate, he seems energetic and indefatigable as ever.

18 January

Shrillness precludes persuasiveness in Gregory Sandow's defense of Glass: "The classical crowd won't grant him the artistic stature of Aaron Copland, say, or even of Pierre Boulez"; "Orthodox classical composers have a problem. . . . Why do they keep writing music nobody listens to?" Sandow implies no middle ground between minimalists and what he calls orthodox composers as embodied in Carter. Where does that leave my sisters and me? Far be it from us to side with orthodoxy, but we tremble at ex cathedra: "The minimalists sound like they took walks, went to movies, and made love; Carter sound[s] like he never did these things, or, if he did, like he never thought of putting them in his music." (Bad grammar also doubtless signifies being alive.) "Music doesn't have to depict everyday life . . . but a musical style that *can't* is only half alive." Then again, a musical style that can't depict intellectual life—or experiences less common than walks and movies and making love—is only half alive.

From the *Village Voice* (Jan. 17, '84) I turn to Renata Adler, to Alice Walker, to my frenzied "duty" which keeps me from my own work, and sigh. If this is the best we've got . . .

22 January

Lemons caught fire, the pears did too, and soon
all gooseberries flamed in the glare of noon.

Stella Adler's secret. The thought: glistening, gorgeous, intelligent, a touch blatant. The reality: she draws attention to herself not through shouting, but by speaking so softly as to command a hush; we lend our ears totally, without ever quite knowing what she's talking about.

Record cold all this week, but bright sunshine. Sky glistens, like Stella.

En souvenir:

Marie Laure's chain-smoking those *Gauloises de famille* drawn forth, at the rate of eight or ten per hour, from a gold *étui*. Her emphysematic hacking, especially at the theater.

The single long white hair emerging from Alvin Ross's forehead.

The memorial for Bill Flanagan (January 1970) when Aaron Copland spoke more of Bill's admiration for him, Aaron, than of his admiration for Bill. And Judge Julius Isaacs's extraordinary remark to the grief-stricken Flanagan parents, simple folk come from Detroit: "Are you in town just for this?"

Measure for Measure as libretto.

Anguished call from young Ken Fuchs wanting me to commiserate about the review—his first in the *Times*, and a bad one—of his string quartet played last week at Juilliard. I assured him calmly that this was but the start of hundreds of such notices he would ultimately be reading about himself. I, the essence of paranoia about precisely what Ken waxed paranoid about (the critic has it in for me), found his words merely paranoid.

28 January

JH wonders that in all of the revisionist controversy about Freud's Seduction Theory, as avidly reported by the *Times*, no one points out its basic fallacy. The claim, that having been seduced as a child provides a basis for adult trauma, assumes mistakenly that the trauma originated in that seduction, real or imagined, rather than recognizing that this real or imagined seduction is merely a mode by which the "traumatized" adult makes use of warped sexual conditioning to dramatize his (her) neuroses. (Child rape is here not the question.) JH perhaps is sensitive on the issue since he and the other church staff members have been advised not to touch the children they work with. No hugs for notes well learned, no kisses for bruised elbows, no fond pats on the back in farewell. He blames Freud's bad theory and its worse misapplications for the current child molestation hysteria.

Every one of us is fondled genitally as a child when adults wash us or change our diapers, and we nurse at the very breasts which, so soon after, are hidden shamefully from us. As for true sexual actions—any involving genitalia—does the child find it traumatic at the time, assuming the action has been forcefully initiated by an adult, because its sexuality is abused, or because its privacy is invaded? Or, if those actions merely satisfy the child's curiosity, will this child grow up a sexual criminal?

I don't know. Child abuse and child love come in all colors. I don't remember ever being "abused," but every member of my family appeared nude before every other member. Rosemary and I were not nudged into finding nakedness shameful, nor were Mother & Father. Yet Mother and Father were—are—quite proper.

A schoolteacher's moral standing is ruined when it's found he's been seduced by a pupil. And his health is ruined by a venereal disease caught from the pupil.

Words that look weird because the division of syllables is ambiguous: molester, goatherd, misled, sightreader.

Dave Brubeck, interviewed about his very sober Mass, states: Only from deep belief can one dredge up a convincing religious music. (Thus does Peter Pan make geniuses of us all.) Knowledgeably he adds: If Bach were alive today he'd be writing jazz. (And Caesar, I suppose, would be using atom bombs instead of bows and arrows.)

Worse than being sexually abused is to hear the well-meaning neighbor: "I overheard you working at the piano and very much enjoyed it."

Germaine Tailleferre says that when Gide came for the weekend he was so shy about being listened to as he practised that he asked the whole household to go into town from 7 A.M. until noon.

Clive Barnes's quip, ten years or so ago. The playwright: "What right have you to call yourself a critic?" Barnes: "What right have you to call yourself a playwright?"

31 January

While watching last night the successfully dreamlike (though less successfully dreamlike than two years ago) decors of David Hockney for *Rossignol*, I of course listened to the beautiful, but finally unsuccessful, music and thought how one thing leads to another, no escape. Elsewhere I've pointed out whence Stravinsky swiped the introductory material. But I hadn't before realized that Honegger's *Pastorale d'été* was swiped from the Fisherman's famous *plainte* in *Rossignol*, with its suave blues and fluted filigree.

Le Sacre having been more embarrassing than ever, with the literal-minded dancers disporting themselves like kindergarteners during a lesson of "The Natives are Restless Tonight," John Gruen and I skipped Oedipus to have a sweet at the Ginger Man and to reconnect after long years *sans tête-à-tête*.

3 February

Just read Mordecai Richler's sophomoric memoir, in *Geo*, of Paris in the fifties. As with all, yes all, American memoirs of Paris in the twenties, Richler, in mentioning what was occurring and who he was seeing during his two years there, mentions not one French name. But there *were* French people there then. I saw them.

To Father, lonely in Cadbury: "Every chapter of our lives is urgent and irreplaceable." Well, this is true, I suppose, but would I have thought to say it to myself?

Am reading ten years after the fact Lenny B.'s generally original, if spasmodic, talks called *The Unanswered Question*. They bow abjectly and needlessly to Chomsky. Which sends me to Mahler's Ninth, and I admit to being caught, but not stung, since there's nothing here as strong (for me) as *Pelléas*—just as nothing in Chomsky is as strong as Lenny, though probably neither of them would rate Debussy higher than Mahler. Anyway, Lenny's colorful words, "And so we come to the final incredible page . . . strands connecting us to life melt away, vanish from our hands even as we hold them. . . . But in letting go, we have gained everything," are echoed uncomfortably (in the program notes for Karajan's record) by one Richard Osborne, who without crediting L.B. informs us that "on the symphony's remarkable last page life appears to slip slowly from the composer's grasp. Yet we should not mourn . . ."

Shouldn't the symphony, if the "dying" theory is correct, narrow down on a single line finally to a single note on a single instrument? That's how I would have ended it, not on a chord as Mahler does.

The piano was of the sort that only non-musicians possess: wood the color of hard cider: blondish red, darker than champagne but frothy, like Marlene's hair.

4 February

Packing to leave tomorrow for three weeks at the Atlantic Center for the Arts in Florida where, with Miriam Schapiro and Lawrence Ferlinghetti, I share the title of Master Artist. We each are given a little house and our own flock of protégés.

The past weeks have been full: affectionate supper at Seymour Barab's, with twenty people around one table, so that friends from forty years ago could reunite. Victor Elmaleh's and Emlen Etting's vernissages in the rain. Birthday for Alger Hiss at Joe Machlis's.

Visit from Henson Markham, insecure in his job with Madame Sills. Maggy and Joe Rosner here to dine, with Lynda Sheldon and Joe LeSueur. Regular trips to Curtis (and to H. McIlhenny).

Party for John Myers's book, *Tracking the Marvelous*. Visit from Ms. Marnie Hall with ten copies of the very well done (by Sharon Robinson, Roz Rees, and Jerry Lowenthal) record of *Last Poems of Wallace Stevens* on her Leonarda (sic) label. Another session as judge on the Academy's Music Awards Committee. Tea with Robert Phelps.

Three concerts at Juilliard, at which the students' works were no less interesting than their mentors', including Shapey's ugly Double Concerto. Lunch with Arthur Peters, of the French-American Foundation, to discuss the impending but much belated publication of the collection of commissioned essays on Cocteau (is he unaware that the essay by me has already been printed thrice: in *Keynote*, in *Christopher Street*, and in *Setting the Tone*?), followed by another picture-taking session with Jack Mitchell, this time at his studio, with JH posing too. Still more photos, by one Steve Ziffer, to accompany Brad Gooch's article on what gayety used to be like, in the *Advocate*.

Rehearsals with Susan Belling and Will Parker for the Paul Jacobs memorial later this month. Visit from Tom Hillbish (about recording recent choral works) and from Kay Kraeft about Arkansas, where I'm to go for an "Art Song Week" this spring. Olivier's *King Lear* (mannered and long, but useful).

Dîner à trois with Ellen Adler & JH here, and at Stephen Koch's with Peter Hujar there. Another chat with Arlene Francis on WOR on the 30th, followed by a visit from Tommy Bogdan who sang my songs to me, and another from Stephen Brewer about my doing an article, probably on Nantucket, for *Geo*.

Drove to Cadbury with JH in a rented car. Corrected proofs of *An American Oratorio* (printed copies will be used for rehearsals). Visit today from a

Mr. Evans Mirages, of Chicago's WFMT, to tape a statement about Paul Jacobs.

It is as though those six brief days of peace in Nantucket at the start of the year were a dream lasting one minute, even without a bathtub.

New Smyrna Beach, Fla.
23 February

Final day of three weeks at the Atlantic Center where in the torpid clime I've nearly completed the piece for The King's Singers, a twenty-minute stark affair with no stops for six unaccompanied male voices and quite chromatic. How they'll stay in tune is . . . . My flock included—besides Daron—Robert Savage, Kenneth LaFave, and William Coble, all noble. We convened an average of fourteen hours a week. (Whatever else they may or may not have gleaned, I did infect them healthily with the nearly lost sense of song.) The rest of the time's been my own, except for two or three interviews and a speech at the university in Orlando. JH came with me, went back to NYC for the church, then, bless him, returned to Florida for several more days. Who knows how bleak it may have been without him.

Ferlinghetti's a second-rate poet trapped in a third-rate mind, as opposed to Ginsberg who's a second-rate poet trapped in a first-rate mind. The Jim Jones of culture surrounded by know-nothings who can't refute his notion of poetry. Will I ever grow accustomed to the ignorance of music by peers in adjoining fields? (L. F., in all his mediocre glory, feels that Ginsberg sheds meaningful light on Blake through that horrid whining.) As Babbitt's willfully fearful convolutions make him and his fans believe that, because of the *care*, he's writing true music instead of subtler mud pies, so Ferlinghetti's inventories, his Brainard-like iterations, reduce him to . . . Not that he simply has nothing to say (poetry's not "about" anything) but that he says his nothing with no urgency.

Critic as frustrated artist? How about artist as frustrated critic? I'm both, and still frustrated.

Jacques Bourgeois years ago wrote that I had "missed the boat," the boat of integral serialism. French idea. But that was *their* boat; can't a composer live by his own rules? Anyhow, which craft did I miss—which of those dozen lifeboats into which musicians flung themselves when Boulez shrieked *Fire*? The great liner on which I remained never sank at all; it chugs along still, watching those burnt ships out there, capsizing.

We saw *Night of the Shooting Stars* with disappointment.

Flat mirthless beaches, surrealist like Dutch waterfronts in winter.

World premiere of my saxophone suite, *Picnic on the Marne,* by John Harle in New York, on the 14th.

Danger of inspiration. Danger of technique. Both dangers are coral reefs, sensuous, rosy, potentially fatal.

Miriam Schapiro's technical inspiration seems not, on the face of it, to resemble her. She's a tried and true feminist, tough, intelligent, one-track-minded. Her symmetrical rugs—or paintings of rugs (one of which hangs at the Orlando depot)—are exquisite. Exquisite means feminine. Miriam would counter that she's not afraid to be feminine, that anyway the greatest men have been exquisite, and that we must change definitions of masculine & feminine or just stop using the terms. That's right. However, her work is only exquisite—which is nice too, except that the exquisiteness, unlike that of Fauré and Cellini and Herrick and other such stalwart males, is not very touching.

Creative interchange, the function of the Atlantic Center for the Arts, although in practice may be a chimera in theory conspires toward a unique pattern of productivity. It could be argued that this pattern contradicts the necessary loneliness of artists (is there a case of a composer who becomes a great songwriter through artificial insemination, rather than from an early, irrepressible urge toward poetry before he's ever met a poet?); yet in looking back I see that I have seldom accomplished so much in so little time, and I like to think that the same holds for my spirited band of young creators.

(There *is* no danger of technique—no such thing as too much of it, as there is of inspiration.)

New York
24 February

The single song that I never tire of practicing isn't one of mine, but Debussy's *Je tremble en voyant ton visage.* I am undone not merely by the perfection of each measure (if no phrase is *de trop,* or misplaced, or slightly atilt harmonically, perfection is still a cultivated and minor virtue, not indispensable to grandeur), but by the melting inspiration of every note. Inspiration is not a word I throw around, nor is it easy to pinpoint, especially as pertaining to the juxtaposition of one man's music on another man's verse.

No sooner off the plane than I rehearsed this and five other songs with Parker and Belling, took a bath, then took a taxi (with Frank and JH) to Symphony Space where, to our surprise, we found a crowd wrapped around the block hoping to procure tickets for Paul Jacobs's memorial.

The memorial lasted nearly five hours; our contribution fell about two-thirds of the way through. I dawdled backstage, listening, sweating nervously, gossiping. Heard from the wings, Bethany Beardslee's *Four Songs of Berg*, accompanied by Yehudi Wyner, was the ultimate in what German singing should be: penetrating, clean, unaccented, silken, granitic, utterly wise and utterly insane. I chatted with James Levine who, despite stitches in a digit (he displayed a bloody forefinger), managed to play Schoenberg's *Six Little Piano Pieces* as though they were music, not "modern music," an appropriate homage to Paul. Chatted also with Bill Bolcom and Joan Morris, who closed the program with a sort of incongruous logic by performing Gershwin's *Our Love is Here to Stay*.

Also logical, though unplanned: the only spoken comments during the evening were by me, Bolcom, and Elliott Carter. For Paul Jacobs, as much as any pianist ever, was aware that composers come first—to a point where, listening to Paul, one heard the music, not him playing the music.

I spoke for about three minutes, describing our shaky relationship in Paris in the fifties and how that relationship solidified through a mutual Debussyan need. The *Trois poèmes de Stéphane Mallarmé* especially, with their rich chords, witty prosody, and almost edible tunes, were a common point. We complained about the misprints still rampant in the Durand edition, and that these songs were virtually never performed, even by French singers. In fact, although Paul knew them backwards, he told me he had never heard them, which is why, I suppose, we programmed them. Susan Belling was not comfortable with the Frenchness of it all, yet (in her foam-green dress) she brought it off, as did Will with the other little cycle which he's sung a thousand times.

While practicing this afternoon it was several times my impulse to dial Paul's number and ask about a fingering, a possible wrong note, a nuance of translation. But if he wouldn't have been at home then, he was certainly with us tonight.

26 February

Last night and tonight, *Pilgrims* conducted by Gerard Schwarz and his string orchestra at the Y. Something about this twenty-five-year-old piece never quite jells. Perhaps it's too rhythmically square for the ambiguous picture I meant to represent (a child's suicide). Have persuaded Schwarz to bring *After Long Silence* to New York next autumn.

Jane Wilson's exhibition, Fishbach.

29 *February*

So Martha Graham, she too, fell into the *Sacre* trap. John Gruen took me last night to witness the premiere of her version. Now, Martha's nothing if not a theatrician; that she should come up with the same old thing—humorless virgin, sacred earth, sacrificial gyration—rather than with, like Paul Taylor, a point of view, means only that she was pulverized like all the others. That no critic has even pointed out that none can withstand the music of *Le Sacre*, and that Martha made a mistake to link herself so literally with her only equal, Stravinsky, is simply another comment on critics. Far from pointing out that Martha should not have tampered with Pandora's box, Kisselgoff declared the event a masterpiece. So much for Martha's Rite. Martha's wrong.

Needless to say, no dance critic mentioned that Martha used Gus Rudolph's reduced score, the so-called "chamber version" of *Le Sacre*, which Stravinsky officially approved without approving of. And how did it sound? They can't tell us. I'll tell you. Surprisingly rich for—how many?—twenty instruments. Impossible to know how small was the orchestra, but it sounded, like Martha, not rite but undecipherably (unlike Martha) wrong.

Thirty-three years ago I hadn't yet the courage of my convictions. The premiere that summer was Stravinsky's *Rake*, and Arthur Weinstein was also in Venice. I thought the *Rake* sounded like Mozart, but didn't dare admit it when Arthur (who knew all) said, "I get sick of all these people who say it sounds like Mozart." Who was I to contradict him? Today I say the *Rake* does sound like Mozart, and I do not bat an eye, for the flux of decades allows.

Re *The Rite* as a dance: the question is not how well, but whether it should be done at all.

Two hours at the dentist. No end in sight.

With Ellen Adler and Joe Machlis to *Painting Churches*, a harmless play featuring a mannered Marian Seldes.

6 *March*

A sometimes mirthless few days.

Rehearsed with Hilda Harris for the concert at the end of next month in memory of Donald Gramm at Rockefeller University on York Avenue. (Originally Donald and I were contracted for the recital. Hilda and Will Parker have graciously agreed to pinch-hit.) We'd planned to include the last piece Debussy ever wrote, *Noël des Enfants qui n'ont plus de Maisons*. Curiously, I never sat down and read the words—the composer penned them himself—until this morning. I told Hilda that although I'm sympathetic to Debussy I'm not sympathetic to his tooth-for-a-tooth sentiments: *Petit Noël, n'allez plus jamais chez eux, Vengez les enfants de France, Punissez-les, Donnez la victoire aux enfants de France.* The so-called enemy was made up of poor teenaged soldiers who didn't know what they were doing any more than the Enfants de France. We've cut the song, though I'm not sure Hilda agrees with my reason.

Thursday afternoon at Columbia, with Ulysses Kay, sifting through the wares of compositional applicants to Yaddo.

Friday, the voice of Frederica von Stade with the Chamber Music Society contains both the famous tear and the infamous waver.

With Morris, a saltless meal.

Last night, gave the first in a series of readings for the new bookstore on Hudson Street, a Different Light. Eugenie and JH helped swell the crowd, which was ample despite the rain. The store's part of the gentrified West Village, a slum, or almost, when we lived there in the 1940s. It's two doors down from what was once Ruby's garage, above which David Diamond lived.

Today, out of friendship for Felicity Dell'Aquila, I gave a class at Rye High School where she teaches. Neither the so-called music faculty nor the students had any idea of what I am, much less who. With no mutual frame of reference, I was at a loss as to how to speak to them. Tried to talk about "contemporary classical music," even played a tape of *Lions*, my most "visual" piece. Still, it was as though they were hearing a lecture on the niceties of Serbo-Croatian *in* Serbo-Croatian.

In the current *Advocate*, my letter about a recent Henze interview:

> We all, to some extent, make ourselves up. But as the occasional subject of interviews (not to mention professional rivalries and love affairs) I have learned that we can also become, against our will, the figment of someone else's imagination. Thus I was inclined to give Hans Werner Henze the benefit of the doubt while reading Patrick Franklin's interview with this German composer (Issue 387). As my host in Naples twenty-seven years ago Henze was generous, open and light-hearted, original, smart, funny, handsome and, of course, brimming with a tangible talent the international approval of which he was en-

joying as a child enjoys a new toy. That he should have grown into the rude and
self-important boor portrayed by your reporter is saddening and hard to grasp.
Yet maybe Henze has become a figment of *my* imagination and it is to Franklin
that I must extend the benefit of the doubt.

Certainly Henze's communism is no more a secret than is his sexuality—a
sexuality which nonetheless seems to contradict the very politics to which he
subscribes. And certainly his alleged replies seem un-thought-through, even
drugged, to questions about the suppression of human rights in Cuba. Any
composer who tries to support, or even to represent, his political leanings
through his art is barking up the wrong tree, and the music of Henze in particular has suffered from this in recent years. Art reflects, it does not dictate. Insofar as it does dictate, it veers away from itself toward propaganda. Art is beyond politics. Civilizations (not to mention ideologies) rise and fade, but their
greatest art survives.

Dear Hans Werner: Should your eye fall upon these words, know that I value
you as a colleague, and value much of your music as the "real thing" in this plastic world. Possibly, so long as we remain strictly musicians, none of us is right
or wrong.

8 March

Linda Sanders invites me to write something on "The New Romanticism"
for the New Horizons program which, like last year, contains all the current
"romantic" composers except me. How can I contribute with a straight face?
It's like not being invited to dance, but kibitzing from the sidelines.

JH, hearing *Canticum Sacrum* on the radio, declares it willfully ugly—a dishonest piece in (as Auden called an earlier period) a dishonest decade. Stravinsky, persuaded he was missing the boat by all the little Crafts, came up
with such stuff.

The hype around Glass and Carter by Rockwell and Porter. They've painted
themselves into a corner and, to save face, pretend publicly to admire the
color of the paint.

It is not my duty to be magnanimous (I am a composer, with everything to
lose), nor does it matter that I am grandly wrong. It is a critic's duty to be
open-minded, and he has not the right to be wrong.

10 March

I can't resist quoting from *The Diaries of Judith Malina*:

December 14, 1952

Party at Jo [*sic*] LeSueur's. We arrive after the rehearsal for *The Age of Anxiety* in time for coffee with Jo and Gianni and George and Paul Goodman and
Don Wyndham [*sic*] and Jim DeVries and Ned Rorem.

When Dicken told me about Ned Rorem's adagio act, I didn't know he meant
that I would find in it some of that demonic beauty that drew me to Lou: I liked
his perverse attractiveness. He listens to music holding a yellow rose with his
head thrown back in a pose as effective as he believes it to be. He is almost entirely turned inward; but if someone more his type had not been determined
to possess him, I might have found a way.

It's not often that we are given "to see oursels as ithers see us"! I do recall the
night at Joe LeSueur's. My date book notes it as December 13 (Judith would
have been writing the morning after), and Frank O'Hara was reduced to
tears by Paul G. who told him, "You're an imitation of me, but you only filch
the froth and not the essence." Judith's journal smells of a milieu of which I
was a peripheral part, and which in retrospect was meaningful. Years later,
while working with the Becks on "The Cave at Machpelah," I learned that,
in that hotbed of exhibitionistic amateurism, Judith alone had the wild electricity of a pro, and she almost "found a way."

15 March

Drive this morning to Cadbury with JH to visit parents and settle Father's
taxes. Father bright as ever at 89, but suffering (not much) from an arthritic
ankle. Mother fat, full of Krön chocolates I brought, in her own world, but
more chipper than a month ago now that she's on just one Meloril per day.
History of Mother's shock treatments. Her foggy madness and Father's crystalline logic merge into my talent.

Father credits his longevity to naps. He now takes three a day, one before
each meal. Including, as he puts it, a nap before breakfast.

I have been personally acquainted with Robert Russell Bennett, Dennis
Russell Davies, Richard Rodney Bennett, Peter Maxwell Davies, Richard
Dyer-Bennet, and Richard Dyer.

Homosexuality is not interesting in itself, any more than heterosexuality.
(There are no plays "about" heterosexuality, i.e., about being heterosexual
as opposed to just sexual.) Homosexuality is interesting only insofar as
homophobes make it a center of interest.

18 March

Last night at Diana Trilling's with JH. Moira and Michael also there, a John Gross from England, and Leo Lerman & Gray Foy. In spite of myself, I'm fond of Leo, though he represents all I despise (high intellect filtered through glossy magazines). Gray, however, at least to me, is cold and rude and pseudo-witty, and he set the tone for a general baiting. Are they disconcerted that *Vanity Fair*, from which Leo's just been released, is sending me next month to Paris? (And why am I filtering myself through a glossy magazine? For the money. At least it's a one-shot deal.)

Tonight, meal with Charles and Sally Jones in their house—yes, their *house*—on East 58th, which could as well be in the suburbs of Omaha. With Vittorio Rieti, Madeleine Milhaud and Louise Dushkin I am, for once, the youngest. But oh, to have one tenth of Madeleine's energy! She's just come from Paris, which she says seethes with a Cocteau revival, and goes tomorrow to Cleveland to teach speech—the impeccable melodrama she used on the records of Darius, which I grew up with.

20 March

Semi-public rehearsal this afternoon at Juilliard of a new song cycle by Leon Kirchner, using Beverly Hoch as model. Milton Babbitt, ever likeable, presided. Leon's not a lucid explicator. It was never clear who wrote the poetry; or why, when he finally permitted poor Miss Hoch to rise, she sang Schumann instead of Kirchner; or why he told us that "our dark era" inspired his muse, rather than how he constructed the thing. When it came time for questions, Milton announced, "Five o'clock. Class is over."

To Paul Taylor Dance Company with Morris and Tim Dlugos. As always with Taylor, and with no other choreographer, something happened. Something spooky and true.

Chicago
24 March

Of the three fertile days in Chicago as guest of the William Ferris Chorale, over and above their flatteringly produced concert of my music (including *Letters from Paris*), the as-always animated interview with Studs Terkel, the aching excursions back to U-High, the delectable suite at the Drake, the signing at the Unabridged Bookstore, and especially the official denotation by Mayor Washington of March 22 and 23 as "Ned Rorem Days," I retain this vignette:

Exhausted during a rehearsal with Katherine and Kristine Ciesinski in Ferris's parlor, I retire to the bedroom from where I hear the sisters as they continue working and am so touched by their English *tutoiement*, the patience and mutual regard with which they listen to each other, aid each other, do not compete with each other, trust and admire each other, that I drift off content.

When occasionally some stranger "recognizes" me—on a beach, say, or in the A & P—and says something flattering and then withdraws, why, although pleased, do I always want to cry? Probably because the recognition is for something now far away: because it's impossible to make further contact with the stranger (my work, stronger than I, has already made the crucial contact, and my self is a shell, removed from that finished work); and because there's nothing I can reply but Thank you, a thank-you uttered for a person (me, earlier) who no longer exists. Also—and this is the truest reason—it's because I don't think I deserve any compliments.

A composer is always on probation.

(TWA flight 375 at six P.M., between Saint Louis and Seattle.) After quitting the Drake this morning, but before boarding the plane at O'Hare, I was whisked to Wheaton College, somewhere in Illinois, for a three-hour master class in song for NATS. Jan DeGaetani had been there all morning and we shared a scanty lunch. On learning that Kristine's husband, Bill Henry, was dying in California, and that Kristine looked gaunt and tired (she follows the same macrobiotic diet as Bill), Jan grew visibly alarmed. "Do you think I could phone her?" she asked.

I caught the tail end of her class. Jan's more patient than I, centering on individual singers and discussing their technical vocal problems (or virtues) in relation to the texts they sing, while I'm inclined to address the audience, using the singers as mannequins whom I publicly reclothe in the memory of how I happened to compose this or that song. Jan, of course, is discussing other people's songs and how to approach them technically, while I (in a classroom situation with singers) almost always discuss just my songs and how to approach them literarily.

(Seattle, Sorrento Hotel.) Arrived here at nine this evening and was immediately taken to a party in honor of the Seattle Men's Chorus, of whom I am the guest. My room—actually an exquisite pair of rooms with huge closets and a bath with phone and heated towels—is filled with the fragrance of roses and pears, gifts of the chorus. What calm. The frank goodwill of the West Coast is a balm on these rare visits here.

Seattle
26 March

When Dennis Coleman invited me to the West Coast premiere of *Whitman Cantata*, it was suggested I "play something" with the chorus. As I had nothing for piano & male chorus, JH suggested I simply accompany, as written, four of my simplest songs, each to be sung in unison by one of the four sections of the choir. The effect proved magical at the rehearsal, as at the performance last evening. The chorus is, above all, devoted and enthusiastic, and it must mean something that Meany Auditorium was crowded to the rafters with a more or less bourgeois audience.

This morning before the plane, sightseeing with Coleman, Jerry Carlson (who'll conduct *Whitman Cantata* with *his* Gay Men's Chorus in Los Angeles later this week), and John David Earnest (whose setting of a poem by Richard Eberhart was on last night's program), mainly to the opulent botanical garden.

New York
30 March

Lukas Foss phoned to ask if I could go, in his place, to Tokyo next week to figure in a conference ("with Xenakis, and other greats") called "Are We in a New Renaissance?" Lukas can't go because of a middle-ear infection, and I can't go because I'll be in Paris. But of course, no one should go. If we *are* in a new renaissance nobody will know it for a hundred years. If someone knew it now, it wouldn't be a composer for whom all renaissance lies only in himself, not in "we." Why should either of us fart around with idle congresses instead of writing our music?

April Fool's Day

Next week I fly from Boston, at *Vanity Fair*'s expense, to Paris where for a fortnight I'll note reactions, diary-style and hour by hour, as during the early fall of 1969. Whatever wrong things happen will still be right simply because it's all to be inscribed. I don't really want to go. Nevertheless, I did write to Claude, and he answered, full of good cheer.

Boston to Paris
5–6 April

TWA FLIGHT 810
Strangers still sometimes ask me how Paris is because of my early journals. But I haven't resided there for twenty-six years.

Sometimes they also ask, Do you still keep a diary? Well, no—at least not from a need to spew forth. But yes, occasionally, as with the present experiment to snare a fortnight.

You can go home again, since every time's a first time (a first time at one's current age), and there's an anticipatory tingle, a harmless thrill, like a child's first sip of ginger ale before he graduates to champagne. Everyone I know in Paris is dead, including the person I once was. Has the Place des Vosges continued to glimmer during my long years away? Did Gallic skies reflect that light, night after night, in tints of fishpond green? Does the world exist if I don't exist? Not my world.

Here in the *New Yorker* is an ad for yet another book on Paris In The Twenties, exhorting us to glean more about Stein and Hemingway and Barnes and Boyle and Thomson and Crosby and Antheil. Why is nary a Frenchman ever listed, as though our expatriates of those days like the Plimptonites in the fifties simply appropriated the town with no interbreeding?

France's mystical lure dissolved in the sixties. Are there Americans in Paris today who've remained through the decades, or who are new and enthusiastic about the scene?

Being twenty-five, in love and in Paris is not the same as being sixty, not in love and in Paris. The red tape of travel is stickier despite the favorable rate of exchange and the inflight magazine's crossword in which I find myself like meeting a long lost friend (clue: Rorem namesakes; answer: Neds).

France, now on daylight savings time, is seven hours older than our East Coast. Every instant of the six-hour trek on this not-filled plane (in whose aisles Jews pray as the sun rises; the ultimate destination of the plane is Tel Aviv) speeds not toward my past but toward a rushed-up future. This noon—yesterday noon?—in Brookline, where for three days I was guest of Phyllis Curtin and Boston University, I panicked and lost my voice. Heartbeat, rain, premonition of being lonely and—not abandoned, exactly, but bored in Paris. Maggie Lee Conroy, still in makeup for a TV soap audition, drove me to Logan Airport in the gloomy rain, calming me considerably with her talk of the opera we may do together based on letters of Maria Mitchell, Nantucket's astronomer heroine. When I speak of fear of fainting in a foreign bathroom, she speaks of *her* fear of *Frank's* fainting in a foreign bathroom, and I feel egotistical for not fearing (except I do) JH's fainting in a foreign bathroom.

I'd like both to retch and to giggle. Do you remember how drunk we used to get on these flights? The French language, here in the sky twixt Boston and Paris, sounds as fresh as Provençal when once we traveled from Paris to Toulon. A Beau Bridges film, half-watched, without a headset. Although cigarets, after thirteen years of abstinence, repel me utterly, an occasional whiff of a fugitive Gauloise can rend the heart no less than Cocteau's snowball. An acid breakfast. Haven't slept a wink. Rain on the portholes. Nerves.

Try to veer from nostalgia to broader issues. Their music now. Politics. The gay milieu. Who is still alive?
    What's the title?
    Settling the Score.
    Is it about placement of proper markings in the conductor's copy of a symphony? Or about tallying the vote?
    It's about getting even.

We coast into Charles de Gaulle airport. The Laughing Man over there, sitting alone bolt upright, for no apparent reason has chuckled frantically and very loudly for six long hours. A steady, raw, and unwelcoming drizzle here too. Guy Ferrand is waving.

7 April

Last fall Virgil Thomson and I, featured stars on the same concert, were seated together in the front row of a small auditorium. Virgil, so deaf now as to find all music pointless and unable to gauge the force of his own voice, remains nevertheless the least foolish man around. The lights dimmed as we chatted of this and that, and I asked him where to stay in Paris. "Hôtel du Quai Voltaire is the only place," said Virgil—whereupon a lady in taupe chiffon emerged onto the stage to play his Violin Sonata. Virgil dropped off. During a hush after the first movement, as the player retuned her fiddle, Virgil awoke and piped resonantly: "But you can't bring anyone up to your room."

    It happens I'm at the Lenox, 9 rue de l'Université, a stone's throw from the no-longer-stylish Flore, in the heart of the *quartier* so dear to us all thirty-five years ago. Room 52 is on the top floor, tiny and bohemian, with a dear gentrified bathroom eleven steps up and a view through the skylight of chimneys like red peppers studded with peppercorns jammed into dirty brie. Above the bed a print from the Reale Piazza di Napoli, "La Morte di Giulio Cesare." Toward noon yesterday I collapsed, jittery, dozed fitfully to the sound of rain and banging doors until five, and arose aching, wanting to go home.
    Phoned Claude.

Walked slowly through the fog to the far tip of Île Saint Louis to dine with Henri Dutilleux, age 67, one of the three living French composers I most admire (with Messiaen, 75, and Henri Sauguet, 83), scarcely noticing Notre Dame—except that the portals are no longer crimson but brown—or indeed any heartbreaking landmark, so quickly are ancient reflexes reclaimed. The Pont Neuf and the quais seemed lined with a hundred new lemon-hued lanterns like radioactive urine specimens swinging in the sky.

Dutilleux, a dead ringer for the handsome André Breton, received me alone, except for his voluble Indian mynah who, like our cat Wallace, is eighteen years old. He gave me a photograph, which I'd never seen, taken for the 1951 Prix de Biarritz, of myself with eleven others (most of them now dead) including Désormière, Marie Laure, Nadia Boulanger, and Marie-Blanche de Polignac. Shoptalk for an hour. He is no gossip.

My sole complaint with the New Romantics (I tell him) is that they crib so predictably from Teuton Giants—Beethoven, Strauss, Mahler—with never a nod toward the French, whereas I've been recomposing Ravel now for forty years. Since there is no French influence in the New Romantics, the question arises: Were the French ever Romantic? But Dutilleux draws a blank, and I realize that not only he but probably all of Paris are not up on our newest silly labels, not to speak of our (to me healthy) tonal backlash.

So, hesitantly, I bring up the subject of the Pompidou-created, Boulez-dominated National Center for Contemporary Art in Paris, a.k.a. IRCAM, an acronym so locally celebrated that the origin—*Institut de Recherche de la Coördination Acoustique/Musique*—has become as remote as that of AIDS. People had hinted that Dutilleux was a lone wolf, unbending to computerized whips. "I think Boulez doesn't dislike my music," said he carefully. But does Boulez perform it? A non-answer: "Boulez would have had to be invented to become the director of IRCAM." Yes, but did IRCAM itself need to be invented? Silence. So we left in his car to dine on a heavy *bourride* at Le Petit Navire near the Halle aux Vins, after which, since my eyes were closing and his knee, recently incised, was aching, he drove me back to the hotel. When I claimed to care less and less about new music, he quoted Valéry: *On juge un artiste à la qualité de ses refus.*

Second night without sleep. Why am I here, tossing and turning, tending to other people's business, nerves shot, arm twitching, limp at 6 A.M.! Do I jump from the skylight? Finally dropping off, only to be shocked by the phone at nine and the solemn diction of Nathalie Sarraute. We make a date for Tuesday.

An hour's stroll through spitting rain all the way to Ethel de Croisset's in the rue Weber. Ethel does things right, as Marie Laure de Noailles, her half-sister-in-law, did before her, with a sumptuous home and capable servants, a *train de vie* now rare. I know Ethel through Francine du Plessix Gray, with whom she shares the urge to be *à la page* in matters artistic. But whereas Francine is herself an artist and thus to some extent invents the rules, Ethel is a fancier and, in the best sense, patronizes others. The lunch guests are book critic Guy Dumur, Mark Rudkin of the American Center, music commentator C. Samuel with his *amie*, Maryvonne Deleau, and Madame Suzanne Tézenas, unchanged since the fifties when she was to Boulez what Marie Laure was to me, and who remains a champion of what the French still call, wistfully, the avant-garde.

Talk is mainly of standard classics (the "new" Massenet, *Werther*, is the rage at the Salle Garnier), but also of Bob Wilson (as he's named here) and his staged inventions with Philip Glass in Rome and Cologne, which Ethel and Mark have witnessed firsthand. Divine! But isn't Philip Glass's public essentially unmusical? Isn't he (I continue to venture) perhaps pretentiously unpretentious, his simplicity being *reaction against*, not *action for*? The great unwashed, by definition, like mud pies, so they can comprehend Glass, but nothing happens with mud pies; they just wash away. My remarks don't go down well, but Ethel, a true lady, makes no attempt to cover up for me. Instead she asks if I know Edmund White: "Francine brought him to lunch with his very young friend. He's really robbing the cradle."

I learn that Massimo Bogianckino, the new boss of the Paris Opera, dreams of presenting operas written for Paris: works of Gluck, Rossini, Bellini, Verdi, Wagner. Not a word about why Bogianckino is not commissioning new operas (even our old white elephant, the Metropolitan, is ahead of him there), but a vague apprehension about his being Italian, since the French don't like foreigners mixing in their musical business.

Monsieur Samuel and Mademoiselle Deleau drive me back to the Lenox in their *six cheveaux*. I make a date with Maryvonne, who works at the Centre Pompidou, for a guided tour of that edifice on Monday, and also of the adjoining IRCAM where I have never been.

Rain.

With James Lord to Bernard Minoret's for an eight o'clock all-male cocktail party at which I am (I think) the guest of honor. James is the same on the surface, strong-jawed and healthy looking, sardonic and opinionated in his French which, though utterly fluent and colloquial, is as heavily accented after forty years as Laurel & Hardy's. His Giacometti book—still unfinished because he can afford for it to be—will be his life's work. Still, one could wish that with his vast knowledge and snobbery, his goyische chutzpah and cruel insolence (I recall on the beach at Cannes, in 1954, his referring to two skinny young men as Miss Dachau and Miss Buchenwald), and his uniquely vested interest and special style, that he would compose a book on Marie Laure. Who else could do it? He tells me of lunching a few months ago at Ethel's. Egmont de la Haye-Jousselin (Marie Laure's anglicized grandson) now in his thirties, was also there. He said to James: Are you still interested in art?

At Bernard's party everyone is *branché*, a new term which seems to mean "with it," or literally "plugged in." A young architect, engaged in resurrecting Marie Laure's ruined château in Provence, asks if we can meet next week *afin de parler du passé*. Then I flee with Edmund White and Gilles Barbedette to the Recamier for a well-balanced meal. Ed pays.

Am I *branché*, Edmund? No, you're *bas bleu*, like Francine.

Ed's dutiful French and Yankee élan remind me of "us" back when. A knack for foreign tongues has nothing to do with a musical ear. Many a fine musician never gets the hang of another tongue, while many a tin-eared dolt speaks many languages flawlessly (while retaining his doltishness in each one). For an American to learn French after childhood, he has to (1) want to, (2) be unafraid, even hammish, and (3) work very hard at discovering the equivalent of his personal English as rephrased by the French *mot juste*. After a year, if he lives in a uniquely French milieu, he'll know the language, so far as accent and grammar are concerned, as well as he ever will. He won't "improve," he'll just augment his vocabulary during the next fifty years. But his children, if he has them in France, will speak better than he does by the age of three: they'll have nothing to suppress.

Ed feels that the French adore us (he means "we" are sexual catches). But the French adore Reagan, too.

To the Flore for ice cream (I paid). AIDS, here known as *Le Sida*, is "style," and so are back rooms, *les salles d'orgie*. They've adopted the word *gai*—with its modifications: *gais, gaie, gaies*—and use it for everything including porno video houses, bars & bistros, and homosexual magazines, of which there seem to be scores more than in the USA. Ed White is a star for them all, being, like Susan Sontag before him, a champion of the up-to-date (which is inherently more French than American), like Foucault, Barthes, now Pina Bausch. But he's right, since (at least for me) he's a semi-major author, and authors are never wrong. He does things right, too, as an intellectual manipulator, the way Ethel does as a hostess. His two translated novels are in store windows.

They walk me back here where now I'm lonely and exhausted and feel I'm learning nothing. In a month, in a year, I'll recall this pain with pleasure, this tedium with interest. But as with Chicago last month, I'll never need to return.

Trees, we are now informed, can communicate with—can warn—each other. If all living things are sentient and by extension have capacity for irony (am I anthropomorphizing?), then does that "viral entity" that causes AIDS relish the notion that we're in a fix?

8 April

After still more panic, finally an acceptable sleep. Habitual *déjeuner*: icy orange juice, hot fresh croissants, firm white butter and gooseberry jelly, jet black coffee and steaming milk. This cramped room I may in a decade far removed think back upon with love. That giant blue pigeon on the drainpipe there, pink-breasted. Letters to JH and to Father.

The Louvre for a while. Looked at Swedes looking at sculpture, and gazed long through the windows at the drizzle drenching the spookily stunted espaliered elms in the central court, and behind them the grafittied barricade around the pit that soon will house Pei's dome, which I'm for and against.

Movie, *Un amour de Swann*. Everything about it is wonderful, except it. Though each frame is deliciously watchable, it's not my Proust, nor yours—it's theirs, and maybe not even theirs. Like Kafka, Proust is unfilmable, but for an opposite reason. Kafka's too general for specification (Joseph K. is Everyman) while Proust is too interior for specification (our pictures evoked while reading *Lost Time* are too personal to share with theirs).

Despicably unProustian are two graphic episodes, both of Jeremy Irons interminably possessing a female *par derrière*. And Delon, though an interesting choice for Charlus, is directed to cast *oeillades* like any dizzy queen at the armed guards. All the famous *répliques* are heavily italicized: "I wasted my life on a woman who wasn't my type," and "Swann, you'll live to bury us all," come out as gag lines.

Still, as the Duchesse de Guermantes, Fanny Ardant, looking like Susan Sontag (on purpose? Nicole Stéphane?) "works," as does Ornella Muti as Odette with the slutty elegance of Cécile Aubry's *Manon* in 1949. Henze's score works too, with his very 1980s string sextet and disembodied soprano encroaching on Debussy's *Arabesque* played on an out-of-tune harp. Henze has solved the problem of the *petite phrase* in the only way possible, with a bold screech played on a fiddle by Ivry Gitlis.

But wouldn't that last freeze-frame of Odette with her parasol in the *bois* (looking here like the Tuileries) be more Proustish if followed by another motionless frame from which Odette has quite disappeared?

It's raining. It began again before dawn, continued vehemently all day so that one wondered at nature's stamina (who would have thought the old sky had so much blood in it!), and now has subsided to a fevered seeping which lends the boulevards an ashy hemorrhaged aspect, not at all unpleasant. Alone in the Café Cyrano. Though it's only six o'clock the street looks like midnight. Sixteen years ago I'd have felt like a Jean Rhys heroine, but in the interim I've had not a drop of alcohol. Snuggly before me sits not a *coup de rouge* or three but a foaming cup of hot chocolate, a brioche, and a jar of hard butter. The solitude is exquisite. Anxious forms beneath umbrellas converge outside like rioting mushrooms toward the Métro, but in here a central stove hisses and I think about Piaf and Simenon and don't feel morose at all, as I write these notes about the Proust movie on the zinc table.

Dined chez Edmund White and John Purcell (he who was robbed from the cradle) in their rented flat, Rue Poulletier, half a block—though light years away—from Dutilleux. Chicken with lemon. No real dessert. Ed's other guests, hand picked from various countries but all like-minded, as they imagine Americans still behave, with leather and chains and promiscuity and no hint of Love, and instruction manuals for *le poingculage*. Their aping of our manners is more dangerous than false. Guy Ferrand on the way from the airport Friday said that *le Sida*, rampant in Zaire, spread from Africa through Haiti to New York quite simply via inflamed rectal tracts, transmitted (like hemophilia in women who are immune carriers) through the semen of *sains porteurs*. Statistics leave the guests indifferent. Guy is the sole Frenchman thus far to indicate aversion for Reagan and sympathy for Mitterand.

Ed and John, who leave tomorrow for Greece, lend me the keys to their flat.

Marlene Dietrich sang of the risks forty-five years ago:

> See what the boys in the back room will have.
> Tell them I sighed, tell them I cried,
> Tell them I died of the same.

Could it be argued that America's reversion to a simpler music corresponds to the current homosexual eschewing, for whatever reason, of promiscuity? If Elliott Carter's quartets parallel the tangled rituals of the Mine Shaft, do Rochberg's quartets parallel the New Sexuality?

9 April

I've not had a full night's sleep in thirty years, and insomnia's almost a friend ("Good morning, heartache, sit down"), but these new bouts are fierce. Scarcely nine hours of sleep since Thursday, wide-eyed conjectures, pained onanism, worry over minutiae. At 6 A.M. after tossing since midnight I phoned Guy hysterically. He'll leave a *somnifère* at the desk later today. The sun seems out. Cool.

A moment in the Église Saint Germain. Knelt and prayed for sleep.

Thorough visit of the Centre Pompidou with the affable Maryvonne Deleau who, though shy, has the innate assurance of European women who know themselves to be on a par with men without being either coy or shrill. Few American women have it, and it has always intimidated and beguiled me, from my piano teacher Nuta Rothschild, with her Russian accent, through visions of Marlene Dietrich, to Yvonne de Casa Fuerte, Virgil's friend, the first French person I ever knew, circa 1943. The Centre Pompidou, known as Beaubourg, is a horrible structure not unlike the Halles it has replaced, except that the glittering livers and lungs hanging on the outside are painted steel, and on the overcrowded inside is a series of ill-hung so-so exhibitions. Except for the gorgeous Bonnard. We cross the square and descend into IRCAM where to my sleepless horror the first person we meet in the corridor is Pierre Boulez. He cannot help but have seen, over the years, my sundry references to him as the Hitler of France. Nonetheless he shakes my hand, says in English "How do you do," and turns and vanishes and that is that.

Through a glass screen in an elaborate studio we watch—listen to—the recording session of a brass piece by a Hungarian composer and conductor unknown to me. Over there two trombones fart dryly, back here a horn farts in reply, then three trumpets fart and are answered by a low fart on the tuba. Then they all fart together, but can't seem really to let loose. Don't true artists grandly shit? Later in the ateliers for computer composers—*ordinateurs*—the same constipation reigns among these well-bred but genderless youngsters solemnly curved over their audio-microscopes. Such expansion of limits! Ah, those bent tones! Oh, that cultured careful madness! Isn't there something old-fashioned about the very notion of progress, of stretching seams, of wishing to be new?—yet not so old-fashioned as to extend back to Bach, or even Schubert, who were hardly concerned with such trends? In broadening the potential of instruments "new" music is all about what the performer can do, not what the creator can do, and so these composers are leaving themselves in the lurch.

IRCAM's literature is garnished with blurbs from the literary likes of Foucault (*Ce n'est pas une musique qui chercherait à être familière; elle est faite pour garder son tranchant. Elle fait irruption toujours aux frontières.*), not from musical savants, demonstrating once again that the French enjoy talking about music more than listening to it.

Barbara Kolb, who is American, spends ten hours a day computing at IRCAM. Does she think it matters? "Oh, what matters?" she retorts in self-defense. But Englishman Nicholas Maw is not, like Barbara, in love with Boulez. "To think of that vast expensive hole in the ground, all to placate the fantasy of one man!"

I emerge from the hole onto the Square Igor Stravinsky, which features a fountain in which glide Disneyesque creatures representing the Firebird, the Nightingale, etc. Nearby in the Église Saint Merri I again pray for sleep.

A step away from IRCAM is the bookstore called *Les Mots à la Bouche*, where I buy a batch of little mags, Genet poems, Sagan's latest, a *récit* by Jouhandeau called *Éloge de l'imprudence*, and the much-discussed Cocteau diary, *Le passé défini*. Back now in Room 52; although it's nearly 8 P.M. a strong yellow glow from a high sun streams through the skylight. One forgets that Paris is on a latitude with Winnipeg.

Some wine doesn't travel. Stephen Sondheim is as unknown here as Juliette Gréco in New York. If music's not a universal language neither are books and pictures. People here don't know John Cheever or Larry Rivers or Bette Midler or Philip Roth, and people there don't know Julien Green or Jean-Louis Curtis or Le Clézio or the venerated Dalida.

10 April

Am writing late in the morning on a table strewn with the *Herald Tribune* sticky with fawn-colored croissant crumbs and cherry (which was brought today instead of gooseberry) marmalade. Pleasant repast last evening with José (Henri Hell) and Richard Négroux, *toujours les mêmes*. Tomato and olive soup with chives, roast lamb, peas and carrots, camembert, huge strawberries and *crème fraîche*. Talk mostly of Poulenc with whom they're both obsessed. And both are pro-Reagan like so many of the French, out of anxiety of actual invasion by human beings.

Phoned JH in New York at midnight and felt better. Took one pill and finally dropped off. If today I feel groggy at least it's normal groggy.

Awoke briefly from the grogginess just before dawn to the sound of sparrows, and recalled, so accurately as though it were an odor in these sheets, the identical sound twelve thousand mornings ago when I would awaken hungover in similar rooms in the arms of strangers who like me stank of booze, or into empty rooms with empty pockets. In the thirteen years that I've not smoked nor touched so much as a drop of vermouth, the smell and the touch are a mere inch away and yes, I do think about it. Yet, knock wood, my trembling frame is more protective than the brain, and the thrilled protective screen that would quickly arise around me in the face of a martini would, next day or next week, fall over to reveal a corpse.

Afternoon. Walked toward the Pont Alexandre. Rain begins again. For protection I enter the Grand Palais. Scattered across these twenty acres are the five thousand paintings of Les Indépendants, all motel-room junk, embellished by an irritating smear of pop music pumped through loudspeakers all about.
    Avenue Georges Cinq. The chestnut trees seem on the edge of bursting but surely won't before I leave ten days hence, whereas the exquisite "forced" pansies at the Rond Point—each one looking like a wee purple plate displaying the yolk of a wren's egg—will have peaked and decayed by then.
    In André Ostier's pretty apartment, rue Bassano, a glass of water only, and an hour's worth of reminiscence, mainly about Valentine Hugo.
    Nathalie Sarraute lives just one block down the hill. At five I ring her bell.

Character is expressed through mouths and eyes (and to some extent hair), which we can alter continually; character is not expressed through chin or nose or those other rocky givens of the head. Yet believing this, can we judge others by pouts and winks? Nathalie Sarraute, who in a drugstore you might not take for the intellectual empress, violently evinces personality through a pair of thick lenses. There she sits, so friendly, even coy, *recroquevillée* on the velour sofa of the small salon (ten years ago it was in the larger room next door), with a slug of scotch—*pour éviter un rhume qui couve*—while I sip tomato juice. Her rugged features clash with her seductive style. Wildly I think of Bill Inge, twice my size, who once sat himself on my lap like an uninvited spaniel.
    "*Comme je vous envie.* I envy you, successful, young, yes young compared to me, living in New York, that city which I adore with a passion. I am passionate about all of North America. I've lectured in every corner from Vancouver to Miami." I fondle a bowl of dried flowers while she leaves to answer the phone, and look from the floor-to-ceiling casements through the dribbly mist to the Musée de la Galleria, and beyond to the rue Freycinet

leading toward Marie Laure's in the place des États-Unis, which once was my only home and which now is a sepulchre.

"It's because I'm Russian that I fear the Russians, and for that reason admire the strength of your president." I can't help but be moved as she talks of her father and mother, divorced and remarried when she was a girl. She knew what Maisie knew, and "dealt with" her parents for decades, never however seeing them together until the end. I bring up JH. "I'm glad," she says, "that one can talk frankly these days about that kind of love. I'm consternated that a close friend of mine has just left his friend of twenty-five years for a worthless boy." So we discuss the merits of fidelity, of longevity, and of fame. "Glory at eighty is not all that exciting, but good reviews are better than bad."

Recalling her once kind words for Mary McCarthy I ask if she still sees her. "Absolutely not. *Elle est vraiment trop méchante*, mean and cruel and not to be trusted," which struck me as a Parisian sentiment, accurate but reversible. Once I wrote that the French for all their fickleness dig deeper than we into friendship, but such a generality is no more than glib—no more, indeed, than French.

In the habit of the war years, when everyone went to cafés to keep warm, she works all morning at the Bar Marceau down the street. Lunches *en famille*. Never goes out, to parties or the theater, in the evening. Though aware of her value and stature, her stardom came too late for her to know how to act the star (she'd like to) as, for example, Françoise Sagan has done all her life.

As a result of her successful cataract surgery she now sees more acutely than even a falcon could desire, or so she contends, examining my gray matter from across the room through heavy spectacles which, combined with her short bob and dated swagger and abrupt tone that she seeks to camouflage with applied charm, make me wonder if she's a lesbian. I doubt it, but wouldn't wish to offend her by being wrong.

"I don't know anything about music," she goes on, "But do you agree that"—she names a composer we both know—"that X's work is a bit force-fed by the Boulez milieu?" Why yes, I do.

But we don't get into esthetics or trends—what do professionals do, after the age of age of reason? She's out to make a nice impression, and does. We sign each other's book. Hers: A *Ned Rorem en souvenir de nos rencontres, avec plein d'amitié*. And *amitié* is what I too feel quickly filled with as we kiss good-bye.

At the pastry shop across the street I buy a pear tart, consume it outdoors

in a shaft of sunshine that pierces the rain, look around in vain for the Bar
Marceau, grab the 63 bus to rue Saint Guillaume, and rush toward the hotel
to take a bath before dining with Claude.

My Paris is both graveyard and slaughterhouse with everyone dead or about
to die, and smelling foul. Can I have been so nurtured here, here in what
now seems a starving metropolis, starving in silk? Any giddy semiotic vogue
assumes an aspect of *grand sérieux*, and the emperor's new clothes are
vended not only by Yves Saint Laurent but by the Saint Laurent of music,
Pierre Boulez. Art is chic. They like everything about art except art, and
maybe the same is true of sex which seems to emerge less through necessity
than through mode. None of this is good or bad.
    But the lavishly costly IRCAM experiments are, it seems to me, just as
much mudpies as the œuvre of Glass. They cut no mustard. In our adolescent Chicago we once had two phonographs, a broken one sounding an octave lower because of a slowed-down turntable, and a normal one. On the
first we played the "rhythmless" *Afternoon of a Faun* simultaneously with,
on the other, *Boy Meets Horn*. Rex Stewart's trumpet with its even beat
against the uneven beat of Debussy's doublebass flute turned out, accidentally on purpose, as inventive, and far cheaper than all the Ircamiana in decades to come.

It's nearly eight. While I was bathing Sarraute phoned, hoping I would never
quote her mention of . . .
    Claude is due in ten minutes. For reasons of art I should never see Claude
again but allow the crazy idyll to throb or expire alone—that is, were I to
compose my life as I compose a symphony. I do recall what I've written about
experiences more than the actual experiences.
    For reasons of history I should write: I did not see Claude again. Old
flames like old friends can't be revived and retain their sparkle, for we are
different persons. But old poems *can* be reread, and yes, love to friendship
often occurs. So I sit now waiting for a knock on the door.

                                                                    11 April

Sarraute called yet again this morning, afraid I might have misunderstood
something she said "about women." For she adores women, is deeply feminist; she just hates screaming from the housetops, that's all. I told her I loved
her (*C'est réciproque*, she affirmed), and probably wouldn't quote anything.
    So, Claude and I dined on the rue du Bac at the old Ministères, smartly
refurbished since 1949 when a waitress named Gaby taught me how to de-

bone a sole. Later, chamomile at the Flore. Our first meeting in twenty years. No fatter, no thinner, no grayer, he looks the same but looks his age. Claims to have spent the past four days in fearful anticipation of this meeting, seemed visibly moved, repentant of the petit bourgeois apprehension about me so very long ago, says he turns red with shame now when looking at *The New York Diary*. *It* was there, but attenuated. A touch of affection, but vapid as the cooling tea before us. That long-ago horror was my own invention and so was the person who provoked it, the person sitting across from me who—he too, with his continuing charm—"doesn't mind Reagan." What has this affable paragon, who even in the burning months was never, as Swann said, "my type," what has he to do with me?

Returned to the hotel toward 1 A.M. and split a pill with my friend Insomnia. Hazy this morning. Thumbing Cocteau's diary.

Lunch chez Robert Veyron-Lacroix, whose apartment, avenue Suffren, is as Frenchly beautiful as Ostier's. Nothing's wrong with it, an impeccable *goût* (which I don't have, but can spot) independent of funds, as distinct from, say, "Falconcrest," which boasts the kind of bad taste only money can buy. Salad of carrot purée and parsley, bouchées à la reine aux champignons, Greek cheese with Spanish oranges, Evian water without ice (ice causes heart attacks), and no coffee. Robert is whiteheaded and too skinny after paralyzing woes which oblige him to withdraw from a performing career while persevering at the Conservatoire. He takes as his due my homage in a recent liner note naming him Europe's only harpsichordist; is more amused than scared by Reagan, nor does he dread a nuclear holocaust since merely to be alive is to be in peril; concurs with the consensus that Messiaen's *Saint François* was a five-hour jerk-off (if a musician as dramatic as Messiaen hasn't written an opera or even a ballet by age seventy-five it's unlikely he'll ever succeed: a sense of drama and a sense of theater are not interchangeable); still worships American beauty, mainly for its cleanliness; is smart and sweet and quick and eroded and just my age.

Well, I don't find much beauty in Americans, I thought as I walked back across the Esplanade des Invalides where the breeze whispered snidely, with its uniquely Parisian accent, of a *découchage* thirty-five years ago when I walked back across the same Esplanade. For it was in May of 1949 that I first came, on the SS *Washington*, to live in France. We were big sexual hits then, but today French youth looks sturdier than ours. And anyway, as I walk and walk—covering how many kilometers each day!—I pass fewer doors behind which I once made love than behind which friends lie dying or dead.

Phoned Yvonne de Casa Fuerte who is honored this week on Radio France-Musique with a retrospective of her fifty-year-old Serenade Con-

certs featuring Sauguet, Rieti, Markevitch, Weill, Milhaud, Nabokov, etc.,
as antidote to the current Boulezian infection.

Apropos of infection, today's *Figaro* reports 125 cases of *le Sida* thus far
in France, versus 3954 in the U.S. And Claude last night told of hearing on
the air that California police are legally raiding saunas.

A touch of sunlight.

Dîner chez Guy. A sensational duck with poached peaches and then the first
wild strawberries of spring served with clotted cream, after which we
watched "Dallas" for one weird hour. The episode was a year old, the dubbing shoddy, with no attempt at regional accents; yet the French are as dazzled as Americans by this and by "Dynasty" and await impatiently the advent
of "Falconcrest," with Reagan's ex-spouse.

To the Deux Magots for tea, having parked in the new labyrinth beneath
Saint Sulpice. Half a sleeping pill. Noisy hallway.

12 April

Went to bed with Cocteau, vaguely disappointing except for the close (to
me) vitality: the journal covers eighteen months beginning in July 1951 (six
more volumes are promised by Gallimard during the next years), in which
nearly every entry brings home an event at which I was present. But the fragmented philosophical gems were all later polished and reset more tellingly
elsewhere. What blinded me yesterday is frayed today: the constant harping
on being read and then forgotten by those few who read. *"On peut dire à
n'importe qui et n'importe où une chose qu'on a déjà écrite. Elle est neuve.
Il n'est pas rare qu'on nous conseille de l'écrire. Même ceux qui nous lisent
ne se souviennent de rien."* Maybe those readers are too polite to say that his
conversation seems a replay of what they've already read. Or maybe, in different contexts, an old *tournure* takes on new light, even new sense. Don't
I reread my own diaries having forgotten that I used a charmed phrase here,
then reused it there? Cocteau was too quick to accuse his public.

In passing he writes of me in an episode which I too have described: our
visit, with Marie Laure, to her mother's at the Villa Croisset in Grasse. I
noted: "On arriving, Cocteau announced to Madame de Croisset, 'It seems
like yesterday that I was bringing Marie Laure back from our outings.' (He'd
not been in this house since the summers of World War I when the adolescent Marie Laure began nursing the love-hate she never forsook.)" *His* entry, though, betrays itself when he tells us that, *"Comme je n'ai aucun sens
du temps, j'ai l'impression d'y revenir après une promenade."* He forever
states that he has "no sense of time," yet isn't it precisely because he does

have a sense of time that he has the *impression d'y revenir?* Again he tells wrong (wrong theatrically) an anecdote—retold in my *Paris Diary*—about Garbo at the Véfour where clients mistook her for Madeleine Sologne. Isn't that irony sufficient? But Cocteau adds what musn't be added: *"Le sens du légendaire est perdu."* Never apologize, never explain.

His pro-Stalin leanings seem naive even for then, as do his generalities about Americans: Americans hate Negroes, yet they all do their best to acquire a suntan.

Around that same season Boulez proclaimed: "Every musician who has not felt the necessity of the serial language is useless." Omit the word *not* and I would agree.

Cold and cloudiness continue. Editorial in *Figaro* by André Roussin about normality of homosexuality today as against 1950 when his *Les Oeufs de l'autruche*—to be revived this week—was first staged. Decision to erect Pei's pyramid in the Cour Napoléon is final and irreversible; the French are as beguiled by this gaudy bauble as by Reagan's jelly beans.

Lunch chez Dino di Méo, just around the corner on the rue des Saints Pères, with Bernard Minoret and Olivier de Magny. Cheese soufflé, flawlessly runny; veal in vinegar; pear compote with almonds; espresso with *sucre de cane.* Dino, looking like a retired boxer with the grin of a Latin saint, is now in the catering business (he will cater Charlotte Aillaud's after-the-opera supper on Monday to which Claude has summoned me), while Bernard and Olivier (whose great-great-great-great-grandfather's verse I once put to music in *Poèmes pour la paix*) are delectably lazy and cultured with a grand gift for chatter. Discussion of some Doré prints which are passed around, and of New York which Dino, refreshingly, hates. More pro-Reaganism, after stasis of Carter; more smirks at mention of AIDS, an American *rigolade*; a nice quote from Peggy Bernier to Georges Bernier about some passing genius: *Mais comment ne peux-tu pas le croire? Il est célèbre.*

Bernard gives me his mauve-covered booklet of recent plays which everyone says are touching and original and underrated.

Late afternoon. Spent a silent hour unpacking at Edmund White's (they're in Athens), glancing through his mail (all literary, nonmusical, in English, nothing on me), looking at snapshots of himself and John, and casing the library (indigestibly pederastic and up-to-date) before going for tea at Marcel Schneider's in the Marais ten minutes away.

Marcel serves linzer cookies with a mint infusion. Pro-Reagan. "If the world does explode—but it won't—such things occur anyway every hundred thousand years, and it will rise again. There's no contemporary music, even bad—no outlet for it. I loathe Sartre and Beauvoir for lending a false idea of socialism to—and hence destroying—a whole generation." (I feel that about Boulez.) "Only great passions sustain me now at seventy." And he bestows upon me his latest book, a collection of stories called *La Lumière du nord* (which he explains doesn't mean northern lights but the influence, in France, of Brahms), with a long inscription suggesting I use one of them for an opera someday. Not that I haven't already used the effects of his vast cultivation that shone in his translation of *Der Jasager* and in the little biography of Schubert.

It seems that roughly forty percent of the whores cruising the shadows of the Bois de boulogne at boulevard Suchet are actually Brazilian males in drag, who earn up to a thousand francs a throw.

There are no cockroaches in France.

To be master in the parlor and slave in the bedroom translates into a perfect alexandrine: *Le bourreau au salon et la victime au lit.*

Acid breath of all the wine-imbibing French . . .

Late evening. Dîner chez Tereska Torres Levin. A crazy cabdriver deposited me ultimately at 65 boulevard Arago but not without a lengthy diatribe, foulmouthed and rasping, on how he was as great a tenor as Pavarotti except that he suffered from chronic catarrh. When, as I got out, I explained that I too am a musician, and American, he said, *Vous voulez dire, comme Samuel Barber?* From the mouths of babes! Last week in New York Elliott Carter, after warmly recalling the SRO audience for his last concert at the Théâtre du Rond Point, had asked: "But what can you write about Paris? Xenakis still reigns supreme, and they know nothing about Americans except Ives."

Tereska has two other guests, both offspring of old friends. The atelier is high and gloomy with her father's sculpture all about and copies of Meyer Levin's books in various translations, as well as those of Mailer whom she admires. We dine in the kitchen. Tereska, who at sixty-three remains a gamine, says that life without Meyer is not life and that she'd kill herself were it not for the children. I say: Given the evidence I cannot believe in the fact of Anne Frank, and add that Meyer's book about Frank is truer than the girl herself. Tereska's own books show as no others have (not Mary McCarthy or Francine du Plessix Gray) what it means to be at once Jewish and Catholic.

Bull session: on beauty; on Meyer's comprehensible paranoia; on God. I say there's no God, no evidence of a caring presence in the universe. He's a human concoction. Animals don't worry about God; but for us, love and art are cursed and illogical, and the processes of war and of aging are disgustingly irrefutable. To be is not to mean, but we force our meagre meaning just to keep going. Still, though I don't "believe," I believe in belief, and envy True Believers if only because they'll die more calmly than I. Then I ask: If confined to a benign international concentration camp, which group will you seek out—intellectual peers speaking a language you don't know, or lingual *semblables* from a lower (or higher) caste? Tereska cuts through this. "I'd seek out the Jews." So, probably, would I.

Bright moon. Am back at Edmund's. Perchance to dream.

Cocteau's diary is hard to put down, not least because I'm continually comparing his version of this or that event with my version. For example, in December of 1951, the notorious debacle at the *Bacchus* gala when Mauriac, a few seats down from us, arose at the final curtain and fled, amongst a battery of flash bulbs and shocked gasps; and his vitriolic attack on Cocteau in *Figaro littéraire* on the twenty-ninth, followed by Cocteau's open reply, JE T'ACCUSE, next day in *France-Soir* (which Cocteau admits to having written *before* Mauriac's article appeared), both men tutoyering each other like beloved enemies. Indeed, I seem to recall—but where is the fact? I've searched everywhere—that he signed his public letter, *Ton ennemi qui t'aime*. This sort of front-page squabble by renowned intellectuals about religious morality versus artistic prerogative, though seeming petty at the moment, is majestically stimulating on rereading, especially in the light of America's know-nothing journalism and a government that eschews literary argument.

Yet who will find himself now in the grip of such reading where Mauriac is unknown and Cocteau but a one-time moviemaker? In this chaotic journal Cocteau resembles his Sphinx—"I secrete my thread, let it out, wind it back and spin it in"—most of whose threads were deknotted into smooth essays the following year, notably in the *Journal d'un inconnu*. As with my unimpeachable Ravel, who dimly showed clay feet a few years back when Orenstein published a batch of his juvenilia, so Jean Cocteau changes—perhaps evolves, and for the better—to my ken.

His words on Proust (on "re-rereading Proust," as he puts it) do ring with the authority of One Who Was There. No such demystification exists in any other article on Proust.

No one has ever written on Proust and music. (Nor, astonishingly, had anyone written on Proust and homosexuality until the recent extraordinary thesis of J. E. Rivers.) How classy, really, and how informed were Proust's notions on music—Proust, whose real-life favorite was Reynaldo Hahn, and in whom the word Pelléas provoked asthma attacks? With jacks-of-all-trades we admire anything *not* our own métier. But Proust on music (and homo-sexuality) embarrasses me, just as perhaps Jane Freilicher is embarrassed by Proust's lengthy asides on the painter, Elstir.

13 April

Decent night's sleep. A sunny morning.

"When a government is refuted by those who help it to power, it fails," states *Figaro* on this cheerful Friday-the-thirteenth as a hundred thousand *sidérurgistes* block the byways in sympathy for thirty-five thousand among them who are being laid off despite the socialists' election promises three years ago. As many citizens, left and right, hate Mitterand as hate Messiaen's opera. *Yentl* a huge success.

I'm a slow reader but I've just consumed in one swoop Françoise Sagan's *Avec mon meilleur souvenir.* For Sagan is a graceful stylist, as addictive as fudge, and her subjects are always engrossing to every class. Yet this collection is weak. Just as Proust, when touching those areas closest to me—music and queerness—seems amateurish, so Sagan when portraying people I've known seems to skirt the point. Her picture of Billie Holiday, for instance, lacks pathos and demonstrates a tin ear, while her picture of Tennessee Williams is colored more by what he thought of her than what she thought of him. As for *her* vision of Proust, she lists him as her favorite of a dozen favorite authors, all French, explaining that he's been her solidest influence for the seemingly negative reason that neither she nor he were ever able to implant every last ramification of a "given" into their work. Wouldn't you think that a better definition of shape is knowing when to stop? Sagan knows when. I admit that I read her now on the off chance she'll be at Charlotte's Monday. She's Charlotte's best friend.

Three o'clock. A glass of tea at Rouquet's with Arlette Katchen coiffed like Falconetti. We rambled for an hour around the neighborhood chatting about: a mutual dependence on A.A.; her Arab lover; her son Stéphane's indifference to sex despite her fitting him out with a call girl; Stéphane's bemusement at his late father Julius's interest in other men, and Julius's sense of rivalry with his son; Arlette's indifference to the piano now that Julius is dead, yet her dismay that Gary Graffman displayed little love for his art in his autobiography. Though contemptuous of Reagan she doesn't mind if the world blows up. When we said goodbye she added: I used to be in love with you.

Aren't you still?

A little.

Five o'clock. Two-hour interview in French for *France-Musique* with the congenial Mildred Clary in my little garret, assisted by a young technician who smelled bad in a good way.

Enough is too much.
A little too much is just enough for me.

La mode c'est la beauté qui devient laide. L'art c'est la laideur qui devient belle.
Et Boulez? C'est la laideur qui reste laide.

Eight o'clock. Dine again at Henri Hell's. Covering the four brief blocks from here to there is to remember how this little area was our village from 1949 through the 1950s when we would awaken in each other's hotel rooms. Here at the Université is where I'd bring Jane Bowles, even drunker than I, of a midsummer dawn; there at the Saint Yves, now razed, is where I lost one of many virginities; beyond, at the Saint Germain, was where S. lost one of her many; and not far up the rue des Saints Pères is where I first knew Marie Laure and Julian Green and "sat" for Cartier-Bresson and how many more! These lanes make me sad, not for the past, but for the present elsewhere— to be back in Nantucket with JH.

José had invited Robert Kanters, blind and extinguished after a long and witty critical career, who breathes scarcely a word all evening; Richard Négroux; and Henri Sauguet and Raphaël Cluzel, both full of vitality, despite the former's diabetic leg which pains him and causes a limp. That Sauguet at eighty-three, after the death of Jacques Dupont, should find another friend half his age, is a comfort to anyone. Raphaël has just published a volume of poems based on a souvenir of Max Jacob—that, and his dialogues for the film a decade ago on *Thomas l'imposteur*, are his claims to fame. Perfect olive soup, roast veal with cèpes, and a thick chocolate mousse.

When Sauguet refers to the tiny place he'll occupy in music's history, everyone protests, but he stands firm and is sincere. None of us knows his eventual place. Yet to be certain of even "the tiny place" seems at once humble and arrogant.

Virgil told me that my most urgent duty in France would be to learn how the production, in the French language, of his *Four Saints in Three Acts* had gone last month in Villejuif. Sauguet, who speaks nothing but French, affirmed that Gertrude Stein's libretto was far more comprehensible in English.

We speak of the melancholy deaths of the Aurics. The beautiful Nora toward the end would go to the bank at midnight in her nightgown, to be escorted home by the police. She fell downstairs and killed herself. Georges a few weeks later married a twenty-eight-year-old Monégasque who bled him dry then returned to the Midi. Eccentric, reclusive, he too died soon after. Georges Auric, at least during the fifties when I saw him every day, was the most intelligent, educated, funny and influential man I'd ever imagined. Nora, the prettiest, most brittle, as a painter the most personal, as a companion the most enjoyable, as a gossip the bitchiest woman I'd ever imagined. Her lover, Georges's chauffeur, the poor handsome foolish Guy de Lesseps, their go-between, has long since vanished with cancer. Thus, sordidly, ends their dynasty. In 1951 Jerry Robbins plotted a ballet that was to open with the emergence on a high platform of a beautiful lady with a whip, as a Liszt concerto runs wild. It was to be called *Madame Auric's Lover*.

In his recent letters Henri Sauguet began to tutoyer me for the first time since we met in 1949 or '50, with Henri Hell, at the terrace of a café near the Luxembourg gardens. I reciprocated. But tonight all is pure *vous* again. Of such is the kingdom of nuance which we Americans are slated forever to ignore.

Full moon. JH so clear on the phone, around midnight.

Finished Cocteau. The man and his work will remain always among the three or four strongest influences that blinded me to other esthetics, other voices. But if childhood loves can never be dislodged like wisdom teeth, they still can grow loose in their sockets in our old age. Cocteau, in repeating to exhaustion his every *bon mot* in case we have never heard it, weakens, by revealing his tricks, the very foundation of his structure. Even Debussy, the nonpareil, when I examined the warmongering text of his very last work, *Noël pour les enfants*, became an average vengeful creature subverting his own art.

14 April

Salade Niçoise near Métro du Bac, followed by an interview for *Magazine* with young Didier Lestrade. Radiant sunshine, pungent hyacinths.

Afternoon concert, with Jay Gottlieb, at the radio. I enjoyed Englishman Nigel Osborne's *Fantasia*, but not Maderna's *Serenata*, nor even especially Messiaen's *Sept Haïkaï*. All is overwrought. (I recall Sauguet's remark last night about the forty-minute section of *Saint François* devoted solely to birdcalls: "It made me want to go home and wring my canary's neck.") Messiaen was present, wrinkled and bent, in a canary-colored sweater. After his piece, he came onstage and smiled and bowed and shook hands with the first violinist and then the cellist and continued to smile and bow and shake hands long after the robust clapping had subsided to a feeble clicking.

I took Jay to a party in Montmartre given by two guests of Ed White's, American fashion models who, after years in Paris, spoke no French, but giggled and were pretty and smoked pot and nibbled raw cauliflower and chattered about fees. We felt out of place and sneaked off to dine Au Manuscrit on the rue des Quatre Fils. *Quenelles de saumon, purée de céléris, gateaux forêt noire.* Jay paid. Much talk of Boulanger with whom Jay began to study, age fourteen, in 1967.

Why do you like Elliott Carter? "Because he brings a necessary peace after all that entanglement." I have no rebuttal for that.

An unforgettable vision of Marie Laure, during the touch–&–go week of Cocteau's heart attack in the mid-fifties, as she crossed and recrossed the Place des États-Unis all through the night, disheveled and on foot, to inquire chez Madame Weissweiller, who lived at No. 3, about the health of him whom she had loved since childhood. (Marie Laure never went out on foot, nor did she habitually show overt concern over the health of friends.)

15 April

Mary Dibbern lives in the core of the still-Zolaesque, still-Arabesque, area near Barbès, in a brand new building decked out with a score of gardens for certain of the lodgers, including her. She is, as she likes to be termed, an accompanist; she came here a half dozen years ago under the auspices of Dalton Baldwin and earns a living playing with soloists, mainly singers, usually Americans. The lunch of quiche with a salad of yellow peppers was engorged near the garden where the bright forsythia, even as we sat there, lured golden finches of a breed new to me. We spoke mainly of the rarity of song in English being heard in this country.

Jay Gottlieb lives, he too, on the Île Saint Louis at the opposite end from Dutilleux and Ed White, in a pair of overcrowded rooms overlooking a quiet inner court. For ninety minutes he gave me a private recital, on his Japanese Atlas piano, in his purposeful and occasionally necessarily (I guess) frenzied manner, of his specialized repertory of new French music.

A case could be made that all present-day French musical composition flows steadily as the Seine out of the Impressionism of 1900 and not out of the seeming Germanisms rampant in 1950. This holds as much for the avant-garde patriarch Pierre Boulez as for the reactionary Poulencophile, Jean-Michel Damase. Now that sudden spurts and splintered dissonances are no surprise, we can hear Boulez and his followers as in a homegrown tradition, a tradition of imprecise rhythms (like the French language, but unlike German speech, which is regular as military drums) and therefore of an apologetically organized method, and of highly differentiated orchestration (again, unlike German chamber music, which features family groups such as string quartets): finger-cymbals, alto flutes, marimbas and violas and guitars and harps. All this would be marvelous if the music also had the guts of the Impressionists. But nothing Jay played has stayed with me.

From Jay's I walk the few blocks down the central thoroughfare that divides, so delicately, the Île Saint Louis into an autonomous village, to Edmund's empty apartment, there to await François Rabaud, who wants to make Marie Laure's home in Hyères—the Château Saint Bernard—into a museum.

An excruciating and wondrous two hours, during which I rose up from this armchair, glided out through the window, and alit several hundred kilometers to the south, and several thousand nights into the past.

For eight hours a day, five months out of the year, all during the 1950s, I worked hard at my music in the Mediterranean mansion of Marie Laure de Noailles, during which time she worked hard at her painting and her books. The rest of the time I played and loved, mildly or suicidally, and grew up. For Monsieur Rabaud I summoned back evenings of smoke curling from distant bonfires across the back-hills of Hyères where one divined, but never perceived, a Giono-like peasant culture as remote as Eden from the clever rambling structure we inhabited, which dominated the knoll overlooking the town. The gallows. Sheepbells in the morning, cowbells at night. As if hypnotized I smelled the citronella used against the August mosquitoes; the hot beach where I went each morning with Nora Auric; the minted drinks imbibed each afternoon with Georges Auric (the Aurics, since the 1930s, were lent a small house on the estate); the steady flow of visitors, some for a night or a week, most for a passing meal. Every July we awaited the fortnight stay of Claus von Bulow, a stay referred to as "fattening Claus," since he always arrived emaciated from a grueling winter as barrister in London, bringing the latest anecdotes. (Cecil Beaton in a crowded hotel elevator is ogled by an awestruck child who asks, Is it true you're a fairy?) Or the promenades with Nancy Mitford. Or Balthus. Or Dora Maar. Or Jean-Louis Barrault and Madeleine Renaud. Et cetera. But I've been told by both James Lord and Robert Veyron-Lacroix, who've visited there since Marie Laure died in 1970, that the formal gardens are waist-high in weeds today, the ceilings are crumbling, and the city has bought the property and will make it a hotel or a museum, or raze it for a tennis court.

Je vais demain à Hyères—a play on words that sounds delicious to French ears. In fact, Monsieur Rabaud was in Hyères just yesterday. He tells me that Henri Perrault, the maître d'hôtel, now an old man, lives alone in the former house of Madame Auric *mère*, and sends me his best regards. So does Madame Rothley, the *pharmacienne*, now an old woman.

It is seven and I'm not due at Noel Lee's until eight. So Rabaud takes me on an architectural tour of the Marais. Then I drop him off near the Louvre. He approves of Pei's dome, thinks it should be even larger. Change is good. . . .

From the standpoint of breadth of repertory if not subtlety of sound, Noel Lee is, now that Paul Jacobs is dead and Jay Gottlieb still a stripling (he wasn't born when Noel moved to France thirty-five years ago), the most important American pianist in Europe. For that reason, not to mention his personal likability, I treasure him as an occasional acquaintance, if not as a close friend—he doesn't, after all, play my music as Katchen did.

The apartment has been enlarged to three times its former size. We dined in the kitchen. I announced that for me this has been a Day of American Pianists; that Jay Gottlieb, who with his twin, percussionist Gordon Gottlieb, was born on my birthday, October 23, says that with all identical twins one is straight and the other gay; and that I'd had lunch with Miss Dibbern. No one was bowled over. Noel is defensively pro-French-music, a right he has earned more than I've earned my anti-French-music stance. He gives me discs of his Debussy *Études* and of the complete piano works of Griffes. He didn't know that the love of Griffes's life was a policeman.

Neither France nor the U.S. presents tempting erotic specimens. It used to be that with the warmth of spring, beauty seeped out of the woodwork and destroyed us. Now, if told I could never have sex again but would remain healthy and productive, it wouldn't make much difference.

16 April

Lunch with Didier Duclos at the Ministères. *Soupe à l'onion* and *tarte tatin*. (I paid, although he should have.) Duclos is the French representative of my music publisher, Boosey & Hawkes, and he brought with him a sheaf of recent reviews of which only the bad ones interested me. The London premiere last week of my new Saxophone Suite was chastised because I "found no new sounds for the instrument." As though I hadn't spent my life avoiding the new! Newness for its own sake is as destructive as is beauty in spring; Pound's "Make it new" is as commercial as "Build a better mousetrap"; Rim-

baud's admonishment, *"Il faut être absolument moderne,"* has disequili-
brated French culture even unto today, and now England. . . .

Duclos is one of the few who loved Messiaen's opera. He explains it's because precisely he doesn't go for vocal music, and thus listened as to a purely
instrumental symphony.

At midnight on the rue du Dragon, Charlotte Aillaud's supper to honor
the final night of *Werther*, and all the stars therein, was of a *mondanité*,
not to mention a lavishness, that resembled the 1950s, or at least "my"
1950s, with princes and duchesses and things. If Françoise Sagan did not
show up, Bogianckino did; but except for him and Alfredo Kraus and
Georges Prêtre, the guests weren't especially musical. They were opera
goers. It was not unpleasant to chat again with Alexis de Redé (who now
looks like Arturo Lopez: divine justice), or with Jimmy Douglas (the subject
being our mutual misrepresentation in the Barbara Hutton biography), or
with many another Rastignac. Nor was I more than passingly offended by
the coarseness of the critic from *Express*, since I learned of her presumed
vested interest in Kraus, and hence understood her nervousness, since
Kraus's wife was also present. And it is always a joy to see François Valéry.
But I am ill at ease in this milieu.

17 April

Death of Ralph Kirkpatrick, surprisingly but correctly covered in the press.
Policewomen abound.

There are as many good bookstores per block in Paris as per avenue in
New York (but no good music stores in either town), and I'd even include the
slightly askew Shakespeare & Company where, after three decades, all the
clients still hope that every time the doors open Jack Kerouac will walk in.

Lunch in an Italian bistro off boulevard Raspail with the affably slim Judith
Pizar who is not unlike (was it Arletty who portrayed her?) the Queen of
Sheba in Guitry's *Story of a Cheat*. We plan together a concert and/or read-
ing at the American Center for a year and a day from today.

Dine again at the Ministères with Guy, also Jean Leuvrais and Georges
Teran. (The spiderweb of relationships is too much to go into.) An ample repast for four, with dessert and wine and *eau de Badoit* (why doesn't America
import this healthful draft instead of the senseless Perrier?) comes to 514.63
Frs. which, with the dollar at nearly nine francs, is not too dear. Exceptionally, Jean is not a Reaganite, but he is otherwise reactionary, feeling a "com-

munist tyranny" creeping through France, as when, for instance, the left-wing National Theater for which he works looks askance at his first-class train tickets. But he also hates Catholics. Guy told a sweet story of how the Holy Fathers in Laos taught Sanskrit to the peasants, and also a course in Laotian history and a course in Buddhism, and then quit the country forever.

18 April

Tribune reports breakthrough in AIDS. Now, if a vaccine were to be developed, would American homosexuals—would *I*—revert to the strenuous promiscuity of the sixties? If cigarettes were proved to be inoffensive would we start smoking again? Shock swerves habit, fear curbs, all quickly; but slow time alters too.

Titles: *Wine, Men and Song; The Lady or the Tigress*
   Meanwhile, according to *Le Monde* this morning, 'tis no longer intellectuals who are heeded by the bourgeoisie in politics, but actors, notably Yves Montand (so notoriously switched to the right), Michel Piccoli, Guy Bédos, and now the palatable Alain Delon.

Simenon still very much in the air, deservedly. Modern France has produced no greater writer.

At 6:15, a drink at Betsy Jolas's, rue Bonaparte. Once I stated that if there were six composers functioning in the world who interested me, three were women, and one of these would be Betsy Jolas. It would be unchivalrous to eat my words. Betsy is half American (her mother is Maria Jolas) but lives in France, and she feels that very little American music, except Ives, holds up. Nobody's tonal anymore, certainly not she, and her students are mostly interested in computers. Would they enjoy, perhaps, listening to Poulenc? "Certainly not." What moves *you*, Betsy? "Well, Josquin moves me." No fair—old Josquin moves everyone. What about now? But I get no clear answer. To be moved is no longer a criterion.
   We're cordial with each other, and not just because we're both to be guests at Boston University next year. Betsy combines the innate assurance of European women with the cool congeniality of American women who try to be European. The result delights me.

Eight o'clock. Dine with Gérard Souzay in the rue du Mail. I am unprepared for his spectral appearance and spectral behavior, this once-dashing genius now as restricted as a slow-motion Caligari, all in black, and huge. Gérard

Souzay is the greatest baritone France ever produced, with a long career in recital and opera copiously represented on records. Now that career is over. Yet sitting across from me in this weird restaurant, fingering the Légion d'Honneur in his lapel and staring through heavy glasses, he says he will never stop, that he means to suppress all his early discs because he knows today so much more deeply than yesterday how this Fauré or that Schubert or those Debussy songs are meant to be interpreted, and next month in Japan, where they still adore him, he will cut some new recordings. At the same time he claims to hate Paris, where he is "forgotten" and where the public in any case is stupid, and where he has no friends, or hardly any, except for Dalton Baldwin and Jacques Leguerney and . . . me! I'm stupified; we are colleagues who meet once every decade, although I suppose a mutual musical communion does make for friendship (it also makes for enmity). Thirty-five years ago I spoke better French than Gérard speaks English now, yet he speaks only English and feigns to flub his native tongue (to the waiter: *Je puis ordonner maintenant?*), offering to help me if I can't understand the menu. Which offends me. Still, his loneliness is moving, as is his admission of a Japanese roommate whom he likes and hates. He proffers the interesting information that thirty-three years ago he fathered a son by X, and told this son only last year of his true identity.

Gérard Souzay's value is beyond rubies. Since the United States, a land of two hundred and fifty million souls, has not one viable French-born coach of vocal literature, Gérard could single-handedly enhance our knowledge of French song literature and thereby change the country. Yet at sixty-seven he claims he is not yet ready.

From place des Victoires by way of the nightmarish little passages near the former Halles I wend my way once more to Île Saint Louis where at 10:30 Jean-Pierre Marty awaits in his little apartment on the rue Regrattier. I'm still discombobulated from the meal with Gérard, possibly because *au fond* I identify with him, so I'm not quite up to the answer to my question: How's your book on Mozart coming, Jean-Pierre? For the past decade Jean-Pierre Marty has been compiling a thesis titled *Tempo Indications in the Music of Mozart,* based on the premise (with which Mozart would concur if he were sitting here with us, JPM assures me—"In fact he'd pat me on the back") that the speeds of various works are absolutes, not decisions according to performers' metabolisms, and JPM has "proved" this by a maniacally canny equation between, or comparisons of, three basic givens: the "Madamina" aria, the first movement of the "Jupiter," and the end of. . . . But who cares? the process seems gratuitous. I'm less concerned that JPM's former madness may be returning than that he's wasting time away from what matters:

his conducting. His conclusions—no more significant than how many angels can dance on the head of a pin—should, to import, obtain to all music, past and present, but do they? I am not inflexible about tempos in *my* music, and I'm here, alive. If I don't know, how can he know what Mozart knew? So, promising him that he can join my farewell *sortie* tomorrow with Ed White whom he admires but doesn't know, I take leave and walk the few blocks to Ed's very flat where now I sit, about to retire.

19 April

Last full day. Phone conversations with those I won't be able to see: Brion Gysin; Jacques Damase; Robert de Saint Jean, who tells me Julian Green is very much in town, although the person who answered Green's phone assured me he was *en voyage*; Juliet Man Ray, who is organizing a retrospective of Man Ray's photographs and has mislaid my portraits. So have I. Like Toklas, Juliet is staying on alone, unlike me, who realized my Americanness after a decade in France and so went home, or Jean-Pierre, who after a decade in America came back here. To reside on foreign soil is not to become a part of that soil, but to see home ground more clearly. Gertrude Stein never really mastered French, while Breton, in New York during World War II, refused to learn English—*pour ne pas ternir mon français.*

Lunch with Claire and Barry Brook in their supermodern garçonnière in rue des Lions Saint Paul. Salade niçoise and a strawberry pie which I ate all of. Barry talked of musicology which he says is low in France where nevertheless the Conservatoire standards are wildly more stringent than ours.

The long taxi trip to Yvonne de Casa Fuerté's recalled the opening verses of the poem Frank O'Hara wrote for my song on Poulenc twenty-one years ago:

> My first day in Paris I walked
>   from Saint Germain to the Pont Mirabeau
> in soft amber light and leaves
>   and love was running out

She lives on the ninth floor of a modern high-rise, rue Rémusat. Except for her trying deafness, Yvonne at ninety is unchanged from the deep-voiced glamourous creature who wore a hat of ostrich plumes to rehearsals of the City Center Orchestra in which she played violin while sweating out the war in New York. Today her head is swathed in bandages and covered with a snood to hide the stitches; two weeks ago, returning from the memorial for Jacques Dupont, she collapsed in the lobby and broke open her skull. Her speech is careful, her opinions . . . strong. But I am growing weary and will report on this in some future diary. (*Yvonne, je vous aime.*) Hurry, hurry.

Five o'clock, and a jump across the river to pick up Michelle Lapautre near the Champs de Mars. Michelle is a redoubtable impressario for authors, not an agent exactly, but the Paris representative for a number of non-French publishers, mostly American. I am hoping she'll arrange for one of my books to be sold here. Meantime, in the taxi carrying us to the Théâtre de la Ville where at 6:30 we're to see the Momix Dance Company, she tells me who does and who doesn't sell, of American writers in French translation. Roth about two thousand, Sontag the same, Styron sells because of the movie of *Sophie's Choice*, et cetera. We enjoyed the flabbergasting suppleness of the Momix Dancers, as well as, I trust, each other.

Edmund White and John Purcell, returned from Crete and none the worse for wear, are filled with tales of carnal exploits that make my hair stand on end. With Jean-Pierre we go to a pretty good restaurant, *À la Grenouille sous l'eau*, and talk about writing an opera together, but nothing will come of it: Ed's pen is not theatrical, nor, probably, is my bent. Later Ed walks me, slowly, back to the hotel, *pour boucler la boucle*, this last night in Paris.

Notre Dame is of unthinkable beauty, as though lit from within by some magic truth, and the route we take—up the rue Saint André des Arts and onto the rue Dauphine, then to the carrefour Buci—is the route of my youth. I've never been more aware of fatality as during these past two weeks. "And love was running out."

> *TWA Flight 801*
> *Paris to New York*
> *20 April*

Do these paragraphs lack fancy and purpose? With France behind me, what of this fortnight would remain had I not written it? How much evaporated before the distillation on this paper, like Odette, jelled in that final freeze-frame? What have I chosen to omit? Would I have gone to Paris without an assignment? or gone, but had other experiences? or the same experiences but with other reactions?

Maybe I am a diarist but certainly not a journalist, for I'm unable to report what I see, only what I feel, and the feelings are made up in advance. Not hating this one or loving that one or being indifferent to some third person there in the far-away past, like Adele H. with her single obsession (or indeed like Meyer Levin), I sleepwalk through time while so much is occurring under my sightless nose. Still, we all guard our lives in cages, cages that clink rustily against each other, emitting thick sighs and hollow coos.

Oh, they're lowering the screen for a movie. And here's some nice coffee. I'm older but no wiser.

New York
26 April

The memorial concert for Donald Gramm was mournful, not because it *was* a memorial, but because the audience in the oddly shaped but acoustically happy hall at Rockefeller University wasn't that aware of the fact of Donald. What's more, my smarmy little speech about his infinite variety was, I realize now, in contradiction to the Debussyan half of the program, since Donald never ever did Debussy songs. Hilda and Will sang nicely, however.

This noon, taped interview with Michael Barrone of Minneapolis Radio about my compositions for organ. Daron, to whom I've entrusted the thankless task of copying the parts of *An American Oratorio*, appeared in the midst of this with a homemade banana cream pie.

Dined at Virgil's with JH. Myrtille Hugnet, pleasant surprise, was there too, looking younger if suaver than twenty-five years ago when Georges Hugnet was still a vital force.

Tomorrow, Cadbury.

Sunday, *Whitman Cantata* by the Gay Men's Chorus of Boston. I cannot attend, but I am honored by the number of hearings the piece has had, thanks mainly to the impressive solidarity of these caring groups across the country.

1 May

Returned from Philadelphia yesterday by train with Vincent Persichetti whose tale of a recent operation discombobulated my suggestible nerves. But the tale of the raccoon that lives, or almost lives, with him and Dorothea was delicious. Vincent is a pure soul.

Annual lunch today, Café des Artistes, with Robert Jacobson, to discuss next season's article on Gershwin. Exhibition of Cornelia Foss at Sutton Gallery. Long chat with Lukas—whose appearance grows ever craggier, like Xenakis—about the anxious state of new music (our criteria are opposed but our conclusions are synonymous, he thinking that New Romanticism doesn't dig deep enough into nostalgia, I scarcely wanting to sully my vocabulary with such a trendy term as New Romanticism), and about my recent Paris visit to the luscious Madame Pizar whose name makes Lukas's eyes shine.

2 May

Ceremonies for the Concert Artists Guild (last year they commissioned my Saxophone suite as a first gesture toward composers as contrasted to strictly performers) at which Martin Bookspan mellifluously introduces me. I give a cogent little plea about the need to recognize living creators, then hand out this year's awards to the young winners, all of them interpreters (in contradiction to my plea). This is followed by an overlong and vaguely sexist *louange* by John Lindsay who, with a wink, tells us he'd love to elope with Ms. Dorothy Dwire, the chairman of the organization.

I've brought along Maggie Paley with whom I then go to Brad Gooch's otherwise all-male party at the Chelsea. Later we dine together in a health store on 19th Street, and I come home by ten o'clock to hear June LeBell's taped conversation with me and the Gregg Smiths on WQXR.

Nantucket
6 May

After heavy rain, clear warmth. Yearly ritual of fertilizing the window boxes and stuffing them with impatiens. Exciting aroma of dirt. Jonquils bursting helter-skelter in the back yard.

Yesterday I broke the middle toe of my left foot, simply by walking into a door. Delightfully discolored, the purple-yellow of a pansy.

As I note this, the first hearing of my new *Dances* is presumably occurring in Detroit. I heard a run-through by the young players—Frederick Moyer, piano, and Jonathan Spitz, cello—a month ago in Boston; they were filled with spontaneous clarity. Interestingly, the Music Study Club, of whose annual competition they are the winners and thus obliged to perform my piece which was commissioned for the group's sixtieth anniversary, was co-founded by Ruth Laredo's mother, Miriam Meckler, with whom I've been in regular touch.

7 May

Death of Bill Ritman yesterday. And Alan Schneider died just a few days ago in London. Bill's sets for the Edward Albee plays are about the most beautiful I've ever seen, and Alan's beautiful direction of these same beautiful plays did for Edward what Kazan once did for Tennessee Williams. What a dumb loss.

Puisque tout passe, faisons une melodie passagère, wrote Rilke in French,

which the German Hindemith and the American Sam Barber then musicalized.

The sky is warm and green. No wind.

Dream of a prisoner in a nest atop a double flagpole. He is free to slide down
either pole, but one will land him in a worldwide epidemic of Karposi's Sarcoma, and the other a worldwide atomic explosion.

Nightly movies on JH's VCR. Claudette Colbert's zany *Midnight*, tight and
clever. Dietrich in *Seven Sinners*, already too old for the part of Bijou, although her rendition of "I've Been in Love Before," a sea breeze stirring
through her white chiffon, is something else again. (I saw it first, with
Maggy, in 1940 at the Tivoli on Cottage Grove.)

13 May

To: *New York Times*, Arts & Leisure
Re: "New York Celebrates the Genius of Jean Cocteau"

To claim, as Annette Insdorf does, that "Cocteau made no secret of his homosexuality and peopled his work with characters whose sexual orientation was
often ambiguous," is to apply today's chic frankness to the oeuvre of an artist
who flourished in the first half of the century. Yet to support the claim by showing that in the movie, *Les Enfants terribles*, a young man's "troubling love interest is portrayed by the same actress who incarnates Dargelos—a boy who
obsesses Paul—at the film's opening" is to equate androgyny with homosexuality, a notion as antique as Freud (whom Insdorf herself quotes Cocteau as
despising).

Jean Cocteau, unlike Gide, never wrote publicly of homosexuality—his own
or anyone else's. (The notorious *Livre blanc* was not "about" either himself or
his friends, nor did it sell over the counter during his lifetime.) The nature of
Cocteau's characters is never more nor less ambiguous than the nature of Balzac's characters, or Hawthorne's or Henry James's or John Cheever's or, indeed,
those of any author of scope.

As for the movie, *Les Enfants terribles*, it was confected by Jean-Pierre Melville whose crucial error (Cocteau later concurred) lay in having a female portray Dargelos, the hero's childhood hero, thus superimposing a Freudian veneer. Men are drawn to other men because they are men, not because they
resemble women; in *Sang d'un poète*, Cocteau's own film, the Dargelos role is
played by a male.

Whatever Jean Cocteau may have "used" of his life in his art, it is not for Insdorf to fathom the method. We must probably assume that he was homosexual

(though what's the difference?), but Cocteau *did* make a secret of it. Nor is it illuminating for Insdorf to inform us that homosexuality and "ambiguous orientation" are the same.

New York
16 May

Whole day with JH at the Academy.

Reviews of *Dances* in Detroit, quite good, and with a certain sense of occasion seldom exuded anymore in New York, where there's an *embarras de pauvresse*. Smaller centers can afford to care.

I came across a file of letters from Denise Duval. These date from 1964 and attest to her extreme desire to create *Miss Julie* at the City Opera, and the desire is corroborated by two letters from Bernard Lefort in the same file. (No copies of my letters to her or to him.) Even with this sheaf before me, I have no remembrance of this correspondence. Why? For me, Duval was the Garbo of opera with a wild touch of vaudeville. She had clarity, intelligence, diction, beauty (with those eyes the size of eagle eggs), and would have been ideal for the role. What happened?

18 May

Visit yesterday from the Australian Broadcasting Company (with the same representatives who had me read about Boulanger into a microphone some time ago) who paid me $120 to discuss, for ten minutes, the mode of the diary in literature.

Buffet then chez Jean-Marie Guéhenno, the cultural attaché, to launch the ambulant Cocteau retrospective now passing through New York. All of us catalogue-contributors were present, as well as the Cocteau entourage (*sans le maître*, like little moons without their planet), including Francine Weisweiller, also Edouard Dermit and his son, who digs rock, here on a first visit. Dermit, Jean Cocteau's gardener and later adopted son and heir, I had remembered as the exact opposite of the poet: rugged, handsome, muscular, simple, shy, and absolutely speechless (not that anyone could get a word in edgewise when Cocteau spoke). Now, like the dog who grows to resemble his master, Dermit is gaunt and quick and very very talkative, punctuating every phrase by pointing his finger to the ceiling, and with the lithe curiosity of a child.

Petit Jean Mountain, Arkansas
25 May

Here for a week as guest of the International Art Song Festival, founded by
Kay Kraeft and Dalton Baldwin. The most delightful attribute of the site is
my personal lodging. Apparently the Winthrop Rockefeller estate allows
this recherché agglomeration to occupy these five thousand acres for one
week a year, the other fifty-one weeks being given over to racehorse breeding. I am assigned a two-story chalet, for me alone, with a vast salon, two
bedrooms (each with a bathroom the size of anyone else's apartment, and
each stocked with an assortment of colognes including Guerlain's *L'Heure
Bleue*, Rochas's *Moustache*, and quart-sized bottles wrapped in green plush
of Balmain's *Vent Vert* from which the emanations bring back like yesterday
the fragrance of Marie Laure's *salle de bain* at Saint Bernard), a studio with
a piano (and a huge loom!), a private garden bordering on a sheer cliff of perhaps a thousand feet, and a view extending indefinitely over a melancholy
Eden checkerboarded with squares of lime-green fields or moss-green for-
ests and dotted with grazing cattle and with fading bonfires. The hitch is that
I'm not allowed to make outgoing calls.

My duties are to give classes and concerts and roundtables and such with
John Stewart, Phyllis Bryn-Julson, and others of their high class. And there's
a regular class of composers, mostly in their thirties, from all over.

The accent: a drawl rawer and longer than in Texas. My Christian name is
Nay-ud. Weird to hear Duparc's settings of Baudelaire discussed with a hill-
billy twang.

All these songs are—indeed, all art is—about death and sex and weather.
Yet academics, who approve Baudelaire, frown on Baudelairean behavior.

Phyllis, pulling off tablecloths, removing chairs, and generally testing the
dining room where she'll sing this evening: "It's not that I don't have a high
D, but does this room have a high D?"

Erlkonig parallels *A Turn of the Screw*.

At the concert of student composers I allow myself to criticize their works
with the aplomb of Jacques Fath approaching Marie Laure during an intermission and adjusting her décolletage.

New York
30 May

Monday, Joe LeSueur, and one of our all-too-rare meals together. Tuesday, *The Rink*, a musical play by Terrence McNally and John Kander, original, stylish, strange, not quite right.

Today at three o'clock, called at Jill Krementz's on East 48th at her friendly urgings. Had she forgotten? She coolly sat me down in a little room with a contact sheet of photos (all hideous) of me taken at the Institute a fortnight ago, and continued her business with two assistants. When I explained that I wasn't here to buy her wares, but on a social call, her mood changed, she summoned Kurt Vonnegut from his study, and the three of us had coffee and a (to me) strained chat for thirty minutes.

Stuart Pope at four o'clock was affability itself.

31 May

At noon today I arose from the dais, on which were seated a dozen special guests of the National Music Council, and uttered the following sentences in praise of Virgil Thomson:

Forty years ago today I had just completed the fifth month of my first paying job, that of Virgil Thomson's in-house copyist, for which I received twenty dollars and two orchestration lessons a week. My daily stint was done on the parlor table within earshot of the next room where—propped in bed, a pad on his lap, an ear to the phone—Virgil ran the world of music. During those brief months, by being accountable for each note of the master, by heeding his ever-lucid but never-repeated dicta on instrumentation, and by eavesdropping on his talk with, say, Stokowski or Oscar Levant on the one hand, or with his colleagues at the *Herald Tribune* on the other, I gleaned as much, esthetically and practically, about the terrifyingly golden milieu of my future vocation as in all my previous years. Nor in all the following years have I ever ceased marveling that, in bed or out, Virgil Thomson had the answers.

Virgil the author, as his dozen books attest, is the world's most informative and unsentimental witness to other people's music. These qualities are enhanced by his addressing the subject from the inside out—from the standpoint of the maker—and by his readability which owes so much to France where, in art as in life, brevity is next to godliness. Beside him, all other critics are superfluous.

Virgil the musician, over and beyond his friendly innovation (based not on new complexity but, ironically, on age-old simplicity), is our sole composer who is as convincing in song as in opera.

If he and I have had at least one grave rift, arising from my urge to lash out, teacher-pupil relationships are never truly dissolved. Though I am now a decade older than Virgil was when we first met, he still intimidates me in the very same way. And I never fail to learn from him. There will be no more rifts, for he is in many ways my oldest friend, and I love him.

His verbal terseness may be French, but socially Virgil Thomson is utterly international, which is why he is so appreciated abroad. Now, that appreciation is precisely due (coming back full circle) to his music which, with its bittersweet recall of hymn tune and folk song, seems as American as the flag. Long may it wave.

During the "luncheon" (the word's not in my vocabulary) the two guests of honor, Virgil Thomson and Lionel Hampton, were introduced to the thousand guests in the Plaza Ballroom. After Hampton's brief bow, Virgil turned to me and asked in a voice loud enough for all to hear: "Who's that?"

1 June

Incongruous assembly:

In the first storms of the end of May (during which, still groggy yesterday morning, JH entered the kitchen with: "As they say in Venice, it's raining catamites and doges"), Father, almost ninety now, has come up from Cadbury for a couple of days so that Blue Cross can videotape him "in depth" discussing the Old Days of medical economics. He's staying with us. Yesterday morning and again today he was called for by the Blue Cross car, which swept him off to a movie career and brought him back again.

At ten A.M. the super sprayed for roaches. At 2:30 Joan Peyser arrived to talk about Leonard Bernstein, of whom she's now the approved biographer. Joan's intense about her subject, almost violent, and was still here when, at 4:30, Robert Ferro and Michael Grumley appeared for tea and crumpets. So the four of us sat down to this fare in the dining room, Joan continuing about Lenny, Robert overflowing with his new book, Michael beaming, when Father arrived with a copy of his just-made video which he was anxious to play for us, but I can't run the machine. Joan left. At 6:30 JH showed up with Frank. Michael and Robert left. Frank and Father and JH and I had supper, during which we ran the video. Before dessert was ingested, Robert Brill of *ASCAP in Action* arrived with a photographer for whom I posed (in the boysenberry-hued sweater), while Brill asked me if I couldn't soften some of the pessimistic remarks in the essay I've written to accompany the photos. Frank left. Meanwhile Gregg and Roz Smith arrived with *their* photographer to shoot a portrait for Roz's song album. Great scramble amidst the electric cords and white parasols photographers like to use, and a balletic conflict of interests, as in the mob scenes of *Petrushka*.

During this time Father remained in the back room reading the recent paragraphs about Paris in this diary.

2 June

JH, without consulting me, purchased a nine-week-old Bichon Frisé which resembles a frisky marshmallow and pees when least expected. He has registered it with the name Sonny Boy. There are now four animals demanding attention in the household.

Editor Karen Sherry, too, exhorts me to amend the essay for *ASCAP in Action*. But the lines she would omit as too problematical are precisely those which I feel are not daring enough. (E.g. "Rock is a quadrillion-dollar business. Even loners on Nantucket beaches bring their transistors—to blot out the historical roar of the waves.") Apparently ASCAP's president, Hal David, was miffed, not just by my "placement" of ASCAP but by my failure to seem misty-eyed about "art." Now, I am not an artist (is anyone?), but a craftsman. That the craft I produce is of better quality than that of those calling themselves artists is not my fault. I write music to keep alive. This said, ASCAP is one of my primary living sources, and I am profoundly grateful. But I am not abject, and I labor hard for what I gain. If I bite the hand that feeds me, and four fingers of that hand point to noisy rock, so be it.

University of Delaware
6 June

Sunday, annual lunch with Edouard Roditi, with latest gossip of Paris. He'd not been there during my visit in April. At four, tea with Wayne Lawson of *Vanity Fair*, who wants to cut vast swatches from my Paris gossip but will nonetheless pay an extra three thousand since the article's so much longer than bargained for.

Monday, noon Metroliner for Wilmington (while, for the record, *After Long Silence* was receiving its London premiere by oboist David Roland), arriving in time to attend recital of Will Parker, abetted by the ineffable expertise of David Garvey's pianism and, in my *Santa Fe Songs*, of three local string players.

Here now I find myself, thirty-six hours later, during the final moment as guest of the Delaware Vocal Arts Festival, similar in format and rarity to the one in Arkansas, except that my lodging is in the upper reaches of a women's concrete dorm furnished without amenities: a bed but no pillow, running water but no paper cup. The festival's the bright idea of Glenda Maurice, a businesslike but subtle mezzo. The one other composer has been John Duke.

One needs to believe that these festivals are useful. Nothing's for nothing, but they seem an ecstatic cry in the wilderness.

Evening, Nantucket. Was driven this morning from Newark, Delaware, to the Philadelphia airport by one Jeff Sharkey, a Corgliano pupil, who during the ride played tapes of his own not unattractive music. Arrived safely on island with a toothache and watched *The Year of Living Dangerously* starring Mel Gibson, who is gorgeous.

Nantucket
8 June

It's Friday, and it's been five days already since I learned of Frazier Rippy's death in Rome yet haven't found a minute to note it here. The fact of death can wait, of course, but the shock of it (ever less shocking, however) is now. Maggy Magerstadt phoned last Sunday with details. The selfish horror is that Frazier is the first of "us"—of comrades from high school—to die. Is it wrong to feel relieved that his death was a suicide, which, although it could come to any of us, is yet, we pretend, a matter of choice?

To forget, but never to forgive.

12 June

Bobby King here for a 48-hour visit. We show him the island's organs (the one in the orange-domed Unitarian church on Orange Street is the oldest continually used instrument in America), and for tea we offer him Mimsi Harbach.

Three new trees from Valero's, two apple (one Delicious and one Mac-Intosh) and a willow.

Reading with disbelief *Ancient Evenings* by our greatest novelist. The style and texture, with at least one exclamation point per page (Frank Conroy: "An author is allowed three exclamation points in his lifetime"), is so giggly and willful that, if I didn't know it was Mailer, I'd say it was by some Vassar undergraduate.

Does any work of art need to be so long? Turning to *Vanity Fair* I learn that, for lack of three million dollars, Robert Wilson, "one of this century's major artists," is rendered impotent in his own land—Wilson, whose twelve-hour spectacles are so adored in France. (One thinks of Schubert without a pittance in Vienna penning his one-page masterpieces, or of Theodore Chanler, a century later in Boston, whose *Eight Epitaphs*—some of them a mere five measures, and all together scarcely more than ten minutes—are as telling as any art.) Alan Rich, who is writing of Wilson, concludes: "That [his] art deserves a showcase in his own country is, I hope, beyond argument. Whether his own country deserves Bob Wilson *or* his art is, however, open to argument." Then again, perhaps France gets what she deserves. But won't she go broke in getting it?

Of course artists should be paid better than street cleaners—but their *art*, in itself, need cost nothing. *Der Jasager* or *Così fan Tutte* are convincing in small productions. Is *Sweeney Todd*?

Nantucket
17 June

My reaction to Susan Sontag when we first met in 1964 was how close she seemed to all those high-IQ Fulbright females around Paris in the early '50s. We never expect well-known people to be like anything we already know. (Copland's first impression of Gertrude Stein: "My God, the woman's Jewish!") But, of course, that for which they are well known is their work; their persona can't afford to have the dazzle. I'm referring, naturally, to creative artists.

JH sometimes makes the rounds of Nantucket night spots. When he returns, and I'm reading in bed upstairs, he always calls out: "It's me." Last evening he called out: "It isn't me." And the night before, "It's eye, said the cyclops."

I wish he didn't have to commute so often. But he replies, "If wishes were whores, beggars would ride."

His rasping tobacco cough is a continuing concern, hour after day after month. Sixteen years younger than I, will he give way sooner? My need is as frightening as my love. He deals with each reality. (Without him could I write checks, let alone know where the various sources represented by the checks are located?)

His bad points? I know of none. But stubbornness is surely his most exasperating trait. Sonny, the dog, is a point in question: I can't deal with him. Is my incapacity stronger than JH's adoration?

Finished finally the essay on Nantucket for *Geo*. It's even more wretched than most of my commissioned prose of the past year: Prosey yet undisciplined, and with no honest—let alone interesting—viewpoint. Well, it's the last prose I'll write for a long while. The concentration necessary for music has suffered because of commitments here and there and everywhere. Has it? The fact is, whatever my worth, nearly every hour of the next twenty months is accounted for. Nice to be wanted.

18 June

I thought of ending *Out of Nantucket* with JH in his basement hideaway re-reading *Out of Africa*, his second favorite writing (after *The Importance of Being Earnest*). Nor did I mention (so I'll mention it here) the quite real possibility of composing an opera on Maggie Lee Conroy's original libretto based on the diaries of eighteenth-century Nantucket women, and centering on the life of Maria Mitchell. Nor did I use my paragraphs from Anton Kuerti's *Whales—A Celebration* ("Whales have always swum in my bloodstream, circling ever nearer the heart. Perhaps it is no coincidence that I now live upon an island shaped like a whale."). Nor did I bring up Francine's hysterical put-down in *Vogue*, claiming that Nantucket was but a land of Lethe. (As sex lurks behind the dozens of doors in Chicago and Paris, death lurks behind the doors of New York and Paris.) Nor that we live here, not all the time, but about a third. Nor that the temperature is cooler in summer and warmer in winter than New York's.

20 June

In the Letters column of *People*, a reader defends Shirley MacLaine's book against the attack that it lacks intellect: "A world that's all intellect and no emotion would be an awful place to live." That'll be the day.

In the fifteen-second TV promo for something called *Heroes*, we see Sally Field, at medium range, saying, "I was against the war, I protested it," and Henry Winkler, in closeup, answering, "And I fought it." He means, of course, that unless she too fought it (in it, or against it?) she has no right to an opinion. But what's the moral?

Insomnia. Making worthless notes at 4 A.M. Sudden light in the middle of the night hurts like sherbet on the incisors.

21 June

As is usual with the American literati, all the painterly names dropped in Updike's new novel are up-to-date types like Rauschenberg, Marisol, Oldenburg, while all the musical names are classical Germans: Bach, Handel, Beethoven. And even the English literati, like Philip Larkin in his new *Required Writing*, when speaking of contemporary music in counterpoint to writers like Ashbery, Pym, Jarrell, Betjeman, speaks not of their formal equivalents (Britten, Carter, Copland) but of Charlie Parker and Fats Waller.

28 June

Tomorrow Richard Dyer flies over from Boston to conduct a forty-eight-hour interview. But what can he write? I am not interesting—only my work is. There's nothing I ever say in talk that I've not said better in books. My work is more intelligent than I.

A note from *The Advocate* inviting another essay on "anything burning" that concerns me right now—but with the hint that for the "new generation," the past, i.e. "the era of one's elders—what was their cultural context," is what they'd appreciate. So I am now an elder.

   With George Chavchavadze in Pigalle, 1950, and the hotel I was afraid to go to with that curly-haired legionnaire, his illiterate odor of Gauloise, brilliantine, brandy, and desire to *tirer un coup*. George said he'd wait downstairs, but I got cold feet. Because I did not experience this experience with the *beau idéal*, he has become the *beau idéal*. (Should that be *bel idéal?*) Unheard melodies are sweeter. Write of connection between liquor and sex. Passivity & shame.

John Ashbery is the one peer whose good reviews don't make me jealous.
   Unfavorites: George Burns; *Under the Volcano* (I don't see what others see in it).

JH contends that Janet Flanner wasn't a good writer but a wonderful rewriter. The notion is clearly from something she would have told him: that her column was based on the translating and readjusting of French newspaper items. Well, in a very real way, all writers are rewriters.

Peter Brook is not a director, he's an undertaker using embalming fluid instead of, like Dr. Frankenstein, hot blood and sparks. Why don't these opera refurbishers simply commission new operas?

Boulez. It's not that he's crazy, but that he's boringly crazy. The IRCAM pit produces music that I don't enjoy, you don't enjoy, and probably he doesn't enjoy. And yes, enjoyment on some level—along with terror and tragedy and force and farce—is a goal and an issue of all art.

With age we gain a certain authority about our own ignorance.

Once I was charming, now I am not. I no longer need to be. However, *n'est pas charmant qui veut*—although that's not for me to say. Still, I have said it.

30 June

Kundera's piece (*NYR*, July 19, 1984), "The Novel and Europe," is admirable and anxious-making, because on the one hand it is so economically cultured and stylish in setting out the thesis that fiction, no less than science and philosophy, describes history, and because on the other it declares what we already know, but in new words: "World unity means: no escape, for anyone, anywhere." Kundera's mind recalls Paul Goodman's (and that is the highest compliment), except that Kundera, unlike Paul, is neither poet nor crank.

But now I open his new novel, and am annoyed twice in the first two pages. Hasn't the idea of Eternal Return become unnegotiable, even in science fiction? (I wrote about this a few years ago re *Time and Again*.) "Will the [meaningless] war between two African kingdoms in the fourteenth century itself be altered if it recurs again and again in eternal return?" Well, that war is certainly different from the vantage of the thirteenth century. But then, in the thirteenth century, how can that war be termed a fourteenth-century war? The Eternal Return means that your life recurs not only every millennium or every month, but is renewed every microsecond; thus it trips over itself, with off-center emphases, like the same movie simultaneously mouthing from different screens in transcontinental 747s. But your top hat and tails contradict the showing for Christ in "his time" no more than Christ himself runs against "our time."

Have I missed the point?—which is, I suppose, metaphoric: We perceive history forever differently according to where we stand, and the flow of time continually alters perspective. (Paul Goodman never spoke metaphors; he meant, literally, just what he said.) But how do we perceive "future" history, like say, 1984 from the vantage of 2184? What did Sappho think of the overlapping lives of, say, Mary Baker Eddy and Logan Pearsall Smith? Is Eternal Return synonymous with E.T.?

Turning the page I read: "But is heaviness truly deplorable and lightness splendid? The heaviest burden crushes us . . . but in love poetry of every age, the woman longs to be weighed down by the the man's body." And what, we may ask, does the man long for? How about the man who longs to be weighed down by a woman's—or, indeed, another man's—body? Perhaps the woman is not, as she sees it, weighed down as much as pulling down. Next paragraph: "The absence of burden causes man to be lighter than air, to soar into the heights." Don't women soar to the heights? Ah, now Kundera uses "man" as "mankind," and thus the two paragraphs form a specious compound. He is good, though, when he asks, "Which one is positive, weight or lightness?" since beauty can reside in superficiality and ugliness in profundity. Yet when *I* say this, people raise their eyebrows: "Poor Ned, his Achilles heel is his notion of prettiness; charm is his downfall." It is no use for me to explain that by ugly I intend force. Even Poulenc is ugly, and so is Bonnard.

It would have been late summer 1952, around four P.M. I was drinking beer with Henri Fourtine on the *terrasse* of Le Select, boulevard Montparnasse. At the next table: an old woman, vague and dark like the "suggestions" of women in Bonnard. Facing us on the sidewalk, another old woman, singing wretchedly and holding out a tin cup. With a sudden grand movement the woman at the table, eyes filled with tears, rose and embraced the one on the sidewalk, then invited her to sit down. The scene came back to me this morning as two sexagenarian males passed the house. Had I addressed them—"people our age"—they would have been amused, not offended. Because they are rich.

As it turns out, those first three pages are the meatiest, the most provocative, of Kundera's whole novel.

1 July

Death of Lillian Hellman.

My first scent of sadness—of wistfulness, not sorrow—would have been the first awareness of autumn. Wasn't it in our backyard, which abutted a pungent no-man's-land, at 16 Rosemary Street in Chevy Chase, in 1930? That feeling of change, of loss, was not unpleasant and couldn't be compared to incomprehensible vacuums produced by the death of my grandmother, and later of friends.

12 July

This morning, finished the orchestration of *An American Oratorio*, curled it into a mailing tube, and sent it by Overnight Express to Boosey & Hawkes who will print up a copy from which Daron Hagen will begin the well-paid chore of extracting the parts. Thus ends a year's work. For the record, during that year I did complete three smaller pieces: the seven waltzes for saxophone & piano called *Picnic on the Marne*, the seven *Dances* for Cello & Piano, and *Pilgrim Strangers* for The King's Singers.

This afternoon, received a clipping (at this late date) from the *National Review* of *Setting the Tone* and the North Point diary reprints. How embarrassing to read again quotes from *The Paris Diary* that, says the reviewer, have made readers squirm for eighteen years. ("The phone: 'But how will I recognize you?' 'I'm beautiful.'")

Just before *The Paris Diary* went into galleys Marie Laure said, "You may publish anything except mention of the Haye-Jousselins, and that . . . ." The "and that" I have respected: it concerned the nature of our relation. Still, it was ML who persuaded me to pursue the diary in the first place.

William Burroughs in *The Advocate* advocates, as a sort of vigilantism against gay-bashers, a system based on a Chinese sect called Tongs who "look out for each other." The premise throughout his oeuvre seems to be that since roughnecks endanger the world, only roughnecks can save the world. Burroughs is now seventy: an old man still playing boys' games, like a queer Hemingway (if the term's not redundant). But Quakers too look out for each other, and turning the other cheek has never provoked war.

Reagan claims "There is no simple way" to deal with warfare. Yes there is: don't fight.

13 July (Friday)

Eric Bentley's contention in the *Voice* last week that "the expression WASP . . . is a racial slur on a level with Yid, Nigger, Wop et al." is unaccountably senile. WASP is not a denigration but a definition (nor is it possible, except with sticks and stones, to wound a power group). As for his explanation that the "structure" is redundant, "there being no non-white Anglo-Saxons," we've all pointed that out years ago.

I first heard *Wozzeck*, or parts thereof, when Ben Weber played me the aircheck he'd made of Eileen Farrell and Bernard Herrmann's midnight performance on WOR. It was around 1944, and I was as bowled over as I'd been eight years earlier by *Le Sacre*. Krasner's performance of Berg's Concerto with Stock in Chicago in 1940 had overwhelmed me, too: those German mysteries were new, and I took the program notes (white virgin, etc.) to heart. Yet Berg has never influenced me, nor do I think of him when he's not there, while Stravinsky has been just across the room every day of my life.

Keeping Quiet	*Keeping Noisy* (a haiku)
Love is fear	As vapors gush from New York sewers
Love is fair	so do I swoon for thee
C'est à dire	Jeannette
C'est à taire	

Bastille Night

In the same issue of *NYR* as the Kundera article, Noel Annan tells us that John Maynard Keynes "was not a congenital homosexual. His psyche and his physique were both bisexual," which explains why Keynes was able to "fall" into marriage with the Russian dancer Lydia Lopokova. Now who is a congenital homosexual? What is the physique of a bisexual? With conjectures like these from the intelligentsia, we don't need the unwashed.

In her frothily readable current best-seller Françoise Sagan quotes Sartre as telling her, "*Vous êtes quelqu'un de très gentil, non? C'est bon signe. Les gens intelligents sont toujours gentils. Je n'ai connu qu'un type intelligent et méchant, mais il était pédéraste and il vivait dan le desert.*" This is meant (by Sagan, if not by Sartre) as humorous; the reader smiles, for yes, of course, homosexuals are never *gentils*. In fact, intelligence and likeability have nothing to do with each other. Sagan's words are from just last year. Such a reflection in America would be taboo, even in the straight press. Or would it? Why is Sagan always so . . . so *superficial* about queers? Didn't she, like Mary McCarthy, ever marry one? She treats them as jesters. In Paris, that still goes.

In Paris there's still the avant-garde notion—that is, the old-hat notion— that because a thing's new it's true.

20 July

Because I go barefoot, and our lawn is rich with clover, I manage at least once each summer to tread on a bee. After the first paralyzing sting there remains for three days an itching both frantic and luscious. Last Tuesday, and again yesterday, I stepped on a bee; then later yesterday, while I was waiting at the airport for Joe LeSueur, an ant bit my midriff (leaving today a scratchy pink disk the size of a quarter), while the back of my left leg is bewelted with mosquito bites. Add to this the incision which Dr. Voorhees performed on Monday to perforate a boil in my right nostril, the maimed gums surrounding my left incisor over which on Tuesday Dr. Slavitz placed a crown, plus a recurrence of my four-year-long prostate "condition," the chronic stomach ache and insomnia, and the gnawing doubts about my so-called talent (can't get any ideas for the Violin Concerto, which is due along with an unbegun Organ Concerto and a Septet for Santa Fe, by the end of October), and you wonder that JH finds me unliveable. Now JH has returned for his obligatory weekend in New York (obligatory because of his weekly service at St. Matthew's & St. Timothy's, where his organ-and-choir manifestations cull silk purses from sows' ears) where he'll be faced by the ordeal of E. on Riker's Island. Then back here to face the carpenter's ineptitude. Meanwhile, Joe LeSueur after our thirty-two years of acquaintance retains both enthusiasms and coppery locks of his youth, and on his first visit to Nantucket keeps his senses open.

Can't work. Perfect weather.

23 July

"You're in trouble only if you stop listening," writes Gregory Sandow of Morton Feldman's new ninety-minute piece, *Three Voices*. "Even if you drop out for only thirty seconds Feldman may have sidled so far from where he began that you'll be lost when you try to jump back in." But how can Sandow know this, unless (as is not the case) he has both been lost and not been lost in the piece?

Dine with Danny Pinkham and entourage. He gives me his new harp suite (I dream of someday finding a harp piece sans glissandos) and a song cycle. Danny uses a device that is the inverse of Britten's. Whereas Britten (in the *Academic Cantata*, for example) uses tunes made from the twelve tones but harmonized diatonically, Pinkham uses diatonic tunes harmonized chromatically. His compositional sense has always been smooth, developmental, evolutionary; yet Danny's conversation is strictly anecdotal.

28 July

As a house gift Richard Dyer sent a cassette of Phyllis Curtin singing Cole Porter, and a volume of poems by his friend Frank Bidart. Now Richard adores Phyllis no more than I, nor is he musically less perceptive, but where he hears a hip lilt I hear a missed beat. As for Bidart's "War of Vaslav Nijinsky" (which Robert Lowell thought was simply a masterpiece), what is it but a collection of other people's history, with no point of view—much less poetry—of Bidart's own?

We hear what we want to hear. If I hadn't been taught that Beethoven's Ninth is a masterpiece it would not have occurred to me. I listen to JH's organ playing as to the utmost finesse, although on a logical level it is not. Andrew Porter is incapable of hearing Elliott Carter's most casual effort as other than holy writ. Because I have not had it appraised, I cannot tell if the red crystal vase sent to me by my invisible friend, Anna Roush of Morgantown, West Virginia, is worth two dollars or two thousand dollars. Even to the most experienced and subtle listeners, best friends can do no wrong.

27 July

Heavy rain chose to fall exactly as JH & Sonny's plane is meant to leave this noon, after two days of seraphic still weather. Now I'm left alone to fume impotently over the Violin Concerto which may never get written.

Lips that touch liquor shall never touch mine.
   Your lips?
   No, my liquor.

It has been over twelve years since I've touched a drop. Not even wine? people ask, as though wine weren't alcohol. Are you as disgusted as I by this dumb question?

The difference between alcoholics and Real People is that when the Real People have ingested their thin slice of bourbon-soaked plum pudding washed down with a single cup of festive punch and are ready to sing carols as pine logs crackle, the alcoholics aren't ready for the carols. The punch is not an ornament to joy but the joy itself. So where's the second cup, and the fifth and the nineteenth—when the joy turns to horror and the party's ruined?

Anyone can get drunk but only I can write my music.

Spoke to John Duffy. I turned down a two-year job to act as advisor to the Atlanta Symphony at forty thousand dollars a year. Can I also afford to turn down Boston U.?

29 July

Composers who teach: The supposition, that because we know how we can show how, is at best risky. (Does the goose know how it lays the golden egg?)

The supposition has been visibly risky for centuries, yet Broadway angels still sink billions into flops, nothing into hits, and great art seems a lottery. Still, Boston University proposes to accord me $60,000 yearly to instruct young composers.

If I "knew how," would I tell? Why not bottle it and sell it and make a mint? Or is there room for another me? Teaching the "art" of composition (unlike the *crafts* of orchestration or counterpoint or ditchdigging) can come only after the fact. Pupils must first produce something that the teacher may criticize.

What can I do? I can smell a rat. And I can intuit who I think the pupil thinks he is and help to clear the debris between himself and his self. A piece results from the taking of your material and stretching and shrinking it, heating and cooling it, weaving and unraveling it, enriching and depleting it, and this according to both textbook and instinct. But if the material itself is second-rate, how can I make it first-rate, even for myself?

30 July

The long rains a month or so ago were record-breaking, but the four-hour deluge last Friday caused more damage. The back and side yards became a lake (gulls paddled there while the pheasant family pecked around the edges), JH's flooded basement retreat was short-circuited, and one of his tenacious butterfly bushes planted two years ago was drowned. We're still raking up crashed branches and wondering about maybe installing a drainage system. Expensive.

As in Ives's song, *Tom Sails Away*, the past assails constantly. For some reason an excursion to Aix-en-Provence shone—a lovable souvenir—from the bedroom wall, as from a TV screen, at three A.M. It would have been in the early 1950s, and Marie Laure and I, just the two of us, motored there from Hyères to dine and to hear a Mozart opera, and came back the same night. During the sixty-mile trek ML had to pee, *rien à faire*, and Bacchat (the famous chauffeur who in earlier years, when ML had a fling with Tom Keogh, had a fling with Tom's wife, Theodora) stopped the blue Buick while the Vicomtesse, already dressed for the evening in a voluminous floor-length skirt of maroon velvet and a snow-white satin bib, descended to trip through a van Gogh field in her silver espadrilles and squat midst the cornstalks, as cars whizzed by on Route 38.

Anxiety about work is like nothing experienced before. I've never been interested in other people's talk of being blocked (nor am I blocked for ideas), but I just can't bring myself to sit down and write the damn concerto. I feel I've proved all I have to prove—but that's frightful to admit. Not that the attitude will necessarily prevent the piece from being "good," if it ever gets composed, but I've little urge, except for the money.

31 July

Last winter Russell Baker, whom I scarcely know, mentioned my songs in his column. At his induction into the Arts & Letters in May I told him I was touched, and he answered, "Actually your song recordings are hard to find." I offered to give him a copy. Which I did, six weeks ago (JH left it on his porch here in Nantucket). But JH, when I ask why Baker never acknowledged the record, says my gesture was pushy—or at best gratuitous. Which makes me feel funny.

Weather opaline. Work going . . . hardly at all. The Jelleme brothers delivered several tons of fertile dirt for the new terrace, submerging in earth, and probably destroying, two azalea bushes.

I worry no less about JH's health because of his two-plus packs a day (he smokes even while shoveling earth) than about my own when—as he does at least once a day—he leaves one or more lighted cigarettes poised on a table's edge as he goes about his business elsewhere.

It was Alvin Ross who told me to go to Drossie's, 1943. I fortified myself with chug-a-lugs from a half-pint of Calvert's Rye, bought (will they or won't they serve me?) from the corner store. I shudder, looking back, to see the incipient alcoholic, but shudder with pleasure, looking forward, at knowing I'll never drink again. Knock wood. It's been twelve years. Actually seventeen. There are no *incipient* alcoholics: you are or you aren't—before you touch that first drink. (Brad Gooch et al. should write on the *forties*.)

I can never think of the word *curry*, though I can always think of chutney. There's another word that I can always never think of, but I forget it.

I wish I were young and dumb and cute again; do my eyes mist over as I type this? They do not. What a horror to be young. Later years are meant for writing romances about what it used to be.

Peach-colored sunsets and sunset-colored peaches. Where does metaphor begin? Cannot a thing resemble itself?

Vogue phoned this morning to ask if I'd do something on Philip Glass, hinting that since Glass is already so broadly and favorably publicized, they wouldn't be against a bit of negativism. I said no. Not because I feel positive, but because I haven't the time. (Nor is it very classy for one composer to put down another in print—unless the print is that of the music engraver.)

It's my parents' 64th wedding anniversary. I sent them Gore Vidal's *Lincoln* and a three-pound box of mixed chocolates from Congdon's Pharmacy.

Later. Dined in Sconset at Mary & Peter Heller's. The other guests: Bill & Frankie Schuman, Paula Robison, and Scott Nickrenz. (Cous-cous with perfectly underdone new carrots & turnips, salad with *real* tomatoes, and fresh fruit drenched in hot chocolate.) Paula, physically svelte and brimming with the goodwill of Bette Midler, asks Bill and me that schoolgirl question, "What are you thinking about when you conceive for the flute?" She wants, of course, to open up talk on esthetics—on metaphors for sound (silky tone, purple trills, Daphnis reflected in a tragic pool, etc.). But Bill, who since his heart attack looks—with his sensual lips and piercing eyes—like Picasso, gives the only answer possible: "I am thinking about what I put on the paper." This doesn't satisfy Paula.

At least twice nightly I get up to pee. Why is this nightly getting-up not accompanied with the same creaks and groans as the morning getting-up?

Today I appeared before the committee of Old North Church to present the case against the ear-splitting carillon (which isn't a carillon but an amplified malfunctioning tape of a syrupy out-of-tune vibraharp oozing versions of *Onward Christian Soldiers* and such) which has plagued the community fifteen minutes a day for the past ten years. The committee was very polite, but they didn't know what I was talking about.

William Schuman, of all American composers of his generation, is the least French. Which is why no one ever points out his affinity to Darius Milhaud. Yet both employ what used to be called bitonality in the same way: their counterpoint is often really harmonic masses moving against each other in contrary motion, masses that are in themselves pure and triadic, but become dissonant (bitonal) when conjoined with each other. I hear this in every one of Bill's pieces, and in Milhaud's, and in nobody else's. But the two composers don't sound alike. Enigma.

Bill gives new meaning to the minor third, an optimistic meaning. The descending C to A is no longer the "dying fall" of Mahler but the rousing street call of Manhattan. Like Robert Schumann, William Schuman is boyish, but boyish with scads of know-how.

20 August

Remember the hammock—the capacious, white-webbed, Chekovian hammock—which for the past nine summers we strung between the elms? Well, it was stolen in the middle of the night. All the creepier in that last night was one of total insomnia. At all hours—at two, at four, at six—I was astir, taking cough drops and aspirin, and could have looked into the back yard toward the furtive form(s). Would I have shouted? This morning we reported it to the police. We feel defiled, public, unprotected.

Far from apprehending thieves, I was centered on myself, the flu, anxieties about deadlines, and confecting aimlessly, by repeating them over and over, little verbal phrases that would be difficult for a foreigner to sight-read:

Though tough, he thought it best to plough right through to Java.

The throne of Cain surrounded by thick prongs.

Think thrice before you bow before the boughs.

22 August

Last night for the first time we dined at The Chanticleer in Sconset as guests of Joan Peyser and Ray Hagel. The site is exquisite. From there on, all downhill. When we arrived at 7:55 for our 8:00 reservation, the cheerless headwaiter resorted to the chintzy ploy, "Would you care to wait in the bar?" We had no wine. The food was mediocre and (we each chose separate menus) undifferentiated, the service bad (an hour's wait between soup and entrée), and the bill cynical (two hundred dollars, which included the disappointing *soufflés aux framboises* and presumably the microscopic bonbons "offered" at the end, but not the bar bill which had to be "taken care of" at the bar). We were in the un-chic upstairs section, to where the efforts of a watery pianist floated intrusively through a dumbwaiter. Last night for the last time we dined at The Chanticleer.

Have definitely decided against accepting the Boston University proposal, on the grounds that there would be no freedom for work, and half my time would be spent waiting in the sleet for the shuttle plane. Which means that, at $60,000 a year, that's $180,000 I will *not* have in 1987. Shall I continue at Curtis, at far less, as my own boss?

Nagging cough that doesn't go away.

25 August

Death of Truman Capote. What a shock. Like a snap of the fingers, the bitterness I've felt toward Truman for the past ten years is gone, and I miss him.

JH to NY for twenty-four hours to get wallpaper. Sonny stays here.

26 August

Plump Mrs. Quigley, who for the past agreeable decade has been our geographically closest neighbor although we exchange scarcely more than a few hellos, was diagnosed last winter with stomach cancer. Now as she sits on the porch on Wesco Place, her little chemotherapy bonnet, like Madame Defarge's, askew on her hairless scalp, she grows visibly skinnier with each passing day and has trouble swallowing, yet smiles and claims to adore watching Sonny romping like a loud moonbeam in our backyard. Last night she went back to the hospital. How long now?

Meanwhile the backyard, like Sonny, grows and grows and the sapphirine sky this morning sparkles with early fall and everything changes. I changed my signature, quite consciously, during the summer of 1952, when Henri Fourtine said that the N of Ned looked like an M. Now I seem to spend more and more time giving interviews not just about myself but about dead friends. During the next month I'm scheduled to chat with the biographers of Dali, Cheever, Griffes, Man Ray, Elizabeth Bishop, and William Kapell, as well as of the still quick Bernstein and Bowles, and dredge up memories and opinions without getting paid even though I'm, in a sense, writing the books. Not to mention writing blurbs, recommendations for friends, and crank letters which, like Paul Goodman's, never get published by newspapers if they're in the least off-center.

Paul compiled a book of such rejected letters, called *The Society I Live in Is Mine*. My missile to the *Times* last May, about Cocteau's personal circumspection, was never acknowledged. Meanwhile the National Institute for Music Theater in Washington has dreamed up a program by which a "younger" composer may apply for a grant to compose an opera, providing he can procure an "older" composer as patron. Kenneth LaFave, one of the students in Florida last February, who earns his board as music critic (quite good) on a Taos paper, has solicited my blessing. I reply:

Dear Kenneth—

You are not the first composer I've refused to sponsor for the National Institute for Music Theater, whose policy, if it were not so ignorant, would seem grasping in the extreme. The so-called Supervisors (presumably established composers—who else would qualify?) are asked to "donate their services to this program," services amounting to "a minimum of three hours per week in private tutorial sessions." (I do note that the Institute, in its infinite generosity, may consider a maximum of $2400 honorarium "where a contribution would constitute a hardship.")

No composer on earth has the energy, let alone the time, to donate one hundred fifty-six unpaid yearly hours to another composer. He'd rather write his own opera, and get paid for it.

The Institute makes two false assumptions: 1) that established composers are financially secure and have time to burn; 2) that established composers know more than the "Intern" about writing operas.

Every serious composer, no matter how famous, needs money (as these Washingtonians ought to know) in a society which grants not even a subsistence to its creative artists who nonetheless glorify, or reflect, that society as no prosperous pop singer or munitions-maker ever will. But no composer, no matter how famous, is equipped to "supervise" another's opera, nor does he even have a formula for his own operas—or why do our Menottis and Bernsteins and Kirchners and Carlisle Floyds, despite their reputations, come up with more flops than hits?

These harsh words are not for you but for the National Institute to whom, now that I think of it, I shall mail a copy. Meanwhile, here's my advice (advanced free of charge): Do not give up your journalism; you're good at it, it's needed, and you should be able to deal with two careers. Find a strong subject and then—much more difficult—have that subject rendered into theatrical, singable, communicable prose. That's half the battle, and no supervisor can help you there. I hope, however, that for your own financial sake, you find a supervisor. And God help him.

1 September

"Can it be played by a conductorless orchestra?" asked Jaime Laredo, whom I'd called in Vermont to announce that his Violin Concerto is done. He was thinking, no doubt, of his Scottish Chamber Orchestra and of other small groups around the country now that he, like so many other string soloists, has been bitten by the baton bug. Well, er, I wasn't quite sure. JH, when I brought this up later, had an answer: "It all depends on who isn't conducting."

JH, who as I write this has just finished laying adobe blocks in the patio (the patio, which he constructed two years ago and which contains a trellis also erected by him, now dripping with new September roses reflecting their crimson onto the freshly hosed bricks below), was an infant prodigy on the fiddle before he specialized in organ, and he directed musicals all through college. He knows in a practical way more than I about violin and podium. Is there nothing he can't do? We do have misunderstandings, but with always the calming therapy of backgammon which we've played nearly every night after supper for the past seven years. My other rigorous habit (it's not a habit, is it? rather, a custom) is the twice-weekly call to Father at Cadbury.

People speak of Debussy's hold on Messiaen but they always mention "late" Debussy. Do you remember Jennie Tourel with foamy green silk protecting her as she emitted *Le Balcon* so long ago? I had assumed, then, that it too was late Debussy, was stunned to learn it dates—like its four fellow *Poèmes de Baudelaire*—from 1887, nearly a century ago. Yet Messiaen last week could have penned the harmonies and tune that fall beneath the verse, *Je sais l'art d'évoquer les minutes heureuses!* (aptly Englished, without the exclamation point, by Richard Howard as: "I know the art of conjuring up delight").

JH refers to me, when speaking to Sonny, as Mister Rosum, the most frequent misspelling of Rorem.

Began the Organ Concerto today.

5 September

JH picked up Doris and Stuart Pope at the ferry yesterday and brought them back to the house just at the moment Rosemary phoned to say that Father had broken his leg. He's at Burlington County Hospital.

Tonight, rambunctious dinner for Aurora Ginastera, Gerrie Feder, the Popes, me & JH, plus Sonny, the life of the party. We used the whole table which with the board insert can seat twelve, candles, and the "good" silver.

Father's leg will be operated on in the early morning. JH, who must return to New York Friday, will visit him next week.

11 September

Sparkling, almost drinkable weather. The Popes have left, rather sadly. Upheavals at B. & H. Doris on hands and knees all afternoon uprooted clumps of crabgrass from our little terrace.

Donald Dervin (and two friends) materialized, still discombobulated with grief and guilt at Donald Gramm's demise.

Working, casually and for the moment without enthusiasm, on the Organ Concerto.

Saturday Rosemary reported that Father was delirious. Result of anesthetic fifty hours earlier? Shock and old age?

12 September

Crutchfield asks in rebuff to my letter about songs, "Mustn't it be conceded that American art-song is simply a brief chapter in music's history—one that, whatever the delights of its best examples and whatever its nourishing potential for singers whose cultural roots it's [sic] are, has not yielded a repertory comparable in scope, variety, whatever, to that that emerged from Germany's longer and earlier one, or France's briefer but more intense one?" Well, gosh. Can Americans know about America, if they are *in* it today when its history is transpiring (rather than in Germany yesterday)? And does this make my forty years of composing songs a superfluous anachronism? If we can write American history so quickly, is it too soon for Crutchfield—who admits to having no ear for him—to declare Elliott Carter simply a brief chapter in that history? Or Cage or Cowell or Copland? Of course, Art Song is not a person but a trend. Still, trends are made by persons, and can resurge.

I've always disliked: "And now to end on a happier note." There is no happier note. Why destroy the effect of what's preceded by trying to end on a happier note? Our history may ultimately show us to be merely in an age of science. But what good has science been up to of late?

13 September

The garden is frantic with growth—a sort of last stand before autumn sets in. These are my last two days alone here, and I should (should?) feel elated and melancholy. I do, yes, I do feel so. But despite the moderate temperature and green sky, everything smells of senility and death. Princess litters the basement with agonizing goldfinches and baby moles. There's blood in my stool (tomorrow I see Voorhees). Chitchat with neighbors—all my age or more—is mainly about other neighbor's cancer. Mother and Father are both sinking, if that's the word, and daily phone talks with JH and Rosemary center on them. Saturday JH will take me straight from La Guardia to Cadbury. There seems nothing redeeming about getting old.

Reading Vivian Perlis's "autobiography" of Copland. With all the glories an artist could hope for, Aaron is apparently unable to remember from day to day that the book exists.

14 September

Last day in Nantucket before the trials of New York and the duties of Philadelphia, where I have four new pupils.

Yesterday, tea at the house with Ursula Colt and her fiancé, and with Noel Sokoloff and his friend, whom I ran across at Bookworks.

Today, saw Voorhees about my bleeding. Tonight late, in the rain which presages Hurricane Diana, Moira Hodgson and Michael Schulan came to call.

To my complete surprise, a cartoon of me by Hirschfeld was in the *Times* today. That, I suppose, is glory.

Lest we not realize how hip he is to gay nuance, Robert Craft, in his review of *Auden in Love*, manages to drop the name of Boy George, allude to *La Cage aux Folles*, concur that Auden's self-reference as Mother infers a maternal feeling toward Chester Kallman, and sum up the biography as "a contribution to the homosexual history of the United States." Auden and Chester must be hooting in their graves.

Long phone talk with JH who found Father lucid and vital; it was the anesthetic that had made him rave. Spoke with Father myself then. He cried. In his ravings he had "seen" Mother, young and beautiful, only to wake up to the "truth" of her remoteness. He'll be in the hospital, and then in convalescence at Cadbury, for several months. But, he says, this is not his "last bout."

New York
19 September

In a 1969 music notebook I find (did I ever use them elsewhere?) these two statements:

"Poets as opposed to lyricists. Lyrics have no life of their own." (Does Ira Gershwin's work have a life of its own?)

"But since conservative poets feel the same way about their words, and since experimental composers are not usually drawn to these poets anyway, one concludes that all music dealing with words will, to communicate (in the broadest sense), necessarily be simple."

Young American composers writing songs today don't seem to know their country's current poetry. They use inevitably Blake, Dickinson, Whitman, Joyce.

Reviews from London for the July performance of *After Long Silence* are so dismissive that David Huntley relinquished them only under pressure. (Nicholas Kenyon: "fatuous powdered-milk dilutions that left their superb poetry quite untouched." Dominic Gill: "in Rorem's familiar cultivated film-score vein which demonstrates only a spectacularly inept response to its chosen words—though maybe anyone who calls Burns and Yeats 'English Poets' has not gone into the field too deeply." Geoffrey Norris: "a monochrome musical evocation of the verse.") JH attempts to comfort me. Isn't all English music monochrome? Don't they all condescend to Americans? Will knowing the homelands of Burns and Yeats deepen my field less mawkishly than Tippett's is deepened by knowing Negro spirituals? Still, I'm felled. *After Long Silence* is one of my best pieces.

Is my "film-score vein" as "cultivated" as Britten's or Walton's? And if I "leave the superb poetry quite untouched," who determines which composers *touch* poetry? The critics, solely—not, surely, the poets.

21 September

Afternoon at Curtis, where the new flock is serious and very young. Then a splendid hour with Todd Duncan at the Barclay, apropos of the article on Gershwin. What a warm, wise, and musically caring man he is.

I like a Gershwin tune, how about you?

What *makes* a Gershwin tune? Intervallic characteristics? But *Somebody Loves Me*'s stepwise ascent of a mere major sixth contrasts radically with the acrobatic disjunct rise of a whole major tenth in *A Foggy Day*, while the anacrusic design of *Embraceable You* (although near to that of *I've Got A Crush On You*) in no way resembles the gradual chromatic descent of *The Man I Love*. Do these disparate relationships distinguish, necessarily, Gershwin from Porter or Kern or Rodgers?

It's rhythm that makes a Gershwin tune.

David Posner phoned recently from Orlando and said, quite simply, "I'm dying, Ned." (Lung cancer, and he never smoked.) Is this one of his masochist self-dramatizations? Pain-in-the-neck though David always was, he was also a mensch when the chips were down. My Buffalo job in 1959 stemmed from him, as did much of the grammar and formality of those Buffalo lectures—the first grown-up prose I ever penned.

Tomorrow, Nantucket for two weeks.
    Father in hospital again: phlebitis.
    A call from Morris: Larry Stanton has AIDS.

> *Nantucket*
> *24 September*

Hot weather.
    Our neighbor Mrs. Quigley died today.

> *27 September*

Last week in New York, a long interview with Cheever's pedagogic biographer, Scott Donaldson. Today, a long interview with a Ms. Gena Dagel, one of a seemingly endless stream of thesis-writers on Paul Bowles.
    Cold weather.

I am offended by something Scott Donaldson revealed—the mean result of a lie. In May of 1977 Cheever wrote me that Max Zimmer, "a very good friend" of his, would be in Yaddo in August. Zimmer did indeed turn up at Yaddo and was aloof. This aloofness, according to Donaldson, was because Cheever had "warned" Zimmer against me—that I would try to seduce him as I had earlier seduced John.

Listening to the new recording of Bill Schuman's two ballets of the late forties, *Judith* and *Night Journey*, and to Elliott Carter's eight-year-old *Symphony of Three Orchestras.* How radically different are these contemporaries. How do I react? Well, there is undeniably more *information* in the Carter, but there is more *appeal* in the Schuman. Still, this appeal doesn't speak to me strongly (as does this same sort of appeal in, say, Copland), nor does Carter's information seem to add up to a declaration. Critics, of course, like information—that's their hook, their field, their crutch. (Their Crutch-field?) The Schuman washes over me, and I get the point quickly. The Carter: I keep looking at the revolving disc, wondering how soon it will all be over.
    One plus in the Carter is: the climax represents the cruelest theatricality (in the good sense) I've ever heard, except perhaps in Bartók's *Mandarin*. When the orchestra, in five crunches, eradicates the infinitely expressive solo strings who, when their whimpering is stopped, are replaced by cries of survivors (?) who in turn are crushed, I am as scared as with "The Day After." (Indeed, I remember telling Elliott in Rome, circa 1954, after his

First Quartet was played there, that it sounded like "The end of the world."
I remember it, because he recently reminded me of it.)

Interesting that E. C. himself, in a program note, says of this moment
only: "The main section is brought to a stop by a series of repeated short,
loud chords for the full orchestra that shatter the previous flow."

There is in the music of Schuman a sort of objective warmth apparent in
everything from the Third Symphony of 1941 to the American Hymn of over
four decades later. Even in the tortured ballets there's the ballsy goodwill of
a well-balanced person. I'd be tempted to call his music heterosexual if that
didn't necessarily pull us into the Gay Sensibility syndrome.

29 September

I am not particularly humble, yet I'm madly insecure about my work. Every
new piece means starting from scratch. As with love affairs, what we learned
with one is no help with the next.

A piece in the *Times* a month or so ago claims that artists who are successful in the world's eyes are no less prone to self-doubt and defeatism than "real
people," and I suppose this is true, although the artists they cite are mostly
recreative, like Richard Burton, and the problem they face is mainly fame,
a problem which any famous person with brains knows is largely a joke. (One
is seldom famous anyway for what one does—even Einstein.) A couple
weeks later another article, by an English "authority," tells us that creative
artists are more prone to need psychiatric care than other people. (This
could only be proved in England.) Generally, it could be argued that artists—true artists—are the least neurotic of citizens. It is they who, in this
vale of tears where almost nobody during a whole lifetime knows what he
wants except to make money, are certain about their aims almost from birth,
and are able to pursue those aims and to be appreciated for them. They know
who they are—which is saying everything. No matter how unhappy, no matter how much of a mess an artist may be in his so-called private life, he is not
a mess while working. And he's working most of the time. He checks his anxieties at the studio door and, while in the act of composing, exists in a limbo
of suspended animation which contains neither sadness nor joy. Still, is
happy music (though what sounds happy to you is the result of convention
and may not have seemed happy to a citizen of tenth-century Albania) the
result of an artist's current happiness, or of what he knows—from his own or
other people's—of happiness of the past?

Artists are the stablest of people.

Nantucket
4 October

Last night a dream. Every time I go into the kitchen to freshen drinks for guests, Larry Rivers is still there arguing with a fellow painter. Clearly their argument will get nowhere since they speak with separate syntaxes, separate frames of reference. In the dream I note: "From completely opposite esthetics they make paintings exactly alike."

Red Ozier Press is about to publish (two years late) my little book, *Paul's Blues*, in a small and expensive edition for which Larry has donated a four-color lithograph. I feel . . . honored isn't quite the word . . . warmed that Larry, over the years, has seen fit, without fuss, to embellish my work every once in a while. Though we hardly know each other and have seen one another only sporadically since a first meeting (at Frank O'Hara's? John Myers's?) in the mid-1950s, I do feel that Larry, exactly my age, is my counterpart in painting, albeit far more reactive to pop than to classical music.

Is a person who has sex with only herself by definition homosexual?
  Is "Have you ever had a bisexual experience?" a legitimate question?

The poet is a prison; his works are prisoners that escape. The image is Cocteau's, and one can empathize. But sometimes the escapees, ignored by the world, run back home.

5 October

The *Boston Globe*'s magazine feature came out last Sunday. Flashy, skillful, thorough, not at all me. (JH think it's very me.) Richard Dyer tells us that at the last moment his editor required him to rewrite the first paragraph. It was not clear (to the editor) that I was a classical composer, or even clear what a classical composer is. Twenty years ago would it have been assumed by the general reader that an article on a living composer would automatically mean pop?
  Reading the Copland biography one is reminded yet again how today (as opposed to yesterday) there is no Koussevitzky, no Mitropoulos—there is not even, so to speak, a Bernstein anymore. No bigtime conspicuous conductor championing the cause of contemporary music. Has the cause been settled? Only for the worse. There is no Copland touring the world in concerts of American music. Even American performers on tours abroad are requested *not* to sing American songs, but rather to sing German lieder.

New York
9 October

Three interviews today: Caspar Citron at 11:00, NPR by satellite to Washington at noon (both of these for the new book), and with Peter Brazeau who came to the apartment at 4:00 to talk about Eliz. Bishop. Jean-Pierre Marty showed up at six, and we went to Erick Hawkins's ballets, O God.

Yesterday, Curtis. Tomorrow, the Perles, and Bruce Phemister to dine. Thursday, Opera Southwest in Washington, D.C., will perform the first of four evenings of my triple bill, *Fables*, *Bertha*, and *Three Sisters Who Are Not Sisters*. They'll mail me a videotape.

11 October

Once I declared: Few subjects inspire unanimous reaction, but one can safely say that everyone likes Mozart. To which John Simon replied, "I loathe Mozart."

And I was impressed last month in Nantucket when Ursula Colt's fiancé said, "I really hate Vermont."

Well, at least there's one unanimity: Everybody loves chocolate. "I can't abide chocolate," says Maggie Paley.

Schoenberg's *Five Pieces for Orchestra*, 1909: The second one inspired not only Stravinsky's *Rossignol* but the opening of Bernstein's *Facsimile*. (The opening also comes from Debussy's *Gigues tristes*, dated 1910–12.)

The third—the so-called "Changing Chord"—is misnamed. The chord is stable, it's the colors that change.

Just as some constitutions are immune to the horrors of certain diseases, so some constitutions are immune to the beauties of serial music, and my constitution is among them.

12 October

A performance last night on Channel 30 of Ravel's *Concerto in G* by Michelangeli, Celibidache conducting. Michelangeli has always represented what I most dislike in piano playing, especially in the playing of Ravel. In "melodic passages" his left hand forever anticipates the right, a nineteenth-century mannerism inappropriate to the concision of harmony innate in Ravel. Celibidache meanwhile is concision personified: the music is a corpse laid out for his exquisite incisions. An elegant sterility imbues each bar, like chloroform by Chanel. Both artists are subject to facial close-ups proving their deep dedication to this Great Music, although the music's nature is (as Ravel would be the first to attest) not Great at all, but very high camp. I've known the concerto backwards since age fifteen. Like all possessions—indeed, like a lover—it's a piece I do and do not want to share: it's mine, but I'd like you to admire it. Only Paul Jacobs, among pianists, has played "my" music in a manner that never outraged me.

Reunion Day at Juilliard, climaxed by Bill Schuman's Violin Concerto stupendously played by Robert Mcduffie.

13 October

Van Gogh at the Met, impossible to see for the crowds.

16 October

Ran into Robert Baksa on Broadway at 69th. We stood a moment in the cold. He says that when he and his music—his delicious and "accessible" music—were recently featured on one of Tim Page's new WNYC programs, an irate listener phoned in: "How can such stuff be justified in the light of *Moses and Aaron!*" But if *Moses and Aaron* (composed in 1930) is the criterion by which ensuing works must be judged, couldn't the listener also question the worth of Ravel's piano concertos, of half of Stravinsky and all of Britten, of Poulenc and Messiaen, of Copland and *Porgy and Bess* and, indeed, the entire American catalogue?

Nantucket
19 October

Working on Organ Concerto for Leonard. It's about two-fifths done. Summery fair skies.

Call from Jacob Druckman, asking me to contest Stuart Pope's being "released" from B. & H., which I willingly do. Phoned London—but the infernal machine is in motion.

JH returned to New York with Sonny and Princess.

26 October

Last full day in Nantucket. Worked on Organ Concerto every day (including program note for same), and watched HBO every night: *Educating Rita* (starring what looked like Stuart Pope and Barbara Kolb), *Terms of Endear-*

ment, the Presidential debate, *The Big Chill* (detestable for its intrusive and incongruous rock score), *Black Sunday*, *Letter to Three Wives*. Truffaut died.

New York
28 October

Visit in morning from Leonard Raver to look over the new concerto. The Davids for dinner: Diamond and Huntley.

30 October

Strained hour at B. & H. wherein Stuart, by some perverse decree, was apparently meant to instruct Jerry Bunke (his successor) in how to deal with contractees. Stuart seemed somnolent and in pain; Bunke, eager to be with-it, kissed me on the cheek—a right he has not earned.

31 October

Judy for supper here. Halloween. Assassination of Indira Gandhi.

2 November

Midafternoon with Kitty Carlisle Hart in the guise of interview for *Porgy and Bess* article. Stylish, energetic, phone constantly ringing, both reticent and forthcoming on Gershwin (she's writing her own book). Says she swims every day.

Late afternoon, wrote up midafternoon.

Evening at Tully Hall, listening to George Perle's new piece. Joanne Cossa presented me with the first copy of the Poulenc two-disc album, *Complete Chamber Music for Wind Instruments and Piano* (performed by The Chamber Music Society of Lincoln Center), for which I provided the very long and very original liner notes.

4 November

Noon rehearsal here of *Ariel* with three members of the Roxbury Arts Group. Sonny, who's never heard a soprano before, sat under the piano and howled.

Evening, premiere of Philip Glass's *Akhnaten*, with JH. We stayed for

only the first act; didn't wish to be seen there. Fled to a party nearby for
George Perle.

Insomnia, rain.

10 November

Interminable flow of visitors, this one and that one, all week, and two radio
interviews—one with Tim Page again, and another at WBAI with Teri
Towe. Zeffirelli's *Pagliacci* on TV, not bad.

11 November

The human baby with the baboon heart. Will the body reject it? Would a
baboon reject a human heart?

Party at Steinway Hall for David Dubal's book, *Reflections from the Keyboard*. Ill at ease. Why? Because, says JH, parties are limbo—like the
baths. Except at the baths you make intimate contact with total strangers,
while at parties you make no contact with old friends.

Earl Wild, who was there, says, "I know this man who had a penis transplant—but his hand rejected it."

12 November

The King's Singers, all six of them, came for lunch with Danielle Woerner.
The nine of us (with JH) sat around the table devouring four quiche Lor-
raines, a giant endive-and-scallion salad, and an expensive chocolate cake—
called a Midnight—from The Country Epicure.

Each one of them is a charmer, with his own strong character and his own
vocal timbre. Extraordinary, how on a stage they can blend as one; and how
they seem to be adored throughout the world, regardless of language. My
first question: In which country do they like you the least? Answer: Canada.
Once in Ottawa, when they asked the local manager if the hall would be free
for a noonday rehearsal, he answered, "What's the matter, haven't you
learned the program yet?"

At *our* rehearsal, after lunch, I was bewitched at how well they knew "the
program." When The King's Singers originally commissioned the piece, my
quick and obvious impulse was to weave them a wreath of flawless posies. A
month later (quite unaware of my impulse) they made it clear that they did
not want yet another wreath of flawless posies; rather, they hoped for an extended through-written drama. So, typecasting flung to the winds, I turned
again to the prose of Whitman who for decades had purveyed my most

heartfelt texts. How interesting it would be to hear old Walt's sturdy Yankee-
isms set into relief by the British diction of this elegant group!

My sole criticism of their impeccable diction, as they ran through *Pilgrim
Strangers* this afternoon, was that they must be careful, at least in American
performances, not to roll the *R* in the word Brooklyn.

13 November

Galbraith presided at the "Fund for Artists Colonies" lunch this noon, and
claimed to find "wonderful" my little speech extolling the virtues of such
colonies. The lunch was far east on Pine Street. I took the wrong subway and
ended up west at Trinity Church where, since I was early, I stopped in to
listen to a very beautiful rehearsal of Larry King's choir, pure as spring
water.

This evening, an overlong Memorial for Tennessee Williams, scheduled for
Books & Company on Madison Avenue, was shifted, because of the crowd,
to the Presbyterian Church down the street. It fell flat, the simplest explanation being that Tennessee, who was surely invited, never showed up.
Ruth Ford, declaiming the final diatribe from *Suddenly Last Summer*, simply couldn't bring it off (no actress could) without a director. Stanley Kauff-
mann's homage, in the garb of a savvy survey, was in fact stale and ignorant,
echoing the identical stance he held eighteen years ago in the very first article he wrote during his stint (short-lived) as drama critic for the *Times*: male
homosexuals write about the general society from their vantage as women-
in-disguise. William Jay Smith, whom I'd not realized was a close friend of
TW in the early Saint Louis days, gave a lively reminiscence of the period;
but my own sermon—culled from the essay *Tennessee Now and Then* and
from notes in this diary—now strikes me as pompous and self-serving.

14 November

Pleasant but exhausting day at Cadbury.

15 November

Michael Boxford, the youngish, dashing new head of the London office of
B. & H. (which, like so many other musical "firms" these days, is playing
musical chairs), came at four for a getting-acquainted drink. (A musician, as
well as a businessman, he knew The King's Singers at Cambridge.) Barbara

Kolb showed up at five, at which time Boxford departed toward his duties as host at the Hampshire House.

At six, Barbara, Charles Moss, JH and I went ourselves to the Hampshire House to grace the Farewell Party for Stuart Pope, a gigantic, noisy, vaguely morbid affair, with perhaps a thousand guests. (At our table: Peggy Jory, Frankie Schuman, Harry Kraut, and Andrzej Panufnik—with his English spouse—whom I'd not seen since Paris in 1951, but whose recent *Arbor Cosmica for Twelve Strings* quite bowled me over. It does what music cannot do: expounds the thoughts of trees.) There's something contradictory about such a lavish party in honor of a much-loved director being relieved of his post.

For twenty years Stuart Pope has been my most valuable friend in the professional world, nor is anyone "in the business" so much the diplomat as he. Stuart has unquestioningly put into print all I've composed during that time. His ear and judgement have never been used to suggest that my own instincts are less than infallible; indeed, his respect for artistic integrity is complete, as others of his musical children would surely agree. When he sleeps I wouldn't know: he's at the office from dawn till dusk, then appears with Doris seemingly every night wherever a piece of contemporary music, no matter how stultifying, is played. He's come to all of our premieres, in whatever city, even as he presides over a catalog of copyrighted music unparalleled in music publishing. Stuart is a publisher who loves music. Profit, of necessity crucial to the job, is something I've never heard him discuss with his composers—the rapports are, like those of the old school (Puccini–Riccordi, Debussy–Durand), of protective camaraderie.

In retrospect, the handwriting on the wall grew visible when Boosey & Hawkes began to be passed among various conglomerates. Yet, his stepping down under pressure is like a lifeboat disappearing in a storm.

16 November

World premiere in Avery Fisher Hall of *Pilgrim Strangers*, delivered to perfection by The King's Singers. In our box: David Diamond, Rosemary, her son Paul Marshall, me and JH. Shirley attended a rehearsal this afternoon and seemed both moved and miffed by the "weird sounds" of the countertenors (or altos, as they call themselves). The weirdest sound tonight—and to me the most tellingly anguished—was the solo wail at the end of the halfway point. "Dear brother Thomas, I have been brave but wicked. Pray for me."

17 November

Two premieres in two days is a coup: This evening Gerard Schwarz conducted *After Long Silence* at the Y with (because Katherine was unavailable) the more than worthy British mezzo, Delia Wallis, and oboist Randall Ellis. Whatever the press will doubtless find wanting in this work, as in last night's *Pilgrim Strangers*, I won't be able to blame it on the performances which were, in both cases, beyond perfection.

Schwarz repeats the program tomorrow. Monday, seventh session of the semester with Curtis protégés. Tuesday, Nantucket for a long quiet Thanksgiving with JH.

Father's ninetieth birthday.

The Barclay
Philadelphia
10 December

Returned from Nantucket on the 6th, Mother's 87th birthday, and dined at Maggy & Joe Rosner's that night. Lunch Friday with Janis Susskind, to ease into a new regime with B. & H.

Two days now in Philadelphia. Saturday, rehearsal with Serebrier in the morning. Two lessons. A series of radio interviews with the Curtis publicist escorting me here & there. Chili at Rosemary's, who then came with me to the 7:30 signing at Giovanni's Room. A mob was predicted. A dozen customers showed up, of whom only four or five bought books. Nervous headache.

Sunday afternoon, José Serebrier's concert with the Curtis Youth Orchestra at the Port of History Museum by the river. A dazzling day. And a dazzling orchestra. My god, they sound like the Philadelphia Symphony, glistening and shimmering and playing smack on pitch. My *Six Irish Poems* (sung by a young soprano, Beth MacLoed, with an agreeable but too-light voice) were revived by Serebrier. No one's done them with orchestra since Nell Tangeman in Paris, with Tony Aubin, in 1951. Dined at Henry McIlhenny's with Rosemary, my niece Rachel, Rachel's fiancé, Mike Purcell, Nancy Grace, the Ettings, and George Dix. Rachel and Mike, both painters, are duly impressed by the McIlhenny collection. Rosemary is seated at Henry's right and I'm at the other end of the table. She'll be leaving soon for Jamaica as a Peace Corps worker. Although I'm talking to Gloria Etting, I overhear Henry saying that when a friend of his had a transfusion once in a Kingston hospital he was pumped full of jigaboo blood. I hold my breath: Rosemary's youngest daughter, Charity, is the mother of two exquisite black infants. But my sister with her usual aplomb smiles sweetly.

Today, two lessons. Then with Rosemary to yet another interview with apparently redoubtable Ms. Terry Gross on WHYY. I'll catch the 5:19 to New
York.

13 December

Phone talk with Carl Apone of Pittsburgh on the subject of *An American
Oratorio*'s premiere there next month. I made no reference to his hot & cold
remarks about me in the past, but *he* did, finally, offering no explanation for
his inconsistency. (In *An Absolute Gift* I had immortalized him by quoting
from his review of *Air Music*, "The Pittsburgh Symphony keeps promoting
Rorem's music even though his orchestral efforts have never deserved the
continued performance he gets here," and from his review of the Piano Concerto five years earlier, "one of the finest new works heard here in years.")
Why should I talk with him now? Because that's how things are done.

Finished Gershwin essay which goes to *Opera News* tomorrow. Picked up
the beautifully bound full score of the new Fiddle Concerto at B. & H. and
took a box of bonbons to the staff.

23 December

Friday, *Aida* at the Met with JH, thanks to Robert Jacobson's gift of two gold
tickets. Leontyne's farewell. We left after the first lackluster act. Last night,
dined with Ellen Adler at Shirley & George's, taking them a present of *Paul's
Blues*, which looks discreetly luxurious.

Today, part of an interview for the Pittsburgh *Post-Gazette*. The critic
Robert Croan happens to be in New York en route for New Orleans, where
I too am headed on the 26th. We'll conclude the interview there.

Gregg and Roz's annual Christmas crush. Tomorrow night, JH's pageant
at St. Matthew's & St. Timothy's. Am practicing the piano two hours a day.

Nagging headaches for weeks.

Bland fare of Beethoven on the radio, year after year, plus the smarm that
goes with it by Karl Haas et alia. Is Beethoven noble? Does his art express
lofty notions? Does he improve us? Has music really anything to do with
goodness? Why not a program on the genius as low sensual being?

New Year's Eve

Back to the slush of Gotham after three interesting days in the heat of Louisiana. Too tired to write of it now.

JH in Nantucket. We'll meet next week in Pittsburgh.

Saw Rossi's film of *Carmen* and was caught up.

With Shirley this bleak afternoon to Saint John the Divine where a crowd of thousands assembled to hear Bernstein conduct "A Concert for Peace." He also spoke from the pulpit with the brevity of genius, the word AIDS ringing bravely into the midst. Later Lenny received in the only area that resembles a dressing room—a little chapel behind the altar—and offered scotch to everyone. (His contract stipulates only a fifth of Ballantine's.)

Walked Shirley home to 93rd Street through the drizzle of that dangerous zone, and then, instead of going to a party, came home myself, supped with the cats, and have collapsed into bed where I'm about to start *Jane Eyre*.

1985

Father's dearest cousin, Chester Ronning, died last night, age ninety.

Three days in New Orleans last week as guest of the National Association of Teachers of Singing. Gave a master class, a "keynote address," an all-Rorem program with Roz Rees and the local cellist, Karen Makas, and a lecture-recital with Leslie Guinn and others, and walked the languid streets of the Vieux Carré for the first time since the visit with Kenward twenty-two years ago. A nice place to visit.

In Martial Singher's class a soprano sang *Green*.

> Voici des fruits, des fleurs, des feuilles et des branches
> Et puis voici mon coeur qui ne bat que pour vous.
> . . . que je dorme un peu puisque vous reposez.

Singher explains the verses as being uttered by a youth who has rushed naked from the bed of love to gather armfuls of verdure for his sleeping mistress. "Why," I wonder aloud, "does the boy address his love as *vous*?" Singher, in his accented but supple English, answers: "That the singer is a naked boy is only my interpretation. He says *vous* out of respect. Indeed, I've known married couples who have exclusively *vouvoyéd* each other all their lives." "Even in bed?" I ask, without facetious intent, while five hundred auditors giggle. (Is it out of respect that we say *vous* to a beggar?) This question, from me to Singher, is as unanswerable as a man asking a woman what it "feels like" to be a woman: there are no terms for explanation. In a language that lacks the second personal singular form of address, the *nuance du tutoiement* can be explained only approximately, without analogy. After thirty-five years of speaking and reading fluently in French, I still don't (and never will quite) know, except in practice, how to exemplify it. By the same token, no foreigner can ever quite know whether translations of his tongue are accurate—e.g., the "false friends" like *sinistre* which is always incorrectly rendered as *sinister* rather than *dreary*. Since, however, later when I introduced myself Singher, without saying hello, instantly kissed me; since he is an idol of my youth; and since he knows singing better than anyone, he—so far as vocal interpretation is concerned—can do no wrong.

A dreary—a *sinistre*—day. JH in Nantucket. No parties; I'm struck with the flu. Phoned David Posner in Florida, and Bob Holton on 93rd Street, because they are stricken and will not outlive the year. The lonely dying, and the rain. I called them not so much because I have a good heart, as because there but for the grace of God.

I get on my nerves.

13 January

Premiere of *An American Oratorio* last week in Pittsburgh. The divergent reviews, because they contrast rather than mesh, teach me nothing. (Critics, wise or dumb, kind or mean, have never been on the receiving end, yet Apone continues to chastise me because I commemorated him in a book.) And how did I like the piece? I like only what JH—who never ever compliments me—said: "It's your most important work." Meanwhile, the Hotel William Penn sprung a leak and I had to change my room at 4 A.M.

Twenty minutes before the premiere Robert Page invited me to the huge rehearsal room to "say a few words" to the chorus. I began by telling them how proud they should be of their director, calling him "the second greatest choral conductor in the universe." I expected someone to ask who the greatest was (answer: there is no absolute, except in the mind), but no one raised a hand. I got sidetracked and didn't return to the question. Sylvia later told me that Page looked crestfallen, and that my quip (it's the first—and last—time I've used it) seemed pointless.

Dîner tête-à-tête chez Lenny B. Friday, our yearly meeting. Can never get used to the declarations of total love, the deep kisses, the abject praise, and the putdown coda. "Ned, you are the most perceptive, intelligent and talented person I know. Why are you such an asshole?" I *think* he means: Why is your conversation so scattered, why can't you stick to subjects? I grow ill at ease like all of his fans, even those who are dearest and most daily.

Lenny is already into a new opera. What's it about? It's about (says he) the same thing as the last one (*A Quiet Place*): "lack of communication—Babel, which is why the sung sentences were so spasmodic, so unfinished, just like we talk. Each scene of the new opera will be in a different language."

Lack of communication—even of just verbal communication (though the minds of the peasants may be as one)—is a good subject for plays and films (e.g., Antonioni) and maybe even for opera. But can lack of communication be communicated by being emitted literally. As for an opera in several languages, has Lenny asked himself honestly whether this is necessary, or merely a histrionic gimmick? He swears it's necessary, he questioned himself with a gun to his head. Hmmm. Lenny longs to be, but isn't, an experimentalist. He's a prime mover maybe, sometimes, but an inventor of new language (by using many languages simultaneously) he's not.

Tea here yesterday for Quentin Crisp and others. QC, exquisitely self-absorbed, has made a unique profession from being a successful outcast. He's uninterested in music ("classical" music), like everyone these days. "Music is a mistake," says he. He may be right, in the sense that everything is a mistake ("Something is missing in man"—Beckett). Yet if everything's a mistake, nothing is.

Everyone's dying, mainly of AIDS. That's now Bob Holton's diagnosis, and Paul Levenglick's.

At Rieti's concert last week (charming, a word I never use, is the only word) Bobby Fizdale introduces Danilova—"You do know Ned Rorem, the wonderful composer, etc." She draws a blank, although this is our eighteenth meeting, and our photo together reposes in Weissberger's book. Though why should she, the idol of my balletic youth, know me?

What are the names on this page, names encountered this past week, names embodying the past forty years, yet unexplained?

More stricken: the painter Larry Stanton, age 32. The cellist Fortunato Arico, 47. Josué Corcos. Kristine Ciesinski's husband, Bill Henry. Bob MacWilliams, of E. C. Schirmer's in Boston. And Calvin Hampton, organist and composer.

Critics hand out grades. Our juniors justify our life.

What interests readers is public names, what absorbs diarists is private drama: untrue.

The grossest (most obvious) miscalculations are those to which famous actors fall prey—are *allowed* to fall prey. Sophia Loren portrays herself, her talented noble self, in the TV dramatization of herself. Now, no one can portray himself. (Even a diarist doesn't portray himself, but renders a biased angle of himself.) It's not that Sophia Loren isn't Sophia Loren (or like Victor Hugo, who was a madman who thought he was Victor Hugo), but she is not an *interpreter* of herself.

Invited to narrate the sound track for a documentary on Colin McPhee (the text from Colin's book, *A House in Bali*), I arrive early at the recording studio, ahead of the producer and his crew, none of whom I've met. The engineer asks, "Are you the talent?" Talent in showbiz parlance means performer. A composer would be referred to as the arranger. (There is no word for the perpetrator of what he arranges.)

The experience is fresh, but frustrating. Everyone tells me how to inflect, and I learn a lot about what not to do into a mike.

Along with refusing BU in Boston and a "composership" with the Atlanta Symphony (several months back) I've just turned down another well-paying job at Queens College, and (after a phone call from John Duffy) a composership with the Houston Symphony. All of which amounts to about a quarter of a million dollars that I won't receive, but it's nice to be wanted.

Robin finds what she seeks, whether it's there or not.

The only food that really satisfies me is sugar.

On being escorted last evening toward the blessed fleet of limousines that fetch us from the annual meetings at the Academy on 155th and drive us home, I was shown into one which contained not only a well-stocked bar and a TV screen, but Elizabeth Hardwick, Saul Bellow, Karl Shapiro, Hortense Calisher and Hugo Weisgall. When Bellow asked Hardwick if she'd read such-and-such recently by Sidney Hook, she answered yes, and they both sneered. Bellow went on: "You know, Hook once asked me if I knew Faulkner. I said, yes, why? He said, because Faulkner's books have no real ideas and I want to write him and tell him so." Everyone in the car laughed. I said, "The idea that Faulkner has no real ideas is itself a real idea, don't you think." Bellow, whom I'd never met before, fixed me glassily, as though to say, "Who's this intruding on his betters!"

Later, when I tell all this to JH, JH says, "Maybe they laughed because they knew that of course Faulkner had no real ideas, and felt that Sidney Hook was just belaboring the obvious."

Tonight, dinner party for Maggie Paley and Virgil Thomson, Sono Osato and Victor Elmaleh, Moira Hodgson and Michael Schulan. Not quite a fair mix, partly because I can no longer, even with JH's help, cook, wait on table, be a witty matchmaker, as well as clean the house and wash dishes. I don't care so much anymore.

Heavy snow. Death of Ruth Orkin.

20 January

The evening could have been just the right length. At the benefit for New Music for Young Ensembles at Merkin Hall we each fit neatly into our fifteen-minute slot: Honi Coles, irresistible as he tapped to jazz improvisations; Jaime and Sharon, flawless in Ravel's duo; Roz and I, perfect in seven of my songs. But then Marvin Hamlisch, unprogrammed and unbidden (so far as I know), usurped the stage and, with charmless vulgarity, showed no signs of leaving after half an hour. So I (now sitting in the hall next to Red Heller who whispered, "Who *is* that man?") got up and left, in full view of the captive audience.

More plaintive and far quieter was Paul Callaway at Albert Fuller's little cocktail last night. He appeared absent, forgetful, weary; the way of all flesh, but his infinite musicality remains.

We decided not to serve ham to Shirley and George. It would have been casting swine before Perles.

Not wishing to pose too tiresome a question—"Do you think I'm a hypochondriac?"—I asked JH if he thought the Pope wore red shoes. "Does the Pope wear red shoes?" he answered.

He reminds me that I said of the frenzied movement called "Yellows" in *Day Music*: I don't mind that it's literally unplayable. I want the effect of someone *trying* to play it.

24 January

At Boosey & Hawkes this afternoon I found Sylvia in her office speaking on the phone. She passed it to me: it was Aaron Copland, his voice weak but lucid. Yet after a minute he repeats, makes little sense. He's just back from the hospital.

Aaron's most beautiful song, at least for me, is a setting of the Dickinson poem that begins:

> The world seems dusty when we stop to die—
> We want the dew then, honors seem dry.

How can one honor any dying friend, until it's too late?

At singers' master classes, including Singher's last month in New Orleans, they don't seem to single out the pianist. Even Casals at Marlboro never, never spoke to the "accompanists" in his classes, even though their parts were on a par with the cellists'.

I too spend more hours before the television than in reading books.

26 January

Eugene and Martita came to dine, plus Janis Susskind and Ellen. All well behaved.

Begin a memoir by describing the glass box, gift of Martita Casals Istomin, and using that box to trace back to first meeting Eugene in Philadelphia. Use other objects, other possessions, that I live with, and detail their provenance. A more than useful device of Mario Praz's in *The House of Life*. How things relate to thoughts.

30 January

After a scratchy run-through in an Omni Park hotel room of *Back to Life*, as effected by Rod Hardesty and a bassist from Boston, I met JH and we went for a meal in Eugenie Voorhees's new cruciform apartment on East Fifty-seventh. Eugenie is the acme of East Coast upper class, liberal division: tactful, good diction with a slight whine, practices what she preaches, modish cook, vastly well-read but unmusical, handsome of form, and (I like to think) a faithful friend.

31 January

Critics seldom fault my music when it is what they call passive or lyrical, especially in word settings. When I venture onto what they call serious ground—war, for example—I don't make it. Michael Walsh describes *An American Oratorio*: "Rorem's style works effectively with gentle poems like Poe's *To Helen*, but it misses the force and majesty of Crane's bitter *War Is Kind. . . .* The reach of the texts generally exceeds the composer's grasp."

A similar reaction greeted *Pilgrim Strangers*. Whitman's prose, like Crane's poetry, is filled with force, majesty, bitterness. Meanwhile, the much earlier *War Scenes*, also based on Whitman prose, are usually described as "powerful." Now, no composer can review his own music (his opinion vacillates even more than the critics'); he can only describe his intent. However, for a critic to declare what a piece should have been rather than whether it succeeds as what it is, is for the critic suddenly to *be* the composer. The critic infers that there are descriptive conventions that a composer must follow. *War Scenes*, with its bombast, observes these conventions; the Crane settings, with their ironic edge, do not.

Has anyone, even Britten in *War Requiem*, made music about war that is as harrowing as the bare bones displayed daily in newscasts? The whole question about what should and shouldn't be set to music (and why one chooses this text and another chooses that text, and how their musical—as well as their literary—approaches differ) is settled only by the realization of the mad illegitimacy of any setting of any text.

Poets in their hearts concur, though it's a bit late in the game for me to be posing the question. But last week, on hearing Wolpe's 1950 setting, for voice & piano, of *Dr. Einstein's Address about Peace in the Atomic Era*, with its constipated and literal-minded clangings on the keyboard, and its corny reiterations (lest you miss the point) of Einstein's straightforward prose ("The basis of trust is loyal give and take . . . give and take, give and take, give and take . . ."), I wanted to throw in the sponge.

Years ago at a drunken party John Myers said to Tom Prentiss, "Be a painter." But Tom *was* a painter, and John knew it, and John was not a painter. Who determines?

Even if he loves you, no critic will ever say what you want him to say about you. We all react differently to the same event, and we all have different needs. Yes, it's part of the New York game—more than a century old—to *be* criticized, but it's hard to swallow when a Londoner comes over the sea to hand out grades.

I've been lauded in *National Criterion*, *Commentary* and *National Review*, possibly on the assumption that since my music is conservative, I am too. In fact, I am a political radical, being an atheistic homosexual pacifist (which, like *humanist*, are vile words in some cliques). But all music is conservative.

Conservative periodicals conserve the fact of serious classical music, while the *Nation*, like so many progressive papers, except for an occasional pop article seems to have dispensed with any music column.

Critics are never on the receiving end. True, they get crank letters which they sometimes publish with a snarl or with silence—a silence that is the last word. But they are seldom, in any real sense, attacked for what they are, in body and soul. In fact, what are they?

Most new music is talentless and it's a critic's duty to say so. But he should say so with sadness, not relish.

1 February

Was Bill Coble less than thrilled when I likened his theme to a tapeworm? All the nourishment and notion was in the head—the first measure—with the following twenty bars trailing like an ever-lengthening parasite.

Sometimes I'm a bit jealous of students. I do what I can for them by allowing them to become fully themselves, then am annoyed when they succeed—not on the page but in the world. There's always room for excellence, isn't there? No.

Recall seeing *She Done Him Wrong*, with Parker Tyler at the Museum of Modern Art, 1945. Afterwards, two spectators declared loudly, "Isn't she a camp." Parker laughed and I found it not funny. I'd missed the point that, of course; that's just what she was. Twenty years later, with Frank O'Hara, looking at Capote's TV rendition of his *Christmas Story* (or whatever is was): when Geraldine Page, gazing wistfully through the window at the frosty pumpkins, says softly to herself, "It's fruitcake time," Frank roared with laughter and I found it not funny. I'd missed the point that, of course, it *was* fruitcake time, my dear.

Michael Blackwood, producer of the *House in Bali* movie, called to say that after a great deal of soul-searching "they" have decided to erase my "voice-over" and hire "a real actor." The trauma for me is identical, but considerably milder, than that caused by getting fired from *Panic in Needle Park* a dozen years ago. Decidedly, I'm not meant for the movies. (They probably want a voice "with expression," always a fatal mistake.)

Some pieces are difficult and sound difficult, and are meant to be and to sound difficult. They are effectively difficult. Chopin's *Études*. Other pieces are ineffectively difficult. Elliott Carter's *Concertos*. (After all that practicing, what have you got?) Still other pieces are impossible, but the effect of the attempt is the effect desired. My *Eighth Étude*, for example.

Tea with Jocy de Oliveira. For seventeen years we've lived in the same building without exchanging more than cool hellos. She brings her book: an expensively got-up *Life's Work* in both English and Portuguese, riddled with misspellings and datedly influenced by "happenings." Also, she can't write. Whatever else John Cage may or may not represent, he does have a high dose of wit. Jocy, in all her Latin glory, takes him seriously and misses the point.

Wallace, at nearly twenty, is epileptic, totally deaf, and skinny to emaciation; he also pees everywhere and limps sideways from room to room. Yet he seems to enjoy life.

To *Wozzeck* with Lenny Bernstein. Picked him up at 7:15 and the house was full of people. At the Met we joined two others in our box. Great embracings later backstage. Then supper in a restaurant on Seventy-fourth. I left him, still going strong, at 2 A.M. Lenny says he cannot be alone, ever.

Bob Holton and David Posner have died, both once so close, now all rot.

Hugo Weisgall for lunch yesterday, just us two, after which Daron showed up with his copy work. (As I to Virgil forty-two years ago, so Daron to me: he's now entrusted with copying all my orchestral parts. Out of Curtis and into Juilliard, with David Diamond, Daron finds this work a useful way of retaining contact.) We all three wonder what young composers are supposed to do these days since publishers want none of them. Start your own publishing house, says Hugo, your own recording company, and stay in school as long as you can, cultivating performers. For after that those performers will desert you.

Blizzard. JH and I made our way through the storm to Rosemarie Beck's vernissage deep in Soho. Becki's paintings are so aggressive they almost jump from the wall. They are remindful of Jacques Dupont's and Veira da Silva's in being constructed from myriad squares—like a quilt—that blend into rounds from afar. Little square clouds. JH attracted to a seascape with people. Robert says, Don't talk to the gallery, call us tomorrow.

At the Astor Gallery of the Library this noon, ASCAP's exhibition of "Seven Decades of American Music," including in its array a little display of my song *Conversation* (on Elizabeth Bishop's poem) in manuscript, in fair copy, and in publication. At the loud lunch I sat between Peggy Jory and Morton

Gould. Always a pleasure to converse with Morton at such functions. He's the very definition of an ASCAP pro. As he chain-smoked Gauloises I told him how in high school my sister Rosemary and I concocted a jitterbug number to a record of his *Pavane*, and he told me of his recent divorce, at 70, which seems to me healthy rather than sad—hopeful, even, if he makes a go of it. He absolutely loves women, he claims, or I *think* he claims—hard to hear what with the live music (a sax, a fiddle, and an accordion) blaring from that corner, in contradiction to the calm that most musicians crave when they eat.

The evening meal was unaccompanied. JH and I partook of it at Frankie and Bill Schuman's on Park Avenue, the four of us, so sweet, with a fire in the grate and little chocolates on the coffee table. How did they mesh in the old days? Frankie is quite strong-minded—"thoroughly modern"—for one who's been married nearly fifty years to the same charmingly childlike yet business-minded musician of quality.

Tomorrow Nantucket.

Nantucket
9 February

Cold bright sun on snow, texture of *crème brulée*.

Ton of mail at the post office, most of it requiring an answer, including galleys of the interesting-looking conversations about Tchaikovsky that Balanchine had, very informally, with Solomon Volkov—the same Volkov who so stunningly edited Shostakovich's memoir, which I reviewed six years ago. I average an hour a day on letters, two hours on reading, a half-hour on exercise, three hours on meals (with reading), nine hours on an attempt at sleeping, twenty-four hours on music.

Have begun composing the Septet for Santa Fe. As with the Violin Concerto, wherein one movement is the instrumentation of an old unpublished song (a setting of Paul Goodman's *Boy with a Baseball Glove*) from which the words are withdrawn, so here I may use the 1950 setting of Yeats' *Do Not Love Too Long* by cutting the text, giving the warm vocal line to a cold piano, and giving the cold piano accompaniment to string quartet. The Septet will be for Quartet with Oboe, French Horn, and Piano. Since I am to be the pianist, the role is being sculpted accordingly.

JH arrives Sunday. Am cleaning the house.

12 February

The Maltese Falcon last evening. Violent rainstorm all night.

This morning I sent off the following, re *Balanchine's Tchaikovsky*, to Simon & Schuster:

Of the lively arts only dance relies upon a fellow muse to complete its identity. We dance *to* something, and that something is music. What we now name "mixed media" has always existed—the product of choreographer working with composer. Sometimes the composer is an active participant, as with most modern dance. Sometimes the composer is long dead, as with so many pieces by George Balanchine who collaborated spiritually (as he put it) with Bach, with Mozart, with Glinka and, most notably, with Tchaikovsky, the musician he adored above all others.

When practitioners of collaborative art speak about method it is inevitably, and understandably, from one side of the fence: how can this decor enhance my play? how can this poem serve my song? how can this symphony impel my dancers? Balanchine is the first such practitioner to express his co-artist's viewpoint—or earpoint. His obsession with what made Tchaikovsky tick is not romantic but practical, cleansing the public notion of "creativity" as random vision rather than as hard work. The choreographer seems to have passed technical scrutiny on each minutia and masterpiece the composer ever penned, but with such wisdom and love that I, for one, am now relistening to Tchaikovsky with new ears. The approach of the book is as novel as would be, say, an essay on Heine by Robert Schumann, or an essay on Apollinaire by Francis Poulenc.

Whether Balanchine's in-depth concern makes, in the long run, for better ballets no one can know. But the fact of such concern, as evinced in these conversations about Balanchine's fellow Petersburger, provides unique insight into the mind of our century's most cultivated choreographer.

Nantucket
Valentine's Day

Finished *Anna Karenina* finally. Marvelous and all-encompassing, though less marvelous and less all-encompassing (can something be less all-encompassing?) than Proust, and too long, like Mahler's Ninth. Both Tolstoy and Mahler say little in their leisurely span that can't be said more tersely—although terser they wouldn't be Mahler and Tolstoy. Everything's too long. Webern is too long. This paragraph is too long.

15 February

We'd planned to spend the long week together in the island's isolation, but JH was called back Wednesday to play a funeral. He and Sonny left by truck in the fog. There's something morbidly satisfying about being utterly alone, reading in bed at midnight while the surrounding yard is blanketed down by snow and the creakings in the cellar conjure up Huck Finn's father.

It's 10:30 in the morning. An hour ago, while ingesting my daily corn flakes with wheat germ and honey, I sat at the window and watched two large white dogs sniffing around the back fence. One, a spitz, was the "follower";

the other, a fluffy sheepdog resembling Sonny but thrice the size, set the tone simply by lying down and chewing at what looked like a root. Then they both walked about slowly, examining this and that, and finally faded away into the leafless landscape stretching over to Lily Street and up toward the sunless sky. That's all. A still life with no point. Except that I was moved. Would I have been less moved if Mahler (the slow part of the third movement of the Ninth) had not been playing in the background? or if it had been Ravel or Billie Holiday or nothing at all, or a Tuesday, or an afternoon, or if I had been five years younger? Anyway, the scene is now gone forever. So are the corn flakes.

The New Romanticism is a term invented after the fact. But after what fact? Rochberg and Del Tredici don't get up each morning and say to themselves, Today I shall compose some more New Romantic music.

If it is a truth not generally acknowledged, that many a dance critic pens many a review without mentioning the music, another truth insists that without music there is no dance. So specialized have we grown that even certain dancers—good ones—are unable to name the composers whose art, night after night, impels their bodies. Choreographers themselves too often are modish, superficial, and none too bright, at least verbally, about the music they choose. Yet wouldn't the question of how music works with dance—as canvas upon which to sketch their pictures, as mere moody background, as kinetic impulse, etc.—seem to be endlessly engrossing? (Endlessly imprecise, too. But if we could explain it, perhaps we'd have no further need for art.)

Balanchine thought so. He was a rare sample (Auden was another) of a creative artist who could dismantle and examine the clockwork of his craft, then put it back together, without ruining it. He belies the notion that creative artists are merely instinctive. Art and intelligence *can* go together. Whatever you may think of Balanchine the choreographer (and I find him overrated, like Beethoven), Balanchine the musician is no fake, though an outsider.

His sexist remarks about women. Ironically, Song and Dance are the two professions—and the only two—where women are used *as* women (and men *as* men), since no man can sing the Queen of the Night, and no woman can sing Boris Godunov; no man can dance Giselle, and no woman can dance Petroushka. Again, ironically, because she is irreplaceable, a woman can here demand—and receive—equal pay. (His naive remarks about homosexuality, re Wilde and Salomé, and also re Tchaikovsky.)

The Tchaikovsky book tacitly assumes, correctly, that dance exists solely through music. True, certain dances—not just primitive rites but sophisticated ballets—have existed without accompaniment; but these are exceptional, and even they produce their own music by rhythms released through body movement.

In the 1960s various choreographers used my *Eleven Studies for Eleven Players*, all excellently, and all predictably. Except for Martha Graham. Whereas the others allowed a dancer to thump when the music thumped, or to swoon when the music swooned (that is, to mickey-mouse the music), Martha went against the sounds. She had Helen McGehee hopping in gyrations against a slow trumpet solo; she had Robert Powell standing motionless while all hell broke loose in the pit. In reconsidering my score, Martha showed me new elements in the music—which, of course, were *not* new, since I'd put them there. Sometimes she had the dancers move, between movements, to no music at all. But this very use of no music was a use of the music. Martha called the ballet *Dancing Ground*.

Now that dance is the major art in America it no longer evolves in tandem with music. Before 1950 most choreographers used scores composed just for them. Today most choreographers use preexisting scores, generally from past centuries.

Philadelphia
The Barclay
19 February

Orchestral concert last night at Curtis of the music of three of my four students: Bill Coble's hyperlush *Eulogy* conducted by himself, Gregory Hall's winsome two-minute Interlude for Strings and Winds, and Jim Helgeson's stylistically uneven but dashing *Divertimento* for Piano and Orchestra. Also David Loeb's two pupils had pieces: Paul Brantley's sober *Tithings*, and Clark Griffith's *Millay Sonnets* (nice to see Millay back in fashion after two generations of near suppression). Proud of them all. It's a semiannual luxury for the composition students to be offered such a program. It should be a biweekly necessity, at all schools.

Not quite nine A.M. In a few minutes, Curtis for two lessons, then a taxi into New Jersey where, at Cadbury, I'll meet JH for lunch with *Père et Mère*. We'll return by rented car to New York.

From the window I can see Eugene Ormandy (the Ormandys reside here at the Barclay) taking the air down in leafless Rittenhouse Square. He is with a black nurse; he's all bundled up, and walking very, very slowly. Thin, extinguished looking. Someone just came up to him, chatted, and he appeared (as I imagine from this distance) to summon a bit of backstage graciousness. I've not seen him since the fall of 1978. What a change.

24 February

Charming, relaxed evening at Judy's Wednesday, the two of us, playing songs, feeling at peace with a sobriety which to me is a fact of life, to her, blessing from above. Thursday at Ellen's with JH and the Gruens. After the meal the women adjourn to the studio to talk about art, while we boys giggle in the parlor about sex and its appended horrors. All day yesterday at Şahan Arzruni's perusing scores by Armenian composers for the Khachaturian Competition. The other judges: Bill Mayer, Louise Talma, Paul Levy and Robert Black. The best of the submissions were by females, clangorous and theatrical. An ample lunch.

Organ recital today by Leonard Raver at Riverside Church, during which I grew hypnotized by the stained glass (as I used to grow hypnotized there at lunch hour in 1945 when a student at nearby Juilliard) in bird colors: cardinal red, canary yellow, finch green, bluebird blue, egret white. During intermission I chatted out on the pavement in the summery sun with Joan Morris and Bill Bolcom, proud to be able to provide them with the lyrics to all the songs Mae West sang in *Klondike Annie*. (Joan is planning a Mae West group for next season's programs.)

Again proof, if proof were needed, that serious music, among elite thinkers, is, if not a pariah, at least something not to be considered:

In the *Village Voice* (26 Feb.) one Carol Sternhall declares: "I don't know much about music, but when I read [Gail] Godwin I feel as if I'm hearing what others mean by symphonies. Or maybe sonatas, fugues—I'm looking these words up—or the music of the spheres." Would any musician claim unembarrassedly: "I don't know much about literature, but now I know what others mean by novels, or maybe short stories, or essays—I'm looking these words up"?

In the *Nation* (23 Feb.) one Charles Molesworth declares of Allen Ginsberg's *Collected Poems*: "The book is a fugue, a massive interweaving of subjects and verse forms that recur and illuminate one another." Laymen often compare literary works to fugue (even Gide, no musical slouch, fell into the trap in describing *Les Faux-monnayeurs*) when sonata would be more appropriate. A fugue by definition has only one theme and uses the same material throughout.

In the *Times* (24 Feb.) one Robert Palmer declares: "Rock is part of adult culture now, to an extent that would have been unthinkable as recently as a decade ago. It is no longer the exclusive reserve of young people sending messages to each other. . . . What does it seem to be telling us about our own time? Part of the message is in the music itself. . . . But lyrics remain the most accurate barometer of what makes *these* times different from . . . the 1960s and 70s." The statement could have been penned in the 60s or 70s by those same people who equated hipness of sentiment with value of creation: if you're against Vietnam, the "being against" is itself art. Palmer, like all pop critics, confuses lyrics with music, nor have any of them ever told how the *music* itself functions.

27 February

Dîner à quatre chez Albert Fuller, with JH and Alice Tully. Albert owns a vast room three blocks away, a forty-foot ceiling, staircases leading to tantalizing cubicles here & there. A photograph of the beautiful cellist Fortunato Arico reminds that AIDS will strike anywhere. Alice speaks at length (for JH's benefit) of her sister's frightful death from emphysema.

We play Nadia Boulanger's forty-five-year-old record of Monteverdi madrigals which Alice does not know. I ask how many requests for money she gets, and how she deals with them. She gets requests daily, not just for musical matters, and deals with them as they come, endowing areas like animal protection and disease control as well as, over the years, commissioning (she recounts this pridefully but without vanity) more new art than we'd supposed—from Messiaen, for instance, and from Louis Malle. Just last month the Academy revived my citation nominating Alice for the Award for Distinguished Service. She'll be "running" against Paul Fromm, Claiborne Pell, and William Shawn.

2 March

Since last night I was to dine in the Village with Janis Susskind, and since I so seldom get downtown anymore now that Mother & Father've left, I made a date to have a drink with Robert & Becki at seven, and before that decided to wander around shedding tears at old stamping grounds. No tears, just tedium. Everything looks the same, but probably I'm different. The Oscar Wilde Bookstore is so loud with rock blazing that browsing's precluded. Julius's (our hangout for so many decades of "restless nights . . . And sawdust restaurants with oyster-shells") is drab and untempting, so I didn't enter, but did recall a restless night, circa 1958, when toward 4 A.M. I took "him" home—the black hair and red lips—not, in my drunkenness, realizing until later that he had an artificial limb, which took ages to remove—no sooner accomplished than I asked him to leave, cowered under the blankets, and heard only his cursing as he clamped the leg back on and clanked down the stairs. The tune at guide-number 13 in *Petroushka* is pilfered not from Slavic folklore but from an air Marie Laure used to sing, *"Elle avait une jambe en bois, Et pour que ça ne se voit pas, . . . La meme chose en caout-chouc."* Who'll supply the lost line? O, she had a wooden leg!

Janis, in their absence, is staying at the Carters' apartment on West Twelfth. I've never been there except for big parties. Now, with only Janis and Tony Fell, I can examine the mirthless spidery layout in an institutional building. It doesn't quite work—like Elliott's music.

People ask if I've a regular work schedule. I'll do anything to put off the moment of organized work. Anything—even the crossword puzzle in *TV Guide*. You don't know what it costs me even to compose this sentence.

Occasionally a whole day goes by without my seeing a roach.

Eugene List died today. He was so very wholesome, one doesn't think of him as dealing in such matters.

4 March

Last night with JH to a concert called "Words Music Words" at St. Mark's Church. I went partly to see what such a thing would be, partly because I seldom attend downtowniana, and partly because poet Norman MacAfee and composer Charles Porter (protégé of George Perle) invited me. Discouraging. The organizer behaved like a standup comic while the know-nothing audience reacted like a laugh-track to verse set to music by mediocre composers performed by mediocre singers (lots of talk, deep feelings, 1960s type) with bad voices and no sense of theater, all in that cheerless auditorium. As with the Philip Glass opera last fall, I suddenly didn't want to be seen there, although everyone saw us leave in the middle, including, I suppose, MacAfee & Porter. Serves them right for getting mixed up with such tackiness. Fled to a restaurant on Thompson Street to meet Roditi who was with Brad Morrow and a female entourage.

JH's first impression of Mother—her eccentricity—circa December 1967, when she said to Marian Van Steenwyck, who professed to pray so as to keep her sanity, "O Marian, you don't!"

There are no reports, none, of lesbians with AIDS.

One never reads of females committing violent crimes, of women who go on shooting sprees or who eviscerate their lovers. Are women incapable of physical mayhem? Does the "appeal" of Lizzie Borden lie in how she managed, or in that she managed at all?

Judging a mass of scores for the New York Gay Men's Chorus contest. Slim pickings. Mostly they're settings of Whitman.

Heavy snow. At six this evening, when I took Sonny for a walk and stopped by the Korean market for radishes and skim milk, Columbus Avenue had the look of Paris of thirty years ago, dark and damp but cheerful with store windows gleaming yellow and the smell of brandy and sex. Blizzards are levelers. As I began to type this a while ago, Wallace, who unbeknownst to me was beneath the chair in this cubicle which JH has finally made into a useful study, had his first seizure in months. His fits are inevitably set off by some steady beat: a typewriter, thunderclaps, a lawn mower. This spasm lasted nearly five minutes (the longest ever), his body stiff and spewing urine. JH held him as he calmed down gradually, eyes glazed, voice wailing, unable to stand. Wallace is nineteen now, totally deaf, boney, unsteady, incontinent and epileptic. Still, it never occurs to us (yes it does) to have him put to sleep. He eats well, sits for hours in the empty bathtub, just staring, is the apple of Sam's eye (Sam, now thirteen, cuddles with Wallace who, though indifferent as an ancient doyenne, remains a walking purr-machine), while Princess seems now, at nearly seven, to have missed out on love. We've never heard her purr. All this livestock!

Wallace very much resembles Mother as she now is. Self-involved utterly.

5 March

City of Gold, Columbus Avenue this afternoon bears no trace of yesterday's slush and has rebecome a glamorous, hardboiled American artery. At Juilliard for first run-through of my Organ Concerto. Leonard has enlisted young Barbagallo as rehearsal pianist, and he plays very nineteenth-centuryishly (left hand always a fraction ahead of the right) which has little (or does it?) to do with my music. Tempos all too fast. The piece seems corny in content and inexact in interpretation, but it has a certain naughty style. Naughty for an organ (waltzes, etc.). It will be pulled together by the 19th, won't it?

Reading a book of Capote interviews which I'll probably review for *Christopher Street*, thus for the first time blowing off steam about Truman. JH hates my doing this, hates even more my self-defense: that the very doing of it is me. Twice only (out of a hundred occasions) have I followed his advice, and felt thwarted. Both times re letters to the *Times*. The one to Schonberg (about "Ideas") and the one to Henahan (about Menotti) were ultimately printed in books, but the bloom had gone and my frustration remained unrelieved.

8 March

What are your influences? That's the question composers most often hear, and the one they most often avoid. A professional composer, because he is quite aware of his thieveries, attempts a disguise—a camouflage—to reshape the stolen goods, or (to switch metaphors) to speak the old tongues with a new accent. This restructuring *is* creation—an act which is no more and no less than covering his tracks. He isn't about to tell a casual questioner about such tricks.

Or so I've always contended. It would be coy at this point to feign. A composer is aware of his influences, but it's not for him to state them; they're nobody's business. Neither is it for him to assess his own music, nor to know where it fits into the general scheme. This said, am I the only American composer of my generation to spring from the French tradition? (What is that tradition? Is America, even out of my generation, still—as always—in the German tradition?) Certainly my new *Scenes from Childhood*, by being vignettes, are in that tradition. True, the most famous previous such Scenes, Schumann's, are German. But they are French, by definition. Even Beethoven used a French word to locate his *Bagatelles*.

I originally planned to name each of the eleven movements after crucial bars of my youth. I've opted for only two: *The San Remo at Six* and *Mary's at Midnight*.

Do we create during or after an experience? From what we are learning or from what we have learned? You can't write about tears in your eyes with tears in your eyes: they leak into the ink and smear the page. Communication is effective only in its clarity.

9 March

Big concert of Lou Harrison's music at Tully Hall, attractive, varied, easy to take, strange for New York—the flavor of California. Waited in line to say hello. Lou shook my hand, "Ah Ned, how nice to see you," and that was that. I was hurt. We meet so seldom, and Lou means much to me. He's one of the three composers (with Paul Bowles and Bill Flanagan) on whom I agreed to write entries for Grove's Dictionary—a lot of work and so little money. Was Lou discontent? Grove does homogenize every entry, like *Time*. The author controls only the factual research.

Opposite in style is the piece on Capote, which I finished this afternoon, for *Christopher Street*. Far from being a review of that dreadful bunch of interviews, it turned out to be a memoir, "What Truman Means to Me," which I hope is spirited without being mean. He was a colorful person and easy to write about, although most of the writing evokes the same colors— his frail stature, weird whine, Agnew-like bon mots.

12 March

Death of Eugene Ormandy. Another branch from my tree falls. (He would have thought I was a branch on *his* tree.) Telegraphed his wife, whom I could never bring myself to call by her first name: "We have lost a great artist. Heartfelt condolences. Your friend, Ned R."

Time draws near for the launching of my two concertos. They'll be premiered in reverse order of their composition: the Organ Concerto next week in Portland, Maine; the Violin Concerto at the end of the month in Springfield, Massachusetts.

14 March

Forty years ago next September this diary opened with (I wince to quote them) these words: "Happiness then is an answering after the heart. Pity the poet of the stock exchange." Has happiness today anything to do with aspiration? Did it then, or was it just a word? Isn't happiness a dim-witted destiny? (Who can want to be happy in this mess?) If so, how many poets get stuck at the stock exchange? And does the stock exchange make them unhappy? What about the stock-exchange executive who's trapped in the body of a poet? Even were happiness a goal, can it be reached by answering after the heart? That way lies madness—as Kahlil Gibran would doubtless not agree.

I've never put much stock in happiness. Happiness is a state incompatible with the dangerous and mediocre globe we inhabit, although a *pursuit* of that state (as the Constitution contends) is probably worthy. But even in the best of times happiness would, for an intelligent person, seem fleeting and peripheral: when in love, during meals, while walking through leaves, or while playing with kittens. (These moments aren't comparable to reading or to listening to music—experiences existing outside of time and which, though thrilling, are also sometimes sad.) I don't seek to be happy so much as to be aware. Yet the condition of awareness precludes regular happiness.

May we wee-wee? Mais oui. We may? Oui, mais . . .
    Therapist. The rapist.

It is not a composer's business, much less duty, to be magnanimous or even fair about the work of colleagues; he's usually wrong anyway. His business is to get his work done. It is a critic's business and duty to keep an open mind, though he too is usually wrong.

15 March

Death of Roger Sessions.
    All composers at all times are influenced by their forebears, close or far. There is no example (save Haydn) of an established "older" composer being influenced, to any effect, by the devices or philosophy of younger composers.
    It is not conceivable that, say, a Babbitt or a Menotti might suddenly see the light of what critics called Minimalism and start writing, convincingly, like Philip Glass. Yes, Stravinsky suffered a *volte face* late in his career, but it's embarrassing. And pieces like *Requiem Canticles* and *Agon* are actually as diatonic, indeed as doggedly ostinatoed, as you please. Poulenc once said, "If only I could be part of the Boulez pointillistic trend" (and he meant it) "but alas, I'm too old."

Been listening to *Sunday in the Park with George*. It's good, rather mild, the way an excellent college show is mild and good. But there's something, well, not quite dirty, but *mean* about Sondheim, and something vain and sophomoric, such as his ideas on art and "the artist." I'm not sure you can make art about art. Nor am I sure that you can express lack of communication through non-communicative sputterings, as in Bernstein's recent opera. You can make art about artists but not art about art, because there is no absolute for a work of art. At the end of Auden's libretto, *Elegy for Young Lovers*, when the Great Poet finally opens his mouth to read his masterpiece, the curtain falls.

Sondheim farms out his scoring. What pleasure he denies himself! What is Seurat if not orchestration?

Sondheim's good but not that good. We've *decided* he's great. We don't feel he's great.

16 March

That's how Bach would have done it if he were alive today, declare the all-knowing arrangers of Bach-With-A-Beat—the two-part Inventions embellished by drums. Then why not take the paintings of Rubens and cut them into squares, or the choreography of Petipa and substitute break dancing? Because, say the all-knowers, Rubens is but one picture, etc. But the "way" of doing things changes every week.

Last night, on impulse, I phoned Marvin Levy who for the last decade has been "undercover." Are you still composing? I ask. "No, I'm tired of that whole scene." I pretend surprise that "that whole scene" should include the delicate duty of creativity, but in reality I'm quite sympathetic to Marvin's decision. By *scene* he means not only the rat race, but the compulsion, feigned or real, for "self-expression." If I could afford it, and if I were like Marvin (or Jean-Pierre Marty) who claims to detest the public part of art, would I stop composing to become a country squire? Still, it's unique: Marvin, who only yesterday was a major name with his splendid opera at the Met, now is seldom mentioned, and doesn't care.

Tomorrow at this hour I'll be in Maine with Sylvia.

The Inn at Park Spring
Portland, Maine
20 March

The Organ Concerto, composed in Nantucket during September and October of 1984 and orchestrated in New York during January, was born right on top of the Violin Concerto. Indeed, the two pieces are siblings in their comparative brevity, modest instrumentation, and coolness of approach. In both cases the solo role is not so much histrionic and competitive as easy and conversational, and the background coloration is that of a chamber ensemble. The Organ Concerto uses only four brass, timpani, and strings. It sounds exactly as I prayed it would.

The rehearsal went smoothly, commencing almost the minute we got off the plane Sunday. Leonard Raver (who'd played *Views from the Oldest House* only last week at Harvard) knew his part cold, and Bruce Hangen, the dashing conductor, led the band enthusiastically in the overly live hall, almost drowning out the historic solo instrument.

We're in a darling pensione at 135 Spring Street. David Huntley showed up in time for the premiere last night with, touchingly, Stuart Pope, who, now that he's no longer with B & H, has no reason beyond sheer friendship for coming. The city is as darling as the pensione: low buildings, brick streets, an excellent museum with lots of Marsden Hartleys. Meals en masse, interviews, panels. (During a "preview" speech I inadvertently referred to Britten's *Young Person's Guide to the Orchestra* as the *Poor Person's Guide to the Orchestra*, and the audience, who'd never heard of the piece, took on an air of great compassion.) *Souper* with Leonard at Baker's Table: very thick shrimp chowder, salad, and lemon meringue pie like your mother used to make. Excursion with Sylvia to L. L. Bean's in Freeport, in the shatteringly bright sun of the north, where I bought some huge plastic marbles to put in the glass box Martita gave me.

At the performance last night, a minor mishap. The concerto opens with six fortissimo blasts from the brass followed immediately by the organ's entrance, quiet and smooth. No organ! Leonard had forgotten to turn on the blowers. A quick flick of the wrist, and all was well. But twixt the blast and the flick, an eternity.

I was very, very pleased with Leonard, with Hangen, and with the whole young orchestra. Bruce and Leonard hope to repeat the piece next year in Omaha, but no other hearings are scheduled yet.

Jacques Février once told me that as a student he played the piano part of the Saint-Saëns Organ Symphony for a rehearsal at which Saint-Saëns was meant to be present. The master was late. Why? Because, from the vantage of his wheelchair stationed just outside the Conservatoire, he was surveying the comings and goings of the *ouvriers* between the pair of *pissotières* at the corner.

New York
26 March

We both have the flu. Insomnia, aches, sinus, rivers of snot and sweat. Watching television in a daze (mostly a K. Hepburn festival). Nonetheless, I'm writing a review for the *Boston Globe* of Jon Bradshaw's quite good biography of Libby Holman, *Dreams That Money Can Buy.* (As usual, everything's on the nose except the few references to me, and they, though correct, are out of kilter. Thus the whole book, like all biographies, must be out of kilter.)

Dragged myself to Jaime Laredo's nine blocks away on Riverside Drive, for a final run-through, with piano, of the Fiddle Concerto for the conductor, Robert Gutter, who's come in specially from Massachusetts. Afterward I walked down Broadway with Gutter toward 70th Street. Now he is a conventional-looking man, not conspicuous, well-dressed, and with a yellow tie. At Seventy-first we passed an elderly couple, of whom the woman, detaching herself from her spouse, pointed a finger at Gutter and screamed, "I'd like to strangle you with that yellow tie." She persisted and approached us, threatening, and passersby, without stopping, evinced a mild curiosity. I was embarrassed and could only apologize: "It's not always like this in New York."

It's Sonny's first birthday.

27 March

Visit from Deborah Davis of Baltimore, one of two persons in that city writing a thesis on my piano music.

Later, visit from Guglielmo Biraghi of Rome, looking as spectacular as he did in the fifties. Claims he's only attracted to orientals, an addiction he likens to Yellow Fever.

Sheraton Inn West
Springfield, Massachusetts
29 March

The Bad Side. Trailways, early morning. Sleepless. Anxiety with JH. Washroom at bus station, a giant naked Negro, epilepsy, latrines filled with unflushed feces. Sadness of the young voyagers who—they too—will die and decay and leave no trace. Death of Chagall. Four dusty hours on the road. Flu turned to bronchitis, with cupfuls of glaucous mucus deep in the chest. Yet I must give a class at Amherst. Hotel lobby, one vast swimming pool brimming with fat people. (The class turned out to be a 75-minute lecture.)

The Good Side. Big attractive hall. Sharon, in her sleek cool warmth, tells me she's doing the *Dances for Cello* next December in New York. Jaime plays so beautifully, and the orchestra too, but underrehearsed.

Saturday. David Huntley and Maury Newberger, like magnets of normalcy, are staying in the same hotel. I've already had my room changed twice because of various kinds of noise and drafts. But now they're here and I feel less . . . foreign.

The premiere was nice. Despite an elaborate note which I penned especially for the program, I was asked to introduce my piece. Told the large audience to take a good look, they may never see a live composer again. That sort of thing. The singular virtue of Jaime Laredo had been constantly in my ear when I was writing the piece: the electric verve of his style, the gentle strength of his intellect, and the unrippable silk of his oceanic tone. Now here were these virtues alive. A rollicking meal afterward, hosted by the orchestra's manager, Wayne Brown, and his wife (who had been a pupil of Margaret Bonds). The concerto's scheduled to be played again on Monday, but I can't stay. It's also contracted for performance by the five other orchestras of the consortium that commissioned it.

New York
2 April

JH came into my room this morning and said, "Wallace is dying." Sure enough, Wallace has passed from his state of hyper-skinny but effortful dilapidation to inert resignation. He refuses and seems unaware of the medicine dropper filled with soup, of water, of the touch of hands; his eyes register nothing. Yet he breathes. (Today is JH's birthday.)

This afternoon, a nice little party at Boosey's for Robin Holloway, and this evening, a dreary dinner at the Academy. The latter was followed by an as-always-ill-advised recital of works by new inductees. Ill-advised, because the members are mostly drunk, musically uncomprehending, and more interested in gossiping with each other. Galbraith prefaces the procedures with a smug, "Of course, I know nothing about music," assured that we all empathize. Imagine a musician declaring—at the American Academy and Institute of Arts & Letters—"Of course, I know nothing about literature, or painting"! It was my luck to be seated for two hours next to George Rochberg, who is as pompous as his music.

Back home we find Wallace unchanged, lying on his side in a neat pile of blankets, breathing imperceptibly, eyes glassy.

JH is now having a violent sinus attack, due as usual to the pre-Easter doldrums rising from the tense demands of his church. His room (which, besides the dying Wallace, contains the two other cats, Sonny the dog, and a bath full of roaches) turns smoggy from his ubiquitous cigarette fumes melting with the vaporizer. He coughs and coughs and coughs and coughs.

As I type, Jaime Laredo is playing the second performance of my Concerto in Springfield, hundreds of miles away. I'm correcting final proofs of *Picnic on the Marne*. We seem on the edge of a worldwide AIDS plague.

3 April

Today I was invited, and declined, to write a twenty-five-hundred-word essay on Peter Serkin for *Esquire*. The premise of the article (one of a series about "artists" under forty) is to laud young Serkin for his service to new music. Inasmuch as he's never touched *my* new music, I'd find it hard to get it up for him. By the same token I refused another dollar-a-word article, this one on Barrault for *Elle*. Proud of myself, I note this for the record. Meanwhile, fool that I am, I reviewed the Libby Holman bio for peanuts for the *Boston Globe*, like the piece about Truman C. for *Christopher Street* for no money at all. At least I have something to say about those two.

Wallace died tonight at 10:25. He will go into the freezer until next Sunday (Easter), when Jim will bury him in Nantucket. Am more bereft than over the deaths of certain humans lately, partly because of the vanished daily marvel that Wallace, with all his dumbness, represented, but mostly because of sympathy for JH's visible grief. JH, who never lets go, cried and cried as he cradled the dead thing on whose jaw the quick rictus formed, even as we watched.

Wallace was younger than we, then our age, then far older. At nineteen he collapsed, a centenarian.

5 April

Because of the flu I postponed, two weeks ago, a visit from Gregory Sandow. Today, still aching and spitting, I hadn't the heart to do it again. Sandow appeared for tea at four, very tall and curly gray-haired and friendly, like Stephen Koch. He said that when *his* cat died he threw it in the Hudson.

Andrew Webber's *Requiem* on TV. Holy cow.

JH dreamed last night that we had put Wallace into the oven, instead of into the freezer, and as he baked, very very slowly, his youth returned.

Am listening to Schubert's A-minor Piano Sonata. So perfect, so boring.

If analyzed on the strictly objective terms of tune and chord, *West Side Story* and Bartók's *Contrasts* would produce much the same result, both works being structured on the tritone. (The devil lurks in an augmented fourth. Title for a novel.)

When my parents used to come to dine on Sunday nights, Wallace would sometimes rush through the dining room at breakneck speed and disappear. "He's streaking," Mother said, using the term for the now forgotten fad of people materializing naked in public places.

Joyce Carol Oates says that her cat, Wallace, in *Bellefleur* was named after ours.

6 April

Truly classy for the *Times* to publish Roger Sessions's obituary on the front page a couple of weeks ago (although the classiness was lessened several days later when their front page featured a puff piece on Liberace).

Sessions was a serious artist, but Sessions was not a saint. (Was he even a composer? that's another story.) Every time Sessions spits, Andrew Porter cries genius (just as Elliott Carter needs only to fart and Andrew has a vision)—neglecting to tell us that he's done a libretto for Sessions based on "The Emperor's New Clothes" (type casting!). Andrew has a right to suggest that "One day, the people will tell of his wisdom, and audiences will show forth his praise" (even as I have a right to say Sessions had a tin ear), but he has no right to suggest that in "*On the Beach at Fontana*, a 1929 song epitomizing what Aaron Copland later said about the First Piano Sonata of 1931: 'Sessions has presented us with a cornerstone on which to base American music.'" Andrew Porter weakens his case, first by quoting what another person said about another piece to strengthen Andrew's case for the song, second by assuming that because Sessions wrote the song it's therefore gold. In fact, *On the Beach at Fontana*—the only song Sessions ever wrote—is demonstrably bad, both as music and as word setting, and Andrew can't help but know this.

So I turn on the TV for consolation and find Michael Korda, in banter with Ted Koppel, telling us that quality is judgeable by financial gain. By this definition Stevie Wonder is a hundred times superior to Sessions. Well, maybe so.

9 April

Yesterday morning, Paul Sperry being abroad, I took over his American Song class at Juilliard wherein seven youngsters sang a dozen of my songs, and I discussed the meaning of it all.

In the evening, rehearsal of *Three Sisters Who Are Not Sisters* in Richard Marshall's original and effective production at the Universalist Church on West 76th. The actual performance tonight was well attended, and preceded by a lecture by me, sponsored by "Meet the Composer." The singers were all good. Bernard Lefort showed up. So did Maury & David, and also Larry Mass. I brought these three back home for ice cream, but they didn't hit it off. David & Maury are less obsessively intrigued with gay rights than Larry. Tom Steele stopped by too.

Tomorrow, Philly again for another student concert.

10 April

JH in Nantucket tells me he's buried Wallace in the patio beneath a beautiful slate slab, the same blue-gray color as Wallace's fur.

12 April

For *Book World* in Washington, on "favorite childhood reading":

We are what we read, and for better or worse we choose our own menu despite the will of parents. Thus I quickly took shelter against *The Wind in the Willows* (whose all-male anthropomorphism slights not only females, but the dignity of the wilds), while venturing into the more abrasive gales of Wilde, Louÿs, and Cocteau.

Oscar Wilde's *Fairy Tales* still seem today, of all "children's literature," the most touching, well crafted, gorgeous and imaginative. Pierre Louÿs's *Aphrodite* (which I had memorized before puberty), in depicting the world's most seductive courtesan who kills and then is killed for the one she adores, reflects any young person's notion of the propriety of love-as-excess. And Jean Cocteau's *Les Enfants terribles*, by portraying a pair of well-off adolescent bohemian siblings who come to what grown-ups call a bad end, swayed a generation of Parisian youth and, by extension, me.

With all my current musical discipline and patient prosifying, I remain— and am thrilled to remain—the condemned nightingale, the fatal vamp, and the self-destructive child.

Although touched that Hugh Ross continues to champion my music after all these years (he premiered *Four Madrigals* at Tanglewood in 1948), it wasn't a hot idea for him to present three extracts (including Emma Lazarus's sonnet "The New Colossus") from *An American Oratorio* on his program Thursday commemorating the Statue of Liberty. My Oratorio is scored, along with the chorus, for ninety-piece orchestra. Hugh used fifteen pieces, plus organ. It's like following a bread recipe faithfully except for the omission of yeast. Henahan was justified in finding that what he heard "lacked . . . distinctive profile."

But Henahan locates himself squarely when he says that Poulenc's *Figure humaine* is "by twentieth-century standards . . . not complex or highly dissonant." Since Poulenc is a maker of manners and not a follower, he *is* twentieth-century standards. Thus, the critic could legitimately state Boulez is "by twentieth-century standards overly complex and highly dissonant." Of course, Henahan, like all Music Lovers, judges our century by the nineteenth. But in the nineteenth, would a reviewer have written—even of Wagner or of Mussorgsky—that a score was not composed according to his century's standards? Meanwhile, as it happens, *Figure humaine* is not overly complex or highly dissonant even by nineteenth-century standards, if such standards exist. Only in our century could a piece be so lean.

Dined in Philadelphia with Andrea and John de Lancie. John is being summarily fired as director of the Curtis Institute, and they're both in a state of acute distress. Is it too soon to assume that this can lead to no good? There's no replacement; Stormy Bok, chairman of the board, seems to have taken matters into her own hands; John's the first director *ever* to have given a hoot about living music.

13 April

Most of yesterday afternoon was passed with Doctor Salomon, lung X rays, etc. He prescribed a strong antibiotic, Septra DS, to clear away the pus I've been spewing for weeks. Thus far it's only cleared away sleep. All night I drifted into the wakeful dreams so silly, so easily recalled. Mozart's piano concertos are twenty-seven able bodies with vigorous erections (the orchestra, with the piano hanging onto it, I guess), like Whitman's "Twenty-eight young men [who] bathe by the shore." Uninteresting, but interesting.

In the essay on Truman C., when I finally stooped to identify "gay sensibility," I forgot to say, simply, that it's camp. Camp's already an out-of-date word. But it's a strictly homosexual (high & low) phenomenon, and it means Get Them Before They Get You, i.e., self-mockery.

Just as no male has a right to adjudicate on the abortion issue, no straight has ever been able to pigeonhole camp. Camp's the wit of the outsider. It's also an esthetic of the past, irrelevant to gay activists. Activists are by definition people of action, while camp, like art, is reaction. Activism has nothing to do with humor: it can't afford it. Larry Mass is quite without humor. That's his strength.

An outsider has the right to determine whether his friend is alcoholic, but he has not the right to say his friend is not alcoholic. E.g. "My Uncle Jake was alcoholic and you're nothing like him. So have another drink."

I've been married nine times, but I've never been divorced.

16 April

David Diamond's seventieth birthday concert last night was powerful and moving. It was moving to see friends of forty years mixed with David's current post-adolescent pupils honestly weeping, not with the frozen pretense we adopt when one we love has just laid an egg. The power rose from the music, four works chosen obviously for their drive and scope rather than for their prettiness and fun. (The concert was short on fun.) Whatever David's notion about himself—I used to annoy him by talking of his Masterpiece Complex—the evening proved him an elder statesman. Something happened. It's never too late to change your mind.

Beforehand I had invited Morris for quiche and salad and cake. Morris has just read Dotson Rader's book about Tennessee Williams, and apparently I'm mentioned, disobligingly, as having taken Tennessee's fancy back in the old days, but not having been well enough endowed to interest him further. Dotson's wrong. I mean, ask anyone! He had only to pick up the phone.

19 April

John Simon in a recent review referred to "faggot nonsense." Soon after, he was reported by Liz Smith as saying, during an intermission, "Homosexuals in the theater! My God, I can't wait until AIDS gets all of them!" Furor in the press from coast to coast, including dissent from the staff of Simon's own *New York Magazine*, which coerced a lukewarm apology out of him. Since Tom Steele knows that I know John, and that this "knowing" is neither hyperthyroid nor bitter, he asked us both if we'd do an "exclusive interview" for the *New York Native*.

Last night, after teaching all afternoon, I trekked downtown, exhausted, to meet John Simon at the Public Theater for a preview of Larry Kramer's *The Normal Heart*. (This would be a perfect curtain-raiser to the interview which was to take place today.) First play I've seen in a year. Impossible to know how, under other circumstances, I might have taken to it—I *wanted* to like it, because I wanted John to like it, and I was pleased and vaguely astounded (can one be vaguely astounded?) when I noticed a tear running down that stony face.

From noon until five this hot afternoon we taped our conversation in my living room. There were interruptions: John Simon had to make two calls; the photographer came with paraphernalia; we had lunch (croissants with Smuckers preserves, California strawberries, Gruyère, decaffeinated espresso); the phone rang incessantly; I had trouble manipulating the tape machine; JH arrived worn out from Nantucket with Sonny who promptly lifted a leg against John's jacket. But my guest was magnanimous about all that, as he was about the cats' dander which brought on an alarming asthma attack. Then there was a thunderstorm, and the room grew dark. Through all we persevered to our seemingly mutual profit.

The tapes will be transcribed by a hireling tonight and tomorrow (easily forty thousand words), edited on Sunday, and will go to press Monday.

20 April

Cogito, ergo sum? We think we think, but perhaps we're robots so finely tuned after the long evolutionary waves, that we only think we think we think. Indeed, we *are* robots, fabricated by what we've chosen to name Nature. We think we feel.

As chance so often has it, I'm reading old friends about other old friends: Donald Windham's classily crabby memoir of Truman Capote, and Harold Norse's crank letters on the biography, *Auden In Love*, from which he's been omitted. Norse and Windham long to set matters straight. The matters turn out to be minute. So what if Norse did coin the term "hideola" credited to Auden, or if Windham's friend, Sandy, did first see Brando in an elongated somnolent stance backstage—a stance that Capote confiscates. Still, the longing is normal: we second-raters need to preen over the disjointed squeaks in the wilderness which our superiors snatch and clamp into place. In today's *New Yorker* Andrew Porter, reviewing Stephen Paulus's new orchestral work whose four movements take their tags from Wallace Stevens's *Sunday Morning*, asks: "How about a suite with titles 'Ambiguous Undulations,' 'The Strings of Our Insipid Lutes' . . . [since] the lines are rich in phrases from which almost any piece of music might be titled?" Doesn't he know my symphonic suite, *Sunday Morning* (one of whose movements is "Our Insipid Lutes"), which predates Paulus's by eight years? We flail about for justice and for proper accreditation. But there is no justice except through art. *Et encore!*

It occurs to me that I've set the words of both Harold Norse and Donald Windham to music: Harold in my very first song cycle, *Penny Arcade* (1948), and Donald in *Poems of Love and the Rain* fourteen years later.

Tomorrow, Oklahoma for three days.

23 April

Flew back this morning from a two-day stint in Tahlequah. During the trek to the Tulsa airport Calvert Johnson played, on the car cassette, his rendition of my organ suite, *Views from the Oldest House.* How weird to hear this Nantucketty music as we sped through the Tulsanian landscape, especially while simultaneously my host divulged that there had been resistance by faculty members to my being invited to Northeastern State University.

In the past two decades I've visited scores of campuses, festivals and workshops, with never a whisper about my wicked ways. Of course, I can't know how many invitations have *not* been extended (and indeed, perhaps Oklahoma should be commended in spite of everything). Nor can I judge how much my two careers, writing and composing, may have, over the years, been mutually interfering, although it's generally un-American to be a jack-of-all-trades. I do know that ninety-five percent of my college visits are as a musician, my hosts being unaware that I've ever published a book. Meanwhile, most of those who read my books have never heard my music.

The postconcert party was hosted by a female instructor of anesthesia. On learning that I once knew Nadia Dubouchet in Paris, she was thrilled and so was I. George Auric's wife's sister was France's greatest specialist in anesthesia.

Nora Auric once explained how her hair, which snowily framed her subtly boned cheeks, had turned color prematurely. In Poland during the war she spent a night in an inn filled with bedbugs. She surrounded the bed with wet rags (water discourages vermin), whereupon the creatures crawled to the ceiling in darkness, and dropped onto her. Next morning Nora's hair was white.

The "anonymous" part of A.A. has always bemused me. Isn't it time now, with other minorities emerging from the closet, for alcoholics to do likewise?

26 April

Two days judging scores by sixty young composers for ASCAP with Barbara Kolb and Richard Felciano chez Peggy Jory, who keeps a huge pet rabbit in the bedroom. Peggy served a succulent salad, homemade brownies, and big oranges with their price stickers still affixed (forty-five cents each). Every one of the scores, unlike those in similar contests ten years ago, was proficient, professional, expertly copied. None of my flock, past and present, made it to the end, nor did any of Barbara's or Richard's. The competition's stiff.

But now what happens to these expert creators in our increasingly Yahoo midst? By some paradox, while fewer and fewer young people listen to anything but pop more and more young composers are writing "serious" music. Just as gays weaned into an AIDS-threatened society must now make their own rules, so musicians of the post-Nagasaki era must decide how best to disseminate their wares. I have no answers anymore.

29 April

Back from the Twin Cities where the local Gay Men's Chorus gave an able rendition of *Whitman Cantata*, while elsewhere on the program I accompanied four songs each sung in unison by one of four sections from the chorus. Also a signing in Odegard's Bookstore, and a speech for Libby Larsen's Minnesota Composers' Forum.

Heartwarming welcome, plus the best room in the Saint Paul Hotel which, alas, was adjacent to a clock-tower which resonantly chimes the quarter-hour ninety-six times a day throughout the year. After I moved to a room (no longer the best) on the hotel's other side, the chimes pursued me. I am the first guest, it appears, to have complained. Without a trace of annoyance the Chorus officials (who during the entire stay treated me like the Hope Diamond) switched me to another inn.

Returning this morning I see on every New York newsstand the *Native* containing the very long John Simon interview, with, on the inner pages, a photo of John and me looking like half-crazed Rasputins. Tom Steele's shortened the piece by about a third, calling it "The Real John Simon," and trimming away all literary divagations from the naughty subject.

Most of the cuts are reasonable, some are good; but together they remove a dimension from a unique document. Not once did I flatly ask, "Are you homophobic?"—since that would be answered implicitly during the course of our talk. But since John spoke at length of his emigration from Yugoslavia just before the war, I did ask the useful question (inexplicably deleted), "Are you Jewish?" Answer: "No."

It's perhaps understandable that one is not attracted to certain individuals, or is even repelled by certain groups: lust and the heart form their own rules, and there's no accounting for taste, etc. But is it acceptable to make a political issue of one's taste? Our *entretien* is interesting by definition, because the right wing has made a problem of homosexuality. Homosexuality is not *of itself* interesting, any more than heterosexuality.

The word "gay" is not in my vocabulary (except in compound formations: gay rights, gay lib) because Chicago jargon favored "queer" when I was growing up, and I shun catch terms. Admittedly, gay's not a catch term like Yuppie, but still. However, to object to the term, as people still do, on the grounds that gays are mostly not merry, is as vain as objecting to black because "they" are mostly lightish. If Whitman and Gide aren't exactly gay, Hazel Scott and Lena Horne aren't exactly black. John Simon, an aristocratic linguist, objects that the word gay's been robbed from the vocabulary (meaning that "they" have kidnapped the word). But many a noun and adjective has many a meaning, and gay, like black, has a new one now. Does Yeats's *Lapis Lazuli* necessarily crumble if read in the new sense?

> Gaiety transfiguring all that dread . . .
> All things fall and are built again,
> And those that build them again are gay.

4 May

Dined last night at Ellen's with, among others, Virgil. He's now an astonishing sight: overweight, good-tempered, brighter than any of us, of high appetite. (Morris used to point out that while Virgil may have concerns he doesn't have anxieties, nor does he agonize about the news. Thus his longevity.) Only his deafness is a growing problem. I've learned where to pitch my voice, and where to angle my mouth toward his loft ear. Still, he's at a loss with more than two people, and especially with the female timbre. He tells me of Yvonne de Casa Fuerte's death last November, at ninety-one, and of recent surgery on the bodies of both Aaron C. and Paul B.

In forty-odd letters from Paul Bowles, only one, the last, has even vaguely offended me. About *Setting the Tone* he said, "What a busy brain! . . . [like] watching a particularly fascinating ant colony." But he's the one who wrote *Without Stopping*.

5 May

Group photo at Tom Victor's of all available East Coast authors with North Point Press. Jack Shoemaker and William Turnbull beam proudly from the sidelines as we weirdos pose for the birdy. (Hoagland, Brazeau, Sandy Friedman, Salter, Richard Howard, Ron Padgett and others.)

Visit, with her pianist, from Danielle Woerner, who intoned *The Nantucket Songs* in a clear soprano. Saw *The Purple Rose of Cairo*, or some of it. It's both original and predictable.

6 May

Humming at the stove, I realized that the tune in my throat was Shirley's *Gentle Lady*. Shirley Gabis a composer? Whoever puts notes on paper is a composer, and what a graceful setting (graceful, and natural as her own easy laugh) is this little song, so many years ago, on the stanza of Joyce. Likewise those useable four-hand hors d'œuvres that she penned for the very young students in her teaching days. Might Shirley have become more of a composer had she spent less of her life sustaining other musicians? Dumb question, for then she wouldn't have been Shirley.

Tonight, her party for George's seventieth birthday.

Tomorrow, Nantucket.

Nantucket
8 May

Rosemary's sixty-third birthday.

A few days' respite from the city. Instantly the phone rings: Dominick Dunne wants to talk about Claus Bulow for *Vanity Fair*. So we talk. My favorite pastime is gazing through the window at JH mowing the lawn—always with that goddamn cigarette in his mouth—clad in overalls, Sonny at his heels. JH just called for me to come out and see how the sun, in hitting just so the buds of the tall hedge, makes it look like a temple of emeralds. (Not half so valuable as his own graying temples.)

TV documentary on concentration camps, timed, no doubt, to synchronize with Reagan's mad visit to Bitburg. The image that struck me even more sharply than the carloads of staring corpses was of the tattered rags *on* the corpses, fluttering in the May breeze of forty sad years ago. That wind seemed still alive tonight.

Misleading, to say the least, how European or Oriental manifestations on television (the demonstrations protesting the Pope in Holland, for example) focus on English-speaking demonstrators toting sloganed banners, written in English, to reassure Americans—if they need such reassurance—that the whole world speaks their language.

Tom Steele says that "our" current issue of *The Native* has sold, coast to coast, better than any of the previous one hundred fourteen issues.

10 May

Afternoon with Mary Hall and William Turnbull (of North Point) who'd spent the morning, on this their first trip here, cycling to Sconset. Conver-

sation inevitably turns to what to call this book, since I've already stretched
possibilities with *The Final Diary* and its North Point rename, *The Later
Diaries*. Anaïs Nin didn't get herself into that bind. I'll give it a real title,
with *Diary* in the subtitle:

Words without Music: The Current Diary of N. R.

The Truth about Lies: The Recent Diary of N. R. (1973–1984)

Or maybe it could be called *The Holy Bible* (like Joan Didion's *Book of
Common Prayer*), since titles can't be copyrighted, as cases in point *Queenie*
by both Calisher and Korda, *American Dream* by both Mailer and Albee
(and others), *Maiden Voyage* by both Denton Welsh and Graham Master-
son.

A Summer Cold
Circle of Fifths

Something about Mary McCarthy, with all her fame and readability, glamour and style, literariness and political devotion, something about her always leaves a bad taste. The *Times* reports the depositing of McCarthy's
papers at Vassar, and confirms via telephone that yes, she did state that
Auden, "an avowed homosexual," proposed marriage to the "recently widowed Hannah Arendt" who was taken aback by the proposal. "He probably
wanted a place to stay." Mary's implication: homosexuals don't marry without ulterior motive. Well, maybe. The ulterior motive in the widowed Auden's marriage to Erika Mann was to facilitate her escape from the horrors
of Germany. Now, what of the marriages of Mary herself?

Another title: *The Sense of Game*. Yourcenar uses it frequently in her essay
on Thomas Mann. As he grew older, as also with Shakespeare, the "pessimism and optimism have been left behind: the world of fixed forms, and
of moving forms, too, order and disorder, life-in-death and death-in-life,
these have become merely aspects of a single *mysterium magnum* grown
thoroughly familiar now to this wise old alchemist; the sense of game inherent in the order of things is gradually supplanting the sense of danger."
In other words, in old age, one sees it all as a solvable puzzle rather than
a lovers' knot or a vale of tears. *Esperons-le.*

New York
13 May

Tonight, in the Grand Ballroom at the Plaza, on the same platform where a
year ago I lauded Virgil Thomson under different auspices, I received, along
with Mathilde Krim and Virginia Apuzzo, a plaque from the Fund for Hu-

man Dignity for my "contribution to the education of the American public about the lives of lesbians and gay men." Well, I'm touched by such an award from the Fund for Human Dignity, especially since I've never thought I was very dignified. But maybe if I'd been more dignified in my youth I wouldn't have been standing there tonight.

Norman Singer surely had everything to do with the honor; I'm the first musician to receive it. But I'm passive politically, although Norman claims I've "helped" him and many others simply by never having made an issue of *not* being gay. He introduced me with just the right tone of serious levity for this unusual assembly, and I gave an acceptance speech that the m.c. compared to Kissinger (meaning, he explained later, classy and dense); certainly it wasn't as infectiously rousing as Apuzzo's charming spiel. My cheering section, assembled by Norman, was a table with Joanne Cossa, Alice Tully, Sheldon Soffer and Geoffrey Charlesworth.

Earlier I attended, with Sylvia Goldstein and Jim Kendrick (the new director of B & H), a memorial for Bob Holton at the Donnell Library. Well done, with Phyllis Curtin and Sheldon Harnick presiding, and live music by Bill Mayer and Carlisle Floyd. Frederica von Stade sang.

From the time I first knew him, at Tanglewood in 1946, Bob was instrumental to my career. He was crucial to my entering Boosey & Hawkes, and two of my major works are dedicated to him. He had an accurate ear, an effective eye, a canny nose and an open heart. I owe him everything.

It's been seven years since Bob's friend Ben Murphy died so hideously. Our paths had all diverged, but they remained friends until the end.

15 May

More unlikely sound-alikes: Ives's *Tom Sails Away* and *Deep River*. The tenor tune in the first movement of Fauré's *Requiem* and the "Lake of Tears" section of Bartók's *Bluebeard's Castle*. Grieg's first *Lyric Piece*, David Del Tredici's *Acrostic Song*, and *Keep the Home Fires Burning*.

Mother and Father are giving way gradually. We drove down to Cadbury this morning to find Father highly excited with his new footwear, and Mother, as always in her own world, ever more preoccupied with minutiae: her hair, meals, bank books, Judy Collins's name. (Yet she remembers everything.) In her militant pacifism for fifty years Mother prescribed a foolproof method for ending wars: Don't wage them. Nobody followed her advice. So she's thrown in the sponge. The world *did* listen to Father. Now, no longer. So he grows sad.

Ned keeps peek den.

Le mousse
is loose
La grue
it's true
La mousse
miss you
The goose
is loose

18 May

Tea party this afternoon (homemade orange cake, garnished with huge sweet strawberries from Argentina) for Robert Phelps and Rosemarie Beck, Joe Machlis, Claire and Barry Brook, Joe LeSueur, and George & Shirley (George bringing his *Lulu* book) so that they could hear the new Violin Concerto. I read the program note aloud. It opens with this: "In the movie *Humoresque* when Joan Crawford, a stylish dilettante, is asked what music she likes, she replies simply: 'Some symphonies, all concertos.' Why is the concerto so universally attractive, not just to dilettantes but to amateurs and connoisseurs as well as to professional performers of every age?"

The tape sounded worn and distant and I felt uncomfortable. Composers hear only what goes wrong, not what goes right, always aware of the slightest cough, fearful that everyone's embarrassed and bored. JH asked me to put on the saxophone suite, *Picnic on the Marne*, as an antidote.

Over tea (coffee, actually) I said to Barry, apropos of the new *Musical Quarterly* for whose launching we yesterday shared lunch at Schirmers with twenty other board members, "When I become editor of that magazine my first act will be to banish all footnotes. There's nothing in the ubiquitous and ever-distracting footnote that a skilled writer can't either incorporate into the body of his text, or eliminate. I'm as allergic to footnotes as to the adjective 'brilliant.'" To which George replied, "Well, the *Lulu* book is full of footnotes, so I'm taking it back."

Joe LeSueur phoned later to say he loved the tea, and also hearing the fiddle piece (at the inception of which he was present last summer), but was I not perhaps mistaken in crediting Joan Crawford's line, "Some symphonies, all concertos," to *Humoresque* when he could have sworn it comes from *A Woman's Face*?

19 May

On impulse I phoned Harold Brodkey (no, not on impulse, but through a chain of circumstances: while reading of Australia I was led to think of Shirley Hazzard, which led me to think of her husband's Flaubert translations, which led me to reread HB's *A Sentimental Education*, and, finding it—in its pure and dated way—good, I called him) and on impulse he came over for a couple of hours this afternoon. It wasn't a mistake exactly. But HB, who looks very well, took up the conversation where he had dropped it twenty-two years ago, with leaden defenses and needling accusations. I had found it necessary to state that "writers write," so where's this chef d'oeuvre we hear about, Harold? (Just publish it, let it sink or swim, and write ten more.) Of course I added, "Literary people know nothing of music," to which he answered, lowering his eyes, "We know about it, we just don't like to talk about it."

He's edgy, like all of us, about AIDS, despite his seemingly workable second marriage (to a woman). He remembered that I'd once said I was incapable, alas, of going to bed with the famous and the rich—that, in fact, I had done so only four times. (What I'd said was that I'd gone to bed with four *Time* magazine covers.) Probably we were both uncomfortable in seeking solely to prove our worth, since the worth engendered from twelve-times-twenty-two months can't be proven in a two-hour chat. Could that chat possibly have taken place between a man and a woman?

20 May

Taped a segment this morning for PBS television honoring Copland on his 85th birthday. Responding to Vivian Perlis's off-camera queries, I covered the following points, more or less:

> It's hard to believe that it was forty-two years ago, and not last month, that I first met Aaron in that famous loft of his, now vanished, on West 63rd.
> Aaron and Virgil: The Rome and Avignon of music in the forties. You had to be in one camp or the other; there were no further choices. But Virgil was more of a presence than an influence, while Aaron stamped virtually every American composer of the 1940s. Even to deny him was to admit him. Yes, his power was manipulative and political. But his artistic persuasiveness stemmed from the

beauty of his music rather than—as with Sessions—the strength of his intellect.

So much has been said about Aaron's generosity and about his even-tempered, almost impersonal friendliness. Was his carnality reserved for his work? Partly true. But I personally never felt his beneficence as much as his benevolence (he never helped me in my career). But I did more than once see him angry, exasperated, sad. He was angry with my *Paris Diary* for its words on Boulanger. He was exasperated, in Rome in 1954, when a piano sonata by Auric seemed to go on forever. ("What a hell of an awful piece," said Aaron, who never swore.) And on two occasions, twenty years apart, I saw him express tearful concern for persons with whom he was (for lack of a better term) in love. It would be to belittle him as artist and as human to deny his temperament, even his lust. Aaron Copland was—is—a man for all seasons, but also a man of high discretion. Unlike Virgil, he doesn't gossip; but he does love to listen to gossip.

Later, the dentist.

Evening, John Gruen's public interview (expert as always) at the Met Museum with the svelte, classy, faintly common, and highly skilled speaker, Maria Tallchief.

21 May

During the Copland filming yesterday I mentioned, as everyone else has doubtless mentioned, Aaron's Americanness, and lamented that younger composers, when writing for voice, often choose every language except their own to set to music. How, I wondered, does Lorca sound to Spanish ears as musicalized by Crumb? Vivian Perlis then asked, "Well, how does *El Salon Mexico* sound to Mexican ears as musicalized by Copland?"

El Salon Mexico is a postcard written by a United States citizen: it is an impression, not an expression, of a Mexico City dance hall, in the same way that Milhaud's ballets of the 1920s or Ravel's concertos of the 1930s are reflections of America, not attempts to speak American. Above all, these pieces are not vocal settings; they are not examples, as Crumb is an example, of a composer stepping inside a foreign language and then speaking out. Does a Madrileño learn something new about Lorca through Crumb the way a Mexicano learns something new about how an outlander sees his country through Copland?

So ever more strongly do I feel about the arbitrary use of word repetitions (the reiteration, sometimes twice, sometimes many times, by the composer, of a word or group of words used only once by the poet) that even such unflawed masterpieces as Britten's *War Requiem* now seem flawed. I speak not of the choral writing (for choral music has its own traditions and necessary conventions) but of the solos on Wilfred Owen's poems.

Nantucket
22 May

I shall remain here now for fifteen weeks (except for three nights in July to Saranac and a fortnight in August to Santa Fe), among the lilacs, the burgundy peonies, the sordid soughing of the mourning doves, and what seems to be more and more tourists, loud, preemptive. JH has built new window boxes and filled them with red impatiens which sprout and spread even as you behold them.

Watched a piece of junk about the wildly rich Beatrice Straight and her son, who is frozen dead for ten years then brought back to life, at great expense, but *without a soul*. This means he's unerringly mean as well as canny. Now, wouldn't a person without a soul, yet sound of mind, be practical and dispassionate, and, if sexual, perfunctory rather than forceful? That is, logical—logic with an erection. Admittedly, sadism, like good manners, comes from the mind, and is developed by custom. What has this man's unleashed viciousness to do with lack of soul? Didn't Hitler and Nero have souls? Don't we all have a soul (whatever the hell that is)? Beatrice Straight is actressy in a dumb way. Her *S* sounds like *Sh*, or rather, like the *Zh* of Zhivago (or the French *J*). Lizabeth Scott had that *S*, many long years ago. The lower-clash version of the upper clash.

Ask your pupil to play a piece (any Chopin Prelude, for example) like iron filings, then like damask roses, then iron roses, then damask filings. Suppose he does; what does it prove? Not that music can resemble these textures, but that your pupil is shrewd enough to adapt your speciousness into manual interpretation—which means he's good enough not to need you anymore.

The merest hint of a transistor down the street is anxious-making. You don't get used to torture (as those marine camps in Idaho proved), you simply go mad. Sam's persistent meow is more annoying with each passing day, after twelve years. Nantucket mopeds and throbbing radios are like the rack, which ends only in permanent maiming and death. Silence is the ultimate luxury. Silence is expensive.

Why am I, a feminist, and in many ways a radical, uneasy at arguments supporting women in the priesthood? Because the arguments go against that which the Church is: a drone-oriented hive founded on the male Christ. The arguments defile the poetry of conservatism: with women calling the shots, the Church would no longer be the Church. Now, although the Church (meaning, of course, the Roman Catholic Church), with its scents and its saints and its silver, its Mediterranean history, Gregorian chant, gaudy inquisitions and ignobly noble rationales, was crucial in shaping the taboo tastes of myself, a midwestern Quaker, it was only the trappings, not the essence, that snared me.

Just as there is something obtuse about male gays wishing to be accepted, on their terms, into the military, when the military is by nature immoral and should be abolished, so there is something contradictory about female believers who wish to be accepted by the Church, on their terms, rather than seeking to abolish the Church.

Even our agony can turn into show biz, as Carol Burnett once quaintly showed in that skit about the lady whose husband was smashed by a car. "How does it feel to be so suddenly a widow?" Frantic tears. "Would you mind repeating that for our cameras, Mrs. Jones?" Tears, but with more aplomb. And so forth.

The parents of the septuplets after three days grow camera-wise. The father, flanked by the press, weeps by rote. The mother declares she's finally chosen names for the five survivors, but will not announce these until the conference Tuesday. Because they're freaks of science, these babies somehow haven't quite earned their fame as the Dionnes—freaks of nature—earned theirs fifty years ago. This reasoning may be unfair.

Daily practicing of *Scenes from Childhood* for Santa Fe.

Daily notes on Mussorgsky for next *Opera News* essay.

On television, the as-always extraordinary Vanessa Redgrave in the comparatively tasteful *Three Sovereigns for Sarah* about the witch hysteria of Salem.

Reading with distaste the preface, which its author calls "Introductory Epilogue," of *Overdrive* by William Buckley. The distaste stems from Buckley's smug indisposition to admit he's wrong (why admit I'm wrong, since I'm always right?), and his assumption in his diary that we're thrilled by every blackhead. Maybe it takes one to know one, and this is probably what makes my own readers—all five of them—climb the wall. But at least I'm self-doubting, am I not?

Buckley attempts the no-win proposition of taking on his critics, every one of them. Like most conservatives he bases his argument on a false premise (or, worse, on an *almost* false premise), and wastes precious time defending his stance rather than listening to yours. For example, on homosexuality. In the book proper he writes: "It is fashionable nowadays to say that a person's sexual 'preference' is not a datum of any consequence. . . . My point here is the discrete one, that the assumption that homosexuality is an enduring condition (like alcoholism) is simply mistaken." In the preface Buckley quotes Eliot Fremont-Smith: "His riff on homosexuality . . . seems deliberately blind to all sorts of subtleties he should, at his age, with his antennae, be less innocent of"; then rather than mulling this notion a bit, Buckley summons, as witness, one Franz Oppenheimer: "Another pernicious myth touched upon in *Overdrive* is the supposed biological and hereditary nature of homosexuality. . . . My father, who practised psychiatry, first in Germany, and, after his emigration, in San Francisco, collected substantial evidence in support of Buckley's impression that homosexuality is a disease that can be cured. During my father's entire professional life he endeavored to find a true 'biological,' i.e., an incurable, homosexual. He never did."

Now, Oppenheimer in these phrases spends more words on the subject than Buckley in his whole book, yet Buckley accepts the findings of Oppenheimer's obscure father to trounce Fremont-Smith. He could have asked me. Four out of five of my male friends, for forty years, have been homosexual, and not one has ever been "cured," or felt the need to change. But the real question's not about whether homosexuality's a disease, but about why Buckley feels that it must be a disease and then offers such limp proof. Had he used the word "sensible," instead of the misleading "fashionable," he'd have had a point.

As for Nora Ephron, because "she imputed anti-Semitism" in her reference to his reference to his landlord as "Shylock," Buckley puts her in *her* place with: "[She] closed by suggesting that my affectations might best be understood by using a little ethnic imagination ('The English used to say, give an Irishman a horse and he'll vote Tory.')." Assuming that he means us to take "ethnic imagination" for "ethnic slur," and that the slur is against the Irish, not the English, is a generality about an Irishman equal to a generality about a Jew? The Irish are not, at least in America, a loathed minority. His tit-for-tat is unbalanced.

(Am I to be indulged, any more than John Simon with his sizing up of actresses according to whether or not he finds them beautiful, if I say that, while many a conservative capitalist can seem sexy, William Buckley physically repels me, especially his tongue, as it darts like a wet snake in and out of those know-it-all lips, while the eyes widen in mock surprise at some pronouncement of a guest on "Firing Line" before coming to rest on the tablet in his lap—a tablet upon which his busy hand still scribbles notes stirring from his ever-active mind?)

Not that I can't sympathize with Buckley's frustration about his critics. In just the past week three critics, *à mon propos*, have said whatever enters their head in direct contradiction to what's before their eyes:

(1) Brandon Judell, on Gay Cable Network, lies about the interview in *The Native* by saying that John Simon, when asked if he'd ever slept with a man, replied that the only time a homosexual made a pass at him Simon slugged him. (Simon actually said he had been mildly flattered.)

(2) Wilfrid Mellers, reviewing my diaries which have just come out in England, lies by saying, with the alliterative grace of an Agnew, that "Rorem flits from cocktails with Cocteau to picnics with Picasso," when in fact I never had, nor wrote that I'd had, cocktails with Cocteau, and never had, nor wrote that I'd had, a picnic with Picasso. Isn't there enough name-dropping in the diary for him to quote without having to fall back on his own poesy? (Has Mellers ever read, over the years, the various admiring sentences I've penned about his musicological gifts?)

(3) The current *Advocate*, in the Gay Trivia Quiz, lies by saying I wrote that Francis Poulenc used "to chase pretty Arab boys through the back streets of French North Africa," and also that Poulenc and Pierre Bernac were lovers. Poulenc never chased, nor did I ever suggest that he chased, pretty boys, nor were Poulenc and Bernac ever more than professional colleagues. (Poulenc's taste ran to overweight gendarmes with handlebar moustaches and to middle-aged businessmen. Governor Thomas E. Dewey, Poulenc once told me, was his ideal.)

Another review from England (unsigned in *Music and Musicians*), this one pretty good, contains a couple of disconcerting phrases. "One will search in vain through these pages for any real insight into the composer's methods. This is all to the good, for Rorem's candid self-analysis is worth reading for his literary and poetic abilities. He is not a great composer—just a very good one—so it is refreshing to read of a man who knows his limitations, and, in the course of his journal, the growing awareness of his limitations, without being bombarded by a self-laudatory attempt to make a musical silk purse out of the proverbial ear." (It's not a proverbial ear, it's a *sow*'s ear, but thanks for the delicacy.) If I don't write here of my "composer's methods" (but surely I do), I *have* filled five books of essays with thoughts on the methods of other composers. But do I know my limitations? And am I not a great composer? Have I expressed such humility? If I'm not great it's because the notion of greatness is fossilized today. I am, however, the best of what there is.

Bosc pears wrapped in ripe Brie. Am trying desperately to get under way with a String Symphony for Atlanta. If I don't here write nowadays of composer's methods, it's because I'm wary of imitating Howard Moss's parody of my diary.

Many Brando reruns on TV. What an unbearable actor—the humorlessness, the *lenteur*, the liberties that fame allows. (My two favorite movies are *The Letter* and *Sunset Boulevard*.) Coppola, like Zeffirelli, seems incapable of simplicity, of producing a work for less than zillions. Our *Miss Julie* in 1979 was, for three thousand dollars, vastly superior to our *Miss Julie* of 1965 for one hundred thousand dollars.

Nor can I any longer bear the "greatness" of Olivier as he rolls, too often, those hooded eyes back into his head.

Altzheimer's Disease rose up seemingly from nowhere, at the same time as AIDS, about four years ago. Had it always existed, like Surrealism, but under a different name? And whatever became of the amoeba scare of 1979–81? Was it replaced by AIDS or merely displaced by AIDS? Did AIDS emerge from it?

What my precious, and probably tragic, mother seems to have, in her luxurious loony bin, is not senility at all, but, with the help of a stabilizing Melaril, indifferent resignation. Tragic, because like Paul Goodman she knew how to save the world but no one listened. Paul died. Mother withdrew.

1 June

Andrew Porter gives Wuorinen the whole first paragraph without offering a value judgement, merely a brief description. With me he doesn't even bother with the brief description. (He doesn't bother to say I'm not worth bothering with.) Andrew has been present at most of my major works of the past decade, including *Assembly and Fall*, *Air Music* (which won the Pulitzer), most recently *Picnic on the Marne*, without mentioning them, though he mentions English works on the same programs.

Has he ever given an English composer a bad review? Has he ever, when there were an English and an American on the same program, not favored the English? Has he ever, except with Sessions, allowed for extenuating circumstances in judging a new work? He hands out demerits to us Yankee hicks as to grammar school students. It's time, as Gandhi said of the colonists, for him to go home.

Yet even so suave a journal as the *New Yorker* labors under the delusion—a delusion shared by Women's Committees of all our big Symphonies—that foreign is better.

The aim of life is to seek life's aim.

. . . as obsessed with Andrew as Meyer Levin with Lillian Hellman . . .

What does it mean to call Roger Sessions—as Andrea Olmstead does in the current (#152) *Tempo*—"America's finest composer," when another with equal justice can claim that Sessions is not a composer at all? Until we can all agree on what is great, we won't be able to construct that computer that will compose masterpieces.

In music there is no finer (is Sessions more fine than Copland?); when that computer comes to be, there will be many "finer" robots.

. . . like explaining to Mother why pianists sometimes "cross hands."

5 June

Paul Theroux's a writer whose natural grace and original mind have always held a tempting appeal. Thus I was felled today by the *Times*'s seemingly admiring remarks about *Sunrise with Seamonsters*. "He notices . . . the incongruous and the obvious that most people overlook. . . . He notices the militaristic organization of so many antiwar groups—'the people who object to ROTC end up marching many more miles than the sophomores on the parade ground.' . . . Mr. Theroux dismisses . . . most pacifists as 'cowards' who are frightened of dying."

Is marching what ROTC is about? Are pacifists (like Gandhi, like the C.O.s who lived in solitary for years, like my own parents who were spit upon) cowards? Is to be frightened of death merely cowardly, or inherent in the structure of all men from Christ to Nero? Aren't heroes frightened of

death—and isn't Paul Theroux himself? And what is a coward? Someone
who turns his back on battle? Simple logic suggests that if we all did that
there would be no more wars.

15 June

JH makes a dozen nine-hour round-trips each season in the truck between
the islands of Nantucket and Manhattan. During every minute of these voy-
ages I calculate: he's getting off the ferry, Sonny's jumped out the window,
they're halfway to New York, they're halfway back, night's falling, a car's
crashed into them, they're in a Providence clinic, no, they're getting back
on the ferry, they've parked on Wesco Place and are moving in the dark
through the backyard. The exhaustion of the trips, the unanswering telephone. Then the late conversations (here peonies are coming forth, there
roaches are out of control, here I procrastinate in the summerhouse, there
the church meetings exasperate) which I depend on to get through the
night. I work better when alone, but the reason for that work is so as not to
be alone. For whom do I compose? Why, for JH (and for those who pay).

He has a trait (not a fault, a trait—a common one) that he ignores. It's crucial for him to be needed, and to this end he will cajole and collapse and rant
and sacrifice and spend a thousand dull hours until the beloved capitulates;
then interest flags as he grows cold and beyond the trail of quizzical hearts.
I've seen the script repeated four times. It takes one to know one. He is as
armored (after the kill) as he used to accuse me of being.

We share different rooms together. I've never been able to share a room,
much less a bed, for a whole night; my sleep's so light, and intimacy of
dreams is more overwhelming, more personal, than the intimacy of love.
Absence *does* make the heart grow fonder. (I've been reading the galleys of
Janet Flanner's letters to Natalia Murray: for forty years they lived more or
less separately, which led to an intensity of pleasure and friendship and—in
Janet's case—of strong literature that is unequaled.) Here in Nantucket JH's
room is two floors below. Every midnight I shudder as he descends. Basement stairs are notorious in any case, but JH approaches them in his floor-
length nightshirt, Sonny under one arm, a lighted cigarette and a glass of ice
water in the other hand, with the two cats shifting underneath his feet on
every unlighted step.

We've both had dreams of mortality lately, each afraid the other may die
first. Life is a terminal disease, says JH cheerfully.

He has a pair of fourteen-year-old protégés from the church here for the
summer, Elvis and Danny, Dominican Republicans, to help with the un-

ending chores. Intellectually they're comic-book level without a reference even to Rita Hayworth, much less to Lewis Carroll. JH tutors them every afternoon: they must learn by heart one poem and read one book each week. They resist this as "stupid." Yet there's something touching about the inverted reactions of these nonrural underprivileged kids. *Alice in Wonderland* is not as good as the movie. Roses smell like soap. And when I call JH to come look at the sky, they ask "What's wrong with the sky?"

Every night after supper for the past eight years JH and I have played backgammon. Our skills are balanced now, but we enjoy it all the same. Good for digestion.

Dream: I murdered, dismembered, and buried a person. I await discovery. No one believes me. Or no one knows. Years pass. The punishment lies in not being punished: in being forced to relive the crime daily, without the release of confession.

17 June

Literally a question of taste. The color of the underside of the new oversized quilt from Buttner's recalls the raspberry bavarians Mother used to make, and my insomnia is less maddening because of it. I can enjoy but do not crave protein and acid, but a day without pie is a day without sun. When alone, I never eat meat; rather, the evening meal consists of a baked potato, a dutiful salad with garlic, a major dessert. Grapefruit and pasta I eat out of discipline, while longing for the final course.

Can this explain my musical taste—and indeed, the music I compose? I simply do not *need* Beethoven, though he may provide a more substantial nourishment than Ravel (though who's to argue that? and how?). Nor can I understand the need of, say, Milton Babbitt, for writing what he writes. Where's the sugar? And why is sugar, like charm, looked at so askance these days?

Whenever you offer a sweet to someone who claims not to eat sweets, he generally devours it gluttonously. Music used to be entertaining. Probably that's what I "need" to express—sad pleasure.

Accompanist is a word I can't abide, and seldom use except in a collaborative sense: singer and pianist accompany each other through the adventure of a song.

20 June

John Myers is in love again. To celebrate this rare condition he sent me a
poem from his own pen, *Triumphal Chant for R.H.*, hoping I'd set it to music as a gift for his friend. I have just done so.

Song is a bastard, a cross between unwedded (unweddable?) genres. Bas-
tards are usually healthy, being a conjoining of separate races. Opposite of
incest.

22 June

Our north bank, as always in late June, is covered—smeared—with ten
thousand wild daisies (or, as the French would say, with savage marguerites)
of a laserlike yellow. Every dawn and every dusk (today, at 3:30 A.M. and at
9:30 P.M.) our elms are so packed with finches that the trees themselves
seem to be singing. Most welcome are the pair of cardinals, of whom the
male is the flavor of those stinging cinnamon drops we used to buy at Sarnets
drugstore, a brutal ruby. Enough colorful writing.

Seventh night since the Lebanese hijacking, an international *cause célèbre*. Then yesterday, four marines gunned down in a Salvador café. Reagan
speaks of reprisals. God knows the hijacking's a nightmare, unforgivable,
dire. Yet haven't the reprisals, to some extent, already occurred? Hasn't the
frustration of the so-called Third World countries, at being occupied by uninvited Yankee bullies, been reprisal enough? In last week's *Times* the
"emancipated" mother of a gay son quotes a soldier: "I was given a medal for
killing a man, and excommunicated for loving one."

The so likeable, and to an extent intelligent, Larry Mass, unable to see
the forest for the trees, keeps writing me about what he feels to be the
responsibility of the gay composer. Yes, at this point I am indeed attracted
by the thought of a "gay libretto" (whatever that might be), but I'm more
strongly drawn to a pacifist libretto. I am as much a Quaker as a gay, and
man's inhumanity and identity and poetry are expressed as much through
common conflict of our fatal globe as through sexual conflict. Perhaps an
opera on a debarred hero? Oscar Wilde? Even Alexander the Great? We
don't permit our sons to grow too big for their britches.

This morning, toilet overflowed. This afternoon, as every June, I trod
barefoot on a bee. This evening I've typed this page, before turning to the
orchestration of the String Symphony. JH in New York for the weekend,
leaving me with his two human protégés, the three animals, and the necessity for finding a plumber on a Saturday.

The night sweats are mental. During insomniac hours (I've not had a good night's sleep in thirty years), ruminations are on the joys of Nantucket—that all this bliss (including the plumbing exasperations) must end. I am afraid to die without JH. But of course I will. Even in the best of times we die alone. ("Strait is the gate"—too narrow to enter two abreast, or whatever it is.) And the hostage crisis in Lebanon seems a microcosm of what will occur. Whatever I wrote earlier about America as bully, it makes a difference when non-abstract relatives are involved. How soon will all the United States be hostage to some Third World land?

Reading Giono again as I read him in the early fifties when he reported on the Dominici trials, pointing out that the very difference in spoken language between the urban judge and the rural accused was the core of the legal stalemate. Like the difference today between the centuries of developed morality of the Lebanese as opposed to the hostages. (North Point has put out a rare series of Giono in English.) But with all his poetic emphasis on the mystery of nature—like the emphasis found in Hamsun and Pasternak—there's a dogged normality to Giono, a heterosexual *donnée*, an assumption that reproduction is more crucial than production. A paradox, since he himself was a producing artist whose "theme" was growth in nature. He made unduplicatable works about the infinite duplicatability of the soil.

30 June

Thirty-five years ago in Fez was the hemorrhoid operation from which I convalesced six months, and I've been bothered down there (the rectum, not Fez) ever since. Yesterday another attack, and panic. *Plus ça change.*

Will Parker arrives Saturday for thirty-six hours of rehearsal. Meanwhile I practice the Ives songs. Although I have a certain respect for some of them (*Tom Sails Away* is as upsetting as a Griffith movie in slow motion), I take no pleasure in working on them. Those random dissonances, with no concept of the hand!

JH, who adores Benchley and Calvin Trillin, says it's because I don't like the homespun. "Humorists" leave me cold, and Ives's songs likewise. Still, I play them well. To dislike something does not preclude an interpretative grasp of that something; indeed, love can becloud viewpoint. The French worship their own music and play it wrong.

The nearby lily pond is being drained by the town. Families of ducks show up in our backyard each morning, discombobulated. To write a letter to the

Inquirer and Mirror could be thought of as a cry in the wilderness, except that there is no wilderness anymore. A cry from an increasingly desiccating urbanization.

An alcoholic binge, at least to me, though sometimes fun during the first years, was a suicide attempt. At the rate of fifty a year for thirty years (some of them lasting three days), that makes fifteen hundred suicide attempts— wear and tear on body and soul. Seventeen years since I've had a drink.

1 July

Larry Mass responds docilely to my ultimatum about discontinuing our, to me, fruitless exchange on gay music, with: "On Thursday Arnie and I are going to see [*sic*] the NYC Gay Men's Chorus, which will feature music by Barber, Bernstein, Copland, Gershwin, Porter, and Rorem. Nowhere—not in the program notes, certainly not in the mainstream press, but probably not even in the gay press or in Ned Rorem's diaries, however, will one read that all of these composers were/are homosexual, or any analysis of what that might mean."

Larry can't stop. Perhaps pink triangles could be placed by appropriate names in the program (although I never knew that Gershwin was homosexual). Doesn't Larry worry about Jewish composers? What has Bernstein's and Copland's (and yes, Gershwin's) Jewishness to do with their music? Larry's Jewish too, but can he tell me why, before Meyerbeyer and Mendelssohn, there were no Jewish composers in Europe? Or why, before Copland, there were none to speak of in America? What would a program note say about, for example, Poulenc? "Poulenc, rumored to be gay (although he sired a daughter upon whom he doted), wrote his mass in . . . ." Or Copland? "Copland, rumored to be gay, was also Jewish, but wrote goyish music all his life, being the first to celebrate cowboys." To dignify Larry's obsessions here is sadistic. Maybe I'll eat my words one day.

Mrs. Roush, the West Virginia fan I've never seen, sends frequent gifts, the latest being a series of Billie Holiday records. Rooms this morning quiver with the plaints of that voice which, way before Jennie Tourel's, was (and for me remains) the most affecting in the world.

Other gifts from Mrs. Roush have been: a ten-pound box of licorice; twenty blood-red tumblers; an expensive facsimile of a Bach manuscript; a Cuisinart.

Does the sunset look like a strawberry sundae or like a butcher shop? The butcher shop looks like a strawberry sundae.

3 July

Frank Conroy, who is doing a study on Peter Serkin for *Esquire*, phoned for a quote. I asked him to call back in half an hour, then typed up the following, which is more or less sincere:

> Fabulous keyboard artists are now a dime a dozen, so competition is stiffer than in the golden age. Still, in the rarefied heights of the Greatest, comparisons remain stable: none is better than another, though each is different from the other. There is no inevitable way to perform a given piece, there are as many true ways as there are true pianists, and the sense of inevitability changes with every generation. Composers themselves can be contradictory about how their music should go from year to year. Since repertory remains pretty stationary while interpreters of that repertory come and go, Peter Serkin cannot be unanimously voted the best of his time, and he would surely be embarrassed, even angry, to win such a vote.
>
> He is nonetheless unique, and his uniqueness may or may not be your dish. The uniqueness lies, as I hear it, in a friendly rather than an overawed approach to classics which he nonetheless plays with the care and brio that's in the family blood, and he's not afraid to be ugly. As to his approach to contemporary music, it is with the same dignity as with the classics, and he is unique among superstars in that he approaches it at all. He's the only big name of his age to feel a duty toward the music of his time, and the duty springs from a need which has elsewhere all but vanished.

5 July

Lenny B.'s *Songfest*, televised live from Washington under his spastic baton, remains buoyant, adroit, honest, delightful, yet fails through striving for grandeur when it's by nature intimate. Lenny's Achilles heel trods molehills as mountains: everything to him is theatrically wide. He proves it most of the time. Never publish this pretentious paragraph.

12 July

Reading *Jane Eyre* finally. Charlotte's novel is more intelligent than Emily's. Still, it is to *Wuthering Heights* what *The Barefoot Contessa* is to *All about Eve*—as capable, touching, and "sophisticated" but more sprawling and thus less telling. Similarly the diction of Philip Glass resembles that masterpiece Jack Nicholson is writing in *The Shining*—the phrase "Now is the time for all good men to come to the aid of their party" (or something like that) restated several thousand times.

Reading also the Glenn Gould collection, which has everything—wit, originality, insight, healthy philistinism, clarity of explanation—except warmth. And his indifference to what he terms "French impressionists" does put me off.

In 1944 I wrote a piece called *Prelude and Adagio* for Organ, Flute, Horn and Viola, and sent it to E. Power Biggs (I'd heard that Biggs, sooner or later, programmed everything he received) who accordingly did it on a Sunday broadcast. When I played an aircheck of this broadcast for Paul Bowles, he declared: "You seem to have gone on where Ravel left off." I looked quizzical, so he added, "I mean, like the way Stravinsky went on where Debussy left off." I swallowed it. To this day, forty-one years later, when I sniff on my palette some pilfered morsel of Ravel, I feel it is no longer his: it is mine as Pierre Menard's Quixote, by dint of passing time and new handwriting, is his. Signatures are unforgeable. (I never met Biggs, although we corresponded for years.)

20 July

One does savor Gould's quip on Beethoven, "He's the one composer whose reputation is based entirely on gossip," which applies as well to Elliott Carter or to Stephen Sondheim. Sondheim, especially, seems a mountain from a molehill, judging by the recent Book-of-the-Month recording. Is there anything, in words or music, he does that Mark Bucci didn't in the fifties?

And Charlotte Brontë's book does have the scope and chutzpah that all great works—sprawling and unsewn though they be—possess, even a tinge, three generations earlier, of Proust in the description of ladies leaving the dining room and entering the parlor. "They dispersed about the room, reminding me, by the lightness and buoyancy of their movements, of a flock of white plumy birds. Some of them threw themselves in half-reclining positions on the sofas and ottomans: some bent over the tables and examined the flowers and books: the rest gathered in a group round the fire." It beats Jean Rhys's *Wide Sargasso Sea*, which I'm reading (after being seduced by her other novels) with chagrin. It has everything but charm. Charlotte makes an error or two. Page 37: "a hungry little robin . . . on the leafless cherry tree" inspecting Jane's crumbs from a roll. Robins migrate in winter; nor do they eat "crumbs," being equipped, as soft-billed predators, only to eat meat.

An "Aid to the Hungry in Ethiopia" display on TV, labeled "concert." This is the music of our world, loved and promoted by all, and written by well-heeled thinkers. I heard nothing but egomaniacal screeching, combos aping static, the mean gaze and dictionless whine of Dylan, the self-promotional eyes (looking in at themselves, not out at their fans) of Tina Turner and Mick Jagger, meaningless, worthless emissions with no sense of occasion; knowing that Russians and Japanese and Mexicans might be digging it, but I wondered what the starving Ethiopians were making of it.

Reagan has cancer. Rock Hudson has AIDS.

JH slaving over my taxes. He says that the only occupational code, out of several hundred given, that I fit into is "Other Entertainment."

3 August

Have been reading with much pleasure *Darlinghissima*, Natalia Murray's awkwardly titled collection of letters, spanning forty years, from Janet Flanner to her.

If asked last week, Who is our most stylish journalist? I'd have quickly answered, Janet Flanner. Today, having read *Darlinghissima*, I must add: So far as nonfiction in English is concerned, she is simply the greatest author of her time. Janet here lends new dimension to the agonized art of epistology, each entry being not only cultured, entertaining, and so very human, but informative on timely matters that do not seem to date. On the technical side, no one handled metaphor like Janet, with all those images—unforced, original, and necessary. On the emotive side, no one was more compelling than she when talking of love—her own as well as other people's; the words are at once tasteful and erotic, and wrenchingly generous. Threading through the letters from start to finish is an attitude, what we now call "feminism," with a lucid strength far ahead of its time.

The relationship of Janet and Natalia, though hardly spelled out in the salacious jargon of our day, is clearly a love affair combining mutual respect with passion, tact with tenderness, and a conjoint intellectuality that rivals Browning & Barrett's. Yet Natalia tells us, by way of postscript, that when Janet was taken by a midnight ambulance to the nearby hospital on November 7, 1978, "a couple of young internists took her away. I tried to follow. 'Who are you?' asked a nurse. 'A friend, the only person she knows in New York . . . she lives with me,' I said, pleading. 'Wait in the entrance,' she retorted." Janet died alone at dawn. The scene reflects *The Well of Loneliness* of sixty years ago.

The more things change the more they stay the same.

Sylvia Goldstein has come and gone—her yearly stay. Of all the hierarchy from the old days of Boosey & Hawkes, Sylvia alone remains a power behind the throne. But who sits on the throne—except, in a way, we few decorative composers? As the Curtis Institute sails rudderless, and many another distinguished music school sinks outright, so the publishing world—literary as well as musical—is now chaotic and exhausted. Sylvia says that in ten, fifteen, years there may be no sheet music as we now know it (photocopying already precludes many a legal sale); instead, buyers will consult a computer about a desired piece, then out it will pop, without the pretty cover composers so love. Forty years ago there was an abundance of sheet-music shops where you could browse for everything new from France, Japan, Finland. Today, not one.

Sylvia at work is a paragon of efficiency: everything having to do with contracts she attends to (as David Huntley attends to orchestra rentals and publicity). Sylvia at play is a paragon of tact: with all her personal problems, she never complains (or expresses a negative opinion about a living composer). Just as certain carpenters pridefully practice the family trade in an age where craftsmanship is near extinction, Sylvia as a musical lawyer fills an even rarer nook.

Three days in Saranac, likeable, but no thanks to the nightmare of plane connections between here & there. Gregg and Roz Smith were again my hosts, contingent with a national conference of the Association for Professional Vocal Ensembles. The conference proved once more that the United States is a land of specialists, even within such specialties as serious music performance. When choral conductors get together they talk about choral music, period. Bring up the question of other kinds of music, not to mention books or butterflies or world famine, and their eyes glaze over in uncomprehending ennui. Yet specialization makes for a keen sense of their craft. General practitioners (Cocteau, Noël Coward, Charles Ives, Wallace Stevens) are, in the nature of things, not as crazy as specialists. Not that their concentration is less intense, but it always entails the breadth of comparison.

Four of the five movements of *String Symphony* are done. No ideas for the fifth, except that it will unfold like a flower into a Rondo.

4 August

Ironic, sad weather. In two hours I leave for Santa Fe, there to launch the new Septet, *Scenes from Childhood*. Thinking of my first meeting with Poulenc thirty-six summers ago, when Henri Hell forced me to sing the cycle *Penny Arcade*, on Harold Norse's words, after which we walked Poulenc to the bus, passing two *art nouveau pissoirs* which then ornamented the outer walk of the Luxembourg across from where he lived, 5 rue de Médicis. He told us that that morning he had entered one and saw a man onanizing, and at noon entered the second one and saw the same man at the same job. I didn't know then that that's what *pissoirs* were for, much less that great musicians talked about such things.

Peggy Jory is dead. Almost since I first knew her, Janet Fairbanks's niece, in the summer of 1946 when she was but a gamine underfoot at Lake Geneva, she was intense about fighting for her belief: that new music in our society is remedially unsteady. All that volatility, suddenly squelched.

More sound-alikes: "Yours" and "Every Night at Eight" (words as well as music). "Easy Come, Easy Go" and "Maybe."

Liquor and the smell of soap in the Midi those many summers ago. . . . One stays sober in order to get drunk. One takes a bath in order to get dirty. (Not the other way around.) The smell of liquor intoxicates, but only for a moment.

815 E. Palace Ave.
Santa Fe
9 August

Fourth full day in Santa Fe. By Sunday, the premiere of *Scenes from Childhood*, we will have had nine hours of rehearsal on this twenty-minute septet. Yet I, the pianist, feel insecure; my colleagues, half my age but twice as knowing in ensemble playing, are deferential, indulgent, and helpful about my faulty entries and splayed roulades. A composer as participating performer of his own new work is at a disadvantage: he can't stand away and hear it whole. The others are quicker than I to catch errors; after all, I've never heard it before either.

Suede landscapes, two daily showers, the smashed apricots all over the sidewalks are as *insolites* as ever, but lusher; the climate is changing. The work and social/interview schedule is ample, and my lodgings acceptable. But I'm lonely. Being far from JH discombobulates; there seems no reason for exertion. Robert Tobin has taken me under his wing and is an affectionate distractor, intelligent (in his new abstinence), and patriarchal with his snowy beard.

Henze's *English Cat* is a worthy failure—worthy, because Henze's a real composer, and because Crosby is right to invest in anything contemporary. But with all his theatrical flare Henze succeeds (for me) only in nonvocal works. A parable to make its point must be succinct; this sprawls. Who cares about symbols for three hours? The tunes, though energetic, never soar; the harmony, though diatonic mostly, seems clogged; the rhythm (as with other Europeans who "jazz it up") is occasionally embarrassing for an American, if always agile. As for the orchestration, it dawdles too much with effects (zither, portative organ, glisses, recorders) that are unneeded, and his percussion is unintegrated punctuation. A composer, as he grows up (does he ever?), should use ever less battery, and if he makes it to fifty, should abandon drums entirely. (The prettiest moment came from a brief bassoon solo which echoes, surely inadvertently, the song "Tonight" from *West Side Story*.) The English singing was incomprehensible. In a month I'll have forgotten I heard it.

10 August

Today is their 65th wedding anniversary. Father tells me that Rosemary, Rachel & Mike came over to Cadbury with pizza and cupcakes, and that Mother recited, by heart, all of "Stopping by Woods on a Snowy Evening."

James Buswell's portrayal (as good a word as any) of Bach's unaccompanied Sonata, the one in C major with the giant fugue, is as satisfying as anything I've heard in ages: controlled yet ecstatic, massively gentle, sensible and accurate. It made me think of Bach, and my mind didn't wander.

With Tobin last night to two-thirds of John Eaton's *Tempest*. The first act bored by being overladen, fussy, loud, needlessly complex, and, so far as diction's concerned, meaningless. But the second act had some (not much, but some) repose, and the hickish jazz may be as kosher a way as another for dealing with buffoons. The conducting of Richard Bradshaw: vibrant to a point of eroticism. Eaton might have displayed a more amusing viewpoint if he'd used the jazz combo for the Elizabethan pastiche pieces, and the sackbutts and violas for the jazz pieces. Next week I'll return for the last act. (We left early so that I could make notes for the Youth Concert speech this morning.)

12 August

Last night, premiere of *Scenes from Childhood*. They played devotedly, I messily, audience warm. Tonight we repeat the piece. On returning home after the party, around midnight, I fell down the bathroom steps. A shock. The sharp flagstone, so typical of Santa Fe dwellings, is more dangerous than quaint. Bruised hand and knee.

Yet it's been years since I've had a drink (barring the three or four binges in my early period with JH; probably my last drink was in 1973). Ditto with cigarettes, after having smoked 328,500 of them (at thirty a day for thirty years). And it's been around three years since, thanks to the specter of AIDS and age, that I've dallied. If God, in whom I don't believe, said, "You will never have sex again, but will remain healthy and productive until the end," the lack would be no big deal.

17 August

Phoned Philadelphia. Rachel and Mike will be married today in Rosemary's garden, and Father will attend. One could weep with pleasure; most news is death.

After our rehearsal (*The Santa Fe Songs*) yesterday, a party at Louise Trigg's. A hundred acres which, because of their green pastures and prim pear orchards, could be in Provence rather than New Mexico. Huge rambling mansion and spacious lawns bedecked with pots of petunias into which peacock feathers are poked. Real peacocks in the acacia trees. Humans sprinkled about, as in India, listening to well-played junk music, Bottesini's *Grand Duo*. Nice and decadent. All the elderly female guests resemble Georgia O'Keeffe. She is to Santa Fe what Melville is to Nantucket. Even as national hotel rooms feature Gideon Bibles, so Santa Fe guests rooms feature O'Keeffe reproductions. (Her work in repro is smoother, speaks better, than in the original.)

Sense of abandonment. But when the phone clangs and someone invites me to lunch, I vaguely resent it. Endlessly saying the same things to different people, or the same things to the same people. The sixty-one years between Debussy and me are the same span as those between me and a composer born yesterday.

Public "conversation" and recital with Will Parker, beginning with *Mourning Scene*, my Opus One from 1947. I could never use that text now (mainly because I used it then), but neither could I write so wistfully. The quartet was impeccable. The Ives group displeases me—I'm so sadly used to Donald Gramm's textures. And they're no fun to play: I work like hell to get all those wrong notes right. Except for maybe Satie, Ives is the only composer in history who can properly be termed a primitive. Paradox, since, unlike poetry or painting, a certain minimum of technical know-how is needed before you can start putting notes together.

19 August

Thinking about librettos. The notion of an Oedipus trilogy sounds dated and dangerous, yet it's never had a musicalization in English, much less in American. It's been done by a Russian (Stravinsky), a Mexican (Chavez), a Franco-Swiss (Honegger), an Italian (Leoncavallo), and a German (Orff). If Shakespeare, why not Sophocles?

The slant is that there is no slant. Except that I'd dispense with *Oedipus Rex*, and congeal *Oedipus at Colonnus* and *Antigone* into a single telegram. A tale of two cities, drawn from three or four translations, but without updating (i.e. no Creon-as-Hitler). Of course, my music by definition updates the play, even as Shakespeare's verse updated Julius Caesar. How does this differ from a director's updating a past piece like, say, Corsaro's setting of Bizet's *Carmen* in the Spain of 1939? Once a piece of music is forged, it hardens permanently, like a sword, *tant bien que mal*, whereas a director, even a "faithful" one, provides merely a momentary sheath.

If you press a doorbell that, unbeknownst to you, is dynamited, are you guilty of the resulting carnage? That's the question throughout Sophocles' trilogy.

25 August

Blurb for Maggie Paley's *Bad Manners*:

If letters are the wings of friendship, as Madame de Sévigné maintained in the eighteenth century, Maggie Paley might claim that in our time the phone is an instrument of enmity. Using that instrument as her mouthpiece in this self-assured first novel, she has confected as wittily wistful and readably strange a version in the American tongue as Ivy Compton-Burnett once confected in the English tongue: a highly stylized milieu of satire where all characters speak identically about crucial horrors. This undifferentiated language is less a liability than an asset since it lends the book its unique tone, or rather, its bad manners. Bad manners, to Maggie Paley, are the camouflage of true feelings in a pre-feminist society where manhunting is the aim of even the most seemingly emancipated women. These women are not far from Clare Boothe's—with an added zest of irony, madness, and, yes, culture—as they pursue, with avid expertise, their shallow goals. Paley's own expertise lies in how she makes these goals alluring to even you and me.

Funny how during the twenty years I've known her I'd not have dreamed that this was the book she'd come up with. Obviously Maggie's wide experience in the world of glossy mags and Estian vogues has provided fodder and (surprisingly) objectivity. I've never read anything quite like it, and I couldn't put it down.

Nantucket
26 August

Jazz is America's classical music, declares Tony Bennett with a wise grin. Which leaves me and my friends just nowhere.

Eighteen years ago I wrote, regarding what I saw as a merger of so-called Art Song and Pop Song, "the best cover-all term is simply *Song*. The only sub-categories are Good and Bad" (a viewpoint Rockwell's been pushing for a decade). Was I wrong! There's difference in kind, and always has been, between music of church and of state, of parlor and of field. Music of medieval aristocracy or church is casually rhythmless and nonsexual like plainchant; music of "the people"—music to labor by—is purposeful, strong-metered, necessarily distracting, and with the regular beat of sexual intercourse. Now Bruce Springsteen is being pushed as music's new Christ, although he's merely another standard hysteric. Because his heart's in the right place he, like Dylan and the Beatles before him, is canonized.

But goodness and greatness are unrelated.

More sound-alikes: Debussy's *La Damoiselle Elue* and Grieg's *Piano Concerto*. Schumann's *Prophet Bird*, Prokofiev's *Third Piano Concerto*, Ravel's *Forlane*.

All the world is queer save thee and me. And even thee . . .

JH made a pecan torte this morning, which was partially ingested at tea-time by Mary Heller and Eva-Maria Tausig. The four of us (they both garbed in white lace and hats) then adjourned to De Marcos's on India Street and dined on the second floor next to an open window through which entered a delicate warmish breeze with already a touch of fall. Conversation low-keyed, more so than if either of these friends had been there alone with us.

28 August

Good reviews of myself, no matter how prestigious, I read only once. Bad reviews twice. Then why do I want reviews? For two reasons: (1) so that old friends and family will read them; (2) so that other composers will read them. Not, you ask, so that performers will read them and then play my music? I long ago learned that performers never read about new pieces, and no amount of publicity, before or after, prolongs the life of a contemporary work. No caring critic, who suggests that this or that deserves to be played again or recorded, has ever, alas, had any effect on the career of this or that.

A singing star (not a rock star who earns unthinkable billions, but an opera star like Price or Domingo) gets as an evening's fee what a composer gets to write a whole opera. Stars are performing seals; what they perform is unimportant.

The past week, back in Nantucket from Santa Fe, has been spent in writing blurbs for other people, and reading possible librettos. *Kiss of the Spider Woman* is *No Exit* with an exit. Probably I'll settle, with JH, on a sort of "Life of Whitman," or "Aspects of Walt," rather like *The Mother of Us All*.

31 August

Party at Bookworks for Frank Conroy's new collection. I balk at the door: slew of unknown faces. (Of course, I'm there to be seen—that is, so as not to be forgotten—and not to see.) I have no circle of intimates in Nantucket, no one I frequent regularly. JH and I spend whole seasons without once being invited anywhere or inviting anyone. Yet this exquisite *embarras du temps* is not passed in "creation." (That's not quite so.)

Nausea of work. Far from flinging myself into it, forgetting to eat and to sleep in an orgy of "self-expression," I now do everything to avoid it (take naps, read want ads), until, nauseated utterly, realizing that a deadline approaches, I cope.

1 September

Cold, rainy. Hurricane in the Gulf of Mexico, preoccupying as South Africa.

To be straight is as mysterious to me as being gay is to, say, my father. I'd never thought it was something grown-ups "did" until—was it 1938, 1939?—Leo Sowerby kissed me. A few years later in New York Ralph Kirkpatrick turned out "that way"; how could a professor in the sober pursuit of analyzing Scarlatti be queer? As late as 1961 in Tangier, when Jane Bowles said, "Homosexual, I wouldn't be anything else," I was relieved (she was like me) but felt, all the same, that she was quite serious. Could serious academicians be prey to broken hearts? All this I note by way of Frank Conroy's stories, every one of them expert and necessary, and heterosexual. Just as Negroes and Chinese and women turn out to be just as dumb as the rest of us, so straights are no less mean and shallow than gays.

The main problem with the Mussorgsky article is that I just don't sit down and do it. Watched *Double Indemnity* instead with JH. Hadn't seen it since

1944, but recalled every frame. Everything's wrong plotwise, but it works, thanks to the Chandler dialogue and to the electricity of the three leads.

The NYT has as many puff pieces this year on Stephen Sondheim as it had last year on Gerard Schwarz.

Rosemary's two-year stint in Jamaica as librarian for the Peace Corps has come to an end after five months. She felt both used and unneeded, a bit fearful and *dépaysée* in that tropical landscape. We're relieved to have her back north.

New York
15 September

Returning after four months I'm stunned by the beauty of the New York apartment. JH repainted, in two shades of white, the walls and ceiling of the living room. He gave away two sofas to a church member and bought new ones with huge ivory-colored cushions. The most startling change is the hanging of the paintings which, in reshuffled relation to one another, take on new meaning.

The biggest, Rosemarie Beck's frantically dappled depiction of Apollo and Daphne given to JH last March, has now a permanent niche above the piano. Two smaller works of Becki are dispersed on other walls among the five Cocteau drawings, three medium-sized pictures by Jane Freilicher, and three by Alvin Ross. Of large paintings, there's one each by Leonid, Gundelfinger, and Jane Wilson. Smaller watercolors, ink sketches, or etchings are by Degas, Larry Rivers, Nell Blaine, Jacques Dupont, Alice Esty, Ruth Kligman, and Tom Prentiss, and there is a little pencil design by Balthus of two heads, made on the paper tablecloth of the Catalan restaurant on March 2, 1952.

The entrance hall contains three hysterical chalk-&-oil-on-paper fantasies by Norris Embry, a calm gouache of irises by Jane Wilson, and a lithograph by Marie Laure. The dining room has paintings by Margot Stewart, Joe Brainard, Maurice Grosser, Robert Dash, Beck, Prentiss, Wilson, plus a shelf of bric-a-brac including the precious glass paperweights from JH on various birthdays and the black onyx box from a group of friends when I was fifty.

In my bedroom, drawings or small paintings by Nora Auric, Tom Keogh, John Heliker, Gene Myers, Beck, Ross, Wilson, Dupont, and Marie Laure, plus photographs of me by Man Ray, Horst, Carl Van Vechten, and Arnold Weissberger. JH's walls, sparser than any others, have mementos of his past. The little study, except for a watercolor by Judy Collins and a color photo of Wallace, is hung only with Quimper crockery, plaques, and framed degrees.

Considering I'm not acquisitive much less a collector or even "visual," these barnacles from the passing years are something to be proud of. (Other "decorations" in the flat: two thousand books, two Persian rugs, seventy boxes of music & manuscripts, and a dozen large filing cabinets.)

17 September

Yesterday, before boarding the train for Philadelphia where I began a sixth season teaching at the Curtis Institute, I learned of the death in Virginia of Muriel Smith, a classmate at Curtis in 1943. From peak stardom as *Carmen Jones* to isolation as pawn of Moral Rearmament, Muriel's trajectory was quixotic, sometimes admirable, and finally sad.

Curtis, still sans director. Demoralization seeping down to the students.

Death today of Julian Beck. Leaves fall ever more rapidly off the family tree.

20 September

JH seems as easy with Sonny and the cats as he does with humans. In many ways I too could choose the island forever more. Certainly the past week's been hyperventilated in contrast to the slow, still summer. People come and play my music for me in preparation for upcoming recitals; it's flattering, sometimes I learn something, but the hours get gobbled up and I feel, doubtless wrongly, imposed upon. Would I use that time to better advantage? *Pourtant je tiens à mes amis.* Paul Goodman wrote that The Master (Confucius) said: "It's impossible to live with birds and beasts as if they were like us. If I do not associate with people, with whom shall I associate?"

Pleasant outing (therefore) on Tuesday with Maggie Paley, longing to talk of the impending publication of her novelette, in a Village restaurant. Tuesday again, another Village restaurant, this one on Hudson Street with David Del Tredici and Joel Conarroe, after hearing a tape of David's shatteringly expert *March To Tonality*, which I'd love to hear once more, but not twice more. Wednesday, taught all day; then a party at the Janis Gallery to launch James Lord's Giacometti biography. (Invited to say a few words, James announced to the forty-odd guests that he wasn't very good at talking but that he could answer questions—"Ned, ask me a question." I was caught off guard.) Then a gathering at Tom Steele's prior to a very expensive party given by Edmund White's publishers for *his* book.

Francine's new novel lambastes the very world from which she springs and of which she is an inseparable appendage: the world of *Vogue*, and thus is as dishonest as her piece on Nantucket six summers ago—in *Vogue*, as it happened. Playing havoc with facts (Jacques Fath had been dead fifteen years when, in *October Blood*, he attends Chanel's funeral) is less important than skirting what does not serve a demolitionary purpose. Even as Francine's Nantucket straw horse was forever fording Lethe, her straw horse here wears blinders. How much more interesting than a narrator who jumps— with a necessary (Francine would say) modernism—from first to third person, would be a depiction of high fashion which in France is as much a part of the good life as politics, painting, cuisine, and the annual bicycle race.

21 September

Four o'clock. Young Michael Torke with tapes of his pieces, which have such instantaneous appeal as to be quite disarming. Who else deserves these words? (JH, however, overhearing from his room, thought it "sounded like party-sex music." Or, as Boulez said of Messiaen, *musique de bordel*.) Torke, as befits his age—or, indeed, the Bernstein-cum-Chomsky age— seems to want to be taken seriously as a Thinker; but his immediate and edible art simply can't bear the weight of the inexact parallel he draws between it and a phrase of Wittgenstein, itself none too startling: Meaning is not in words themselves but in grammar of words used. "You drop the name of Wittgenstein," I tell him, "but you don't pick it up."

Anaïs Nin wrote in 1969 apropos of *The Paris Diary*: "The Ned Rorem diary had brilliant moments and he could have written a fascinating one, but remained on the surface . . . and also in spite of appearances, indiscreet but not open, not really. Some parts are striking. He never went fully into anything. He falls apart. Certainly his life is in shreds, and wilfully superficial. Scattered. No courage and no core. A shame. I don't know his music. I am sure there was more there than he gave."

Six o'clock. Detailed phone conference with Robert Shaw in Atlanta. We went over every note in *String Symphony*, which he now knows better than I.

22 September

The elaborate service, at the Church of St. Matthew & St. Timothy for the 175th anniversary of the parish, began extraordinarily. I joined the followers in the procession, led by Father Gordon with Bishop Paul Moore, with JH conducting an ambulant brass quartet in appropriate and continual anthems as it advanced west on 84th, wound south on Amsterdam around to 83rd, proceeded east to Columbus, and thence back to the church door. We could have been in a Mediterranean city, so unrelievedly squalid was this open-windowed slum where Hispanics gathered to watch the passing crimson robes and silver crosses but did not tune down their thunderous transistors in deference to the little marching band.

23 September

As Is at the Lyceum, after which Bill Hoffman takes me down the block to Charlie's, a showbiz hangout known to everyone but me. Unlike Paris in the 1950s, the milieus of music and of stage in New York today are autonomous and mutually exclusive. Charlie's is as replete with big actors as it is with young hopefuls, all unaware of classical music. Bill's an overnight star in a way composers can never be, although he's not being hyped the way Edward Albee was a generation ago. Thousands see his play nightly, he's rich and in demand, fans and friends approach our table obsequiously (glancing at me obliquely and without interest, if at all) to gush at him. He's quite aware of his worth, knows how to drive a bargain, is less intellectual than I'd thought but canny as hell, and not about to scratch out a mere libretto, for me or anyone, without top billing and equal pay. (His undertaking with Corigliano predates his stardom; he's stuck with it.) Nor is he interested in other than favorable reactions to his play—that play, after all, being foolproof because it's a success. (I'd quietly suggested that for such a careful, such a "musical," script, there was maybe a bit too much obscenity for impact; wouldn't one well-placed "fuck" be worth the barrage of *fucks* offered undifferentiatedly? Also, isn't the reference to sex on a tombstone in Marrakech, like Charlotte Brontë's robin in winter, incongruous, since Arabs don't have tombstones?)

As Is is as nice as a ballet by Jerry Robbins: terse and tight, everything counts, the sentimentality's unabashed. Yet it moved me less than Larry Kramer's play, which is twice as ungainly, perhaps partly because at *The Normal Heart* I was with John Simon and wanted *him* to be moved, and partly because I saw *The Normal Heart* first. I go to a play every two years; suddenly in only five months I've seen two. And such two! Bill voiced the standard reaction to Larry: a playwright mustn't cast himself. Yet for those unaware (like me) that Kramer's chief character is himself, no self-promotion seems in question, whereas Bill Hoffman's play, as voiced by his eight protagonists, seethed with Bill Hoffman. If an author doesn't write about himself, who does he write about? I scarcely know him, but Bill says we met twenty-one years ago during his first night in Paris. Elliott Stein introduced us, both drunk, in a bar, and we hit each other.

After Charlie's we walked up Eighth Avenue through a tender drizzle, talking of his fame and fortune and that of other playwrights. When I allowed as to how I don't get the point of Sam Shepard, Bill explained that it's because Shepard suffers from an overdose of heterosexuality. One might say the same for Jacob Druckman. At the corner of Columbus and 70th he grabbed a cab and I came home.

Final night in New York. Tomorrow, back to Nantucket, after nine days here getting the Curtis class started and visiting Mother & Father at Cadbury. The city after four months' absence has seemed scary—not hostile, exactly, but indifferent. On the train from Philly I read Paul Fromm's not unintelligent essay on criticism from which my name unexpectedly jumped out at me, as from a crossword puzzle. "Ned Rorem has said that it is easier to recognize the real thing when you hear it than to recognize the absence of the real thing." Did I? Couldn't I as easily have said the reverse? The absence of the real thing seems more evident than its presence. Gide once wrote that he wasn't sure he'd recognize *d'emblée* the genius of Rimbaud without the sway of indoctrination (that's how I feel about much of Beethoven), and his initial rejection of Proust is notorious.

JH's skin is still young, complexion mostly healthy, and eyes wise, especially when he discourses enthusiastically on some project (our Whitman libretto, maybe, or his programs at the church). I watch those eyes, and pray that I will die before they grow dim.

> *Nantucket*
> *27 September*

Noon. The sound began at 4:30 A.M. I was expecting it. Was I already awake, or vaguely asleep but waiting for the alarm? It was like the roar during August 1971 at Fire Island, except that that was a typhoon from Bengal, while Hurricane Gloria comes from Africa. I'm alone. JH drove with Sonny last night to New York, a city in a state of emergency. Spent the morning in town. Main Street's battened down as for an air raid. People chuckle nervously. Last midnight the stars were so utterly benign, the air so windless, there was no suspicion of the great octopus whirling through the sky.

One P.M. Day is stifling. Taped the windows. Eugenie and Carl Norman offered to come now to fetch me, but I can't leave the cats. Wind rising, rain begins spattering the glass. I've dismantled the birdbaths. Branches fall. Eugenie phones again to say the worst is now, and that we'll dine together at seven, as planned, barring flooding. Looks bad. But not too bad. Panic has lasted forty-eight hours, mainly because the TV keeps announcing the storm in the same agitated terms as the Mexican earthquake and AIDS.

Three P.M. Feel rather silly. Very little downpour, and the "gusts" (as meteorologists call them) are less strong than in many an unannounced gale. Vast relief. Remote disappointment.

Five-thirty. Nagging wind, like the sirocco, or the mistral that drives you mad. Weary, aching. Until this morning it had never struck me that for eleven years I've been living in Massachusetts as well as in Nantucket.

28 September

Nary a shard of yesterday's over-hyped frenzy in today's warm green calm except a few dead twigs and the souvenir of that fame-hungry born-again Christian TV weatherman in Florida who gave seventy-two interviews in one day and kept the nation shuddering for seventy-two hours. Spent the morning trying to concentrate on Bruckner's Eighth, but as usual with that man's art I hear nothing but fustian punctuated throughout with only exclamation points, the sophomore's trademark. Margaret Hillis last July in Saranac claimed this particular symphony as her breakthrough, her *Sacre*, her change of life. Well, each to his own. But why, except with me, is it always German stuff that fells them? More important was getting to know Margaret again. After our friendship via Nell Tangeman in the late forties, and her championing of my choruses in the mid-fifties, we never met again till now, and now she'll do *An American Oratorio* in my home town in April. Everything returns if you live long enough. We're as incongruous, yet as congruous, a union as Madame Verdurin and the Prince de Guermantes, but which of us is whom?

Blow-up on the telly. Although this is surely my fifth viewing since 1966, except for the few great scenes and the general ambiance I recall little of the flow each time and none of the minor details. (*Double Indemnity*, seen but once, had remained indelible.) Everything rusts. Antonioni tonight seems less crucial—though not embarrassingly so—than during the decade when he seemed to be our globe's one great artist.

1 October

Dick Cavett began a new series last night, appeared uneasy. His was the most alert talk show going while it went; now it seems merely showbiz chatter. When he mentioned W. C. Fields, I heard Debussy Fields.

Death of Simone Signoret.

Forrest Smith has brought me the dangerously welcome gift of eighty Simenon paperbacks. As with desserts I can't get enough, devouring three simultaneously (*Betty, Le passage de la ligne* and *Strip-tease*) without even savoring the as-always-squalid details, so avid am I for the net effect. Simenon, with Proust and James and Maggie Paley, is my favorite writer, but unlike them he's the soul of economy, never a word too many, and scarcely an adjective. His global popularity is curious in that he's so unrelentingly depressing and French, without ornamentation or humor.

Death of Rock Hudson.

Gorbachev in Paris.

Already days grow so noticeably shorter that I switch on lamps at four. Nantucket's two hundred miles east of New York, on the edge of Ocean Standard Time.

Trying to compose a Trio for Clarinet, Violin and Piano. To be called *End of Summer*.

In the fifty-thousand-word entry on *Song* in the new Grove's Dictionary— British to the gills—there is an eight-line coda on U.S. composers who have contributed to the genre: Ives, Thomson, Diamond, Copland, Babbitt. But neither me nor Barber. (In the entry on *Song cycle* I *am* included, with Copland as the only other American.)

Vindication lies in *The Concert Guide to Song* by Charles Osborne—also British to the gills—who lists me as one of three composers (the others are Tippett and Britten) "who are now, in the mid-1970s, making important contributions to song" and elsewhere as "one of the best living American song composers." Osborne, you may recall, once co-authored, with Brigid Brophy, a thesis entitled *Fifty Masterpieces We Could Do Without*.

4 October

Criticism, despicable employment, with no top-notchers today. Yet some of my best friends have been music critics, starting with Virgil, then Bill Flanagan and Jay Harrison, and virtually all the stringers on the long-defunct *Tribune*. They were, each of them, critics only secondarily; primarily they were practising musicians, a professional activity which lent them . . . not an authority so much as a *poignance* (no other word) of viewpoint. It takes one to know one. On the other hand we have Jacob Druckman, a composer who, if not exactly a critic, is a loud arbiter making the rules for other composers, as Boulez did before him. When Druckman declares that a composer must be forward-looking (i.e., not backward-looking), he settles an issue that he himself has made an issue, then sits back. Now, all music is at all times backward-looking; how can it not be? That which is good (advisable, according to Druckman) for a composer is to be present-looking. But since every composer, good or bad, looks at the present despite himself, his act is not an aspiration but a fact in the process of continual accomplishment. What's unhealthy is for a Druckman to be out on the town laying down laws rather than home writing music. The present is made up of the past (and so, of course, is the future, except that the future is that which by definition does not exist), and the past changes focus with every breath we draw.

6 October

On PBS last evening a two-hour Juilliard jubilee to celebrate its eightieth birthday. Two hours, without a word about composers. Indeed, nothing on creative music, although Paul Taylor was represented by a big ballet, Tennessee Williams by an uncomfortable bit from *Streetcar*, the Juilliard Quartet, with two students in tow, by a dull sextet of Brahms, and Leontyne (mannered to a point of parody, as though if it were learned she wasn't a Lady she might commit suicide) by a soliloquy of Barber who had nothing to do with Juilliard and everything to do with Curtis. Music begins with composers. This fact is ignored not only by the great unwashed, but alas by the most prestigious centers of all: Juilliard and Curtis.

10 October

Long day at Curtis yesterday, and again this morning. Went with Rosemary to the new black opera, "X," too long by half as far as force of text goes, although since it's all based, like Glass, on ostinato, any scene musically would have the same effect thrice longer or thrice shorter. Spent the night at Henry McIlhenny's, always the ultimate host.

Dined tonight chez Shirley and George. Chicken and a celery stew, salad and cheese, and (especially for me; most people don't serve sweets) kiwi tarts. I say that Copland has influenced every composer in America, even those who hate or repudiate him—since the very act of hate or repudiation is an admission of his force. I've said this so often it's dogma, so I'm disconcerted when George says, "He never influenced me. In fact, I've influenced him. Copland, like Stravinsky, in their dotage finally came over to serial technique, while I never 'went over' to their side. I never even hated him." Of course his point is clear. As for Copland and Stravinsky "coming over," today it can be seen as hysteria: not wanting to get left behind.

13 October

The best way isn't always the shortest way. Oh yes it is. But the shortest way isn't always terse. Or rather, that which is terse isn't necessarily brief. Or rather, brevity is a question of saying the maximum with the minimum. *The Rite of Spring*, the *Matthew Passion*, or *Pelléas* would not be the same (would not be "as good") with even one note changed. (This paragraph would improve if I cut all but the first three phrases.)

15 October

Dined chez Christopher Blake (up from New Orleans to launch a play) with Virgil and Maurice, both in top form. Discussing Simenon, I say how revealing he can be with scarcely an adjective. "Oh, he uses adjectives all right," says Virgil, "but specific ones, not the general ones that critics throw around, like *magnificent* or *superb*—always misused, what's more." *Superb* really means *haughty*, interjects Maurice. Simenon on the first page will set the tone by describing with all five senses the dawn fog of a village as it blends with the sweat of a bedroom.

"I like to teach, yes," says Maurice, "even though I never really know who's talented." I feel the same. Why would a real artist be studying with me, or, indeed, be in school at all? Except that schools today, unlike yesterday, are almost the sole outlet for a young composer.

17 October

When it comes to prizes there is no right choice, although with hindsight every choice can seem inevitable. Most witnesses are uncomfortable, especially the losers, and even the Nobel Prize is a raffle. In honoring Claude Simon the Nobelists now show themselves to admire the trend of form over content which has been festering in all French art for three decades, and which at its most extreme becomes the very definition of decadence. It makes me sad.

If they had to choose a Frenchman, why not Simenon?

Long talk with Joe LeSueur about how J. J. Mitchell is coping (is that the verb for how you handle an avalanche?) with AIDS. Apparently A.A. friends plus gay activists have rallied, are "saintly," and remain unflappable during his seizures, although neighbors shun him. Joe says that J. J. "knows" something—that through that layer of horror there gleams some information, some lesson about death, that we, *nous autres*, can't know.

Death? I'm too old for a new experience.

The TV documentary on Copland last night was unsatisfactory, like the Juilliard documentary. Fragmented, furtive, skittish about playing too much music. Each bit of the music was just that, a bit. I knew, of course, that I was to appear in a cameo, but had forgotten what I had said. I liked my stressing of Aaron's vulnerabilities (you can't be a saint without having been a sinner), not by negative observation but by shaking pepper over the treacle voiced by others.

Sympathetic as I am to even Henahan's plaints about the updating viewpoints of so many opera directors, starting with Corsaro (Why make an alternative version of a work which, simply by being revived a century later, is already an alternative to what it was?), I still wonder why no one mentions the fact that an opera, any opera, is by definition a radical alternative. Verdi's *Otello*, Bizet's *Carmen*, Puccini's *Manon* expiring of thirst in the "deserts" of waterlogged Louisiana are weird rewrites of literary pasts which, even in their originals by Shakespeare and Mérimée and Prévost, were weird rewrites.

20 October

For Andrew Porter the importance of a piece can lie in its density, its inherent request to be diagnosed ("When [Stockhausen's] 'Licht' is complete, it will keep analysts busy for decades as they trace and define the musical processes, the symbolism, the mythology, anima and ego aspects."). Indeed, a critic is flattered to be asked to use his head, even as a pianist—one breed of pianist—is flattered to be asked to master *Night Fantasies*. What's there to say or learn about a mere Poulenc song? Yet that song will keep singers busy for decades as they trace and define the processes of text and tune for rapt listeners.

Just as Elliott Carter no longer needs exposure so much as to be exposed, so Fred Astaire is due for a dressing-down. He's old-time America's notion of continental sophistication, but what a one-dimensional hick he seems today, clunky as Keeler. Ginger Rogers outdanced him. Astaire belongs with the plodding George Burns, low on the totem pole.

Asking an author to elaborate on an epigram is like dismantling a watch in search of lost time.

Visit from Sharon Robinson and pianist Margo Garrett, who play lustrously (with the embarrassingly out-of-tune Baldwin) the *Dances for Cello*. I never get used to performers who *interpret* my music, with their imperceptible pressures, their added strokes of "meaning," their classically studied hesitations. For me to assume that my expression rests on the page is not to deny their legitimacy, and in fact I'm flattered they care. It's just that I never get used to it.

Ani Kavafian shows me polaroids of her two-month-old child. Most infants to me resemble wizened octogenarians but Ani's son is simply gorgeous. Is she offended when I say that he looks like JH's dog Sonny?

Evening alone with David Diamond. Moved, not only by the looks of the thirty-pound score of his *Ninth Symphony* (surely what he intends it to be: a masterpiece, as well as a piece by a master, though such terms are out of sync with our times), but by David himself, seventy now, pale, not rich, dedicated to the roots in a way I'm not, speaking with such tenderness of his sister, Sabina, who in her Rochester clinic has assumed a permanent fetal position though her heart is strong and she prevails. We talk as always of the good old days and of the narrowing future. Not a morning goes by that I don't, while squinting half awake toward the gray light through the curtain or walking past overturned garbage cans in the rain on Amsterdam Avenue, ask myself how this would seem with the stink of a hangover or the authority of ten rye whiskies. All these sober years. Yet I remain as close to a blackout as that bottle across the room. DD's patience, and my exasperation (I'd roll my eyes & sigh in front of other students), with our mutual pupil, old Gladys Fisher, twenty-five years ago in Buffalo.

22 October

Lunch by Blue Cross honoring Father in a dining hall of a Philadelphia skyscraper. Guests included former colleagues of Father's and current vedettes in Blue Cross. Rosemary and I went together. (I found myself saying, "We're the Rorem children," although she's 63 and I'll be 62 tomorrow.) Father, although still the most intelligent man I know, ambulates now solely with a "walker." After a lavish *éloge* by a cohort, he was asked "to stand and acknowledge his accomplishments." Rosemary helped him to his feet and he said, "My main accomplishment is that I *can* stand."

Did June slip in prune whip?
or George gorge on fudge flip?
There's a tom cat where Mom sat
and a fall breeze o'er all these.

C'est clair et net: nous n'irons plus hautbois.

An hour with Stormy Bok to discuss the fate of Curtis, and my fate therein.

23 October

I'm 62, the age Ravel died. Allen Hughes called to ask if I'd write two thousand words for Copland's birthday. I said two hundred, but only if the *Times*
asked five others to provide valentines; otherwise I wasn't the one—why not
Arthur Berger? He called back to say, okay, two hundred words, but it would
be just me, plus a poem by Lenny Bernstein, which he then read aloud. So
I'll do it, using Lenny's poem as pivot.

Tonight the Gruens will come to dine, also the Perles and Ruth Ford, plus
beforehand for champagne David Del T. and Joel Conarroe (whose birthday
it also is—as well as that of Maurice Grosser, Miriam Gideon, Sarah Bernhardt, Johnny Carson, Franz Liszt, and Jay & Gordon Gottlieb).

24 October

Spent the afternoon at City College conferring with the dean, Virginia Red,
and members of the music faculty. Verbally I've agreed to take over David
Del T.'s spring semester. What with Curtis, and three musical and three
prose commissions due, perhaps I'll be chewing more than I can spit out.

Returned and wrote in one fell swoop a little profile on Aaron for the
Times.

25 October

Death of Bill Elliott, of AIDS, at only 41.

Atlanta
Halloween

So as not to repeat the gaffe of last January in Pittsburgh, I took care this
evening, when Robert Shaw presented me to his vast chorus, to make three
studied comments: (1) Francis Poulenc is our century's first composer; (2)
Poulenc once said, "Shaw conducts my *Stabat Mater* at the same speed as
the blood in my veins. He is my ideal, and should be America's President";
(3) Mr. Shaw told me last night that you, chorus, are the best he's ever
directed.

They loved it. After which Shaw led the world premiere of my *String Symphony* in such a way that, although future performances by others may be
different and even as good as, none will ever be better than. (I kissed him
onstage, which flustered him.) I concur with Francis. Shaw was an idol of
yore, but we'd never met until now.

With the ever-staunch Sylvia, arrived last night in time for dress rehearsal. On the backstage bulletin board hung an interview in the local paper with these words underlined by an orchestra member: "Mr. Rorem claims he is always surprised when he hears southern accents uttering anything intelligent, just as he is surprised when he hears English accents uttering anything stupid." Lecture at noon to a subscription audience, after which a bearded man in the crowded elevator thrust a number and name into my hand and said firmly, "This person admires you. He couldn't come today because he's in the hospital, diagnosed with AIDS. Could you phone him?" I did.

Tomorrow, lunch chez Robert & Caroline Shaw whose enthusiasm matches mine, at least for now. They've scheduled the Symphony for Washington and Carnegie Hall in April, as well as for Paris in June. Shaw thinks that with my glasses on I look like Donald Gramm.

3 November

Returned on Air Atlanta (half filled, exquisite, dying) in time for JH's choral concert (half filled, exquisite, vital) this afternoon at St. Matthew's & St. Timothy's, with Chuck Turner and Frank Benitez. To say that JH's way with a choir is no less persuasive than Shaw's is to say all. He leaves tomorrow for Nantucket with Sonny. I'll profit from the loneliness by finishing the Trio.

9 November

Went Monday to Donald Collup's stylish if bland recital. My shyness is pathological when I'm alone in intermissions—needlessly vicious to strangers who say hello (the more beautiful they are the more vicious I am). Thursday, Will Parker's distinguished and stimulating all-French program (like Collup, his sung French is flawless, though neither speaks it) accompanied by Dalton Baldwin.

Tonight with Rosemary, yet another choral concert, Gregg Smith's all-American affair including my *Missa Brevis* which he premiered twelve years ago. In the taxi, as Willie Nelson bleated over the too-loud radio, I said to Rosemary that such sound was everything I despised: the nasal whine belittled excellence and catered to know-nothings. She nodded coolly, her son Per being a country singer of sorts (I've never heard him). What, then, is she (or am I, for that matter) to make of Gregg's aristocratic choristers in pink and black as for twenty minutes they intone unvaryingly Lukas Foss's text: A-E-I-O-U?

Reading, with the dwindled hope of finding a libretto, *The Waltz of the Toreadors*. The Samuel French edition is so strewn with stage directions that you can't see the forest. Cocteau used to *tutoyer* whole rooms full of people. JH helps fill out the "acceptance" blanks for the new NEA grant, a hopeless maze of red tape.

Daron came by with the parts of the new Trio, which we corrected together, and also with an advance copy of Section Two of tomorrow's NYT. My article on Aaron is on the front page (sandwiched between Streisand and Horowitz) and retitled "A Songfilled Rock of Gibraltar."

12 November

With Shirley to Argento's *Casanova*. No worse, *en fin de compte*, than the Henze and the Eaton operas last summer, though a good deal vulgarer. Audience, goaded by useful surtitles, responded like a laugh track. Argento's weakness is Henze's too: given their "accessible" style, they have no tuneful gift to burnish it. Later, hot fudge sundae with S. and Robert Savage.

This afternoon, ran into Jack Gottlieb on Broadway and Sixty-ninth. For five minutes, poised on the edge of a chasm where once stood the noble A & P, we gossiped amiably. Jack says Lenny's feeling awful (health, plus the impending Diamond symphony) and that I should phone him. I do. Lenny indeed is in a crisis, with no singer for the Diamond Sunday. Also dysentery. When he claims that "friends" found my reference to him (in the Copland essay) as a "versifier" bitchy I'm shocked that either he missed my affectionate wit, or that the wit fell flat. When I tell him what I'm doing these days, he says, slightly censorious, "Oh Ned, you're so prolific." I reply, "Well, that's why I'm here." Long pause. Then with the saddest of voices he says, "That's why I'm here too, but I've got these concerts to conduct."

Tomorrow Father flies to Chicago, just three days shy of his 91st birthday, to attend a ceremony at which the Blue Cross and Blue Shield Association will present to Bob Sigmond its first "C. Rufus Rorem Health Service Award." Father has already left a deep dent on the world's hard surface.

15 November

Eugenie Voorhees came with me to Aaron's 85th birthday concert last night, a once-in-a-lifetime affair, and not just for Aaron, but for our grandchildren and the television medium.

16 November

JH has found an answer to Bible-thumping homophobes of mid-America. Only in our century—certainly not in the Old Testament—has homosexuality been given a name and a quasi definition. There was not in ancient Israel a homosexual *way of life* to be reviled, only acts. Those acts were taboo to all (that is, also to "heterosexual") Jews, but did not obtain to Gentiles. Indeed, the act of copulation with a Gentile was itself taboo. Moral Majority WASPs could do better than to cite Leviticus, and many a proper homosexual is himself repelled by the cynical ways of Sodom.

The world is mine, as well as Jerry Falwell's.

I did not discuss this last midnight on a well-meaning little Cable Network program, although there was a great deal of discussion of the decay of the musical public—how we composers are not even ignored: we don't exist. The Midnight Muse on Channel Six has a call-in format. The first caller immediately missed the point with: "You, Ned Rorem, are known to more people than Bach in his day." Well, yes, because Cable Network for sixty minutes brings me to fifteen hundred people. But what's that to, say, Mick Jagger, who is known to five hundred million? Yet neither Mick nor Ned are functioning necessities, like Bach; our new cantatas are not played Sunday after Sunday.

17 November

Yesterday, the first snowfall—sleetfall—through which I trudged to a pleasant run-through at Columbia of *Three Sisters Who Are Not Sisters*, the third separate production of this little drama in less than a year. I'll be in Nantucket next Thursday when the American Chamber Opera Company gives the first of four performances co-billed with Weisgall's *The Stronger*.

This afternoon, with JH after church, to Carnegie Hall for David Diamond's *Ninth Symphony*, a fifty-minute two-movement dead-serious masterfully scored Masterpiece—if perhaps not a masterpiece—in the shape of a big tombstone weighing upon a still-living consciousness. If that sounds grandiose, it should. Except for the Michelangelo sonnets, set in English, which seemed superfluous, incomprehensible, and unlyric (meaning syllabic, disjunct, not fun to sing), the piece, as heroically conducted by Lenny Bernstein, is a *tour de force* in the Mahlerian mode, and worth its weight . . . Could David anymore compose, say, a terse song like those unornamented gems of the mid-fifties, which simply *were*? This symphony, unlike those tunes, is filled with fancy but devoid of charm.

Tomorrow, dentist for four hours. Then Nantucket for a holiday.

Nantucket
23 November

Cold, wet, gloomy. JH to New York for weekend. Joined Eugenie for *dîner à cinq* with Russell and Mimi Baker ("on island" for the winter), and statuesque Virginia Vanocur who, among other things, vends furniture on Center Street. Mimi has an appeal, at least to me, that's vaguely cold yet whimsical, like Jane Freilicher (whom she doesn't know): a very American juxtaposition of traits, nonexistent in France. Russell's chief conversational frame of reference is journalism (more, I think, than mine is music): when he talks of a writer, the writer is usually a fellow columnist. That too is American specialization, as opposed to the general practice of all French writers. Yet Russell at his best is Voltairian in concision, and one of the rare authors (with Alexander Cockburn and Gore Vidal) with whom I'm politically at one.

We speak of fan mail and hate mail. Does Russell ever get gifts from readers? Yes, he did once receive, care of the *Times*, a box of three dozen "sticky buns," made from pecans and caramel, which he says were delicious. Wasn't he afraid of poison? "Well," says Russell, "I first passed them around to the researchers on the floor below."

Eugenie made, as always, a perfect meal. We sat around a fire.

In 1936, returning from Cherbourg on the *Aquitania*, Rosemary threw a message overboard in a bottle; months later in Chicago she received a reply from someone in Johannesburg. Publication is a bottle flung to the waves, intimacy with a total stranger.

Can anyone, once part of his diary is published, just go on *comme si de rien n'était*? No author, no composer, can tell you, finally, who he writes for. The same compulsions, the same *lubies*, the very same laments dot this page tonight as dotted it 160 seasons ago.

"Only mediocrities progress—masters revolve." Richard Howard places the epigram on the tongue of Wilde. As an epigraph it could suit my title page, except that epigraphs, like dedications, are for finished works; a diary is by definition an ongoing unpolished affair which doesn't end but, as Valéry liked to say, is only abandoned.

28 November (Thanksgiving night)

JH is back, with Sonny. The three of us had turkey and a squash pie with a mess of pure whipped cream. Reading *Le Testament Donadieu*, an early Simenon and rather too wordy for him.

New York
4 December

New York premiere in Alice Tully Hall of *Dances for Cello & Piano* as performed without flaw by Sharon Robinson and Margo Garrett. Also on the program was an attractive Rhapsody by one William Bland, unknown to me, who was present. Alice Tully herself came with us, and as we gazed down from her box, did she notice the layers of unswept dust upon the stage? Sharon sat on a platform, back to Margo, not untheatrical, but no eye contact between the players and hence no intimacy. Nor was her music stand very pretty. For chamber music in that hall, why not a lamp instead of the over-head worklights? (Sharon fools with her hair between movements, even be-tween phrases. Since every nuance in a performer counts, we ask ourselves what this gesture represents.)

Park Avenue party later at the home of a well-bred couple whom Sharon didn't know, but who are apparently contributors to Pro Musicis, the orga-nization that sponsored the recital and that is run by a French priest, Fr. Eu-gène Merlet. Father Merlet was so delirious at the sight of Alice, whom he'd never met, that he expropriated her from me, gave a long self-congratulatory speech about his organization, proposed a toast to Miss Tully (who had noth-ing to do with tonight's music), with nary a nod to me or William Bland. Of such is the kingdom of heaven.

The kingdom of music is a bit tighter. Ironic to realize that Sharon's spouse, Jaime Laredo, who premiered my Violin Concerto last March, was previously married to, and recorded my *Day Music* with, the wondrous pi-anist Ruth Laredo, whose mother commissioned the *Dances for Cello*.

6 December

Mother's 88th birthday.

Authorities, on page 36 of today's *Times*, declare the Shakespeare poem, whose discovery was bruited on the front page a month ago, to be not by Shakespeare because it's "not good enough." Is that a reason? All great men have written stuff (not just juvenilia) which they suppressed before publi-cation. If we knew Ravel solely by those posthumous works issued by Or-enstein a decade ago, we'd vote no. Or Beethoven: the ordinariness of his germinal ideas, as evidenced in the notebooks (and not even organists play his numerous organ works). Or the banality of Elliott Carter's early ballets. In the Bard's case, the point is not whether it's Shakespeare, but whether it's bad Shakespeare or bad someone else.

Does writing it get rid of it? Do poets only seem to suffer more gorgeously? Philosophers who investigate each cranny of suicide end up killing them-selves all the same. The "Letter to Claude" merely gave me something to do. If now I'd rather anytime agonize in mind than in body, does it only mean I'm getting on?

After five years, symptoms recur: a blue-hot icicle lodged in the urethra, scrotum a sirocco. A dozen doctors nod sagely and mutter: prostate.

It's hard to feel another's physical pain. Reading of torture, I relate this solely to my own—the all-consuming ego of an ailing person, more boring than a man in love. More boring than the recital of another's dream is the recital of his illnesses—the organ recital. One's very soul centers on the body; a flame that curls the black leaf . . . and no, metaphors are no relief.

It's easy to feel another's mental pain. But one's own bodily anguish, once it's gone, is, thank God (for God must have something to do with it), impossible to revive in the imagination.

8 December

Marvelously rehearsed and produced revival of the pruned *Lord Byron* in its semi-staged production at Tully Hall (if that stage can look so elegant for Virgil on Saturday, why not for Sharon on Wednesday?), and both the music and Jack Larson's libretto seemed paradoxically less dated than at the world premiere in 1972. Everyone there, everyone content; the show lasted just long enough. What an enigma is Virgil the composer, the studied innocent. Except he's never been innocent; wisdom governs his options. He opts for expertise, which in musical composition is always simplicity. (Boulez, insofar as he is worthy, is by definition the essence of simplicity in the tongue he speaks.)

11 December

Cadbury yesterday. Each monthly visit resembles the previous one, like a movie replay, for the lives of Mother and Father are not socially varied, and their healths seem stable. (Who can know what variety runs beneath the surface?)

Replays. When I returned home it turned out JH had bought a video camera. After experimenting on Sonny and the cats, he did a four-minute number called "Ned Shows You the Kitchen." I take to it like a duck . . .

14 December

Shirley had the generous yet inevitable idea, two weeks after the fact, of throwing a sixtieth birthday feast for Eugene Istomin, and of almost accidentally choosing such a combination of souls—around three dozen—as would provide an atmosphere of *le temps retrouvé*. If the atmosphere felt *retrouvé* too soon, well, it *could* someday be too late, and there'll never be the right moment; most of us have perhaps just one more decade in us. Many of the guests had often been in the same room together over the past forty years, but never all at once.

Pleasant to chat for half an hour—plates poised on knees and too-loud laughter jamming our antennae—with Isaac Stern who, as intelligent performers go, is at the other end of the rainbow from me. He seemed miffed, for example, that my recent Fiddle Concerto was composed less from inner urge than from practical need, and that I'd used the small orchestra, not primarily because chamber sonorities were throbbing for release, but because I was sick of the large orchestra. Isaac, our most experienced interpreter, seems still respectful of the phenomenon called inspiration, a phenomenon that composers see solely as a tool. I do recall something from the first time we met: In the early 1950s with Eugene we were sitting at a Rond Point terrace. Isaac had a cold and was worried about the evening's concert: "Even at my worst I must be better than everyone else." What an aspiration! Tonight I told him I'd enjoyed his dubbing of John Garfield playing the violin in *Humoresque*, and he revealed to me—or rather, to us, for Gary Graffman had joined us on the sofa, and JH too—how his arms were filmed with Garfield's body, by his standing behind the actor whose own hands were pulled behind his back.

Whereupon Vera Stern, a strapping lass and hardly timid, planted herself room-center and proposed a pattern for the evening. (It was ten o'clock now, everyone had eaten and was wine-filled, though cake & coffee were yet to come. If Shirley had planned her own scenario, it was now tacitly forfeited.) Each guest was to rise, one by one, and deliver an homage to Eugene. I froze, as I used to freeze in fourth grade when Miss Burris sprang an unannounced oral exam for which I was unready. Gary instantly got up and read a charming little speech. He had always looked up to Eugene (he said) since they first met at Curtis, when he was ten and Eugene was twelve. That crucial age difference set the pattern for the next half century, during which, while everyone else became more dissolute, Eugene grew more svelte. I first heard Gary play (it was the A-flat Ballade) at Curtis in 1943; I first heard Seymour Lipkin play (Ravel's *Tombeau*) at the same place, same year. Seymour now evoked those Curtis days, as did David Lloyd (he was David Jenkins then, and his tenor *lied* singing was a model for my vocal writing ever since), and Marie.

Ken McCormick talked of the solidarity of baseball. Anna Lou Kappell (stylish, like a still-vital actress from yesterday) revived the specter of Willy. Ellen Adler spoke too, as did Lillian Kallir, Anne McCormick, Martita, John Gruen, and nearly everyone else, even George Perle whose past was not linked to the guest of honor's. My head ached nervously, I scrunched my shoulders and shyly sat low, hoping to be overlooked; indeed, Vera, saving best for last, now solemnly called on her husband. Isaac, without rising (a *coup de théâtre*, forcing us to heed him with care) spoke in generalities, movingly if a touch pompously, about Eugene's dedication, beauty of spirit, sense of responsibility to great art, and so forth. After which I'd have sighed with relief, had not Eugene himself announced, "I want Ned to say something." So I stood up.

Unlike Gary, I've always looked down upon Eugene, being two years his senior. Thus, although I was to learn as much from him as from any other executant I've ever known (I sensed this already at nineteen), when I made the Saturday rounds of Philadelphia bars I wasn't about to let Eugene tag along. During my first month at Curtis I lived above the florist shop on 21st & Locust, and the Istomins lived just above me. One day I went up to see Eugene, and found instead Shirley, swathed in her Persian lamb, toying at the keyboard. Although we'd never met, she threw me a smile of such radiance that to this day I'm a bit blinded. A week later I moved into the spare room of her mother's apartment on Delancey Place. Coming from a midwest family where meals were downed in peace, I'd never known anyone quite like Shirley and Rae Gabis and their extrovert milieu, which extended to all the semi-European child prodigies of Curtis. What was retained from my single year at that Institute was not the dusty wisdom of Maestro Scalero but the ever-active comradeship of young pianists, notably Eugene and Shirley. Shirley has in many ways remained my best friend—despite passing exasperations (surely mutual) that all friendship withstands—with her unshielded warmth, beautiful face and figure forever intact, instant comprehension of music new and old, and a fidelity of spirit which can't be feigned or bought. Similarly Eugene. As David Lloyd's accurate and easy vocalism influenced my writing for the human voice (an early song, *Catullus: On the Burial of His Brother*, is dedicated to him), Eugene's easy and accurate pianism influenced my writing for, yes, the human voice. Like all interpretive artists worthy of the name, there is something *wrong* with Eugene (at these words the interpretive artists in the room all stiffened): meaning his individual divergence from the True Way—there is no one true way—and the involuntary eccentricity that makes him him. That can't be bought or feigned, either. But my very attempt to copy in composition Eugene's mannerism of performance has given, for better or worse, a certain style to a certain aspect of my life's work.

Precious friends.

Visit Wednesday from the Verdher Trio, who commissioned *The End of Summer*, which they plan to play first . . . in Burma!

Thursday, dentist. Cozy tea party at Robert Ferro's. Then an orgy at the Astor Gallery where the American Music Center presented annual awards to Peggy Jory (posthumously) and Gunther Schuller. Judy Collins came to dine on quiche and a mocha cake (left over from the Verdhers), which she needs to eat more of. Talked till midnight.

Tree-trimming party Friday at the Gruens' to whom we offer *en cadeau* Colette's biography-in-photographs. Apartment swarming with dancers who, as Virgil once wrote, "are auto-erotic and have no conversation," but who talk up a storm and look beautiful as they hover about Jane's groaning buffet, itself a contradiction of her Spartan still lifes. Background music too loud, thanks to young Julia's milieu. John, perfect host, tunes it down.

At 4 A.M. JH went to the kitchen for a glass of water and surprised a small rat on the table. Other tenants in the building, it turns out this morning, have reported rats.

Spoke with Joe Machlis, abed with a quadruple bypass, and, typically, quite merry about it.

Visit today from Richard Howard, with a book of Florine Stettheimer's poems which he thinks might be songs (they are not); from cousin Sara Watts, with a mug for Father from his hometown of Radcliff, Iowa; and from Maggy Magerstadt, fresh from *Tango Argentino*.

Christmas Day

Morris came for a sandwich, then to JH's Midnight Mass, before which the organ broke down completely but was fixed at literally the eleventh hour. For a Christmas gift Sonny gave to me (i.e., to Mister Rosum) a twelve-pound yellow-&-blue platter in the same Quimper pattern that Mother collected when we were children. And I composed a *Serenade for Two Paws* for JH to teach to Sonny on rainy days. (Sonny's black eyes are like Picasso's, but guileless.)

Party at Judy's. Spoke mainly to Nan Talese (who's editing Judy's memoirs) and her sensational daughters who, with their etched, charcoal eyes, look like profiles on Etruscan pottery; and to Martin Duberman, docile and still handsome after his two heart attacks, and writing a biography of Paul Robeson. Very very cold. Nantucket alone tomorrow.

Nantucket
31 December

Days alone, snowed in. Dreamed that Wallace, who had been hanging dead on the wall, came back to life, young and furry and purring. *Arrivés* Sunday, JH and Sonny. The Cat Lady, as she calls herself, will stop by the apartment daily while we're gone.

Death of Audrey Wood after five years in a coma. (I was Audrey's sole musical client during the end of the 1950s, and although she didn't know quite what to do about it, beyond creditably getting the operatic rights for *Mamba's Daughters*, she was loyal, industrious, and one of a kind.)

In December the sun sets here at three. Pitch dark at 4:30 when Eugenie and her daughter, Evan, stopped by for a cup of almond infusion with which to toast out the old year, calmly.

Such a toast, however fugitive, is an important counteraction to my now frequent bouts of what the French call *àquoibonisme* (what difference does it make?). Not just the ambiguous prostate that casts a shadow (can prostates cast shadows?), but also: What to aspire to? I do love life, and life does seem short now—three hundred years wouldn't be enough for all I'd like to finish. I've had great performances of all my pieces, and regular appreciation, in public, in private, for what I intrinsically am, by nature and by ambition. Yet I go to bed most nights with a weary heart, am eased by an hour or two of reading, fret with insomnia till sunrise, then praise the stars I'm alive for another dawn. I approach that day as though treading a spider web: what shocks, deaths, disappointments will arrive before dark? Will the world ever be a better place?

Sometimes, though, the day becomes a pleasure, usually, but not always, because of the fact of JH without whom life wouldn't be a life at all. The pleasure can even be unalloyed:

> Not the longing for a lover
> or the sentiment of starting over
> but this clear and refreshing rain
> falling without haste or strain.

Paul Goodman also felt that "So effortlessly we are not given / to move on earth as these in heaven / clouds, nor without desire / to tend whither the airs conspire."

Still, we *can* be effortlessly given to move. Sometimes, for a brief span—while sweeping the basement, watching crows on the snow, playing backgammon with JH—I'll experience a surge of absolute happiness.

INDEX OF NAMES